The Chronicles of Medieval Wales and the March

MEDIEVAL TEXTS AND CULTURES OF NORTHERN EUROPE

General Editor
Rory Naismith, *University of Cambridge*

Editorial Board
Elizabeth Boyle, *Maynooth University*
Aisling Byrne, *University of Reading*
Sharon Kinoshita, *University of California, Santa Cruz*
Carolyne Larrington, *University of Oxford*
Erik Niblaeus, *University of Cambridge*
Emily V. Thornbury, *Yale University*

Previously published volumes in this series are listed at the back of the book.

Volume 31

The Chronicles of Medieval Wales and the March

New Contexts, Studies and Texts

Edited by

Ben Guy, Georgia Henley,
Owain Wyn Jones, and Rebecca Thomas

BREPOLS

British Library Cataloguing in Publication Data

A catalogue record for this book is available from the British Library.

© 2020, Brepols Publishers n.v., Turnhout, Belgium

All rights reserved. No part of this publication may be reproduced, stored in a retrieval system, or transmitted, in any form or by any means, electronic, mechanical, photocopying, recording, or otherwise, without the prior permission of the publisher.

D/2020/0095/86
ISBN: 978-2-503-58349-5
e-ISBN: 978-2-503-58350-1
DOI: 10.1484/M.TCNE-EB.5.116607
ISSN: 1784-2859
e-ISSN: 2294-8414
Printed in the EU on acid-free paper

Contents

List of Illustrations	vii
List of Abbreviations	ix
Preface	xiii
1. Chronicling and its Contexts in Medieval Wales HUW PRYCE	1
2. Historical Writing in Europe, *c.* 1100–1300 BJÖRN WEILER	33
3. Historical Scholars and Dishonest Charlatans: Studying the Chronicles of Medieval Wales BEN GUY	69
4. Meet the Ancestors? Evidence for Antecedent Texts in the Late Thirteenth-Century Welsh Latin Chronicles HENRY GOUGH-COOPER	107
5. *Bonedd y Saint*, *Brenhinedd y Saesson*, and Historical Scholarship at Valle Crucis Abbey BARRY J. LEWIS	139

6. The Continuation of *Brut y Tywysogyon*
   in NLW, MS Peniarth 20 Revisited
   DAVID STEPHENSON   155

7. *O Oes Gwrtheyrn*: A Medieval Welsh Chronicle
   OWAIN WYN JONES   169

8. The Cardiff Chronicle in London,
   British Library, MS Royal 6 B XI
   GEORGIA HENLEY   231

9. The Chronicle of Gregory of Caerwent
   JOSHUA BYRON SMITH   289

10. A Forgotten Welsh Chronology in Aberystwyth,
    National Library of Wales, MS 5267B, in
    MS Peniarth 50, and in the Red Book of Hergest
    REBECCA TRY   341

11. *Brut Ieuan Brechfa*: A Welsh Poet Writes the Early Middle Ages
    BEN GUY   375

Appendix: List of the Chronicles of Medieval Wales and the March   421

Index of Manuscripts   431

General Index   433

List of Illustrations

Henry Gough-Cooper

Table 4.1: b1241–b1255 (AD 1219 to 1234). 113

Table 4.2: b1225–b1233 (AD 1203 to 1211) 114

Table 4.3: c577–c562 (AD 1237 to 1241). 117

Table 4.4: **C** between 1214 and 1219 117

Table 4.5: Parallels between the structuring of the universal chronicle and the later annals in **C** 118

Table 4.6: **B** and **C** between 1202 and 1210. 120

Table 4.7: **B**, **C**, **P**, and **S**, epitome 1176–87. 123

Table 4.8: *Chronicle of 1151. 125

Table 4.9: Chronology from 1101 to 1114. 129

Table 4.10: Chronology from 1114 to 1135 130

Table 4.11: Chronology from 998/1000 to 1016 134

Table 4.12: Chronology from 983 to 998. 136

Barry J. Lewis

Figure 5.1: Stemma of the third branch of *Bonedd y Saint*. 152

Owain Wyn Jones

Figure 7.1: The relationship between different manuscripts
of *O Oes Gwrtheyrn*... 179

Table 7.1: The relative and absolute chronology of *O Oes Gwrtheyrn* . . 207–08

Georgia Henley

Figure 8.1: The Cardiff chronicle's relationship
with the Annals of Tewkesbury.................................. 244

Figure 8.2: The transmission of sources from Tewkesbury
to Glamorgan, and from Glamorgan to North Wales................. 251

Table 8.1: Close correspondence in the Neath chronicle
and Cardiff chronicle entries for 1258–1268,
with comparison to the Annals of Tewkesbury 240–43

Table 8.2: Examples of the Cardiff chronicle's
closer agreement with the Annals of Tewkesbury 245–46

Table 8.3: Examples of the Cardiff chronicle's
closer agreement with the Neath chronicle...................... 246

Table 8.4: The Cardiff chronicle's tailoring of its Tewkesbury source 247

Rebecca Try

Figure 10.1: Stemma of *Blwydyn Eiseu*................................. 358

Table 10.1: Annals 21 and 22 in *CB*................................... 345

Table 10.2: The four annals that appear in *CB*
and MS Peniarth 50 but not RBH 349

Table 10.3: A comparison of the dates in the
three primary witnesses to *Blwydyn Eiseu*...................... 368–73

Ben Guy

Figure 11.1: A stemma of the witnesses to *Brut Ieuan Brechfa*. 387

List of Abbreviations

AC	*Annales Cambriae*, ed. by John Williams ab Ithel, Rolls Series, 20 (London: Longman, Green, Longman, and Roberts, 1860).
AM	*Annales Monastici*, ed. by Henry Richards Luard, Rolls Series, 36, 5 vols (London: Longmans, Green, Reader and Dyer, 1864–69).
Auct. ant.	Auctores Antiquissimi.
BBCS	*Bulletin of the Board of Celtic Studies.*
BL	The British Library.
BS	*Brenhinedd y Saesson: BM Cotton MS Cleopatra B v and The Black Book of Basingwerk, NLW MS. 7006*, ed. and trans. by Thomas Jones (Cardiff: University of Wales Press, 1971).
BT (Pen. 20)	*Brut y Tywysogyon: Peniarth MS. 20 Version*, ed. by Thomas Jones (Cardiff: University of Wales Press, 1941).
BT (Pen. 20 trans.)	*Brut y Tywysogyon or The Chronicle of the Princes: Peniarth MS. 20 Version*, trans. by Thomas Jones (Cardiff: University of Wales Press, 1952).
BT (RB)	*Brut y Tywysogyon or The Chronicle of the Princes: Red Book of Hergest Version*, ed. and trans. by Thomas Jones, 2nd edn (Cardiff: University of Wales Press, 1973).
CCR	*Calendar of the Close Rolls Preserved in the Public Record Office*, 47 vols (London: Her Majesty's Stationery Office, 1892–1963).

CPR	*Calendar of the Patent Rolls Preserved in the Public Record Office*, 52 vols (London: Her Majesty's Stationery Office, 1891–1916).
CMCS	*Cambridge Medieval Celtic Studies* (Summer 1981–Summer 1993); *Cambrian Medieval Celtic Studies* (Winter 1993–).
DD	Diplomata regum et imperatorum Germaniae.
DMLBS	*Dictionary of Medieval Latin from British Sources*, ed. by Ronald E. Latham, David R. Howlett, and Richard K. Ashdowne (London: Oxford University Press for the British Academy, 1975–2013), <clt.brepolis.net> [accessed 17 April 2018].
HC	*Historia et Cartularium Monasterii Sancti Petri Gloucestriae*, ed. by William Henry Hart, Rolls Series, 3 vols (London: Longman, Green, Longman, Roberts, and Green, 1863–87).
HSJ	*The Haskins Society Journal: Studies in Medieval History.*
HW	John Edward Lloyd, *A History of Wales from the Earliest Times to the Edwardian Conquest*, 3rd edn, 2 vols (London: Longmans, Green & Co, 1939).
MA	*The Myvyrian Archaiology of Wales*, ed. by Owen Jones, Edward Williams, and William Owen Pughe, 3 vols (London: Rousseau, 1801–07).
MA²	*The Myvyrian Archaiology of Wales*, ed. by Owen Jones, Edward Williams, and William Owen Pughe (Denbigh: Gee, 1870).
MHB	*Monumenta Historica Britannica: or, Materials for the History of Britain, from the Earliest Period. Volume I, Extending to the Norman Conquest*, ed. by Henry Petrie and Thomas Duffy Hardy ([London]: [Record Commission], 1848).
MGH	Monumenta Germaniae Historica.
NLW	The National Library of Wales.
NLWJ	*National Library of Wales Journal.*

PL	*Patrologiae cursus completus: Series Latina*, ed. by Jacques-Paul Migne, 221 vols (Paris: Migne, 1844–64).
RG	*Rhyddiaith Gymraeg 1300–1425*, ed. by Diana Luft, Peter Wynn Thomas, and D. Mark Smith (Cardiff: Cardiff University, 2007–13) <http://www.rhyddiaithganoloesol.caerdydd.ac.uk> [accessed 28 June 2018].
RMWL	J. Gwenogvryn Evans, *Report on Manuscripts in the Welsh Language*, 2 vols (London: Her Majesty's Stationery Office, 1898–1910).
SS	Scriptores.
SS rer. Germ.	Scriptores rerum Germanicarum.
SS rer. Merov.	Scriptores rerum Merovingicarum.
THSC	*Transactions of the Honourable Society of Cymmrodorion*.
WG 1	Peter C. Bartrum, *Welsh Genealogies AD 300–1400*, 8 vols (Cardiff: University of Wales Press on behalf of the Board of Celtic Studies, 1974).
WG 2	Peter C. Bartrum, *Welsh Genealogies AD 1400–1500*, 18 vols (Aberystwyth: NLW, 1983).
WG 3	Michael Powell Siddons, *Welsh Genealogies A.D. 1500–1600* (Aberystwyth: CMCS Publications, 2017).

Preface

This volume is the culmination of the collaborative work undertaken by the Welsh Chronicles Research Group. Founded in 2014 by the present editors, the group has since striven to realize the research potential of the vastly understudied body of annalistic chronicles composed in medieval Wales. Annalistic chronicles form one of the most important categories of narrative source surviving from the period. The group aims to establish the study of these sources as a priority in the study of medieval Wales. They provide much of the narrative background for our understanding of Wales in this period, but they must be studied in their own right rather than being used simply as repositories of information.

The group has established a website, hosted by Bangor University (<http://croniclau.bangor.ac.uk>), which has acted as a useful repository for bibliographic information and new editions of Latin chronicles by our colleague Henry Gough-Cooper. Three conferences have also been organized, at which some of the chapters in the present volume were first aired: these took place at Bangor University in 2014 (Chapter 5), at the University of Glasgow in 2015 (Chapter 10), and at the University of Cambridge in 2016 (Chapters 4, 8, 9, and 11). We owe much gratitude to all the participants in those events, whose collective insights have contributed enormously to the formation of this book.

This volume is divided into three parts. Part I, 'Synopses', offers three overviews of the subject from three different standpoints: the national, the international, and the historiographical. Huw Pryce surveys the entirety of Welsh chronicle writing against the backdrop of historical developments in medieval Wales, beginning with the earliest annals surviving from the eighth, ninth, and tenth centuries and ending with the poet, genealogist, and textual scholar Gutun Owain in the latter half of the fifteenth century. In doing so, he describes the development of ideas of the past in medieval Wales through which the following studies and discussions must be understood. Björn Weiler focuses chronologically on the twelfth and thirteenth centuries, but takes a much broader geographical view, highlighting commonalities in chronicle writing from across medieval Europe. The specificities and idiosyncrasies of Welsh historical writing must be understood as part of this common European textual culture, where ideas were more often shared than guarded. Ben Guy takes a historiographic approach to the study of medieval Welsh chronicles, outlining the key developments in the field since the early nineteenth century. He identifies particular points of contention in addition to areas that might profit from further attention, and demonstrates the place of this volume in the overall development of the field.

Part II, 'Detailed Studies', contains three chapters with important implications for our understanding of the two foremost groups of Welsh chronicles, known as *Annales Cambriae* and *Brut y Tywysogyon*. Henry Gough-Cooper innovatively traces the stages in which the Breviate and Cottonian chronicles (the *Annales Cambriae* B- and C-texts) were compiled over time, working backwards from the extant manuscripts and paying close attention to matters of chronological structure. Barry J. Lewis identifies a textual link between the chronicle known as *Brenhinedd y Saesson* and the well-known collection of Welsh saints' genealogies known as *Bonedd y Saint*, a link which has important ramifications for the dating of *Brenhinedd y Saesson*. David Stephenson undertakes a detailed analysis of the continuation of Peniarth 20 version of *Brut y Tywysogyon* for the years 1282–1332, suggesting that it might have been compiled in multiple stages, and that the information for the annals from 1320 onwards may have been supplied by Madog ap Llywelyn, an *uchelwr* from north-east Wales.

Part III, 'Editions', serves to expand the field of study considerably by presenting five new studies, editions, and translations of previously unpublished chronicles. Owain Wyn Jones produces the first critical edition of the thirteenth-century vernacular chronicle *O Oes Gwrtheyrn*, probably the earliest extant manifestation of vernacular chronicle writing surviving from medieval Wales. Jones argues that the text was composed in multiple stages in the Cistercian abbey of Aberconwy in Gwynedd, rendering *O Oes Gwrtheyrn* one of the only examples of northern Welsh chronicling surviving from the central Middle Ages. Chapters by Georgia Henley and Joshua Byron Smith direct attention to the southern March of Wales and to the tantalizing nexus of chronicle writing centred on the monasteries of the Severn valley. Henley edits and translates the chronicle of Cardiff Priory, and explores its textual connections with the *Annals of Tewkesbury* and with a set of annals associated with the Cistercian abbey of Neath. Smith rescues the chronicle of Gregory of

Caerwent from the sixteenth-century antiquarian copy in which it uniquely survives, thereby facilitating access to one of the most important witnesses to the chronicling tradition of St Peter's Abbey, Gloucester. Two chapters by Rebecca Try and Ben Guy then address aspects of chronicle writing from the later Middle Ages. Rebecca Try identifies a short vernacular chronicle in three manuscripts of the late fourteenth or fifteenth centuries and attempts to unpick some of the knotty chronological problems that it presents. Ben Guy rends a vernacular chronicle known as *Brut Ieuan Brechfa* away from the grasp of the late eighteenth- and early nineteenth-century romantic forger Iolo Morganwg and restores it to Ieuan Brechfa, a poet and genealogist of the late fifteenth and early sixteenth centuries, who appears to have endeavoured to rewrite the Red Book version of *Brut y Tywysogyon*, with somewhat bizarre consequences.

Lastly, an appendix to the volume provides a list of the chronicles of medieval Wales and the March, from the Harleian chronicle in the tenth century to the *Cronica Walliae* of Humphrey Llwyd in the sixteenth. For each chronicle listed, information is given about the years covered by the chronicle, the primary manuscripts containing the chronicle, and the most important editions of the chronicle. It is acknowledged that this list of twenty-seven texts can only be preliminary prior to the full uncovering of the textual riches of early modern Welsh manuscripts.

Several different approaches are used below to extend and define the study of these chronicles. The detailed studies, editions, and contextual discussions clarify the work that has already been done on the chronicles and outline possible directions for further research. This collection of essays will not be the last word on the chronicles of medieval Wales and the March, indeed far from it; it is our sincere hope that the collection will serve to stimulate further ideas about the material under study, especially when that material has received little previous attention. More generally, it is hoped that the collection will render Welsh chronicle writing more accessible to scholars working in the broader field of medieval historical writing.

The Welsh Chronicles Research Group owes several debts of thanks to those who have helped us along the way. We would like to thank the universities of Bangor, Glasgow, and Cambridge, as well as St John's College in Cambridge, for kindly hosting our three conferences. We are very grateful to the bodies that funded the Cambridge conference in particular: St John's College, Pembroke College, the University of Cambridge's Faculty of English, and the Chadwick Fund. Many thanks too to the speakers at those conferences whose contributions could sadly not be included in this volume: Professor J. Beverley Smith, Professor Dauvit Broun, Dr Denis Casey, Dr John Reuben Davies, Dr

Nicholas Evans, Dr Roy Flechner, Professor Chris Given-Wilson, Scott Lloyd, and Professor Paul Russell. We would like to thank Bangor University for hosting the Research Group website, and especially Nerys Boggan for patiently responding to our website requests. Finally, we gladly acknowledge the many careful observations of this book's anonymous reviewer, which much improved the final version, and we are grateful to Dr Elizabeth Boyle for very kindly shepherding the book through the press.

Ben Guy, *University of Cambridge*
Georgia Henley, *Saint Anselm College*
Owain Wyn Jones, *Bangor University*
Rebecca Thomas, *Bangor University*

20 February 2020

1. Chronicling and its Contexts in Medieval Wales

Huw Pryce

Chronicles, works that presented their account of past events in a year-by-year format, were the principal type of historical narratives written in medieval Wales.[1] By contrast, other kinds of historical narratives were few: the early ninth-century *Historia Brittonum* ('History of the Britons'), saints' Lives, one medieval biography of a Welsh ruler, *Vita Griffini filii Conani* ('The Life of Gruffudd ap Cynan'), and Geoffrey of Monmouth's *De gestis Britonum* ('Concerning the Deeds of the Britons') or *Historia regum Britanniae* ('History of the Kings of Britain'), completed *c.* 1138. In its Welsh versions, known as *Brut y Brenhinedd* ('The History of the Kings'), Geoffrey's *De gestis Britonum* was the most popular history book in medieval Wales. Moreover, by the early fourteenth century it was repurposed to provide a prequel and framework for chronicle writing that had originated in the late eighth century and had continued to 1282. To a significant degree, later medieval scribes and patrons sought to conserve this earlier chronicle writing and give it a canonical form as part of a historical continuum that traced the origins of the

---

[1] The definition of chronicles as works adopting an annalistic or year-by-year structure is used here for analytical convenience, although the distinction between 'chronicles' and 'histories' that eschewed this structure became increasingly blurred from the twelfth century onwards: David N. Dumville, 'What Is a Chronicle?', in his *Celtic Essays, 2001–2007*, 2 vols (Aberdeen: Centre for Celtic Studies, University of Aberdeen, 2007), II, 1–24 (first publ. in *The Medieval Chronicle II*, ed. by Erik Kooper (Amsterdam: Rodopi, 2002), pp. 1–27). For doubts about the usefulness of drawing any generic distinction between chronicles and histories, see Chris Given-Wilson, *Chronicles: The Writing of History in Medieval England* (London: Hambledon and London, 2004), p. xix. See also Björn Weiler, Chapter 2, below.

Welsh from Troy to the eve of the Edwardian conquest of 1282–1284. In addition, spasmodic and generally brief attempts were made, in either continuations of existing texts or independent works, to extend the chronological coverage of chronicles beyond the conquest.

This chapter offers an overview of chronicle writing in medieval Wales intended to complement the introductory chapters by Björn Weiler and Ben Guy which follow. It thus aims to chart the development of the chronicles over time as well as to consider some of their characteristics and the contexts in which they were produced. The discussion will focus in turn on the early Middle Ages, the two centuries from the first Norman incursions in Wales to Edward I's conquest of 1282–1284 that witnessed the consolidation of both Marcher lordships and Welsh principalities, and post-conquest Wales down to the early sixteenth century, including an assessment of the significance of the chronicles copied and edited by the scribe and poet Gutun Owain (fl. *c.* 1451– *c.* 1500). This leads to a brief conclusion that offers some general observations on developments over the medieval period as a whole.

The Early Middle Ages

The earliest evidence for chronicle writing in Wales appears in the collection of historical texts in London, BL, MS Harley 3859, copied *c.* 1100 from an exemplar written in south-west Wales, very probably St Davids, between 954 and 988.[2] This comprises three works: the *Historia Brittonum* ('History of the Britons'), as the work is conventionally known,[3] composed in Gwynedd in 829/30 and ascribed in some manuscripts to Nennius, together with a chronicle and a set of genealogies which have been interpolated into it. Here, attention will focus on the Harleian chronicle, also known as the A-text of *Annales Cambriae* ('The Annals of Wales'). This records events down to the death of Rhodri ap Hywel in 954,[4] and contains entries made contemporaneously at St Davids from the late eighth century onwards, which were combined with material from two

---

[2] Ben Guy, 'The Origins of the Compilation of Welsh Historical Texts in Harley 3859', *Studia Celtica*, 49 (2015), 21–56.

[3] On the title, see David N. Dumville, '*Historia Brittonum*: An Insular History from the Carolingian Age', in *Historiographie im frühen Mittelalter*, ed. by Anton Scharer and Georg Scheibelreiter (Vienna: Oldenbourg, 1994), pp. 406–34 (pp. 415–17).

[4] Although blank annals continue to 977, it is likely that the Harleian annals were not continued after *c.* 954: Egerton Phillimore, 'The *Annales Cambriae* and Old-Welsh Genealogies from Harleian MS. 3859', *Y Cymmrodor*, 9 (1888), 141–83 (p. 144).

other sources. One was a chronicle from Gwynedd, quite possibly written at the church of Abergele, covering the period from the mid-fifth century to 858, which probably began to be written in the late eighth century and derived some of its entries down to the later seventh century from a northern British source also used by the *Historia Brittonum*. A revised version of the Gwynedd chronicle was then inserted as an appendix to the *Historia Brittonum* in the third quarter of the ninth century. The other source consisted of a version of the Annals of Clonmacnoise in Ireland, datable to 911 × 954, which supplied retrospective entries back to the mid-fifth century as well as other additions.[5] It is likely that an important stimulus for writing the Gwynedd chronicle was the adoption in 768 by the Britons of Wales of the Roman method of calculating the date of Easter followed by the other churches of Western Europe, a change ascribed to Elfoddw, termed 'archbishop of Gwynedd' in his obituary notice in 809.[6] This brought the Britons of Wales into line with the other churches of Britain and Ireland, which had adopted the Roman Easter at various stages between the early seventh century and its acceptance by the monastery of Iona in 716.[7]

The Harleian chronicle indicates, then, that the earliest known Welsh chronicles — at both St Davids and a centre in North Wales, very probably Abergele — date from the late eighth century onwards, and thus considerably later than their Irish and English counterparts: the Chronicle of Ireland originated in the later sixth century at the Hebridean monastery of Iona, while annals were composed in Northumbria from the early eighth century and in Wessex quite possibly from the mid-seventh century.[8] This contrast may, of course, simply be an optical illusion resulting from the loss of sources. At the very least, though,

---

[5] Kathleen Hughes, 'The Welsh-Latin Chronicles: *Annales Cambriae* and Related Texts', *Proceedings of the British Academy*, 59 (1973), 233–58 (references given here to the reprinted version in her *Celtic Britain in the Early Middle Ages*, ed. by David N. Dumville (Woodbridge: Boydell, 1980), pp. 67–85 (pp. 68–73)); Guy, 'Origins', pp. 27–45; Kathryn Grabowski and David N. Dumville, *Chronicles and Annals in Medieval Ireland and Wales: The Clonmacnoise-Group Texts* (Woodbridge: Boydell, 1984), pp. 207–26.

[6] Phillimore, 'The *Annales Cambriae*', pp. 162, 163.

[7] Thomas M. Charles-Edwards, *Early Christian Ireland* (Cambridge: Cambridge University Press, 2000), ch. 9, esp. pp. 408–10; David N. Dumville, '*Annales Cambriae* and Easter', in his *Celtic Essays*, II, 25–33 (first publ. in *The Medieval Chronicle III*, ed. by Erik Kooper (Amsterdam: Rodopi, 2004), pp. 40–50); Guy, 'Origins', pp. 38–39, 42.

[8] *The Chronicle of Ireland*, trans. by Thomas M. Charles-Edwards, 2 vols (Liverpool: Liverpool University Press, 2006), I, 8–9; Barbara Yorke, *Kings and Kingdoms of Early Anglo-Saxon England* (London: Seaby, 1990), pp. 73, 128; Kenneth Harrison, 'Early Wessex Annals in the Anglo-Saxon Chronicle', *English Historical Review*, 86 (1971), 527–33 (p. 530).

it appears that any earlier chronicles kept at Welsh churches were not available to the compilers of the Harleian chronicle and its antecedent texts. The impact of the adoption of the Roman Easter is evident in the structure of the Harleian chronicle, probably deriving in turn from the Gwynedd chronicle interpolated into the *Historia Brittonum*, which was modelled on that of late antique Easter tables and chronicles. This is suggested by the Harleian chronicle's chronological framework, which consists of a sequence of 533 years from 445 to 977 based on the 532-year great cycle of the 19-year Easter cycle introduced by Elfoddw, as well as by the system of giving a number every ten years that is also used in Prosper of Aquitaine's *Epitoma chronicon*. The latter was a history of the world down to 455, and ultimately derived from the chronicle of Jerome (*c*. 380), which in turn was a translation and adaptation of the early fourth-century chronicle of Eusebius.[9]

The Harleian chronicle conformed, then, to a well-established type of Western European historical writing. Its contents were also typical of early medieval chronicles elsewhere. To begin with, though not adopting a system of AD dating, through its use of Dionysiac reckoning the chronicle recorded the passing of time within a Christian framework designed to facilitate the correct calculation of the date of Easter, correlated with Christ's Incarnation.[10] From this perspective, arguably the most significant aspect of the Harleian chronicle, as it survives from the tenth century, is that over 70 per cent of its annals are blank: that is, they only record the passing of a year (L. *annus*).[11] The events which are recorded in the remaining annals thus make only fitful appearances in the text as a whole. They are also usually brief, mainly concern the religious and secular elites or plagues and unusual natural phenomena, and range across the Insular world.[12] While their geographical scope partly reflects the assimilation of sources from northern Britain and Ireland, especially for the period down to

---

[9] *Annales Cambriae, A.D. 682–954: Texts A–C in Parallel*, ed. and trans. by David N. Dumville (Cambridge: Department of Anglo-Saxon, Norse, and Celtic, University of Cambridge, 2002), p. xiii; Guy, 'Origins', pp. 39–42.

[10] For Dionysius Exiguus's use of the birth of Christ as the fixed point for his Easter cycle, see Rosamond McKitterick, *History and Memory in the Carolingian World* (Cambridge: Cambridge University Press, 2004), p. 91.

[11] The blank annals are included in Phillimore's edition of the Harleian chronicle. Cf. Sarah Foot, 'Finding the Meaning of Form: Narrative in Annals and Chronicles', in *Writing Medieval History*, ed. by Nancy Partner (London: Arnold, 2005), pp. 88–108 (pp. 95–96).

[12] Plagues: Phillimore, 'The *Annales Cambriae*', pp. 154, 155, 159 (s.aa. 537, 547, 682, 683). Other natural phenomena: Phillimore, 'The *Annales Cambriae*', pp. 157, 158, 159, 160, 163 (s.aa. 624, 650, 676, 684, 689, 714, 721, 812, 814).

the mid-eighth century, these notices were evidently considered appropriate for inclusion in the chronicle and thus throw light on their authors' assumptions about what merited inclusion in Welsh churches' records of the past.

Unsurprisingly, in view of the text's clerical authorship, one prominent theme is the progress of Christianity and the history of individual churches, witnessed not only by annals concerning the adoption of the Roman Easter, but by obits of numerous Irish and British religious figures, including Brigit, Patrick, Columba, Gildas, and David, by references to the conversion of the English and the death of Bede, and by notices of destruction suffered by the church of St Davids.[13] The world of secular politics also receives considerable coverage, with annals recording conflicts among the Britons and their neighbours and the deaths of secular rulers in the kingdoms not only of the Britons but also of the English, Irish, Picts, and, in one case, the Franks.[14] The occasional appearance of terms in Old Welsh suggests that some of these entries derive from material transmitted in the vernacular, notably the use of *gueit(h)* or, in two instances, *cat*, rather than the more frequently used Latin *bellum*, for a 'battle', followed by an Old Welsh place name — as in '*Gueith Cam lann* ['the battle of Camlann'], in which Arthur and Medrawd were killed'.[15] (Arthur is also described as participating in the British victory at Badon).[16] Another example is the notice of *Gueit Conguoy* ('the battle of Conwy'), followed by an explanatory phrase that uses another Welsh term to present this in terms of a feud: *Digal Rotri a Deo* ('God's revenge for Rhodri').[17] The appearance of such Welsh phrases, together with the frequent use of Welsh forms of proper nouns, show that the compilers of the Harleian chronicle were able to write in the vernacular as well as Latin, which in turn suggests that they were open to the native historical culture also cultivated by poets — an impression reinforced by the references to Arthur.

---

[13] Phillimore, 'The *Annales Cambriae*', pp. 153, 155, 156, 161, 163, 167 (s.aa. 454, 457, 562, 595, 601, 735, 810, 906).

[14] See e.g. Phillimore, 'The *Annales Cambriae*', pp. 156, 157, 158, 160, 161, 166 (s.aa. 607, 617, 644, 714, 736, 887).

[15] Phillimore, 'The *Annales Cambriae*', p. 154 (s.a. 537). For the examples of *cat*, see Phillimore, pp. 160, 165 (s.aa. 722, 869).

[16] Phillimore, 'The *Annales Cambriae*', p. 154 (s.a. 516).

[17] Phillimore, 'The *Annales Cambriae*', p. 166 (s.a. 880). For other annals using *gueith* as the only word for 'battle', see Phillimore, 'The *Annales Cambriae*', pp. 156, 157, 160, 164, 165, 166, 167, 168 (s.aa. 613, 630, 722, 817, 848, 873, 876, 906, 921); and for its use as a gloss on *bellum*, Phillimore, 'The *Annales Cambriae*', p. 161 (s.aa. 750, 760).

From Norman Invasions to Edwardian Conquest, c. 1070–1282

Although the Harleian chronicle ends in 954, a chronicle continued to be written at St Davids for over three centuries thereafter.[18] The St Davids manuscript containing a version of the chronicle down to 1288 is but one instance of the significant growth in the number of surviving chronicles written in twelfth- and thirteenth-century Wales — in turn part of the wider pattern of growth across Europe discussed elsewhere in this volume by Björn Weiler. In Wales, this increase resulted largely from ecclesiastical changes precipitated by foreign conquest and domination from the late eleventh century onwards, namely the foundation of monastic houses by both Anglo-French settlers and Welsh rulers. This in turn meant that chronicle writing in Wales belonged to two overlapping contexts: on the one hand, the continuation of a pre-Norman Welsh tradition best represented by the Harleian chronicle; on the other, the expansion of monastic chronicling in Britain and Ireland, especially among the Cistercians.[19] Thus the chronicles under consideration here exemplified — and, in some cases, were closely connected with — wider historiographical trends extending beyond Wales. Moreover, in contrast to the pre-Norman period, chronicles were composed in Wales by foreign settlers as well as by the Welsh. One aspect of this, as we shall see shortly, was the appropriation of chronicles that continued the annalistic tradition at St Davids. However, these continuations marked a significant change in interest and allegiance. Divergence from the native tradition was clearer still in new chronicles created in Glamorgan, which developed into a major Marcher lordship after its conquest by the Normans in the late eleventh century, namely the annals down to 1235 written at Margam Abbey (a Cistercian house founded in 1147 whose library contained the histories of both William of Malmesbury and Geoffrey of Monmouth) as well as late thirteenth-century adaptations of the Annals of Tewkesbury at the Cistercian abbey of Neath and the Benedictine priory of Cardiff.[20] To a great

---

[18] Hughes, 'The Welsh-Latin Chronicles', pp. 73–76, 84–85; *Annales Cambriae*, ed. and trans. by Dumville, pp. x–xii.

[19] Antonia Gransden, *Historical Writing in England*, 2 vols (London: Routledge and Kegan Paul, 1974–82), I: *c.550 to c.1307* (1974), 143–48, 318–45, 395–438; Julian Harrison, 'Cistercian Chronicling in the British Isles', in *The Chronicle of Melrose Abbey: A Stratigraphic Edition. Volume I: Introduction and Facsimile Edition*, ed. by Dauvit Broun and Julian Harrison (Woodbridge: Boydell, 2007), pp. 13–28.

[20] Hughes, 'The Welsh-Latin Chronicles', pp. 81–82; J. Beverley Smith, 'Historical Writing in Medieval Wales: The Composition of *Brenhinedd y Saesson*', *Studia Celtica*, 52 (2008),

extent, these were derived from monastic chronicles in England and reflected the Anglocentric outlook of the communities where they were produced: thus their chronology is structured around the reigns of kings of England, and several begin with the death of Edward the Confessor and the Norman conquest of England in 1066.[21] By contrast, there is only limited evidence of cross-fertilization between these texts and native Welsh chronicle writing before the end of the thirteenth century.[22] However, like monastic chronicles elsewhere, those in Glamorgan also recorded events in their localities, including Welsh attacks on the possessions of Margam and Neath.[23] These events were in turn affected by developments originating farther afield in Wales, especially the dominance achieved by Llywelyn ab Iorwerth (d. 1240), Prince of Gwynedd, who receives considerable attention in the Annals of Margam, most notably after he led forces into South Wales in the early 1230s.[24]

Nevertheless, the most substantial and geographically extensive body of chronicles written in Wales in this period were those which continued the St Davids tradition represented by the Harleian chronicle that ended in 954. Two of these are extant in manuscripts of the late thirteenth century: the Breviate chronicle (the B-text of the *Annales Cambriae*), copied at the Cistercian abbey of Neath, which contains annals down to 1286, and the Cottonian chronicle (the C-text of the *Annales Cambriae*), copied at St Davids, the provenance of

---

55–86 (pp. 67–70); Frederick George Cowley, *The Monastic Order in South Wales, 1066–1349* (Cardiff: University of Wales Press, 1977), p. 144; Robert B. Patterson, 'The Author of the "Margam Annals": Early Thirteenth-Century Margam Abbey's Compleat Scribe', *Anglo-Norman Studies*, 14 (1992), 197–210; Marvin L. Colker, 'The "Margam Chronicle" in a Dublin Manuscript', *HSJ*, 4 (1992), 123–48; Georgia Henley, Chapter 8, this volume.

[21] *Annales de Margan*, in *AM*, I (1864), 1–40 (p. 3); Georgia Henley, Chapter 8, below (which argues that down to 1244 or possibly 1246 the Cardiff Chronicle is based on the Annals of Tewkesbury). Another Glamorgan chronicle opens with Augustine's mission to the English in 600 but then continues from the death of Edward the Confessor to 1298: 'Chronicle of the Thirteenth Century: MS. Exchequer Domesday', [ed. by Harry Longueville Jones], *Archaeologia Cambrensis*, 3rd ser., 8, no. 32 (1862), 272–83 (p. 273, s.aa. 600, 1066). For this chronicle, see Smith, 'Historical Writing', pp. 67–68.

[22] Smith, 'Historical Writing', pp. 67–71.

[23] *Annales de Margan*, pp. 34–37 (s.aa. 1223–1224, 1226–1227, 1229).

[24] *Annales de Margan*, pp. 31–32, 38–39 (s.aa. 1211–1212, 1230–1232). See also Georgia Henley's edition of the Cardiff Chronicle in this volume (s.aa. 1211, 1228, 1230, 1231, 1232, 1240); 'Chronicle of the Thirteenth Century', p. 278 (s.a. 1231); Smith, 'Historical Writing', pp. 69–70.

the chronicle as a whole, which ends in 1288.²⁵ Both derive from a St Davids chronicle down to *c.* 1202, but thereafter the Breviate chronicle drew its material from Welsh Cistercian houses, quite possibly Whitland (Dyfed) and (at least ultimately) Strata Florida (Ceredigion), and also almost certainly Cwmhir (Maelienydd in mid-Wales) for the period 1257–1263; the final section was composed *c.* 1300 at Neath, when retrospective additions of English events recorded in annals from Waverley Abbey (Surrey) were also made.²⁶ These differences are related to the changing political orientation of the churches at which the chronicles were written. From the 1160s the Cottonian chronicle offers an English perspective on events reflecting the Marcher environment of St Davids and the integration of its bishops in the province of Canterbury, whereas the composite nature of the Breviate chronicle reveals shifting views: thus for the period 1189–1263, whose narrative is largely derived from Welsh Cistercian houses, it 'speaks with the voice of independent Wales', while its final part, written at Neath, an abbey patronized by the Braose lords of Gower, supports Edward I (r. 1272–1307).²⁷

In one respect, however, the ancestors of both chronicles shared a common historical perspective after they diverged *c.* 1202, as they subsequently combined their annals with a universal history — an independent work composed after the completion of Geoffrey of Monmouth's *De gestis Britonum c.* 1138 — extending from the creation of the world to the reign of the Emperor Heraclius (610–42), derived principally from Isidore of Seville's *Chronica minora*, to which was added material on early British history from Geoffrey and also, in

---

²⁵ Unsatisfactory editions in *AC*, which is cited here for convenience. For full and accurate transcriptions, see *Annales Cambriae: The B Text, from London, National Archives MS E164.1, pp. 2–26*, ed. by Henry W. Gough-Cooper (The Welsh Chronicles Research Group, 2015) and *Annales Cambriae: The C Text, from British Library Cotton MS Domitian A. i. ff. 138r–155r*, ed. by Henry W. Gough-Cooper (Welsh Chronicles Research Group, 2015), both available at <http://croniclau.bangor.ac.uk/editions.php.en> [accessed 5 April 2018].

²⁶ Here I follow Hughes, 'The Welsh-Latin Chronicles', pp. 73–76, 79–84, with the modifications proposed by David Stephenson, 'Gerald of Wales and *Annales Cambriae*', *CMCS*, 60 (2010), 23–37; David Stephenson, 'The Chronicler at Cwm-hir Abbey, 1257–63: The Construction of a Welsh Chronicle', in *Wales and the Welsh in the Middle Ages*, ed. by Ralph A. Griffiths and Phillipp R. Schofield (Cardiff: University of Wales Press, 2011), pp. 29–45; and David Stephenson, 'In Search of a Welsh Chronicler: The *Annales Cambriae* B-Text for 1204–30', *CMCS*, 72 (2016), 73–85.

²⁷ Hughes, 'The Welsh-Latin Chronicles', pp. 76, 79 (quotation), 81–83. For a detailed analysis of the likely stages in the evolution of both the Breviate and Cottonian chronicles, see Henry Gough-Cooper, Chapter 4, this volume.

the Breviate chronicle, the *De temporibus* of Bede.[28] In the case of the ancestor of the Cottonian chronicle, this involved extensive chronological restructuring of the text, probably in or shortly after 1216.[29] The retrospective expansion of the chronicles was designed to give them greater chronological depth and to integrate them with universal Christian history. It is also significant as marking one of the earliest attempts to connect Geoffrey's account of the kings of Britain with a chronicle that continued beyond the late seventh century and focused predominantly on events in Wales, albeit less explicitly than in the case of *Brut y Tywysogyon* discussed below.[30]

Two other texts provide further evidence of chronicle writing by Welsh Cistercians in the thirteenth century. The *Cronica de Wallia*, extant in a late thirteenth-century manuscript, was probably written at Whitland Abbey (quite possibly in 1277) and covers the period 1190–1266, providing fairly full narratives of many years down to 1255.[31] It bears close resemblances to the Welsh-language *Brut y Tywysogyon*, some of whose lost Latin sources were probably very similar, as well as to parts of the Breviate and Cottonian chronicles.[32] By contrast, the other work, *O Oes Gwrtheyrn* ('From the Age of Vortigern'), a title derived from its opening words and whose earliest surviving copies were written *c.* 1400, is unique among chronicles of this period. As Owain Wyn Jones argues, this appears to be a new work deriving from the Cistercian abbey of Aberconwy, patronized by the princes of Gwynedd, and to have been first composed in the second decade of the thirteenth century, during the reign of Llywelyn ab Iorwerth, before being updated in the late 1260s. True, the work derives material from the Latin chronicle originating at

---

[28] Caroline Brett, 'The Prefaces of Two Late Thirteenth-Century Welsh Latin Chronicles', *BBCS*, 35 (1988), 63–73.

[29] Henry Gough-Cooper, 'Decennovenal Reason and Unreason in the C-Text of *Annales Cambriae*', in *The Medieval Chronicle 11*, ed. by Erik Kooper and Sjoerd Levelt (Leiden: Brill, 2017), pp. 195–212.

[30] It is uncertain whether the connection was made before the use of Galfridian material in *O Oes Gwrtheyrn*, datable to the second decade of the thirteenth century: see below.

[31] '"Cronica de Wallia" and Other Documents from Exeter Cathedral Library MS. 3514', ed. by Thomas Jones, *BBCS*, 12 (1946–48), 27–44 (pp. 29–41); J. Beverley Smith, 'The "Cronica de Wallia" and the Dynasty of Dinefwr', *BBCS*, 20 (1963–64), 261–82; Hughes, 'The Welsh-Latin Chronicles', pp. 77–79; Julia Crick, 'The Power and the Glory: Conquest and Cosmology in Edwardian Wales', in *Textual Cultures: Cultural Texts*, ed. by Orietta Da Rold and Elaine Treharne (Cambridge: Brewer, 2010), pp. 21–42.

[32] *BT (Pen. 20)*, pp. xi–xiii; *BT (Pen. 20 trans.)*, p. xl; Smith, '"Cronica de Wallia"', pp. 274–76.

St Davids, presumably via a version kept at Aberconwy's mother house of Strata Florida. However, it was not conceived as a continuation of that chronicle. Instead, it adopts a different chronological structure and also, in contrast to all other Welsh chronicles before the fourteenth century, was very probably composed in Welsh rather than Latin. It may therefore be seen as part of a broader pattern of vernacular historiographical endeavour at early thirteenth-century Aberconwy also represented by the copying of genealogies focused on Llywelyn ab Iorwerth and other texts.[33] As its title indicates, the work fixed its dating with reference to the time since the reign of Vortigern, named in the *Historia Brittonum* and elsewhere as the British tyrant who had invited the Saxons into Britain, and, while some sections are written in a sequential year-by-year form, it also included calculations of the years that had elapsed since the coming of various peoples to Britain.[34] This allowed the chronicler to set recent events, however disastrous, against the backdrop of an ancient history which played on the long-established notion that the Welsh, as successors of the Britons, were the rightful proprietors of Britain. One example is the description of Llywelyn ab Iorwerth's surrender of his son Gruffudd as one of the terms of the prince's surrender to King John in 1211:

> O'r pan doeth Kymry gyntaf y ynys Prydyn yny doeth Ieuan urenhin Aber, ac yny aeth Grufut ab Llewelin ygwystyl, ij. m. ccccc. xvj.
>
> From when the Welsh first came to the island of Britain until King John came to Aber and until Gruffudd ap Llywelyn was taken hostage, two thousand five hundred and sixteen years.[35]

---

[33] See Owain Wyn Jones, Chapter 7, this volume; Ben Guy, 'A Lost Medieval Manuscript from North Wales: Hengwrt 33, the *Hanesyn Hên*', *Studia Celtica*, 50 (2016), 69–105, esp. pp. 85–86.

[34] A precedent for, and thus possible influence on, this formulation is a statement in the *Historia Brittonum*, originally composed in Gwynedd in 829/30, that 428 years had passed 'from the first year in which the English came to Britain until the fourth year of King Merfyn' ('A primo anno, quo Saxones venerunt in Brittanniam, usque ad annum quartum Mermini regis'): *Historia Brittonum*, § 16, in Edmond Faral, *La légende Arthurienne: études et documents*, 3 vols (Paris: Champion, 1929), III, 4–62 (p. 13). This in turn seems to have been modelled on the work's summary of the Six Ages of the World (*sex aetates mundi*), an influential periodization devised in Late Antiquity: *Historia Brittonum*, §§ 1–4, in Faral, *La légende Arthurienne*, III, 5. For a similar scheme, see, for example, Bede, *De temporum ratione*, §§ 1–6, ed. by Theodor Mommsen, MGH, Auct. Ant. (Berlin: Weidmann, 1898), pp. 247–48, and discussion in Paul Merritt Bassett, 'The Use of History in the Chronicon of Isidore of Seville', *History and Theory*, 15 (1976), 278–92 (pp. 281–87).

[35] See Owain Wyn Jones's edition, Chapter 7, below, § 63.

The work is significant, then, in showing how long-established understandings of the Brittonic past helped to structure new historiographical writing in the thirteenth century. Moreover, this occurred in the context of a Cistercian monastery patronized by the most powerful Welsh ruler, presumably in collaboration with poets or other members of the native learned orders who cultivated genealogy and other aspects of Welsh historical culture.

The fullest evidence for chronicle writing in this period occurs in *Brut y Tywysogyon* ('The History of the Princes'), the conventional title for chronicles extant in manuscripts from the mid-fourteenth century onwards which covered the years from 682 to early 1282 and were intended as a continuation of Geoffrey of Monmouth's *De gestis Britonum*.[36] These were also the most influential of the medieval Welsh chronicles, since they formed the basis for the earliest histories of Wales written in the Elizabethan period which in turn retained their authority as authoritative accounts of the Welsh past into the nineteenth century.[37] The chronicles survive in two main versions, Peniarth 20 and the Red Book of Hergest, named after manuscripts containing copies of them. These versions are datable respectively to 1286 × c. 1330 and 1307 × c. 1350; another version, *Brenhinedd y Saesson* ('The Kings of the English'), probably datable to 1282 × c. 1330, is closely related.[38] The extant texts are thus important evidence for Welsh history writing in the period after the Edwardian conquest, and their significance in that context will be assessed below. However, they are also highly relevant to a discussion of chronicling in the twelfth and thirteenth centuries, as it is generally agreed that the Welsh texts are translations of one or more sources in Latin on account of their preservation of Latin declensional forms, errors explicable as resulting from a misconstruing of Latin, and close similarities of some sections to surviving Welsh-Latin chronicles, especially the *Cronica de Wallia*.[39] True, the extent to which the translations keep to the wording of their

---

[36] *Historical Texts from Medieval Wales*, ed. by Patricia Williams (London: Modern Humanities Research Association, 2012), pp. xxv–xxxii; Owain Wyn Jones, 'Historical Writing in Medieval Wales' (unpubl. doctoral thesis, Bangor University, 2013), ch. 4.

[37] Robert T. Jenkins, 'William Wynne and the *History of Wales*', *BBCS*, 6 (1931–33), 153–59.

[38] *Brenhinoedd y Saeson, 'The Kings of the English', A.D. 682–954: Texts P, R, S in Parallel*, ed. and trans. by David N. Dumville (Aberdeen: Department of History, University of Aberdeen, 2005), pp. v–x. For the dating of *Brenhinedd y Saesson*, see also Barry Lewis, Chapter 5, below.

[39] John Edward Lloyd, 'The Welsh Chronicles', *Proceedings of the British Academy*, 14 (1928), 369–91 (pp. 378–79); *BT (Pen. 20 trans.)*, pp. xxxvi, lvi; *BT (RB)*, pp. li–lii; Smith, 'Historical Writing', pp. 57–58.

Latin sources has been debated. An influential interpretation posits the creation shortly after the Edwardian conquest of a 'Latin *Brut*', a literary composition which adapted — and in parts significantly elaborated — earlier Latin chronicles and was subsequently translated into Welsh.[40] However, this view has been persuasively challenged by recent textual studies which have instead argued that *Brut y Tywysogyon* essentially reproduces, albeit in translation, the wording of Latin chronicles written at different stages from the eleventh to thirteenth centuries.[41] It should be noted, however, that even proponents of an embellished 'Latin *Brut*' accept that the vernacular chronicles are a palimpsest beneath which earlier stages of Latin chronicle writing remain visible.[42] The following discussion will proceed, then, on the assumption that *Brut y Tywysogyon* provides valuable evidence for chronicle writing before the Edwardian conquest.

J. E. Lloyd argued that *Brut y Tywysogyon* — and thus its Latin original — was based primarily on a sequence of annals written at St Davids, then at Llanbadarn Fawr (*c.* 1100–*c.* 1175), and finally at the Cistercian abbey of Strata Florida in Ceredigion (albeit drawing on material from other Welsh Cistercian houses).[43] This sequence has been largely accepted by subsequent scholars.[44] However,

---

[40] Lloyd, 'Welsh Chronicles', pp. 382, 384, 386; *BT (Pen. 20 trans.)*, pp. xxxv–xxxvi, xxxviii–xxxix and n. 3; J. Beverley Smith, *The Sense of History in Medieval Wales* (Aberystwyth: University College of Wales, 1989), p. 7; Smith, 'Historical Writing', p. 56. See further Ben Guy's discussion of these issues in Chapter 3 in this volume.

[41] David Stephenson, *Medieval Powys: Kingdom, Principality and Lordships, 1132–1293* (Woodbridge: Boydell, 2016), pp. 25–28; David Stephenson, 'The "Resurgence" of Powys in the Late Eleventh and Early Twelfth Centuries', *Anglo-Norman Studies*, 30 (2008), 182–95 (pp. 184–89); David Stephenson, 'Welsh Chronicles' Accounts of the Mid-Twelfth Century', *CMCS*, 56 (2008), 45–57 (pp. 51–57); David Stephenson, 'Entries Relating to Arwystli and Powys in the Welsh Chronicles, 1128–32', *Montgomeryshire Collections*, 99 (2011), 45–51 (pp. 47–49); Owain Wyn Jones, '*Brut y Tywysogion*: The History of the Princes and Twelfth-Century Cambro-Latin Historical Writing', *HSJ*, 26 (2015), 209–27 (pp. 215–27). This does not mean that all the events were recorded shortly after they occurred. For example, the detailed account in *BT (Pen. 20 trans.)*, p. 12 (s.a. 1022) may well be a retrospective entry composed in the late eleventh century: Stephenson, *Medieval Powys*, pp. 27–28; see also Jones, '*Brut y Tywysogion*', pp. 213–14.

[42] For example, *BT (Pen. 20 trans.)*, p. xli.

[43] Lloyd, 'Welsh Chronicles', pp. 382–86.

[44] For example, *BT (Pen. 20 trans.)*, pp. xxxiv, xli. David N. Dumville, review of Kathleen Hughes, *The Welsh Latin Chronicles* (1974), *Studia Celtica*, 12/13 (1977–78), 461–67 (p. 465), argues that a version of the St Davids chronicle passed directly to Strata Florida, without an intervening period at Llanbadarn Fawr, but recent work has reinforced Lloyd's case for the importance of the latter: above, n. 41.

those who argue that the vernacular chronicles consistently adhere closely to their underlying Latin sources allow for a more complex and sophisticated picture of Latin chronicle writing, especially in the late eleventh and twelfth centuries, than the advocates of late thirteenth-century literary elaboration by the author of a 'Latin *Brut*'. Thus, to take a particularly significant example, it has been convincingly argued that the account of the years 1100–1126, which occupies about a sixth of *Brut y Tywysogyon* and is notable for its lengthy rhetorical passages, essentially represents a Latin chronicle written in the early twelfth century by a cleric from Llanbadarn Fawr in Ceredigion, quite possibly Daniel (d. 1127), a son of Sulien (*c.* 1012–1091), twice Bishop of St Davids in the later eleventh century.[45]

Authorship by Daniel ap Sulien is plausible in view of his public role as archdeacon of Powys and 'mediator between Gwynedd and Powys concerning any between whom there was trouble in those lands' as well as of the historical interests of other members of Sulien's family.[46] Indeed, this dynasty offers a rare glimpse of the ecclesiastical milieu in which chronicles were written in the late eleventh and early twelfth centuries, before the introduction of Cistercian monasticism in native Wales. Rhygyfarch ap Sulien (d. 1099) wrote a Life of St David as well as a Latin verse 'Lament' (*Planctus*) that portrays the Norman conquest of Ceredigion in 1093 in Gildasian terms as the destruction of an established order by foreign oppressors visited upon the Britons as divine punishment for their sins; he may also have contributed to chronicle writing in the late eleventh century.[47] Another poem was composed by Rhygyfarch's brother

---

[45] *BT (Pen. 20 trans.)*, pp. 21–50; *BT (RB)*, pp. 38–111; *BS*, pp. 92–143. See Stephenson, '"Resurgence" of Powys', pp. 184–89; Jones, '*Bruty Tywysogion*', pp. 215–27. However, the author of the 'Llanbadarn History' may have relocated to the church of Meifod in Powys after monks from Gloucester Abbey occupied Llanbadarn Fawr *c.* 1116 (and his successor was possibly based at Llandinam in Arwystli (mid-Wales) in 1128–1132): David Stephenson, 'Entries Relating to Arwystli and Powys', pp. 47–49.

[46] *BT (Pen. 20 trans.)*, p. 50. Sulien ap Rhygyfarch (d. 1146) was also described as 'a mediator for various kingdoms': *BT (Pen. 20 trans.)*, p. 54.

[47] 'Rhygyfarch's *Life* of St David', ed. and trans. by Richard Sharpe and John Reuben Davies, in *St David of Wales: Church, Cult and Nation*, ed. by J. Wyn Evans and Jonathan M. Wooding (Woodbridge: Boydell, 2007), pp. 107–55; 'Planctus Ricemarch', ed. and trans. by Michael Lapidge, 'The Welsh-Latin Poetry of Sulien's Family', *Studia Celtica*, 8/9 (1973–74), 68–106 (pp. 88–93), and also edited by Sarah Elizabeth Zeiser, 'Latinity, Manuscripts, and the Rhetoric of Conquest in Late-Eleventh-Century Wales' (unpubl. doctoral dissertation, Harvard University, 2012), pp. 334–36, with discussion at pp. 209–20, 304–06; Stephenson, *Medieval Powys*, pp. 26–28.

Ieuan in honour of their father Sulien that set the latter's biography against the backdrop of the early British past. This celebrated not only the author's descent from 'the famous race of the Britons (which) once withstood the Roman army energetically' but also the 'homeland' (L. *patria*) of Ceredigion, location of the 'city' (L. *metropolis*) of Llanbadarn, where St Padarn had lived and Sulien was born.[48]

After its relocation to Strata Florida by the late twelfth century, the chronicle detectable in *Brut y Tywysogyon* was continued in a very different ecclesiastical institution from Llanbadarn: a Benedictine monastery belonging to the international Cistercian order peopled by celibate monks and lay brothers rather than an early medieval foundation controlled by ecclesiastical and lay kin groups.[49] Nevertheless, the maintenance of the chronicle at Strata Florida signalled a continuity of cultural outlook between the old and the new, reflecting a broader accommodation with Welsh society also attested in the monastery's close association with princely dynasties perceptible both in its historical writing and in other sources.[50] One symptom of this, in chronicles written at both Strata Florida and other Welsh Cistercian houses from the later twelfth century onwards, was the frequent emphasis on the unity of Wales in phrases such as '(all) the princes of Wales', while the *Cronica de Wallia* even refers to 'the monarchy of all Wales' (L. *tocius Wallie monarchiam*).[51] This greater emphasis on Wales as a political unit was facilitated by the connections ensuing from the shared filiation of Welsh Cistercian houses patronized by Welsh rulers, which set them apart from Cistercian houses such as Margam and Neath patronized

---

[48] 'Carmen Iohannis de uita et familia Sulgeni', ed. and trans. by Lapidge, pp. 80–89; quotations from lines 55, 57, 69; also ed. and trans. by Zeiser, 'Latinity, Manuscripts, and the Rhetoric of Conquest', pp. 326–31, with discussion at pp. 34–49, 262–63.

[49] See J. Wyn Evans, 'The Survival of the *Clas* as an Institution in Medieval Wales: Some Observations on Llanbadarn Fawr', in *The Early Church in Wales and the West*, ed. by Nancy Edwards and Alan Lane (Oxford: Oxbow, 1992), pp. 33–40.

[50] See, for example, Daniel Huws, *Medieval Welsh Manuscripts* (Cardiff: University of Wales Press, 2000), pp. 14–15; Cowley, *The Monastic Order in South Wales*, pp. 25–27, 195, 210–12; Jemma Bezant, 'The Medieval Grants to Strata Florida Abbey: Mapping the Agency of Lordship', in *Monastic Wales: New Approaches*, ed. by Janet Burton and Karen Stöber (Cardiff: University of Wales Press, 2013), pp. 73–87; David Stephenson, 'The Rulers of Gwynedd and Powys', in *Monastic Wales*, ed. by Burton and Stöber, pp. 89–102.

[51] For example, *AC*, p. 50 (1165); *BT (Pen. 20 trans.)*, pp. 70, 79, 85, 89, 91, 104, 105, 114, 117 (s.aa. 1175, 1198, 1211, 1215, 1238, 1240, 1264, 1275). 'Monarchy of all Wales': '"Cronica de Wallia"', p. 36 (s.a. 1215 = 1216). Cf. '"Cronica de Wallia"', p. 32 (s.a. 1201); *BT (Pen. 20 trans.)*, p. 81 (s.a. 1201).

by Marcher lords whose political perspective, as we have seen, was very different.[52] But above all it reflected political changes, especially the ambitions of the expansionist thirteenth-century princes of Gwynedd, one of whom, Llywelyn ap Gruffudd (d. 1282), was recognized by the English crown in 1267 as 'Prince of Wales' ruling a 'Principality of Wales'.[53] Accordingly, during the thirteenth century the Strata Florida chronicle, in common with some other related chronicles written at Welsh Cistercian houses, assumed some of the characteristics of a national history. This in turn helps to explain why it subsequently came to be regarded as a history of the Welsh that could be reconfigured to form a sequel to the history of the Britons related by Geoffrey of Monmouth.

The Later Middle Ages

Two important themes emerge in considering Welsh chronicle writing in the period from Edward I's conquest of Wales to Henry VIII's 'Acts of Union' and the Protestant reformation in the 1530s and 1540s. One, just mentioned, is the creation of *Brut y Tywysogyon*, a vernacular chronicle based on earlier Latin chronicles and intended as a continuation of Geoffrey of Monmouth's *De gestis Britonum*. The other is the adaptation and continuation of this chronicle beyond 1282 together with the composition of other chronicles that cover events from the late thirteenth to early sixteenth century.

While sketchy on the course of the Edwardian conquest, historical writing in late thirteenth- and early fourteenth-century Wales may be seen as responding to its consequences. A likely case in point is the compendium of historical texts contained in Exeter Cathedral Library, MS 3514, very probably all written in a Welsh scriptorium, quite possibly at Whitland Abbey, and completed between 1285 and the early fourteenth century.[54] The manuscript combines widely known texts — Pseudo-Methodius, Dares Phrygius, Geoffrey of Monmouth, and Henry of Huntingdon — with genealogies of Anglo-Saxon, Norman, French, and Welsh dynasties, and concludes with the *Cronica de*

---

[52] In these cases, then, ethnic and political loyalties appear to have mattered more than membership of the same religious order: cf. Björn Weiler, Chapter 2, this volume.

[53] *The Acts of Welsh Rulers 1120–1283*, ed. by Huw Pryce (Cardiff: University of Wales Press, 2005), no. 363; *BT (Pen. 20 trans.)*, p. 115 (s.a. 1267); R. Rees Davies, 'The Identity of "Wales" in the Thirteenth Century', in *From Medieval to Modern Wales: Essays in Honour of Kenneth O. Morgan and Ralph A. Griffiths*, ed. by R. Rees Davies and Geraint H. Jenkins (Cardiff: University of Wales Press, 2004), pp. 45–63.

[54] Crick, 'The Power and the Glory'.

Wallia and another short chronicle covering the period from the fall of Troy to 1285.[55] It thus places Welsh views of the past, from Trojan origins to the age of Llywelyn ap Gruffudd, against a backdrop of universal history beginning with the creation of the world and embracing the island of Britain as well as, to some extent, France. Moreover, while some of the texts may have been copied before 1282, the collection was completed later in the thirteenth century and may be seen as a historiographical response to conquest that affirmed the special place of the Welsh in Britain after the extinction of princely rule.[56] The same may be true of the short chronicle in Welsh, known from its opening words as *Oed yr Arglwydd* ('The Age of the Lord'), that spans events from the death of Arthur to the accession of Edward II, and thus compiled after 1307, possibly at Valle Crucis.[57]

Contemporary political events also stimulated the insertion *c.* 1300 of historical texts into a copy of an abbreviated version of Domesday Book at Neath Abbey, namely, the Crown's challenge to the Marcher status claimed by the monastery's patrons, the Braose lords of Gower. The most substantial of these texts was the Breviate chronicle, discussed above, but they also included a short chronicle, based on Tewkesbury annals, which covers the period 1066 to 1298 with a focus on events in Glamorgan, and memoranda on native rulers in south-west Wales.[58] At least one chronicle was also written at another religious house in the March of Wales, namely the Cistercian abbey of Tintern, in the thirteenth and early fourteenth centuries, and included notices of events both at the abbey and in the surrounding area in south-east Wales.[59]

However, the most influential post-conquest development in the historiography of Wales was the consolidation of a master narrative extending from the Trojan origins of the Welsh to 1282. This was accompanied by a decisive shift from Latin to Welsh as the main language of historical writing. The chronicle kept at Strata Florida perceptible in *Brut y Tywysogyon* petered out

---

[55] Contents listed in Crick, 'The Power and the Glory', pp. 36–38. For the last two texts, see also Georgia Henley, 'The Use of English Annalistic Sources in Medieval Welsh Chronicles', *HSJ*, 26 (2014), 229–47 (pp. 240–42).

[56] Crick, 'The Power and the Glory', pp. 30–35.

[57] Edited and translated in Guy, 'A Lost Medieval Manuscript', pp. 101–04, with discussion at pp. 82, 84, 86–87; O. W. Jones, 'Historical Writing', pp. 291, 293, 296–97.

[58] Smith, 'Historical Writing', pp. 72–74; 'Chronicle of the Thirteenth Century'. See also Georgia Henley, Chapter 8, this volume.

[59] Julian Harrison, 'The Tintern Abbey Chronicles', *The Monmouthshire Antiquary*, 16 (2000), 84–98.

in early 1282, while the Breviate and Cottonian chronicles ended respectively in 1286 and 1288. True, translations of Geoffrey of Monmouth and the *Vita Griffini filii Conani* were made in or by the early thirteenth century, an important indication of the kinds of historical writing which appealed to (presumably lay) Welsh readers and listeners of that period who were unfamiliar with Latin. And, as we have seen, *O Oes Gwrtheyrn* probably represents a pioneering attempt to compose a Welsh-language chronicle in the age of Llywelyn ab Iorwerth. However, the use of the vernacular was extended significantly in the early fourteenth century with the creation of *Ystorya Dared*, a translation of the *De excidio Troiae historia* attributed to Dares the Phrygian,[60] as well as of *Brut y Tywysogyon* and the related chronicle known as *Brenhinedd y Saesson* ('The Kings of the English'). Welsh was likewise the language of almost all other historical texts composed in fourteenth- and fifteenth-century Wales, which formed an integral part of a wider vernacular literary culture patronized by the gentry.[61] Until the mid-fourteenth century, texts continued to be produced mainly in Cistercian monasteries, symbols of the old order whose memory they served to perpetuate, most visibly as the burial places of their princely patrons and benefactors. Thereafter lay scribes and patrons were largely responsible for book production, although some maintained close links with religious houses: Gutun Owain is a notable example in the second half of the fifteenth century, as we shall see.[62]

The creation of *Brut y Tywysogyon* affords further evidence of Geoffrey of Monmouth's continuing, indeed growing, influence on medieval Welsh historiography. As argued above, it is uncertain whether the conception of the chronicle as a work beginning in 682 as a continuation of Geoffrey's *De gestis Britonum* originated in a lost Latin chronicle (sometimes referred to as the 'Latin *Brut*') completed shortly after the Edwardian conquest. The idea could equally well have originated with the first compiler of *Brut y Tywysogyon* itself,

---

[60] Helen Fulton, 'Troy Story: The Medieval Welsh *Ystorya Dared* and the *Brut* Tradition of British History', in *The Medieval Chronicle VII*, ed. by Juliana Dresvina and Nicholas Sparks (Amsterdam: Rodopi, 2011), pp. 137–50. For editions of *Ystorya Dared*, see Benjamin G. Owens, 'Y Fersiynau Cymraeg o *Dares Phrygius* (*Ystoria Dared*), eu Tarddiad, eu Nodweddion, a'u Cydberthynas' (unpubl. MA thesis, University of Wales, 1951).

[61] Helen Fulton, 'Literature of the Welsh Gentry: Uses of the Vernacular in Medieval Wales', in *Vernacularity in England and Wales c. 1300–1550*, ed. by Elisabeth Salter and Helen Wicker (Turnhout: Brepols, 2011), pp. 199–223.

[62] Huws, *Medieval Welsh Manuscripts*, p. 16; Andrew Abram, 'Monastic Burial in Medieval Wales', in *Monastic Wales*, ed. by Burton and Stöber, pp. 103–15 (pp. 104, 109).

adapting one or more Latin chronicles beginning before 682, at some point between 1282 and *c.* 1330. Be that as it may, the work survived only in Welsh. The author was evidently familiar with one or more Welsh versions of Geoffrey's *De gestis Britonum* (*Brut y Brenhinedd*) as well as with earlier Welsh chronicles maintained at Cistercian houses and ultimately deriving from St Davids.

Both the Peniarth 20 and Red Book of Hergest versions of *Brut y Tywysogyon* open with an annal which adapts the notice in the Harleian chronicle of Cadwaladr ap Cadwallon's death in 'a great plague' in 682 and draws on the conclusion of Geoffrey's work, faithfully translated in the earliest versions of *Brut y Brenhinedd*, to relate that Cadwaladr died in Rome, before declaring, to quote the Peniarth 20 version, that 'thenceforth the Britons lost the crown of kingship, and the Saxons obtained it, as Myrddin [Merlin] had prophesied to Gwrtheyrn Wrthenau [Vortigern the Very Thin]' (W. 'Ac o hyny allan y kolles y Brytanyeid goron teyrnas, ac y kafas y Saesson hi, megys y proffwydassei Uerðin wrth Wrtheyrn Wrtheneu').[63] The passage continues by relating how Cadwaladr was succeeded by Ifor, son of Alan, King of Brittany, 'not as king but as leader' (W. 'nid megys brenin namyn megys tywyssawc'), who 'held dominion over the Britons for forty-eight years' (W. 'a gynhelis pennaduryaeth ar y Brytannyeid wyth mlyneð a deugeint'), before being succeeded in turn by Rhodri Molwynog.[64] The reference to prophecy echoes the passage in Geoffrey which states that God did not wish the Britons to rule any longer in Britain 'until the time came which Merlin had foretold to Arthur' (L. 'antequam tempus illud uenisset quod Merlinus Arturo prophetauerat').[65] However, rather than reproduce that passage, with its hope of ultimate deliverance, *Brut y Tywysogyon* emphasizes the finality of the Britons' loss of sovereignty and, instead of naming Arthur, alludes to Geoffrey's account of Merlin's prophecies to Vortigern, the king blamed in medieval Welsh literary and historical texts

---

[63] *Brenhinoedd y Saeson*, pp. 4–5. See also *BT (Pen. 20 trans,)*, p. 1, and notes at pp. 129–30; and cf. *Annales Cambriae*, ed. and trans. by Dumville, p. 2.

[64] *BT (Pen. 20 trans.)*, p. 1 (s.a. 682); *BT (Pen. 20)*, p. 1.

[65] Geoffrey of Monmouth, *The History of the Kings of Britain: An Edition and Translation of De gestis Britonum [Historia Regum Britanniae]*, ed. by Michael D. Reeve, trans. by Neil Wright (Woodbridge: Boydell, 2007), p. 279 (§ 205); *Brut Dingestow*, ed. by Henry Lewis (Cardiff: University of Wales Press, 1942), p. 206; Aberystwyth, NLW, MS Llanstephan 1, p. 204 (incomplete), in *Rhyddiaith y 13eg Ganrif: Fersiwn 2.0*, transcribed, reformatted, and emended by Graham R. Isaac and others (2013), downloaded from <http://cadair.aber.ac.uk/dspace/handle/2160/11163> [accessed 6 April 2018], p. [120].

as the traitor responsible for inviting the English to Britain.⁶⁶ The description of Cadwaladr's successor as *tywyssawc* ('leader' or 'prince') rather than *brenin* ('king') likewise underlines the Britons' defeat, albeit by developing a distinction between Welsh 'leaders' and English 'kings' drawn in *Brut y Brenhinedd* but lacking in Geoffrey's *De gestis Britonum*, which states that both peoples were ruled by *reges* ('kings') after the English conquest.⁶⁷ The clear implication, then, was that the events thereafter related in *Brut y Tywysogyon* concerned the Britons, or Welsh, after their loss of sovereignty over the island of Britain; *Brut y Tywysogyon* was thus explicitly linked to a cardinal tenet of historical thinking in Wales from the time of Gildas onwards.

In terms of their length, different versions, and the number of surviving manuscripts, the Welsh translations of Geoffrey's *De gestis Britonum* were by far the most popular and influential historical works in later medieval Wales.⁶⁸ It is quite likely that Dares Phrygius was translated specifically in order to provide a prequel to Geoffrey of Monmouth, just as *Brut y Tywysogyon* was conceived as its sequel, and that the three vernacular works — *Ystorya Dared*, *Brut y Brenhinedd*, and *Brut y Tywysogyon* — were a cultural response to conquest that emphasized the deep roots and distinctive history of the Welsh people.

---

⁶⁶ Geoffrey of Monmouth, *History*, pp. 144–59 (§§111–17). Cf. *Trioedd Ynys Prydein: The Triads of the Island of Britain*, ed. and trans. by Rachel Bromwich, 2nd edn (Cardiff: University of Wales Press, 1978), pp. 392–96. It should be noted, though, that Gwrtheyrn is substituted for Arthur in a Welsh version of Geoffrey extant in London, BL, MS Cotton Cleopatra B V (s. xiv¹), copied at Valle Crucis by the same hand as Aberystwyth, NLW, MS Peniarth 20 containing *Brut y Tywysogyon*: *Brut y Brenhinedd, Cotton Cleopatra Version*, ed. by John Jay Parry (Cambridge, MA: The Mediaeval Academy of America, 1937), p. 216; cf. *BS*, pp. xvi–xviii; Huws, *Medieval Welsh Manuscripts*, pp. 53, 59. This could, perhaps, suggest that the adaptation of the passage in *Brut y Tywysogyon* originated with the Valle Crucis scribe who wrote both the Cotton Cleopatra version of *Brut y Brenhinedd* and the Peniarth 20 version of *Brut y Tywysogyon* (the text of *Brenhinedd y Saesson* copied by the same scribe in MS Cotton Cleopatra B V omits the prophecy altogether and links the chronicle to Geoffrey's *De gestis Britonum* differently from *Brut y Tywysogyon*, as explained below).

⁶⁷ *Brut Dingestow*, p. 208; *Brut y Brenhinedd: Cotton Cleopatra Version*, pp. 217–18; Geoffrey of Monmouth, *History*, pp. 280–81 (§ 208).

⁶⁸ At least four versions of *Brut y Brenhinedd* have been identified, extant in about twenty-two manuscripts datable between *c.* 1300 and *c.* 1540: Patrick Sims-Williams, 'The Welsh Versions of Geoffrey of Monmouth's "History of the Kings of Britain"', in *Adapting Texts and Styles in a Celtic Context: Interdisciplinary Perspectives on Processes of Literary Transfer in the Middle Ages*, ed. by Axel Harlos and Neele Harlos (Münster: Nodus Publikationen, 2016), pp. 53–74, esp. pp. 58–59, 62–64; *Liber Coronacionis Britanorum*, ed. by Patrick Sims-Williams, 2 vols (Aberystwyth: CMCS Publications, 2017), II, 1–2; O. W. Jones, 'Historical Writing', p. 431.

Archbishop Pecham's call in 1284 for the Welsh to be weaned from their belief in their Trojan origins evidently fell on deaf ears.[69] Moreover, some scribes and patrons, at least, understood the three works as forming a historical continuum that narrated the making of the Welsh from Troy to the end of the age of the princes, since they follow each other in several manuscripts from the mid-fourteenth century onwards, or else combine *Brut y Brenhinedd* with just one of the other works.[70] Despite being first attested as preceding *Ystorya Dared* in a late fifteenth-century manuscript, discussed below, it is also possible that *Y Bibyl Ynghymraec*, the Welsh translation datable to *c*. 1300 of the *Compendium Historiae in Genealogia Christi* attributed to Peter of Poitiers, which provides an account of biblical history beginning with the Creation, was conceived from the outset as forming part of the historical continuum, as it adds a passage making Aeneas a descendant of Japhet son of Noah and refers to both *Brut y Brenhinedd* and *Ystorya Dared*.[71]

One indication of the central position occupied by the Welsh versions of Geoffrey in the later Middle Ages is the survival of manuscripts copied by members of the laity, apparently for their own use. Thus in 1444 Dafydd ap Maredudd Glais copied a text of *Brut y Brenhinedd*, to which he appended his own Welsh translation of a Latin version of *Brenhinedd y Saesson*, tasks quite possibly undertaken while banished from Aberystwyth following his murder of two members of a rival family, and it is likely that an Anglesey landowner produced the extensively illustrated copy of *Brut y Brenhinedd* in Aberystwyth, NLW, MS Peniarth 23, datable to *c*. 1500.[72] The continuing appeal of Geoffrey's *De gestis Britonum* was probably both aesthetic and ideological, as its fast-

---

[69] *Registrum Epistolarum Fratris Johannis Peckham, Archiepiscopi Cantuariensis*, ed. by Charles Trice Martin, Rolls Series, 77, 3 vols (London: Longman, 1882–85), II (1884), 741–42.

[70] For the earliest examples, see O. W. Jones, 'Historical Writing', p. 431.

[71] *Y Bibyl Ynghymraec, sef Cyfieithiad Cymraeg Canol o'r "Promptuarium Bibliae"*, ed. by Thomas Jones (Cardiff: University of Wales Press, 1940), esp. pp. xlvi–xlvii, 63; Thomas Jones, 'Historical Writing in Medieval Welsh', *Scottish Studies*, 12 (1968), 15–27 (pp. 17–18); O. W. Jones, 'Historical Writing', pp. 49–50. For the title *Compendium Historiae in Genealogia Christi* (rather than *Promptuarium Bibliae*), see Philip S. Moore, *The Works of Peter of Poitiers, Master in Theology and Chancellor of Paris (1193–1205)* (Notre Dame, IN: [University of Notre Dame], 1936), ch. 4. My thanks to Ben Guy for drawing this point to my attention and for the reference.

[72] Katherine Himsworth, 'Dafydd ap Maredudd Glais: A Fifteenth-Century Aberystwyth Felon and Scribe', *Welsh History Review*, 28 (2016–17), 269–82; Katherine Himsworth, 'A Fifteenth-Century *Brenhinedd y Saesson*, Written by the Aberystwyth Scribe, Dafydd ap Maredudd Glais', *Studia Celtica*, 51 (2017), 129–49; *Liber Coronacionis Britanorum*, II, 5–6.

paced narrative of the Britons' triumphs, betrayals, and eventual loss of the sovereignty of Britain provided not only entertainment but an explanation for the position of the Welsh in the present.

Further evidence of an attempt to connect Geoffrey's *De gestis Britonum* to later history is provided by *Brenhinedd y Saesson* ('The Kings of the English').[73] This may be seen as a variant of *Brut y Tywysogyon* which sought to combine the histories of the Welsh and English kings, thereby combining in one text the two separate tasks Geoffrey left respectively to Caradog of Llancarfan and to Henry of Huntingdon and William of Malmesbury.[74] The work survives in several versions. The earliest occurs in London, BL, MS Cotton Cleopatra B V, a manuscript written *c.* 1330 at Valle Crucis Abbey, where it follows a version of *Brut y Brenhinedd* by the same translator and in the same hand.[75] This version covers the years 682–1198, though it may have originally continued further, as the manuscript is incomplete and breaks off at that point.[76] Two later versions copied by Gutun Owain, which continue to 1461, will be considered below.[77] As we have seen, a related Latin text was translated into Welsh in 1444 by Dafydd ap Maredudd Glais.[78] The Cotton Cleopatra version of *Brut y Brenhinedd* was clearly intended to precede *Brenhinedd y Saesson*, as it alters Geoffrey's conclusion, accurately reproduced in other Welsh translations, by naming Caradog of Llancarfan as the writer to whom was left the history, not only of the Welsh princes, but also of the kings of the English, thereby removing the reference to Henry of Huntingdon and William of Malmesbury as the preferred authors of the latter. Likewise, the allusions to Geoffrey at the beginning of *Brenhinedd y Saesson* are much fuller than those that provide a link with him in *Brut y Tywysogyon*, mainly by providing details of the Saxon conquests of Britain.[79]

Brenhinedd y Saesson resembled *Brut y Tywysogyon*, then, by conceiving of the history of the Welsh after the late seventh century as a continuation

---

[73] *BS*; Smith, 'Historical Writing'. See also Barry Lewis, Chapter 5, this volume.

[74] Geoffrey of Monmouth, *History*, pp. 280–81 (§ 208).

[75] *BS*, pp. xvi–xviii.

[76] *BS*, pp. xxxix–xl. See also Ben Guy's discussion, Chapter 3, this volume.

[77] *BS*, pp. xiv, 329.

[78] Himsworth, 'Fifteenth-Century *Brenhinedd y Saesson*'. The text in Dafydd's manuscript is incomplete, breaking off in the reign of Edward the Confessor.

[79] *Brut y Brenhinedd: Cotton Cleopatra Version*, pp. 217–18; *BS*, pp. 2–5; Smith, 'Historical Writing', pp. 59–60, 61, 65–66.

of the history of the Britons related by Geoffrey of Monmouth. In its earliest Cotton Cleopatra version, *Brenhinedd y Saesson* falls into two main sections. The first covers events in Wales and England from 682 to 1095, and draws on three principal sources: a Welsh Latin chronicle similar to that underlying *Brut y Tywysogyon*, Winchester annals, and William of Malmesbury's *Gesta regum Anglorum* ('Deeds of the Kings of the English'). This preserves the entries from the Latin sources of *Brut y Tywysogyon* virtually intact, in contrast to the second section, a continuation that breaks off in 1198 and that focuses mainly on Wales, where they are condensed. Here, the attempt to combine Welsh and English history is largely abandoned, though some entries are still derived from English sources; these have particularly close parallels with the Latin chronicle from Glamorgan that ended in 1298 mentioned above.[80] In his comprehensive study, J. Beverley Smith has argued that the different Latin sources had already been combined *c.* 1300 in a Latin chronicle, possibly at the Cistercian monastery of Neath in South Wales, whence a copy reached Valle Crucis by *c.* 1330, where it was translated into Welsh as *Brenhinedd y Saesson*.[81]

Accounts of events after the Edwardian conquest provide further evidence of the continuing salience of the framework provided by Geoffrey's *De gestis Britonum*. Most of these are set against the backdrop of the ancient history of the Britons, either as continuations of chronicles in turn conceived as continuations of the Welsh versions of Geoffrey (*Brut y Brenhinedd*), or as short independent texts. The former occur in the Peniarth 20 version of *Brut y Tywysogyon*, composed at Valle Crucis, and the versions of *Brenhinedd y Saesson* written by Gutun Owain, discussed below. The Peniarth 20 continuation, whose scribe is also that of the Cotton Cleopatra version of *Brenhinedd y Saesson*, narrates events from the outbreak of war on Palm Sunday 1282 to Edward Balliol's attempt to gain the throne of Scotland in 1332.[82] David Stephenson has argued that the continuation falls into two main parts, one extending to 1319, followed by annals for 1320–1329 indebted to information provided by Madog ap Llywelyn (d. 1332), a prominent Welsh magnate and office-holder, who also contributed to subsequent entries made for 1330–1331; the last entries were written in 1332 after Madog's death.[83] The section covering 1282–1332 throws significant light on historical thinking at Valle Crucis

---

[80] *BS*, pp. xiii–xiv; Smith, 'Historical Writing', pp. 60–67, 70–72.

[81] Smith, 'Historical Writing', esp. pp. 60, 81–86.

[82] *BT (Pen. 20 trans.)*, pp. lxii–lxiii, 120–27; *BS*, pp. xvi–xviii.

[83] See David Stephenson, Chapter 6, this volume.

c. 1330 in its insistence that the history of the Britons and Welsh that originated in Troy had continued beyond the Edwardian conquest to the scribe's own day.[84] In addition, three independent chronicles set post-conquest events in a Galfridian framework. *Brut y Saeson* ('The History of the English'), versions of which are extant in three related manuscripts of the late fourteenth or early fifteenth century, gives an account of the kings of England from the death of Cadwaladr to the reign of Richard II (1377–1399), and provides a striking witness to how long-established notions in Wales of the Britons' loss of sovereignty over Britain could sustain an interest in English as well as Welsh history.[85] Two other short chronicles adopt an even longer timeframe. One, a Latin text composed in Glamorgan, and also extant in an abridged version datable to 1404, extends from the coming of Brutus to Britain in 1230 BC to 1375.[86] The other, in Welsh, extant in manuscripts from *c.* 1400 onwards and known as *Blwydyn Eiseu* (after its opening words), sets the history of the Britons in the context of Christian history, opening with the Creation and Incarnation before recording Brutus's arrival, likewise placed in 1230 BC. This survives in two versions, of which the earlier continued to 1321.[87] However, several early modern manuscripts contain a later version, which they attribute to a 'book of William Llŷn' (presumably the poet of that name who died in 1580), which extends the narrative to the coronation of Henry VI in 1422 and provides the fullest Welsh account of the rising of Owain Glyndŵr.[88]

---

[84] Gifford and Thomas M. Charles-Edwards, 'The Continuation of *Brut y Tywysogion* in Peniarth MS. 20', in *Ysgrifau a Cherddi Cyflwynedig i / Essays and Poems Presented to Daniel Huws*, ed. by Tegwyn Jones and E. B. Fryde (Aberystwyth: NLW, 1994), pp. 293–305 (pp. 300–04).

[85] *Brut y Saeson*, in *The Text of the Bruts from the Red Book of Hergest*, ed. by John Rhŷs and J. Gwenogvryn Evans (Oxford: Evans, 1890), pp. 385–403. The other complete version, in Aberystwyth, NLW, MS Peniarth 32, fols 125ᵛ–32ᵛ, is transcribed in *RG* <http://www.rhyddiaithganoloesol.caerdydd.ac.uk/en/ms-page.php?ms = Pen32&page = 251> [accessed 5 April 2018]. The version in Aberystwyth, NLW, MS Peniarth 19 breaks off in AD 979. See O. W. Jones, 'Historical Writing', pp. 43–44, 282; Huws, *Medieval Welsh Manuscripts*, p. 60.

[86] *Epitome Historiæ Britanniæ*, in *Lives of the Cambro British Saints*, ed. and trans. by William J. Rees, Society for the Publication of Ancient Welsh Manuscripts, [4] (Llandovery: Rees, 1853), pp. 278–86, 612–22; Diana Luft, 'The NLW Peniarth 32 Latin Chronicle', *Studia Celtica*, 44 (2010), 47–70.

[87] See Rebecca Try, Chapter 10, this volume.

[88] Aberystwyth, NLW, MS Cwrtmawr 453, pp. 91–109; NLW, MS 2023B, pp. 409–19; NLW, MS 1992B (Panton 23), pp. 210–29; NLW, MS Peniarth 135, pp. 49–65 (without attribution to the 'book of William Llŷn'). The Annals of Owain Glyndŵr attributed to a book of

In addition, three short chronicles open in the thirteenth century without reference to Galfridian origins: notices of events focused on south-east Wales from 1294 to 1348 composed in Latin at Abergavenny Priory, extant in a manuscript copied *c.* 1400;[89] brief Latin annals copied by the antiquary Robert Vaughan of Hengwrt (1591/92–1667) covering the period from the death of Llywelyn ap Gruffudd in 1282 to 1448;[90] and an eighteenth-century copy of annals in Welsh from 1251 to 1501.[91] Also relevant in this context is a collection of historical notices written in various fifteenth-century hands in or near Oswestry. These mostly record events between 1400 and 1461 (among them the rising and death of Owain Glyndŵr) but also include references to the deaths of Thomas Becket in 1170 and 'Llywelyn Prince of Wales' (L. 'Lewelini principis Walie') in 1282.[92]

Gutun Owain

The continuing vigour in late medieval Wales of the master narrative of the Britons and Welsh and its use as a framework for the history of recent events is vividly attested by the work of Gutun Owain.[93] A member of a Welsh gentry

---

Lewys Morgannwg (the bardic name of Llywelyn ap Rhisiart, fl. 1520–1565) copied by Evan Evans *c.* 1776, cover only 1400–1415: NLW, MS 1991B (Panton 22), fols 1–4. For editions and translations of the annals for 1400–1415, based mainly on MS Peniarth 135, see John Edward Lloyd, *Owen Glendower: Owen Glyndŵr* (Oxford: Clarendon Press, 1931), pp. 149–54; *Owain Glyndŵr: A Casebook*, ed. by Michael Livingston and John K. Bollard (Liverpool: Liverpool University Press, 2013), pp. 172–75, 371–79.

[89] Eric St John Brooks, 'The *Piers Plowman* Manuscripts in Trinity College, Dublin', *The Library*, 5th ser., 6.4–5 (1951), 141–53 (pp. 141, 144–51); David Stephenson, Chapter 6, this volume.

[90] Aberystwyth, NLW, MS 9092D: <https://archives.library.wales/index.php/brut-y-tywysogion-10> [accessed 5 April 2018].

[91] Aberystwyth, NLW, MS 2008B (Panton 40): *RMWL*, II (1902–10), 849–50. See also Ben Guy's discussion of other chronicles in early modern manuscripts that continue to the sixteenth century in Chapter 3 of this volume.

[92] J. R. S. Phillips, 'When Did Owain Glyn Dŵr Die?', *BBCS*, 24 (1970–72), 59–77 (pp. 67–69, 73–76 (quotation at p. 74)); Gruffydd Aled Williams, *The Last Days of Owain Glyndŵr* (Talybont: Y Lolfa, 2017), pp. 46–48.

[93] Gruffydd Aled Williams, 'Owain, Gutun [Gruffudd ap Huw ab Owain]' (*fl. c.*1451–1498)', *Oxford Dictionary of National Biography*, <https://doi.org/10.1093/ref:odnb/20982>; J. E. Caerwyn Williams, 'Gutun Owain', in *A Guide to Welsh Literature 1282–c.1550*, ed. by A. O. H. Jarman and Gwilym Rees Hughes, rev. by Dafydd Johnston (Cardiff: University of Wales Press, 1997), pp. 240–55; Huws, *Medieval Welsh Manuscripts*, p. 62;

family from the Welsh-speaking border with Shropshire who held land in the lordship of Oswestry and enjoyed close links with the abbey of Valle Crucis, Gutun was a poet and a prolific scribe whose manuscripts, written over more than four decades, included works of medicine, astrology, hagiography, and grammar as well as genealogy, heraldry, and history. Moreover, since a significant number of his manuscripts were produced for Welsh gentry patrons, both laymen and Cistercian abbots in north-east Wales, they attest to a wider interest in the learning they contained among contemporaries of a similar social background.[94] The same is true, on a more limited scale, of Gutun's South Walian contemporary, the poet Ieuan Brechfa (fl. *c.* 1490–*c.* 1520), whose works included genealogical manuscripts and a chronicle based on the Red Book of Hergest version of *Brut y Tywysogyon* for 720–1079, supplemented by other sources.[95] In the context of the present discussion, Gutun is particularly significant as a representative of Welsh bardic learning and culture who sought to preserve the legacy of medieval interpretations of the past and make them serviceable for the native elites of his own time. Thus, while deeply conservative, he developed a dynamic approach based on an increasing mastery of the texts he read and brought his own editorial imprint to bear on the manuscripts he copied. In addition, Gutun expanded the boundaries of Welsh-language learning by assimilating historical writing and other material, notably medical texts, from England.

Gutun wrote at least three manuscripts containing historical narratives. The best known is the Black Book of Basingwerk (Aberystwyth, NLW, MS 7006D), probably written at Valle Crucis Abbey. This contains texts of Dares Phrygius (*Ystorya Dared*), *Brut y Brenhinedd*, and *Brenhinedd y Saesson*, thereby exemplifying the historical continuum extending from Troy to medieval

---

Ann T. E. Matonis, 'A Case Study: Historical and Textual Aspects of the Welsh Bardic Grammar', *CMCS*, 41 (2001), 25–36; Ann T. E. Matonis, 'Gutun Owain and His Orbit: The Welsh Bardic Grammar and Its Cultural Context in Northeast Wales', *Zeitschrift für celtische Philologie*, 54 (2004), 154–69; Morfydd E. Owen, 'Prolegomena i Astudiaeth Lawn o Lsgr. NLW 3026, Mostyn 88 a'i Harwyddocâd', in *Cyfoeth y Testun: Ysgrifau ar Lenyddiaeth Gymraeg yr Oesoedd Canol*, ed. by R. Iestyn Daniel and others (Cardiff: University of Wales Press, 2003), pp. 349–84; O. W. Jones, 'Historical Writing', pp. 47–51, 59–60, 76–77, 108, 114–18, 121.

[94] For Gutun's patrons, see Glanmor Williams, *The Welsh Church from Conquest to Reformation*, rev. edn (Cardiff: University of Wales Press, 1976), pp. 263, 284; David J. Bowen, 'Guto'r Glyn a Glyn-y-Groes', *Ysgrifau Beirniadol*, 20 (1995), 149–83 (pp. 158–60); Owen, 'Prolegomena i Astudiaeth Lawn o Lsgr', pp. 351–52, 372–74.

[95] See Ben Guy, Chapter 11, this volume.

Wales.⁹⁶ The version of *Brenhinedd y Saesson* largely reproduced the material down to 1198 found in the early fourteenth-century Cotton Cleopatra version of *Brenhinedd y Saesson*, which Gutun very probably copied. It is uncertain whether he added the section covering 1198–1332 derived from the Peniarth 20 and Red Book versions of *Brut y Tywysogyon*, as this may originally have been contained in the now lacunose Cotton Cleopatra manuscript whose narrative breaks off in 1198. If the latter, Gutun was responsible only for the final section from 1346 to the accession of Edward IV in 1461; he also added further details to the account of the period down to (at least) 1198.⁹⁷ Second, the lost paper folio manuscript held at Llannerch (Denbighshire) in the eighteenth century contained a similar combination of texts, namely *Ystorya Dared* followed by versions of both *Brenhinedd y Saesson* and *Brut y Tywysogyon*.⁹⁸ Third, and most ambitious in scope, is a paper volume (Oxford, Jesus College, MS 141), written 1471 × c. 1500, probably for Gutun's personal use.⁹⁹ Now misbound and incomplete, this assembled a compendium of historical texts in Welsh comprising a world chronicle beginning with Adam (including part of *Y Bibyl Ynghymraec*), followed by *Ystorya Dared*, an expanded version of *Brut y Brenhinedd*, and a version of *Brenhinedd y Saesson* that continued to 1461.¹⁰⁰ The manuscript also contains a description of Britain (*Disgrifiad o*

---

⁹⁶ *BS*, pp. xviii–xx; O. W. Jones, 'Historical Writing', pp. 47, 59–60, 75–76, 114. Gutun copied about 75 per cent of the manuscript, the texts of *Ystorya Dared* and the first part of *Brut y Brenhinedd* being in the hand of an older contemporary.

⁹⁷ *BS*, pp. xiv, 272–77; O. W. Jones, 'Historical Writing', pp. 47–49; Ben Guy's discussion of *Brenhinedd y Saesson* in Chapter 3.

⁹⁸ A. O. H. Jarman, 'Lewis Morris a Brut Tysilio', *Llên Cymru*, 2 (1953), 161–83 (pp. 174–78).

⁹⁹ *RMWL*, II, 35–38. For the date, see Daniel Huws, *A Repertory of Welsh Manuscripts and Scribes* (forthcoming), s.n. Jesus 141 (which corrects the dating of c. 1499 proposed in Daniel Huws, 'Rhestr Gutun Owain o Wŷr wrth Gerdd', *Dwned*, 10 (2004), 79–88 (p. 81)). See also *Y Bibyl Ynghymraec*, pp. lix–lxi; Phillips, 'When Did Owain Glyn Dŵr Die?', pp. 69, 73; Brynley F. Roberts, '*Ystoriaeu Brenhinedd Ynys Brydeyn*: A Fourteenth-Century Welsh Brut', in *Narrative in Celtic Tradition: Essays in Honor of Edgar M. Slotkin*, ed. by Joseph F. Eska, CSANA Yearbook, 8–9 (Hamilton, NY: Colgate University Press, 2011), pp. 217–27 (p. 223); O. W. Jones, 'Historical Writing', pp. 49–51.

¹⁰⁰ Digitized images of the manuscript available at 'Digital Bodleian: Welsh Chronicles', <https://digital.bodleian.ox.ac.uk/inquire/p/65e8406f-265c-47f2-ae09-d2c860d6e671> [accessed 5 April 2018]. Although the continuation of *Brenhinedd y Saesson* in Jesus College, MS 141 breaks off in 1459 (fol. 123ᵛ), a stray folio now bound in Aberystwyth, NLW, MS 1585D, fol. 132ʳ⁻ᵛ shows that it originally continued at least to the accession of Edward IV in 1461: cf. Benjamin G. Owens, 'Llawysgrifau N.L.W. 1585 a J.C. 141', *NLWJ*, 7 (1951–52), 271–72.

Ynys Brydain) originally translated into Welsh in 1471 from Ranulf Higden's Latin *Polychronicon*, together with other material on early British history as well as the oldest surviving copy of the fifteenth-century heraldic treatise *Llyfr Dysgread Arfau*.[101]

The versions of *Brenhinedd y Saesson* in the Black Book of Basingwerk and Jesus College, MS 141 throw valuable light on Gutun's approach to history writing. Comparison of the former version with that in MS Cotton Cleopatra B V, its source down to 1198, shows that Gutun engaged critically with the text, as he not only rephrased passages but also provided further details concerning both English and Welsh rulers.[102] Particular attention was paid to kinship ties. For example, the annal recording the death of Rhodri Mawr in 878 adds the names of his parents, traces his mother's pedigree back to Cadwaladr the Blessed, and corrects the identification of the kinsman killed with Rhodri as his son (rather than brother).[103] Likewise, in observing that the West Saxon dynasty ended with Edward the Confessor, Gutun traced his pedigree back to Ecgberht, 'the first king of the English who brought the kingdoms of England under one rule' ('y brenhin kyntaf o'r Saesson a oresgynnws teyrnas Lloegyr yn vn'), while, most strikingly, the version of *Brenhinedd y Saesson* in the lost Llannerch manuscript reportedly included 'Pedigrees of the Kings beautifully

---

[101] Jesus College, MS 141, fols 124ᵛ–50ᵛ; Michael D. Siddons, *The Development of Welsh Heraldry*, 4 vols (Aberystwyth: NLW, 1991–2006), I (1991), 31–33; Thomas Jones, 'Syr Thomas ap Ieuan ap Deicws a'i Gyfaddasiad Cymraeg o "Fasciculus Temporum" Werner Rolewinck', *THSC*, 1943–1944 [1946], 35–61 (pp. 46–49). The 'Description of Britain' is preceded by a statement that the work had been translated in 1471 for the benefit of those lacking books. The date therefore does not refer, as implied in *RMWL*, II, 35, to the last year of the continuation of *Brenhinedd y Saesson* (which appears to have ended in 1461): Jones, 'Syr Thomas ap Ieuan ap Deicws', p. 48. It is unknown whether Gutun was the translator or simply copied an earlier translation.

[102] For differences between the texts of the chronicle down to 1198 in NLW, MS 7006D and MS Cotton Cleopatra B V, see the textual notes in *BS*, pp. 2–195. To judge by its legible portions, the version of *Brenhinedd y Saesson* in Jesus College, MS 141 was a different adaptation of the Cotton Cleopatra text from that in NLW, MS 7006D: Jesus College, MS 141, fols 48ᵛ–58ᵛ, 102ʳ–03ᵛ.

[103] *BS*, p. 24 and n. 13 (trans. in *BS*, p. 25 and n. 1). For other examples of additional genealogical detail, see *BS*, pp. 78 and n. 19, 162 and n. 17, 168 and n. 19 (trans. in *BS*, pp. 79 and n. 1, 163 and n. 2, 169 and n. 2). Although such additions seem to be mostly accurate, Gutun misidentified two notables in south-east Wales as members of the dynasty of Gwynedd: *BS*, p. 158 and nn. 22–23.

drawn'.[104] These examples highlight the importance Gutun attached to genealogy as a means of apprehending the past. As Ben Guy has shown, his growing mastery of this material is demonstrated by his four surviving genealogical manuscripts, written between c. 1456 and 1497, which reveal Gutun's increasing skill and sophistication as an editor who adapted existing accounts to serve the needs of his own day.[105] As well as rearranging material from earlier collections these manuscripts contain numerous innovations, especially new sections on the pedigrees of the gentry and the earliest copies of the lists of the 'Five Kingly Tribes of Wales' and 'Fifteen Tribes of Gwynedd', schemes attributing medieval founders to the dynasties and families concerned.[106] Furthermore, his latest extant genealogical collection, Manchester, John Rylands Library, MS Welsh 1 (1497), explicitly linked the pedigrees from Brutus 'to the old tribes which were before this age' (W. 'hyd yr hen llwytha6 a v6ant kynn yr oes honn'), extant in a collection originating in the age of Llywelyn ab Iorwerth, to 'the nobility of this age' (W. 'vonedd yr oes honn') — the gentry pedigrees of contemporaneous kin-groups — that followed in the text.[107]

In addition, Gutun continued the narratives in both versions of *Brenhinedd y Saesson* to the accession of Edward IV in 1461. True, much of the material he recorded for the fourteenth and fifteenth centuries focused on kings of England. Moreover, the much fuller continuation from the accession of Richard II in 1377 onwards in Jesus 141 derives in large measure from the Middle English prose *Brut* chronicle. This originated as a translation of the Anglo-Norman *Brut* towards the end of the fourteenth century, but Gutun appears to have used the first printed edition, which continued to Edward IV's accession in 1461 and was published in 1480 by William Caxton, who almost certainly compiled the work's continuation beyond 1419.[108] The debt to the

---

[104] *BS*, pp. 72–75 (also Jesus College, MS 141, fol. 57[r–v]); Jarman, p. 175.

[105] Ben Guy, 'Medieval Welsh Genealogy: Texts, Contexts and Transmission', 2 vols (unpubl. doctoral thesis, University of Cambridge, 2016), I, 113–18. See also Francis Jones, 'An Approach to Welsh Genealogy', *THSC*, 1948, 303–466 (pp. 352–56); Owen, 'Prolegomena i Astudiaeth Lawn o Lsgr.', pp. 352–54.

[106] Jones, 'Approach to Welsh Genealogy', p. 353; Siddons, I, 381.

[107] Guy, 'Medieval Welsh Genealogy', I, 115.

[108] Jesus College, MS 141, fols 109[r]–23[v]; NLW, MS 1585D, fol. 132[r–v]; William Caxton, *The Cronicles of Englond* (Westminster: Caxton, 1480). For the English *Brut* and Caxton's continuation, see Lister M. Matheson, 'Printer and Scribe: Caxton, the *Polychronicon*, and the Brut', *Speculum*, 60 (1985), 593–614; Lister M. Matheson, *The Prose Brut: The Development of a Middle English Chronicle* (Tempe, AZ: Medieval and Renaissance Texts and Studies, 1998),

Middle English *Brut* is clear, for example, in Gutun's accounts of the Peasants' Revolt in 1381, Jack Cade's rising in 1450, the invention of printing in Mainz (placed around 1456), and the deposition of Henry VI in 1461.[109]

Yet Gutun, in common with the authors of other Welsh chronicles covering the fourteenth and fifteenth centuries, did not present the Welsh as having been completely subsumed in the history of England after the Edwardian conquest. While the English *Brut* seems to have provided a framework for his account of events from 1377 to 1461, Gutun was both highly selective in the passages he translated and supplemented its narrative by drawing on other sources, including material concerning events in Wales. As in his versions of the earlier part of *Brenhinedd y Saesson*, this was largely a matter of supplying additional details such as the names of the Welshmen who captured the Lollard leader Sir John Oldcastle in Powys.[110] However, Gutun went further with respect to Owain Glyndŵr's rising, as he declined to follow the Middle English *Brut*'s hostile treatment and instead reproduced the short account he had already included in the Black Book of Basingwerk.[111] Even so, like Welsh annals charting the rising composed earlier in the fifteenth century, Gutun's account is circumspect and avoids conferring legitimacy on Glyndŵr by referring to him as Prince of Wales.[112]

Gutun Owain thus exemplified a wider assumption among late medieval Welsh writers of history that the canonical narratives of the Welsh past, extending from Troy to the age of Llywelyn ap Gruffudd, should be both conserved and continued. That accounts of events beyond the Edwardian conquest focused mainly on the kings and kingdom of England does not weaken the case

---

pp. 47–49, 157–59, 164–66; Daniel Wakelin, 'Caxton's Exemplar for The Chronicles of England?', *Journal of the Early Book Society for the Study of Manuscripts and Printing History*, 14 (2011), 75–113. The conclusion in 1461 of the short continuation in the Black Book of Basingwerk may indicate that Gutun was acquainted with Caxton's edition by *c.* 1481; however, the verbal parallels with the latter are too few to establish a direct debt and the common terminal date may be coincidental.

[109] Jesus College, MS 141, fols 109^{r-v}, 120^v–21^v, 122^v; NLW, MS 1585D, fol. 132^v; Caxton, sig. r5^v–r6^v, x6^v–x7^v, y1^v, 5^v; cf. Matheson, 'Printer and Scribe', pp. 599–600.

[110] Jesus College, MS 141, fols 113^v–14^r; cf. Caxton, sig. u1^v–u2^r.

[111] *BS*, pp. 274–75; Jesus College, MS 141, fols 114^v–15^r; cf. Caxton, sig. s8^v. Both the passage in Jesus College, MS 141 and the account in a continuation of the English *Brut* to 1419 are edited and translated in *Owain Glyndŵr: A Casebook*, pp. 174–77, 212–13. See also Phillips, 'When Did Owain Glyn Dŵr Die?', pp. 69, 76–77.

[112] See n. 88 above.

for their having been regarded as continuations of an ancient story. To begin with, as we have seen, those accounts still paid some attention to Wales. More fundamentally, though, their Anglocentric emphasis was itself consistent with aspects of Welsh historical writing earlier in the Middle Ages, especially understandings of the past that situated the history of the Welsh and their British ancestors within the orbit of Britain. Indeed, kings of England were arguably an integral component of medieval Welsh historiography. After all, *Brenhinedd y Saesson* had originally been designed as a continuation of Geoffrey of Monmouth's *De gestis Britonum* that combined both Welsh and English history, while, more generally, Welsh chroniclers had long been concerned with the kings of England and their deeds, especially but not exclusively in relation to Wales.[113] After the Edwardian conquest, English political and military history was all the more relevant to readers of Welsh historical texts, as many of the Welsh gentry served the Crown as administrators or soldiers: the episodes in the Hundred Years War with France narrated by Gutun Owain could be seen as pertaining to the history of the Welsh not merely because they were subjects of the king of England but because they fought in royal armies.[114] For Gutun Owain, then, the history of the Welsh in the fourteenth and fifteenth centuries was inextricably linked to the kingdom of England and predicated on loyalty to its monarch, but nevertheless retained a distinctively Welsh inflection — a balance encapsulated in his description of Henry V as 'king of England and Wales' (W. 'vrenin Lloegr a Chymry').[115]

Conclusion

Gutun's historical works provide an instructive vantage point from which to survey Welsh chronicle writing over eight centuries. Their language reflected a wider shift to the use of the vernacular instead of Latin in Welsh historical texts that had begun by the early thirteenth century but gathered momentum from

---

[113] See, for example, Jones, '*Brut y Tywysogion*', pp. 218–22.

[114] *BS*, pp. 272–75; Jesus College, MS 141, fols 115^r–16^v. Cf. R. Rees Davies, *Conquest, Coexistence, and Change: Wales 1063–1415* (Oxford: Oxford University Press, 1987), pp. 409–10, 415–17; M. M. N. Stansfield, 'Prosopography and the Principality of Wales, 1284–1536: The Second Stage', *Medieval Prosopography*, 12 (1991), 1–33, esp. pp. 28–31; Adam Chapman, *Welsh Soldiers in the Later Middle Ages, 1282–1422* (Woodbridge: Boydell, 2015); Antony D. Carr, *The Gentry of North Wales in the Later Middle Ages* (Cardiff: University of Wales Press, 2017), pp. 34–59.

[115] *BS*, pp. 274–75.

the early fourteenth. This in turn was connected to the development in the later Middle Ages of gentry patronage of and participation in a diverse Welsh vernacular literary culture in which chronicles and other historical works, notably genealogies, were a key component. An associated change was the appearance, especially from the later fourteenth century, of professional lay scribes — such as Gutun Owain — and the concomitant decline in the importance of monastic scriptoria as centres for manuscript production. At first sight, the context and purpose of Latin chronicle writing in Wales from the late eighth to late thirteenth centuries were very different. As elsewhere in Europe, chronicles originated as ecclesiastical records of the passing of sacred time, based on tables created to help calculate the correct date of Easter, and indeed for much of the medieval period they reflected the concerns of their ecclesiastical authors, especially in notices of the deaths of churchmen and other events pertaining to churches. Yet neither the early medieval churches nor, from the late eleventh century onwards, Benedictine (predominantly Cistercian) monasteries which kept chronicles in Wales were isolated from the world around them. As in other medieval societies, ecclesiastical communities were dependent on secular rulers and other lords for their lands and protection, and the chronicles they produced paid considerable attention to secular affairs. More specifically, clerical families like that of Sulien at Llanbadarn Fawr shared many of the values of their lay counterparts and negotiated with secular powers, while Cistercian houses founded and endowed by Welsh rulers seem largely to have comprised Welsh monks and lay brothers and aligned themselves politically with their princely patrons and benefactors. Conversely, monasteries in Welsh Marcher lordships had different allegiances that informed their perspectives on the past. The multifaceted relationship of ecclesiastical institutions and the wider society to which they belonged merits further attention in future work on the chronicles. While Gutun Owain is a conspicuous example of a lay scribe and poet in later medieval Wales copying and editing texts written in monastic scriptoria, manuscripts containing Welsh poetry and law were produced in religious houses before the Edwardian conquest, indicating interaction with Welsh poets and lawyers.[116] Such interaction has implications for chronicle writing, too, as it provides further evidence of the porous boundaries between religious houses and lay society, and invites us to think about the writing of chronicles

---

[116] Huws, *Medieval Welsh Manuscripts*, pp. 70–75, 169–92; Huw Pryce, *Native Law and the Church in Medieval Wales* (Oxford: Clarendon Press, 1993), pp. 17–19, 22–28, 29–36; Huw Pryce, 'Lawbooks and Literacy in Medieval Wales', *Speculum*, 75 (2000), 29–67 (pp. 42–43, 46–47).

as collaborative enterprises, involving not only the combined efforts of contemporaneous or successive ecclesiastical scribes but also a close engagement with ruling elites and learned orders in the secular world.[117]

---

[117] I am grateful to Ben Guy for his helpful comments on an earlier version of this chapter.

2. Historical Writing in Europe, *c.* 1100–1300

Björn Weiler

The immediate aim of this chapter is to convey a sense of the European context within which medieval Welsh chronicles were situated. It builds on the premise that historical culture in high medieval Europe was a trans-European phenomenon.[1] Texts by Welsh authors surface in Acre and Champagne, and ones from Germany in Denmark and Croatia. Similarly, there was an expectation that geographical horizons of reporting, and of the sources consulted, extended across the West. That writers of history operated within a shared framework does not, of course, mean that they did so in an identical fashion. Ubiquity does not equal uniformity. We are dealing with a set of patterns, frequently modified, inherently flexible and able to accommodate diverse expectations, genres, languages, as well as the varying preferences, ambitions, and skills of authors, their peers, patrons, and public. However, we will be able to identify what was distinctive about the Welsh experience only once we are aware of how it relates to broader European examples and conventions.

Historical writing was both a social and a cultural practice. It depended on routes and networks of communication for materials to be compiled and consulted, and on an educational and literary infrastructure being in place for writers, readers, and consumers to be instructed and trained.[2] We are, there-

---

[1] For the conceptual framework employed here: Peter Lambert, 'What is Historical Culture?', in *How the Past Was Used: Historical Cultures, c. 750–2000*, ed. by Peter Lambert and Björn Weiler (Oxford: Oxford University Press, 2017), pp. 6–16; and Björn Weiler, 'Themes in Historical Culture', in *How the Past Was Used*, ed. by Lambert and Weiler, pp. 16–48.

[2] I have learned much from Howard S. Becker, *Art Worlds: 25th Anniversary Edition, Updated and Expanded*, 2nd rev. edn (Berkeley: University of California Press, 2008).

fore, dealing not only with individuals, but with whole communities who viewed themselves — and who desired themselves to be seen — as embedded in a wider European culture. That, in turn, required that historical writing was presented in a manner that conformed to general expectations about how history ought to be constructed, verified, and communicated. Sources had to be recognized as such, and standards of truthfulness adhered to. While many of the authors to be discussed here wrote about a distinctive community (a monastery, cathedral, dynasty, or realm), they still did so in relation to, and by drawing on, a culture that transcended in equal measure medieval polities and modern nations.

Let me add a few remarks about the premises on which this chapter builds. Most importantly, it will use 'chronicles' and 'historical writing' interchangeably. After all, the distinction between annals, histories, and chronicles, famously drawn by Gervase of Canterbury, was honoured, even by his contemporaries, largely in its breach. Distinctions of genre were subordinate to the practicalities of recording and recovering the past. Furthermore, this chapter is interested less in interpretations of the past, than in the tools employed to retrieve it. The focus is on how authors compiled the information from which renditions of the past were subsequently fashioned, and on the shared practices they employed in assessing and evaluating that evidence. What follows builds on (and develops further) an important strand in recent scholarship, where greater emphasis has been placed on the training received by chroniclers, the dissemination and reception of history, and on the actual processes by which particular accounts had initially been compiled.[3] However, most studies have centred on just one text or community. That allows for considerable depth of coverage and greatly enhances our understanding of that particular example. Inevitably, though, the broader European framework within which authors and communities operated is in danger of being overlooked. It will take centre stage in this chapter. What, then, was this framework, and how did it come about?

---

[3] See, for instance, Benjamin Pohl, *Dudo of St Quentin's Historia Normannorum: Tradition, Innovation and Memory* (Woodbridge: York Medieval Press, 2015); Piotr Górecki, *The Text and the World: The Henryków Book, Its Authors, and Their Region, 1160–1310* (Oxford: Oxford University Press, 2015); *Medieval Cantors and Their Craft: Music, Liturgy and the Shaping of History, 800–1500*, ed. by Katie Ann-Marie Bugyis, A. B. Kraebel, and Margot E. Fassler (Woodbridge: York Medieval Press, 2017); Miriam Weiss, *Die Chronica maiora des Matthaeus Parisiensis* (Trier: Kliomedia, 2018).

Models and Origins

A start can be made by outlining the models and sources on which writers drew. Let me use the classical texts and Bible as examples,[4] not least because they will help contextualize the remainder of this chapter. Probably around 1120, the English chronicler William of Malmesbury composed the *Polyhistor*, a compilation of passages from classical, biblical, and patristic literature.[5] Among the authors excerpted were St Augustine, Cicero, Pliny the Elder, Valerius Maximus, Ambrose, Aulus Gellius, Martianus Capellanus, Vitruvius, Jerome, Macrobius, Seneca, and Cassiodorus.[6] Who these were and what specific part of their oeuvre William copied is, for the moment, less significant than their range, which stretched from the Late Roman Republic to the end of Empire. They included writers on rhetoric, natural history, theology, philosophy, poetry, history, and architecture. This does not mean that William knew these materials in their entirety. In fact, several passages seem to have been gleaned from summaries in other texts or from florilegia. When introducing Pliny's *Natural History*, for instance, William noted its use by Solinus (a third-century compiler) and Isidore of Seville,[7] while most references to Vitruvius (the first century BCE writer on architecture) were likely taken from a now-lost florilegium.[8] The use of such compilations is by no means uncommon.[9] Here, I would like to focus on the kind of information that William

---

[4] See also: Matthew Kempshall, *Rhetoric and the Writing of History, 400–1500* (Manchester: Manchester University Press, 2011); Ernst Breisach, *Historiography: Ancient, Medieval and Modern*, 3rd edn (Chicago: University of Chicago Press, 2007); Jennifer Harris, 'The Bible and the Meaning of History in the Middle Ages', in *The Practice of the Bible in the Middle Ages: Production, Reception, and Performance in Western Christianity*, ed. by Susan Boynton and Diane J. Reilly (New York: Columbia University Press, 2011), pp. 84–104.

[5] William of Malmesbury, *Polyhistor*, ed. by Helen Testroet Ouelette (Binghamton, NY: Center for Medieval and Early Renaissance Studies, 1982). On William: *Discovering William of Malmesbury*, ed. by Rodney M. Thomson, Emily Dolmans, and Emily A. Winkler (Woodbridge: Boydell, 2017); Rodney M. Thomson, *William of Malmesbury*, rev. edn (Woodbridge: Boydell, 2003).

[6] William of Malmesbury, *Polyhistor*, pp. 157–61.

[7] William of Malmesbury, *Polyhistor*, p. 45.

[8] William of Malmesbury, *Polyhistor*, p. 22.

[9] James Willoughby, 'The Transmission and Circulation of Classical Literature: Libraries and Florilegia', in *The Oxford History of Classical Reception in English Literature*, ed. by David Hopkins and Charles Martindale, 5 vols (Oxford: Oxford University Press, 2012–), I: *800–1558*, ed. by Rita Copeland (2016), pp. 95–120; Mary A. Rouse and Richard H. Rouse,

collated. Obviously, the *Polyhistor* was not a straightforward historical narrative. Most of it provided a compendium of curious facts, like a list of the seven marvels of the ancient world,[10] or matters suitable for contemplation, such as extracts from Seneca's *Epistolae moralium*.[11] This does not mean that it lacked historical content: William recounted the deaths of Alexander the Great and of Socrates,[12] the reign of Tiberius,[13] and the campaigns of Julius Caesar.[14] It was not, however, concerned with providing a continuous narrative of the past, and it certainly did not stray far even into the history of imperial Rome. It is thus all the more striking that pretty much the same set of sources surfaces in William's more conventionally historical works.[15]

William is considered to be among the foremost Latinists of the twelfth century, at least in England. Yet his reading was unusual not its range, but in its depth. Cosmas of Prague, who completed his *Chronica Boemorum c.* 1123, consulted Virgil, Ovid, Horace, Lucan, Cicero, Pliny the Elder, Sallust, St Augustine, Gregory the Great, Isidore of Seville, and the tenth-century chronicler Regino of Prüm.[16] The so-called 'Gallus Anonymus', in turn, who composed the *Gesta principum Polonorum c.* 1110, drew on Sallust, Virgil, Ovid, Horace, and Regino,[17] as well as the eleventh-century German chronicler Thietmar of

---

'Florilegia of Patristic Texts', in *Les genres littéraires dans les sources théologiques et philosophiques médiévales. Définition, critique et exploitation*, ed. by Robert Bultot (Louvain-la-Neuve: Institut d'études médiévales, 1982), pp. 165–80.

[10] William of Malmesbury, *Polyhistor*, p. 22.

[11] William of Malmesbury, *Polyhistor*, pp. 104–05.

[12] William of Malmesbury, *Polyhistor*, pp. 106 (Alexander), 107 (Socrates).

[13] William of Malmesbury, *Polyhistor*, p. 75.

[14] William of Malmesbury, *Polyhistor*, p. 72.

[15] William of Malmesbury, *Gesta regum Anglorum*, ed. and trans. by R. M. Thomson, Michael Winterbottom, and R. A. B. Mynors, 2 vols (Oxford: Clarendon Press, 1998–99), II (1999), 458–63.

[16] Cosmas of Prague, *Chronica Boemorum*, ed. by Bertold Bretholz, MGH, SS rer. Germ., NS, 2 (Berlin: Weidmann, 1923), pp. xxvi–xxxii. On Cosmas: Lisa Wolverton, *Cosmas of Prague: Narrative, Classicism, Politics* (Washington DC: The Catholic University of America Press, 2015).

[17] Regino's text was immensely popular: the nineteenth-century editor counted *c.* 30 manuscripts from the eleventh and twelfth centuries. *Reginonis abbatis Prumiensis Chronicon cum continuatione Treverensi*, ed. by Friedrich Kurze, MGH, SS rer. Germ. (Hanover: Hahn, 1890), pp. xi–xiv.

Merseburg.¹⁸ This list included exemplars of classical Latin (Virgil, Horace, Ovid, Juvenal), ancient and late antique historians and writers of miscellanies (Sallust, Valerius Maximus, Martianus Capellanus, Solinus) or rhetoricians (Cicero), and early Christian authors (Augustine, Gregory, Isidore). A similar range of sources was employed by Otto of Freising (*c.* 1145),¹⁹ Godfrey of Viterbo (*c.* 1190),²⁰ Alberic of Troisfontaines (*c.* 1250),²¹ and Martin of Troppau (*c.* 1280).²² That is, chroniclers from Germany (Otto), Italy (Godfrey), France (Alberic), and Bohemia (Martin) drew on the same materials and models (though not necessarily in the same versions) to fashion their renditions of the past.

A similar picture emerges once we turn to vernacular sources. There, direct quotations from Latin are, of course, more difficult to trace. Yet a lack of immediately recognizable borrowings does not denote a lack of familiarity. Quite to the contrary. The Bryggen Museum in Bergen (Norway) holds a wooden tablet with a runic inscription combining Old Norse with a Latin quotation from Virgil.²³ Likewise, among the earliest texts produced in Iceland was *Trójumanna saga*, a history of Troy based on Dares Phrygius's *De excidio*

---

¹⁸ *Gesta principum Polonorum*, ed. and trans. by Paul W. Knoll and Frank Schaer, with a preface by Thomas N. Bisson (Budapest: Central European University Press, 2003), pp. xxxviii–xl.

¹⁹ Otto of Freising, *Chronica sive historia de duabus civitatibus*, ed. by Alfred Hofmeister, MGH, SS rer. Germ., 2nd edn (Hanover: Hahn, 1912), pp. xcii–xciv: among others, Jerome, St Augustine, Gregory the Great, Isidore of Seville, Boethius, Cicero, Seneca, Virgil, Horace, Ovid, Juvenal, Orosius, Eusebius, Sallust, Dares Phrygius, Josephus, Regino of Prüm.

²⁰ Godfrey of Viterbo, *Opera*, ed. by Georg Waitz, MGH, SS, 22 (Hanover: Hahn, 1872), pp. 3–4: Virgil, Seneca, Juvenal, Ovid, Horace, Jerome, Isidore of Seville, Valerius Maximus, Orosius, Dares Phrygius.

²¹ Alberic of Troisfontaines, *Chronicon*, ed. by Paul Scheffer-Boichorst, MGH, SS, 23 (Hanover: Hahn, 1874), pp. 656–57: Jerome, Augustine, Ambrose, Solinus, Eusebius, Josephus, Orosius, Gregory of Tours, while Regino was replaced by Flodoard of Rheims (the editor did not list literary influences).

²² Martin of Troppau, *Chronicon pontificum et imperatorum*, ed. Ludwig Weiland, MGH, SS, 22 (Leipzig: Hahn, 1872), pp. 391–93: Virgil, Juvenal, Livy, Orosius, Solinus, Isidore of Seville, St Augustine, Gregory the Great, Paul the Deacon.

²³ <http://skaldic.abdn.ac.uk/db.php?if = default&table = mss&id = 15060> [accessed 6 March 2018]. I am grateful to Mark Philpott for this reference. For related examples see Paul Russell, '"Go and Look in the Latin Books": Latin and the Vernacular in Medieval Wales', in *Latin in Medieval Britain*, ed. by Richard Ashdowne and Caroline White (Oxford: Oxford University Press, 2017), pp. 213–46; Birger Munk Olsen, 'Comment peut-on déterminer la popularité d'un texte au Moyen Âge? L'exemple des oeuvres classiques latines', *Interfaces*, 3 (2016), 13–27.

Troiae historia,²⁴ perhaps the most widely read text on Trojan history in the high medieval West.²⁵ In popularity, *Trójumanna saga* was closely followed by Old Norse versions of the Alexander legend.²⁶ Classical influences were not, however, limited to the translation or retelling of texts. Torfi Tulinius has thus pointed to echoes of Cicero in Sturla Þórðarson's thirteenth-century *Íslendinga saga*.²⁷ Finally, alongside classical motifs, Christian motifs can easily be traced.²⁸ It is difficult to read *Njáls saga*, for instance, without noticing the parallels between the eponymous hero, famed for his legal expertise and refusal to engage in violence, and the hagiography of Gerald of Aurillac, a lay lord who

---

²⁴ Randi Eldevik, 'Troia Redux: A Medieval Tradition, an Old Norse Mystery', *Proceedings of the Medieval Association of the Midwest*, 2 (1993), 34–46.

²⁵ Frederic N. Clark, 'Reading the "First Pagan Historiographer": Dares Phrygius and Medieval Genealogy', *Viator*, 41.2 (2010), 203–26. For the wider context: František Graus, 'Troja und trojanische Herkunftssage im Mittelalter', in *Kontinuität und Transformation der Antike im Mittelalter*, ed. by Willi Erzgräber (Sigmaringen: Thorbecke, 1989), pp. 25–43; and (though focusing on specific references to Troy) Kordula Wolf, 'Troja und Europa. Mediävistische Mythosforschung im Visier', in *Gestiftete Zukunft im mittelalterlichen Europa. Festschrift für Michael Borgolte zum 60. Geburtstag*, ed. by Frank Rexroth and Wolfgang Huschner (Berlin: Akademie, 2008), pp. 165–92; Kordula Wolf, *Troja — Metamorphosen eines Mythos: Französische, englische und italienische Überlieferungen des 12. Jahrhunderts im Vergleich* (Berlin: Akademie, 2008).

²⁶ Torfi H. Tulinius, 'Langues scandinaves et adaptations du Latin sur Alexandre le Grand', in *La fascination pour Alexandre le Grand dans les littératures européennes (Xe–XVIe siècle): réinventions d'un mythe*, ed. by Catherine Gaullier-Bougassas (Turnhout: Brepols, 2014), pp. 589–95. Generally: Randi Eldevik, 'What's Hecuba to Them? Medieval Scandinavian Encounters with Classical Antiquity', in *Scandinavia and Europe 800–1350: Contact, Conflict, and Coexistence*, ed. by Jonathan Adams and Katherine Holman (Turnhout: Brepols, 2004), pp. 345–54.

²⁷ Torfi H. Tulinius, '*Skaði kennir mér minni minn*: On the Relationship between Trauma, Memory, Revenge and the Medium of Poetry', in *Skandinavische Schriftlandschaften. Vänbok til Jürg Glauser*, ed. by Klaus Müller-Wille and others (Tübingen: Narr Francke Attempto, 2017), pp. 129–35 (p. 133). I am grateful to Lars Kjaer for this reference.

²⁸ Haki Antonsson, 'The Present and the Past in the Sagas of Icelanders', in *How the Past Was Used*, ed. by Lambert and Weiler, pp. 69–90 (pp. 76–79); Haki Antonsson, 'Salvation and Early Saga Writing in Iceland: Aspects of the Works of the Þingeyrar Monks and Their Associates', *Viking and Medieval Scandinavia*, 8 (2012), 71–140; Haki Antonsson, 'Christian Themes', in *The Routledge Research Companion to the Medieval Icelandic Sagas*, ed. by Ármann Jakobsson and Sverrir Jakobsson (London: Routledge, 2017), pp. 279–91; Torfi H. Tulinius, 'Honour, Sagas and Trauma: Reflections on Literature and Violence in 13th Century Iceland', in *Literature and Honour*, ed. by Aasta Marie Bjorvand Bjørkøy and Thorstein Norheim (Oslo: Universitetsforlaget, 2017), pp. 81–94 <https://www.idunn.no/literature-and-honour> [accessed 6 March 2018]. I owe this reference to Lars Kjaer.

famously shunned the spilling of blood.[29] Such parallels need not be rooted in direct borrowing. They do, though, point to a shared cultural framework of values, norms, and textual practices.

That framework further constituted itself in *how* texts were used. Medieval authors assessed, questioned, and verified their sources. Writing in the 1130s, Heimo of Bamberg did not shy away from lambasting even the Church Father Eusebius: the only explanation why the saint had miscalculated biblical dates must be that he had been asleep while reading.[30] Around 1280, the Hungarian chronicler Simon de Kéza similarly took issue with Orosius, 'for he concocted many apocryphal stories in his pages'. In particular, Orosius had claimed that the Hungarians descended from incubi who had impregnated Scythian women abducted by the Goths. This, Simon claimed, was preposterous: 'One must dismiss it as against nature and quite contrary to the truth when he maintains that spirits can beget when they are not supplied with the natural organs which could provide the procreative ability and function capable of creating the true form of an embryo.'[31] More commonly, authors weighed up and compared. When recounting the destruction of Troy and the subsequent travails of its erstwhile inhabitants, Otto of Freising listed Homer, Pindar, Dares Phrygius, and Virgil among those who had described these events. And when summarizing Virgil's account of the Trojan origins of Rome, Otto also referenced a more uncomplimentary image of Aeneas as traitor and necromancer that survives in Dares Phrygius.[32] Otto concluded his account with a discussion of Virgil's and Dares' respective merits as historical sources.[33] At other times, classical texts provided a means with which to structure a narrative. Between 1200 and 1230, an anonymous notary at the Hungarian court composed a history of the early Magyars, recounting their deeds from their origins in Scythia to just before the conversion of St Stephen (*c.* 1000). In his preface, the author recounted how he had composed a history of Troy, based on Dares and other texts. The anonymous recipient of his narrative had repeatedly asked for an account of

---

[29] Paul Beekman Taylor, 'Njáll grómr: Christian Morality and Norse Myth in Njál's Saga', *Mediaeval Scandinavia*, 13 (2000), 167–80.

[30] Heimo of Bamberg, *De decursu temporum*, ed. by Hans Martin Weikmann (Hanover: Hahn, 2004), p. 182.

[31] Simon de Kéza, *Gesta Hungarorum*, ed. and trans. by László Vészpremy and Frank Schaer, with a study by Jenö Sczücs (Budapest: Central European University Press, 1999), pp. 4–7.

[32] Otto of Freising, *Chronica*, p. 56.

[33] Otto of Freising, *Chronica*, p. 58.

the Hungarians in the manner of Dares, which the author now provided.[34] Importantly, he did not claim Trojan descent for the Hungarians: the Magyars originated in Scythia.[35] And they most certainly were not forced into exile; rather, faced with overcrowding, they sent out an army to conquer a new homeland. However, partly because Dares Phrygius's account was so well known, it provided a useful model on which to base a narrative of communal origins. Of course, the notary's account both echoed the history of the Trojans and established a clear contrast with it. Here, the practice matters because it reflected — and thus, even in its seeming rejection, reinforced the normative nature of — a common European cultural framework that derived many of its reference points from the narratives of Antiquity and the writings of the Fathers.

The Bible must be added to these sources. Its uses do, of course, pose particular problems.[36] Most importantly, the veracity of the Bible was never in question. That did not, however, mean that every reference to biblical characters conferred a sacral character upon the matter described. In fact, sometimes style and imagery were more important than the specific biblical passage from which references had been gleaned. Let me use as an example the *Vita Griffini filii Conani*, an anonymous Latin life, produced probably between 1137 and 1148, of Gruffudd ap Cynan, ruler of Gwynedd (d. 1137).[37] Gruffudd is reported as refusing to use his full force against the invading Normans just as David had held back against Saul (I Samuel 24. 1–8); the Welsh are described as hiding in marches and caves to avoid the English, with language taken from I Samuel 12. 6, where the Israelites similarly took refuge from the Philistines; and, on his deathbed, Gruffudd assembled his children to instruct them 'just as Ezekias had done' (II Chronicles 29–32). In each instance, the biblical reference placed the events described in line with hallowed precedent. Gruffudd imitated the

---

[34] Anonymous notary, *Gesta Hungarorum*, in Anonymus and Master Roger, *The Deeds of the Hungarians and the Epistle to the Sorrowful Lament upon the Destruction of the Kingdom of Hungary by the Tatars*, ed. and trans. by János M. Bak and Martyn Rady (Budapest: Central European University Press, 2010), pp. 2–3.

[35] See, though, Alberic of Troisfontaines, *Chronicon*, p. 675, for the Scythian origins of the Trojans.

[36] Julie Barrau, *Bible, lettres et politique: l'écriture au service des hommes à l'époque de Thomas Becket* (Paris: Classiques Garnier, 2013); Philippe Buc, 'Crusade and Eschatology: Holy War Fostered and Inhibited', *Mitteilungen des Instituts für Österreichische Geschichtsforschung*, 125 (2017), 304–39.

[37] *Vita Griffini filii Conani: The Medieval Latin Life of Gruffudd ap Cynan*, ed. by Paul Russell (Cardiff: University of Wales Press, 2005).

rulers and prophets of Israel, while the Welsh were implicitly likened to God's chosen people. But then matters were not always this straightforward.

Rather more allusive use is also made of the Bible. When Gruffudd ordered a rival to be killed, he was told that the deed had been done by a young man, who was then likened to the Amalekite who had brought Saul's sceptre and armband to David (II Samuel 1).[38] Unlike in the Bible, however, the messenger was not killed for having raised his hand against the Lord's anointed. Instead, he was rewarded with a royal bride. Perhaps most strikingly, the *Vita* reports how, at one point, the English king had raised an army, with the intention of wiping out Gruffudd's people without even leaving 'a dog pissing against a wall' ('ut ne canem mingentem ad parietem relinqueret'). It is impossible to link this quote directly to any particular passage in the Old Testament. This is not for a lack of options, though. In I Samuel 25. 34, for example, David, having been appeased by Abigail, declared: 'if thou hadst not quickly come to meet me, there had not been left to Nabal by the morning light, any that pisseth against the wall'. The image recurs in I Kings 14. 10, 16. 11, 21. 21, and II Kings 9. 8. Those threatened with extinction were associates of tyrants, usurpers, and other enemies of God's people. This, however, was hardly the meaning proposed by the *Vita*'s anonymous author. Consequently, he either possessed a weak grasp of the Bible or, more plausibly, Scripture provided a pool of imagery that could be employed to convey a sense of Gruffudd's deeds as echoing without necessarily replicating those of the leaders of Israel. That certainly seems to have been the case with Henry's threatened canicide: the image conveyed was not one of Henry I unleashing his righteous wrath upon the Welsh but of the severity of the slaughter that he desired to inflict upon them. Henry resembled David not in the legitimacy of his actions but in the bloodshed that he proposed.

Moreover, just like the history of Troy or Rome, the Bible provided narrative models for constructing an account. Cosmas of Prague's account of the origins of ducal power in Bohemia borrowed extensively from that of the beginnings of Israelite kingship in I Samuel 8. To recap: the Israelites had been ruled by Samuel, the last of the judges. Partly because he was old and his sons unsuitable, the Israelites demanded to have a king just like other nations did. Samuel warned that the king would have complete power over them. Their daughters would become servants, and their sons eunuchs and soldiers, while their king would tax and oppress them all. Still, the Israelites persisted, and Samuel picked a king for them: a young man, who had lost his way searching for

---

[38] *Vita Griffini*, pp. 62–63.

an errant flock of sheep. That man was Saul. Now to twelfth-century Prague: the early Bohemians, Cosmas informs us, had lived in innocent bliss. As they became wealthier, divisions increased, exacerbated by the fact that they had no prince or lord to do justice for them. Instead, the Bohemians turned to rich men. One of these, Krok, had three daughters, among them Libuŝe, a prophetess. One day, when Libuŝe decided a case, one of the claimants felt insulted at being judged by a woman. Libuŝe responded that, just as the doves had chosen the kite as their king, so the Bohemians would acquire a new ruler in the husband she was now going to take. The prophetess and her sisters convened an assembly, where Libuŝe explained just what it meant to have a duke: he would be easy to appoint, but difficult to depose; everything the Bohemians owned would be his; they would live in perpetual fear; he would make some of them peasants, some millers, some tax collectors; he would enslave their children and raid their possessions. Still, the people persisted, and so Libuŝe directed them that they would find their duke ploughing his fields close to a nearby town.[39]

Cosmas's approach to the Bible has much in common with that of the *Vita Griffini*. Clearly the dukes of Bohemia were not the kings of Israel. To begin, the image of ducal power was rather more positive: it formed part of a civilizing mission of the Czech that, the Old Testament made clear, was most certainly not required in the case of Israel. Equally, while the Israelites were God's people, the Bohemians were pagans, ruled by rich men, not judges, and so on. It may even be possible to detect an echo of an Ovidean scheme of human society in steady decline from a golden age to the present. In fact, Cosmas constructed the passage with the aid of quotations from and allusions to Boethius, Juvenal, Horace, Ovid, Virgil, St Augustine, Regino of Prüm, Terence, Prudentius, and Sallust.[40] In short, the Old Testament was but one in a series of models employed to construct a narrative of communal origins. It mattered because it provided an exemplary plot device, but without bestowing upon either the Bohemians or their leaders a status equivalent to any Old Testament forebears.

---

[39] Cosmas of Prague, *Chronica Boemorum*, pp. 6–18.

[40] Cosmas of Prague, *The Chronicle of the Czechs*, trans. by Lisa Wolverton (Washington DC: Catholic University of America Press, 2009), pp. 37–47, nn. 38–85; Jacek Banaskiewicz, 'Königliche Karrieren von Hirten, Gärtner und Pflügern', *Saeculum*, 33 (1982), 265–86; Jacek Banaskiewicz, 'Slavonic *origines regni*: Hero the Law-Giver and Founder of Monarchy (Introductory Survey of Problems)', *Acta Poloniae Historica*, 69 (1989), 97–131; Octav Eugen de Lazero, 'The Dynastic Myth of the Przemyslids in the *Chronica Bohemorum* by Cosmas of Prague', *Ollodagos: Actes de la Société Belge d'Études Celtiques*, 12 (1999), 123–75.

Sketching the pool of sources and models available, tracing the extent to which they circulated across the West, and outlining how they were used is essential for understanding the common cultural framework within which the writing of history unfolded. We can assume a shared familiarity with the inheritance of classical literature: over a two-hundred-year period, a largely identical set of authors was consulted by writers in Wales, England, Germany, Bohemia, Poland, Italy, France, Hungary, Norway, Iceland, and Denmark. The examples of Dares Phrygius and the Old Testament, in turn, illustrate how exemplars constituted a tool, not a rigid template. Invoking Troy and the Old Testament did not constitute an attempt to reduce modern affairs to a mere re-enactment of a more glorious past. The Hungarians were most certainly not Trojans, and Bohemia was not Israel. For this approach to work, it was, however, necessary that these materials served as both a rhetorical tool and a repertoire of useful information. The past provided an incentive for thinking about the present. This inherently critical engagement, in turn, formed the essential precondition for a trans-European textual culture to emerge. Only because of this shared foundation was it possible for the writings of Regino of Prüm, to give but one example, to be consulted in England, Poland, Bohemia, and Germany. They could be used as a historical source because there were shared expectations as to what history should look like and how it was meant to be written. Equally, there needed to be a clear sense that authors would question, test, verify, and compare in order to get at pieces of information with which they could illuminate the rather different past that they sought to recover and retrieve. In this regard, drawing upon a biblical or classical heritage and engaging with a European textual culture were not distinct, but mutually dependent and reinforcing aspects of literary production. What, though, did this mean in practice?

Historical Writing as a European Social Practice

In high medieval Europe, the writing of history was a truly international undertaking. Not only classical, but also contemporary and earlier medieval texts were shared across Latin Christendom. Until the late twelfth century, most universal chronicles circulating in England, for instance, were those by Marianus Scottus (d. 1082), produced for the imperial court, and by Hugh of St Victor, penned for the benefit of his brethren and students in twelfth-century Paris.[41]

---

[41] Martin Brett, 'The Use of Universal Chronicle at Worcester', in *L'historiographie médiévale en Europe*, ed. by Jean-Philippe Genet (Paris: Éditions du Centre national de la recherche

The international dimension continued to shape the efforts of Ralph Niger and Ralph de Diceto, who composed the first indigenous English renditions of a universal past. Ralph Niger's *Chronica*, written *c.* 1195–1197, drew not only on Eusebius, Jerome, Orosius, Bede, and Paul the Deacon, but also on Adam of Bremen and Sigebert of Gembloux, Hugh of Fleury, Orderic Vitalis, and Danish informants.[42] That is, alongside late antique and early medieval writers, he consulted an eleventh-century history of the archbishops of Hamburg (Adam), an early twelfth-century universal chronicle (Sigebert), a history of West Francia written at around the same time (Hugh), and an account of the Norman Church (Orderic), as well as oral testimony from Scandinavia. When Ralph de Diceto (d. 1200/01), in turn, compiled the *Abbreviatio Chronicarum*, a series of excerpts from earlier writers like John of Worcester, Gregory of Tours, or Sigebert of Gembloux, he redacted these to insert materials taken from the history of the counts of Anjou, the forebears of King Henry II (r. 1154–1189). That he amended his sources is less significant than that he had access to and deemed worth including in a collection on Christian, imperial, and British history an account of the king's comital ancestors.[43] Two of the *Abbreviatio*'s manuscripts also open with an exchange of letters between Ralph and Archbishop John of Lyon,[44] and a list of 113 ecclesiastical provinces mistakenly attributed to Bishop Burchard of Worms (d. 1025).[45] The correspondence had come about because the list excluded Britain and because Ralph hoped that the metropolitan might be able to shed light on peculiarities in the ecclesiastical structure of France. In order to restore England and its neighbours to their rightful place

---

scientifique, 1991), pp. 277–85; Julian Harrison, 'The English Reception of Hugh of Saint-Victor's *Chronicle*', *Electronic British Library Journal*, 2002, 1–33; Elizabeth Tyler, 'Writing Universal History in Eleventh-Century England: Cotton Tiberius B. i, German Imperial History-Writing and Vernacular Lay Literacy', in *Universal Chronicles in the High Middle Ages*, ed. by Michele Campopiano and Henry Bainton (York: York Medieval Press, 2017), pp. 65–94.

[42] Hanna Krause, *Radulfus Niger — Chronica. Eine englische Weltchronik des 12. Jahrhunderts* (Frankfurt am Main: Lang, 1985), pp. 42*–99*; Mia Münster-Swendsen, 'Lost Chronicle or Elusive Informers? Some Thoughts on the Source of Ralph Niger's Reports from Twelfth-Century Denmark', in *Historical and Intellectual Culture in the Long Twelfth Century: The Scandinavian Connection*, ed. by Mia Münster-Swendsen, Thomas K. Heebøll-Holm, and Sigbjørn Olsen Sønnesyn (Toronto: Pontifical Institute of Mediaeval Studies, 2016), pp. 189–210.

[43] Ralph de Diceto, *Historical Works*, ed. by William Stubbs, Rolls Series, 2 vols (London: Longman, Green & Co., 1876), i, 135, 161–65. On Ralph: Michael Staunton, *The Historians of Angevin England* (Oxford: Oxford University Press, 2017), pp. 67–81.

[44] Ralph de Diceto, *Historical Works*, i, 5–6.

[45] Ralph de Diceto, *Historical Works*, i, 6–10.

among the universal Church, an English cleric corresponded with a French prelate to amend materials believed to have originated in Germany.

Comparable practices are evident across the West. Around 1138–1139, those commissioning or writing the *Chronicon Roskildense*, the first indigenous history of Denmark, acquired a manuscript of Adam of Bremen's *History of the Archbishops of Hamburg* (*c.* 1075/76).[46] They also appear to have had access to Abbo of Fleury's *Passio* of St Edmund, and to the first recension of Henry of Huntingdon's *Historia Anglorum*, completed *c.* 1133.[47] It might even be possible to identify the particular manuscript of Adam's text acquired by the canons.[48] In short, the anonymous author and his patrons went to considerable lengths to secure the most current and up-to-date information, wherever they might find it. Their approach was not unusual. The author of the anonymous *Historia Norwegie* (*c.* 1170) had access to copies of Adam of Bremen and Honorius Augustodonensis (d. 1140), and might have consulted a version of Merlin's prophecy,[49] while, in Denmark, Saxo Grammaticus drew on Dudo of St Quentin's tenth-century *Deeds of Norman Dukes*, John of Salisbury's *Policraticus*, and Walter of Châtillon's *Alexandreis*.[50] Moving beyond Scandinavia, Gerald of Wales was cited by both Archbishop Jacques de Vitry of Acre[51] and Alberic of

---

[46] Adam was widely consulted around the Baltic: Anne Katrine Gade Christensen, *Studien zur Adam von Bremen Überlieferung* (Copenhagen: University of Copenhagen, 1975). I am grateful to Erik Niblaeus for this reference. Christoph Dartmann, 'Die Rezeption der Frühgeschichte des Erzbistums Hamburg-Bremen bei Adam von Bremen, Helmold von Bosau und Albert von Stade: ein Beitrag zur norddeutschen Geschichtsschreibung des Hochmittelalters', *Rotenberger Schriften*, 92 (2012), 289–312.

[47] Michael H. Gelting, 'Henry of Huntingdon, the *Roskilde Chronicle*, and the English Connection in Twelfth-Century Denmark', in *Historical and Intellectual Culture*, ed. by Münster-Swendsen, Heebøll-Holm, and Sønnesyn, pp. 104–18 (pp. 117–18). Generally on the circulation of German and English materials in Denmark and Norway: Münster-Swendsen, 'Lost Chronicle'; Paul Gazzoli, 'Anglo-Danish Connections in the Later-Eleventh Century' (unpubl. doctoral thesis, University of Cambridge, 2010); Rodney M. Thomson, 'William of Malmesbury and the Scandinavians', in *Historical and Intellectual Culture*, ed. by Münster-Swendsen, Heebøll-Holm, and Sønnesyn, pp. 91–103 (pp. 97–103); Edward Carlson Browne, 'Roger of Howden and the Unknown Royalty of Twelfth-Century Norway', *Quaestio Insularis: Selected Proceedings of the Cambridge Colloquium in Anglo-Saxon, Norse and Celtic*, 11 (2010), 75–96.

[48] Gelting, 'Henry of Huntingdon', p. 109.

[49] *Historia Norwegie*, ed. by Inger Ekrem and Lars Boje Mortensen, trans. by Peter Fisher (Copenhagen: Museum Tusculanum, 2003), pp. 17–20.

[50] Saxo Grammaticus, *Gesta Danorum*, ed. by Karsten Frijs Jensen, trans. by Peter Fisher, 2 vols (Oxford: Clarendon Press, 2015), II, 1702.

[51] Jacques de Vitry, *Historia Occidentalis*, ed. by John Frederick Hinnebusch (Fribourg:

Troisfontaines in Champagne.[52] In the Balkans, Thomas of Split consulted Adam of Bremen and the *Liber pontificalis* (a collection of papal biographies),[53] and, in Hungary, Simon de Kéza utilized Godfrey of Viterbo, Jordanes, and German epic poetry to write the *Gesta Hungarorum* (c. 1282).[54] No credible approach to high medieval historical writing and culture can afford to overlook this trans-European framework. How, though, did chroniclers get this information?

We have already seen how the cathedral clergy at Roskilde collated the materials necessary to write a history of Denmark. A generation later, seeking to secure Charlemagne's canonization, their peers at Aachen procured texts from Santiago de Compostella to compile a record of Charlemagne's saintly deeds.[55] Likewise, the anonymous compiler of the *Warenne Chronicle*, a history of England and Normandy from c. 1035–1120, used Robert of Torigni's version of the *Gesta Normannorum ducum*, William of Malmesbury's *Gesta regum Anglorum*, and might have had access to the works of John of Worcester or Henry of Huntingdon — all of them, it is worth noting, active contemporaneously with the chronicler. Like the canons at Roskilde, he seems to have been embedded in a network that allowed him access to the most current and up-to-date renditions of the past.[56] These cases help contextualize Thomas of Split. The archdiocese was by no means blessed with resources: when Archbishop

---

University Press, 1972), p. 186. On Acre as a cultural centre, see also Jonathan Rubin, *Learning in a Crusader City: Intellectual Activity and Intercultural Exchanges in Acre, 1191–1291* (Cambridge: Cambridge University Press, 2018).

[52] Alberic of Troisfontaines, *Chronicon*, p. 861.

[53] Thomas of Split, *Historia Salonitanorum atque Spalatinorum pontificum*, ed. and trans. by Olga Peric and others (Budapest: Central European University Press, 2006), pp. 36 (Adam of Bremen), 21, 44 (*Liber*).

[54] Simon de Kéza, *Gesta Hungarorum*, p. xlviii.

[55] Ludwig Vones, 'Heiligsprechung und Tradition: Die Kanonisation Karls des Großen 1165, die Aachener Karlsvita und der Pseudo-Turpin', in *Jakobus und Karl der Große. Von Einhards Karlsvita zum Pseudo-Turpin*, ed. by Klaus Herbers (Tübingen: Narr, 2003), pp. 89–106. For the context: Knut Görich, 'Karl der Große — ein "politischer Heiliger" im 12. Jahrhundert?', in *Religion und Politik im Mittelalter: Deutschland und England im Vergleich*, ed. by Ludger Körntgen and Dominik Waßenhoven (Berlin: De Gruyter, 2013), pp. 117–55.

[56] *The Warenne (Hyde) Chronicle*, ed. by Elisabeth M. C. van Houts and Rosalind C. Love (Oxford: Clarendon Press, 2013), pp. xliv–xlviii. See, for parallel cases, Benjamin Pohl, 'The "Bec Liber Vitae": Robert of Torigni's Sources for Writing the History of the Clare Family at Le Bec, c. 1128–54', *Revue Bénédictine*, 126 (2016), 324–72; Benjamin Pohl, '(Re-)Framing Bede's *Historia ecclesiastica* in Twelfth-Century Germany: John Rylands Library, MS Latin 182', *Bulletin of the John Rylands Library*, 93 (2017), 67–119.

Ugrinus died in 1248, it was a token of his wealth that, while a student in Paris, he had acquired a 'whole bible together with commentaries and glosses, such as the masters in the schools are wont to read'.[57] Even so, Thomas not only gained access to Adam of Bremen and the *Liber pontificalis*,[58] but also demonstrated familiarity with Isidore of Seville, Virgil, Florus's *Epitome bellorum annorum*, Ovid, Horace, and Lucan.[59] Remoteness did not equal a lack of access to networks and sources.

Modern readers of medieval chronicles have not always taken this aspect fully into account.[60] This is understandable: we normally lack the evidence that we have, for example, for the twelfth-century abbey of Cluny, where Abbot Peter the Venerable corresponded widely to gather manuscripts,[61] or letters like

---

[57] Thomas of Split, *Historia Salonitanorum*, pp. 356–57. To put this in context: in the second half of the twelfth century, Abbot Gebhard of Windberg thus spent half a talent for a psalter with glosses, 30 pence for a Gospel of St John with glosses, 3 talents for a missal with the New Testament, for another missal and lectionary in two volumes 20 shillings, and 2 talents for a two-volume exegesis of St Augustine. Max Manitius, 'Drei ungedruckte Bibliothekskataloge', *Neues Archiv der Gesellschaft für ältere deutsche Geschichtskunde*, 32 (1907), 243–51 (p. 249).

[58] Thomas of Split, *Historia Salonitanorum*, p. xxxii.

[59] Thomas of Split, *Historia Salonitanorum*, pp. xxxiii–xxxvii. See also pp. 2–12 (classical references). For the parallel case of Henry of Livonia: Leonid Arbusow, 'Das entlehnte Sprachgut in Heinrichs "Chronicon Livoniae". Ein Beitrag zur Sprache mittelalterlicher Chronistik', *Deutsches Archiv für Erforschung des Mittelalters*, 8 (1951), 100–53.

[60] See, for contrasting practices in other fields of medieval studies, Elma Brenner, 'The Transmission of Medical Culture in the Norman Worlds *c.* 1050–*c.* 1250', in *People, Texts and Artefacts: Cultural Transmission in the Norman Worlds of the Eleventh and Twelfth Centuries*, ed. by David Bates, Edoardo D'Angelo, and Elisabeth van Houts (London: Institute of Historical Research, University of London, 2018), pp. 47–64 <http://humanities-digital-library.org/index.php/hdl/catalog/book/normanworlds> [accessed 18 February 2018]; Pascale Bourgain, 'The Circulation of Texts in Manuscript Culture', in *The Medieval Manuscript Book: Cultural Approaches*, ed. by Michael R. Johnston and Michael Van Dussen (Cambridge: Cambridge University Press, 2015), pp. 140–59; Rodney M. Thomson, 'The Place of Germany in the Twelfth-Century Renaissance: Books, Scriptoria, and Libraries', in *Turning Over a New Leaf: Change and Development in the Medieval Manuscript*, ed. by Erik Kwakkel, Rosamond McKitterick, and Rodney M. Thomson (Leiden: Leiden University Press, 2012), pp. 127–44; Bernice M. Kaczinsky, 'The Authority of the Fathers: Patristic Texts in Early Medieval Libraries and Scriptoria', *Journal of Medieval Latin*, 16 (2006), 1–27; Rosamond McKitterick, 'The Audience for Latin Historiography in the Early Middle Ages: Text Transmission and Manuscript Dissemination', in *Historiographie im frühen Mittelalter*, ed. by Anton Scharer and Georg Scheibelreiter (Vienna: Oldenbourg, 1994), pp. 96–114.

[61] Peter the Venerable, *Letters*, ed. by Giles Constable, 2 vols (Cambridge, MA: Harvard University Press, 1967), I, nos 24, 132, 169–70.

those of Bern of Reichenau, who, a century earlier, had sent treatises to the emperor for them to be added to the imperial library.[62] Works of history also rarely feature in medieval library catalogues.[63] Even so, we should not overlook the evidence that does exist. Sometimes, copies of specific texts were commissioned. In the middle of the thirteenth century, Thomas Foerster has recently suggested, both the English and the Castilian royal courts took an interest in Godfrey of Viterbo's *Pantheon*, a world chronicle centring on the deeds of the Western emperors. Either might have commissioned a copy now surviving in the municipal archives of Bordeaux, and feasibly did so in the context of the 1257 German imperial election, which pitched the Earl of Cornwall against the King of Castile.[64] Sometimes, chroniclers travelled to gather information, as when William of Malmesbury visited Worcester Cathedral to consult its library.[65] William's Norman contemporary Orderic Vitalis of St Evroul likewise reported how, while staying at Croyland Abbey, he had received information about the community's past, which he duly included in his history of the Norman Church.[66] At Worcester, he met his fellow-historian John, and recorded John's efforts to continue the world chronicle of Marianus Scottus.[67] While at Worcester and Cambrai, Orderic also inspected copies of Sigebert

---

[62] *Die Briefe des Abtes Bern von Reichenau*, ed. by Franz-Josef Schmale (Stuttgart: Kohlhammer, 1961), no. 27. On Bern: Dieter Blume, *Bern von Reichenau (1008–1048): Abt, Gelehrter, Biograph. Ein Lebensbild mit Werkverzeichnis* (Ostfildern: Thorbecke, 2008).

[63] Max Manitius, 'Geschichtliches aus mittelalterlichen Bibliothekskatalogen', *Neues Archiv der Gesellschaft für ältere deutsche Geschichtskunde*, 16 (1891), 171–74; 32 (1907), 647–709; 36 (1911), 755–74; 41 (1919), 714–32; and 48 (1930), 148–56.

[64] Thomas Foerster, 'Twilight of the Emperors: Godfrey's *Pantheon* and the Hohenstaufen Inheritance in Thirteenth-Century Castile and England', in *Godfrey of Viterbo and His Readers: Imperial Tradition and Universal History in Late Medieval Europe*, ed. by Thomas Foerster (Farnham: Ashgate, 2015), pp. 67–88.

[65] William of Malmesbury, *Polyhistor*, pp. 14–17. I am grateful to Caitlin Naylor for pointing out the Worcester connection. On the holdings of Worcester Cathedral: Rodney M. Thomson, with Michael Gullick, *A Descriptive Catalogue of the Medieval Manuscripts in Worcester Cathedral Library* (Woodbridge: Brewer, 2001). See, for a parallel case, David W. Rollason, 'Symeon of Durham's *Historia de regibus Anglorum et Dacorum* as a Product of Twelfth-Century Historical Workshops', in *The Long Twelfth-Century View of the Anglo-Saxon Past*, ed. by David A. Woodman and Martin Brett (Farnham: Ashgate, 2015), pp. 95–112.

[66] Orderic Vitalis, *Historia ecclesiastica*, ed. and trans. by Marjorie Chibnall, 6 vols (Oxford: Clarendon Press, 1969–80), I (1980), 48–77; II (1968), 338–50. See also II, xxv–xxix. I am grateful to Charles Rozier for his advice on Orderic.

[67] Orderic Vitalis, *Historia ecclesiastica*, II, 186–89.

of Gembloux's *Chronicle*, not available at St Evroul.[68] We know this because William dedicated copies of his *Life of St Wulfstan* to the canons of Worcester, and because Orderic mentioned how he gathered information. Over a century later, Simon de Kéza appears to have refashioned the past partly so as to be able to incorporate information gathered from materials collated during his travels to Sicily in 1270/71. He invented a series of campaigns by the Huns, and recounted tales from several of the places that he added to their itinerary, often unrelated to Attila and his hordes. But Simon never explicitly stated how he had found this information. Still, that he referred to works of history written in Strasbourg and Venice, for example, and that it is possible to identify several of his putative sources, suggests that, like William and Orderic, he consulted local libraries.[69]

All these authors tapped into existing networks of patronage and exchange. Those, in turn, were by no means limited to monastic houses. At St Albans, Matthew Paris received information about the Anglo-Saxon past from royal administrators, who were themselves engaged in writing about pre-Conquest English history — a perhaps useful reminder that, by the middle of the thirteenth century, Latin historical writing was no longer an exclusively clerical pursuit.[70] Alberic of Troisfontaines, in turn, reported on matters as diverse as the legend that Trier's foundation predated Rome's by 1252 years, which first surfaced in the twelfth-century *Gesta Treverorum*;[71] the appearance of St Ursula in a vision to the mystic Elisabeth of Schönau (d. 1164);[72] or how, in 274, a certain Mercurius, also known as Wotan, came to rule the island of Gotland, from whom the kings of the English descended — a genealogy sur-

---

[68] Orderic Vitalis, *Historia ecclesiastica*, II, 188–89.

[69] Simon de Kézai, *Gesta Hungarorum*, pp. xcix–ci. For a putatively parallel case see Godfrey of Viterbo, *Memoria seculorum*, in *Opera*, ed. by Waitz, p. 105.

[70] Matthew Paris, *Chronica majora*, ed. by Henry Richards Luard, Rolls Series, 7 vols (London: Longman, 1872–83), VI: *Additamenta* (1882), 519; Richard Vaughan, *Matthew Paris* (Cambridge: Cambridge University Press, 1958), p. 196.

[71] Alberic of Troisfontaines, *Chronicon*, p. 675; *Gesta Treverorum*, ed. by Georg Waitz, MGH, SS, 8 (Hanover: Hahn, 1848), p. 130. On Alberic: Mireille Schmidt-Chazan, 'Aubri de Trois-Fontaines, un historien entre la France et l'Empire', *Annales d'Est*, 5th ser., 36 (1984), 163–92 (see also Alberic's list of early Trier prelates: *Chronicon*, p. 681). The *Gesta* were among the most widely read of medieval urban chronicles, with at least thirty surviving manuscripts: *Gesta Treverorum*, pp. 122–26; Johannes Kramer, 'Edition der Trierer Handschrift 1342b/97 der "Gesta Treverorum" (12. Jh.)', *Kurtrierisches Jahrbuch*, 55 (2015), 77–121.

[72] Alberic of Troisfontaines, *Chronicon*, p. 683.

viving in the Anglo-Saxon Chronicle, and preserved by Henry of Huntingdon (d. *c.* 1157).[73] We do not know how, precisely, Alberic obtained this information. However, networks of Cistercian houses seem a plausible source,[74] especially once we take into account how widely Cistercian collections of exempla, visions, and miracles circulated among constituent houses.[75] Both Alberic and Matthew provide a useful reminder as to the importance of networks for the circulation of manuscripts and the forging of a European textual culture.

In this context, attention must be paid to patrons who commissioned or who were expected to take an interest in the past. Yet their precise role is sometimes difficult to ascertain: that someone was the dedicatee of a particular chronicle did not mean that they also took an active role in sharing it. Even if they did, those copying, adapting, revising, or continuing a text might not acknowledge from whom it had originally been received. All we can do is highlight patterns. Still, those point to the importance of association with particular patrons in ensuring a narrative's dissemination. William of Malmesbury, for instance, had begun the *Gesta regum Anglorum* at the behest of the Queen and dedicated it to Henry I's (d. 1135) daughter, his illegitimate son (Earl Robert of Gloucester), and the King of Scotland.[76] The presence of Earl Robert among the *Gesta*'s recipients is worth noting, given his household's association with the works of Gaimar, who produced the first Anglo-Norman history of England, and Geoffrey of Monmouth.[77] How actively Robert promoted the writings of

---

[73] Alberic of Troisfontaines, *Chronicon*, pp. 684, 736–37. See also his borrowings from Pseudo-Turpin at pp. 724–25. Henry of Huntingdon, *Historia Anglorum* (*History of the English People*), ed. and trans. by Diana Greenway (Oxford: Clarendon Press, 1996), pp. 246–47; Elizabeth M. Tyler, 'Trojans in Anglo-Saxon England: Precedent without Descent', *Review of English Studies*, 64 (2013), 1–20.

[74] Janet Burton, 'The Monastic World', in *England and Europe in the Reign of Henry III (1216–1272)*, ed. by Ifor W. Rowlands and Björn Weiler (Aldershot: Ashgate, 2002), pp. 121–36.

[75] Stefano Mula, 'Geography and the Early Cistercian "Exempla" Collections', *Cistercian Studies Quarterly*, 46 (2011), 27–43; Stefano Mula, 'Twelfth- and Thirteenth-Century Cistercian Exempla Collections: Role, Diffusion, and Evolution', *History Compass*, 8 (2010), 903–12; Bernhard Meehan, 'Durham Twelfth-Century Manuscripts in Cistercian Houses', in *Anglo-Norman Durham 1093–1193*, ed. by David Rollason, Margaret Harvey, and Michael Prestwich (Woodbridge: Boydell, 1993), pp. 439–49.

[76] William of Malmesbury, *Gesta regum*, I (1998), 2–15.

[77] John Gillingham, 'Kingship, Chivalry and Love: Political and Cultural Values in the Earliest History Written in French: Geoffrey Gaimar's *Estoire des Engleis*', in his *The English in the Twelfth Century: Imperialism, National Identity and Political Values* (Woodbridge: Boydell,

either William or Geoffrey is impossible to determine, though with roughly forty twelfth-century manuscripts of the *Gesta regum* and almost eighty for Geoffrey's *Historia*,[78] they certainly rank among the most widely copied of contemporary historical narratives. Royal and papal associations in particular seem to have helped a text's dissemination. Otto of Freising's *Chronica*, of which he had dedicated a copy to Emperor Frederick Barbarossa, thus remains extant in over forty medieval copies;[79] Godfrey of Viterbo's *Pantheon*, dedicated to Emperor Henry VI and Pope Urban III, in at least fifty-nine;[80] while the nineteenth-century editor counted at least twenty copies of Martin of Troppau's (d. 1278) chronicle of popes and emperors (a mere fraction of the total).[81] The evidence, while circumstantial, nonetheless suggests a mutually reinforcing relationship between a text's popularity and the prestige of its patrons.

This was likely the result of a patron's standing enhancing that of author and oeuvre but also of easier access to networks of distribution, and of expectations about the kind of work that patrons would receive. Each of these texts offered something distinctive and innovative. William of Malmesbury had penned the first comprehensive history of England since Bede, and did so in a manner that proudly displayed its Latinity. Geoffrey of Monmouth did something similar

---

2000), pp. 233–58; Jean-Guy Gouttebroze, 'Robert de Gloucester et l'écriture de l'histoire', in *Histoire et literature au moyen âge. Actes du colloque du Centre d'Études Médiévales de l'Université de Picardie (Amiens 20–24 mars 1985)*, ed. by Danielle Buschinger (Göppingen: Kümmerle, 1991), pp. 143–60.

[78] William of Malmesbury, *Gesta regum*, I, pp. xxi–xxv; Geoffrey of Monmouth, *The History of the Kings of Britain: An Edition and Translation of the De gestis Britonum [Historia Regum Britanniae]*, ed. by Michael D. Reeve, trans. by Neil Wright (Woodbridge: Boydell, 2007), pp. xxxi–xlix.

[79] Otto of Freising, *Chronica*, pp. xxiii–lxxxviii.

[80] Godfrey of Viterbo, *Opera*, pp. 13–20. The number fifty-nine is based on Loren J. Weber, 'The Historical Importance of Godfrey of Viterbo', *Viator*, 25 (1994), 153–95 (pp. 192–95).

[81] Martin of Troppau, *Chronicon*, pp. 380–90. But see also Anna-Dorothee von den Brincken, 'Studien zur Überlieferung der Chronik des Martin von Troppau (Erfahrungen mit einem massenhaft überlieferten historischen Text)', *Deutsches Archiv für Erforschung des Mittelalters*, 41 (1985), 460–531; Wolfgang-Valentin Ikas, 'Neue Handschriftenfunde zum *Chronicon pontificum et imperatorum* des Martin von Troppau', *Deutsches Archiv für Erforschung des Mittelalters*, 58 (2002), 521–37. For Martin's reception history: Wolfgang-Valentin Ikas, 'Martinus Polonus' Chronicle of the Popes and Emperors: A Medieval Best-Seller and Its Neglected Influence on English Medieval Chroniclers', *English Historical Review*, 116 (2001), 327–41; Wolfgang-Valentin Ikas, *Martin von Troppau (Martinus Polonus), O.P. (gest. 1278) in England. Überlieferungs- und wirkungsgeschichtliche Studien zu dessen Papst- und Kaiserchronik* (Wiesbaden: Reichert, 2002).

for the period not covered by William. Godfrey produced a universal history that helpfully recorded and excerpted the most important medieval and classical writers. Martin of Troppau's *Chronicon*, in turn, offered new means of textual presentation that provided an easy-to-access compendium of the most important events since the coming of Christianity. In order to be associated with powerful patrons, something special had to be offered. Humdrum history would not do.[82] That distinctiveness, in turn, might well have reinforced the popularity of any particular text.

We should not, however, overlook otherwise often uncredited institutions that acted as mediators and multipliers in a narrative's transmission. Elisabeth van Houts has highlighted the importance of dynastic networks in the commissioning of regnal history.[83] Likewise, Mia Münster-Swendsen has drawn attention to the overlapping literary circles associated with the court of the archbishop of Sens.[84] The archbishops of Lund appear to have played a similar role: not only did Saxo Grammaticus dedicate the *Gesta Danorum* to Archbishop Absalon,[85] but Absalon's successor also ensured the instruction of missionaries in the eastern Baltic. It has even been suggested that this was how Henry of Livonia had become familiar with common European models of writing about the past.[86] When tracing networks of intellectual exchange, we must therefore consider not only where texts were initially composed, but also the means by which they might have been disseminated or — as in the case of Worcester — by which they might have become knowable.

Importantly, functioning as a hub need not require the composition (as opposed to the copying) of narratives. Until the later thirteenth century, the monks of Glastonbury relied on others to write history on their behalf. They did, however, copy texts. In particular, they played a pivotal role in collating and disseminating materials on King Arthur (who, they claimed, was buried in their abbey) and the legend of St Joseph of Arimathea (attested in the New Testament as having been in charge of Christ's burial, and claimed

---

[82] See also Hugh of Fleury's *Historia*, commissioned by Adela of Blois, daughter of William the Conqueror: *PL*, CLXIII (1854), col. 821.

[83] Elisabeth van Houts, 'The Writing of History and Family Traditions through the Eyes of Men and Women: The *Gesta principum Polonorum*', in *Gallus Anonymous and His Chronicle in the Context of Twelfth-Century Historiography from the Perspective of the Latest Research*, ed. by Krzysztof Stopka (Kraków: Polish Academy of Arts and Sciences, 2010), pp. 189–204.

[84] Münster-Swendsen, 'Lost Chronicle'.

[85] Saxo Grammaticus, *Gesta Danorum*, I, 2–5.

[86] Arbusow, 'Das entlehnte Sprachgut', p. 101.

by the brethren as their community's founder).⁸⁷ What mattered was therefore that those receiving a text preserve it and facilitate its dissemination. Alongside royal patrons, prelates or communities other than the one to which an author belonged played a major part in the preservation and passing on of manuscripts. Cosmas of Prague sent copies of his *Chronica Boemorum* to Provost Severus of Melnik,⁸⁸ Archdeacon Gervase of Prague,⁸⁹ and Abbot Clement of Brevnov.⁹⁰ While none of these manuscripts survive, fifteen later copies,⁹¹ including one from the Bavarian abbey of Niederaltaich,⁹² testify to the *Chronica*'s continuing reception, ensured in part, we might assume, by Cosmas's readers. Similarly, where the high medieval origins of the surviving manuscripts for Otto's *Chronica* can be identified, they seem to have been produced in southern German monasteries,⁹³ rather than in cathedrals or houses of secular canons. For us, this means that we need to be aware of the social dimension of manuscript circulation. It was, after all, key in bringing about the textual culture at the heart of this chapter. We have already seen that networks of dissemination and reception could overlap. So did both the types of text most frequently consulted and the uses to which these were put. The phenomenon reflected both necessities and cultural conventions.

Historical Writing as a European Cultural Practice

Most importantly, just because manuscripts circulated widely did not mean that information was easy to come by. Writing history all too often meant plugging gaps and reconstructing from fragmentary evidence a plausible rendition of what might have happened. Sources might have fallen victim to

---

[87] Antonia Gransden, 'The Growth of the Glastonbury Traditions and Legends in the Twelfth Century', *Journal of Ecclesiastical History*, 27 (1976), 337–58.

[88] Cosmas of Prague, *The Chronicle of the Czechs*, pp. 29–30; *Chronica Boemorum*, pp. 1–2.

[89] Cosmas of Prague, *Chronicle*, pp. 30–33, 182–83; *Chronica*, pp. 2–4, 159–60.

[90] Cosmas of Prague, *Chronicle*, pp. 109–10; *Chronica*, pp. 80–81.

[91] Cosmas of Prague, *Chronica*, pp. xlv–lxxxiv.

[92] Cosmas of Prague, *Chronica*, pp. lxvii–lxviii. Niederaltaich seems to have been a nodal point in its own right: <http://www.geschichtsquellen.de/kloestersuche.html?kloesteralph = Niederaltaich> [accessed 25 February 2018].

[93] Otto of Freising, *Chronica*, pp. xxiv (Heiligenkreuz), xxv–vi (Zwettl), xxx (St Ulrich and Afra at Augsburg), xxxvi–xxxix (Weihenstephan), xxxix (Admont), xl (Tegernsee), li–v (Neuburg near Hagenau), lx (St Lambert in Carinthia), lxiii (Niederaltaich).

Viking incursions and Magyar raids.[94] They might also have been written in a script or language no longer decipherable or in a style no longer fashionable. The trope was famously employed by Geoffrey of Monmouth,[95] yet it long predated him. In the ninth century, Hincmar of Rheims described the fate that had befallen an earlier *vita* of the community's patron saint: one of the abbots had commissioned Venantius Fortunatus to produce a shorter verse summary of the — rather lengthy — original. The new version proved popular, and the original fell into neglect. In the eighth century, the monks had become so poor that they had to beg for money, and they wrapped the coins that they received in leaves torn from the manuscript. Thus, by the time Hincmar began writing, only scraps of the original text survived, which he had collated and on which his own *vita* was based.[96] There could even be something magic about the appearance of old texts: in the tenth century, the *Gesta abbatum* of St Albans (*c.* 1178) inform us, a book written in 'Old British' had been found, containing a life of St Alban, as well as several pagan hymns dedicated to Diane and Mercury. Once the sections about St Alban had been translated into Latin, the manuscript turned to dust.[97] Finally, sources might perish by accident. In England, Abbot Geoffrey (1119–1146) had first joined the community of St Albans after he had accidentally burned some of its books.[98] In *c.* 1136/37, Abbot Peter the Venerable of Cluny wrote to the monks of La Grand Chartreuse, requesting a new copy of St Augustine's letters, since much

---

[94] See generally: Rudolf Schieffer, 'Zur Dimension der Überlieferung bei der Erforschung narrativer Quellen des Mittelalters', in *Von Fakten und Fiktionen. Mittelalterliche Geschichtsdarstellungen und ihre kritische Aufarbeitung*, ed. by Johannes Laudage (Cologne: Böhlau, 2003), pp. 63–78; Thomas Haye, *Verlorenes Mittelalter. Ursachen und Muster der Nichtüberlieferung mittellateinischer Literatur* (Leiden: Brill, 2016); Julia Barrow, 'Danish Ferocity and Abandoned Monasteries: The Twelfth-Century View', in *The Long Twelfth-Century View*, ed. by Brett and Woodman, pp. 77–94; Christofer Zwanzig, 'Heidenheim and Samos: Monastic Remembrance of the "Anglo-Saxon Mission" in Southern Germany and the "Mozarabic Resettlement" of Northern Spain Compared', in *Churches and Social Power in Early Medieval Europe: Integrating Archaeological and Historical Approaches*, ed. by José Carlos Sánchez Parda and Michael G. Shapland (Turnhout: Brepols, 2015), pp. 269–96.

[95] Geoffrey of Monmouth, *History*, pp. 4–5.

[96] Hincmar of Rheims, *Vita sancti Remigii*, ed. by Bruno Krusch, MGH, SS rer. Merov., 3 (Hanover: Hahn, 1896), pp. 250–52. I am grateful to Ed Roberts for this reference.

[97] Thomas of Walsingham, *Gesta abbatum monasterii sancti Albani*, ed. by H. T. Riley, Rolls Series, 3 vols (London: Longman, Green, Reader, and Dyer, 1867–69), I: *A.D. 793–1290* (1867), p. 26.

[98] Thomas of Walsingham, *Gesta abbatum*, I, 73.

of the manuscript kept at one of Cluny's dependencies had been eaten by a bear.[99] The past was inherently fragile.

The resulting gaps could be considerable. Even at St Albans, which, by the early thirteenth century, had emerged as a centre of historiographical production, Matthew Paris still complained that no account of the community's reputed eighth-century founder had been written.[100] Indeed, he discovered only by accident how, in the ninth century, the Danes had pillaged St Albans and carried the saint's relics away with them to Odense, from whence they had to be retrieved in a clandestine mission.[101] Much historical writing, in short, was a matter of retrieving evidence with which to fill lacunae, with which to contextualize and assess new information that had come to light, and with which to satisfy shifting expectations of what was newsworthy. This background is essential for understanding both how chronicles were used and what kind of narratives proved popular. There was, of course, a didactic aspect to the writing of history.[102] But first the information had to be gathered that then allowed moral lessons to be drawn. This requirement is essential for understanding episodes like the one that occurred in 1167 during one of Frederick Barbarossa's Italian campaigns. Before issuing a charter to confirm that Emperor Otto II (d. 993) had indeed transferred the relics of St Bartholomew to the eponymous church in Rome, members of Barbarossa's court first consulted Otto of Freising's *Chronica* to check that this had indeed been the case.[103] This did not mean that Otto's more exalted claims for the *Chronica* had been dismissed — reading history would enable Frederick Barbarossa to imitate brave and pious deeds, to be a just ruler, and to gain divine favour. Rather, it reflected the fundamental need for information to be gathered wherever it could be found.[104] Chronicles

---

[99] Peter the Venerable, *Letters*, I, no. 24.

[100] Matthew Paris, *Chronica majora*, VI, 519.

[101] Thomas of Walsingham, *Gesta abbatum*, I, 12–18.

[102] See, for instance Otto of Freising, *Chronica*, pp. 3–6, where Otto encouraged the imperial chancellor, Rainald of Dassel, to act as interpreter and exegete of the *Chronica* for Frederick Barbarossa. See also: Henry Bainton, 'Literate Sociability and Historical Writing in Later Twelfth-Century England', *Anglo-Norman Studies*, 34 (2011), 23–40.

[103] *Die Urkunden Friedrichs I.*, ed. by Heinrich Appelt, MGH, DD, 10, 5 parts (Hanover: Hahn, 1975–90), pt 2: *1158–1167* (1979), no. 534; John B. Freed, *Frederick Barbarossa: The Prince and the Myth* (New Haven, CT: Yale University Press, 2016), p. xxiii. I am grateful to Ryan Kemp for this reference.

[104] Otto of Freising, *Chronica*, pp. 1–3. See the comparable episodes in eleventh-century Freising and twelfth-century Durham: Steffen Patzold, 'Wie bereitet man sich auf einen

served as depositories of useful information, be that the factual detail they contained, or the moral lessons that were to be drawn from it.

We might even imagine how the process unfolded in practice. It seems likely that Ralph de Diceto's *Abbreviatio* had initially been conceived as a collection of useful information which could then be utilized for the writing of a fully blown narrative. This is most likely also how Heimo of Bamberg (fl. 1108/9–36) had envisaged his *De decursu temporum* to be used,[105] and it was, Thomas Foerster has suggested, one of the reasons why the *Pantheon* of Godfrey of Viterbo proved popular as a comprehensive and wide-ranging compendium of history, mixing reliable information with anecdotes that were both entertaining and instructive.[106] Comparable factors underpinned the wide dissemination of universal chronicles by Marianus Scottus and Sigebert of Gembloux,[107] which offered short, precise and universal coverage.[108] The latter was especially important. Godfrey of Viterbo might have exaggerated when he promised in his *Memoria seculorum* to cover the deeds of Franks, Italians, Sicilians, Tuscans, Lombards, Swabians, Saxons, Gauls, Goths, Vandals, Huns, Hungarians, Spanish, Britons, English, Danes, Scots, Frisians, Welsh (*Gualensium*), and Russians.[109] But he is still representative of an expectation that chroniclers reported widely, especially

---

Thronwechsel vor? Überlegungen zu einem wenig beachteten Text des 11. Jahrhunderts', in *Die mittelalterliche Thronfolge im europäischen Vergleich*, ed. by Matthias Becher (Ostfildern: Thorbecke, 2017), pp. 127–57; Simon MacLean, 'Recycling the Franks in Twelfth-Century England: Regino of Prüm, the Monks of Durham, and the Alexandrine Schism', *Speculum*, 87 (2012), 649–81.

[105] Heimo of Bamberg, *De decursu temporum*, pp. 89–95.

[106] Foerster, 'Godfrey of Viterbo and His Readers', in *Godfrey of Viterbo*, ed. by Foerster, pp. 1–12 (pp. 4–5).

[107] Of Sigebert's Chronica, at least sixty copies survive: Sigebert of Gembloux, *Chronica*, ed. by Ludwig C. Bethmann, MGH, SS, 6 (Hanover: Hahn, 1844), p. 284. See also Manitius, 'Geschichtliches' (1907), pp. 694–95. Marianus Scottus, by contrast, has not received a critical edition: <http://www.geschichtsquellen.de/repOpus_03350.html?pers_PND=PND100952984> [accessed 5 March 2018]. On Sigebert: Anna-Dorothee von den Brincken, '"Contemporalitas regnorum": Beobachtungen zum Versuch des Sigebert von Gembloux, die Chronik des Hieronymus fortzusetzen', in *Historiographia Mediaevalis: Studien zur Geschichtsschreibung und Quellenkunde des Mittelalters. Festschrift für Franz-Josef Schmale zum 65. Geburtstag*, ed. by Dieter Berg and Hans-Werner Goetz (Darmstadt: Wissenschaftliche Buchgesellschaft, 1988), pp. 199–211.

[108] Sigebert knew Marianus's chronicle: Sigebert, *Chronica*, p. 364.

[109] Godfrey of Viterbo, *Memoria seculorum*, p. 97. See also Godfrey of Viterbo, *Pantheon*, in *Opera*, ed. by Waitz, pp. 127–28.

when they wrote about more than just their local or regnal community. Sigebert of Gembloux, for instance, referenced the works of Liudprand of Cremona and Widukind of Corvey, Ruotger's Life of Bruno and Lantbert's of Heribert of Cologne, but also Peter Damian's *vita* of Odilo of Cluny and Wibert's of Pope Leo IX, Rodulfus Glaber, Anselm's *Gesta* of the bishops of Liege, Marianus Scottus, the account of Humbert of Silva Candida's mission to Constantinople, John's account of the translation of St Nicholas to Bari, and various crusading letters.[110] With materials drawn from Italy, Flanders, Burgundy, and Germany, including saints' Lives, chronicles, and letters, this was about as broad a coverage as was possible around the year 1100. It also set a standard for successors and continuators.

These materials were added to and revised in turn. Indeed, it is worth keeping in mind the lines of transmission linking many of these texts: Marianus Scottus was read by Sigebert of Gembloux, Sigebert by Otto of Freising, Otto by Godfrey of Viterbo, and Godfrey by Alberic of Troisfontaines, Thomas of Split, and Martin of Troppau. Inevitably, new sources also entered the fold. In particular, the kind of regnal history so popular from the early decades of the twelfth century filtered through into the writing of universal history, with Godfrey of Viterbo referencing Geoffrey of Monmouth,[111] or Alberic of Troisfontaines Hugh of Fleury.[112] On one level, this complicates matters: knowledge of particular texts might well have spread because they were referenced by other chroniclers or because passages had been included in historical compendia. When Alberic of Troisfontaines cited William of Malmesbury, it was probably not because he was fully familiar with the English monk's oeuvre, but because it had been excerpted by Hélinand of Froidmont, whose *Chronicon* circulated widely among Cistercian houses.[113] Similarly, the twelfth-century denizens of Durham Cathedral focused their reading of Regino of Prüm on a selection of useful passages that they then compiled in a separate manuscript,[114] while in late medieval Denmark Saxo Grammaticus's *Gesta Danorum* seems to

---

[110] Sigebert, *Chronica*, p. 275.

[111] Godfrey of Viterbo, *Memoria seculorum*, p. 99.

[112] Alberic of Troisfontaines, *Chronicon*, pp. 656–59.

[113] Alberic of Troisfontaines, *Chronicon*, p. 658. Erik L. Saak, 'The Limits of Knowledge: Hélinand de Froidmont's *Chronicon*', in *Pre-Modern Encyclopaedic Texts*, ed. by Peter Binkley (Leiden: Brill, 1997), pp. 289–302.

[114] MacLean, 'Recycling the Franks'.

have circulated in simplified Latin synopses for easier reading.[115] But then, in the present context, the use of compilations, and the access to writers through florilegia and excerpts, only serves to highlight the degree of interconnectedness that is so integral a feature of high medieval historical culture. Writers of history drew on the same rhetorical models and they mostly read the same authors.

More importantly still, they also adopted similar approaches to establishing the reliability of the past that they recorded, and the uses to which it might be put. Compiling useful information was not, after all, the only reason why historical compendia and universal histories proved popular. Many of these texts gave access to conflicting opinions and interpretations. Heimo of Bamberg tended to use as many authorities as possible to validate (or question) particular pieces of information.[116] So did Sigebert of Gembloux and Alberic of Troisfontaines.[117] Indeed, scouting for information was among a chronicler's most important tasks. Writing history was *meant* to be hard work. The historian, Matthew Paris explained, was a careful searcher for truth (*indagator*) who sweated (*persudare*) to compile a trustworthy account of the past.[118] Much of that labour involved collating information and engaging with it critically. At Roskilde, Henry of Huntingdon's *Historia Anglorum* was consulted to find out about the raids of Ragnar Lodbrok's sons in ninth-century England. In Croatia, Adam of Bremen's text provided Thomas of Split with the number of Polish and German tribes believed to have aided the Goths in the destruction of Salona in the sixth century. And in Hungary, Simon de Kéza consulted Venetian sources to insert an account of the city's reputed Trojan origins in his account of Attila's conquests.[119]

Research also involved assessing and, if necessary, revising and amending sources, however authoritative those might otherwise have been. We have

---

[115] A. L. Knudsen, 'The Use of Saxo Grammaticus in the Later Middle Ages', in *The Birth of Identities: Denmark and Europe in the Middle Ages*, ed. by Bernard P. McGuire (Copenhagen: Reitzel, 1996), pp. 147–60.

[116] Heimo of Bamberg, *De decursu temporum*, pp. 89–95.

[117] Sigebert of Gembloux, *Chronica*, pp. 509–10, 541, 546–47; Alberic of Troisfontaines, *Chronicon*, pp. 701, 716, 722–23. These are not comprehensive lists. See also Saxo Grammaticus, *Gesta Danorum*, I, 1. 1: the Danes received their name from their first ruler (Dan), but he still cited Dudo of St Quentin's tenth-century suggestion that they received their name because they were Greeks (*Danai*).

[118] Matthew Paris, *Chronica majora*, I: *The Creation to A.D. 1066* (1872), p. 3.

[119] Simon de Kéza, *Gesta Hungarorum*, pp. 58–59.

already seen what this meant in practice, as when Heimo of Bamberg criticized Eusebius for his faulty chronology, or when Simon de Kéza lambasted Orosius for fantasizing about genitally challenged genies impregnating Scythian women. The process of redaction also involved checking and revising information. In his account of the origins of the Slavs, Helmold of Bosau might have drawn extensively on Adam of Bremen, yet he paraphrased, condensed, and rewrote as much as copied the earlier chronicler. When dealing with the mission of St Anskar (d. 865) to Sweden, he freely mixed information from Adam, the *Vita Anskari*, and his own findings,[120] while in his account of the conversion of King Harold Bluetooth of Denmark (d. 985/86), Helmold not only abridged Adam's text, but also added a reference to the Danes paying tribute to the Holy Roman Empire.[121] If necessary, written sources had to be complemented by linguistic or material evidence. Just before 1200, the monks of Göttweig in Lower Austria traced the community back to a leader of the Goths, who had been named after a sword that Attila had received, which had once belonged to an even more ancient warrior called Mars (*Wich* in the language of the Goths), later mistaken for a god. Göttweig, it was asserted, had been named after this leader (*Wich*) and his people (the Goths).[122] The author of *Heimskringla*, in turn, referenced archaeological evidence to describe ancient burial rites,[123] while Simon de Kéza, on recounting the first major defeat suffered by the Huns, reported that their leader had been buried 'at a place by the highway where a stone statue is erected'.[124] Chroniclers, in short, were not just copyists. They investigated and assessed, revised and collated, questioned and amended the materials at their disposal, and they sought out new ones. They built on, and thereby reflected and reinforced, a shared cultural framework.

---

[120] Helmold of Bosau, *Chronica Slavorum*, ed. by Bernhard Schmeidler, trans. by Heinz Stoob, with an afterword by Volker Scior, 6th edn (Darmstadt: Wissenschaftliche Buchgesellschaft, 2002), pp. 50–51.

[121] Helmold of Bosau, *Chronica Slavorum*, pp. 62–63. See also: Thomas Zotz, 'Kaiserliche Vorlage und Chronistenwerk. Zur Entstehungsgeschichte der *Gesta Frederici* Ottos von Freising', in *Geschichtsvorstellungen: Bilder, Texte und Begriffe aus dem Mittelalter*, ed. by Steffen Patzold, Anja Rathmann-Lutz, and Volker Scior (Vienna: Böhlau, 2012), pp. 153–77.

[122] *Vita Altmanni episcopi Pataviensis*, MGH, SS, 12 (Hanover: Hahn, 1856), p. 237. I am grateful to Ryan Kemp for alerting me to the Göttweig example.

[123] Snorri Sturluson, *Heimskringla*, trans. by Lee M. Hollander (Austin: University of Texas Press, 1964), pp. 3–4.

[124] Simon de Kéza, *Gesta Hungarorum*, pp. 36–37.

Let me use Latin as an example. Its use formed an integral part of a wider European cultural framework. Latin was an international language that facilitated the exchange of texts and information across Western Europe, and it provided a set of models and examples for writers to use. It also held religious connotations as the language of the Bible and the liturgy, and mastery of Latin was an inevitable prerequisite for and consequence of Christianization, itself a marker of civilization. Moreover, its cultural cache was both rooted in and reinforced by its association with Rome. For a community's past to be recognized as legitimate, and for that community to be deemed part of a family of civilized nations, a Latin record of its past was needed. Such thinking likely underpinned the first wave of historical writing in post-Conquest England: between *c.* 1080 and *c.* 1130, Eadmer and Osbern at Canterbury, William of Malmesbury, Simeon of Durham, and John of Worcester, as well as the abbots and abbesses commissioning Goscelin of St Bertin,[125] aimed to procure a Latin record of Anglo-Saxon saints and kings. Here, a further impetus was provided by foreign elites, who needed to be instructed and familiarized with the past and customs of their people. Similar patterns surface elsewhere, however, especially in realms that had been converted fairly recently.[126] After all, possessing and knowing one's history was a mark of civilization. Only brutes, Henry of Huntingdon explained, refused to know their past.[127] Both the ability and the desire to recover one's past demonstrated familiarity with classical authors, the Bible, and a growing body of writings from across the Latin West. This also required that authors muster the approaches, display the erudition, and show the command of Latin that allowed a work of history to be recognized as such.[128] The ostentatiously classicizing idiom employed by William of Malmesbury, Vincent Kadlubek, or Saxo Grammaticus might well have been chosen with these concerns in mind: the past of the English, Poles, and Danes

---

[125] Bernhard Pabst, 'Goscelin von St. Bertin und die literarische Biographie', in *Scripturus vitam: Lateinische Biographie von der Antike bis in die Gegenwart. Festgabe für Walter Berschin zum 65. Geburtstag*, ed. by Dorothea Walz (Heidelberg: Mattes, 2002), pp. 933–47.

[126] *Historia Norwegie*, pp. 50–51; Saxo Grammaticus, *Gesta Danorum*, i, 2–3. See also: Björn Weiler, 'Tales of First Kings: Narratives of Royal Origin in the West, c. 1000–c. 1200', *Viator*, 46.2 (2015), 101–28.

[127] Henry of Huntingdon, *Historia Anglorum*, pp. 4–5; Theodoricus Monachus, *Historia Norwegiae*, in *Monumenta Historica Norvegiae: Latinske Kildeskrifter til Norges Historie i Middelalderen*, ed. by Gustav Storm (Kristiana: Brogger, 1880), p. 4.

[128] Theodoricus Monachus, *Historia*, p. 4; Anonymous notary, *Gesta Hungarorum*, pp. 4–5; Cosmas of Prague, *Chronica Boemorum*, pp. 1–3.

2. HISTORICAL WRITING IN EUROPE, c. 1100–1300

merited efforts rivalling those of the ancients. Their modern descendants, in turn, practised a standard of literacy and erudition that emulated, and perhaps even surpassed, the best that the Romans had to offer. They might not *be* Romans, but they certainly could *write* like them.

Of course, that authors invoked the cultural legacy of Rome did not mean that they laid claim to its political inheritance. Indeed, in most communities, writers eschewed postulating any descent from Rome at all. This extended to rejecting Trojan connections. Indeed, before the thirteenth century, few claimed Trojan ancestry, apart from the rulers of France and Germany and the inhabitants of Wales.[129] Instead, they sought to situate a community's origins in a more distinctive form of antiquity. According to Simon de Kéza, the Hungarians were thus Egyptians, who, after the fall of the Tower of Babel, had moved to Persia, before overpopulation forced them to expand into Scythia, from whence they (or, rather, the Huns) conquered most of Europe, before eventually settling in Hungary.[130] To Vincent Kadlubek, writing in Kraków c. 1200, the Poles were actually Gauls: some of them attacked and conquered Rome, while others, having defeated the Danes, settled in Poland.[131] Saxo Grammaticus, in turn, fashioned a narrative of Danish history inverting that of Rome: whenever the latter suffered reversals, the former triumphed.[132] And c. 1100 a most elaborate tale was spun at Trier: Trebeta, the son of King Ninus of Assyria, fled to Europe to escape the advances of his lascivious stepmother.

---

[129] With the exception of Sicard of Cremona, the sole other source to do so: Wolf, *Troja*. See, though, the passing allusion in Dudo of St Quentin's *Historia Normannorum*, written c. 996–1015, to Antenor, a Trojan exile who, according to Virgil, ended up founding Padua, as the forefather of the Danes: Dudo of St Quentin, *De moribus et actis primorum Normanniae Ducum*, ed. by Jules Lair, new edn (Caen: Le Blanc-Hardel, 1865), p. 130.

[130] Simon de Kéza, *Gesta Hungarorum*, pp. 8–25. Simon mentioned Troy only once: the Venetians, having fled Troy, first settled in Pannonia, before the Huns forced them to move yet again (pp. 58–59). Rome similarly appears only when Pope Leo offered submission to Attila (pp. 60–63).

[131] Vincent Kadlubek, *Die Chronik der Polen*, ed. and trans. by Eduard Mühle (Darmstadt: WBG, 2014), pp. 94–97. On Vincent: *Writing History in Medieval Poland: Bishop Vincentius of Cracow and the 'Chronica Polonorum'*, ed. by Darius von Güttner-Sporzyński (Turnhout: Brepols, 2017).

[132] Karsten Frijs Jensen, 'Saxo Grammaticus's Study of the Roman Historiographers and His Vision of History', in *Saxo Grammaticus: Tra storiografia e letteratura*, ed. by Carlo Santini (Rome: Il Calamo, 1992), pp. 61–81; Lars Boje Mortensen, 'Saxo Grammaticus' View of the Origin of the Danes and His Historiographical Models', *Cahiers de l'Institut du moyen-âge grec et latin (Université de Copenhague)*, 55 (1987), 169–83.

He eventually reached the Mosel valley, where he came to rule a tribe called the Gomer — as the chronicler noted, the most ancient people in Europe — and where he founded Trier in the seventh year of the patriarchate of Abraham, and 1250 years before the foundation of Rome.[133] All these authors drew on familiar models: Orosius, Isidore of Seville, St Jerome, Lucan, the epitome of Justin, Cicero, and the Bible. They also made indirect reference to Rome: their communities were peopled by the descendants of those who had conquered Rome, whose deeds were greater than those of the Romans, or whose cities long predated Rome. Similarly, with the exception of Saxo, these accounts, perhaps echoing Virgil and the Bible, involved either a leader or a people of distant origins (Egypt, Assyria, or Gaul). However, unlike in Exodus or the *Aeneid*, while their leaders might be exiles (Trebeta), the people themselves were either long-established in their homeland (Danes and Gomer), or its conquerors (Hungarians and Poles). Across the Latin West, communal identities were shaped in relation to a common European textual culture.

It might be tempting to view the rejection of Roman or Trojan origins as reflecting political considerations: most of these realms at one point or another faced claims to overlordship from German prelates and emperors, who *did* invoke Trojan ancestry.[134] Precisely because they were *not* Trojans, by contrast, Poles, Hungarians, Danes, and Czechs remained beyond the purview of their Frankish neighbours. However, the phenomenon cannot be reduced to one of political expediency alone. Part of the aim of these accounts was to fashion a version of the communal past that conformed to contemporary expectations of what a reliable and truthful history should look like. This, as we have seen, involved engagement with familiar models. But it also depended on finding and selecting reliable evidence. And there were no trustworthy sources that linked these communities to Troy. Most of the materials on which Scandinavian reconstructions of the past were based either made no reference to Troy at all or

---

[133] *Gesta Treverorum*, p. 130.

[134] Matthew J. Innes, 'Teutons or Trojans? The Carolingians and the Germanic Past', in *The Uses of the Past in the Early Middle Ages*, ed. by Yitzhak Hen and Matthew Innes (Cambridge: Cambridge University Press, 2000), pp. 227–49; Jonathan Barlow, 'Gregory of Tours and the Myth of the Trojan Origins of the Franks', *Frühmittelalterliche Studien*, 29 (1985), 86–95; Alheydis Plassmann, *Origo Gentis: Identitäts- und Legitimitätsstiftung in früh- und hochmittlelalterlichen Herkunftserzählungen* (Berlin: Akademie, 2006), pp. 153–55; Wolf, *Troja*, pp. 264–75. Examples: Otto of Freising, *Chronica*, pp. 56–57 (see also the Germans as *Teutonici Franci*: pp. 7, 272, 277, 278, 285, 288, 315); Wipo, *Gesta Chuonradi imperatoris*, ed. by Harry Bresslau, MGH, SS, 3rd edn (Hanover: Hahn, 1915), p. 16.

contained a wholly different set of origin stories. Adam of Bremen, a key source for the *Chronicon Roskildense*, Sven Aggesen, Saxo Grammaticus, and the *Historia Norwegie*, referred to Troy not even once. In Hungary, plausibly influenced by Orosius, the connection between Huns, Magyars, and Hungarians provided a well-attested version of communal origins. Even Geoffrey of Monmouth fits this pattern: he embellished and added to the ninth-century *Historia Brittonum*, where the reference to the Trojan origins of the Welsh first surfaced.[135] In short, emphasizing a community's non-Trojan roots often meant simply following the evidence. That was, after all, precisely what chroniclers were meant to do. It was how they claimed membership of a wider European textual and cultural community.

It was also how they established truthfulness. History was meant to record only what had verifiably happened.[136] Only then could moral lessons be drawn, rights be defended, and a community's distinctiveness be ascertained. In practice, matters were, of course, less rigid. Moral frequently trumped historical truth: what should have been might prove more instructive than what had actually been. Sometimes, there simply was not enough evidence, but gaps still had to be filled with what seemed likely to have occurred.[137] At other times, insufficient evidence existed for that which authors and patrons just knew to be true, and a suitable record had to be fashioned.[138] And in many an instance, especially where property rights, legal privileges, the possession of relics, or the deeds of a patron saint were concerned, alternative pasts had to be put into writing to refute the claims of rivals and competitors.[139] Even then, though, authors

---

[135] *Historia Brittonum*, ed. by Theodor Mommsen, MGH, Auct. ant., 13 (Berlin: Weidmann, 1889), pp. 111–222 (pp. 149–53); Geoffrey of Monmouth, *History*, pp. lvii–lix; Wolf, *Troja*, pp. 171–87.

[136] Isidore of Seville, *Etymologies*, ed. and trans. by Stephen A. Barney (Cambridge: Cambridge University Press, 2006), p. 67.

[137] Björn Weiler, 'Tales of Trickery and Deceit: The Election of Frederick Barbarossa (1152), Historical Memory, and the Culture of Kingship in Later Staufen Germany', *Journal of Medieval History*, 38 (2012), 295–317.

[138] Denis Drumm, *Das Hirsauer Geschichtsbild im 12. Jahrhundert: Studien zum Umgang mit der klösterlichen Vergangenheit in einer Zeit des Umbruchs* (Ostfildern: Thorbecke, 2016).

[139] See, for an especially striking example, *Die jüngere Translatio S. Dionysii Aeropagitae*, ed. by Veronika Lukas, MGH, SS rer. Germ., 80 (Wiesbaden: Harrassowitz, 2013). Generally: *Fälschungen im Mittelalter. Internationaler Kongreß der Monumenta Germaniae Historica München, 16.-19. September 1986*, 6 vols (Hanover: Hahn, 1988–90).

employed an established set of tools with which to convey rigour, learning, and truthfulness. They constructed verisimilitude.[140]

That, in turn, was accomplished by employing a series of textual markers: the language employed, the references made to familiar sources and events, or that a text had been cited by trusted authorities. Naturally, these markers changed over time. New texts were added, and others forgotten. What might once have been deemed credible, was considered plausible no longer, while erstwhile flights of fancy could, with the proliferation of similar accounts, become established truths. At St Albans, for instance, the patron saint's cloak (*amphibalus*), became, in Geoffrey of Monmouth's rendering, which was then adopted by the monks, St Amphibalus, Alban's trusted companion, and a prolific worker of miracles.[141] Similarly, with new actors emerging as patrons, informants, and audiences, new types of writing emerged that both echoed and transcended established genres and conventions.[142] Theodoricus Monachus had felt the need to compose a Latin chronicle because Norwegian history had thus far been written only in Old Norse. Latinity carried with it both credibility and cultural caché. A century later, Simon de Kéza used the Middle High German *Nibelungenlied* to gather information about the Huns. That the *Lied* also drew on a shared canon of sources, such as Statius, Prosper of Aquitaine, Fredegar, and Godfrey of Viterbo's *Pantheon*, likely reinforced its credibility.[143] Indeed, the extent to which vernacular texts employed the rhetorical markers of Latin historiography is worth noting. Reflecting classical handbooks on rhetoric, Orosius, Caesar, and Pliny the Elder, and in line with writers as diverse as Thietmar of Merseburg and Ralph de Diceto, *Heimskringla* opens with a short geography of the world and of Norway.[144] For his *Weltchronik* (*c*. 1250), Rudolf

---

[140] Ruth Morse, *Truth and Convention in the Middle Ages: Rhetoric, Representation, and Reality* (Cambridge: Cambridge University Press, 1991); Kempshall, *Rhetoric*, pp. 350–427.

[141] Matthew Paris, *Chronica majora*, II: *A.D. 1067 to A.D. 1216* (1874), pp. 301–05, 306–08; Thomas of Walsingham, *Gesta abbatum*, I, 219; Geoffrey of Monmouth, *History*, pp. 94–95. I owe this point to Tom O'Donnell.

[142] Gert Melville, 'Spätmittelalterliche Geschichtskompendien — eine Aufgabenstellung', *Römische Historische Mitteilungen*, 22 (1980), 51–104; Björn Weiler, 'Historical Writing and the Experience of Europeanisation: The View from St Albans', in *The Making of Europe: Essays in Honour of Robert Bartlett*, ed. by John G. H. Hudson and Sally Crumplin (Leiden: Brill, 2016), pp. 205–43.

[143] <http://gottfried.unistra.fr/nibelungen/deutsche-fassungen/nibelungenlied/> [accessed 21 March 2018]; Simon de Kéza, *Gesta Hungarorum*, pp. 66–69.

[144] *Heimskringla*, p. 6; Kempshall, *Rhetoric*, pp. 305–07.

of Ems, in turn, drew on Peter Comestor, the Bible, and Godfrey of Viterbo,[145] while the *Estoria de Espanna*, a history of Castile to 1253, cited Godfrey alongside Pliny, Josephus, and Statius.[146] In consulting the *Nibelungenlied*, Simon applied familiar criteria for assessing the validity of information. Yet he did so in a rapidly changing environment, where even the imaginary tale of Siegfried, Hagen, and Kriemhild could don the accoutrements of Latin historiography.

This is not to suggest that Simon had been duped by the *Lied*. Rather, I suggest, his example alerts us to the social and material context of cultural practices. It was all well and good to try writing verifiable history, but what was to be done if the evidence was lacking? The wealth of mutual borrowing, shared sources, and common approaches that has been outlined here should not let us forget the earlier observation about the fragility of the past. In fact, Simon faced a dual challenge. First, his main source, the anonymous notary, required updating. Dares Phrygius might have been an appropriate model for the notary's contemporaries, but two generations later it would no longer suffice: too much new information had come to light, so much more was known, and expectations of Latin composition had changed. That the notary had ended his account with a short reference to the conversion of St Stephen also meant that there existed no narrative record of the intervening (almost) three centuries. His *Gesta* required both revision and continuation. Second, there remained the problem that little was known about the Huns and early Magyars. There was Orosius, of course, but his account, as we have seen, was clearly deemed to be faulty and flawed. Hence Simon's quest for new materials, his scouting the libraries of Strasbourg and Venice, his gleaning of information from Godfrey and Jordanes. Hence, too, his consultation of the *Nibelungenlied*.[147] His was a case not of credulity, but of a desire to recover and preserve an inherently fragile past, one that was in constant danger of fading from memory, or of being known only through inaccurate and faulty sources, and to present it in a manner that was recognizable, and that would be accepted, as truthful and reputable.

---

[145] Rudolf von Ems, *Weltchronik. Aus der Wernigeroder Handschrift*, ed. Gustav Ehrismann (Berlin: Weidmann, 1915); Christoph Thierry, 'Écrire l'histoire universelle à la cour de Konrad IV de Hohenstaufen: la Weltchronik de Rudolf von Ems (milieu XIIIe siècle)', in *Universal Chronicles*, ed. by Campopiano and Bainton, pp. 141–78.

[146] <http://estoria.bham.ac.uk/blog/> [accessed 21 March 2018].

[147] Indeed, where possible, he was careful to verify what he found with other types of evidence. Simon de Kéza, *Gesta Hungarorum*, pp. 36–37.

Conclusion

Simon was not alone in facing such challenges. In Poland, Vincent Kadlubek rewrote and updated the history of the Poles composed almost a century before by the so-called Gallus Anonymus; in Denmark, Saxo Grammaticus did likewise with the *Chronicon Roskildense*; and William of Malmesbury in England, or Godfrey of Viterbo in the Holy Roman Empire similarly set out to update, rewrite, and fill the gaps in the works of their predecessors. This required that they search for and incorporate new information and that they refashion the past to meet the shifting expectations of an expanding range of readers and patrons. Most strikingly, though, while each author remained distinctive in style and subject matter, collectively they nonetheless formed part of a recognizable European literary and textual culture. They drew on similar models, read similar texts, employed similar approaches to verify information, and dealt with similar challenges in forging — from always fragmentary and often disparate elements — a plausible rendition of the past. Furthermore, their efforts shed light on the social reality within which the writing of history unfolded. They allow us to identify networks of communication and intellectual exchange that spanned the whole of Christendom. They finally point to intellectual fashions that emerged independently from but in close chronological proximity to each other, such as the first Latin records of the regnal past (or at least the first in several centuries) being produced within a generation of each other in Poland (*c.* 1110), Bohemia (*c.* 1123), England (*c.* 1125), and Denmark (*c.* 1139), or the classicizing refashioning of these accounts that occurred within a decade in the Empire (*c.* 1190), Poland (*c.* 1200), and Denmark (*c.* 1200).

Let me conclude by outlining how these findings might help shape our approach to high medieval historical writing more broadly. I do not presume to be comprehensive, and will focus on just three aspects. Most immediately, we should keep in mind that what has been sketched here is a framework. Variations clearly existed: in Catalonia and Hungary, charters often took the place occupied in Germany or France by chronicles and histories,[148] while the rich corpus of communal and local narratives in Italy or Germany had no real equivalent in England. The social and material context outlined here might provide a path towards understanding and analysing such peculiarities. Second,

---

[148] Adam Kosto, 'The Elements of Practical Rulership: Ramon Berenguer I of Barcelona and the Revolt of Mir Geribert', *Viator*, 47.2 (2016), 67–94; László Veszprémy, 'Historical Past and Political Present in the Latin Chronicles of Hungary (12th–13th Centuries)', in *The Medieval Chronicle*, ed. by Erik Kooper (Amsterdam: Rodopi, 1999), pp. 260–68.

it is worth pondering whether a comparative approach might not benefit from setting social groups alongside one another, or even prioritizing them over geographical divisions. The tendency, still prevalent in some modern scholarship, to approach medieval narratives of the past in neatly compartmentalized sections based on nineteenth-century political geography (with distinct Castilian, German, French, etc., traditions), clearly does not reflect the evidence. Given the importance, for instance, of Cistercian networks in collating and disseminating texts and information, could it be that regional peculiarities could be more easily ascertained when reading Cistercian histories from across the Latin West both alongside each other, and in combination with other texts from the same region? Similar questions might be asked about genres of writing that built on shared foundational texts and patterns of composition. Episcopal *vitae* and *gesta* thus looked back to a common corpus of models rooted in the New Testament and Late Antiquity and normally followed a comparable narrative structure. Yet they also reflected their immediate political and social environment. Would this enable us to trace broader differences and commonalities? Finally, the model sketched here encourages us to move beyond a quest for the peculiar and particular. The material and social framework of writing history points to concrete realities that can be traced more easily through redactions of the past: networks of communication, education, reading, and for procuring texts. The cultural dimension, in turn, shows a fruitful route into debates and developments that otherwise remain hidden from view. Why, for instance, was it that, around 1200, writers across Europe decided to refashion the communal past in so ambitiously classicizing a manner? Likewise, what does the extent to which communal distinctiveness was asserted along very similar lines across the West reveal about concepts of Christendom, regnal identity, and so on? In short, adopting the approach proposed here will allow us to gain a deeper understanding both of the peculiar and the general. It also points to a world remarkably rich and varied, just waiting to be explored.

3. Historical Scholars and Dishonest Charlatans: Studying the Chronicles of Medieval Wales

Ben Guy

During the past two centuries, the chronicles of medieval Wales and, most especially, the families of chronicles known loosely as *Annales Cambriae* and *Brut y Tywysogyon*, have become the most frequently cited sources for the history of medieval Wales. This is not surprising; a great deal of their subject matter is entirely absent from other extant sources, especially matter concerning the activities of the native Welsh princes. But how many users of these texts truly understand what it is that they are reading? The annalistic format of the chronicles certainly lends them a user-friendly appearance, even if the dates that appear beside the annals in the editions are usually editorial insertions of disputable accuracy. Less immediately clear, however, is the perspective of the texts. Any student of history will know that a source is of limited use if its point of view cannot be discerned and contextualized. This is a problem of particular complexity for annalistic chronicles. On the one hand, they claim to offer straightforward accounts of political events of the kind sought by historians to lend order and structure to their historical narratives, but, on the other hand, they can purport to cover multiple centuries and can draw upon several sources of different hues, resulting in the reader being subjected to a veritable cacophony of unidentifiable, discordant voices.

Much of the modern scholarly work on the chronicles of medieval Wales has sought to erect a framework within which these various difficulties can be comprehended, but not all modern interventions have succeeded in clarifying matters. An obvious example is provided by the amorphous family of chronicles known, since 1848, as *Annales Cambriae*. Various choices made by the 1848 editors have had unfortunate, lasting consequences. For a start, their generic and non-committal title ('Annals of Wales') has become reified in scholarship, to the extent that some can talk of '*Annales Cambriae*' as if it were itself a 'text'. As is discussed in greater detail below, the 1848 editors created a composite edition of a chronicle covering 444–1066 from three different sources, one belonging to the tenth century and the two others to the thirteenth. Although for the period from 444 (actually 445) to 1066 the three chronicles share a common source, following their annals for 1202/03 the two thirteenth-century texts develop quite differently. If a name for the common source is required, the 'Annals of St Davids' would be preferable to '*Annales Cambriae*', giving non-specialists a much clearer idea about the text's perspective.

The chronicles of medieval Wales have also been subject to a wider scholarly trend that has, until recently, served to hinder proper understanding of the subject. Since chronicles have often been viewed as repositories of useful information rather than as deliberate literary productions, there has been a tendency to edit and print only those sections of the chronicles that contain unique information, leaving other sections unedited and inaccessible. Such was the case, for example, with *Cronica ante aduentum Domini* in Exeter Cathedral Library, MS 3514. This text covers the years 1132 BC to AD 1285, but only the final section, encompassing the years 1254–1285, was printed by Thomas Jones, because, as he saw it, 'its earlier entries have no historical value'.[1] By this he meant that the earlier items preserved no information that could not be found in other readily available sources. However, we would now recognize that the earlier part of the text could be of great historical value indeed, depending on the questions asked of it: it could inform us about the medieval organization of historical time, about the teaching of history in monastic houses, and more broadly about the purpose and function of chronicles.[2] Recently, a less restricted approach to medieval chronicles in Wales has been yielding insightful results, as shown, for example, by Henry Gough-

---

[1] '"Cronica de Wallia" and Other Documents from Exeter Cathedral Library MS. 3514', ed. by Thomas Jones, *BBCS*, 12 (1946), 27–44 (p. 29). The entire text is now available in a transcription by Henry Gough-Cooper, published on the website of the Welsh Chronicles Research Group: <http://croniclau.bangor.ac.uk/editions.php.en> [accessed 15 March 2019].

[2] For annalistic chronicles as didactic tools, see *The Winchcombe and Coventry Chronicles: Hitherto Unnoticed Witnesses to the Work of John of Worcester*, ed. and trans. by Paul Anthony Hayward, 2 vols (Tempe: Arizona Center for Medieval and Renaissance Studies, 2010), I, 37–48.

Cooper's important study of the organization of the six ages of the world in the thirteenth-century St Davids chronicle.[3] It has also allowed other, generally later chronicles, which would previously have been deemed to possess 'no historical value', to enter the discussion for the first time, often throwing unexpected light on previously inscrutable difficulties.

Despite such obstacles, it remains true that significant advances have been made in the field over the past two centuries. Entrenched historiographical myths have been dispelled, such as the idea that the hagiographer Caradog of Llancarfan was the author of *Brut y Tywysogyon* up to the mid-twelfth century. Fine editions have appeared, including Phillimore's exacting reproduction of the Harleian chronicle and Jones's indispensable (though not infallible) editions of *Brut y Tywysogyon* and *Brenhinedd y Saesson*. Some complex textual relationships have been discerned, involving the vernacular and Latin chronicling traditions of 'native' Wales, the Marcher chronicles of the monasteries of South Wales, and external chronicles of the Irish and English traditions. And some attempts have been made, however fleetingly, to peer beyond textual matters and produce qualitative judgements about the intentions, motivations, and perspectives of chronicle writers in Wales across the medieval period.

Much remains to be done, but it seems timely to take stock of where matters currently stand. The purpose of this chapter is thus to survey the activities of scholars who have studied the annalistic chronicles of medieval Wales during the past two centuries and more. It is hoped that the exercise will highlight certain strands of debate that might not otherwise be immediately apparent to casual users of the chronicles, drawing attention, in the process, to quite how few are the elements of certainty in the subject. The discussion proceeds chronologically, addressing in turn the shaky foundations laid by nineteenth-century scholars, the formation of the modern consensus during the twentieth century, and the various strands of further enquiry that have been pursued in recent decades. In light of the discussion, certain suggestions are made as to where attention might productively be turned in the future.

---

[3] Henry Gough-Cooper, 'Deconnovenal Reason and Unreason in the C-Text of *Annales Cambriae*', in *The Medieval Chronicle 11*, ed. by Erik Kooper and Sjoerd Levelt (Leiden: Brill, 2017), pp. 195–212. See below, pp. 93–94.

Faltering Beginnings

For the Welsh scholarly community, it has always been the vernacular manifestations of chronicling in Wales that have held the greatest appeal, and which have engendered the largest volume of attention. This is partly due to the literary qualities of some of the vernacular texts and the comparative ease with which they can be read by modern speakers of Welsh. Such factors were already at work among Welsh antiquarians during the early modern period. In general, very few Latin manuscripts survive that can be securely attributed to medieval Wales, and even fewer of those preserve Latin chronicles.[4] Far more chronicle-bearing manuscripts survive written in Welsh, and it was these manuscripts that were extensively copied by Welsh antiquarians between the sixteenth and eighteenth centuries. Little wonder, then, that the first chronicles of medieval Wales to be printed fully, in the pages of the second volume of *The Myvyrian Archaiology of Wales* (1801), were various versions of the important vernacular chronicle *Brut y Tywysogyon*, alongside its reworked relative *Brenhinedd y Saesson*.[5] According to the volume's preface, these texts were printed because they 'were deemed, by the Editors, most important, towards the elucidation of British History'.[6] The editors rightly drew attention to the fact that *Brut y Tywysogyon*[7] was deliberately written as a continuation of 'the history of the kings of Britain', meaning *Brut y Brenhinedd*, the medieval Welsh translation of Geoffrey of Monmouth's *De gestis Britonum*.[8] They also repeated the early modern idea that the bulk of the chronicle should be attributed to the twelfth-century scholar Caradog of Llancarfan. This idea originated in David Powel's *Historie of Cambria*, published in 1584, in which Powel printed an expanded version of Humphrey Llwyd's English history of Wales, *Cronica Walliae*.[9] Powel

---

[4] Daniel Huws, *Medieval Welsh Manuscripts* (Cardiff: University of Wales Press, 2000), p. 3.

[5] *MA*.

[6] *MA*, II (1801), p. v.

[7] I shall continue to use the medieval spelling of *Brut y Tywysogyon* (ending with *-yon*) employed by Thomas Jones, the text's editor, rather than the modern spelling (ending with *-ion*) favoured by some writers, including the editors of the *Myvyrian Archaiology*.

[8] *MA*, II, p. vii.

[9] David Powel, *The Historie of Cambria, now called Wales: A Part of the Most Famous Yland of Brytaine, written in the Brytish Language aboue two hundred years past* (London: Newberie and Denham, 1584), preface, fol. v^r, and p. 206. The attribution of *Brut y Tywysogyon* to Caradog of Llancarfan had been considered and rejected by John Leland earlier in the sixteenth century: see Caroline Brett, 'John Leland, Wales, and Early British History', *Welsh History Review*,

knew that Geoffrey of Monmouth, in the famous epilogue to his history, had requested that his contemporary Caradog of Llancarfan should continue the story for the rulers of Wales, and Powel assumed that *Brut y Tywysogyon* was the product of that request. The myth of Caradog's authorship would linger on for a further century after the publication of the *Myvyrian Archaiology*, before it was finally laid to rest by J. E. Lloyd in 1928.[10]

The editors of the *Myvyrian Archaiology* printed four annalistic chronicles written in medieval Welsh.[11] First came the text now known as the Red Book version of *Brut y Tywysogyon*, taken from the Red Book of Hergest itself.[12] Following this, three similar texts were printed in parallel: the text now known as *Brenhinedd y Saesson* (misleadingly called *Brut y Saeson* in the *Myvyrian Archaiology*), taken from London, BL, MS Cotton Cleopatra B V; the infamous 'Aberpergwm' or 'Gwentian' *Brut* (also labelled simply as *Brut y Tywysogion*); and the interpolated version of *Brut Ieuan Brechfa*.[13] The *Gwentian Brut* would prove highly influential in nineteenth-century historical writing, even though its authenticity was doubted by such scholars as Thomas Stephens, who proved in 1858 that it contained at least one interpolation dateable no earlier than the mid-sixteenth century.[14] But it was only through the efforts of G. J.

---

15 (1990), 169–82 (pp. 176–77). Humphrey Llwyd's original work can now be accessed in Humphrey Llwyd, *Cronica Walliae*, ed. by Ieuan M. Williams and J. Beverley Smith (Cardiff: University of Wales Press, 2002). Among Llwyd's sources were several versions of *Brut y Tywysogyon*: see Humphrey Llwyd, *Cronica Walliae*, pp. 20–22.

[10] John Edward Lloyd, *The Welsh Chronicles*, The Sir John Rhŷs Memorial Lecture, British Academy (London: Milford, 1928), pp. 5–9; also printed as 'The Welsh Chronicles', *Proceedings of the British Academy*, 14 (1928), 369–91 (references are to the pamphlet).

[11] For more details, see my chapter (Chapter 11) below on *Brut Ieuan Brechfa*.

[12] *MA*, II, 391–467.

[13] *MA*, II, 468–582. All four texts appear as discreet items in the single-volume edition of the *Myvyrian Archaiology*: *MA²*, pp. 602–51 ('Brut y Tywysogion'), 652–84 ('Brut y Saeson'), 685–715 ('Brut y Tywysogion'), 716–20 ('Brut Ieuan Brechfa'). In medieval manuscripts, *Brut y Sae(s)son* is a title given to a separate text, as mentioned below; it is never applied to *Brenhinedd y Saesson*. Cf. Egerton Phillimore, 'The Publication of Welsh Historical Records', *Y Cymmrodor*, 11 (1890–91), 133–75 (p. 156).

[14] Thomas Stephens, 'The Book of Aberpergwm, improperly called The Chronicle of Caradoc', *Archaeologia Cambrensis*, 3rd ser., 4, no. 13 (1858), 77–96 (p. 95). Aneurin Owen had made the same observation, seemingly independently, prior to his death in 1851, and his reasoning is laid out in his introduction to *Brut y Tywysogyon*, published posthumously in 1864: *Brut y Tywysogion: The Gwentian Chronicle*, trans. by Aneurin Owen (London: Smith and Parker, 1863), p. ix; this publication may be found appended to the 1864 volume of *Archaeo-*

Williams in the twentieth century that the *Gwentian Brut* and the interpolated version of *Brut Ieuan Brechfa* were definitively proved to be literary concoctions of the romantic forger Edward Williams (Iolo Morganwg, 1747–1826), and they have consequently been ejected from the canon of medieval Welsh historical writing.[15]

In the second quarter of the nineteenth century the debate was broadened, and put on a firmer scholarly footing, by Aneurin Owen, son of the *Myvyrian* editor William Owen Pughe. Aneurin Owen is best known as the author of the foundational work on medieval Welsh law, *Ancient Laws and Institutes of Wales*, published in 1841.[16] Fortunately, Aneurin Owen also applied his skill as a textual critic to the chronicles of medieval Wales. His work on this subject was first published in 1848 as part of the first (and only) volume of *Monumenta Historica Britannica* (hereafter *MHB*), an epic collection of source materials for the history of England and Wales from the earliest times to the Norman conquest.[17] The volume was prepared for the Record Commission by Henry Petrie, Keeper of the Records of the Tower of London. However, owing to the suspension of the project in 1834 and Petrie's death in 1842, it was eventually brought to completion by Petrie's successor, Sir Thomas Duffus Hardy.[18] Although Owen's contribution is never explicitly recognized, it is clear from various footnotes that Owen was Petrie and Hardy's primary authority for Welsh chronicles, and it was he who supplied them with the edited texts.[19] Two such texts appear in

---

logia Cambrensis. However, when ab Ithel reworked Owen's introduction for the Rolls Series edition of *Brut y Tywysogyon*, he carefully suppressed the evidence against the authenticity of the *Gwentian Brut*: cf. Anon. [Harry Longueville Jones], review of John Williams ab Ithel, *Brut y Tywysogion* (1860), *Archaeologia Cambrensis*, 3rd ser., 7, no. 25 (1861), 93–103 (pp. 96–97); Phillimore, 'Publication', p. 165 n. 6. For ab Ithel's hostility towards criticism of 'bardic' texts like the *Gwentian Brut*, see Griffith John Williams, *Agweddau ar Hanes Dysg Gymraeg*, ed. by Aneirin Lewis (Cardiff: University of Wales Press, 1969), p. 259.

[15] Griffith John Williams, 'Brut Aberpergwm: A Version of the Chronicle of the Princes', *Glamorgan Historian*, 4 (1967), 205–20.

[16] *Ancient Laws and Institutes of Wales*, ed. and trans. by Aneurin Owen ([London]: [Public Record Office], 1841).

[17] *MHB*.

[18] See Albert Frederick Pollard, 'Petrie, (Frederick) Henry', rev. by Bernard Nurse, in *Oxford Dictionary of National Biography* <https://doi.org/10.1093/ref:odnb/22052>.

[19] For example, *MHB*, pp. 94 n. 2, 95 n. 2. See Owen's 1829 letter to Petrie, printed in *Brut y Tywysogion: The Gwentian Brut*, pp. xix–xxiv. Cf. Phillimore, 'Publication', pp. 140, 144; Williams, *Agweddau*, p. 267.

MHB: one called 'the anonymous Annals of Cambria',[20] or *Annales Cambriae* in Latin, and the other called *Brut y Tywysogion*. Because the first volume of *MHB* was intended to address only the pre-Norman period, neither edition goes beyond 1066 (the edition of *Annales Cambriae* covers 444–1066, and the edition of *Brut y Tywysogyon* covers 681–1066), even though no significant breaks occur in the texts at that year.[21] The edition of *Annales Cambriae* was taken from three manuscripts considered together for the first time in *MHB*: London, BL, MS Harley 3859; London, The National Archives, MS E 164/1 (the chronicle at fols 1ʳ–13ʳ); and BL, MS Cotton Domitian A I. In relation to the *MHB Annales Cambriae*, these three texts were respectively assigned the sigla A, B, and C, which is why they are now generally known as the A-, B-, and C-texts of *Annales Cambriae*.[22] The *MHB Brut y Tywysogyon*, like the version in the *Myvyrian Archaiology*, was based on the text in the Red Book of Hergest, but it was furnished with variants from four other medieval manuscripts.

It is remarkable how many basic tenets concerning these texts were first established in the introduction to the *MHB* editions.[23] With respect to *Annales Cambriae*, it was established that the earlier part of the A-text was taken from an Irish chronicle; that the world history at the beginning of the B-text was derived primarily from the works of Isidore of Seville, Bede, and Geoffrey of Monmouth; that the latter part of the B-text was probably composed at the Cistercian abbey of Strata Florida; that the B- and C-texts generally agree with each other to 1203;[24] that the C-text thereafter becomes briefer and more par-

---

[20] *MHB*, p. 92.

[21] Note that 444, the lower dating terminal for the edition of *Annales Cambriae*, is an error; the edition took for its first date the first annal of the Harleian chronicle, which is actually equivalent to 445. The error was perpetuated in *AC*, p. xxiv; Egerton Phillimore, 'The *Annales Cambriæ* and the Old-Welsh Genealogies from *Harleian MS. 3859*', *Y Cymmrodor*, 9 (1888), 141–83 (p. 152); Egerton Phillimore, 'Publication', p. 40; and *BT (Pen. 20 trans.)*, p. lxiv, but corrected in Alfred Anscombe, 'The Exordium of the "Annales Cambriae"', *Ériu*, 3 (1907), 117–34 (pp. 123–24 n. 2) and Alfred Anscombe, 'Mr. E. W. B. Nicholson and the "Exordium" of the "Annales Cambriae"', *Zeitschrift für celtische Philologie*, 7 (1910), 419–38 (p. 422).

[22] Despite the imprecision of the terminology, I employ this system of labelling below where it is necessary to avoid ambiguity.

[23] Introduction to 'Annales Cambriae' at *MHB*, pp. 92–94; introduction to 'Brut y Tywysogion' at *MHB*, pp. 94–95.

[24] Note that Kathleen Hughes expressed a slightly different view when she noted that the final instance of substantial verbal agreement between the B- and C-texts occurs in the annal for 1202. David Stephenson has more recently restated the significance of the annals for 1203, supporting the original proposition offered in *MHB*. See Kathleen Hughes, *Celtic Britain in*

tial towards England; and that the C-text was interleaved with annals culled from a Worcester source. Similarly, with respect to *Brut y Tywysogyon*, it was recognized for the first time that the language of the text betrays a Latinate origin (even though, notably, Owen found it difficult to decide whether the *Brut*'s compilation took place in Latin or in Welsh), and that *Brenhinedd y Saeson* (again called *Brut y Saeson*, following the *Myvyrian Archaiology*) had been amalgamated with the Annals of Winchester.[25] In his original introduction to *Brut y Tywysogyon*, printed after his death, Owen also argued that *Brut y Tywysogyon* was probably compiled in the Cistercian abbey of Strata Florida.[26]

Although Owen was inclined to create variorum editions where parallel editions might have been more appropriate, his textual work was generally sound, and, had he lived to see the completion of his work, the incipient discipline of Welsh history might have been furnished with serviceable editions of some of Wales's most significant medieval chronicles.[27] Unfortunately, Owen died in 1851, and the work that he had undertaken in preparation for full editions of *Annales Cambriae* and *Brut y Tywysogyon* was released to the world only through the distorting filter of the Reverend John Williams ab Ithel.[28] Ab Ithel published the fruits of Owen's labours under his own name and without any acknowledgement of Owen in the two Rolls Series editions of 1860.[29] The reaction was almost immediate. In the first number of *Archaeologia Cambrensis* for 1861, an anonymous reviewer (known to be Harry Longueville Jones) of ab Ithel's *Brut y Tywysogion* lambasted ab Ithel for publishing Owen's entire text and translation without due acknowledgement and for distorting Owen's original introduction, as found in his notes, through the addition of 'irrelevant discussion of the triads, and some notes of little value', derived for the most part from the pseudo-historical bardic matter appearing in the publications of Iolo

---

the Early Middle Ages, ed. by David N. Dumville (Woodbridge: Boydell, 1980), p. 74; David Stephenson, 'Gerald of Wales and *Annales Cambriae*', *CMCS*, 60 (2010), 23–37 (pp. 25–27).

[25] This latter fact seems to have been first observed by Henry Petrie: see *Brut y Tywysogion: The Gwentian Brut*, p. xxiii.

[26] *Brut y Tywysogion: The Gwentian Brut*, pp. xv–xvi; cf. pp. xx–xxi. Owen's conclusion was reproduced without acknowledgement in *Brut y Tywysogion; or, The Chronicle of the Princes*, ed. by John Williams ab Ithel (London: Longman, 1860), pp. xxxvi–xxxvii.

[27] Though for criticism of Owen's editorial work, see Phillimore, 'Publication', p. 147.

[28] For ab Ithel, see Williams, *Agweddau*, pp. 253–77 (his work on the chronicles noticed at pp. 256, 266–67).

[29] *AC*; *Brut y Tywysogion*, ed. by Williams ab Ithel. Other publications from ab Ithel were the products of similar plagiarism: Williams, *Agweddau*, pp. 260–66.

Morganwg and his son Taliesin Williams.[30] To prove the point, the reviewer printed extracts from ab Ithel's preface and Owen's original preface in parallel, highlighting the sections that ab Ithel had plagiarized from Owen and the sections that he had added himself.[31] Ab Ithel responded to the review with a series of excuses, but this did nothing to placate the reviewer.[32] In a second review, further aspects of the edition were attacked, especially the glossary, the bardic matter in the preface, and the inexplicable transposition of phrases in the edition by comparison with Owen's original text.[33] In a third review, it was the turn of ab Ithel's *Annales Cambriae* to come under fire.[34] The reviewer made an important observation: that the text down to 1066 is generally correct, due to its close reliance on Owen's *MHB* edition, whereas the succeeding part down to 1288 is full of errors, and was probably ab Ithel's own work, based on transcripts made by others. The terrible inaccuracy of ab Ithel's text is important to recognize, because, remarkably given the circumstances, ab Ithel's edition of *Annales Cambriae* remains the standard edition used today.

More fundamental criticisms of ab Ithel's method of editing *Annales Cambriae* were published thirty years later by Egerton Phillimore.[35] Phillimore was well aware of the deficiency of Owen's use of the title '*Annales Cambriae*' for the common source of the three chronicles edited for the period 444–1066 in *MHB*, referring to it as a 'loose generic title'.[36] What concerned him far more, though, was ab Ithel's extension of Owen's title and editorial method to the entirety of the three chronicles concerned, beyond even the point where

---

[30] Anon. [Longueville Jones], review of Williams ab Ithel, *Brut y Tywysogion*, p. 95. For Harry Longueville Jones, see Huw Pryce, 'Harry Longueville Jones, FSA, Medieval Paris and the Heritage Measures of the July Monarchy', *The Antiquaries Journal*, 96 (2016), 391–414.

[31] Owen's original preface was later printed in *Archaeologia Cambrensis* as an introduction to his English translation of the *Gwentian Brut*, which had been prepared originally for publication in *MHB*: *Brut y Tywysogion: The Gwentian Brut*, pp. vii–xviii. See *BT (Pen. 20 trans.)*, pp. xxix–xxx.

[32] John William [*sic*] ab Ithel, 'Brut y Tywysogion', *Archaeologia Cambrensis*, 3rd ser., 7, no. 26 (1861), 169–71.

[33] Anon. [Harry Longueville Jones], 'Brut y Tywysogion (Second Notice)', *Archaeologia Cambrensis*, 3rd ser., 7, no. 27 (1861), 263–67.

[34] Anon. [Harry Longueville Jones], 'Annales Cambriæ', *Archaeologia Cambrensis*, 3rd ser., 7, no. 28 (1861), 325–32.

[35] Ben Guy, 'Egerton Phillimore (1856–1937) and the Study of Welsh Historical Texts', *THSC*, new ser., 21 (2015), 36–50 (pp. 45–46).

[36] Phillimore, 'Publication', p. 133; cf. p. 139.

they cease to share any common source. One can do no better than quote Phillimore's own words on the subject:

> Now the two later Chronicles [i.e. the B- and C-texts], during the period common to them and the older *Annales* [i.e. the A-text], viz., between 444 [*recte* 445] and 954, differ little in substance from the latter or from one another, but very much in phraseology and the orthography of proper names. As they proceed, however, the differences of every kind become progressively greater and greater, till finally, after 1203, they part company and become entirely different. This being the case, it will be clear that any one text formed by a fusion and collation of the three must largely constitute a mere mosaic of disjointed fragments, without entity or unity of its own; from the like of which it is absolutely impossible for any one to take a bird's-eye view, far less form a comparative and critical estimate, of any one of the separate works, its nature or value. The plan of adopting one MS as the text, and putting the variants of other MSS in the notes, is of course an excellent one when the collated MSS are substantially identical; but when they are very substantially different, and especially when, as with our *Annales*, each text contains orthographical peculiarities of the highest value for the history of the little-known stages of a language, the system is an utterly inadequate one. The process of forming one text out of such discordant materials may be compared to that of making an elaborate knot with threads of various colours. The trouble of making the knot is vast, but the trouble of undoing it when once made is so much vaster, that there is little likelihood of its ever being undone to any purpose. The only adequate plan in such a case is to print the various texts in parallel columns.

Phillimore eloquently expresses the problem at the heart of the matter: that the three so-called '*Annales Cambriae*' chronicles are separate texts sharing a common source, and so should not be combined together into a single variorum edition. Phillimore's plea for a parallel edition was sound and has been repeated by subsequent scholars, but the project has still not been fully realized.[37]

Forming a Consensus

Real progress in the subject began to be made in the second half of the nineteenth century with the publication of reliable editions of individual chronicles. Already in the 1860s, competent editions of two chronicles from the Cistercian monasteries of the southern March had appeared. In 1862, ab Ithel's erstwhile antagonist, Harry Longueville Jones, published a chronicle now known to be

---

[37] See below, pp. 92, 100–01.

associated with Neath Abbey.[38] Two years later, in the first volume of *Annales Monastici*, Henry Luard edited the Annals of Margam ('Annales de Margan').[39] In 1888, Egerton Phillimore published a precise and helpfully annotated edition of the so-called A-text of *Annales Cambriae*, otherwise known as the Harleian chronicle.[40] Phillimore's edition was gladly received; when the eminent Welsh historian J. E. Lloyd published his parallel edition of the B- and C-texts of *Annales Cambriae* for the years 1035–1093 a little over ten years later, he said of Phillimore's edition that it 'gives the student all that he can desire'.[41]

The Welsh-language chronicles were also granted renewed attention by the palaeographer J. Gwenogvryn Evans. Evans's contribution was two-fold. Firstly, working alongside John Rhŷs, Professor of Celtic at Jesus College, Oxford, he produced accurate editions of the most substantial vernacular chronicles in the Red Book of Hergest.[42] Although this entailed the nineteenth century's third printing of the Red Book's text of *Brut y Tywysogyon*, it was the first time that the text had been printed with adequate accuracy. Rhŷs and Evans also published the first editions of two further vernacular annalistic chronicles found in the same manuscript: *Brut y Saesson*, which in the Red Book cov-

---

[38] 'Chronicle of the Thirteenth Century: MS. Exchequer Domesday', [ed. by Harry Longueville Jones], *Archaeologia Cambrensis*, 3rd ser., 8, no. 32 (1862), 272–83. Note that the text of Longueville Jones's edition was accidentally printed out of order: the content of page 281 needs to be transposed with that of page 282.

[39] *AM*, I (1864), 1–40. The Annals of Margam had previously been printed by Thomas Gale in 1687 under the title *Annales Marganenses*: Thomas Gale, *Historiae Anglicanæ scriptores quinque* (Oxford: Sheldonian Theatre, 1687), pp. 1–19.

[40] Phillimore, '*Annales Cambriæ*'. Phillimore's text of the annals was reproduced in *Les Mabinogion du Livre rouge de Hergest avec les variantes du Livre blanc de Rhydderch*, trans. by Joseph Loth, rev. edn, 2 vols (Paris: Fontemoing et cie, 1913), II, 370–82. Phillimore's article was reprinted in its entirety in John Morris, *Genealogies and Texts*, Arthurian Sources, 5 (Chichester: Phillimore, 1995), pp. 13–55. Another edition of the A-text was published by Edmond Faral in 1929: *La légende arthurienne: études et documents*, 3 vols (Paris: Champion, 1929), III, 44–50. Faral's text, with light corrections and additions from the B- and C-texts, was printed, alongside a translation, in *Nennius: British History and Welsh Annals*, ed. and trans. by John Morris, Arthurian Sources, 8 (London: Phillimore, 1980), pp. 45–49, 85–91.

[41] John Edward Lloyd, 'Wales and the Coming of the Normans (1039–1093)', *THSC*, 1899–1900 [1901], 122–79 (p. 165). Lloyd's parallel edition appears at pages 165–79 as an appendix to his article.

[42] *The Text of the Bruts from the Red Book of Hergest*, ed. by John Rhŷs and J. Gwenogvryn Evans (Oxford: Evans, 1890). For a vernacular chronicle in the Red Book that Rhŷs and Evans did not edit, see Rebecca Try, Chapter 10, below.

ers the period from Cadwaladr Fendigaid in the seventh century to the sixth year of Richard II's reign in 1382, and *O Oes Gwrtheyrn*, a thirteenth-century chronicle which in the Red Book ends prematurely, during the reign of King John.[43] Secondly, and more importantly, Evans's extensive study of Welsh-language manuscripts allowed him to present to the world the true extent of their historical riches, including their chronicles. This may be seen in his pioneering attempt to list and date the various manuscript witnesses to the chronicles edited from the Red Book in the preface to the edition. It is there that the first clear attempt to differentiate between the Red Book and Peniarth 20 versions of *Brut y Tywysogyon* may be found.[44] This line of enquiry was taken to its logical conclusion in Evans's four-volume *Report on Manuscripts in the Welsh Language*, published between 1898 and 1910, where the earliest notices of (and various extracts from) many of the vernacular chronicle manuscripts mentioned in the discussion below may be found.[45]

The stage was now set for J. E. Lloyd to lay the groundwork for the future consensus about Wales's best-known chronicles in his British Academy lecture of 1928.[46] Lloyd dismissed the spurious *Gwentian Brut* and rebuked the theory about Caradog of Llancarfan's authorship of *Brut y Tywysogyon*. Instead, he focused his attention on the provenances of the main versions of *Annales Cambriae* and the *Brutiau*. He supported the conjecture made in *MHB* that the latter part of the B-text was a Strata Florida chronicle, and affirmed Phillimore's conclusion that the A-text was the product of St Davids, suggesting further that the affinity with St Davids begins around the year 770.[47] Lloyd also independently came to a conclusion that Henry Wharton had reached in

---

[43] The former is the text to which the name *Brut y Saesson* properly pertains (despite the name being bestowed upon *Brenhinedd y Saesson* by the editors of the *Myvyrian Archaiology*). For a full study and edition of *O Oes Gwrtheyrn*, see Owain Wyn Jones, Chapter 7, below.

[44] *Text of the Bruts*, pp. xxi–xxiii. Evans unhelpfully labelled the Red Book version as the 'Strata Florida' version; in fact, both versions derive from a Strata Florida original: cf. *BT (Pen. 20 trans.)*, p. lxiii; *BT (RB)*, p. xi.

[45] *RMWL*. For example, Evans was the first to print the continuation of *Brut y Tywysogyon* for the years 1283–1332 found in Aberystwyth, NLW, MS Peniarth 20: *RMWL*, I (1898), 343–46.

[46] Lloyd, *The Welsh Chronicles*. For Lloyd's life and intellectual context, see Huw Pryce, *J. E. Lloyd and the Creation of Welsh History: Renewing a Nation's Past* (Cardiff: University of Wales Press, 2011).

[47] Kathleen Hughes (*Celtic Britain*, p. 68) later wrongly claimed that Lloyd saw the St Davids affinity as beginning precisely with the annal for 796.

1691, that the C-text is essentially a St Davids chronicle.[48] With respect to *Brut y Tywysogyon*, Lloyd supported Aneurin Owen's hesitant notion of the text's Latinate origin, expressing his view in a strongly evocative metaphor:[49]

> Not only is the name of each earl [in the *Brenhinedd y Saesson* annal for 1098] given in the Latin form, but in one case the ablative inflexion has been retained, as infallible a mark of origin as the morsel of cheese which betrayed the fact that the specimen lump of coal, displayed for the benefit of investors, though it had indeed come from the mine, had first gone down the shaft in the miner's dinner basket.

Lloyd's view on the matter was more strident than Owen's: Lloyd saw good reason to believe that the three versions of the Welsh text, namely the Peniarth 20 and Red Book versions of *Brut y Tywysogyon* as well as *Brenhinedd y Saesson*, all preserve independent translations of an original Latin chronicle.

The primary contribution of Lloyd's lecture, however, was his elucidation of the chief chronicling centres responsible for recording the matter that would find its way into the *Brut*. Three particular sources were delineated. Up to 1099, the chronicle was seen to be predicated on the same St Davids source witnessed by the three *Annales Cambriae* chronicles. For the portion from 1100 to *c*. 1175, including the spirited narrative from 1100 to 1121, and again from the end of 1135, Lloyd discerned a Llanbadarn Fawr source. From *c*. 1175, finally, Lloyd identified the Cistercian abbey of Strata Florida as the primary chronicling centre, supporting Aneurin Owen's view that the *Brut*, in its extant form, was compiled in that house. Somewhat less clear, however, was Lloyd's view of

---

[48] Wharton printed extracts from the C-text in his *Anglia Sacra* under the title *Annales ecclesiæ Menevensis* and attributed the text to a canon of St Davids: Henry Wharton, *Anglia Sacra*, 2 vols (London: impensis Richardi Chiswel, ad insigne rosæ coronatæ in cœmeterio s. Pauli, 1691), II, 648–51; cf. *MHB*, p. 27. Similarly, more recent commentators have taken to referring to the C-text as the 'Annals of St Davids' or the like: e.g. David Stephenson, 'Welsh Chronicles' Accounts of the Mid-Twelfth Century', *CMCS*, 56 (2008), 45–57 (p. 49); David Stephenson, 'The Chronicler at Cwm-hir Abbey, 1257–63: The Construction of a Welsh Chronicle', in *Wales and the Welsh in the Middle Ages*, ed. by Ralph A. Griffiths and Phillipp R. Schofield (Cardiff: University of Wales Press, 2011), pp. 29–45 (p. 32). It was apparently from a closely related sister copy of the C-text that John Leland copied annals covering the period from the sixth century to 1233 into his *Collectanea*: *The Itinerary of John Leland in or about the Years 1535–1543*, ed. by Lucy Toulmin Smith, 5 vols (1964), IV, 168–77; cf. Brett, 'John Leland', pp. 178–79.

[49] Lloyd, *The Welsh Chronicles*, p. 13.

the relationship between *Brut y Tywysogyon* and the *Annales Cambriae* chronicles. He set out his opinion in somewhat cryptic terms:[50]

> Let me now revert to the Brut. The position that I have endeavoured to establish is that its forms, as found in the Red Book, Peniarth MS 20 and 'Brenhinedd y Saeson', are translations of one Latin archetype, no longer extant. What was the relation of this archetype to the Latin texts printed as *Annales Cambriae*? It was very much fuller, as may be seen at once from the marked difference in the size of the two volumes in the Rolls edition. Nor is the difference due to verbiage or the accumulation of trivial detail; at hundreds of points, the Brut adds material statements which will bear critical examination. One must conclude, therefore, either that the compiler of the Latin original of the Brut had many other sources before him beyond the three which have survived or — and this is the view to which I incline — that the two principal texts in *Annales Cambriae* [i.e. the B- and C-texts] began as mere skeletons or outlines of the chronicle which was then being built up as the foundation of the Brut.

In other words, Lloyd seems to have inclined to the view that the two thirteenth-century *Annales Cambriae* chronicles were abstracted from a draft of the Latin original of the *Brut*. He supported this argument with a further observation: 'it is an argument in favour of the derivation of *Annales Cambriae* from the Latin *Brut* that the two MSS both have this gap between 1132 and 1135', a gap found also in the *Brut*.[51] Furthermore, in his earlier parallel edition of the B- and C-texts of *Annales Cambriae*, Lloyd had observed the following: 'that B and C had a common source different from and (at least in places) inferior in authority to the Latin original of the *Brutiau*, appears from the fact that the two MSS [of B and C] have in exactly the same place (events of 1151–1153) a hiatus of which the *Brutiau* show no trace'.[52] As is discussed further below, it is worth taking note of Lloyd's carefully phrased judgements on this matter, because the question of the relationship between the *Brutiau* and the B- and C-texts of *Annales Cambriae* has been the subject of more recent debate.

Building on the foundation laid down by Lloyd, two other scholars were able to establish a working orthodoxy for the interpretation of the chronicles of medieval Wales: Thomas Jones and Kathleen Hughes. Following the various misadventures of the nineteenth century, it was Thomas Jones who was responsible for producing definitive editions and translations of the two versions of

---

[50] Lloyd, *The Welsh Chronicles*, p. 16.
[51] Lloyd, *The Welsh Chronicles*, p. 18.
[52] Lloyd, 'Wales', pp. 170–71 n. 1.

Brut y Tywysogyon (the Red Book and Peniarth 20 versions) and of the related text *Brenhinedd y Saesson*. These were published originally between 1941 and 1971.[53] He affirmed the idea, first clearly expressed by Gwenogvryn Evans, that the Peniarth 20 and Red Book versions of *Brut y Tywysogyon* were independent witnesses to the same text. He also judged that *Brenhinedd y Saesson* preserves a third independent witness to the text of the *Brut* as far as 1197, though up to the annal for 1092 the text has been interposed rather crudely with matter taken from a copy of the annals by Richard of Devizes related to the Annals of Winchester, close to the copy found in Cambridge, Corpus Christi College, MS 339 (a manuscript dated to *c.* 1200 containing a chronicle ending in 1139).[54] Jones deduced that, after its annal for 1197, *Brenhinedd y Saesson* is based on other sources: for 1197–1282, it is an amalgam of the Peniarth 20 and Red Book versions of *Brut y Tywysogyon*; for 1282–1332, it is based solely on MS Peniarth 20's continuation; and, thereafter, it is an independent but meagre set of annals to the end of the text in 1461.

Jones was clear that, in his view, all three versions of the *Brut* preserve independent translations of different copies of an original Latin *Brut*, itself created in Strata Florida sometime after 1286.[55] In his opinion, MS Peniarth 20 preserved the most complete version of the original, whereas the Red Book version was generally the most correct.[56] He deduced that the Red Book version was translated sometime between Edward I's death in 1307 and the writing of the earliest manuscript witness, Aberystwyth, NLW, MS Peniarth 18, which Jones dated to the first half of the fourteenth century but which is now dated

---

[53] *BT (Pen. 20)*; *BT (Pen. 20 trans.)*; *BT (RB)*; *BS*. Jones's views on the texts are summarized in Thomas Jones, 'Historical Writing in Medieval Welsh', *Scottish Studies*, 12 (1968), 15–27.

[54] For Richard of Devizes as probable author of these annals, see John T. Appleby, 'Richard of Devizes and the Annals of Winchester', *Bulletin of the Institute of Historical Research*, 36 (1963), 70–77 (pp. 72–73) and *The Chronicle of Richard of Devizes*, ed. by John T. Appleby (London: Nelson, 1963), pp. xxiv–xxv.

[55] For the date, see *BT (Pen. 20 trans.)*, p. xxxix n. 3, where Jones notes that both versions of the *Brut*, in their annals for 1280, refer to a fire at Strata Florida which, according to the B-text of *Annales Cambriae*, occurred in 1286. Daniel Huws has noted, however, that the fire recorded in the latter source might be a misdated reference to the fire at the end of 1284, which would alter the *terminus post quem* of the final version of the Latin *Brut*: *Medieval Welsh Manuscripts*, p. 216 n. 36. Elsewhere, however, Jones suggested that the *Brut*'s reference to the fire may have originated as a gloss, and that the original Latin *Brut* may have been compiled in 1282, prior to the death of Llywelyn ap Gruffudd on 11 December of that year: 'Historical Writing', pp. 23–24.

[56] *BT (Pen. 20 trans.)*, p. lx.

to the mid-fourteenth century.⁵⁷ He also pointed to linguistic evidence suggesting that *Brenhinedd y Saesson* was translated by the same person who translated the version of *Brut y Brenhinedd* (the Welsh translation of Geoffrey of Monmouth's *De gestis Britonum*) in MS Cotton Cleopatra B V, the earliest witness to *Brenhinedd y Saesson*, written around 1330.⁵⁸ Jones seems not to have identified any specific evidence allowing the translation of the Peniarth 20 version to be dated any more precisely than sometime between 1286 and the date of the manuscript, which Jones accepted as the second half of the fourteenth century but which is now understood to be *c.* 1330.⁵⁹

Jones was the first (and only) scholar to undertake a full examination of the many manuscript witnesses to *Brut y Tywysogyon* and *Brenhinedd y Saesson*. He confirmed that MS Peniarth 20 is the sole independent witness to the Peniarth 20 version of *Brut y Tywysogyon*. He expressed considerable uncertainty about the date and provenance of the manuscript, but more recent work, focused especially on MS Peniarth 20's continuation of *Brut y Tywysogyon* for 1282–1332, has helped to establish that the manuscript was written in the Cistercian abbey of Valle Crucis in the years around 1330.⁶⁰ Jones identified many independ-

---

⁵⁷ *BT (RB)*, pp. xxii, liii–lv. One of the two scribes responsible for MS Peniarth 18 has now been identified as the famous Anchorite of Llanddewibrefi, who may have written the manuscript with his colleague at Strata Florida Abbey: Huws, *Medieval Welsh Manuscripts*, pp. 49, 59, 76, 239, 243.

⁵⁸ *BS*, pp. xii, xvi, xlvii. This view retains the support of Brynley Roberts: 'Ystoriaeu Brenhinedd Ynys Brydeyn: A Fourteenth-Century Welsh Brut', in *Narrative in Celtic Tradition: Essays in Honor of Edgar M. Slotkin*, ed. Joseph F. Eska, CSANA Yearbook, 8–9 (Hamilton, NY: Colgate University Press, 2011), pp. 215–27 (p. 223). For the date of the manuscript, see Huws, *Medieval Welsh Manuscripts*, pp. 53, 59. Note, however, that in Chapter 5 Barry Lewis produces evidence to suggest that *Brenhinedd y Saesson* had been translated into Welsh by *c.* 1300.

⁵⁹ *BT (Pen. 20 trans.)*, p. xlvii; Huws, *Medieval Welsh Manuscripts*, pp. 47, 59, 76; and see the following note.

⁶⁰ *Y Bibyl Ynghymraec*, ed. by Thomas Jones (Cardiff: University of Wales Press, 1940), pp. lxxxviii–xc; *BT (Pen. 20)*, pp. xvi, xix; J. Goronwy Edwards, review of *Brut y Tywysogyon: Peniarth MS. 20*, ed. by Thomas Jones (1941), *English Historical Review*, 57 (1942), 370–75; *BT (Pen. 20 trans.)*, pp. xlvi–xlix, lxii–lxiii; Gifford and Thomas M. Charles-Edwards, 'The Continuation of *Brut y Tywysogion* in Peniarth MS.20', in *Ysgrifau a Cherddi Cyflwynedig i / Essays and Poems presented to Daniel Huws*, ed. by Tegwyn Jones and E. B. Fryde (Aberystwyth: NLW, 1994), pp. 293–305; Owain Wyn Jones, 'Historical Writing in Medieval Wales' (unpubl. doctoral thesis, Bangor University, 2013), pp. 241–48. For MS Peniarth 20's continuation, see now David Stephenson, Chapter 6, below.

3. HISTORICAL SCHOLARS AND DISHONEST CHARLATANS

ent witnesses to the Red Book version, including four medieval manuscripts.[61] He concluded that, contrary to the prominence given to the Red Book of Hergest in the nineteenth century, it is the earliest manuscript, MS Peniarth 18, that preserves the best text of the Red Book version.[62] The manuscripts of *Brenhinedd y Saesson* proved more of a headache. Jones identified two independent witnesses, both medieval: MS Cotton Cleopatra B V, part i, written in the second quarter of the fourteenth century, and Aberystwyth, NLW, MS 7006D (the Black Book of Basingwerk), written by Gutun Owain and a collaborator sometime after 1461 (though Jones believed that the collaborator worked before Gutun Owain, in the fourteenth century). Following much discussion, Jones came to the same conclusion as J. J. Parry and B. G. Owens, who had respectively examined the texts of *Brut y Brenhinedd* and *Ystorya Dared* common to these same two manuscripts: that, while the texts in the two manuscripts were closely related, the later Black Book of Basingwerk was not copied from the earlier Cotton manuscript.[63] This conclusion forced Jones to proffer a second, more questionable view. The text in MS Cotton Cleopatra B V breaks off abruptly in its annal for 1197 (with events really belonging to 1198), due to an indeterminable number of leaves having been lost from the end of the manuscript. According to Jones, this is also the point where the version of *Brenhinedd y Saesson* in the Black Book of Basingwerk switched from its independent *Brenhinedd y Saesson* source to its Red Book- and Peniarth 20-type sources. Jones was therefore required to explain why the switch would have occurred at exactly this point had the Black Book of Basingwerk not been based on MS Cotton Cleopatra B V up to 1197. His solution was that the original text of *Brenhinedd y Saesson* was never continued much beyond 1200, meaning that

---

[61] See the stemmas at *BT (RB)*, pp. xxxvii, l.

[62] Nevertheless, some of Jones's textual arguments require reconsideration. For example, he concludes that P and M share a common exemplar that was separate from the common exemplar of R and T, but the evidence presented in his textual discussion seems to suggest otherwise. At *BT (RB)*, pp. xl–xlii, he shows that M and R share errors that are absent from P. At pp. xlvii–xlix, on the other hand, it is suggested that certain readings show that P and M share errors that are absent from R and T. In my view, the latter evidence is much weaker than the former, which could mean that M should be placed on the stemma closer to RT than to P. Alternatively, there may have been more contamination in the textual tradition than Jones allowed.

[63] This view is accepted by J. Beverley Smith: 'Historical Writing in Medieval Wales: The Composition of *Brenhinedd y Saesson*', *Studia Celtica*, 42 (2008), 55–86 (pp. 55, 62 n. 41). Brynley Roberts has expressed greater uncertainty: Roberts, '*Ystoriaeu Brenhinedd Ynys Brydeyn*', p. 222.

only a few leaves have been lost from MS Cotton Cleopatra B V.[64] However, this view has more recently been doubted.[65] Nevertheless, a solution, pending more detailed examination, may have been offered by Beverley Smith, who has observed that *Brenhinedd y Saesson* assumes the derivative character exhibited later in the Black Book of Basingwerk by no later than its annal for 1172, and may have been drawing on one or more separate texts of *Brut y Tywysogyon* already by that year.[66] If this is correct, Jones's problem disappears, for the apparent change of source in the Black Book of Basingwerk would no longer seem to occur at the point at which the Cotton manuscript becomes lacunose.

On the question of the relationship between the *Brut* and the B- and C-texts of *Annales Cambriae*, Jones came to a rather different view from Lloyd. He suggested that the compiler of the original Latin *Brut* combined aspects of the B- and C-texts of *Annales Cambriae* together.[67] Nevertheless, the examples given by Jones could just as easily be interpreted as supporting Lloyd's view that the B- and C-texts represent independent versions of an abstraction from a draft of the Latin *Brut*. Jones also expressed the view that the more literary aspects of *Brut y Tywysogyon*, particularly in its early twelfth-century portions, were the product of the compiler of the *Brut* in the late thirteenth century, rather than an aspect of one or more of the compiler's sources.[68] According to this view, therefore, the more laconic items in the Latin chronicles would be closer to the original records than the translated and elaborated items in the *Brut*. Jones perceived a similar situation with the chronology of the texts. He was the first scholar to attempt to analyse the chronology of the Welsh chronicles critically.[69] Previous scholars, including editors of the Latin chronicles, had been content either to follow the dates in the texts or, for the earlier portions that lack

---

[64] *BS*, pp. xxxix–xl.

[65] *Brenhinoedd y Saeson, 'The Kings of the English', A.D. 682–954: Texts P, R, S in Parallel*, ed. by David N. Dumville (Aberdeen: Department of History, University of Aberdeen, 2005), p. ix n. 44.

[66] Smith, 'Historical Writing', p. 71. However, I do not understand Smith's reason for thinking that 'this consideration may strengthen the possibility that the text in the earlier manuscript was never taken beyond what is found in the folios of Cotton MS Cleopatra B v' (n. 102). If there is no change in the Black Book of Basingwerk's source around 1197, there seems no basis on which to doubt that the Cotton manuscript did not once contain a full text of *Brenhinedd y Saesson* extending into the fourteenth century.

[67] *BT (Pen. 20 trans.)*, pp. xli n. 5, xliii; cf. T. Jones, 'Historical Writing', p. 25.

[68] *BT (Pen. 20 trans.)*, p. xliii.

[69] *BT (Pen. 20 trans.)*, pp. lxiv–lxxiv; *BT (RB)*, pp. lv–lxi; *BS*, pp. xlviii–l.

explicit dates, to attribute dates to events without addressing the irregularities of each chronological apparatus. Jones adduced that in certain instances the chronological irregularities of the three Welsh chronicles derive from differing interpretations of the chronological structure found in the Latin chronicles. This is an argument for the three Welsh texts being independent versions of a common original and for the Latin chronicles preserving aspects of that common original that are no longer apparent in the extant Welsh texts. Further sustained attention to the chronological structuring of all the relevant chronicles would no doubt repay the effort.

Jones's other major contribution to the subject was his publication and discussion of two further Latin chronicles from medieval Wales preserved in a previously unnoticed late thirteenth-century manuscript: Exeter Cathedral Library, MS 3514.[70] The importance of the manuscript had been ascertained by Robin Flower, who communicated his findings to Thomas Jones. The two chronicles have become known respectively as *Cronica de Wallia* and *Cronica ante aduentum Domini*.[71] Jones printed the entirety of *Cronica de Wallia* (which covers 1190–1266) but only the last portion of *Cronica ante aduentum Domini* (for 1254–1285), because, as was said above, the preceding part was seen to be derivative and therefore of 'no historical value'.[72] From Jones's point of view, the foremost reason for interest in the texts, beyond their importance for Welsh history more generally, was the close parallels between some sections of *Cronica de Wallia* and *Brut y Tywysogyon*, especially in its Peniarth 20 version, seemingly confirming his view that the substance of the *Brut* existed in Latin form before it was translated on three separate occasions into Welsh.

---

[70] For the Exeter manuscript, see now Julia Crick, 'The Power and the Glory: Conquest and Cosmology in Edwardian Wales', in *Textual Cultures: Cultural Texts*, ed. by Orietta Da Rold and Elaine Treharne (Cambridge: Brewer, 2010), pp. 21–42.

[71] Julia Crick noted that the abbreviation *cronic'* in the title of *Cronica de Wallia* that appears in the manuscript's early fourteenth-century contents list could just as validly be read as *cronicon*: Crick, 'The Power and the Glory', p. 38 n. 45. The title *Cronicon de Wallia* was adopted in Georgia Henley, 'The Use of English Annalistic Sources in Medieval Welsh Chronicles', *HSJ*, 26 (2014), 229–47 (cf. p. 240 n. 47). *Cronica ante aduentum Domini* is sometimes known as *Cronica de Anglia*, again because that is the title found in the early fourteenth-century contents list: cf. Georgia Henley, 'Rhetoric, Translation and Historiography: The Literary Qualities of *Brut y Tywysogyon*', *Quaestio Insularis: Proceedings of the Cambridge Colloquium in Anglo-Saxon, Norse and Celtic*, 13 (2012), 78–103 (p. 83 n. 20).

[72] '"Cronica de Wallia"', ed. by Jones, also published as *Cronica de Wallia and Other Documents from Exeter Cathedral Library MS. 3514*, ed. by Thomas Jones (Oxford: Oxford University Press, 1946).

A historical study by J. Beverley Smith, published in 1964, concluded that *Cronica de Wallia* was probably redacted in the Cistercian abbey of Whitland between 1277 and 1283, perhaps specifically in 1277.[73] *Cronica ante aduentum Domini*, on the other hand, may have been redacted a few years later, between 1285 and 1287.

While Jones's comprehensive discussions of three of the most important Welsh vernacular chronicles established the parameters of future debate for those texts, it was Kathleen Hughes's groundbreaking British Academy lecture of 1973 that provided the touchstone for all subsequent work on Latin chronicles written in medieval Wales.[74] Hughes conducted a succinct but detailed survey not only of the well-known '*Annales Cambriae*' chronicles but also of various chronicles linked to the Marcher monasteries of South Wales. Much of the lecture was devoted to establishing the sources and textual interrelationships of the chronicles. She suggested that the Irish source of the *Annales Cambriae* chronicles, first identified in *MHB*, was used up to 613, and she postulated that a hypothetical 'northern chronicle' (whose source material was available to the *Historia Brittonum*) lies behind a number of the *Annales Cambriae* annals from the early seventh to the late eighth century.[75] She established that the common

[73] J. Beverley Smith, 'The "Cronica de Wallia" and the Dynasty of Dinefwr', *BBCS*, 20 (1963–64), 261–82. Kathleen Hughes was sceptical of Smith's argument but agreed that Whitland is a likely candidate for the centre responsible for the compilation of *Cronica de Wallia*: see her *Celtic Britain*, pp. 77–79 (esp. p. 78 n. 67). She also considered it likely that *Cronica ante aduentum Domini* came from the same house. Julian Harrison is similarly sceptical of Smith's argument, suggesting that *Cronica de Wallia* could equally belong to either Whitland or Strata Florida: Julian Harrison, 'Cistercian Chronicling in the British Isles', in *The Chronicle of Melrose Abbey: A Stratigraphic Edition. Volume I: Introduction and Facsimile Edition*, ed. by Dauvit Broun and Julian Harrison (Woodbridge: Boydell, 2007), pp. 13–28 (p. 16 n. 23). David Stephenson, however, is inclined to favour Smith's argument: 'In Search of a Welsh Chronicler: The *Annales Cambriae* B-Text for 1204–30', *CMCS*, 72 (2016), 73–85 (p. 83 n. 54).

[74] Kathleen Hughes, 'The Welsh Latin Chronicles: *Annales Cambriae* and Related Texts', *Proceedings of the British Academy*, 59 (1973), 233–58, also published as Kathleen Hughes, *The Welsh Latin Chronicles: 'Annales Cambriae' and Related Texts* (London: Oxford University Press, 1974). The essay was reprinted and lightly revised by David N. Dumville in Hughes, *Celtic Britain*, ch. 5. Hughes's more detailed study of the A-text of *Annales Cambriae* was published posthumously as ch. 6 of the latter volume, with footnotes provided by the volume's editor, David N. Dumville.

[75] Prior studies of the relationship with the Irish annals may be found in James Carney, *Studies in Irish History and Literature* (Dublin: Dublin Institute for Advanced Studies, 1955), pp. 339–50, 371–73; Nora Kershaw Chadwick, 'Early Culture and Learning in North Wales', in *Studies in the Early British Church*, ed. by Nora Kershaw Chadwick (Cambridge: University

source of the B- and C-texts of *Annales Cambriae* up to 1202[76] was a St Davids chronicle, though she noted that the B-text begins to diverge at 1189.[77] The differences between the two versions of the St Davids chronicle preserved in these texts, she implied, were due mostly to the B- and C-texts having abbreviated the common source in different ways.[78] She divided the remainder of the B-text into four sections, and characterized them as follows:

1. 1189–1231: Betrays evidence of a Cistercian milieu, with an interest in the area of Whitland Abbey.

2. 1231–55: Displays an interest in Strata Florida, and a strong affinity with *Cronica de Wallia*.

3. 1256–63:[79] Displays an interest in the area of Cwm-hir Abbey, a daughter house of Whitland.

4. After 1263: Derives its main structure from a version of the Winchester chronicle augmented at Waverley, similar to that found in London, BL, MS Cotton Vespasian E IV, from which source items have been added to other parts of the chronicle.[80]

Press, 1958), pp. 29–120 (pp. 50–58). A northern source had previously been suggested by the Chadwicks, followed by Kenneth Jackson: Hector Munro Chadwick and Nora Kershaw Chadwick, *The Growth of Literature*, 3 vols (Cambridge: University Press, 1932–40), I: *The Ancient Literatures of Europe* (1932), pp. 148–49; Nora Kershaw Chadwick, 'Early Culture and Learning', pp. 58–73; Kenneth Jackson, 'On the Northern British Section in Nennius', in *Celt and Saxon: Studies in the Early British Border*, ed. by Nora Kershaw Chadwick (Cambridge: Cambridge University Press, 1963; rev. edn 1964), pp. 20–62 (pp. 48–49). A recent and authoritative survey of the issue may be found in Thomas M. Charles-Edwards, *Wales and the Britons 350–1064* (Oxford: Oxford University Press, 2013), pp. 346–59.

[76] Possibly 1203: see above, n. 24.

[77] Note that Hughes called the B-text the 'PRO chronicle', because in 1973 the manuscript was deposited in the Public Record Office.

[78] Hughes, *Celtic Britain*, pp. 74–75.

[79] Stephenson ('The Chronicler at Cwm-hir Abbey', pp. 30–31) has argued that this section should properly begin with the annal for 1257, because the annal for 1256 'shows considerable phraseological similarities to the *Brut*', another Strata Florida text.

[80] For MS Cotton Vespasian E IV, see Neil Denholm-Young, 'The Winchester-Hyde Chronicle', *English Historical Review*, 49 (1934), 85–93, repr. in his *Collected Papers on Medieval Subjects* (Oxford: Blackwell, 1946), pp. 86–95. The manuscript is now thought to have been written in Reading Abbey: see Alan Coates, *English Medieval Books: The Reading Abbey Collections from Foundation to Dispersal* (Oxford: Oxford University Press, 1999), pp. 70, 72, 157–58.

She suggested that sections 1–3 were added to a version of the St Davids annals ending in 1202, possibly by someone at Strata Florida. All of this material was then inherited by Neath Abbey, where the material of section 4 was added. Overall, therefore, the B-text emerges from Hughes's discussion as a pivotal text, with different sections showing close affinities with the other two *Annales Cambriae* chronicles, *Cronica de Wallia*, and the *Brutiau*.

Hughes also refined our understanding of the two Exeter MS 3514 chronicles. She argued that the portion of *Cronica de Wallia* for 1190–1255 came from a Strata Florida source, confirming Thomas Jones's earlier perception of a Strata Florida connection.[81] Due to the common Strata Florida connections, *Cronica de Wallia* has a strong affinity with *Brut y Tywysogyon* in the annals for 1190–1216, a slightly weaker affinity with *Brut y Tywysogyon* in the annals for 1228–1230, and is almost identical to the B-text of *Annales Cambriae* in the annals for 1231–1246. Towards the end of the Strata Florida source, Hughes detected that most of the remaining text, from 1254 to 1266, was a conflation of extracts from the St Davids annals (as represented by the C-text of *Annales Cambriae*) and the Bury St Edmunds chronicle of John of Taxster, which originally ended in 1265.[82] This is significant because the bulk of *Cronica ante aduentum Domini* is formed from the same two sources: the Bury chronicle from 1172 to 1265 and the St Davids annals thereafter until 1285. Hughes noted that the same extracts appear in both Exeter texts.[83]

Hughes drew attention to other chronicles composed in South Wales. She makes brief mention of the Cardiff chronicle discussed by Georgia Henley below (Chapter 8).[84] She noticed two further chronicles that appear in the Breviate of Domesday manuscript, the manuscript containing the B-text of *Annales Cambriae*. The more substantial of these (edited in 1862 by Longueville Jones)[85] maintains a perceptible interest in Glamorgan, and though many of

---

[81] Cf. *BT (Pen. 20 trans.)*, p. xl.

[82] For the Bury chronicle of John of Taxster, see *The Chronicle of Bury St Edmunds 1212–1301*, ed. and trans. by Antonia Gransden (London: Nelson, 1964). For the termination date of 1265, see pp. xvii, xix.

[83] For further thoughts on the use of the Bury chronicle in the Exeter texts, see Henley, 'Use of English Annalistic Sources'.

[84] Hughes, *Celtic Britain*, p. 82 n. 81. Cf. Robert B. Patterson, 'The Author of the "Margam Annals": Early Thirteenth-Century Margam Abbey's Compleat Scribe', *Anglo-Norman Studies*, 14 (1991), 197–210 (p. 200 n. 27); Smith, 'Historical Writing', p. 69; *The Winchcombe and Coventry Chronicles*, I, 133–35.

[85] See above, pp. 78–79.

its items are paralleled in the Annals of Margam (from 1081) and Tewkesbury (1142–1240s), the text contains independent items of Welsh interest from 1256, and Hughes suggested that it was compiled in the Cistercian abbey of Neath.[86] The other, briefer set of annals in the same manuscript is relevant to the conquest of Carmarthen and Gower by the De Braose family, the patrons of Neath Abbey.[87] Hughes identified Neath as the place responsible for these additional texts in the Breviate manuscript, and furthermore she postulated that the latter parts of the B-text of *Annales Cambriae* contained in the same manuscript were composed by a Neath scribe.[88]

Hughes's lecture was the subject of an early review by David Dumville, which is still frequently cited in modern scholarship.[89] He attempted further refinement of some of Hughes's conclusions. For instance, he suggested that the *Historia Brittonum* may have drawn directly upon the so-called 'northern chronicle' that Hughes had perceived underlying the seventh- and eighth-century sections of the *Annales Cambriae* chronicles, rather than upon the hypothetical memoranda used to compile that 'northern chronicle', as Hughes had thought. Less happily, however, Dumville argued that the B-text displays evidence for a Welsh chronicle covering the period 1189–1263, which existed before it was combined with the St Davids annals ending in 1202 (or 1203). His reasoning was that the additions from the Waverley chronicle were only

---

[86] It had previously been suggested that the text was compiled at either Neath or Margam: J. Beverley Smith and Thomas B. Pugh, 'The Lordship of Gower and Kilvey in the Middle Ages', in *Glamorgan County History*, ed. by Glanmor Williams, 6 vols (Cardiff: University of Wales Press, 1936–88), III: *The Middle Ages*, ed. by Thomas B. Pugh (1971), pp. 205–65 (p. 241). Hughes (*Celtic Britain*, p. 82 n. 83) argued against the Margam attribution. Marvin Colker noted the significance of this chronicle's apparent preservation of Margam annals as late as 1245 and 1288, implying that chronicling activity continued at Margam later than 1232, when the extant Annals of Margam end: Marvin L. Colker, 'The "Margam Chronicle" in a Dublin Manuscript', *HSJ*, 4 (1992), 123–48 (p. 127).

[87] More recently, J. Beverley Smith ('Historical Writing', p. 79) has deduced that most of the annals in this short text were taken from the B-text.

[88] It had previously been suggested that this manuscript was written by a scribe of Neath Abbey: Smith and Pugh, 'The Lordship of Gower and Kilvey', p. 241 n. 197 (the note is on p. 620). See now Daniel Huws, 'The Neath Abbey *Breviate of Domesday*', in *Wales and the Welsh in the Middle Ages*, ed. by Griffiths and Schofield, pp. 46–55.

[89] David N. Dumville, review of Hughes, *The Welsh Latin Chronicles: 'Annales Cambriae' and Related Texts* (1974), *Studia Celtica*, 12/13 (1977–78), 461–67, repr. with the same pagination and additional notes in David N. Dumville, *Histories and Pseudo-Histories of the Insular Middle Ages* (Aldershot: Variorum, 1990), ch. 3.

added to the annals for 1189–1263. However, it had been shown by Hughes, and it has recently been re-emphasized by David Stephenson, that the Waverley chronicle was the source for many B-text annals earlier in the twelfth century too, suggesting that the annals for 1189–1263 were amalgamated with the St Davids annals to 1202 (or 1203) prior to the interpolation of the Waverley annals.[90] Dumville also repeated Phillimore's call, made over eighty years before, for a parallel edition of the interrelated Welsh Latin chronicles. To this end, he assigned *Cronica ante aduentum Domini* the letter D and *Cronica de Wallia* the letter E, extending the *Annales Cambriae* sigla of *MHB*.

Focusing the Lens

Following the erection of a workable framework for the interpretation of Welsh chronicles by Lloyd, Jones, and Hughes, scholarship has advanced on a number of fronts, particularly with regard to the interrelated chronicles in the *Annales Cambriae* and *Brut y Tywysogyon* families. Much work has been done on the early centuries of Welsh chronicling, as reflected to some extent in all these texts. A fascinating and important study of the natural phenomena recorded in the annals for the early medieval period has been published by Erik Grigg, who attempted to correlate the annalistic record with modern scientific data.[91] Other work has focused on the sources used by the early chroniclers. It has been demonstrated that the substantial Irish element in the tenth-century St Davids source underlying all extant Welsh chronicles covering the early Middle Ages was entered into the St Davids record between 911 and *c.* 954 from the Clonmacnoise recension of the Chronicle of Ireland.[92] This Irish source was ulti-

---

[90] Cf. Hughes, *Celtic Britain*, p. 81 n. 76; Stephenson, 'Welsh Chronicles' Accounts', pp. 49–51. Dumville's view on this matter caused him to doubt the role that Hughes had given Strata Florida in the assembly of the B-text. For this reason, Dumville omitted from his reprint of Hughes's article the relevant statement about Strata Florida's role (compare point 8 in Hughes, 'The Welsh Latin Chronicles', p. 257, and Hughes, *Celtic Britain*, p. 85. Another change was made to point 12: cf. Caroline Brett, 'The Prefaces of Two Late Thirteenth-Century Welsh Latin Chronicles', *BBCS*, 35 (1988), 63–73 (p. 64 and n. 3)). As is discussed below, p. 96, David Stephenson similarly doubts the role of Strata Florida in this process, but for different reasons.

[91] Erik Grigg, '"Mole Rain" and Other Natural Phenomena in the Welsh Annals: Can *Mirabilia* Unravel the Textual History of the *Annales Cambriae*?', *Welsh History Review*, 24 (2009), 1–40.

[92] David N. Dumville, 'When was the "Clonmacnoise Chronicle" Created? The Evidence of the Welsh Annals', in Kathryn Grabowski and David N. Dumville, *Chronicles and Annals of*

mately responsible for many items in the chronicles beyond the 613 terminus perceived by Hughes. Hughes's northern source, however, has fared a little less well. Nicholas Evans successfully countered her proposition that the northern source common to the *Historia Brittonum* and the Welsh annals also underlies the Chronicle of Ireland.[93] A consequence of this argument, viewed alongside the recent work on the Irish source of the Welsh annals, suggests that most of the eighth-century annals that Hughes had perceived to be derived from a northern source were probably taken instead from the Irish annals.[94] The hypothetical 'northern' source, therefore, may have only addressed the seventh century. One further source of the tenth-century St Davids annals has been postulated by scholars working since Hughes. This source was a northern Welsh chronicle extending to *c.* 858, which may have been compiled at the church of Abergele.[95]

Fresh interest in using medieval chronicles as sources for medieval ideas about history, rather than simply as sources for new historical facts, is shown by the attention granted to the world chronicles forming the first parts of the B- and C-texts of *Annales Cambriae*. Caroline Brett has demonstrated that the world chronicles are based chiefly on Isidore of Seville's *Chronica minora*, Bede's *De temporibus*, and Geoffrey of Monmouth's *De gestis Britonum*, and she confirmed Dumville's view, expressed in his review of Hughes's work, that the two world chronicles, though deriving from a common original, were joined to the annals of the B- and C-texts on separate occasions.[96] Henry Gough-Cooper has argued persuasively that the C-text was restructured in 1216 in

---

Medieval Ireland and Wales (Woodbridge: Boydell, 1984), pp. 209–26; Ben Guy, 'The Origins of the Compilation of Welsh Historical Texts in Harley 3859', *Studia Celtica*, 49 (2015), 21–56 (pp. 30–37). Cf. Charles-Edwards, *Wales and the Britons*, pp. 352–53.

[93] Nicholas Evans, 'The Irish Chronicles and the British to Anglo-Saxon Transition in Seventh-Century Northumbria', in *The Medieval Chronicle VII*, ed. by Juliana Dresvina and Nicholas Sparks (Amsterdam: Rodopi, 2011), pp. 15–43. Charles-Edwards (*Wales and the Britons*, p. 352) arrived at the same conclusion, seemingly independently.

[94] Guy, 'Origins', p. 43.

[95] Molly Miller, 'Final Stages in the Construction of the Harleian *Annales Cambriae*', *Journal of Celtic Studies*, 4 (2004), 205–11 (p. 211); *Annales Cambriae, A.D. 682–954: Texts A-C in Parallel*, ed. and trans. by David N. Dumville (Cambridge: Department of Anglo-Saxon, Norse and Celtic, University of Cambridge, 2002), p. ix (esp. n. 46); David N. Dumville, '*Annales Cambriae* and Easter', in *The Medieval Chronicle III*, ed. by Erik Kooper (Amsterdam: Rodopi, 2004), pp. 40–50, repr. in his *Celtic Essays, 2001–2007*, 2 vols (Aberdeen: The Centre for Celtic Studies, University of Aberdeen, 2007), II, 25–33 (p. 32); Charles-Edwards, *Wales and the Britons*, pp. 350–51; Guy, 'Origins', pp. 27–30.

[96] Brett, 'The Prefaces'.

order to present the rise of Llywelyn ab Iorwerth as the culmination of a period of 532 years (equivalent to the Easter great cycle) beginning in 684.[97] As part of this restructuring, the chronology of the fifth age of the world in the world chronicle was revised so that it likewise sums to 532 years, creating a parallel between the birth of Christ at the end of the fifth age and the rise of Llywelyn ab Iorwerth later in the text.

Another aspect of the broader interest in medieval historical writing shown by modern students of Welsh chronicles may be seen in the new interest taken in the chronicles' English sources. Georgia Henley has examined the ways in which *Brenhinedd y Saesson* and the two Exeter, MS 3514 chronicles made use of the Annals of Winchester and the Bury St Edmunds chronicle respectively.[98] J. Beverley Smith has drawn attention to *Brenhinedd y Saesson*'s use of William of Malmesbury's *Gesta regum Anglorum*, particularly for its survey of the kingdoms of the English, and he has noted the relevance of a twelfth-century manuscript, then in the possession of Margam Abbey, in which William of Malmesbury's work sits alongside Geoffrey of Monmouth's *De gestis Britonum* (London, BL, MS Royal 13 D II).[99] In this connection, it is significant, as Smith points out, that the Annals of Margam, like *Brenhinedd y Saesson*, made use of both William's *Gesta regum Anglorum* and annals of the Winchester-Waverley affiliation.[100] Smith also discussed the sources of the second substantial chronicle in the Breviate of Domesday manuscript, the composition of which Hughes had assigned to Neath Abbey.[101] He suggested that the basis of this Neath chronicle was a text close to the Annals of Tewkesbury, though this suggestion may need to be revised in light of Paul Hayward's argument that the Annals of Tewkesbury were dependent on the chronicling tradition of St Peter's Abbey,

---

[97] Gough-Cooper, 'Deconnovenal Reason'.

[98] Henley, 'Use of English Annalistic Sources'.

[99] Smith, 'Historical Writing', pp. 62–67.

[100] Smith, 'Historical Writing', p. 68; *AM*, I, xiii–xiv; Robert B. Patterson, *The Scriptorium of Margam Abbey and the Scribes of Early Angevin Glamorgan: Secretarial Administration in a Welsh Marcher Barony, c. 1150–c. 1225* (Woodbridge: Boydell, 2002), p. 66.

[101] Smith, 'Historical Writing', pp. 69–70. Smith calls this chronicle 'the Breviate annals', risking confusion with the B-text of *Annales Cambriae*, sometimes called the 'Breviate chronicle' (e.g. J. Beverley Smith, 'Castell Gwyddgrug', *BBCS*, 26 (1974–76), 74–77 (p. 75)). It might be preferable to call the text either the 'Glamorgan chronicle', with Hughes, or else the 'Annals of Neath', with Julian Harrison: 'The Tintern Abbey Chronicles', *The Monmouthshire Antiquary*, 16 (2000), 84–98 (p. 84 n. 4).

Gloucester.[102] Hayward has also devoted attention to the Worcester annals interleaved in the manuscript of the C-text of *Annales Cambriae*.[103] He has shown that the additions to the C-text were taken from a version of the Worcester source lying behind the Winchcombe and Coventry chronicles, a version that had been continued with additional material from the Annals of Tewkesbury for the period after 1121. A very similar version of the same Worcester source, continued with elements drawn from the Annals of Tewkesbury, was used to augment the Annals of Worcester Priory, explaining why Hughes perceived a connection between the C-text additions and the latter chronicle.[104] Further detailed work on the textual interrelations of chronicles connected with Worcester, Tewkesbury, and the Marcher houses of South Wales would no doubt yield significant new insights into the area's networks of communication.[105]

Among the Welsh Latin chronicles, it is the B-text of *Annales Cambriae* that has seen most attention in recent years, primarily from David Stephenson.[106] Stephenson has made several pertinent observations. He has emphasized the extent to which the B-text, particularly in its mid-twelfth-century section, has been compressed, comparing the related but fuller material in *Brut y Tywysogyon*.[107] He has also convincingly dismissed Julian Harrison's suggestion that the St Davids source of the B-text ends in 1202 because the source was contained in one of the manuscripts that Gerald of Wales apparently lost to the monks of Strata Florida in that year.[108] Instead, Stephenson has put for-

---

[102] See *The Winchcombe and Coventry Chronicles*, I, 133–35. I owe thanks to Paul Hayward for responding graciously to my enquiries on this matter. For another possible source of the Neath chronicle, see Georgia Henley, Chapter 8, below. For Gloucester's chronicling tradition, see too Joshua Byron Smith, Chapter 9, below.

[103] *The Winchcombe and Coventry Chronicles*, I, 173–76. Hayward prints the interleaved annals at II, 709–16, with commentary at I, 349–53.

[104] *The Winchcombe and Coventry Chronicles*, I, 169–73; Hughes, *Celtic Britain*, p. 76 n. 58. The Worcester connection was originally noticed in *MHB*: see above, pp. 75–76.

[105] It is also relevant that, as mentioned above, the B-text of *Annales Cambriae* was augmented, seemingly in Neath, with material taken from a chronicle similar to that in MS Cotton Vespasian E IV. The latter was the direct source for the base text of the *Annales prioratus de Wigornia*, as Luard showed: *AM*, IV (1869), pp. xxxvi–xxxix.

[106] See especially Stephenson, 'Welsh Chronicles' Accounts'; 'Gerald of Wales'; 'The Chronicler at Cwm-hir Abbey'; 'In Search of a Welsh Chronicler'.

[107] Stephenson, 'Welsh Chronicles' Accounts', pp. 48–49.

[108] Julian Harrison, 'A Note on Gerald of Wales and *Annales Cambriae*', *Welsh History Review*, 17 (1994), 252–55; Stephenson, 'Gerald of Wales'.

ward an alternative argument, that the latter portion of that St Davids source, from the 1180s to *c.* 1201, might have been somehow influenced by Gerald.[109] Furthermore, he suggested that the ending of the B-text's St Davids source in 1203 might be related to administrative changes and alterations to the composition of the cathedral chapter brought about by the arrival of a new bishop of St Davids (Geoffrey de Henlaw) at the end of 1203.[110] Stephenson has also attempted to realign the view advocated by Hughes about the B-text's relationship with the Cistercian abbeys of Strata Florida and Whitland. According to Hughes, Strata Florida may have been responsible for assembling the B-text as far as 1263, using sources from St Davids, Whitland, and Cwm-hir, in addition to its own annals.[111] Stephenson would instead see Whitland as responsible for this process, at least until 1259, seemingly because (a) the 1204–1230 section contains annals compiled at Whitland, partially retrospectively;[112] (b) the 1231–1256 section, though containing Strata Florida material, has been copied selectively;[113] and (c) the 1257–1259 part of the section linked to Cwm-hir (1257–1263) contains material probably composed in Whitland.[114] Stephenson would agree with Hughes, nevertheless, that the final phase

---

[109] Compare Henry Gough-Cooper's comments below in Chapter 4, p. 122.

[110] Stephenson, 'Gerald of Wales', p. 30.

[111] This is why Harrison designates the B-text as a 'Strata Florida Chronicle' in 'Cistercian Chronicling', pp. 16, 25, 27 n. 66.

[112] Stephenson, 'In Search of a Welsh Chronicler', esp. pp. 76–77, 81–83. Somewhat misleadingly, Stephenson denies the 'Cistercian' milieu of this section, even though he argues that much of it was written at the Cistercian abbey of Whitland. This is because the annals that Hughes used to support her claim of a Cistercian milieu for this section were probably additions made later in the Cistercian abbey of Neath using a Waverley source: see Hughes, *Celtic Britain*, p. 80 n. 73; Stephenson, 'Gerald of Wales', p. 27; Stephenson, 'In Search of a Welsh Chronicler', p. 78.

[113] Stephenson, 'The Chronicler at Cwm-hir Abbey', p. 31.

[114] Stephenson, 'The Chronicler at Cwm-hir Abbey', pp. 31–34. Stephenson is inconsistent at this point though. At pages 32–33, he suggests that there are distinctive stylistic characteristics connecting the 'Whitland' annals of 1257–1259 with the 'Cwm-hir' annals of 1260–1263. At page 34, however, he suggests that Whitland borrowed the Strata Florida text of 1231–1256, added the annals for 1257–1259, and then passed the full package along to Cwm-hir. In this latter scenario, it is difficult to see why there would be distinctive stylistic characteristics for the period 1257–1263. If the latter are to be given any weight, it would be consistent with Stephenson's argument to imagine that all the material for 1257–1263 was edited as a unit, probably in Whitland, before being combined with the material for the preceding years.

3. HISTORICAL SCHOLARS AND DISHONEST CHARLATANS

of redaction took place at Neath Abbey, where the text was copied into the Breviate of Domesday manuscript.

Related matters have been discussed in great detail by J. Beverley Smith in his magisterial analysis of *Brenhinedd y Saesson*.[115] Smith identified an additional source used for the composition of *Brenhinedd y Saesson* that was overlooked by Thomas Jones: the Neath chronicle discussed above. This observation enabled Smith to suggest that the original Latin version of *Brenhinedd y Saesson* might have been assembled in Neath (or possibly Whitland), though his discussion is ultimately inconclusive.[116] Nevertheless, Smith emphasizes that the very idea of synchronizing Welsh and English history, as exhibited in *Brenhinedd y Saesson*, concurs with wider sentiment around the year 1300.[117]

Although *Brut y Tywysogyon* has received only limited attention in recent decades, a certain degree of scepticism towards Thomas Jones's views has arisen. Vague doubts have been expressed about Jones's opinion (following Lloyd) that the two versions of *Brut y Tywysogyon* in addition to *Brenhinedd y Saesson* represent three independent translations of different copies of an archetypal Latin *Brut*.[118] Further doubts have been expressed about the very existence of such a Latin archetype, Julian Harrison suggesting instead that the *Brut* was originally compiled in Welsh, albeit from multiple Latin sources.[119] These assertions do not fundamentally challenge Jones's view of the textual relationships between the different versions of the *Brut*, but rather restate the original uncertainty expressed by Aneurin Owen about precisely when (and how many times) during the process of compilation the material was translated from Latin into Welsh. Unfortunately, none of the sceptics has offered a detailed case against Jones's view.[120]

More fundamental disagreement has emerged concerning the detailed and elaborate narrative offered by the *Brut* for the first two thirds or so of the twelfth

---

[115] Smith, 'Historical Writing'.

[116] Smith, 'Historical Writing', pp. 77, 80.

[117] Smith, 'Historical Writing', p. 60; cf. Henley, 'Use of English Annalistic Sources', pp. 238–39.

[118] *Brenhinoedd y Saeson*, ed. by Dumville, p. vi; David Stephenson, 'The "Resurgence" of Powys in the Late Eleventh and Early Twelfth Centuries', *Anglo-Norman Studies*, 30 (2007), 182–95 (p. 183); cf. Henley, 'Rhetoric, Translation and Historiography', p. 82 n. 18.

[119] Harrison, 'Cistercian Chronicling', p. 27 n. 66.

[120] Beverley Smith ('Historical Writing', pp. 58–59), on the other hand, agrees with Jones that the process of compilation happened in Latin, and that *Brenhinedd y Saesson*, at least, preserves an independent translation of the Latin material into Welsh.

century, and especially for the first three decades up to 1126. Two contrasting views seem to have developed. One, which has yet to be argued at any length, is sceptical about the proposed association between this section of the *Brut* and Llanbadarn Fawr. In 1978, David Dumville stated assertively, but without supporting argumentation, that 'we have no reason to continue to sustain Lloyd's theory that the annals for the period 1100–1175 derive from a chronicle kept at Llanbadarn Fawr'.[121] Similarly, Beverley Smith has more recently suggested that 'explanation of the peculiarities in the content of the chronicle for these years may lie not with the location of the early twelfth-century annalist but with the interests and inclinations of the late thirteenth-century author of the Latin *Brut*', presumably based in Strata Florida, not far from Llanbadarn Fawr.[122] It would seem to be the economy of this argument that would recommend it to its proponents: since St Davids is indisputably the ultimate source for all the material in the relevant chronicles for the period before the twelfth century, it is simpler to argue that a St Davids source continues to underlie the narratives for the first three quarters of the twelfth century, rather than that St Davids chronicles (like the C-text of *Annales Cambriae*), having previously supplied the Llanbadarn/Strata Florida tradition with material for the early Middle Ages, were later themselves supplied with twelfth-century material from the Llanbadarn/Strata Florida tradition. However, the argument's economy does not necessarily make it correct.

The second view, propounded chiefly by David Stephenson, agrees with Lloyd and Jones that the narrative for these years is based on a Llanbadarn Fawr source, but rejects the notion that the denser factual detail, the verbosity, and the literary elaboration of this section were the products of the thirteenth-century compiler of the *Brut*. Instead, Stephenson would attribute this narrative to the Llanbadarn compilers, and, for the earlier sections, specifically to the Llanbadarn cleric Daniel ap Sulien (d. 1127) and to members of his household resident in Arwystli in the period 1128–1132.[123] Stephenson perhaps over-

---

[121] Dumville, review of Hughes, *The Welsh Latin Chronicles*, p. 465.

[122] Smith, 'Historical Writing', p. 57 n. 13.

[123] Stephenson, 'The "Resurgence" of Powys', pp. 183–89; Stephenson, 'Welsh Chronicles' Accounts' (esp. pp. 47–57); David Stephenson, 'Entries Relating to Arwystli and Powys in the Welsh Chronicles, 1128–32', *Montgomeryshire Collections*, 99 (2011), 45–51; David Stephenson, *Medieval Powys: Kingdom, Principality and Lordships, 1132–1293* (Woodbridge: Boydell, 2016), pp. 25–28. Stephenson thought that Daniel ap Sulien composed the chronicle away from Llanbadarn Fawr after *c.* 1116, once the latter had been granted to Gloucester Abbey: 'Entries', p. 47. Owain Wyn Jones, however, argues that Daniel wrote in Llanbadarn Fawr

states the extent to which earlier historians saw the *Brut* as nothing more than a literary elaboration of brief Latin annals like those preserved in the *Annales Cambriae* chronicles.[124] J. E. Lloyd was clear in his view that the difference between the *Brutiau* and the *Annales Cambriae* chronicles was not 'due to verbiage or the accumulation of trivial detail', because 'at hundreds of points, the Brut adds material statements which will bear critical examination'.[125] Much the same was later observed by Beverley Smith.[126] In fact, Stephenson's view of the *Brutiau* seems to accord rather closely with that of Lloyd. For instance, because of his view about the primacy of the account in the *Brutiau* in the twelfth century, Stephenson concurs with Lloyd that the two thirteenth-century *Annales Cambriae* chronicles may have begun as abstractions from one of the primary Latin sources of the *Brutiau*.[127]

Further detailed work by Georgia Henley and Owain Wyn Jones has tended to support Stephenson's view, casting further doubt upon Jones's inclination to envisage the thirteenth-century compiler of the *Brut* as more of a literary redactor than a simple translator. Henley compared the *Brutiau* with *Cronica de Wallia* for the period 1190–1216, when their narratives correspond most closely, and she concluded that, for these years, almost all of the literary and rhetorical language found in the *Brut* narratives was present already in the Latin before it was translated into Welsh.[128] Owain Wyn Jones argues in favour of Stephenson's view that the narrative in the *Brutiau* for the years 1100–1127 represents near contemporary history writing at Llanbadarn Fawr rather than thirteenth-century literary elaboration, and he goes so far as to dub this section of the *Brutiau* 'the Llanbadarn History'.[129] This notion is amply justified through a sensitive consideration of the way that the author of the narrative for these years portrays political power among the Welsh and the

---

while it was under Anglo-Norman control: '*Brut y Tywysogion*: The History of the Princes and Twelfth-Century Cambro-Latin Historical Writing', *HSJ*, 26 (2014), 209–27 (p. 225).

[124] Most noticeably in Stephenson, *Medieval Powys*, p. 25. A similar sentiment is expressed in O. W. Jones, '*Brut y Tywysogion*', p. 211.

[125] Lloyd, *The Welsh Chronicles*, p. 16.

[126] Smith, 'Historical Writing', p. 57.

[127] Stephenson, 'Welsh Chronicles' Accounts', p. 57; Stephenson, 'Entries Relating to Arwystli and Powys', p. 51 (esp. n. 38). For Lloyd's view, see above, p. 82.

[128] Henley, 'Rhetoric, Translation and Historiography'. A similar conclusion is reached in O. W. Jones, 'Historical Writing', pp. 223–25.

[129] Jones, '*Brut y Tywysogion*'.

Anglo-Normans. Significantly, Jones argues that the political mindset exhibited in the 'Llanbadarn History' can be seen to inform the rewriting of certain earlier annals for the late tenth and eleventh centuries, such as the obituaries of Maredudd ab Owain, Rhys ap Tewdwr, and Bleddyn ap Cynfyn, and the account of the invasion of Rhain the Irishman in 1022.[130] Further detailed consideration of these matters will no doubt help to solve the ongoing puzzle of the relationship between *Brut y Tywysogyon* and the B- and C-texts of *Annales Cambriae*.

New Horizons

In addition to further work engaging with the issues discussed above, there would seem to be three chief areas of the subject that would benefit from further sustained attention.

Firstly, it has long been recognized (since 1891) that a new edition of the chronicles in the Latin *Annales Cambriae* family, presented in parallel columns, would be an enormous benefit not only to the study of Wales's chronicles, but to the study of medieval Wales in general. Efforts have been made in this direction, but they can only be regarded as preliminary to the comprehensive treatment required. David Dumville has edited the three chief Latin chronicles available for the period 682–954, and has made some headway in addressing their chronological problems.[131] He has produced a similar edition for the three primary Welsh chronicles covering the same period.[132] For

---

[130] In the latter case, Jones criticizes an earlier attempt to elucidate the surviving accounts of Rhain the Irishman: David Ewan Thornton, 'Who was Rhain the Irishman?', *Studia Celtica*, 34 (2000), 131–48. Jones's point about the annal for 1022 is made again, from a different angle but apparently independently, in Stephenson, *Medieval Powys*, pp. 27–28.

[131] *Annales Cambriae*, ed. and trans. by Dumville. Further consideration of chronological matters for the period 956–1063 may be found in Charles-Edwards, *Wales and the Britons*, pp. 579–80.

[132] *Brenhinoedd y Saeson*, ed. by Dumville. Due to his belief that the title '*Brut y Tywysogion*' is not found in any manuscript prior to the sixteenth century, Dumville proposed in this volume that the title '*Brenhinoedd y Saeson*', as found in the fourteenth-century MS Cotton Cleopatra B V, should be attributed to the whole *Brut* family, rather than just to the conflated text usually known as *Brenhinedd y Saesson*. The same point is made in *Annales Cambriae*, ed. and trans. by Dumville, p. v. Owain Wyn Jones, however, has pointed out that the title *Brut y Tywysogyon* does in fact occur in a medieval manuscript, contrary to Dumville's belief, for it is found in the *explicit* to the text of the Red Book version of *Brut y Tywysogyon* in Aberystwyth, NLW, MS Peniarth 19: 'Historical Writing', p. 186; cf. Smith, 'Historical Writing', p. 58 n. 16.

the earlier period, Henry Gough-Cooper has published a parallel edition of the Latin texts to 682, complementing Dumville's work.[133] More recently, Gough-Cooper has published a series of new transcriptions on the website of the Welsh Chronicles Research Group. These transcriptions comprise the five texts of *Annales Cambriae*, A–E, allowing easy access for the first time to the full texts of the B- and C-texts and of *Cronica ante aduentum Domini* (the so-called 'D-text').[134] Gough-Cooper has also begun to produce new parallel editions of the Latin texts on the model proposed by Dumville in 1977/78.[135] It should be stressed that, though these editions are a great stride forward, they are no replacement for a complete, integrated, and indexed scholarly edition and translation of all the chronicles concerned. But they are an admirable and much appreciated start.

Secondly, there is much to be gained from further work on the various chronicles of the Anglo-Norman monasteries of South Wales and the borders, which have been mentioned occasionally in the preceding discussion. These received some attention in 1991–1992, when Marvin Colker and Robert Patterson published similar studies on the textual relations of the Annals of Margam.[136] The two scholars were apparently working independently, and each came to a different conclusion about the textual relationships of the relevant manuscripts.[137] Both scholars compared chronicles in four manuscripts: Cambridge, Trinity College, MS O.2.4, which contains the copy of the Annals of Margam edited by Henry Luard, covering 1066–1232; Trinity College Dublin, MS 507, another witness to the Annals of Margam identi-

---

[133] Henry Gough-Cooper, 'Annales Cambriae, from Saint Patrick to AD 682: Texts A, B & C in Parallel', *The Heroic Age: A Journal of Early Medieval Northwest Europe*, 15 (October 2012) <http://www.heroicage.org/issues/15/gough-cooper.php> [accessed 11 December 2017].

[134] Available at <http://croniclau.bangor.ac.uk/editions.php.en> [accessed 11 December 2017]. Unreliable translations of all these chronicles, in addition to the Neath chronicle in the Breviate of Domesday manuscript, were published by Paul Remfry in 2007: Paul Martin Remfry, *Annales Cambriae: A Translation of Harleian 3859; PRO E. 164/1; Cottonian Domitian, A1; Exeter Cathedral Library MS.3514 and MS Exchequer DB Neath, PRO E. 164/1* ([Shrewsbury]: Castle Studies Research & Publishing, 2007).

[135] Available at <http://croniclau.bangor.ac.uk/parallel-editions.php.en> [accessed 11 December 2017].

[136] Colker, 'The "Margam Chronicle"'; Patterson, 'The Author of the "Margam Annals"'.

[137] Patterson, 'The Author of the "Margam Annals"', p. 210; Colker, 'The "Margam Chronicle"', p. 123 n. 1.

fied by Colker, with a short continuation for 1232–1235;[138] the Breviate of Domesday manuscript, and in particular its Neath chronicle (though neither writer recognized the Neath connection); and London, BL, MS Egerton 3088, which contains the annals of the Cistercian abbey of Dore, covering the period from the Incarnation to 1243, and later continued to 1362.[139] Colker deduced that the Dublin manuscript of the Annals of Margam shares a common source with the Annals of Dore, a source which included the Dublin manuscript's continuation for 1232–1235, which is partially reproduced in the Annals of Dore. Colker suggested that the common source was written at Grace Dieu Abbey, a daughter house of Dore, which may have been where the continuation was compiled.[140] A somewhat less satisfactory textual discussion is offered by Patterson, who did not perceive any particular relationship between the Dublin manuscript of the Annals of Margam and the Annals of Dore. Patterson did, however, succeed in identifying the scribe of the Cambridge manuscript of the Annals of Margam, and indeed the annals' probable author, as one of the early thirteenth-century scribes of extant Margam documents (Patterson's 'scribe 24').[141] The chronicles of the Cistercian abbey of Tintern have received separate treatment from Julian Harrison.[142] Harrison identified three extant chronicles or chronicle fragments associated with Tintern, covering events between the twelfth and fourteenth centuries.[143] Much remains to be done on all these texts, particularly, one suspects, on the Annals of Margam and the Neath chronicle.

Thirdly, it may have been noticed that the bulk of the discussion above has focused on the twelfth- and thirteenth-century chronicles of a select few religious establishments in south and west Wales: St Davids, Llanbadarn Fawr, Strata Florida, Whitland, Neath, and Margam being the chief among them. What of Wales's non-monastic chroniclers? In the later Middle Ages, a few

---

[138] Colker printed the continuation in 'The "Margam Chronicle"', pp. 132–41, and gave a collation of the two manuscripts for 1066–1232 at pp. 143–48.

[139] The Annals of Dore (*Annales Dorenses*), for 687–1362, are partially edited by R. Pauli, MGH, SS, 27 (Hanover: Hahn, 1885), pp. 514–31.

[140] The Grace Dieu connection is accepted in Julian Harrison, 'The Troubled Foundation of Grace Dieu Abbey', *The Monmouthshire Antiquary*, 14 (1998), 25–29; Harrison, 'Cistercian Chronicling', pp. 16, 24–25.

[141] Patterson, 'The Author of the "Margam Annals"', p. 203; Patterson, *Scriptorium of Margam Abbey*, pp. 63–66.

[142] Harrison, 'The Tintern Abbey Chronicles'.

[143] See the Appendix to this volume.

3. HISTORICAL SCHOLARS AND DISHONEST CHARLATANS 103

such individuals stand out: Adam Usk, most notably, in his highly individualized chronicle covering 1377–1421, but also Elis Gruffydd, who completed a massive history of the world in 1552, lavishing upon the reader detailed anecdotes of especial value for the period 1510–1552. Chris Given-Wilson has ensured that modern study of Adam Usk's chronicle rests on solid foundations, but more attention might productively be given to Elis Gruffydd.[144] In particular, an edition of the final portion of Gruffydd's chronicle, that which recounts his personal experiences and observations at great length, would be enormously useful for the study of Welsh chronicle literature and Tudor history.[145] What of the chronicles of North Wales?[146] Such chronicles do exist, but they have not, until recently, been granted much attention, probably because they are generally late and often contain little of what earlier scholars would have deemed to be of historical value. Some have received modern attention by virtue of their preserving unique information about the Glyndŵr rebellion. Such has been the case with the fifteenth-century vernacular chronicle known as the 'Annals of Owain Glyndŵr', compiled around 1422 and preserved by Gruffudd Hiraethog and others in the sixteenth century, and the miscellaneous fifteenth-century annals for the years 1400–1461 compiled in the Oswestry area and preserved in Aberystwyth, NLW, MS Peniarth 26.[147] A small portion of the chronicle in Gutun Owain's manuscript Oxford, Jesus College, MS 141 has also been

---

[144] *The Chronicle of Adam Usk 1377–1421*, ed. and trans. by Chris Given-Wilson (Oxford: Clarendon Press, 1997); Chris Given-Wilson, 'The Dating and Structure of the Chronicle of Adam Usk', *Welsh History Review*, 17 (1995), 520–33.

[145] For Elis Gruffydd as a chronicler, see Thomas Jones, 'A Welsh Chronicler in Tudor England', *Welsh History Review*, 1 (1960–63), 1–17; Prys Morgan, 'Elis Gruffudd of Gronant: Tudor Chronicler Extraordinary', *Flintshire Historical Society Journal*, 25 (1971–72), 9–20; Ceridwen Lloyd-Morgan, 'Elis Gruffydd a thraddodiad Cymraeg Calais a Chlwyd', *Cof Cenedl*, 11 (1996), 31–58; Jerry Hunter, *Soffestri'r Saeson: Hanesyddiaeth a Hunaniaeth yn Oes y Tuduriaid* (Cardiff: University of Wales Press, 2000).

[146] Or indeed mid-Wales. Stephenson has argued that a fragment of a chronicle from Strata Marcella survives in the *Brutiau*: David Stephenson, 'A Possible Glimpse of Annals from Strata Marcella: Events at Welshpool, 1196', *Montgomeryshire Collections*, 104 (2016), 7–16.

[147] For the former, see J. E. Lloyd, *Owen Glendower* (Oxford: Clarendon Press, 1931), pp. 147–54; *Owain Glyndŵr: A Casebook*, ed. by Michael Livingston and John K. Bollard (Liverpool: Liverpool University Press, 2013), pp. 172–75, 371–79. For the latter, see J. R. S. Phillips, 'When Did Owain Glyn Dŵr Die?', *BBCS*, 24 (1970–72), 59–77. The text prefaced to the Annals of Owain Glyndŵr in most manuscripts would seem to be a version of *Blwydyn Eiseu*, the subject of Rebecca Try, Chapter 10, below. See *RMWL*, I, 847, and II, pt 3 (1905), 833, Huw Pryce, Chapter 1, above (p. 23), and the Appendix to this volume.

printed because it addresses the Glyndŵr rebellion.[148] The latter text was called *Teyrnassedd y Saesson* by Thomas Jones, and was described by Gwenogvryn Evans as 'a sort of paraphrase of *Brut y Tywysogion*'.[149] The text is now recognized as an abbreviated but independent copy of *Brenhinedd y Saesson*.[150] The historical value of the text's later annals, ending in 1461,[151] and the value of the text overall as a substantial product of a fifteenth-century north-eastern poet's historical enterprise, shows that the text is worthy of further consideration.

Recently, attention has been granted to other chronicles identified as products of North Wales, with a view to understanding them as texts rather than simply as repositories of information. The most substantial of these is *O Oes Gwrtheyrn*, which has been edited and subjected to a full study for the first time by Owain Wyn Jones.[152] Jones has identified the chronicle as a product of the Cistercian abbey of Aberconwy in Gwynedd. Two versions of the text survive, one redacted in about 1265, and the other sometime thereafter. The text bears an interesting relationship to another short set of annals transmitted alongside it in one of the two branches of its textual tradition. That text was named *Oed yr Arglwydd* by Owain Wyn Jones, and has been edited and studied by the present writer.[153] This text may have been assembled at the Cistercian abbey of Valle Crucis, also in North Wales, shortly after the death of Edward I in 1307, and seems to have drawn upon the relative chronology of *O Oes Gwrtheyrn* for the dating of its earliest annals. In its mid-thirteenth century section, however, it notices similar events to *O Oes Gwrtheyrn* but provides more precise dating information.

Another chronicle associated with Aberconwy is the so-called 'Aberconwy Chronicle', which was edited by Henry Ellis in 1847 and thoroughly discussed by David Stephenson in 2002.[154] Though the text does contain various series

---

[148] Phillips, 'When Did Owain Glyn Dŵr Die?', pp. 76–77.

[149] *BT (Pen. 20 trans.)*, p. xii; *RMWL*, II, pt 1, 37.

[150] Cf. O. W. Jones, 'Historical Writing', pp. 50–51, 123–24; Roberts, '*Ystoriaeu Brenhinedd Ynys Brydeyn*', pp. 223, 227. See Huw Pryce, Chapter 1, above.

[151] See Huw Pryce, Chapter 1, n. 100, above.

[152] Initially in O. W. Jones, 'Historical Writing', pp. 287–316, 409–30, and now in Jones, Chapter 7, below.

[153] Ben Guy, 'A Lost Medieval Manuscript from North Wales: Hengwrt 33, the *Hanesyn Hên*', *Studia Celtica*, 50 (2016), 69–105 (study at pp. 82–83 and 86–87, text and translation at pp. 101–04).

[154] *Register and Chronicle of the Abbey of Aberconway from the Harleian MS. 3725*, ed. by Henry Ellis ([London]: Camden Society, 1847); David Stephenson, *The Aberconwy Chronicle*,

of annals, it is not a simple chronicle, since it contains a number of documents linked not only to Aberconwy, but also to other Cistercian abbeys in Wales. Stephenson concluded that the compilation was actually assembled at Hailes Abbey in Gloucestershire towards the end of the fifteenth century. Intriguingly, the earlier sections of the 'chronicle', drawn primarily from the works of Geoffrey of Monmouth and Gerald of Wales, are almost identical to the relevant sections of another late medieval Latin chronicle from Wales, known as *Epitome historiae Britanniae*.[155] This chronicle seems to have been assembled late in the fourteenth century, and survives in three versions: two full versions, dated respectively to 1399 (London, BL, MS Cotton Nero A IV) and 1429 (London, BL, MS Cotton Titus D XXI), and an abbreviated version, dated to 1404 (Aberystwyth, NLW, MS Peniarth 32).[156] Diana Luft has characterized it as 'a short and selective history of Britain written from a Glamorgan perspective beginning with the coming of Brutus to Britain in 1230 BC'.[157] Luft suggests that the abbreviated version of the text in MS Peniarth 32 might be associated in particular with the Cistercian abbey of Llantarnam, a daughter house of Strata Florida. It was presumably through such Cistercian links that the text became available in Hailes Abbey in the late fifteenth century.

It may finally be noted that there are a number of chronicles concerning the Middle Ages in early modern Welsh manuscripts that have received very little attention to date. Two may be noticed here.[158] One appears in Aberystwyth, NLW, MS Peniarth 212, written by the poet Wiliam Cynwal between 1565 and 1587. On pages 249–309 is a substantial chronicle in Welsh described as 'Y koronigl o Gadwaladr Vendigaid y brenin diwaethaf o'r Brytaniaid hyd at y frenhines Elssabeth' ('The chronicle from Cadwaladr the Blessed, the last King of the Britons, as far as Queen Elizabeth'). Gwenogvryn Evans said of it that it 'has no particular merit, and is very meagre from the reigns of Henry VIII, Edward VI, and Mary, as well as the early years of Elizabeth'.[159] However, given

---

Kathleen Hughes Memorial Lecture, 2 (Cambridge: Hughes Hall and Department of Anglo-Saxon, Norse and Celtic, 2002).

[155] Diana Luft, 'The NLW Peniarth 32 Latin Chronicle', *Studia Celtica*, 44 (2010), 47–70 (pp. 54–55).

[156] For relevant editions, see the Appendix to this volume.

[157] Luft, 'The NLW Peniarth 32 Latin Chronicle', p. 49.

[158] Others are mentioned by Huw Pryce, Chapter 1, p. 24.

[159] *RMWL*, I, 1034 (cf. *Text of the Bruts*, p. xxii). Evans also suggested that the text might have been composed by Gruffudd Hiraethog, Wiliam Cynwal's bardic teacher. According to

that Evans also said of the very interesting text *O Oes Gwrtheyrn* that 'it is a waste of time to inquire into worthless compilations of this kind with the Eisteðvodic stamp on them', his judgement should perhaps be taken lightly.[160] The second chronicle is found in Aberystwyth, NLW, MS Peniarth 138, pages 243–49, written by the sixteenth-century genealogist Thomas ap Llywelyn ab Ithel of Bodfari in north-east Wales.[161] The text, written in Welsh, begins with Jasper Tudor's burning of Denbigh in 1468 and ends with the decapitation of Edward Seymour, Duke of Somerset, on 22 January 1552 (1551 by the text's reckoning).[162] It may provide an interesting insight into the perspective of the gentry of north-east Wales on contemporary political events.

Conclusion

The chronicles of medieval Wales have been much discussed, albeit by a select few, during the past two centuries of scholarship. Much has been learned, but with each step forward new questions have arisen. Since discussion has necessarily been dominated by textual matters, some core questions have remained inconclusively answered. How did the purpose of chronicling in Wales change over time, between the eighth and sixteenth centuries? What were the similarities and differences between chronicling in Wales and Wales's neighbours, especially England and Ireland? How were chronicles used at different stages of Wales's history, and by whom? Such questions can only be answered with reference to the broadest possible range of evidence, and it is hoped that the studies which follow can provide some of this evidence, productively building upon the work surveyed above.[163]

Phillimore, there was a compilation of this kind among the manuscripts of Shirburn Castle, so perhaps there is another copy to be found among the Llanstephan manuscripts: 'Publication', p. 160. Thomas Jones does not mention it in his notice of this manuscript at *BT (RB)*, pp. xxx–xxxi.

[160] *Text of the Bruts*, p. xxiv. It is notable, however, that Aneurin Owen recognized the potential value of *O Oes Gwrtheyrn* in his 1829 letter to Henry Petrie: *Brut y Tywysogion: The Gwentian Chronicle*, p. xx.

[161] For Thomas ap Llywelyn ab Ithel, see Ben Guy, 'Writing Genealogy in Wales, *c.* 1475–*c.* 1640: Sources and Practitioners', in *The Production of Genealogical Knowledge in Pre-Modern Times*, ed. by Jost Eickmeyer, Volker Bauer, and Markus Friedrich (Berlin: De Gruyter, 2019), pp. 99–125 (pp. 113–16).

[162] Extracts are given in *RMWL*, I, 872.

[163] My thanks to Rebecca Thomas for her helpful comments on a draft of this chapter.

4. Meet the Ancestors? Evidence for Antecedent Texts in the Late Thirteenth-Century Welsh Latin Chronicles

Henry Gough-Cooper

Introduction

The three principal Welsh Latin annalistic chronicles are all written in single hands: the Harleian chronicle (henceforth **A**) in a hand of *c.* 1100; the Breviate chronicle (henceforth **B**) in a hand of the late thirteenth century; and the Cottonian chronicle (henceforth **C**), also in a hand of the late thirteenth century.[1] The relationship between these chronicles was the subject of a comprehensive analysis by Kathleen Hughes in a lecture read to the British Academy in 1973.[2] Hughes focused on **A**, which appears to represent a mid-tenth cen-

---

[1] *Annales Cambriae, A.D. 682–954: Texts A–C in Parallel*, ed. and trans. by David N. Dumville (Cambridge: Department of Anglo-Saxon, Norse and Celtic, University of Cambridge, 2002), pp. vii–viii. **A**: London, BL, MS Harley 3859, fols 190^r–193^r. **B**: London, The National Archives, MS E 164/1, pp. 2–26. **C**: BL, MS Cotton Domitian A I, fols 138^r–155^r. The editions used here: *Annales Cambriae: The A Text, from British Library, Harley MS 3859, ff. 190r–193r*, ed. by Henry W. Gough-Cooper (The Welsh Chronicles Research Group, 2015) <http://croniclau.bangor.ac.uk/documents/AC_A_first_edition.pdf> [accessed 4 April 2018]; *Annales Cambriae: The B Text, from London, National Archives MS E164.1, pp. 2–26*, ed. by Henry W. Gough-Cooper (The Welsh Chronicles Research Group, 2015) <http://croniclau.bangor.ac.uk/documents/AC%20B%20first%20edition.pdf> [accessed 4 April 2018]; *Annales Cambriae: The C Text, from British Library Cotton MS Domitian A. i. ff. 138r–155r*, ed. by Henry W. Gough-Cooper (Welsh Chronicles Research Group, 2015) <http://croniclau.bangor.ac.uk/documents/AC%20C%20first%20edition.pdf> [accessed 4 April 2018]. The alphanumeric tags used are of these editions.

[2] Kathleen Hughes, 'The Welsh Latin Chronicles: *Annales Cambriae* and Related Texts', in her *Celtic Britain in the Early Middle Ages: Studies in Welsh and Scottish Sources by the Late*

tury recension of a St Davids chronicle,[3] and on **B**,[4] the most complex of the chronicles, but she devoted little more than two brief paragraphs to **C**.[5] Hughes considered that **B** and **C** represented independent recensions of a St Davids chronicle down to 1202, after which they diverged.[6] Recent scholarship has also focused largely on **A** and **B**,[7] to the comparative neglect of **C**, while the Welsh vernacular chronicles, the *Brutiau*, have long benefitted from excellent commentaries, editions, and translations.[8] The neglect of **C** can perhaps be explained as a result of its more localized character which renders it of slighter interest to historians, but this neglect cannot be justified when looking for evidence of the origins and development of the *Annales Cambriae* and the *Brutiau* as a corpus of interrelated texts, as the following preliminary study will attempt to show.

Much of the history of the gradual compilation of **C** can be deduced from chronological disjunctions and disruptions that have been preserved as it was copied, recopied, and edited over the course of several centuries and by comparing its chronological structure with that of **B** and the Welsh vernacular chronicles, the *Brutiau* (**P**, **R**, and **S**).[9] The two thirteenth-century Welsh

Kathleen Hughes, ed. by David N. Dumville (Woodbridge: Boydell, 1980), pp. 67–85 (first publ. in *Proceedings of the British Academy*, 59 (1973), 233–58). References to Hughes are to the pagination of the reprint.

[3] Hughes, 'The Welsh Latin Chronicles', pp. 68–73.

[4] Hughes, 'The Welsh Latin Chronicles', pp. 79–83.

[5] Hughes, 'The Welsh Latin Chronicles', p. 73.

[6] Hughes, 'The Welsh Latin Chronicles', p. 74.

[7] These include Owain Wyn Jones, '*Brut y Tywysogion*: The History of the Princes and Twelfth Century Cambro-Latin Historical Writing', *HSJ*, 26 (2014), 209–27; J. Beverley Smith, 'Historical Writing in Medieval Wales: The Composition of *Brenhinedd y Saesson*', *Studia Celtica*, 52 (2008), 55–86; David Stephenson, 'The "Resurgence" of Powys in the Late Eleventh and Twelfth Centuries', *Anglo-Norman Studies*, 30 (2007), 182–95; David Stephenson, 'Welsh Chronicles' Accounts of the Mid-Twelfth Century', *CMCS*, 56 (2008), 45–57; David Stephenson, 'Gerald of Wales and *Annales Cambriae*', *CMCS*, 60 (2010), 23–37; David Stephenson, 'The Chronicler at Cwm-hir Abbey, 1257–63: The Construction of a Welsh Chronicle', in *Wales and the Welsh in the Middle Ages*, ed. by Ralph A. Griffiths and Phillipp R. Schofield (Cardiff: University of Wales Press, 2011), pp. 29–45; David Stephenson, 'In Search of a Welsh Chronicler: The *Annales Cambriae* B-text for 1204–30', *CMCS*, 72 (2016), 73–85.

[8] *BT (Pen. 20)*; *BT (Pen. 20 trans)*; *BT (RB)*; *BS*; *Brenhinoedd y Saeson*, 'The Kings of the English', A.D. 682–954: Texts P, R, S in Parallel, ed. and trans. by David N. Dumville (Aberdeen: Department of History, University of Aberdeen, 2005).

[9] This alphabetical designation follows *Brenhinoedd y Saeson*, ed. and trans. by Dumville.

Latin witnesses represent final surviving recensions and can be referred to as the Chronicle of 1286 (**B**) and the Chronicle of 1288 (**C**). **B** was almost certainly copied into the Neath Breviate flyleaves later than the year of its last annal, 1286 (a date of *c.* 1300 has been suggested for the latest of the collection of miscellanea in which it is found).[10] **C** was most likely last worked on, and then abandoned, in or shortly after the last of its annals, which is for the year 1288 (see below). **B** is the final form of a synthetic chronicle compiled from disparate sources in the late 1270s, to which the last three isolated annals (1282, 1283, and 1286) were added as a postscript at a later date. Both **B** and **C** include recensions of a St Davids chronicle extant in the early thirteenth century, which ran from the mid-fifth century up to 1202 or 1203. **C** is the final form of a cumulative chronicle updated at St Davids from time to time. Conjectural ancestors of these chronicles are marked with an asterisk, for example '**B** *Chronicle of 1277'. I will give a brief resumé of the development of **B** after 1202, and then pass on to a more detailed consideration of the St Davids chronicle, **C**, as a whole, comparing it with **B** and the *Brutiau* from the early thirteenth century back to the mid-tenth century.[11]

B: The Chronicle of 1286

B is one of a collection of items copied into the flyleaves of the Neath Breviate of Domesday *c.* 1300. These items were copied by thirteen distinct hands, and they all show de Braose interest, the principal purpose of which was to support the de Braose faction at a time when the lordship of Gower was under dispute.[12] Neath Abbey, although in the Clare lordship of Glamorgan, had become, by 1300, a virtual *Eigenkloster* of the de Braose family.[13] The witness to the Chronicle of 1286 (**B**) is a very clean copy, showing no signs of being a

---

The standard editions of the texts are *BT (Pen. 20)* and *BT (Pen. 20 trans)* (**P**); *BT (RB)* (**R**); *BS* (**S**).

[10] Daniel Huws, 'The Neath Abbey *Breviate of Domesday*', in *Wales and the Welsh*, ed. by Griffiths and Schofield, pp. 46–55 (p. 49).

[11] **C** begins with a World Chronicle derived from Isidore of Seville's *Etymologiae*, but its annals do not commence until the late seventh century. The annals in **C** are based on a source that was also common to **A** and **B**. Only the annals in **B** and **C** that act as a continuation of **A** after that chronicle ends in the mid-tenth century are examined here.

[12] Huws, 'The Neath Abbey *Breviate*', pp. 47–49.

[13] Smith, 'Historical Writing', p. 74.

'work-in-progress'.[14] David Stephenson, following Kathleen Hughes, sees the chronicle falling into five major periods from the late twelfth century onwards: 1189–1203, 1204–1230, 1231–1256, 1257–1263, and 1264–1286.[15] **B** concludes with a brief codicil of three annals for the years 1282, 1283, and 1286,[16] noting the deaths of the last native princes of Wales and a fire at Strata Florida. The previous annal is for 1277 (b1298) and is the last in an almost continuously dated set of annals running from 1097 (b1119),[17] and concerns Edward I's invasion of North Wales and the subsequent peace treaty agreed between the King and Llywelyn ap Gruffudd, here called 'Prince of North Wales' ('princeps Nortwallie'). Thus, Stephenson's last period should be divided into two sections: 1264–1277 and 1282–1286 (or 1284). The immediate ancestor of **B**, therefore, would appear to be a chronicle that ended in 1277. Although the series of dated annals in **B** is almost continuous from 1097 down to 1277, with only the year 1232 omitted, the apparatus is demonstrably artificial. The compiler of 1277 introduced extracts from English chronicles going back to the early twelfth century, most of which can be identified as coming from a source related to the extant Winchester, Waverley, and Tewkesbury annals, particularly as exemplified by the chronicle in London, BL, MS Cotton Vespasian E IV,[18] a set of Winchester annals augmented at Waverley (henceforth Winchester-Waverley), and these parallel items are closely associated with the AD dating apparatus.[19] Even where the chronology of **B** is otherwise in advance or in arrears, these reciprocals of English annals fall in the correct nominal year.[20]

---

[14] There is a late fourteenth-century copy of **B** in London, BL, MS Harley 848, fols 96ʳ–114ᵛ. This copy follows **B** very closely, even to the extent of leaving a gap of twelve lines where there is still a damaged area of the manuscript of **B** today (b1118), suggesting it was very probably copied directly from **B**.

[15] Stephenson, 'In Search of a Welsh Chronicler', p. 73.

[16] Possibly a scribal error for 1284, see Smith, 'Historical Writing', p. 74 n. 114.

[17] The annals in **B** run from Julius Caesar's invasion of Britain (b1), sixty years before the Nativity (b60), but AD dates only appear in the annal headers from 1097 onwards.

[18] See Felix Liebermann, *Ungedruckte Anglo-Normannische Geschichtsquellen* (Strassburg: Trübner, 1879), pp. 173–202; *AM*, II (1865); IV (1869).

[19] There are some sixty-four such items between 1101 and 1275, the great majority of which can be identified as parallels of passages in the Waverley, Winchester, or MS Cotton Vespasian E IV annals.

[20] A striking example is the duplication of a note on the capture of Robert, Duke of Normandy, by his brother, King Henry, in 1106, which appears in both b1127 (AD 1105) and b1128 (AD 1106). Here the chronology in **B** is running a year in arrears, so the note in b1127

4. MEET THE ANCESTORS? 111

Therefore, they were probably copied from a source with an AD dating apparatus, and synchronized by the compiler with the artificial dating system in **B**, whether agreeing with the chronology of the surrounding annals or not.[21] The first of the many parallels with items also found in the Winchester-Waverley chronicle is in the annal for 1101 (b1123.3), the last is in the annal for 1271 (b1292), but there are two further annals where an English chronicle source is possible, but not yet identified: 1274 (b1295.1)[22] and 1275 (b1296.1).[23] There is a sparse period in **B**, between 1264 and 1273, where nearly all the annals are parallels of those in the Winchester-Waverley chronicle. It must be concluded, therefore, that, as these Winchester-Waverley parallels are found in the chronicle from the early twelfth century right down to the 1270s, the ancestors of **B** before the *Chronicle of 1277 did not have these items from English annals and did not have the closely associated AD dating apparatus as it now appears in the Chronicle of 1286.

In contrast to **C**, whose annals are sparse between 1256 and 1270, **B** has some of its most extensive annals between 1255 and 1263,[24] some of which consist of quite lengthy narratives, and there are few identifiable extracts corresponding to the Winchester-Waverley annals in this section. It is, in effect, a chronicle of the 'Great War in Wales' noted by **C** in its annal c576 ('magna guerra in Wallia'). Stephenson has argued that the annals for 1257 to 1263 were written by a chronicler associated with Cwm-hir Abbey, a daughter house of Whitland, who edited two sections of text (the first for 1255–1259, the second for 1260–1263) into a common form.[25] There is certainly an abrupt cut-off from the extensive accounts of warfare from 1257 to 1263 to a very brief annal at 1264 of a disagreement between Cîteaux and Clairvaux (a garbled paraphrase corresponding to a passage in the Waverley annal for that year),[26] and no further Welsh events are recorded until 1270. However, it is more difficult to determine where this 'Cwm-hir' compilation begins. **B** has a series of empty annals from 1247 to 1250, into which has been inserted a note, also

---

appears under the correct year ('1105' = 1106), but it also appears in b1128, '1106', in a form almost identical to that in MS Cotton Vespasian E IV, fol. 170ʳ, s.a. *mcvi*.

[21] This artificiality is particularly noticeable in the annals for 1134–1155.

[22] The return of Edward, son of Henry III, from France, and his coronation.

[23] Edward I's first parliament at Westminster.

[24] See Stephenson, 'The Chronicler at Cwm-hir Abbey'.

[25] Stephenson, 'The Chronicler at Cwm-hir Abbey', pp. 33–34.

[26] *AM*, II, 357.

found in the Winchester–Waverley annals,[27] about the capture of Damietta by King Louis IX of France in 1249. The annal for 1251 is very slight, recording only two obituaries, and the annals for 1252 to 1254 are not much more expansive, but the annals for 1252, 1254, and 1255 all make reference to Maelgwn Ieuanc and the deaths of his children who predeceased him, marking the end of the line of Maelgwn ap Rhys. One possible explanation for the empty annals from 1247 to 1250 is that the compiler had one source that ended in 1246, and another that began in 1251, with obituaries for Gwladus ferch Llywelyn and Morgan ap Rhys, but his chronological apparatus obliged him to recognize that there were four years wanting between the two. There is a close resemblance between the annals in **B** and those in the *Cronica de Wallia* (**E**)[28] from 1231 to 1249, even to the extent that they both omit 1232 entirely. Their annals for 1246 are almost identical, except that **B** has added the deaths of Walter and Anselm Marshal after the last of **E**'s items. But their annals for 1247 and 1248 are different. The annal in **B** for 1247 is empty, whereas **E** has the same items, but in a different order, to those in **P**, **R**, and **S**; and **E** places the capture of Damietta under 1248, where **B** has it under the correct year, 1249.

The series of annals that ends in 1246 seems to have run from about 1230, where order is restored following a period of considerable chronological disruption. Despite what its AD apparatus indicates, **B** has no annals for 1220, 1221, 1225, 1226, or 1227: its annals labelled as such are, in fact, for events of 1223 to 1224, and 1228 to 1230, after which there is an empty annal (b1250) labelled '1228' and then two slight annals for the years labelled '1229' and '1230', neither of which record Welsh events. The chronology is altogether very haphazard from b1242 ('1220') to b1250 ('1228'). Therefore, there would appear to have been a lacuna from 1225 to 1228, which has been silently repaired by a later editor by filling it with events of 1228 to 1230.

B goes a year ahead at b1237 ('1215') recording an event of 1216, and there is no annal for events of 1215, and its annals labelled '1216' to '1218' are possibly for 1217 to 1219.

---

[27] *AM*, II, 91.

[28] '"Cronica de Wallia" and Other Documents from Exeter Cathedral Library MS. 3514', ed. by Thomas Jones, *BBCS*, 12 (1946), 27–44. See also *Annales Cambriae: The E Text, from Exeter Cathedral Library MS 3514, pp. 507–19*, ed. by Henry W. Gough-Cooper (The Welsh Chronicles Research Group, 2016) <http://croniclau.bangor.ac.uk/documents/AC_E_First_Edition%20%20.pdf> [accessed 4 April 2018].

4. MEET THE ANCESTORS? 113

Table 4.1: b1241–b1255 (AD 1219 to 1234).

Stated chronology	Actual chronology
b1241 '1219'	Events of 1220 and 1219 (death of William Marshal the elder).
b1242 '1220'	An event of 1222.
b1243 '1221'	Events of 1223 and 1221.[29]
b1244 '1222'	An event of 1224 (William Marshal the younger goes to Ireland).
b1245 '1223'	An event of 1223?
b1246 '1224'	An event of 1224 (capture of Bedford Castle).
b1247 '1225'	An event of 1228.
b1248 '1226'	An event of 1229.
b1249 '1227'	An event of 1230 (May).
b1250 '1228'	(Empty).
b1251 '1229'	An event of 1230 (October).
b1252 '1230'	An event of 1230 (25 October).
b1253 '1231'	An event of 1231 (William Marshal, Earl of Pembroke, died.).
	(No annal for '1232').
b1254 '1233'	An event of 1233?
b1255 '1234'	An event of 1234.

David Stephenson has undertaken a comprehensive analysis of the annals from 1204 to 1230,[30] concluding that this represents two periods of compilation, the first covering 1204 to 1219, the second 1220 to 1230.[31] During the first of these, 1204 to 1219, there are stylistic repetitions that are found nowhere else in **B**,[32] but the annals for 1204 to 1210 are fragmentary, while those for 1211 to 1219 are fuller, suggesting that 1219, noting the death of William Marshal, represents the end of a period of compilation that was retrospective for 1204 to 1210. After 1219 the annals again become fragmentary, and their chronology largely erroneous, representing an attempt by the compiler to bring the chronicle down from 1219 to the chronologically more secure

[29] A parallel of a Winchester-Waverley annal. *AM*, II, 84; Liebermann, *Ungedruckte Anglo-Normannische Geschichtsquellen*, p. 189.
[30] Stephenson, 'In Search of a Welsh Chronicler'.
[31] Stephenson, 'In Search of a Welsh Chronicler', pp. 76–77.
[32] Stephenson, 'In Search of a Welsh Chronicler', p. 75.

material at 1231. Stephenson considers the construction of the text for 1220 to 1230 may have taken place many years later.[33]

This period of retrospective compilation to 1231 may be summarized as in Table 4.1 on the previous page. Stephenson's view of the earlier section (1204 to 1219), dividing it into a retrospective section (1204 to 1210) and a more detailed compilation (1211 to 1219), is put in doubt by the structure of the chronicle to 1211, which may be summarized as in Table 4.2:

Table 4.2: b1225–b1233 (AD 1203 to 1211)

Chronology	Events
b1225 '1203' (1203)	Geoffrey consecrated Bishop of St Davids (December 1203).
b1226 '1204' (1203, 1204)	Arthur of Brittany dies (April 1203); Robert, Earl of Leicester, dies (October 1204).
b1227 '1205' (1205, 1206)	Hubert, Archbishop of Canterbury, dies (July 1205); King John goes to Picardy (June 1206); change of coinage (parallel of Winchester, s.a. 1205).[34]
b1228 '1206'	(Empty).
b1229 '1207' (1207)	Parallel of Waverley;[35] no Welsh event.
b1230 '1208' (1208?)	Rhys Fychan (*paruus*) burns *Luchewein* (Llangadog or possibly Llyn Llech Owain).[36]
b1231 '1209' (1209)	No Welsh event.
b1232 '1210' (1210)	(= **P** 1210) King John expels the de Lacys from Ireland.
b1233 '1211' (1211)	King John campaigns in North Wales.

There may be some slight evidence here arguing for a hiatus at 1206–7. This is supported by a feature of the Welsh vernacular chronicle (**P**) at this point, where it omits 1207 and then puts events of 1212 under two years.[37] The crowding of events of 1203 and 1204, and 1205 and 1206 in **B** into two annals, followed by an empty annal for 1206, may indicate a period of compilation that ended in 1206, or perhaps just further evidence of the divergence after 1203. After 1206, as Stephenson notes, the annals continue to be quite minimal until

---

[33] Stephenson, 'In Search of a Welsh Chronicler', p. 77.

[34] *AM*, II, 79.

[35] *AM*, II, 258–59.

[36] See *HW*, II, 621, n. 50.

[37] *BT (Pen. 20 trans.)*, pp. 86 and 195.

b1233, '1211', where a relatively extensive account is given of King John's campaign and its outcome. 1202 or *c*. 1203 has been suggested as the date at which the common ancestor of the **B** and **C** chronicles ended, and where the texts finally diverge.[38]

C: The Chronicle of 1288

For its last eighteen years or so, **C**, the St Davids chronicle, is quite clearly a work-in-progress. This final period of compilation begins with a new annal on a fresh *recto* leaf of a new bifolium at about the year 1270 (c592).[39] Unlike the annals to 1256 (c576) which are written almost continuously, one or two lines are left blank between annals, and the last two leaves (154^v and 155^r) are quite untidy, with crossings-out, marginal corrections, and the final four 'Annus' headings left without rubricated capitals. The last noted annal (c609) records the solar eclipse of 2 April 1288, after which, twelve lines further down, the scribe has written '(a)nn*us*' without even a small 'a' to remind the rubricator where to insert the capital, showing that the intention was to continue the chronicle. The compiler of 1288 was also preparing to interpolate extracts from a Worcester chronicle for the years 1016 to 1199, but the project was left in note form, interleaved with the bifolia of the chronicle on two bifolia and a singleton, with its items tagged to the Welsh annals by a system of *signes-de-renvoi*.[40] AD dates appear only in the last few annal headers (c605, 1284;[41] c607, 1286; c608, 1287; c609, 1288), and in two of these (c605 and c608) the date has been added *post-scriptum* above the line.[42]

---

[38] As discussed below (pp. 121–22), **B** and **C** show signs of independence from 1189 onwards, but Kathleen Hughes ('The Welsh Latin Chronicles', p. 75) identified 1202 as the last annal that **B** and **C** have in common. David Stephenson ('Gerald of Wales', p. 27) has argued that the final divergence occurred after the entries for 1203.

[39] The first externally datable event here is the death of Henry III of England in 1272, noted in c594.

[40] See *The Winchcombe and Coventry Chronicles: Hitherto Unnoticed Witnesses to John of Worcester*, ed. and trans. by Paul Anthony Hayward, 2 vols (Tempe: Arizona Center for Medieval and Renaissance Studies, 2010), I, 173–76; II, 709–16.

[41] Erroneously annotated *Millio .cc. lxxxiii°*.

[42] Few other AD dates appear in **C**, and none in the annal headers, so that these must be an innovation of the 1280s.

C: *Chronicle of 1256

As noted above, the first page of the last bifolium begins at 1270 (c592), but the fifth from last annal on the previous bifolium, the last notated annal on that page, is itself also for 1270 (c587), and so the last empty annal (c591) is ostensibly for 1274. The annals on this page, back to 1256 (c576.2: 'Et incepit magna guerra in Wallia', 'and a great war began in Wales') are sparse. There are seven, brief, notated annals to eight empty ones, and all — except for the last empty pair (c590 and c591) — have one or two blank lines between them, leaving room for additional items which were never supplied. This suggests a chronicle which ended in 1256, to which were added a few scattered entries, with room left to insert further material, with enough 'annus' headings to take the entries down to 1274. That this was a provisional draft is evidenced by the chronological disjunction between c591, the last notated annal of folio 153^v (for 1274), and c592, the first annal of folio 154^r (by deduction, for 1270).[43] This *Chronicle of 1256 perhaps begins at 1240 or 1241, as there are signs of a chronological disjunction between 1237 and 1241 (see below).

Both **B** and **C** become laconic after the extinction of the Marshal line in the mid-1240s, both having had a strong Marshal interest for the period from *c.* 1219 to 1245–1246.[44]

C: *Chronicle of 1237

It is not certain that the **C** *Chronicle of 1256 went any further back than 1240, where **C** shows evidence of a minor disruption in its chronology between 1237 (c557) and 1241 (c562). The sequence of annals is as appears in Table 4.3: There are no annals for 1238 and 1239, and the chronology is uncertain until 1241 (c562). However, prior to that, the chronology is cogent back to 1219 (c538), except perhaps for the synchronization of the death of Rhys Gryg (placed by **B** at 1234)[45] with the very dry summer of 1232 (c552).[46]

---

[43] The last notated annal on fol. 153^v (c587) is for an event of 1270, but this is followed by four empty annals (c588–c591).

[44] **C** records the apportioning of the Marshal lands between the three Marshal heiresses (c569.1; 1248) and then leaps three years from an event of 1250 (c572) to one of 1254 (c574).

[45] This is also the date given in *Handbook of British Chronology*, ed. by E. B. Fryde and others, 3rd edn (Cambridge: Cambridge University Press, 2003), p. 53.

[46] See J. Titow, 'Evidence of Weather in the Account Rolls of the Bishopric of Winchester 1209–1350', *Economic History Review*, 12 (1960), 360–407 (p. 367).

4. MEET THE ANCESTORS?

Table 4.3: c577–c562 (AD 1237 to 1241)

C	Events	Dates
c557	Otto the Legate arrives.	1237
c558	(Empty).	(1238–1239?)
c559	Prince Llywelyn dies; Walter Marshal builds the keep (*turrim*) at Cardigan.	1240
c560	(Empty).	?
c561	Walter Marshal takes the lands of the honour of Carmarthen on behalf of Gilbert, his brother.	?
c562	Gilbert Marshal dies; Walter made Earl of Pembroke.	June/October 1241

C: *Chronicle of 1216–17

C exhibits evidence of a radical revision made between 1216 and 1219, probably in 1217. There are four annals for 1215 and 1216–1217, after which it leaps directly to an annal for 1219. Table 4.4 shows the recursion around the years 1215–1216, followed by the leap to 1219.[47]

Table 4.4: C between 1214 and 1219

Year	Events	
1214	c534 The Papal Interdict is relaxed (July 1214). Geoffrey, Bishop of St Davids, dies; Gervase succeeds him. King John crosses to Poitou. Battle of Bouvines (July 1214).	
1215	c535 Discord arises between the King and the barons.	c537 Discord arises between the King and the barons. King John takes the cross (March 1215). Papal legate sent to England (May 1216). The legate excommunicates Prince Louis who, after absolution, returns to France (autumn 1217).
1216	c536 First year of a decennovenal cycle (1216). Lateran council. Pope Innocent III dies (July 1216).	c538 At the end of the year, King John dies (October 1216). Prince Henry crowned. Llywelyn was at Wolfsdale in Rhos.
1219	c539 Damietta is captured by the Christians (November 1219). William Marshal the elder dies (May 1219).	

---

[47] In Tables 4.4 and 4.5 the content of the annals has been abbreviated for the sake of concision.

The two annals c537 and c538 might be taken to represent proxies for the two missing years 1217 and 1218, although this is not what their content says. The first, c537, covers events of 1215 to 1217; the second, c538, events of 1216, with which is synchronized the statement about Llywelyn ap Iorwerth being at Wolfsdale, about fourteen miles east of St Davids.

At this time, a World Chronicle based on Isidore's *Chronica minora* was joined to the annals by means of a sophisticated revision of the last part of Isidore's Sixth Age (into which were incorporated pre-680s items extracted from a source similar to that for the same period in **A** and **B**, and from Geoffrey of Monmouth's *De gestis Britonum*), as shown in Table 4.5.[48]

Table 4.5: Parallels between the structuring of the universal chronicle and the later annals in **C**

The last item of Fourth Age: cw58.3 Temple of Jerusalem burnt.	The last item of Sixth Age: cw132.3 Monastery of St Davids burnt.
First item of Fifth Age: cw59.1 Hebrews in captivity.	**C** Annals (second item of first annal): c3.2 Cadwaladr abandons Britain and goes to Armorica.
Fifth Age edited to sum to 532 years.	The first decennovenal marker in **C**: c8, first year of a 19-year cycle (684).
The last item of Fifth Age: cw80 Octavian reigns for fifty-five years, in the fortieth year of which Christ is born. The Fifth Age ends lasting 533 (*sic*) years (the items in fact sum to 532 years).	The last decennovenal marker in **C**: c536, first year of a 19-year cycle (1216). (thus framing a 532-year cycle).

The burning of Jerusalem at the end of the Fourth Age, the Hebrews being led into captivity, and a Fifth Age carefully edited to sum to 532 years (leading up to the birth of Christ, the saviour of mankind), prefigures the burning of St Davids at the end of the World Chronicle, Cadwaladr abandoning Britain, and the 532-year frame for the annals from 684 to 1216, after which 'Llywelyn was at Wolfsdale in Rhos' (c538.2 'Lewelinus fuit [apud] Woluedale in Ros'). The purpose of this complex recension of 1216–1217 seems to have been to celebrate Llywelyn ab Iorwerth (*c.* 1172–1240) at the zenith of his career: Llywelyn, the saviour of the Welsh.[49]

---

[48] Isidore of Seville, *Etymologiarum sive originum libri XX*, V. 39, ed. by W. M. Lindsay, 2 vols (Oxford: Clarendon Press, 1911), I.

[49] For a full analysis, see Henry Gough-Cooper, 'Decennovenal Reason and Unreason in the C-text of *Annales Cambriae*', in *The Medieval Chronicle 11*, ed. by Erik Kooper and Sjoerd Levelt (Leiden: Brill, 2017), pp. 195–212.

The recension of 1216–1217 almost certainly altered the overall form of the St Davids chronicle;[50] to what extent it affected the contents of the preceding annals is uncertain. Nevertheless, it is possible to detect the broad outlines of a common source behind **B** and **C** up to 1203.

Evidence for a Common Source behind the Breviate (B) and Cottonian (C) Chronicles prior to 1203

*Chronicle of 1202–03

1202 was the year identified by Kathleen Hughes as the point at which the **B** and **C** chronicles diverge completely.[51] The annals in **B** and **C** for 1202 (b1224 and c523) have almost identical wording, signalling the point before which the **B** and **C** texts show evidence of a common ancestor:

> [b1224] Anus .m.ccii. Arthurus dux Armoricanorum Britonum a rege Iohanne in belli conflictu cum multis baronibus et militibus · Philippo regi Francorum fauentibus captus est · et Alienor soror eius cum ipso.

> The year 1202. Arthur, duke of the Armorican Britons, was captured in battle with many barons and knights loyal to Philip, King of the French, and Eleanor his sister with him.

> [c523] Annus. Arthurus dux Armoricanorum Britonum a Iohanne rege Anglie in belli conflictu cum multis baronibus et militibus Philippo regi Francorum fauentibus captus est.

> A year. Arthur, duke of the Armorican Britons, was captured in battle by John, King of England, with many barons and knights loyal to Philip, King of the French.

From this annal for 1202 back to 1187 (b1209, c507), of the sixteen annotated annals (**C** has an extra empty annal at c510) there are eleven in which can be detected close parallels, although the annals in **B** tend to be fuller than those in **C**. Where the chronicles have very different annals, **B** has items of Welsh interest while **C** has items of English interest, most of which concern King Richard I (b1211, c509; b1212, c511; b1216, b515; b1221, c520).[52]

---

[50] It seems probable that this is the stage at which the World Chronicle was fused with the annals. See Gough-Cooper, 'Decennovenal Reason and Unreason', pp. 199–208.

[51] Hughes, 'The Welsh Latin Chronicles', p. 74.

[52] **C** has a curious error at c518 (AD 1197) where it announces the death of Richard I of England two years before a further, correct, notice of his death at c520 (AD 1199).

If this is the juncture at which **B** and **C** began to be maintained separately, there might be signs of a *Chronicle of 1202 when the copy was made that left St Davids. The annals for this period can be compared as in Table 4.6:

Table 4.6: **B** and **C** between 1202 and 1210

Date	B	C
1202	b1224 '1202' Arthur captured.	c523 Arthur captured.
1203–04	b1225 '1203' Bishop Geoffrey consecrated (December 1203).	c524 Arthur dies (April 1203); Bishop Geoffrey consecrated.
	b1226 '1204' Arthur dies (April 1203); King Philip takes Normandy (1203–1204); John de Courcy is expelled from Ireland; William Marshal takes Cilgerran; Robert, Earl of Leicester, dies (October 1204).[53]	
1205–06	b1227 '1205' Death of Archbishop Hubert (July 1205); John campaigns in Poitou (June to December 1206); Rhys Parvus (Rhys Fychan) burns Llangadog Castle; new coinage is introduced (1205).[54]	c525 John loses Rouen and Normandy (by 1204); Death of Archbishop Hubert (July 1205); Canterbury election dispute (1205–1206); Langton consecrated by the Pope (July 1207); Death of Henry, Bishop of Exeter (November 1206).
	b1228 '1206' (empty).	c526 The Prior of Canterbury goes to Rome (October 1205 × December 1206).
1207	b1229 '1207' Taxation for recovery of Normandy (1207).[55]	c527 Stephen Langton consecrated by the Pope (1207).
1208	b1230 '1208' Rhys Parvus (Rhys Fychan) burns Llangadog Castle a second time (1208).[56]	c528 Papal Interdict on England (March 1208); banishment of William de Braose.
1209	b1231 '1209' Birth of Richard; John goes to Scotland (1209).	c529 (empty).
1210	b1232 '1210' John expels the de Lacys from Ireland, Wales, and England (1210).	c530 John goes to Ireland to expel the de Lacys (1210); captures Maud de Braose and her son.

[53] Winchester-Waverley: *AM*, II, 256, s.a. 1204.
[54] Winchester-Waverley: *AM*, II, 79, s.a. 1205.
[55] Winchester-Waverley: *AM*, II, 258–59, s.a. 1207.
[56] **P** has this under the year 1207, but **P**, **R**, and **S** have omitted 1207.

C has the death of Arthur and the consecration of Geoffrey, Bishop of St Davids, in the correct order and in the same year (April and December 1203), whereas **B** has these in the wrong order and under different years (1203, 1204). The rest of **B**'s items for 1204 seem cogent, but it then conflates items for 1205 and 1206 in its annal for 1205, leaving 1206 as an empty annal. Its next annal, for 1207, is an item which has a parallel in the Waverley annals, and is therefore probably a late insertion, implying that **B**'s ancestor had no annals for 1206 and 1207. **C**, on the other hand, has put the loss of Normandy (1204) into its annal covering the events of 1205–1207, and thus has no separate annal for 1204. **C** then reiterates under its annals for 1206 and 1207 information already given in its compendious annal for 1205 (c525). There are no clear signs of the end of a chronicle here, but there is a certain amount of disruption. **C** probably reflects contemporary records at St Davids down to 1203 (c524), after which the lengthy account of the disputed election at Canterbury and its aftermath is almost certainly a retrospective interpolation. But **C** continues without a break until its empty annal for 1209. **B** has had obvious problems from 1203 until 1210, which perhaps reflects retrospective compilation to fill a lacuna. The only convincingly contemporary annal here in **B** before 1210 is that for 1208. The evidence supports David Stephenson's suggestion that 1203 may have been the year after which the ancestor of **B** was moved away from St Davids.[57]

In the long decade from 1187 to 1203, **B** and **C** start to show signs of dissimilarity. In 1187 (b1209/c507), to the note in **C** on Archbishop Baldwin's entry into Wales to preach the Crusade, **B** adds a brief gloss noting his visit to St Davids and his circuit through North Wales and back to England, most of which was accomplished in 1188. Both **B** and **C** note the appearance of a comet in 1188, but **B** adds a learned note paraphrasing Lucan's *Pharsalia*.[58] They then have completely different annals for 1189 (b1211/c509), **B** ignoring the death of Henry II in favour of describing events in Wales. Thereafter, **B**'s and **C**'s annals for 1190, 1193, and 1199 are very different, those for 1191, 1195, 1201, and 1202 very similar, and the remainder share some similar items but **B** is fuller, **C** quite brief. **C** here seems to reflect the underlying source, the St Davids chronicle, where **B** shows signs of retrospective editing. David Stephenson has presented an interesting case for associating this

---

[57] Stephenson, 'Gerald of Wales', p. 27.
[58] Lucan, *The Civil War*, I. 526–29, ed. and trans. by J. D. Duff, Loeb Classical Library, 220 (Cambridge, MA: Harvard University Press, 1923), p. 40.

editing of **B** with the presence of Gerald of Wales at St Davids,[59] but it may be noted that, between 1189 and 1196, **B** shows an interest in William de Braose, whose power was growing in South Wales at this period and for whose family the collection of historical memoranda and charters was copied into the Neath Breviate of Domesday; this interest is not shared by **C**.[60] It is possible that **B**'s focus on William de Braose was the result of retrospective selectivity at Neath.

*Chronicle of c. 1180

There are two major instances of chronological disjunction in the twelfth-century annals of the **B** and **C** chronicles, providing evidence for an underlying source chronicle, or chronicles.

The first falls in the 1180s where both **B** and **C** have a lacuna between 1183/84 and 1187.[61] Here, **B** simply has a series of empty annals which it labels '1183' to '1186', while **C** has a rather confused series of annals for the events of 1179 to 1184. After this, the chronicles resynchronize with a very similar notice of the disastrous battle at the Horns of Hattin ('apud mare tyberiadis'; 'at the Tiberiad Sea') of 1187, and its consequences. Table 4.7 below shows the period as covered in **B** and **C**, and also shows the same period as it appears in the Welsh vernacular texts, **P** and **S** (**S** labels every year, **P** only specifies 1180). For ease of comparison of the chronology, the information in the annals has been summarized as footnotes to the table.

As can be seen, **B**'s chronological apparatus is running a year in advance in the 1170s: this is due to **B** having overcompensated for missing years in the period 1135–1154 (see below). Nevertheless, the relative chronology is cogent at 1176 (**B** '1177'). **B** and **C** have the same number of annals over this period (**P**, **R**, and **S** have gained an extra year), but their distribution is quite differ-

---

[59] Stephenson, 'Gerald of Wales'. The indications of Gerald's influence are, however, qualified as 'faint': p. 30. Furthermore, there seems to be no particular reason to suppose that the variant annals in **B** between 1187 and 1203 were compiled at St Davids.

[60] William is noted in 1174 (b1197), 1189 (b1211), 1192 (b1214), 1195 (b1217), and 1196 (b1218); his son, Giles, in 1199 (b1221).

[61] **P**, **R**, and **S** may also show some evidence of this: their annals for 1177 to 1184 are unusually brief, and for 1180 (**P** and **S**) 'there was nothing that might be placed on record in that year'. **P**: 'Pedwarugeint mlynet a cant a mil: ny bu dym a ellit y dwyn ar gof' (*BT (Pen. 20)*, p. 129a); **S**: 'Anno Domini .m.c.lxxx. ny bu dim o'r a dyckit ar gof yn y vlwydyn honno' (*BS*, p. 184).

4. MEET THE ANCESTORS?

Table 4.7: **B**, **C**, **P**, and **S**, epitome 1176–87

B	C	S
[b1199] '1177' (1176)[1]	[c497] (1176)[1]	'Anno .vi.' (1176)[1]
[b1200] '1178'[2]		'Anno .vii.'[3]
[b1201] '1179' (1178)[4]	[c498] (1178)[4]	'Anno .viii.'
	[c499] (1178)[5]	
[b1202] '1180' (empty)	[c500] (Aug 1179–Sept 1180)[6]	'Anno .ix.'
[b1203] '1181' (1180–1182)[7]		'1180' ('there was nothing which might be placed on record') (= **P**)
[b1204] '1182' (1182)[8]	[c501][8]	
	[c502] (1181)[9]	'Anno .i.' (1181)[9]
	[c503] (1182–1183?)[10]	'Anno .ii.'
[b1205] '1183' (empty)	[c504] (1183–1184)[11]	'Anno .iii.' (1183–1184)[11]
	[c505] (empty)	
[b1206] '1184' (empty)	[c506] (1184)[12]	'Anno .iiii.'
[b1207] '1185' (empty)		'Anno .v.' (1185)[13]
[b1208] '1186' (empty)		'Anno .vi.' (1185)[14]
		'Anno .vii.'
[b1209] '1187' (1187)[15]	[c507] (1187)[15]	'Anno .viii.' (1187)[15]

[1] Richard de Strigoil and Maurice fitz Gerald (**B**, **C**), and David, Bishop of St Davids, (**B**, **C**, **P**, **R**, **S**), died.
[2] Morgan Patta died.
[3] Morgan ap Maredudd was slain (of Rhwng Gwy a Hafren?).
[4] The first year of a decennovenal cycle.
[5] An eclipse of the sun, on the Ides of September (13 September 1178, NASA eclipse website: <https://eclipse.gsfc.nasa.gov/eclipse.html> [accessed 4 April 2018]).
[6] Louis, King of France, came to St Thomas (August 1179); King Louis died (18 September 1180); he was succeeded by his son Philip (crowned 1 November 1179).
[7] The king changed the coinage at Martinmas (11 November 1180); Philip, King of the French, expelled the Jews from France (April 1182).
[8] The church of St Davids was demolished and built anew (**B**, **C**); King Henry sent 42,000 marks to Jerusalem (**B** = MS Cotton Vespasian E IV, s.a. 1182).
[9] Pope Alexander died (30 August 1181); Lucius succeeded him.
[10] Discord between King Henry and his son.
[11] Henry the Young King died (11 June 1183); Richard, Archbishop of Canterbury, died (16 February 1184).
[12] Bartholomew, Bishop of Exeter, died (15 December 1184).
[13] The Patriarch came from Jerusalem to seek support from Henry, King of England (MS Cotton Vespasian E IV, s.a. 1185). On the Calends of May, the sun changed its colour and was under an eclipse (MS Cotton Vespasian E IV, s.a. 1185; 1 May 1185, NASA eclipse website: <https://eclipse.gsfc.nasa.gov/eclipse.html> [accessed 4 April 2018]).
[14] Pope Lucius died (25 November 1185), and after him Urban III succeeded as pope.
[15] The Battle at the Horns of Hattin, or 'at the Tiberiad Sea' (4 July 1187) (**B**, **C**; MS Cotton Vespasian E IV, s.a. 1187). The siege of Jerusalem (September–October 1187) (**P**, **R**, **S**).

ent, and **C**'s annals jump from 1184 to 1187, having simply clumped a series of miscellaneous annals into the period from 1177 to 1184.[62] **B** and **C** resynchronize at AD 1187 (with **B**'s chronological apparatus now correct, but **C** having lost a year) with very similar annals for the events of that year. This strongly suggests that the source chronicle was lacunose from at least 1184 until 1187, more probably from *c.* 1180, with some additional notes of subsequent events. **B**'s last annal in the sequence is for 1182, and is a reciprocal of a note in MS Cotton Vespasian E IV, thus probably added in the 1270s (see above).[63] As with the next chronological disruption to be considered, it is important to note that the compilers of the **B** and **C** chronicles had different solutions to the problem they faced.

*Chronicle of 1151

The next major chronological disjunction in the source of **B** and **C** was simply covered up. The compilers of **B** and **C** must have known that the reign of King Stephen covered a decennovenal cycle (1135–1154),[64] but their source appears to have had only seventeen annals. J. E. Lloyd noted the hidden lacuna in the Welsh Latin chronicles from the middle of 1151 to 1153,[65] which appears to indicate a discrete chronicle running from 1135 to 1151, and this sequence is also preceded by a lacuna in both the Latin and the vernacular chronicles (see Table 4.8).

Both **B** and **C** attempt unsuccessfully to supply the missing two years. **B** supplies three, leaving it a year in advance until the lacuna *c.* 1180 × 1187. **B**'s chronological apparatus is misaligned with items of Welsh origin, but synchronized with items from English chronicles. In Table 4.8, **B**'s chronological apparatus is cogent up until 1146–1149, where it acquires two extra years, so that

---

[62] **C** has a minimal chronological apparatus, but c498 is an exception in stating the first year of a decennovenal cycle (by deduction, AD 1178). Decennovenal years were always reckoned from 1 January, so they are in conflict with Annunciation years, which begin on 25 March. c498 might therefore be an annal for the Annunciation year 1177. Otherwise, **C** has no annal for 1177.

[63] **C**'s positioning of the other event noted, the demolition and rebuilding of the church of St Davids, suggests that it may have happened in 1180 (c501), not 1182 (b1204).

[64] **C** notes both the decennovenal year of Henry's death and that of Stephen in the fifteenth year of successive cycles.

[65] J. E. Lloyd, 'The Welsh Chronicles', *Proceedings of the British Academy*, 14 (1928), 369–91 (pp. 381–82).

Table 4.8: *Chronicle of 1151. *Italics* indicate surplus annals to be removed; **bold** indicates annals requiring division (c461, c462) or amalgamation (b1168–b1171 and c466–c469).

B	C	S
[b1157] '1135' (1135)[1]	[c456] (1135)[1]	'1134' (1135)[1]
[b1158] '1136'	[c457]	'1135'
[b1159] '1137'	[c458]	'1136'
–	*[c459] (unique)*	–
[b1160] '1138'	[c460] (1139/40)[2,3]	'1137' (1139/40)[2,3]
[b1161] '1139' (1139)[2]	**[c461a]**	'1138'
[b1162] '1140' (1140)[3]	**[c461b]**	'1139'
[b1163] '1141' (1141)[4]	**[c462a]**	'1140' (= **P**)
[b1164] '1142'	**[c462b]**	'1141'
[b1165] '1143' (1143)[5]	[c463] (1143)[5]	'1142' (1143)[5]
[b1166] '1144' (1144)[6]	[c464]	'[Anno] .iii.'
[b1167] '1145' (1145)[7]	[c465]	'Anno .iiii.'
[b1168] '1146'	**[c466]**	'Anno .v.'
[b1169] '1147'	**[c467]**	
[b1170] '1148'	**[c468] (1148)[8]**	'Anno .vi.' (Summer 1147–January 1148)
[b1171] '1149' (1147/8)[9]	**[c469] (erroneous)**	
[b1172] '1150' (1148)[10]	[c470] (1148)[10]	'Anno .vii.' (April 1148)[10]
[b1173] '1151'	[c471]	'Anno .viii.'
[b1174] '1152' (1152)[11]	*[c472] (empty)*	–
[b1175] '1153' (1153?)[12]	[c473]	'Anno .ix.' (1150)[13]
[b1176] '1154' (1153)[14]	[c474] (1153)[14]	'1150' (= **P**)
–	–	'Anno .i.'
–	–	'Anno .ii.' (1153)[15]
[b1177] '1155' (empty)	[c475] (1154)[16]	'Anno .iii.' (1154)[16]
[b1178] '1156'	[c476]	'Anno .iiii.' (1155)[17]

[1] Death of Henry I of England (1 December 1135); accession of Stephen.
[2] The Empress comes to England (30 September 1139).
[3] Solar eclipse (20 March 1140; NASA).
[4] King Stephen is captured by the Earls of Chester and Gloucester (2 February 1141), and later released (Nov. 1141).
[5] Miles, Earl of Hereford, is killed in a hunting accident (24 December 1143).
[6] A boy is crucified by the Jews of Norwich (*AM*, II, 230, s.a. 1144).
[7] The king takes the Earl of Chester into his court (*AM*, IV, 379, s.a. 1145).
[8] Earl Gilbert *Stragore* ('Strongbow') dies (6 January 1148).
[9] Earl Robert, son of King Henry, dies (31 October 1147); Earl Gilbert 'Strongbow' dies (6 January 1148).
[10] The Bishops of Llandaf and St Davids (**B**, **C**, **P**, **S**) and Hereford (**C**, **P**, **S**) die.
[11] Henry besieges Malmesbury between January and March 1153 (*AM*, IV, 380, s.a. 1152).
[12] The Empress and her son, Henry, who was Duke of Normandy and Count of Anjou, land at Wareham (erroneous; possibly referring to Henry's expedition of 1153).
[13] Battle of Coleshill.
[14] Rhys ravages Cyfeiliog (**B**); deaths of David of Scotland (**B**, **C**) and Ranulf, Earl of Chester (**B**).
[15] Rhys ravages Cyfeiliog; deaths of David of Scotland and Ranulf, Earl of Chester.
[16] Death of Stephen of England, 'anno decennouennalo . cicli . iiii^{or} . concurrentes' (c475) (24 October 1154).
[17] Geoffrey (of Monmouth), 'Bishop of Llandaff', and Roger, Earl of Hereford, die.

its annal for '1150' actually notes events of 1148. It then has a further extra annal, possibly either b1174 or b1175, so that after its leap to b1177 it is a year in advance, and remains so until *c.* 1180 (see above). **C**, on the other hand, acquires an extra annal at c459, an account not found in any of the other chronicles, but then amalgamates into two annals the events of four years (c461 and c462), and divides the events of two years into four annals (c466–c469), as can be seen by comparison with the annals in the vernacular chronicles (**S** 'Anno V' and 'Anno VI'). Even though the vernacular annals are a year in arrears here (and remain so until 1170), their relative chronology is correct. The fact that the Welsh vernacular annals (shown here as **S** and **P**) are able to fill the chronological gap correctly shows that they were not using **B** or **C** as their source at this point, and that **B** and **C** were not aware of **P**'s and **S**'s chronology. This indicates that **P** and **S** were compiled from a source or sources that did have the correct chronology, not available to **C** in 1216 or to **B** in 1277 (where we might surmise the major efforts of retrospective editing of the chronicles occurred). It may be noted that if the material from English chronicles inserted later into this sequence of annals in **B** is removed, we are left with purely Welsh events.[66] The original source chronicle, before it was reorganized by **B** and **C**, may have looked something like this:

Annal 1 (1135): The death of Henry I of England (**B**, **C**, **P**, **R**, **S**). Discord between the Britons and the French (**C** only).

Annal 2 (1136): The same events as **B**, **P**, **R**, and **S**, but possibly in less elaborate language than **P**, **R**, and **S**.

Annal 3 (1137): Gruffudd ap Rhys's 'uniting' of Rhos, and Anarawd's killing of Letard Litelking without his father's knowledge (**B** only). Death of Gruffudd ap Rhys. Third attack on Ceredigion (and death of Gruffudd ap Cynan?) (**B**, **C**, **P**, **R**, and **S**).

Annals 4–6 (1138–1140): As **C**, **P**, **R**, and **S** (**B** revised order when AD years were added?).

---

[66] **B** reflects Winchester–Waverley in its annals for 1135 (b1156), 1139 (b1161), 1140 (b1162.3), 1141 (b1163.1), 1143 (1165.3), 1144 (b1166.2–3), 1145 (b1167.4), and 1152 (b1174). **C** probably preserves the original version of the annal for 1135, noting after the death of Henry I the 'great discord between the Britons and the French' ('Et maxíma discordia fuit inter britones et francos'), and that 'the Britons were victorious' ('sed britones uictores fuerunt').

4. MEET THE ANCESTORS?

Annal 7 (1141): Hywel (ap Maredudd) ap Rhydderch killed.

Annal 8 (1142): Hywel (ap Maredudd) ap Bleddyn killed. (Hywel ap Madog ab Idnerth and Cadwgan his brother slain; not in **B**).

Annal 9 (1143): Anarawd ap Gruffudd ap Rhys killed by Cadwaladr ap Gruffudd ap Cynan (but not the aftermath in **P**, **R**, and **S**). Miles, Earl of Hereford, killed.

Annal 10 (1144): Cadwaladr's rebellion against, and rescue by, Owain.

Annal 11 (1145): Rhys ap Hywel seized by Hugh de Mortimer. Hywel ab Owain and Cynan his brother ravage Aberteifi. Carmarthen and Mabudryd Castles are built (**B**, **P** and **R**, and **S** all differ on who built them).

Annal 12a (1146): Maredudd ap Madog ab Idnerth killed by Hugh de Mortimer.

Annal 12b (1146?): Cadell ap Gruffudd and his brothers take Dinefwr. Hywel ab Owain helps them take Carmarthen, and they take Llanstephan Castle and give it to Maredudd as custodian. They burn Wyddgrug Castle by night. Rhun ab Owain dies (**P**, **R**, and **S** have this in a different order).

Annal 12c (1146/47?): Hugh de Mortimer blinds Rhys ap Hywel.

Annal 13a (1147): Cadell ap Gruffudd and his brothers, with William fitz Gerald and his brothers, with the help of Hywel ab Owain, destroy Wizo's castle.

Annal 13b (1147?): Earl Robert, son of Henry I, dies. Earl Gilbert Strongbow dies. (Cynan and Hywel ab Owain take Meirionydd by force from Cadwaladr?).

Annal 14 (1148): Uchdryd, Bishop of Llandaf, dies. Bernard, Bishop of St Davids, dies, and David, son of Gerald, succeeds him.

Annal 15 (1149): Cadwaladr builds Llanrhystud Castle, and gives his part of Ceredigion to his son, Cadfan (*Catwano*; Cadwgan in **P**). Madog ap Maredudd gives Cyfeiliog to Owain and Meurig ap Gruffudd (his nephews).

Annal 16 (1150): Cadell ap Gruffudd devastates Cydweli. Hywel ab Owain seizes Cadfan, his cousin, and takes his land and castle. Cadell and his brothers come to Ceredigion and take Is-Aeron (*infra Ayron*).

Annal 17 (1151): Cadell and his brothers attack Hywel's castle around 2 February, but cannot take it, so make off with plunder and captives. They take Llanrhystud Castle after a long siege and give it to its garrison to guard. But Hywel ab Owain in fury sets fire to the castle, killing them all. Cadell and his brothers rebuild Ystrad Meurig Castle. Cadell ap Gruffudd is assaulted by the men of Tenby while out hunting and left for dead. Maredudd and Rhys destroy Aberllwchwr Castle.

Endnotes: Rhys devastates Cyfeiliog, possibly added at a later stage. David, son of Malcolm, dies; Ranulf, Earl of Chester, dies.

The fact that **B** and **C** proposed different solutions to the same problem suggests that the insufficiency of years between 1135 and 1154 was not recognized until much later, perhaps not until the latter part of the thirteenth century.

*Chronicle of 1131

C and the *Brutiau* both have a series of empty annals before their annals for 1135. **C** shows three empty annals while **P** and **R** imply four 'empty' years, and **S** fills its fourth year after three empty years with the same erroneous note as **B** (b1156) on the death of Earl Robert.[67] The explicit AD chronology of **B** looks coherent from where it starts at 1097, down to 1135, but both **B** and the *Brutiau* have omitted a year, and the year **B** calls '1104' is in fact 1105; the year 1104 is represented in **C** by an empty annal, c425. There are problems with the chronology of both **B** and the *Brutiau* from 1101 to 1114, as shown in Table 4.9.

S notes the first year of a nineteen-year cycle at the year that the *Brutiau* call '1100' (the first year of this decennovenal cycle was 1102). There is clear evidence of the later editing of **B** in the duplication of its note about Earl Robert being captured by his brother, King Henry, in September 1106. This first appears under the year that **B** calls '1105' (b1127), but is then duplicated under the year that it calls '1106' (b1128). The duplication is an exact parallel

---

[67] **B** and **S** both echo the error in MS Cotton Vespasian E IV in claiming that Earl Robert died at Gloucester (**B** 'in carcere', 'in prison') and was buried at Cardiff (**S** 'ac y clathpwit yNgaerdyf'), whereas the opposite is true: Robert had been incarcerated in Cardiff Castle, where he died, and was buried in Gloucester.

4. MEET THE ANCESTORS?

Table 4.9: Chronology from 1101 to 1114

Actual AD years	B 'declared years'	C (notional years)	S 'declared years'
1101	b1123 '1101'	c422 (1101)	'1099'
1102	b1124 '1102'	c423 (1102)	'1100' (= **P**) (**S**: 'there was a first *decemnouenalis*')[68]
1103	b1125 '1103'	c424 (1103)	'1101'
1104		c425 (1104)	
1105	b1126 '1104'	c426 (1105)	'1102'
1106	b1127 '1105'	c427 (1106)	'1103'
1107	b1128 '1106'	c428 (1107)	'1104'
1108	b1129 '1107'	c429 (1108)	'1105'
	b1130 '1108'[69]		
	b1131 '1109'[70]		
1109	b1132 '1110'	c430 (1109)	'1106'
1110	b1133 '1111'	c431 (1110)	'1107'
1111	b1134 '1112'	c432 (1111)	'1108'
1112	b1135 '1113'	c433 (1112)	'1109'
1113		c434 (1113)	'1110' (= **P**)
1114	b1136 '1114'	c435 (1114)	'1111'

to the same passage in the Winchester-Waverley annals for 1106.[71] **B** inserts two anachronistic notes of events of 1113 and 1119 under the years that it calls '1108' and '1109', but then includes items for 1112 and 1113 under the year that it calls '1113', thus bringing it back into synchronization with the actual AD year, 1114. So, for the period 1101 to 1114, the only chronicle with a coherent chronology is **C**, the *Brutiau*'s omission of 1104 having gone unnoticed and uncorrected by the compilers.

For the period 1114 to 1135, it is more difficult to see what may have been the structure of the original source for the chronicles (compare Table 4.10).

[68] See below, pp. 131–32.
[69] An event of 1113.
[70] An event of 1119.
[71] *AM*, IV, 374.

Table 4.10: Chronology from 1114 to 1135

B 'declared years'	C (notional years)	S 'declared years'
b1136 '1114'	c435 (1114)	'1111'
b1137 '1115'	c436 (1115)	'1112'
b1138 '1116'	c437 (1116)	'1113'
b1139 '1117'	c438 (1117)	'1114'
b1140 '1118'	c439 (1118)	'1115'
b1141 '1119'	c440 (1119)	'1116'
b1142 '1120' (empty)	c441 (1120)	'1117'
b1143 '1121'	c442 (1121)	'1118' '1119' ('there was peace')
b1144 '1122'		'1120' (= **P**)
b1145 '1123'	c443 (1122)	'1121'
b1146 '1124'	c444 (1123)	'1122'
b1147 '1125' (empty)	c445 (1124; empty)	'1123'
b1148 '1126' (empty)	c446 (1125; empty)	
b1149 '1127'	c447 (1126)	'1124'
b1150 '1128'	c448 (1127)	'1125'
b1151 '1129'	c449 (1128)	'1126'
b1152 '1130'	c450 (1129)	'1127'
b1153 '1131'	c451 (1130)	'1128'
b1154 '1132'	c452 (1131)	'1129'
b1155 '1133' (empty)	c453 (1132; empty) c454 (1133; empty)	'1130' (empty) (= **P**) '1131' (empty) '1132' (empty)
b1156 '1134' (Earl Robert d.)	c455 (1134; empty)	**S**: '1133' (**P** and **R** empty; **S** = **B**)
b1157 '1135' (King Henry d.)	c456 (1135; = **B**)	**S**: '1134' (= **B**)

C has an annal for King Henry's 1122 campaign in Powys, but not for the killing of Gruffudd ap Sulhaearn (b1144; **P**, **R**, and **S** s.a. 1120). Neither **B** nor **C** has an equivalent of **P**'s and **S**'s 'year in which there was peace'.[72] **B** and **C** both

---

[72] **P**: 'Bloidyn y bu he[duch]' (*BT (Pen. 20)*, p. 81b; *BT (Pen. 20 trans.)*, p. 170, notes that this phrase was 'added in the margin by the early corrector of the text'). **S**: 'Pan oyd oed Crist .m.c.xix. hedwch uu y vlwydyn honno' (*BS*, p. 140).

have a pair of empty annals (b1147/c445 and b1148/c446), against which the *Brutiau* have only one year, '1123'. Finally, **B** has an empty annal against two in **C** and three in the *Brutiau*, after which **C**, **P**, and **R** have a further empty annal against an annal in **B** and **S** noting the death of Earl Robert,[73] before the chronicles all arrive at an annal for 1135 concerning the death of Henry I of England and the accession of Stephen of Blois (b1157/c456). Although differing over the distribution of their annals for this period (1101 to 1135), both **B** and **C** have the correct number of years, while the *Brutiau*, starting off two years in arrears and becoming at times three years in arrears, end up having one too many years. In any event, **B** and **C** cannot have taken their structure from the *Brutiau*, since there is no equivalent in the *Brutiau* to the pair of empty annals in **B** and **C** for 1124 and 1125, but the *Brutiau*, in staring a series of empty years before 1135, may have been influenced by the same feature in the St Davids annals. In short, **B** appears to have been influenced by the structure of both **C** and the *Brutiau*, but **C** looks unlikely to have been influenced by either. If this is correct, then **C** must best represent the chronology of the St Davids source chronicle for this period, while **B** has undergone a greater degree of editing at a later time. The source chronicle might be referred to as the *Chronicle of 1131.

*Chronicle of 1091

Before 1091, the eleventh-century annals in **B** and **C** are sparser than those of the twelfth century; almost half of them are empty, and there are frequent groups of two or three consecutive empty years. But this seems to end with the annals for 1089–92: the annal for 1089 (b1111, c410) records the plundering of St David's shrine — to which **C** appends, perhaps pointedly, the note of a significant earthquake ('terremotus ingens'), and the annals for 1090 and 1092 are empty, bracketing the annal for 1091 (b1113, c412) which records the destruction of St Davids by the Norse (**B** and **C**) and the death of Bishop Sulien (**C**). After 1092, there are far fewer empty annals.

The annals in **B** and **C** for the eleventh century are chronologically very similar to those in the vernacular chronicles **P**, **R**, and **S**, but these latter are provided with a framework of decennovenal markers which can be deduced as indicating the 'primus decennouenalis' years 1007, 1026, 1064, 1081, and (**S**

---

[73] b1156: 'Anus ·m·cxxxiiii · Robertus dux · Normannie iussu · Henrici fratris sui pelue excecatus est et postea obiit apud Gloucestriam in carcere' ('The year 1134: Robert, Duke of Normandy, was blinded while washing by the order of his brother Henry, and afterwards he died at Gloucester in prison'). This is another reciprocal of the Winchester-Waverley annals: Liebermann, p. 182.

only) 1102.⁷⁴ The first year of the decennovenal cycle of 1045 is not noted. The AD apparatus is misaligned with these decennovenal markers, generally being two years in arrears, so that 1007 is shown as '1005', 1102 as '1100'. This suggests that the decennovenal markers were the primary chronological apparatus in the source, the AD system being adopted later. The translators of the Latin source or sources of the *Brutiau* did not seem to know what was meant by these statements in their Latin source, considering that their translations read 'the first year that was called decennouenalis' (for example, 'y bu y vlwyn gyntaf a elwid decemnoue*n*nalis')⁷⁵ rather than 'the first year of a decennovenal cycle' (for example, 'primus decennouenalis cicli', or similar; *cicli* is often omitted). The presence of decennovenal markers can only indicate one thing: the knowledge and use of paschal tables. As we have seen, **B** only has one decennovenal marker, for 1178, with which its AD apparatus is also misaligned. But this may point to a remnant of a deleted decennovenal system, as it is the only notation for that year in **B**, and appears to be an otherwise pointless anomaly. **C** indicates a Great Cycle from 684 to 1216, 532 years plus a year, also pointing to an understanding and use of paschal tables.⁷⁶ Evidence for the knowledge and use of the paschal tables in eleventh-century Wales is provided by the Psalter and Martyrology of *Ricemarch* (Rhygyfarch), dated to between 1064 and 1082, which includes a series of chronological tables exemplifying various aspects of the Easter *computus*, including a complete Great Cycle of 532 years running from 1064 to 1595.⁷⁷ The table is not without errors, however, and certain of these suggest that the scribe was updating an exemplar written between 1026 and 1044.⁷⁸ The *Ricemarch* for whom the Psalter and Matyrology were written has been identified as Rhygyfarch ap Sulien. Sulien was Bishop of St Davids from *c.* 1072 to 1078, when, according to **C**, he resigned, and again from 1080

---

⁷⁴ It is significant that the compiler(s) of the vernacular chronicles used variants of the Latin term for the nineteen-year cycle, for example 'decemnoue*n*nalis' (*BT (Pen. 20)*, p. 13b), rather than a Middle Welsh version of the term. The Old Welsh version of the term ('circhl naunecant') is attested in the fragment of an Old Welsh *computus* in Cambridge University Library, MS Add. 4543; see John Armstrong III, 'The Old Welsh Computus Fragment and Bede's *Pagina Regularis*', *Proceedings of the Harvard Celtic Colloquium*, 2 (1982), 187–272.

⁷⁵ *BT (Pen. 20)*, p. 13b.

⁷⁶ For a fuller account of **C**'s decennovenal reasoning, see Gough-Cooper, 'Decennovenal Reason and Unreason'.

⁷⁷ Hugh Jackson Lawlor, *The Psalter and Martyrology of Ricemarch*, 2 vols (London: Henry Bradshaw Society, 1914), II, plate XLIX.

⁷⁸ Lawlor, *The Psalter and Martyrology*, I, 113.

to 1085 when he resigned a second time. He died on 1 January 1091 at the age of 80.[79] This suggests that he would have been born in 1011 and have been of age by 1030, and he may well have written, or supervised the writing of, the *computus* exemplar of 1026 × 1044 from which the tables in the Martyrology were updated towards the end of his life.[80] The purpose of annalistic chronicles was not for writing narrative history as such, but for plotting key events over long periods of time. The adoption of the Bedan-Dionysian tables, with their 532-year span comprised of twenty-eight decennovenal cycles, provided an ideal basis for doing so. However, the nature of cycles is that one can begin anywhere on the cycle, and the cycle closes when one returns to the point on the cycle where one began. Thus, the evidence of the **C** text appears to outline a cycle starting at 684 and closing at 1216. There can be, therefore, no certainty as to what the era of the paschal tables being employed by the various compilers of the chronicles might have been, only that it must certainly have consisted of decennovenal cycles and probably spanned 532 years, and was probably a version of the Bedan-Dionysian Great Cycle.

It is remarkable that the decennovenal years noted in **P** all fall on years which are otherwise empty, and are also empty annals in **B** and **C**; furthermore, two of them, 1026 and 1064, are noted in a year following the death of a bishop of St Davids (1025, Morgynnydd, **B** only; 1063, Joseph, **B** and **C**). The rather sparse annals for the eleventh century down to 1090 may represent a chronicle extracted from notes in the margin of a paschal table kept at St Davids during the time of Bishop Sulien and his predecessors.[81]

*Chronicle of 1005

There are two substantial lacunae on the cusp of the tenth and eleventh centuries. The first consists of a series of empty annals in both **B** and **C** covering the second half of the first decade of the eleventh century (*c.* 1006–1011), and it is only by comparison with the vernacular annals (**P** and **S**) that the first year of the decennovenal cycle of 1007 can be defined as a probable chronological reference point, as shown in Table 4.11.

---

[79] **P**, s.a. 1089 (*recte* 1091); **C**'s *Lxxv* (c412) is perhaps an error for *Lxxx*.

[80] A mark against one of the years in the table, 1079, may point to the year in which the *computus* was written; see Lawlor, *The Psalter and Martyrology*, I, pp. xxi–xxii.

[81] In the eleventh century, other bishops beside Sulien noted in the chronicles are Morgynnydd (d. 1025), Erfyn (d. 1040), Joseph (d. 1064), Bleiddudd (d. 1072), and Abraham (d. 1080).

Table 4.11: Chronology from 998/1000 to 1016

Putative or *actual* AD date	B	C	S
1000[1] / S '998'	[b1021][2]	[c324][2]	'998'[2]
1001 / S '999'	[b1022][3]	[c325][3]	'999'[3]
1002 / S '1000'	[b1023][4]	[c326] (empty)	'1000' (= **P**)[4]
1003 / S '1001'	[b1024] (empty)	[c327] (empty)	'1001'[5]
1004 / S '1002'	[b1025] (empty)	[c328] (empty)	(year missing)
1005 / S '1003'	[b1026][6]	[c329][6]	'1003'[6]
1006 / S '1004'	[b1027] (empty)	[c330] (empty)	'1004'[7]
1007	[b1028] (empty)	[c331] (empty)	'1005'[8]
1008 1009 1010 1011	[b1029] (empty) [b1030] (empty) [b1031] (empty) [b1032] (empty)	[c332] (empty) [c333] (empty) [c334] (empty)	(five years missing?)
1012	[b1033][9]	[c335][9]	'1011' (= **P**)[9]
		[c336] (empty)	
		[c337][10]	'1012'[11]
1013	[b1034][12]	[c338][13]	'1013'[14]
1014	[b1035] (empty)	[c339] (empty)	(year missing)
1015	[b1036][15]		'1015'[15]
1016	[b1037][16]	[c340][16]	(year missing in **S**)[16]

[1] Working backwards from the year that **S** calls AD 1005 and says is the first year of a decennovenal cycle, that is, AD 1007.

[2] Maredudd ab Owain dies; St Davids ravaged by the heathen; Bishop Morgenau dies.

[3] Cynan ap Hywel holds Gwynedd.

[4] The heathen ravaged Dyfed.

[5] Mor ap Gwyn and Imhar of Waterford died.

[6] Cynan ap Hywel was slain.

[7] *Gwlfach* and *Ubiad* (i.e. Wulfheah and Ufegeat) were blinded (on this see Elizabeth Boyle, 'A Welsh Record of an Anglo-Saxon Political Mutilation', *Anglo-Saxon England*, 35 (2006), 245–49).

[8] The first year of a decennovenal cycle.

[9] St Davids ravaged by Eadric and *Ubis*; the shipwreck of Sweyn, father of Cnut (**B** only); Iarddur of Bardsey died (**P**, **R**, and **S** only).

[10] Brian (*Bianus*), King of Ireland, was killed with his son *Ascuthin*, that is, by the King of Dublin (April 1014).

[11] Sweyn Haraldsson, father of Cnut, invaded the territory of Æthelred, son of Edgar, and drove him from his kingdom, and in the same year he died (1013–February 1014).

[12] Sweyn approached the region of the English. Æthelred, son of Edgar, was driven from his kingdom which Sweyn took over. But in the same year he died (1013–February 1014).

[13] Sweyn, King of England.

[14] Brian, King of Ireland, and Murchad, his son, and many other kings, led a host against Sitric and Máel Mórda, and Brian and Murchad were slain (April 1014).

[15] Owain ap Dyfnwal was slain.

[16] Cnut Sweynsson gained the kingdom of the English (**B** and **C**; 'and Denmark and Germany', **P** and **R**; 30 November 1016).

It should be noted that, although considering b1028 and c331 to equate to AD 1007 seems to fit with what follows, a simple count backwards to the year of Maredudd ab Owain's death (b1021, c324) reveals a discrepancy of two years with the stated year in **S**, 998, which, as we will see, is perhaps the correct date.

*Chronicle of 996

There is a lacuna in all chronicles at AD 997 (b1020 and c319–c323; **S** leaps from '995' to '998'). In a continuation of the mid-tenth-century chronicle from 954 (b976; c278), **B** has seven unique entries; **C** has three. Although **B** and **C** have the same number of annals from 954 to 998 (**B** has forty-six, **C** has forty-six if the extra annal at c297 is not counted), they deal differently with the distribution of the annals here, so that **C** ends with a series of five empty annals against one in **B**.[82] At the same point, **P** claims to jump three years, while **S** jumps two ('995' to '998'). It is impossible that **C** could have been developed from **B**, but quite likely that **B** has added to the source of **C**, and has smoothed the chronicles to fill the lacuna visible in **C** (c319 to c323, inclusive). **C**, then, reflects the structure of the source chronicle, which may have broken off at AD 995–96. However, the year AD 998, onto which all the chronicles appear to converge (b1021, c324, **S** '998'), seems to have been a known fixed point to the early chronographers (see Table 4.12).[83]

Conclusion

The **B** and **C** texts have been compiled in very different manners, but they developed from a common stock which is detectable up to and just beyond the end of the twelfth century. **B** is a composite text, heavily edited, which has been shown to draw on numerous sources: a St Davids chronicle and material from

---

[82] There is some similarity here with the way the annals for **B** and **C** are treated between 1132 and 1135: **B** only has one empty annal between 1132 and 1134, whereas **C** has three empty annals between 1131 and 1135 (see above). **B** has smoothed its annals to fill the period 1101 to 1134, where **C** has left a series of empty years at the end, even though both chronicles cover exactly the same number of years.

[83] Which does not necessarily invalidate earlier authorities (*BT (Pen. 20 trans)*, p. 10; *Handbook*, p. 52; Thomas M. Charles-Edwards, *Wales and the Britons 350–1064* (Oxford: Oxford University Press, 2014), p. 554) regarding the events as of AD 999, if an Annunciation year March 998 to March 999 is what is being stated here, as seems to be the case for many of the tenth- and eleventh-century annals.

Table 4.12: Chronology from 983 to 998

AD	B	C	S
983	[b1005][1] (**S** '982')[2]	[c308][2,3] (982?)	'982'[2]
984	[b1006] (**S** '983')[3]		'983'[3]
985	[b1007] (**S** '984')[4]	[c309][4,5] (983?)	'984'[4]
986	[b1008] (**S** '985')[5]		'985'[5]
987	[b1009] (**S** '986')[6]	[c310][6] (984?)	'986'[6]
988	[b1010] (**S** '987')[7]	[c311][7] (985?)	'987'[7]
989	[b1011] (**S** '988')[8]	[c312][8] (986?)	'988'[8,9]
990	[b1012] (**S** '989')[10]		'989'[10]
991	[b1013] (**S** '990')[11]	[c313][11] (987?)	'990'[11] (= **P**)
	[b1014] (991?)[12]		
992	[b1015] (992?)[13]	[c314][13] (988?)	'991'[13]
993		[c315] (empty) (989?)	'992'[14]
994	[b1016] (**S** '993')[15]	[c316][15] (990?)	'993'[15]
995	[b1017] (**S** '994')[16]	[c317] (empty) (991?)	'994'[16]
	[b1018] (995?)[17]		
996	[b1019] (996?)[18]	[c318][18] (992?)	'995'[18,19]
997	[b1020] (997?) (empty)	[c319] (empty) (993?) [c320] (empty) (994?) [c321] (empty) (995?) [c322] (empty) (996?) [c323] (empty) (997?)	
998	[b1021][20] (**S** '998')[21]	[c324][21] (998)	'998'[21,22]

[1] b997; c300 'Eadgar saxonum rex obiit' (8 July 975). b1005 = c308 = AD 983.
[2] Hywel ab Ieuaf and Ælfhere ravage Brycheiniog and all the lands of Einion ab Owain.
[3] Einion ab Owain was slain by the men of Gwent.
[4] Hywel ab Ieuaf was slain by the English.
[5] Maredudd ab Owain slew Cadwallon ab Ieuaf and gained possession of his territory, that is, Gwynedd.
[6] Godfrey, son of Harold, with the black heathens, ravaged Anglesey.
[7] Ieuaf ab Idwal and Owain ap Hywel died. And the heathens ravaged St Davids, Llanbadarn, Llanilltud, Llancarfan, and Llandudoch.
[8] Maredudd ab Owain gave a penny from every person to the black heathens. Mortality of men through famine.
[9] **P**, **R**, and **S**: Glúniairn, son of Amlaíb, was slain (*Annals of Ulster*, 989.3, ed. by Seán Mac Airt and Gearóid Mac Niocaill (Dublin: Institute of Advanced Studies, 1983), pp. 420–21).
[10] Owain ap Dyfnwal was slain.
[11] Maredudd ab Owain ravaged Maesyfed.

(Table footnotes continued opposite)

4. MEET THE ANCESTORS?

(Table footnotes continued)

[12] Only in **B** (empty annal), not in **C**, **P**, **R**, or **S**.

[13] Edwin ab Einion and *Edylfi* (i.e. Æthelsige) the Saxon and with him a great host, ravaged all the territory of Maredudd in Deheubarth, that is, Ceredigion and Dyfed and Gower and Cydweli. For a third time St Davids was ravaged.

[14] The sons of Meurig besieged (were in; **P**) Gwynedd, and the island of Anglesey was ravaged on Ascension Thursday.

[15] There was famine in the kingdom of Maredudd. A battle between the sons of Meurig and Maredudd ab Owain near Llangwm, in which the sons of Meurig were the victors. Tewdwr ab Einion was slain.

[16] Sweyn, son of Harold, ravaged Man.

[17] Only in **B** (empty annal), not in **C**, **P**, **R**, or **S**.

[18] Idwal ap Meurig was slain.

[19] Armagh was ravaged and burnt (*Annals of Ulster*, s.a. 995 [*recte* 996]: 'Tene di ait do ghabail Aird Macha connafarcaibh dertach na dam liac na herdamh na fidnemedh ann cen loscadh', 'Lightning struck Armagh and It did not leave unburnt an oratory, stone church, vestibule, or wooden sanctuary').

[20] b1037 = 30 November 1016; b1034 = autumn 1013–3 February 1014; b1021 = 1000? (but there is a further series of empty annals at b1027–b1032 and c330–c334).

[21] St Davids was ravaged by the Heathen, and Bishop Morgenau was slain by them. King Maredudd ab Owain died.

[22] **S** leaps from '995' to '998'.

Whitland, Strata Florida, Cwm-hir, and elsewhere. **C** (at least as far as its post-950 annals are concerned) is considered to be entirely a product of St Davids,[84] and therefore much more unified than **B**, and the even more eclectic *Brutiau*. Of the two late thirteenth-century *Annales Cambriae* Welsh Latin chronicles, scholarly interest has tended to focus on the major chronicle copied into the Neath Breviate of Domesday, not least because of its unique account of the events of the years 1257–1263. But a critical reassessment of **C** is indispensable in seeking relatively uncorrupted traces of some of the later tenth-, eleventh-, and twelfth-century ancestors of the chronicles of the late thirteenth century.

[84] Hughes, 'The Welsh Latin Chronicles', p. 76.

5. *Bonedd y Saint*, *Brenhinedd y Saesson*, and Historical Scholarship at Valle Crucis Abbey

Barry J. Lewis

The genealogical tract, *Bonedd y Saint*, gives the pedigrees of many of the saints of Wales. This short work was intensively copied and studied, and occurs in more than eighty manuscripts ranging from the second half of the thirteenth century to the eighteenth. Although the number and order of the items in the tract are quite variable, there is an identifiable common core of entries, those numbered §§1–63 in the standard edition.[1] These sixty-three entries represent a stage in the evolution of the text which had been reached probably quite a short time before our earliest extant witnesses appear. For, within this common core, one entry stands out as an obvious interpolation: the one that deals with St Peris of Llanberis in Caernarfonshire (§ 41). If this entry is recognized as a late addition, then certain important conclusions follow. The fact that it is found in all of the early copies would indicate that the interpolation was made before even the earliest of our surviving texts. Furthermore, all of the surviving copies of *Bonedd y Saint* must ultimately go back to a single, lost text, the one in which § 41 had been incorporated. Hence we can talk with confidence of an archetype behind the whole visible transmission of *Bonedd y Saint*. The date and place of origin of this archetype will concern us in this chapter. They are quite separate matters from the actual compilation of the tract, which certainly took place somewhat earlier,[2] but here I

[1] *Early Welsh Genealogical Tracts*, ed. by Peter Bartrum (Cardiff: University of Wales Press, 1966), pp. 51–67.

[2] *Bonedd y Saint* cannot be older than the work of Geoffrey of Monmouth (d. 1155), to which it is indebted in various ways. On the other hand, the early copies show hints of Old

am concerned not with the origins of *Bonedd y Saint* but with a section of its subsequent history from around the middle of the thirteenth century to the middle of the fifteenth. It will be argued below that *Bonedd y Saint* was read, copied, and worked over during this period at the Cistercian abbey of Valle Crucis in north-east Wales, as part of a wider engagement with Welsh historical texts. I must begin, however, by justifying the claim that the entry on St Peris is not original, for the remainder of the argument rests on this foundation.

The Entry on St Peris in Bonedd y Saint *and its Source in* Brenhinedd y Saesson

I give first the entry in question, together with the two surrounding entries. The text is based on the oldest witness (A = Aberystwyth, NLW, MS Peniarth 16, fol. 54ᵛ):³

> § 40. Tutclyt a Guynnoedyl a Merin a Thudno yg Kyngre*a*udyr a Senne*u*yr, meibyon Seithennin 6renhin o 6aes Gwydno a oresgynnwys mor eu tir.
>
> § 41. Peris Sant, cardinal o Ru*u*ein.
>
> § 42. Bodo a Gwy*nn*in a Brothen Sant, meibyon Glanna6c m. Helic 6oel o Dyno Helic, g6yr heuyt a oresgynnwys mor eu tir.

> § 40. Tutglyd and Gwynhoedl and Merin and Tudno in the Great Orme and Senefyr, sons of King Seithennin of Maes Gwyddno whose land the sea overwhelmed.
>
> § 41. St Peris, a cardinal of Rome.
>
> § 42. Bodo and Gwynnin and St Brothen, sons of Glannog son of Helig Foel of Tyno Helig, likewise men whose land the sea overwhelmed.

The usual format of entries in *Bonedd y Saint* is as follows: a saint's name, followed by the name of the father and, usually, the grandfather. Epithets and place names can be attached to the saint or his ancestors, although many entries lack them. Several saints can be grouped together if they are regarded as sons of

---

Welsh orthography which suggest that it was compiled not later than the early part of the thirteenth century. These issues will be discussed in depth in my forthcoming new edition of the text (Barry J. Lewis, *'Bonedd y Saint': An Edition and Study of the Main Collection of Welsh Saints' Genealogies*).

³ Entry numbers, punctuation, and capitalization have been supplied. Italics indicate emendation based on other versions, all of a minor nature and not relevant to the present discussion. My translation.

the same father, as is the case in both § 40 and § 42. These two entries are in fact fairly representative of the rest of *Bonedd y Saint*, whereas § 41 is not. Firstly, it is not a pedigree. All of the other entries in the common core of *Bonedd y Saint* are true pedigrees except the second part of § 20, which lists the companions of St Cadfan (himself the subject of the preceding entry, § 19). Secondly, it attributes a markedly exotic origin to St Peris. All of the other saints in the common core of *Bonedd y Saint* are assigned a Brittonic origin, with the exception of St Gwyddfarch of Meifod (§ 37) and St Germanus (§ 61). Thus, although each of these unusual features is paralleled in at least one other entry, the combination is not, and the unusualness of §§20, 37, and 61 can be accounted for: the companions of Cadfan belong naturally alongside him, while Gwyddfarch was the teacher and older companion of St Tysilio (§ 33) and is included within a run of saints connected with southern Powys. Germanus, the quasi-apostle of the Britons, is a case apart.[4] None of this applies to § 41, which is unrelated to the entries around it. Furthermore, the very position of § 41 is suspicious, since it interrupts two entries which naturally belong together. Entries 40 and 42 deal with saints whose origins are traced to the legendary drowned lands off the coast of Wales. One of these drowned lands was supposed to lie underneath Cardigan Bay, off the west coast, while another was imagined to lie off the north coast. The saints in both entries largely represent churches that are close to these two coastlines, though the division between the two entries is not neat, reflecting the fact that there was considerable confusion over the location of the drowned lands.[5] Nevertheless, the connection between the entries is clear, and

---

[4] On Germanus's importance for Brittonic writers, see Thomas M. Charles-Edwards, *Wales and the Britons 350–1064* (Oxford: Oxford University Press, 2013), p. 618; Barry Lewis, 'The Saints in Narratives of Conversion from the Brittonic-Speaking Regions', in *The Introduction of Christianity into the Early Medieval Insular World: Converting the Isles I*, ed. by Roy Flechner and Máire Ní Mhaonaigh (Turnhout: Brepols, 2016), pp. 431–56 (especially pp. 451–52).

[5] Tudno's church overlooks the northernmost of the supposed drowned lands; so does the church of Bodo and Gwynnin further west at Dwygyfylchi. The churches of Gwynhoedl and Merin are on the Llŷn Peninsula, which forms the northern shore of Cardigan Bay, while St Brothen at Llanfrothen is near the eastern shore of the bay. Bodo, if the same as Bodfan, was also culted at Abergwyngregyn on the north coast and at Llanaber on the Cardigan Bay coast. There are further suggestions of a cult of Bodo and Gwynnin on the Llŷn; see Peter C. Bartrum, *A Welsh Classical Dictionary: People in History and Legend up to about A.D. 1000* (Aberystwyth: NLW, 1993), pp. 48, 357. Only Tutglyd of Penmachno is not near either coast, while Senefyr is not certainly identified. On the confusion between the various drowned lands, see Rachel Bromwich, 'Cantre'r Gwaelod and Ker-Is', in *The Early Cultures of North-West Europe*, ed. by Cyril Fox and Bruce Dickins (Cambridge: Cambridge University Press, 1950),

even extends to a similarity of wording: 'men whose land the sea overwhelmed' in § 40 is answered by 'likewise men whose land the sea overwhelmed' in § 42. Bunching together of related entries is very common in *Bonedd y Saint*; indeed, much of the text follows a clear plan.[6] These two entries must surely have been consecutive in an older version. Entry 41 is therefore at best misplaced, and more likely, given how divergent it is from the rest of the entries, it is an entirely new addition. We can speculate that it was made in the margin of a lost manuscript of *Bonedd y Saint*, somewhere near § 40 and § 42 though unconnected with them, and that subsequently another scribe took it into the main body of the work, establishing it in this inappropriate position.

Interestingly, the source from which § 41 was deduced has survived. It is the entry in the Welsh chronicle known as *Brenhinedd y Saesson* for the year 1072.[7] In that year, the Archbishop of Canterbury, Stigand, was deposed:

> Yn y vlwydyn honno y duc Stigandus, archescob Keint, i ar escob Caer Wint y escobaut am na chyvarchws well idaw. Ac y doeth yntev y'r kwnssyli hyt yng Kaer Wint y gwynaw yngwyd y brenhin a holl esgyb Lloegyr a legat o Rvuein a deu effeiriat y'r cardinalieid, Jeuan a Pheris. Ac yna y ducpwyt y archescobaut i arnaw, ac y dodet yngharchar yny uu varw.

> In that year Stigand, Archbishop of Canterbury, took from the Bishop of Winchester his bishopric because he did not greet him. And he came to Winchester to the council to complain in the presence of the King and all the bishops of England and a legate from Rome and two priests of the Cardinals, John and Peter. And then his archbishopric was taken from him, and he was placed in prison till he died.[8]

---

pp. 215–41 (pp. 224–25 n. 4); Bartrum, *A Welsh Classical Dictionary*, pp. 362–63.

[6] That is, it first lists saints traced back to the Old North (§§1–18), then saints from Brittany (§§19–25), Cornwall (§ 26–27), and elsewhere, chiefly Wales (§ 28 onwards). The structure becomes more disparate further on, suggesting that there has been accumulation of entries over time. Some smaller blocks are discernible. For instance, §§30–38 list saints of Powys or of the Powys dynasty; the saints of §§46–47 are closely related to one another; §§46–49 (and arguably § 50) list saints of Anglesey; §§59–60 list descendants of Caw; §§58–60 list saints of Arwystli in mid-Wales; and there are further examples.

[7] The parallel was first noted by S. Baring-Gould and John Fisher, *The Lives of the British Saints: The Saints of Wales and Cornwall and Such Irish Saints as Have Dedications in Britain*, 4 vols (London: Honourable Society of Cymmrodorion, 1907–13), IV (1913), 91–92 n. 4, but they did not realize that the chronicle entry must be the source of the item in *Bonedd y Saint*.

[8] Text and translation from *BS*, pp. 78–79. The date 1072 is corrected from 1070 in the manuscript.

Peris, the form in the original text here translated as 'Peter', is a very unusual name in Welsh, and when we further observe that the Peris of this entry was a priest of, or attached to, the cardinals of Rome, then it seems that we have found the source of the information in the interpolated entry in *Bonedd y Saint*. Somebody, reading this section of the chronicle, leapt to the conclusion that it explained, or could be made to explain, the mysteriously named St Peris of Llanberis, and noted down his discovery in the margin of a copy of *Bonedd y Saint*.

The direction of borrowing must have been from the chronicle to the genealogy, as the history of the chronicle makes clear. It is well-established that *Brenhinedd y Saesson* is a composite of two main sources: a Welsh-Latin chronicle similar to the one that underlies the related Welsh chronicle *Brut y Tywysogyon*, and a set of annals from Winchester.[9] The Stigand entry derives from the latter and is not found in either of the two recensions of *Brut y Tywysogyon*. Here is the original Winchester text:

> Co[n]cilium celebratum apud Wintoniam presente rege Willelmo, presidente Hearmenfredo Sedunensi episcopo et summi Pontificis legato cum duobus presbiteris cardinalibus Johanne et Petro. Stigandus archiepiscopus qui et Wentanus episcopus non enim ualedixerat uni sedi pro altera in hoc concilio degradatus utriusque sedis honore privatus est, quem comprehensum post mori permisit in ui[n]culis.[10]

> A council was held at Winchester in the presence of King William and presided over by Bishop Ermenfrid of Sion, Papal legate, along with two cardinal priests, John and Peter. Archbishop Stigand, who was also Bishop of Winchester (he had not resigned the latter see even though he also held the former), was deprived of both sees. He was arrested and [the King] allowed him to die whilst still in chains.

From this it is apparent that *Peris* was chosen by the Welsh translator of *Brenhinedd y Saesson* to translate Latin *Petrus*. Moreover, the translator's use of the name *Peris* can be shown to have been motivated.

---

[9] See *BS*, pp. xl–xlviii; J. Beverley Smith, 'Historical Writing in Medieval Wales: The Composition of *Brenhinedd y Saesson*', *Studia Celtica*, 42 (2008), 55–86 (pp. 60–62).

[10] Cited in *BS*, p. xlv, from Cambridge, Corpus Christi College, MS 339, fol. 22ᵛ. My translation. The annals were probably the work of Richard of Devizes; see John T. Appleby, 'Richard of Devizes and the Annals of Winchester', *Bulletin of the Institute of Historical Research*, 36 (1963), 70–77; *The Chronicle of Richard of Devizes of the Time of King Richard the First*, ed. by John T. Appleby (London: Nelson, 1963), pp. xxiv–xxv. This would place them towards the end of the twelfth century.

Peris is a form of the French *Piers*, i.e. *Peter*, Latin *Petrus*.[11] It is noteworthy that the translator of *Brenhinedd y Saesson* chose this form, rather than the older Welsh form *Pedyr*. He uses *Perys* again s.a. 1176 for Bishop Peter de Leia of St Davids and once more when recording the death of Abbot Peter of Clairvaux s.a. 1186; the Welsh form *Pedyr* he reserves for St Peter.[12] Evidently, then, the French-derived form was his preferred translation for any *Petrus* who was not the apostle. In this he agrees with the Peniarth 20 recension of *Brut y Tywysogyon*, which uses *Pyrs* for Peter of Clairvaux and Peter de Leia, but *Pedyr* for St Peter, and for the most part with the Red Book of Hergest recension as well, though the latter admits *Pedyr* for the abbot of Clairvaux.[13] The preference for the French-derived form may reflect the strong tendency in medieval Welsh society for saints' names to be restricted to the saints who bore them. Early medieval Welsh people were not normally named after saints, biblical or otherwise, nor are the names of Welsh saints such as Cadog or Teilo generally found attached to any other individual.[14] The creators of *Brenhinedd y Saesson* and *Brut y Tywysogyon* seem to have preferred to respect the uniqueness of *Pedyr*. Thus, the connection of the 'Peter' of 1072 with the Roman cardinals derives from the Winchester chronicle, and not from any pre-existing tradition associated with Peris of Llanberis. The creator of the entry in *Bonedd y Saint* must have been drawing on a copy of *Brenhinedd y Saesson*; even the Winchester chronicle will not do, because it used the Latin *Petrus*.

St Peris and Llanberis

I have argued above that the French-derived *Peris* was used to refer to men from the contemporary French-speaking world in which a taboo against reus-

---

[11] Cf. the Middle English forms *Peris*, *Peres*; see P. H. Reaney and R. M. Wilson, *A Dictionary of English Surnames*, 3rd edn (London: Routledge, 1991), p. 347 s.n. *Peter*, p. 351 s.n. *Piers*.

[12] *Perys*: BS, pp. 182, 186; *Pedyr*: BS, pp. 19, 57, 158, 170, 208.

[13] *BT (Pen. 20)*, pp. 127b, 130b, 145a; *BT (RB)*, pp. 166, 168, 182.

[14] Under Norman and English influence *John* (*Ieuan*, *Siôn*, etc.) became popular in the later Middle Ages, but even then other saints' names remained remarkably rare among individuals who can be identified as ethnically Welsh. A similar prohibition operated in Irish, where proper names could be made out of saints' names only through the medium of such formulae as *Céle Petair* 'adherent of Peter', *Máel Brigte* 'devotee of Brigit', or *Gille Pátraic* 'servant of Patrick'. On the chronology of these, see the brief remarks in M. A. O'Brien, 'Old Irish Personal Names', ed. by Rolf Baumgarten, *Celtica*, 10 (1973), 211–36 (pp. 229–30). Welsh *Gwas Padrig* and Cumbric *Gospatrick* are comparable Brittonic forms.

ing saints' names did not exist as it seems to have done among the Welsh. If so, then it is extraordinary that it should have come to be the name of a Welsh saint. Both the name *Peris* and the dedication of Llanberis are mysterious. The church is in the heart of Gwynedd and seems unlikely to have been named after a French speaker, though that is not impossible since Gwynedd was under Anglo-Norman occupation for a period in the 1080s and 1090s. A much more likely answer, however, is that the name of the saint has a different, native derivation, as suggested by Melville Richards, who offered a plausible etymology.[15] The suspicion that Peris was not a Norman latecomer is strengthened by the fact that he was also culted at Llangïan on the Llŷn Peninsula and by his deep penetration of the local topography: there is a Nant Peris, a Llyn Peris, a Llwyn Peris, a Gorffwysfa Beris, and a Ffynnon Beris.[16] There is another stream called Nant Peris in Cardiganshire.[17] Proof, finally, that the name itself is old is found in the *Historia Brittonum* of 829/30, in which one of the ancient cities of Britain, Portchester, is named as *Kaer Peris*.[18] The likelihood, therefore, is that *Peris* is an old and native name, but when under Anglo-Norman influence the French name *Piers* became known in Wales, the two would have fallen together.

The earliest mentions of Llanberis in Melville Richards's online archive date to 1283.[19] There is a reference to *Sedes Peris*, that is, Gorffwysfa Beris, in a char-

---

[15] Melville Richards, *Enwau Tir a Gwlad* (Caernarfon: Gwasg Gwynedd, 1998), p. 137. He suggests that the root is the same as the verb *paraf* – *peri* 'to cause', while the suffix is that seen in the name *Ceris*. This latter possibility, however, is weakened by the likelihood that *Ceris* was earlier *Cerist*; see Patrick Sims-Williams, *The Celtic Inscriptions of Britain: Phonology and Chronology, c. 400–1200* (Oxford: The Philological Society, 2003), p. 110 n. 603. On a possible suffix *-is*, see further Sims-Williams, *The Celtic Inscriptions*, p. 31 n. 50.

[16] Arthur W. Wade-Evans, 'Parochiale Wallicanum', *Y Cymmrodor*, 22 (1910), 22–124 (p. 66); Baring-Gould and Fisher, *The Lives of the British Saints*, IV, 92–93; Hywel Wyn Owen and Richard Morgan, *Dictionary of the Place-Names of Wales* (Llandysul: Gomer, 2007), pp. 220, 299, 340. Local topographical legends concerning St Peris were published in 'Lhwydian Correspondence', ed. by Robert Williams, *Archaeologia Cambrensis*, 3rd ser., 6 (1860), 237–40; they were provided to Edward Lluyd by a certain 'G. R.'.

[17] It is mentioned by the fifteenth-century poet Guto'r Glyn; see Poem 11, line 46 <www.gutorglyn.net/gutorglyn/poem/?poem-selection = 011> [accessed 1 November 2017].

[18] Text in Edmond Faral, *La légende arthurienne: études et documents*, 3 vols (Paris: Champion, 1929), III, 57.

[19] <http://www.e-gymraeg.co.uk/enwaulleoedd/amr/cronfa.aspx>, under *Llanberis* [accessed 23 October 2017]. Two documents were issued from Llanberis in that year by Dafydd ap Gruffudd and one by Gruffudd ap Maredudd; see *Littere Wallie Preserved in 'Liber A' in the Public Record Office*, ed. by J. Goronwy Edwards, History and Law Series, 5 (Cardiff:

ter allegedly of 1199, but it seems that the document is actually no older than 1283.[20] These references must be quite close in date to the archetype of *Bonedd y Saint*, so they do not help to push back the date of the origin of the cult. All that we can say is that St Peris was culted from the later thirteenth century. The likelihood is that he is a pre-Norman figure, though there is no proof.

Bonedd y Saint *at Valle Crucis Abbey*

When and where, therefore, was the Peris entry in *Bonedd y Saint* created? The dates of the early manuscripts of *Bonedd y Saint* are palaeographically determined and thus only approximate. The oldest witness (A) is dated to the second half of the thirteenth century, but we must posit an earlier compilation, now lost, which lies behind A and the slightly later witness, B.[21] Further behind that was the archetype of *Bonedd y Saint*, perhaps directly, perhaps not. On current dating, therefore, the archetype, including § 41, cannot be later than the second half of the thirteenth century. The diagram opposite illustrates the textual stages postulated here. It will be seen that this requires the date of the Latin original of *Brenhinedd y Saesson* and the extant Welsh version to be placed some time before *c.* 1300, which is the date favoured for the creation of the Latin text in J. Beverley Smith's recent and lucid study of

---

University of Wales Press, 1940), pp. 75, 77, 133. The spelling is in each case *L(l)anperis*. Note that the medieval Llanberis was located at what is now Nant Peris, a couple of miles east from the present-day town of Llanberis, which is a modern settlement.

[20] The document is a supposed charter of Llywelyn ab Iorwerth in favour of Aberconwy Abbey. See *The Acts of Welsh Rulers 1120–1283*, ed. by Huw Pryce (Cardiff: University of Wales Press, 2005), p. 354 (item xv in the charter); for the date, resting on arguments made by Charles Insley, see p. 359. It is quite likely that the charter was concocted from earlier documents, but this cannot be proved.

[21] A is Aberystwyth, NLW, MS Peniarth 16, fols 53ᵛ–54ᵛ, a detached portion of NLW, MS 5266B (the Dingestow Court manuscript); B is MS Peniarth 45, pp. 286–91 (early fourteenth century). For their dates, see Daniel Huws, *Medieval Welsh Manuscripts* (Cardiff: University of Wales Press, 2000), pp. 58–59. A and B form a branch of the stemma on their own. There is ample internal evidence that B does not derive from A, but from a common source; for instance, A has suffered eyeskip in § 9, whereas the text is whole in B. The same situation precisely applies to other texts shared between the two manuscripts, as Brynley Roberts has demonstrated for *Brut y Brenhinedd* ('Fersiwn Dingestow o Brut y Brenhinedd', *BBCS*, 27 (1977), 331–61) and Rachel Bromwich for the Triads (*Trioedd Ynys Prydein: The Triads of the Island of Britain*, 4th edn (Cardiff: University of Wales Press, 2014), pp. xviii–xx). Thus, there must have been at least one manuscript between the archetype of *Bonedd y Saint* and A.

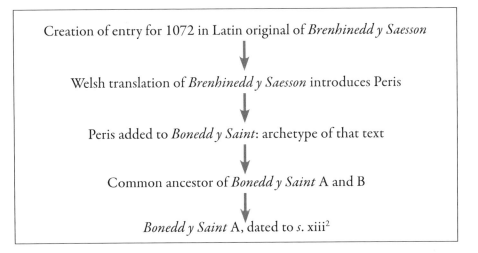

the making of *Brenhinedd y Saesson*.²² Smith's article has advanced our understanding of the creation of the work beyond the point reached by its editor, Thomas Jones. He reaffirms that it is a Welsh version of a chronicle made originally in Latin. The main sources that contributed to the making of its Latin original were: (1) a Welsh-Latin chronicle closely related to the original of *Brut y Tywysogyon*; (2) the Winchester annals; (3) the *Gesta regum Anglorum* of William of Malmesbury; and (4) a Marcher chronicle very similar or even identical to the so-called 'Breviate annals', which are found in a manuscript of the early fourteenth century written at Neath Abbey.²³ The identifying of this last element has led Smith to put forward a strong argument that the Latin original of *Brenhinedd y Saesson* depended partially on material assembled at Neath Abbey around 1300; even if not itself a Neath product, it seems to reflect sources that were gathered in that house around that time, when the monks were engaged in historical research connected with the dispute between the Crown and William de Braose, Lord of Gower, regarding the legal status of that lordship, a dispute that culminated in 1306. The Breviate annals themselves extend to 1298. There is thus a need to consider the implications of the Peris entry in *Bonedd y Saint* for the dating of *Brenhinedd y Saesson*. I cannot resolve the question here, but one answer might be to consider the

---

²² Smith, 'Historical Writing', pp. 60, 83–84.

²³ Elsewhere in this volume these 'Breviate annals' are called the 'Neath chronicle'. See the Appendix, item 10.

Neath materials as having been gathered over a longer period, extending some time before the turn of the century; the chronology would be more comfortable if we were to posit an earlier version of the Breviate annals than the version extending to 1298 that we find in the Neath manuscript. Certainly a date for the Latin original of *Brenhinedd y Saesson* in, say, the later 1280s would match the considerable historical activity that was ongoing in those years, to judge from the terminal dates of *Annales Cambriae* B (1286), *Annales Cambriae* C (1288), *Cronica ante aduentum Domini* (= *Annales Cambriae* D) (1285) and the Latin *Brut* behind *Brut y Tywysogyon* (probably 1284). The Peris entry must also be taken into account for the dating of the extant Welsh version of *Brenhinedd y Saesson*, which Smith would tentatively place close to the date of the manuscript itself, so *c.* 1330.[24] Again, to judge from the existence of the Peris entry in the earliest copy of *Bonedd y Saint*, we may have to push the date of the Welsh *Brenhinedd y Saesson* back into the thirteenth century. The only other possibility would seem to be to reconsider the palaeographical dating of manuscript A of *Bonedd y Saint*.

If the Neath connections of the Latin original of *Brenhinedd y Saesson* remain to be confirmed, it is more certain that the Welsh text was created at the Cistercian abbey of Valle Crucis in north-east Wales. Indeed, there is no indication that it ever circulated far beyond the walls of the abbey. The only surviving copies are linked to Valle Crucis by strong circumstantial evidence.[25] It is thus very likely that the Peris entry in *Bonedd y Saint* was made at Valle Crucis too. As we shall see, this fits with other circumstantial evidence linking *Bonedd y Saint* to that abbey.

The stemma of *Bonedd y Saint* divides into three branches. Of these, the third branch is very plausibly linked to Valle Crucis. The oldest text in this branch, Dd (Cardiff, Central Library, MS 1.363, fols 209ᵛ–212ʳ), follows on from a Welsh translation of Geoffrey of Monmouth's *De gestis Britonum*. There were several such translations, all known under the umbrella-term *Brut y Brenhinedd*. The particular version in Cardiff 1.363 is the so-called Llanstephan 1 version, and it has been described as 'almost identical with that in Llanstephan 1, linguistically and orthographically', such that the pair are probably 'independent

---

[24] Smith, 'Historical Writing', p. 83.

[25] Summarized in Smith, 'Historical Writing', pp. 81–82, especially n. 144, with references to previous work by Thomas Jones, Daniel Huws, and Brynley Roberts. The second copy (Aberystwyth, NLW, MS 7006D) probably passed at some point to the other Cistercian house of north-east Wales, Basingwerk.

but faithful copies of the same original'.[26] The manuscript Aberystwyth, NLW, MS Llanstephan 1 itself was almost certainly a product of Valle Crucis Abbey.[27] There is a prima facie case, therefore, that Cardiff MS 1.363 was also written there.

Further evidence emerges in later texts of the third branch. All texts below Dd in the stemma of the third branch contain a set of additional entries (§§64–70). These are strongly biased towards north-east Wales and the adjacent borderlands.[28] The additional entries are first apparent in a lost medieval exemplar which was used by John Jones of Gellilyfdy when he copied *Bonedd y Saint* in 1640; it was textually still close to Dd.[29] Another, quite similar exemplar, but a little more divergent, was copied by Huw Pennant in the early sixteenth century.[30] What seems to be the same exemplar was used by Gutun Owain in the fifteenth century to make E (Llanstephan 28), which is the oldest surviving copy to contain the new entries, but clearly was not the place where they originated since it is visibly further down the stemma as well as having its own idiosyncratic readings and errors.[31] Gutun seems to have found his text in the lost manuscript, Hengwrt 33, known as 'Hanesyn Hen', since MS Llanstephan

---

[26] *Brut y Brenhinedd: Llanstephan MS. 1 Version*, ed. by Brynley F. Roberts, Medieval and Modern Welsh Series, 5 (Dublin: Dublin Institute for Advanced Studies, 1984), p. xxxvii.

[27] The case for this is complex; see in particular Huws, *Medieval Welsh Manuscripts*, pp. 189–92, on another manuscript by the same scribe, London, BL, MS Cotton Caligula A III, for which there is strong circumstantial evidence of a Valle Crucis origin.

[28] Saeran (§ 65) and Cynhafal (§ 68) belong to the Vale of Clwyd. Chad (§ 66) and Oswald (§ 70) belong to the neighbouring borderlands within the diocese of Lichfield, but had a significant cult in north-east Wales too. Ffraid (Brigit, § 67) is of more general interest but she does have a church at Llansanffraid Glyn Ceiriog, close to Valle Crucis and appropriated to the abbey by the middle of the thirteenth century (David Stephenson, *Medieval Powys: Kingdom, Principality and Lordships, 1132–1293*, Studies in Celtic History, 35 (Woodbridge: Boydell, 2016), p. 272). Only Elfod of Holyhead (§ 64) and Cadfarch of Llŷn (§ 69) are north-western saints, but Elfod was also associated with Abergele, as attested in a poem by the early thirteenth-century poet Einion ap Gwalchmai (*Gwaith Meilyr Brydydd a'i Ddisgynyddion*, ed. by J. E. Caerwyn Williams and others, Cyfres Beirdd yr Uchelwyr, 1 (Cardiff: University of Wales Press, 1994), poem 27, line 93: 'Mal dyuod Eluod eluyt Geleu'). See further Ben Guy, 'A Lost Medieval Manuscript from North Wales: Hengwrt 33, the *Hanesyn Hen*', Studia Celtica, 50 (2016), 69–105 (pp. 88–91).

[29] His transcript is in Cardiff, Central Library, MS 3.77, pp. 32–39 (siglum Hb). The lost original is the one called 'Y' by Bartrum.

[30] In Aberystwyth, NLW, MS Peniarth 182, pp. 63–74 (siglum H).

[31] Aberystwyth, NLW, MS Llanstephan 28, pp. 69–75 (siglum E).

28 contains a whole series of texts that match the surviving contents lists for Hengwrt 33 very closely. Through Gutun Owain, though not directly from E, the 'Hanesyn Hen' text fed also into G, the work of Thomas ab Ieuan ap Deicws, and through successive stages of accretion it gave rise to most of the numerous early modern copies from north-east Wales.[32] The lost Hengwrt 33 was a highly influential manuscript. It was a compilation of historical texts, of which *Bonedd y Saint* was merely one, and it gave rise to a large progeny of descendants. Ben Guy has made a strong case that Hengwrt 33 must have been put together at Valle Crucis, notably because one of the texts which it contains, a short chronicle named *Oed yr Arglwydd*, shows an interest in the region of north-east Wales, and because the various people who copied from Hengwrt 33 — including Gutun Owain, Huw Pennant, Gruffudd Hiraethog, and John Jones — were all associated with the north-east.[33] It is well-established that Gutun Owain, in particular, had access to manuscripts from Valle Crucis. If both Dd and Hengwrt 33 were from Valle Crucis, it is very likely that so were the intermediate stages between them, of which we have a representative in the lost exemplar transcribed by John Jones in Hb, and there were others too.[34] In other words, the third branch developed at Valle Crucis from some point in the later thirteenth century down to the time of Gutun Owain. Only from his time onwards did descendants of the 'Hanesyn Hen' copy multiply beyond the walls of Valle Crucis, in the hands of Gutun's successors who inherited his manuscripts.[35] Even then, we have later testimony from Gruffudd Hiraethog stating that Peniarth 127 (containing G) was written using manuscripts that belonged to the Abbot of Valle Crucis.[36]

---

[32] G is Aberystwyth, NLW, MS Peniarth 127, pp. 43–49. For representatives of the later tradition emanating from this node of the stemma, see the readings of J and K in Bartrum's edition of *Bonedd y Saint*. There are many more among the other early modern copies.

[33] Guy, 'A Lost Medieval Manuscript', pp. 84–91. Apart from *Oed yr Arglwydd*, he also cites the north-eastern additions to *Bonedd y Saint*.

[34] The very corrupt copies in Aberystwyth, NLW, MSS Peniarth 118, Peniarth 137, and Peniarth 183 derive from versions that branched off the stemma below John Jones's exemplar but above Hengwrt 33.

[35] Readings in common between E, G, and the later copies such as J and K make it likely that all derive from a transcript of the 'Hanesyn Hen' made by Gutun Owain. E, apparently an early copy by Gutun, has its own peculiar errors; it seems that Gutun did not reproduce all of those errors in his later work on *Bonedd y Saint*.

[36] 'wrth gyfarwyddyd llawer o awduriaid o achav yr abad Jhon o Lan Egwestl'; cited in Thomas Jones, 'Syr Thomas ap Ieuan ap Deicws a'i gyfaddasiad Cymraeg o "Fasciculus Tempo-

It is thus possible to trace the development of *Bonedd y Saint* at Valle Crucis Abbey from the creation of the archetype with the Peris entry, through the third branch from Dd downwards to E in the middle of the fifteenth century. Scholarly work on *Bonedd y Saint* at Valle Crucis thus did not end with the creation of the archetype: further copies were made and the text was subsequently extended through the addition of §§64–70, reflecting an interest in local saints. It is not possible, however, to date this expansion precisely. Frustratingly, the earliest third-branch text, Dd, cannot be read beyond the bottom of fol. 212[r] (the middle of § 61). The palaeographer John Gwenogvryn Evans was of the view that the faded and unreadable text on the verso of the same leaf is not part of *Bonedd y Saint*, but this seems a strange situation.[37] It is more likely that it is the end of Dd, in which case it probably had room for §§61–63 but not for the new entries. If so, then the new entries were not yet added when Dd was copied in the first half of the fourteenth century. On the other hand, they cannot have been added much later, since Guy has shown that Hengwrt 33 must have been made in the same period.[38]

The derivation of the other two branches cannot presently be attached to any locality. The first branch is certainly of northern origin, but cannot be linked to any particular part of North Wales. The second branch consists mainly of southern manuscripts and was enlarged by the addition of more saints from Ceredigion in south-west Wales, but it has northern representatives too. The only thing that links these two branches of *Bonedd y Saint* to Valle Crucis is, thus, the presence of Peris, showing that they descend from the Valle Crucis archetype. Yet they do not contain the north-eastern-focused additions of §§64–70, and may have developed elsewhere, assuming that a copy or copies of the Valle Crucis archetype passed out of the abbey at an early date.

The early manuscript contexts of *Bonedd y Saint* are interesting for what they suggest about its reception. It occurs alongside Welsh versions of Geoffrey of Monmouth in A, B, and Dd, and the Triads of the Island of Britain in A, B, and C. This suggests that it was appreciated as a piece of historical scholarship on the Welsh or British past. The creation of the Peris entry on the basis of *Brenhinedd y Saesson* indicates much the same set of interests. Hengwrt 33

---

rum" Werner Rolewinck', *THSC*, 1943–1944 [1946], 35–61 (p. 37).

[37] *RMWL*, II, pt 1 (1902), p. 301: 'The text [...] is incomplete at the end, being apparently left unfinished by the scribe.' Alternatively, Evans's phrasing may suggest that he missed the text on fol. 212[v].

[38] Guy, 'A Lost Medieval Manuscript', pp. 84–85, 91.

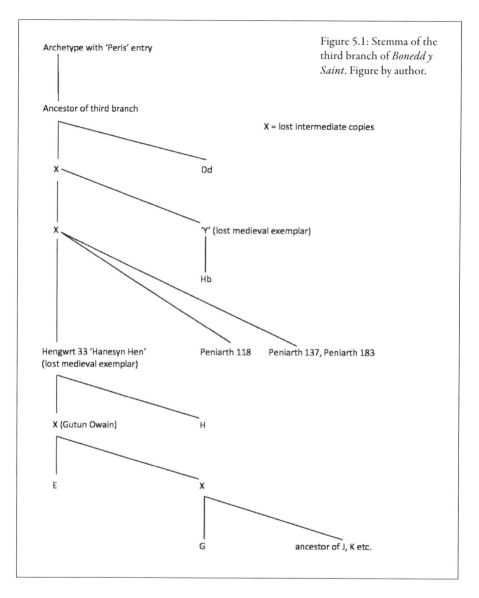

Figure 5.1: Stemma of the third branch of *Bonedd y Saint*. Figure by author.

was also a historical compilation. From Gutun Owain's time, however, *Bonedd y Saint* was generally subsumed into larger genealogical collections (a process that had already begun in Hengwrt 33). It is striking how rarely it is found alongside religious or devotional works. Here the southern, second-branch manuscript D (Cardiff, Central Library, MS 3.242, pp. 110–12), a compilation of mainly devotional prose, is a rare exception.

Conclusion

The archetype and third-branch texts of *Bonedd y Saint* can be attributed to a particular religious house through a web of inferences that are compelling yet do not quite amount to proof. The same could be said of other hypotheses which link Welsh literary activity of the later thirteenth and early fourteenth centuries to Cistercian abbeys, such as the attribution of the Hendregadredd manuscript of court poetry and the lost Latin chronicle behind *Brut y Tywysogyon* to Strata Florida, or the ascription of *Brenhinedd y Saesson*, the Peniarth 44 and Llanstephan 1 versions of *Brut y Brenhinedd*, and the Peniarth 20 texts of *Brut y Tywysogyon* and the bardic grammar, to Valle Crucis.[39] Each of these cases is convincing, and yet there is no definitive proof such as could be provided by a colophon. It is a frustrating situation, but the evidence does not admit of certainty.

Though it is highly probable that all of our extant versions of *Bonedd y Saint* derive from a version made at Valle Crucis in the second half of the thirteenth century, this version, which included the new entry for St Peris, was not identical to the original *Bonedd y Saint*. The latter can only be located by extrapolating from its contents, especially the first forty or so entries which follow a plan that looks reassuringly deliberate. These strongly suggest that *Bonedd y Saint* was compiled further west and at one of the older, substantial churches that are loosely known as *clas* churches to historians of medieval Wales. It was to these churches and their dependents that the many local saints of *Bonedd y Saint* were attached. The tract survived, however, through being valued and copied in one of the new Cistercian abbeys. Many other texts must have made a similar journey from the library of a *clas* church to a Cistercian scriptorium: the *Mabinogi* tales, the *Gododdin* and other early verse, the poetry of the twelfth-century *Beirdd y Tywysogion*, indeed virtually everything composed in Welsh before the thirteenth century. There must be a strong suspicion that the Cistercian abbeys of Welsh Wales maintained close links with the older *clas* churches, adopting and ultimately inheriting their role as creators and preservers of Welsh lit-

---

[39] On these hypotheses, see Huws, *Medieval Welsh Manuscripts*, pp. 189–92, 213–22; J. Goronwy Edwards, review of *Brut y Tywysogyon: Peniarth MS. 20*, ed. by Thomas Jones (1941), *English Historical Review*, 57 (1942), 370–75; Gifford and Thomas M. Charles-Edwards, 'The Continuation of *Brut y Tywysogion* in Peniarth MS. 20', in *Ysgrifau a Cherddi Cyflwynedig i / Essays and Poems Presented to Daniel Huws*, ed. by Tegwyn Jones and E. B. Fryde (Aberystwyth: NLW, 1994), pp. 293–305.

erature.[40] We may further suspect that the early Welsh Cistercians recruited a proportion of their monks from the established ecclesiastical families who had controlled the *clas* churches. That is intrinsically likely, even if it remains to be demonstrated from firm evidence. If the more traditional view were true — that the new Cistercian houses represented a brutal rupture with the older ecclesiastical arrangements — then we would not now be able to read the corpus of older Welsh literature, since barely any books survive from the libraries of the *clas* churches.

[40] A series of studies by Patrick Sims-Williams has begun to open up the question of attributing texts to particular *clas* churches. See, e.g., his important examination of the church of Clynnog Fawr in 'Clas Beuno and the Four Branches of the Mabinogi', in *150 Jahre Mabinogion — deutsch-walisische Kulturbeziehungen*, ed. by Stefan Zimmer and Bernhard Maier (Tübingen: Niemeyer, 2001), pp. 211–27.

6. The Continuation of *Brut y Tywysogyon* in NLW, MS Peniarth 20 Revisited

David Stephenson

The continuation of *Brut y Tywysogyon* found in Aberystwyth, NLW, MS Peniarth 20 is the most substantial chronicle of Welsh origin dealing with the decades after 1282, though it is not the only one.[1] It has been the subject of several studies since Thomas Jones published his edition of the Peniarth 20 version of the *Brut* in 1941, notably by Jones himself in his translation of 1952, by J. Goronwy Edwards in his review of Jones's text in 1942, by Gifford and Thomas Charles-Edwards in a paper of 1994, and most recently in a wide-ranging and important study by Owain Wyn Jones in 2013.[2] Nevertheless, there are grounds for re-examining this section of the chronicle; close textual examination and the establishment of a probable political context for its composition will refine, and perhaps challenge, aspects of the prevalent views about the construction of the continuation.

---

[1] The continuation runs from 1282 to 1332; another chronicle of Welsh origin, the *Epitome historiae Britanniae*, originating in large measure in Glamorgan, also runs into the fourteenth century; see the description and references to texts and editions in the website of the Welsh Chronicles Research Group (<http://croniclau.bangor.ac.uk/hist-britanniae.php.en> [accessed 14 April 2018]. For extracts from annals compiled at Abergavenny which also extend into the fourteenth century, see below.

[2] *BT (Pen. 20)*; *BT (Pen. 20 trans.)*; J. Goronwy Edwards, review of *Brut y Tywysogyon: Peniarth MS. 20*, ed. by Thomas Jones (1941), *English Historical Review*, 57 (1942), 370–75; Gifford and Thomas M. Charles-Edwards, 'The Continuation of *Brut y Tywysogion* in Peniarth MS. 20', in *Ysgrifau a Cherddi Cyflwynedig i / Essays and Poems Presented to Daniel Huws*, ed. by Tegwyn Jones and E. B. Fryde (Aberystwyth: National Library of Wales, 1994), pp. 293–305; Owain Wyn Jones, 'Historical Writing in Medieval Wales' (unpubl. doctoral thesis, Bangor University, 2013), chs 2 and 4.

The most comprehensive depiction of the development of this section of the *Brut* is that provided by Gifford and Thomas Charles-Edwards. A careful analysis of changes of script and ink and the adoption at one point of a new chronological system enabled them to suggest the following sequence of development of the continuation. Latin annals compiled at Strata Florida and extending to the spring of 1282 were continued at the same abbey up to and including the record of the capture of the rebel Lord of Dryslwyn, Rhys ap Maredudd, recorded under the year 1290. A separate set of annals, constructed at some unknown place, but not at Strata Florida, included entries for the period 1291–1329. These last annals are:

> 'evidently compiled from sources inadequate for the purposes of an annalist, perhaps even in part mere memories, as is shown by the serious chronological dislocations, by the appearance of runs of years without any record, and by the general sparcity of information. Not until the 1320s and the period of Despenser power is there a sequence of reasonably well informed annals'.[3]

The 'Strata Florida annals' and those for 1291–1329 were translated into Welsh at Valle Crucis. That translation is represented by the Peniarth 20 version of *Brut y Tywysogyon*. Finally, annals for 1330–1332 were added, in Welsh, to the translated *Brut*.[4] It was further suggested that the references in the continuation to the bishops of St Asaph were 'likely to have been added well after the event', and that the annals up to 1329 might be based on a source which did not derive from Valle Crucis.[5]

Aspects of the above scenario have, however, been modified by Owain Wyn Jones. He points out that the 1282–1290 section shows no special connection with Strata Florida, and notes the occurrence of just the same sorts of errors in dating as those which characterize the entries for the following years. These include the dating of the birth of Edward of Caernarfon to 1283 when it actually occurred in 1284, the misdating to 1289 of the revolt of Rhys ap Maredudd in 1287, as well as a reference to the building of the castle of Beaumaris in 1283, when it was not begun until 1295.[6]

---

[3] G. and T. M. Charles-Edwards, 'The Continuation of *Brut y Tywysogion*', p. 302.

[4] G. and T. M. Charles-Edwards, 'The Continuation of *Brut y Tywysogion*', pp. 302–04.

[5] G. and T. M. Charles-Edwards, 'The Continuation of *Brut y Tywysogion*', p. 301. For further discussion of the St Asaph material, see below, p. 162.

[6] Jones, 'Historical Writing', pp. 241–47, especially p. 243 where a 'Venedotian focus' in the annals for 1282–1290 is noticed, and p. 244, where it is acknowledged that a change of dating system after the annal for 1290 'could indicate that [the account of 1282–1290] was

In addition, Jones is understandably cautious on the attribution of the (Latin) annals which underlie the continuation to Valle Crucis, as he points out that the references to St Asaph may indicate an origin there, though he does ultimately incline towards Valle Crucis and also emphasizes the importance of that house as a repository for historical texts.[7] In the present study it is accepted that Valle Crucis is the most probable place of composition of most of the Peniarth 20 continuation. But it remains possible that we may ultimately have to consider one of the major churches of Maelor as a place of composition.

The first point which requires some scrutiny is the argument that the section covering the years 1291–1329 represents, or is based on, annals written somewhere other than at Valle Crucis. Gifford and Thomas Charles-Edwards did not suggest what the place of production of that chronicle might have been, and, in terms of their primarily palaeographical focus, they did not perhaps need to do so. But a footnote in the translation of the Peniarth 20 version of *Brut y Tywysogyon* published by Thomas Jones in 1952 appears at first sight to give a valuable lead. Jones noted the following:

> Mr. E. St. John Brooks has called attention to the agreement between the annalistic memoranda at the end of Trinity College, Dublin, MS D. 4. 1 and some of the entries in the continuation of the Pen. MS 20 version [of the *Brut*]. He suggests that the former were written at Abergavenny.[8]

This note distorts to some degree what St John Brooks actually wrote — though he did indeed describe the Trinity College Dublin annals as 'related' to the continuation and he suggested that they 'were in all probability drawn from a set of monastic annals *such as* [my italics] those used by the continuator of the Peniarth version of the *Brut*'.[9] This gives a rather different impression from

composed separately from the following section'. To the slips in dating noted by Jones we may add the dating of the capture of Dafydd ap Gruffudd to the autumn of 1283, when that event took place in June of that year, and the placing of the capture of Rhys ap Maredudd in Mallaen in 1290 rather than in 1292. The reference to the building of Beaumaris in 1283 may simply be a failure of concentration on the part of the annalist: it comes in a list of Edwardian castles, from which Conwy is notably absent. If written shortly after 1295, it may be that the annalist thought too readily of the newly-founded Beaumaris rather than Conwy.

[7] Jones, 'Historical Writing', pp. 74–78.

[8] *BT (Pen. 20 trans.)*, p. lxiii n. 2. It should be noted that Trinity College Dublin, MS D. 4. 1 was the reference current when St John Brooks was writing, but it is now MS 212.

[9] Eric St John Brooks, 'The *Piers Plowman* Manuscripts in Trinity College, Dublin', *The Library*, 5th ser., 6.4–5 (1951), 141–53 (p. 151).

either Brooks's own description of the Trinity College Dublin annals as 'related' to the continuation, or Jones's 'agreement' between the two sets of annals.

In order to resolve the issue of the relationship between these two sets of annals it will be necessary to examine those in Trinity College Dublin (henceforth TCD), MS 212 in some detail.[10] The TCD annals are therefore given here in translation; dating formulae and names have been modernized.

> ***Memorandum*** that [on] 26 September AD 1294 Geoffrey Clement was killed by the men of Cardigan.
>
> ***Item***, in the same year the Welsh rose up against the peace and the aforesaid men of Cardigan made Maelgwn ap Rhys [*Maylgonem ap Rees*] their lord.
>
> ***Item***, the North Welsh [*Norwalences*] made Madog ap Llywelyn [*Madocu[m] ap Lewelyn*] their lord.
>
> ***Item***, the men of Glamorgan made Morgan ap Maredudd [*Morganu[m] ap Moredith*] their lord.
>
> ***Item***, the Welsh of Gwent [*Walences vero Wencie*] made Meurig ap Dafydd [*Mauricium ap David*] their lord.
>
> ***4 August, AD 1265***, Simon de Montfort was slain.
>
> ***AD 1312***, Piers de Gaveston [*Petrus de Gavereston*] was beheaded.
>
> ***AD 1315***, about 2 February, Llywelyn Bren [*Lewellinu[s] Pren*] rose against the king's peace.
>
> ***AD 1321***, many magnates were hanged, to wit Lord Thomas of Lancaster was beheaded, 22 March.
>
> ***Item***, the Earl of Hereford was killed, 24 November.
>
> ***AD 1326***, Hugh le Despenser was drawn and hanged at Hereford.
>
> ***AD 1327***, 21 September, Edward, who was King of England, died at Berkeley, [and was] buried at Gloucester.

---

[10] The translation given here is a slightly amended version of that given by Eric St John Brooks ('The *Piers Plowman* Manuscripts', p. 145); the form of Welsh names given in TCD, MS 212, fol. 89ᵛ is given in brackets. Though some Welsh personal names were partially Latinized, the consistent use of *ap* to introduce the patronymic, and the fact that Welsh names were not subjected to serious mangling, may possibly suggest a scribe familiar with Welsh.

> *AD 1330*, 29 November, Roger de Mortimer, Earl of March, was drawn and hanged at London.
>
> *AD 1295*, about 29 September, there was mortality of men through hunger, so that their bodies, like the corpses of dogs, lay everywhere unburied; then Thomas de Turberville was drawn and hanged.
>
> *AD 1348*, about 29 August, Laurence de Hastings, Lord of Abergavenny [*Bergeveny*] died. Item, in the same year there was mortality of men at Abergavenny [*Bergeveny*], and in the following year in the parts of England and in the year of grace the mortality ceased.[11]

Perhaps the first thing to note is that the TCD annals were certainly compiled at Abergavenny. Meurig ap Dafydd, the leader of a rising in Gwent in 1294, can be identified as a man with particular interests in Abergavenny,[12] and the last two entries in the annals make specific reference to the Lord of Abergavenny in 1348, and to the effects of plague there. There is a more generalized interest in events in south-east Wales, though some of the more striking political developments in the reign of Edward II are also noticed.

Even making allowance for the difference of language (Latin in TCD, MS 212, Welsh in the continuation), there does not appear to be any verbal similarity between the two sets of annals, nor does there seem to be any but the most superficial correspondence between them in terms of content. It is unsurprising that none of the references in the continuation to episcopal succession at St Asaph appears in the annals compiled at Abergavenny, in the diocese of Llandaf. Both sources note the murder of Geoffrey Clement in 1294, but while the Abergavenny annals have him killed by the men of Cardigan, the continuation notes that he was killed at Y Gwmfriw in Builth. Again, both refer to the risings of 1294–1295, but the Abergavenny annals give the name of the leader in Gwent, Maurice (i.e. Meurig) ap Dafydd, while MS Peniarth 20,

---

[11] See St John Brooks, 'The *Piers Plowman* Manuscripts', p. 145, and TCD, MS 212, fol. 89ᵛ. I am most grateful to the staff of Digital Imaging Services of the Library of Trinity College Dublin for providing me with a fine image of the relevant part of the manuscript.

[12] Meurig ap Dafydd was in dispute with the burgesses of Abergavenny in 1279: see *The Welsh Assize Roll, 1277–1284*, ed. by James Conway Davies (Cardiff: University of Wales Press, 1940), pp. 272–73. In 1285 he was amongst the witnesses of a charter issued by John de Hastings, Lord of Abergavenny: *CCR: Edward I. A.D. 1279–1288* (1902), p. 366; and in 1292 he was one of the chief taxators of Abergavenny: Francis Jones, 'The Subsidy of 1292', *BBCS*, 13 (1950), 210–30 (p. 215).

along with all other known annalistic texts, does not mention either the Gwent uprising or its leader.[13] On the other hand, the continuation includes Cynan ap Maredudd as a leader, along with Maelgwn ap Rhys, in Deheubarth, whereas the Abergavenny annals contain no reference to him. They do however refer to the execution of Thomas Turberville, which is ignored by MS Peniarth 20, and also describe a widespread mortality in 1295, which is not mentioned in MS Peniarth 20. Between 1295 and 1312 entries are made in the Peniarth 20 continuation for eleven years, and these are not given in the Abergavenny annals. The continuation gives significantly more detail of the death of Piers Gaveston in 1312, and fuller references to the rising and the capture of Llywelyn Bren under the erroneous dates of 1317 and 1318; the Abergavenny annals give a simple notice of his insurrection under the possibly correct date of 1315.[14] The continuation notices the battle of Bannockburn; the Abergavenny annals do not. From 1319 onwards, as will be seen below, the continuation becomes much fuller, and this fullness is not reflected in the Abergavenny annals. Both sets of annals do agree on 22 March as the date of Thomas of Lancaster's execution; they both note the death of Hugh Despenser in 1326, and give the same date (29 November) for the execution of Roger Mortimer in 1330. But these events were amongst the most dramatic of the period, and news of them surely circulated widely. In contrast, the Abergavenny annals give 21 September as the date of the death of Edward II, whereas the continuation refers only to his being taken prisoner, without noting his death. The Abergavenny annals stop in 1348–1349, after a silence for the years after 1330, while the material in the continuation ends in 1332, with notably detailed entries covering the last few years. The annals copied into TCD, MS 212 are marked by some very precise, and with one apparent exception accurate, dating across their chronological range, perhaps suggesting that the entries in the annals from which they appear to have been extracted were made very close in time to the events recorded.[15] They are not set out in chronological order, which perhaps sug-

[13] The Abergavenny annals in TCD, MS 212 appear to be the only source to refer explicitly to a rising in Gwent in 1294, though it now seems probable that a (vacated) grant of August 1295 to John de Hastings of 'the forfeitures of all his Welsh men and tenants lately in arms against the king in the late war in Wales' refers to events in Abergavenny rather than (or perhaps as well as) the Hastings lordship of Cilgerran: *CPR: Edward I. A.D. 1292–1301* (1895), p. 144.

[14] As Llywelyn Bren's uprising took place in January–March 1316, a date of 1315 is correct if we assume that the annalist was reckoning the start of the year on 25 March, as is clearly the case with the record of Thomas of Lancaster's execution, placed under 1321.

[15] They may result from chronological memoranda, but they seem more likely to be extracts

gests that they were copied from fuller materials. Thus, while the Abergavenny annals are an interesting source, previously unexploited, they do not appear to be related to the material in the continuation in any meaningful way.

Having discounted any suggestion of a link between the continuation of the Peniarth 20 *Brut* and the Abergavenny annals (and having in the process pointed to the interest of the latter) we have now to examine the content of the continuation and to probe some important structural aspects which have been overlooked or not given due weight in previous analyses. These include a marked shift in the character of the entries, which takes place with the entry for 1320. Most of the annals for the two decades up to and including the entry for 1319 (*recte* 1317) are either very brief or consist solely of a note of the date (given as a number in a ten-year cycle). But in contrast to this sporadic pattern, from 1320 onwards entries are made for every year, and are frequently significantly more substantial than in the previous section of the continuation. In addition, entries from 1321 onwards are correct in terms of chronology.[16] Entries for the middle years of the 1290s tend to lag one year behind the actual date of the events recorded, while the time lag is greater in the early years of the fourteenth century.[17] The situation is rectified in the annal for 1306, but, with one exception (that is, the chronicler's 1312), the annals for 1311 to 1314 once again lag one year behind actual dates. The chronicler's annals for 1317 to 1319 on the other hand appear to be two years in advance of actual dates.[18]

---

from a longer original set of annals. The exception to the generally accurate dating of the Abergavenny annals is the apparent misdating to November 1322 of the death of Humphrey de Bohun, Earl of Hereford, who was killed at Boroughbridge in March 1321/22. But this is clearly a copying error, quite probably made by the scribe who copied the annals into TCD, MS 212: the date given for Humphrey de Bohun's death (24 November, *viii kalend. Decemb'*) is placed at the end of the record for 1321. It has been placed there in error, as it should form part of the following entry, recording the execution in 1326 of Hugh Despenser the Younger which indeed took place on 24 November. Humphrey de Bohun's death was thus originally given without a precise date, but in a context which clearly connected it to Boroughbridge.

[16] The entry which *BT (Pen. 20 trans.)*, p. 123 ascribes to 1320 in fact appears as *Anno domini m⁰. ccc⁰. xix⁰*. But the incident which it describes apparently relates to the crisis of August 1321, for which see Seymour Phillips, *Edward II* (London: Yale University Press, 2011), pp. 389–94. If so, the annal is displaced by some two years. It may have been written up at a later date, from the memory of the compiler or that of his informant.

[17] *BT (Pen. 20 trans.)*, p. 122 corrects to 1304 dates given in the original text as 1300 and 1301, and to 1305 a date given as 1302.

[18] *BT (Pen. 20 trans.)*, p. 123.

A further, and potentially important, point is that in the period 1320–1330 we have, as part of an emphasis on the 'high politics' of the realm of England, a number of specific references that indicate an interest in the lay and ecclesiastical lords who controlled Bromfield and Yale and neighbouring territories: there are references to the Warenne earls of Bromfield and Yale, under 1300 (*recte* 1304), 1324, 1325, and 1329; to the Earl of Arundel, Lord of Oswestry, which bordered Bromfield, under 1326; and to his successor in 1330.

References to the bishops of St Asaph are notable. We have noted that it has been suggested that the St Asaph references are a late intrusion into a text which has no close relationship to Valle Crucis.[19] The late intrusion of the St Asaph material is possible, but by no means certain: it is just as likely, for instance, that it originally took the form of notes which were written up together with items derived from memory and/or similar notes about more secular events, many of which concerned north-east Wales. The entries relating to the bishops of St Asaph are not concerned simply with their deaths: the entry for 1313 (*recte* 1314) records the death of Bishop Llywelyn and the election of his successor, Dafydd ap Bleddyn, while that for 1314 (*recte* 1315) records Dafydd's consecration.[20]

Much of the content of the continuation for the years before 1331 is geographically diffuse. In places the continuation certainly shows an interest both in the Clare earls of Gloucester, lords of Glamorgan, and in that lordship. References to them occur under 1291, 1297 (*recte* 1295), and 1313 (*recte* 1314); there are references to Morgannwg under the years 1293 (*recte* 1294), 1321, and 1326; and there are references to Llywelyn Bren, the lord of part of Senghennydd, under 1317 (*recte* 1315) and 1318 (*recte* 1316).[21] But that interest is not a consistent one, nor is it particularly emphatic. The clash between Gilbert de Clare and Edward I in the early 1290s is not recorded; Morgan ap Maredudd's rising in Morgannwg in 1294–1295 is recorded last in a list of the risings of that period and there is no notice of its outcome; important developments in the lordship of Glamorgan in 1297 are ignored; the revolt in Morgannwg following Gilbert de Clare's death in 1314 is not mentioned; the succession of Hugh Despenser to the lordship of Glamorgan in 1317 is

---

[19] See above, p. 156.

[20] The election of Dafydd ap Bleddyn is omitted from the table in G. and T. M. Charles-Edwards, 'The Continuation of *Brut y Tywysogion*', p. 301.

[21] It should be noted that if this annal (for which see *BT (Pen. 20)*, p. 231b: 'Anno. viij. y delijt llywely bren') relates to the death of Llywelyn Bren, it does not require correction.

not noted. It is thus possible that some elements of the continuation may have derived from material emanating from Morgannwg and subsequently incorporated in that text, but it seems unlikely that such material formed the original basis of an entire section of the continuation. An interest in Glamorgan and its lords, particularly the de Clare family, who are noticed in markedly positive terms, may reflect the possibility of a southern origin of the man, now resident in north-east Wales, responsible for writing up the continuation in its present state in *c.* 1330–1332.[22] That possibility is strengthened by the occurrence of South Walian characteristics in the language of the text.[23] The omissions of incidents relating to Glamorgan noted above, and the misdating of Bogo de Clare's death to 1291 instead of 1294 and Gilbert de Clare's death to 1297 instead of 1295, make it unlikely that a set of annals from Glamorgan lay behind the de Clare-related entries in the continuation: it seems more likely that the Glamorgan entries were inserted from memory.

In some respects, the final entry, for 1332, is not in line with the entries for the previous two years. It contains no 'local' information of the sort that led Goronwy Edwards to attribute the continuation to Valle Crucis. Instead it consists mainly of 'gossip' about the discovery of the uncorrupted body of King Harold II of England at Chester, to which is added a note on Edward de Balliol's expedition to Scotland. In 1332 the continuation appears to be entering a new phase, at which point it terminates, though whether this was the result of the compiler's death or distraction, or whether it reflects the loss of an important source of information is uncertain. There is however a good case for emphasizing this last possibility. The 'local' element had been pronounced in the entries for 1330 and 1331, and had ended with the record of the death of Madog ap Llywelyn, 'the best man that ever was in Maelor Gymraeg'.[24] The remarkable nature of this entry has never been fully explored. With the exception of the record of the death in 1331 of Goronwy ap Tudur, one of the greatest supporters of the English Crown in Wales, Madog ap Llywelyn is the only notable Welsh layman to be accorded an obituary notice in the continuation for the

---

[22] Bogo de Clare, so often vilified in chronicles, is 'the foremost person in England, and the most powerful'; Gilbert de Clare is 'the man of gentlest blood and the most powerful of the English': *BT (Pen. 20 trans.)*, pp. 121–22.

[23] *BT (Pen. 20 trans.)*, pp. xlviii–xlix; G. and T. M. Charles-Edwards, 'The Continuation of *Brut y Tywysogion*', pp. 301–02, 305 n. 22.

[24] *BT (Pen. 20 trans.)*, p. 126. The translation 'in Bromfield' is rather misleading: the original (*BT (Pen. 20)*, p. 237b) has 'Maelor Gymraec'. It seems that the compiler thought in old regional terms rather than in terms of the more recent lordship name.

period after 1290.²⁵ This alone suggests that there was something remarkable about Madog, a suspicion deepened by the reference to him as the best man that ever was in Maelor Gymraeg. If we accept that the last part, at least, of the continuation — the entries for 1330–1332 — was compiled at Valle Crucis, or at a location with very close links to it, then this fulsome reference to a man from a region adjacent to the abbey probably suggests some special relationship between him and that house.

It will be useful at this point to set out in some detail the known facts about Madog ap Llywelyn. He was born into one of the largest and most prominent kin-groups of north-east Wales, the descendents of Tudur Trefor. His father, Llywelyn ap Gruffudd, was one of the more prominent *uchelwyr* of Bromfield.²⁶ Madog's mother was Angharad, daughter of Maredudd ap Madog ap Gruffudd, the granddaughter of the Lord of Northern Powys and the daughter of the Lord of Iâl. Maredudd ap Madog's wife, the mother of Angharad, was Catrin, a sister of Llywelyn ap Gruffudd, Prince of Wales.²⁷ So Madog ap Llywelyn was of very distinguished lineage. But there was more to his eminence than his ancestry. He was also a man who had evidently risen high in the service and estimation of the post-conquest lords of Bromfield and Yale. The lord in the early years of the fourteenth century was John de Warenne, Earl of Surrey, and in 1308 Madog witnessed a grant that Warenne made of a knight's fee at Hem to one John de Wysham; of the eleven witnesses Madog was the only Welshman.²⁸ Seven years later the Survey of Bromfield and Yale revealed that Madog was the holder of substantial and widespread lands in the lowland areas of the lordship.²⁹

By 1318 Warenne had been forced to conclude an agreement with the increasingly powerful Thomas, Earl of Lancaster, whereby the latter became the new Lord of Bromfield and Yale. Amongst the appointments that Lancaster

---

²⁵ The death of Goronwy ap Tudur is given without comment, in contrast to that of Madog ap Llywelyn.

²⁶ Michael Rogers, 'The Welsh Marcher Lordship of Bromfield and Yale, 1284–1485' (unpubl. doctoral thesis, University of Wales, 1992), p. 326.

²⁷ *WG 1*, IV, 'Tudur Trefor 22–24'; for Angharad see I, 'Bleddyn ap Cynfyn 4', and for Catrin see III, 'Gruffudd ap Cynan 5'. For Maredudd ap Madog ap Gruffudd, Lord of Iâl, see David Stephenson, *Medieval Powys: Kingdom, Principality and Lordships, 1132–1293* (Woodbridge: Boydell, 2016), pp. 110, 118, 120.

²⁸ *CPR: Edward II. A.D. 1307–1313* (1894), p. 405.

²⁹ T. P. Ellis, *The First Survey of Bromfield and Yale, A. D. 1315*, Cymmrodorion Record Series, 11 (London: Honourable Society of Cymmrodorion, 1924), pp. 40, 46, 60, 64, 126. See Rogers, 'The Welsh Marcher Lordship', pp. 326–27.

made, possibly in 1319, was that of Madog ap Llywelyn to the powerful and important post of Receiver of the lordship.[30] Madog's importance, and perhaps his political agility, were emphasized in February of 1322 when Thomas of Lancaster's steward of Bromfield and Yale was ordered to hand over levies from that lordship to Madog and a colleague, who would escort them to the king at Coventry.[31] It would appear that Madog had moved into the service of the king.

Lancaster was executed later in that year, after the defeat of his forces at Boroughbridge, and Warenne successfully petitioned for restoration to the lordship. The fact that Madog ap Llywelyn had served the man who had ousted him in 1318 does not seem to have caused Warenne to exclude him from his inner circle, for in 1323 Madog and four other Welshmen, including his brother Gruffudd, witnessed a Warenne grant issued at Reigate.[32] This is important in that it provides an instance of Madog's travelling within England, and mixing in the company of the Warenne entourage in the heart of his earldom of Surrey. As late as 1330 Madog witnessed a further Warenne grant, this time at Holt, the caput of the lordship of Bromfield and Yale.[33] And in a most interesting record of December of 1330 he appears, along with four English officials, charged with carrying out a commission of *Oyer et Terminer* consequent on a petition of the community of the land of North Wales to the king and his council, complaining of oppressions committed by William de Shaldeford while he acted as deputy to Roger Mortimer, former Justice of North Wales.[34] Madog

---

[30] Rogers, 'The Welsh Marcher Lordship', p. 327.

[31] *CCR: Edward II. A.D. 1318–1323* (1895), p. 521; it is significant that the troops were needed for action against the Scots and the contrariants, the latter led by Thomas of Lancaster.

[32] Rogers, 'The Welsh Marcher Lordship', p. 327.

[33] Rogers, 'The Welsh Marcher Lordship', p. 327.

[34] *CPR: Edward III. A.D. 1330–1334* (1893), p. 61. The other members of the commission were John de Wysham, Justice of North Wales until August 1331 (*CPR: 1330–1334*, p. 181), probably to be identified with John de Wyshin, described in 1333 as late keeper of Anglesey (*Calendar of Ancient Correspondence Concerning Wales*, ed. by J. Goronwy Edwards (Cardiff: University of Wales Press, 1935), p. 221); William de Ercalu (?Ercal in Shropshire), who, *inter alia*, received a commission of the peace in 1331 for Shropshire, was keeper of the peace for Salop, a supervisor of ships, South Wales, 1332, and acted as a commissioner of array for Salop and Staffs in 1333 (see *CPR: 1330–1334*, pp. 136, 294, 323, 419; see also a petition that he and others should keep the peace in Salop on account of danger from the Welsh, 1330 × 1332, *Calendar of Ancient Petitions Relating to Wales*, ed. by William Rees (Cardiff: University of Wales Press, 1976) p. 239); Nicholas de Acton, who was a commissioner of array, and supervisor of ships for North Wales in 1332 (*CPR: 1330–1334*, pp. 321, 323); and the final member of the

ap Llywelyn's eminence is confirmed by the military effigy which adorns his tomb at Gresford church.[35] The form of the effigy points to a military involvement which is only occasionally hinted at in the documented episodes in his career. We thus see a man involved in baronial politics and administration at a notably high level, a man who travelled widely on official business, both for the lords of Bromfield and Yale and for the royal government, so that his horizons were not limited by the bounds of his native territory. More specifically in the present context, it is notable that the density of the Peniarth 20 continuation entries increases and their chronological accuracy becomes much more precise as soon as we have evidence that Madog was undertaking important high-level official duties in Bromfield and beyond.

The possibility that Madog was in some way connected with the development of the Peniarth 20 continuation cannot be ignored. His background and career were such that he was well placed to glean information about the aristocratic politics of the English realm from his contacts with the Earl Warenne and the Earl of Lancaster, with their leading officials and with royal administrators. One of the features of the continuation is the growing incidence of precise dates for events. The annals for 1283–1306 contain only two exact dates; between 1307 and 1320 they contain four such dates.[36] From the entry for 1321 to that for 1329 the occurrence of precise dates becomes much more pronounced, with twenty such instances.[37] The annals for 1330–1332, which have been argued to reflect effectively contemporary recording, contain fourteen instances.[38] It is of particular interest, and almost certainly of significance, that the start of the phase 1307–1317 closely coincides with the first known

group, Roger de Pulesdon, who was a member of a prominent ministerial family. The official involvement of Madog's colleagues suggests his eminence.

[35] Colin Gresham, *Medieval Stone Carving in North Wales* (Cardiff: University of Wales Press, 1968), pp. 184–86.

[36] For 1283–1306 exact dates are given under 1283, 'the fifth day from the end of April', and under 1293, 'on that feast of Michael', though in both cases the event concerned is given under the wrong year: 1283 should be 1284, and 1293 should be 1294; for the period 1307–1320 there are exact dates under (corrected) 1307 (twice), 1312, 1314.

[37] Exact dates given in the following annals: 1321 (three times, with the third instance being 'the Monday following the feast of Benedict the abbot' — i.e. 23 March, suggesting that the annalist begins the year on 25 March, as Thomas of Lancaster's death was in 1322 by modern reckoning); 1324; 1325; 1326 (six times); 1327; 1328 (five times); 1329 (three times).

[38] Exact dates are given in the annals for 1330 (eight instances); 1331 (four instances); 1332 (two instances).

appearance in 1308 of Madog ap Llywelyn in the entourage of Warenne, and the beginning of the phase 1320–1329 comes after his elevation to the post of Receiver in the lordship of Bromfield and Yale under Thomas of Lancaster and subsequently his evident importance in the entourage of the Earl of Surrey when the latter was restored to the lordship. The growing incidence of precise dates suggests an initial period when the annals were being supplied by reference to scraps of information and perhaps largely from memory, followed by a period when more certain information was available, but perhaps not always close in time to the events being recorded, and finally a period when news was passing to the annalist more rapidly and accurately.

Most strikingly, the obituary notices in the entry for 1331 of men associated with Gwynedd — Goronwy ap Tudur and the Archdeacon of Meirionnydd — come at the precise period when Madog had been sent into Gwynedd on royal business. Here, then, was a perfect context in which he may have picked up such information. The developments in the career of Madog ap Llywelyn as traced above seem thus to coincide to a marked degree with changes in the structure and characteristics of the continuation between about 1307 and 1332, and prompt a suspicion that he may have been a crucial informant of the Valle Crucis annalist. Such a role would, of course, help to explain the praise accorded to Madog ap Llywelyn in his obituary notice in the *Brut*, the fulsome character of which outdoes any other such notice in the continuation.

It is now perhaps possible to suggest, however tentatively, a process of development of the continuation of the Peniarth 20 version of *Brut y Tywysogion* which differs in several respects from that previously prevailing. The suggested process of development is as follows:

i. Annals running from late March of 1282 to 1319, based on both memory and rough notes, were added to Latin annals subsequently translated into Welsh as *Brut y Tywysogion*. It remains possible, but by no means certain, that some of the early material in this continuation, particularly the detailed annal for 1282, may have come from Strata Florida. Some additions in this phase may have been derived from materials emanating from Glamorgan, or from memories of events there, but it is probable that many entries were based on material collected at Valle Crucis.

ii. Entries for the period 1320–1329 were more detailed, and seem to have been based on information supplied by someone with first-hand knowledge of the 'high politics' of the period. It is suggested that this person was probably Madog ap Llywelyn, who may also have been responsible for suggesting some of the material for the period 1307–1319. It is possible that the materials in phases i and ii were written into the continuation at the same period.

iii. Annals were entered year by year at Valle Crucis, 1330–1332, with Madog ap Llywelyn once more the main source for the entries for 1330–1331. The entries under 1332, after Madog's death, no longer contain material of local significance.

The centrality in this sequence not only of the scribe responsible for work on *Brenhinedd y Saesson* and the Peniarth 20 continuation of *Brut y Tywysogyon*, but also of Madog ap Llywelyn, a man memorialized in writing in the latter text and in stone at Gresford Church, reminds us that chronicles, along with other categories of literature, were developing a new importance as responses to the demands of an emergent class of Welsh magnates prominent in the society of post-conquest Wales.[39]

---

[39] I should like to thank Owain Wyn Jones for his helpful comments on a draft of this chapter. I am solely responsible for the errors and misapprehensions which remain.

7. *O OES GWRTHEYRN*: A MEDIEVAL WELSH CHRONICLE

Owain Wyn Jones

The purpose of this chapter is to provide an edition and discussion of the medieval Welsh chronicle *O Oes Gwrtheyrn*. Although a relatively short text which has seen little discussion in the past, *O Oes Gwrtheyrn* is notable in several important ways. Firstly, it is the only monastic chronicle to survive from medieval Gwynedd, the most politically important kingdom of medieval Wales. This edition establishes that the text most likely derives from the Cistercian monastery of Aberconwy and was first compiled in the second decade of the thirteenth century. Secondly, the likelihood that this chronicle was written originally in Welsh would make it an innovative new departure in vernacular historical writing. This gives the short text a wider significance not only in the development of medieval chronicles in Wales, but also in terms of the development of European vernacular historical writing and the relationship of international monastic orders such as the Cistercians to this process.

The third notable aspect of the chronicle is its unique recording of some events. Although much of the material contained in the chronicle is drawn from other sources, its fuller account of some years in the early thirteenth century offers a unique perspective on known events, and it records some otherwise unattested events. The most notable of these is the death of the Norwegian Erlendr píkr at Llanfaes in 1209, which can be considered the last viking raid on Wales and brings Wales briefly into the history of the Norwegian civil wars.

This chapter will first discuss the manuscript witnesses to the chronicle, which will then lead to a textual discussion of the edition which follows. Attention will be given to the chronicle's provenance, which will enable a more general discussion of the work's historical significance and its place in medieval Welsh historical writing. Some of the most important events noted in the chronicle will then be discussed, in particular the 1209 raid on Anglesey and the broader implications of this event. While *O Oes Gwrtheyrn* is short and has been neglected as a historical source, this discussion and critical edition establishes its uniqueness and importance to medieval Welsh history and to medieval chronicle writing more generally.

It is clear from the manuscripts listed below that *O Oes Gwrtheyrn* was fairly well-known to Welsh antiquarians in the early modern period, and Robert Vaughan's translation of the work into English also seems to have had a relatively wide distribution. A version of the text with a translation into Latin and notes was included in Moses Williams's 1731 edition of Humphrey Llwyd's *Britannicæ descriptionis commentariolum*. This version contained the *Llyfr Coch Hergest* (A) text until its end, and continued with the text of Aberystwyth, NLW, MS Llanstephan 28 (C).[1] The *Llyfr Coch Hergest* version of the work was published in J. Gwenogvryn Evans's edition of the *Brutiau* from that manuscript, but as discussed below this version is incomplete.[2] Gwenogvryn Evans gave an extremely unkind and indeed untrue characterization of the work when he said that 'it is a waste of time to inquire into worthless compilations of this kind with the Eisteðvodic stamp on them'.[3] It is hoped that this discussion will give the lie to that statement.

The work was used fairly extensively by J. E. Lloyd in his *History of Wales*, and he refers to it frequently for corroboration of the events of the late twelfth and early thirteenth centuries.[4] It appears that Lloyd relied on Gwenogvryn Evans's edition of A and on consultation of Cardiff, Central Library, MS 3.11 (F) as well as on the Moses Williams edition of Humphrey Llwyd's work.[5] Since then the work has undergone little discussion. The reasons for this are unclear, but must have something to do with the fact that the only accessible published version of the work was incomplete, and that there has been no recent English translation.

The chronicle begins by noting the number of years from the time of Gwrtheyrn/Vortigern (*O Oes Gwrtheyrn*) until Arthur's battle with the Saxons at Badon. It goes on to note the number of years between Badon and the battle

---

[1] *Humfredi Llwyd, armigeri, Britannicæ descriptionis commentariolum: necnon de Mona insula et Britannica arce, sive armamentario Romano disceptatio epistolaris. Accedunt æræ Cambrobritannicæ*, ed. by Moses Williams (London: Bowyer, 1731), pp. 141–64.

[2] *The Text of the Bruts from the Red Book of Hergest*, ed. by John Rhŷs and J. Gwenogvryn Evans (Oxford: Evans, 1890), pp. 404–06.

[3] *Text of the Bruts*, p. xxiv.

[4] *HW*, II, 499, 587–90, 592, 616, 632, etc. Lloyd's longest assessment of the work of which I am aware is in his 'Wales and the Coming of the Normans (1039–1093)', *THSC*, 1899–1900 [1901], 122–79 (pp. 135–36 n. 3).

[5] *HW*, II, 499, 632.

of Camlan, and continues with this method of dating significant events in relation to the previous noted event, a relative chronology spanning a number of centuries. The events noted are generally Welsh, with the occasional exception, and most are familiar from other Welsh chronicles such as the Welsh Latin annals collectively known as *Annales Cambriae* and the family of vernacular chronicles entitled *Brut y Tywysogyon*.

From the mid-twelfth century onwards, a number of events are noted which do not appear in any other surviving chronicle, and at the end of the first decade of the thirteenth century the character of the text changes somewhat, briefly becoming a more detailed and sequential, year-by-year chronicle narrative. The focus of these years, and of the unique events which precede them, is North Wales. After a few such annals, however, the text returns to the brief relative chronology with which it began, although with a continuing focus on the royal dynasty of Gwynedd to the early years of Llywelyn ap Gruffudd's reign in the 1260s.

The work closes with a series of notices which establish the time between a date towards the end of the text and various significant milestones in the history of the Britons, such as the settlement of Britain, its conversion and invasions. One group of manuscripts relates these events to the hostageship of Gruffudd ap Llywelyn in 1211, whereas the other group relates them to the battle of Bryn Derwin in 1255. This is the most significant difference between the different manuscripts of the chronicle and divides them clearly into two groups.

Overall, these manuscripts show *O Oes Gwrtheyrn* to have been a relatively popular text, though one that was perhaps somewhat unloved, often hurriedly scrawled and abbreviated. The present study and edition will demonstrate the work's usefulness as a historical source, but attention will first be given to the different surviving manuscript versions.

Manuscripts

Manuscripts containing *O Oes Gwrtheyrn*:

    A Oxford, Jesus College, MS 111 (*Llyfr Coch Hergest*), c. 1382 × c. 1410.
    B Aberystwyth, NLW, MS Peniarth 32 (*Y Llyfr Teg*), c. 1404.
    C Aberystwyth, NLW, MS Llanstephan 28, 1455–1456.
    D Aberystwyth, NLW, MS Peniarth 182, 1509 × 1513.
    E Aberystwyth, NLW, MS Peniarth 135, 1556–1564.

F Cardiff, Central Library, MS 3.11, *c.* 1572–*c.* 1580.
G Aberystwyth, NLW, MS Peniarth 212, 1565 × 1587.
H Aberystywth, NLW, MS Peniarth 183, *c.* 1582–1586.
I Aberystywth, NLW, MS Peniarth 137, *c.* 1550 × 1600.
J Aberystwyth, NLW, MS Cwrtmawr 453, *c.* 1615 × 1630.
K Aberystwyth, NLW, MS 4973B, 1620 × 1634.
L1 and L2 Aberystwyth, NLW, MS Llanstephan 80, *c.* 1710 × 1720.
M1 and M2 Aberystwyth, NLW, MS 1984B, 1757.
N Aberystwyth, NLW, MS 2024B, *c.* 1762.
O Aberystwyth, NLW, MS 1992B, >1768.

In August 2019, a manuscript was discovered in Northamptonshire Archives containing a copy of *O Oes Gwrtheyrn* (Northampton, Northamptonshire Archives, MS FH7), at too late a stage for its inclusion in this edition. It is discussed in more detail below.[6]

Description of the Manuscripts

The following descriptions are based on my own inspection of the manuscripts as well as the descriptions in Daniel Huws's *Repertory of Welsh Manuscripts and Scribes* (forthcoming).

A Oxford, Jesus College, MS 111, *Llyfr Coch Hergest* (*c.* 1382 × *c.* 1410)

O Oes Gwrtheyrn occurs on fol. 254^{r-v}, preceded by *Brut y Saeson* and followed by *Hengerdd*.[7] The text, though the earliest of *O Oes Gwrtheyrn*, is incomplete, breaking off midway through what is given as item 48 in the following edition. It is likely that knowledge of this influenced the scribe of MS Peniarth 137 (I) (see below). Its incomplete character is original to the period of the production of the manuscript.

---

[6] Gruffudd Antur, pers. correspondence.

[7] For the manuscript more generally, see Daniel Huws, 'Llyfr Coch Hergest', in *Cyfoeth y Testun: Ysgrifau ar Lenyddiaeth Gymraeg yr Oesoedd Canol*, ed. by R. Iestyn Daniel and others (Cardiff: University of Wales Press, 2003), pp. 1–30 (esp. pp. 6, 12, 20).

B Aberystwyth, NLW, MS Peniarth 32, *Y Llyfr Teg* (*c.* 1404)

Roughly contemporary with A as it shares with it a scribe, Daniel Huws's *X91*, who wrote the *Llyfr Coch* text of *O Oes Gwrtheyrn* but not the text in MS Peniarth 32. *O Oes Gwrtheyrn* is on fols 114^v–116^v, written by a scribe writing in 1404, termed hand *B* by Huws. It is preceded by some Latin annals in the same hand,[8] and followed by *Breuddwyd Pawl* in a different hand. The end of *O Oes Gwrtheyrn* coincides with the end of the quire and ends incomplete, midway through item 64.

C Aberystwyth, NLW, MS Llanstephan 28 (1455–1456)

Written by the poet Gutun Owain for Phylip ap Madog ab Ieuaf. *O Oes Gwrtheyrn*, on pp. 86–92, is preceded by a number of genealogical tracts and immediately followed by *Oed yr Arglwydd*, a related chronological work which also follows it in D and G.[9] The text is complete though rather abbreviated, especially in comparison to D, its closest relative.

D Aberystwyth, NLW, MS Peniarth 182 (1509 × 1513)

A commonplace book of Huw Pennant, curate of Dolwyddelan. *O Oes Gwrtheyrn* is on pp. 24–34, preceded by pedigrees and followed by *Oed yr Arglwydd*. There is some disorder in the text, with the correct order indicated by marginal notes.

E Aberystwyth, NLW, MS Peniarth 135 (1556–1564)

Most of the manuscript, including this text, is in the hand of the poet Gruffudd Hiraethog of Llangollen. *O Oes Gwrtheyrn*, on pp. 66–71, is preceded by annals and finishes incomplete, missing the date at the end of the chronicle for the arrival of the Normans.

---

[8] For which see Diana Luft, 'The NLW Peniarth 32 Latin Chronicle', *Studia Celtica*, 44 (2010), 47–70.

[9] For *Oed yr Arglwydd* as a text dependent on *O Oes Gwrtheyrn* but written subsequently, see Ben Guy, 'A Lost Medieval Manuscript from North Wales: Hengwrt 33, The *Hanesyn Hên*', *Studia Celtica*, 50 (2016), 69–105, and below.

F Cardiff, Central Library, MS 3.11 (*c.* 1572–*c.* 1580)

O Oes Gwrtheyrn occurs on pp. 149–54 in David Powel's hand, preceded by a tract on coinage and followed by *Vita Griffini filii Conani*, a version of the Latin biography of Gruffudd ap Cynan.[10] A heading describes the text as taken *Ex lib Dñi Jo Prise militis*, indicating that it was taken from a now lost manuscript in the possession of Sir John Prise (*c.* 1500–1555). The recently discovered manuscript at the Northamptonshire Archives, MS FH7, is in John Prise's hand, and its text of *Oes Gwrtheyrn* was David Powel's source here. Though substantially complete, the text is abbreviated throughout and ends at item sixty. The half-page after the text's end contains disjointed statements, sometimes repeated two or three times, pertaining to the Glyndŵr revolt, and some of these also appear at the end of G, suggesting a common exemplar.

G Aberystwyth, NLW, MS Peniarth 212 (1565 × 1587)

A manuscript in the hand of Wiliam Cynwal, a pupil of Gruffudd Hiraethog (see above, E). *O Oes Gwrtheyrn*, on pp. 514–23, is preceded by a list of names used by *brudwyr* and followed by a chronicle of the fifteenth century and other chronological calculations. The text itself is idiosyncratic in its combination of Roman and Arabic numerals, the Arabic numeral generally occurring in the right-hand margin and sometimes giving a different number (noted in the apparatus to the edition, for example at n. 4). Several of the pages are torn towards either the upper-right or upper-left corners, with consequent lacunae in the text. The text is somewhat disordered.

H Aberystywth, NLW, MS Peniarth 183 (*c.* 1582–1586)

A composite manuscript, with *O Oes Gwrtheyrn* occurring on pp. 268–72 in the hand of Wiliam Dyfi, preceded by a text of *Bonedd y Saint*. The manuscript's Radnorshire associations, as well as the stemmata of the other texts it contains, indicates that it shared an exemplar with I, probably a sister of the lost manuscript Hengwrt 33.[11] The text of *O Oes Gwrtheyrn* is incomplete, breaking off at item 30.

---

[10] For more on the manuscript, see Huw Pryce, 'The Church of Trefeglwys and the End of the Celtic Charter Tradition in Twelfth-Century Wales', *CMCS*, 25 (1993), 15–54 (pp. 19–24, 52–54); *Vita Griffini filii Conani: The Medieval Latin Life of Gruffudd ap Cynan*, ed. by Paul Russell (Cardiff: University of Wales Press, 2005), pp. 4, 11–15.

[11] Guy, 'A Lost Medieval Manuscript', p. 88.

I Aberystwyth, NLW, MS Peniarth 137 (*c.* 1550 × 1600)

A composite manuscript, the third part (pp. 159–316) containing *O Oes Gwrtheyrn* on pp. 194–95. Preceded by genealogies and followed by the chronological text *Oed yr Arglwydd*, the text of *O Oes Gwrtheyrn* is incomplete, beginning at the end of item 47 and proceeding to the end of the text. The reason for this is apparent when considering the circumstances of the manuscript's composition. The genealogies it contains relate to Elfael, and it is in the hand of John ap Rhys of Llanfihangel Nant Melan. By this time *Llyfr Coch Hergest* (A) was at Hergest, about six miles from Llanfihangel. It seems likely that John ap Rhys knew of the incomplete text of A, and coming across a fuller text of *O Oes Gwrtheyrn*, almost certainly the exemplar of H and a sister of the lost manuscript Hengwrt 33, copied it from the point at which A broke off. The text is rather rushed, with a tendency to abbreviate and condense.

J Aberystwyth, NLW, MS Cwrtmawr 453 (*c.* 1615 × 1630)

In the hand of Robert Vaughan of Hengwrt, this short manuscript consists of brief annals, opening with *O Oes Gwrtheyrn* on pp. 9–24, followed by blank pages before *Oed yr Arglwydd*. The text is preceded by the rubric 'allan o hen llyvrae memrron y wedi eu scrivennu ers gwell no 300 mlynedh y cawd y cofion hynn' ('these notices were taken from old parchment books written more than three hundred years ago'), and it is likely that one of the manuscripts referred to here was the lost Hengwrt 33, *Hanesyn Hen*.[12] The rubric's suggestion of multiple sources is borne out in the text itself, which gives some alternative readings in square brackets and dates the final chronological section with reference to both Gruffudd's imprisonment (as in BG) and the battle of Derwin (as in CDE).

K Aberystwyth, NLW, MS 4973B (1620 × 1634)

In the hand of John Davies of Mallwyd, *O Oes Gwrtheyrn*, on fols 405–06, was copied from A (*Llyfr Coch Hergest*), and is preceded by a list of the contents of that manuscript. It reflects its source in being incomplete.

---

[12] Guy, 'A Lost Medieval Manuscript', p. 83.

L1 and L2   Aberystwyth, NLW, MS Llanstephan 80 (*c.* 1710 × 1720)

In the hand of Moses Williams, it contains two versions of *O Oes Gwrtheyrn* as well as extracts from *Brut y Tywysogyon*, which precede the first version, L1, appearing on fols 14–16. This version is taken from *Llyfr Coch Hergest*, A, though it finishes at item 39. It is immediately followed by the second version, L2, on fols 17–21, which is given the heading, 'out of Sir Tho. S. Sebright's MS Nº 13'.[13] This version appears to be derived directly from F.

M1 and M2   Aberystwyth, NLW, MS 1984B (1757)

In the hand of Evan Evans, it contains mainly *hengerdd* but opens with prose, including an incomplete *O Oes Gwrtheyrn* on fols 10–13, derived from A, *Llyfr Coch Hergest*. When A ends at item 48 it is continued with ten lines from the relevant section of J (MS Cwrtmawr 453).

N   Aberystwyth, NLW, MS 2024B (*c.* 1762)

A manuscript compiled from miscellaneous papers of Evan Evans, with a complete text of *O Oes Gwrtheyrn* on fols 213–18, taken from a copy of J made by Lewis Morris.

O   Aberystwyth, NLW, MS 1992B (>1768)

Another paper manuscript in Evan Evans's hand, with *O Oes Gwrtheyrn*, complete, on pp. 155–68, again derived from Lewis Morris's copy of J.

Lost manuscripts of *O Oes Gwrtheyrn* include Hengwrt 33, discussed in more detail below. It is likely that the MS Peniarth 182 text of *O Oes Gwrtheyrn* is derived directly from Hengwrt 33, whereas the MS Llanstephan 28 text perhaps derives from a copy of Hengwrt 33. The version of *O Oes Gwrtheyrn* belonging to the CDE branch of the tradition combined by Robert Vaughan of Hengwrt into the conflated J text of *O Oes Gwrtheyrn* was also very probably derived from Hengwrt 33.[14] F also notes a now-lost manuscript which

---

[13] The Sebrights secured possession of Edward Lhuyd's manuscripts after his death, and Moses Williams was allowed access to the collection at Beechwood in Hertfordshire. Huws, *Repertory* (forthcoming).

[14] Edward Lhuyd, *Archæologia Britannica* (Oxford: Lhuyd, 1707), p. 256; for an independent list of contents, see *Ymddiddan Myrddin a Thaliesin (o Lyfr Du Caerfyrddin)*, ed. by Alfred O. H. Jarman (Cardiff: University of Wales Press, 1951), p. 20, where it is listed

belonged to Sir John Prise, and the exemplar of H and I, a sister of Hengwrt 33, is also lost.

There exists a seventeenth-century translation of the work into English by Robert Vaughan, which is not discussed here. The following manuscripts contain this English version, though the list is not exhaustive:

Aberystwyth, NLW, MS Wynnstay 12 (1653–1672).

Aberystwyth, NLW, MS Bodewryd 103 (*c.* 1700).

Aberystwyth, NLW, MS Llanstephan 74 (38C) (1728).

Several preliminary conclusions can be drawn from the manuscripts discussed above. The texts can be divided into two broad groups depending on their formulation of the chronicle's conclusion. One group, ABFG, dates the closing chronological section with reference to the imprisonment of Gruffudd ap Llywelyn, while the second, CDEHI, dates it with reference to the battle of Derwin. The division of these two groups can be further demonstrated with reference to the apparatus at items 13, 24, 34, and 47.

The further relationship between these texts can be established with some confidence. The important points of comparison are noted as follows (references are to the item numbers of the edition below):

B is not derived from A: 47, 48.

G is not derived from A: 34, 47, 48.

G is not derived from B: 27, 37, 61.

F is not derived from A: 47, 48.

F is not derived from B: 27, 37.

F is not derived from G: 26, 43, 47.

G is not derived from F: 60, 46.

F and G may be derived from a common exemplar: 25, 46, 47, and the notes on the Glyndŵr revolt which follow both.

Whether FG's exemplar was closer to A or B could be indicated at items 27, 33, 37, and 47. It might be argued that it was closer to A, but overall it is impossible to decide with any certainty.

as *Chronologieth yn dechreu Oes Gwrtheürn Gwrtheneu*; Guy, 'A Lost Medieval Manuscript', pp. 69–70.

D is not derived from C: 7, 8, 20, 27, 28, etc. The shortenings and omissions of C make DE better representatives of the common source of CDE. In addition, the fact that both C and D are followed by the same work make it likely that *Oed yr Arglwydd* followed *O Oes Gwrtheyrn* in their common source.

E is not derived from C, and is closer to D: 7, 20, 28, 34, 52, etc.

E is not derived from D: 46, 52.

That CDE were derived from Hengwrt 33 and H was derived from a sister of Hengwrt 33 is suggested at 24.

Determining J's relationship to the earlier manuscripts is difficult given its derivation from more than one source, but Ben Guy has demonstrated that its source from the CDEHI branch must be the lost Hengwrt 33. Its source from the ABFG group is more difficult to determine.[15] It cannot have been derived from AB since they lack most of the chronological calculations present in J's conclusion, and dependence on FG is perhaps precluded by the unlikelihood that Vaughan would have described these as three centuries old.

An edition of *O Oes Gwrtheyrn* was included as part of my doctoral thesis, and since then two new manuscripts of the text (MS Peniarth 183 and MS Peniarth 137) have been brought to my attention.[16] This means that the sigla for manuscripts have changed slightly in this new edition. These changes are as follows: H was previously used to signify MS Cwrtmawr 453, but is now MS Peniarth 183, MS Cwrtmawr 453 now being J. Similarly, I was previously used to signify NLW, MS 4973B, but is now MS Peniarth 137, with NLW, MS 4973B now being K. Correspondingly, the sigla of later manuscripts have changed as follows from the thesis edition to the current one: what was K is now M; what was L is now N; what was M is now O. Given that only ABCDEFGH were used in the first edition, and ABCDEFGHIJ are used for the current one, the only really significant differences in the edition itself are the addition of H and I and that the sigla for MS Cwrtmawr 453 is now J rather than H.

The manuscript of *c.* 1550 recently unearthed in the Northamptonshire Archives in the hand of Sir John Prise of Brecon, MS FH7, contains a text of *O Oes Gwrtheyrn* which has not been used in the preparation of this edition, but preliminary conclusions can be drawn as to its relationship with other manu-

---

[15] Guy, 'A Lost Medieval Manuscript', pp. 82–83.

[16] My thanks to Ben Guy for this.

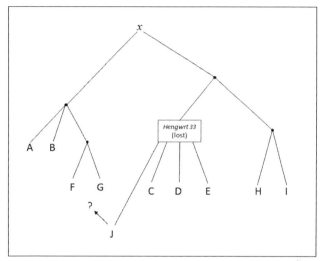

Figure 7.1: The relationship between different manuscripts of *O Oes Gwrtheyrn*. Figure by author.

scripts. It appears to have been the source of F and was also probably the source of G, therefore its place in the stemma is immediately above these. As it drew on the same source as A and B, the second of which is used as the main text for the following edition, the authority of its text is therefore considerable. It could be used to fill the brief lacuna in B after item 64, as its authority is greater than that of G and J, which are used below. However, a preliminary survey of the text does not suggest any important differences.[17]

Date and Provenance

The form that the chronicle takes is one which prioritizes the transmission of chronological data. It begins with a series of notices apparently derived originally from the St Davids chronicle, which now survives in the three versions of *Annales Cambriae* as well as in *Brut y Tywysogyon*.[18] It opens with the time between the reign of Vortigern and Arthur's battles, and this pattern of counting the years between one event and the other continues, with the occasional extra detail and chronological anchor, until item 47. Around this point the nature of the chronological calculation changes, and the formula *o'r pan [...]*

---

[17] Thanks to Gruffudd Antur, who drew my attention to this discovery and provided me with photographs of the Northamptonshire manuscript's text of *O Oes Gwrtheyrn*.

[18] The versions of *Annales Cambriae* are generally known as A, B, and C, although I refer to C as the Cottonian chronicle and B as the Breviate chronicle.

yny [...], 'from when [...] until [...]' is abandoned in favour of introducing events with *yn y 6loythyn rac 6yneb*, 'in the next year'.[19] In this section, then, it moves from being a mere series of chronological calculations to more of a chronicle proper, with particular attention given to interactions between Llywelyn Fawr and King John. This relatively detailed section continues to item 52, where there is a return to the brevity of the opening section along with some errors in dating indicative of later addition.

Structurally, then, there are several indications that the chronicle was originally compiled in the early thirteenth century and was updated in the mid-thirteenth century. The first of these is the level of detail for the years 1208–1212/16, this detailed section being followed simply by notices of the deaths of prominent members of the Gwynedd dynasty until some details concerning the early campaigns of Llywelyn ap Gruffudd.[20] Secondly, in the group of broad chronological calculations with which the work ends, one branch of the tradition (CDEI) calculates from the battle of Bryn Derwin (1255) whilst the other (BG) calculates from the captivity of Gruffudd ap Llywelyn in 1211. Although the latter group also contains the annals from 1211 to *c.* 1265, it can be suggested that the original work ended in 1211/12[21] but was later extended to *c.* 1265, keeping the chronological calculations referring to the captivity of Gruffudd. This version would now be represented by BG. This version was then updated, with the chronological calculations changed to centre on the battle of Bryn Derwin, as in CDE.

This interpretation of the work's date gains support from what can be surmised about the chronicle's origins. The places mentioned in the text show that the chronicle is centred on Gwynedd, with over a third of the thirty or so places mentioned being there, including more than half of those places named after the mid-twelfth century. There is also a tendency towards the northern coast of Gwynedd, on both sides of the Conwy. Three places on Anglesey are mentioned, along with Bangor, Abergwyngregyn, the river Conwy, Degannwy (three times), Creuddyn, Diserth, Rhuddlan, and Mold.

The prominent role of the Cistercian order in the keeping of chronicles in Wales would therefore lead one to suspect Aberconwy Abbey, at the centre of

---

[19] I am indebted to David Stephenson for bringing this difference of terminology to my attention.

[20] See below for the ambiguity of this end-date.

[21] The last detailed notice of the fuller section of the text relates to the year after Gruffudd's captivity.

these locations, as a place of composition. This suspicion is fortified when considering those Venedotian dynasts the chronicler chooses to mention, albeit briefly. The prominence of Llywelyn ab Iorwerth and his family is quite clear, but mention of the members of the generation before Llywelyn, and of his contemporaries, may be significant. These include obituaries of Rhodri ab Owain Gwynedd and his brother, Dafydd, as well as their nephews Gruffudd and Maredudd ap Cynan. All these figures were involved in the struggle for control of Gwynedd after Owain Gwynedd's death, a struggle from which Llywelyn ab Iorwerth emerged the victor, and although the chronicler's interest in them could simply reflect his interest in Llywelyn himself, it is likely that their connections with the abbey of Aberconwy was also a factor. Rhodri and Dafydd probably acted as joint founders of the abbey, and Gruffudd ap Cynan granted it lands on Anglesey.[22] Gruffudd was buried at the abbey after assuming the habit of the order. His son, Hywel, is mentioned twice in *O Oes Gwrtheyrn*, once accompanying Llywelyn ab Iorwerth to Scotland and again at his death, and he was also buried at Aberconwy.[23] Llywelyn ab Iorwerth and his sons, Dafydd and Gruffudd, were also buried there.[24]

The impression of an Aberconwy origin is further confirmed when comparing the places mentioned in the work to the granges held by the abbey.[25] There is little correlation between places mentioned on Anglesey and the abbey's lands there.[26] The chronicle's mention of the battle of Bryn Derwin is an outlier from the general rule that places named in Gwynedd are on or near its northern coast, as it lies inland on the border of Arfon and Eifionydd. Aberconwy's lands at Cwm and Nant Call, however, lie on either side of Bwlch Derwin, where the battle of 1255 was fought.[27] While the battle's significance in the

---

[22] Foundation: Colin A. Gresham, 'The Aberconwy Charter: Further Consideration', *BBCS*, 30 (1982–83), 311–47 (pp. 314–16); Charles Insley, 'Fact and Fiction in Thirteenth-Century Gwynedd: The Aberconwy Charters', *Studia Celtica*, 33 (1999), 235–50 (pp. 236–38). Gruffudd ap Cynan's grant: *The Acts of Welsh Rulers 1120–1283*, ed. by Huw Pryce (Cardiff: University of Wales Press, 2005), pp. 338–39.

[23] *BT (Pen. 20)*, pp. 145–46, 173; *BT (RB)*, pp. 182, 210; *BS*, pp. 196, 216.

[24] *BT (Pen. 20)*, pp. 198, 201, 204; *BT (RB)*, pp. 236, 238–40, 242; *BS*, pp. 232, 236, 238.

[25] This approach is used with reference to Cwm-hir by David Stephenson, 'The Chronicler at Cwm-hir Abbey, 1257–63: The Construction of a Welsh Chronicle', in *Wales and the Welsh in the Middle Ages: Essays Presented to J. Beverley Smith*, ed. by Ralph A. Griffiths and Phillipp R. Schofield (Cardiff: University of Wales Press, 2011), pp. 29–45.

[26] David H. Williams, *The Welsh Cistercians* (Leominster: Gracewing, 2001), p. 178.

[27] Gresham, 'The Aberconwy Charter', map between pp. 312–13.

chronicle, probably a result of updating in the mid-thirteenth century, could be explained simply through interest in Llywelyn ab Iorwerth's descendants (particularly Llywelyn ap Gruffudd, son of the Gruffudd given as hostage in 1211), its occurrence almost within the abbey's lands may also be relevant.

The abbey held no other lands close to places mentioned in the chronicle with the exception of Degannwy and the Creuddyn. Here, the level of detail is near proof of the chronicle's Aberconwy origin. The mention of Earl Ranulf of Chester's use of the timber of the barn of Creuddyn in his fortification of Degannwy in 1210 must refer to the barn of the monastery's Creuddyn grange near Degannwy Castle, the Aberconwy lands lying closest to the abbey itself.[28] This level of detail, combined with the abbey's links of patronage with the men mentioned in the work and the fact that its chronicle sources circulated among Cistercian monasteries, indicate that *O Oes Gwrtheyrn* is a product of the Cistercian abbey of Aberconwy.

Purpose

An Aberconwy origin makes *O Oes Gwrtheyrn* the only thing approximating a native chronicle to have survived from Gwynedd, since David Stephenson has demonstrated that the so-called 'Aberconwy Chronicle' is a later compilation undertaken at Hailes Abbey. Stephenson has suggested that although historical writing was probably undertaken in thirteenth-century Gwynedd, none survived the conquest.[29] Whilst *O Oes Gwrtheyrn* cannot be categorized as a chronicle on the same level of detail as *Brut y Tywysogyon* and most versions of *Annales Cambriae*, it certainly represents a form of historical writing. The other significant vernacular chronicles from northern Wales are continuations of *Brut y Tywysogion* associated with Valle Crucis, written in the fourteenth and fifteenth centuries and much later in their focus than *O Oes Gwrtheyrn*.[30] The survival rate of medieval manuscripts from north-eastern Wales is much better than from Gwynedd Uwch Conwy,

---

[28] Gresham, 'The Aberconwy Charter'. pp. 315–18.

[29] David Stephenson, *The Aberconwy Chronicle*, Kathleen Hughes Memorial Lecture, 2 (Cambridge: Hughes Hall and Department of Anglo-Saxon, Norse and Celtic, 2002), pp. 17–18.

[30] For the first of these, in the Peniarth 20 manuscript, see David Stephenson, Chapter 6, this volume. The second, Gutun Owain's updating of *Brenhinedd y Saesson/Brut y Tywysogyon* to 1461, is discussed in Huw Pryce, Chapter 1, above.

and this is indicated by the north-eastern provenance of these later chronicles as well as the association of the *CDE* version of *O Oes Gwrtheyrn* itself with north-eastern Wales.[31]

One of the chief concerns of the work would appear to be chronology, and it is possible that it represents something of a middle stage in the work of historical writing at Aberconwy. To clarify, if we consider the events noted in recent history from the point of view of the original compiler, the years 1187–1212, it is striking that the majority of notices concern either patrons of the abbey (Dafydd and Rhodri ab Owain; Gruffudd ap Cynan ab Owain; Llywelyn ab Iorwerth; Hywel ap Gruffudd) or events closely involving the abbey (Ranulf of Chester's activities in Degannwy; John's invasion of 1211). It may be that the reason for including events such as the obituaries of prominent patrons in a chronological work of this nature was to establish their place in relation to the corpus of annalistic material we know Cistercian houses to have shared. Put another way, it may be that *O Oes Gwrtheyrn* represents an intermediate step when notes relating to the affairs of the abbey's patrons were fitted into a chronological framework derived from a chronicle brought to Aberconwy from another abbey, a chronicle related to the group of texts now known as *Annales Cambriae* and *Brut y Tywysogyon*.[32] The most likely source of chronicle material used at Aberconwy would be the monastery's mother house of Strata Florida in Ceredigion, as there was an expectation that a mother house would provide its daughters with such materials.[33]

There are indications of a similar approach to chronicle writing in a text associated with Strata Florida. Around the late twelfth century, *Brut y Tywysogyon* ceases to be a chronicle written at Llanbadarn Fawr and begins to assume the character of a chronicle compiled at Strata Florida. The last of the stylistic formulae that David Stephenson took as indications of contemporary chronicling

---

[31] As discussed above, CDE were derived from Hengwrt 33, which Ben Guy has shown to have been a Valle Crucis manuscript.

[32] For detailed studies of the exchange of this chronicle material between Welsh (especially Cistercian) monasteries, see J. Beverley Smith, 'Historical Writing in Medieval Wales: The Composition of *Brenhinedd y Saesson*', *Studia Celtica*, 42 (2008), 55–86; Stephenson, 'The Chronicler at Cwm-hir Abbey'; David Stephenson, 'Gerald of Wales and *Annales Cambriae*', *CMCS*, 60 (2010), 23–37; Kathleen Hughes, *Celtic Britain in the Early Middle Ages*, ed. by David N. Dumville (Woodbridge: Boydell, 1980), pp. 67–85.

[33] Janet Burton, *The Monastic Order in Yorkshire, 1069–1215* (Cambridge: Cambridge University Press, 1999), pp. 281–82.

at Llanbadarn occurs in 1170.[34] From that point on, notices of the burial of laity at Strata Florida occur in 1175, 1185, and 1191. There are additionally notices of the death of an abbot in 1185 and the founding of a daughter house in the following year. The relatively full coverage of events characteristic of previous decades comes to an end in 1176, giving way to relatively sparse chronicling from 1177 to the mid-1180s, with no events at all recorded in 1180. This may indicate the end point of the material in the chronicle derived from Llanbadarn.[35]

The above suggests that when the chronicle of Strata Florida, which is the textual basis of *Brut y Tywysogyon*, was combined with the chronicle of Llanbadarn Fawr at the close of the twelfth century, the material used for this process was comparable in nature to the material contained in *O Oes Gwrtheyrn*, such as notices of the deaths of prominent patrons buried at the abbey.[36] This further strengthens the impression that *O Oes Gwrtheyrn* represents an intermediate step in the process of chronicle compilation.

The closely detailed section of the text comes to an end after noting the death of Maredudd ap Cynan in 1212, and although the close of this section notes the release of Gruffudd ap Llywelyn in 1216, it is unclear whether this particular notice is part of the original text or the later, mid-thirteenth century updating. The same can be said of the notice of the length of the Papal Interdict of 1208, which misdates the length of the interdict but was clearly written at some point after 1213.[37] This mid-thirteenth century updating is characterized by fairly sparse notices of the deaths of prominent members of the Gwynedd dynasty in the 1230s and 1240s until some more detailed notes about the early career of Llywelyn ap Gruffudd in the 1250s. Why the fuller account of the original compiler was not continued is an intriguing question. It is suggested below that the chronicle was originally compiled in Welsh, and this would make it something of a new departure, an experiment which may not have been continued enthusiastically after its original compiler, for whatever reason, left it around 1212.

---

[34] David Stephenson, 'Welsh Chronicles' Accounts of the Mid-Twelfth Century', *CMCS*, 56 (2008), 45–57 (pp. 52–54).

[35] *BT (Pen. 20)*, pp. 71–74; *BT (Pen. 20 trans.)*, pp. 127–33; *BT (RB)*, pp. 166–73; *BS*, pp. 182–89.

[36] The lack of notices of abbatial succession should be noted, although we know of no named abbot of Aberconwy until Anian in 1258. It may be that there was no change of abbot between the monastery's establishment in 1186 and the compilation of *O Oes Gwrtheyrn* around 1212 ′ 1216. David H. Williams, 'Fasti Cistercienses Cambrenses', *BBCS*, 24 (1970–72), 181–229 (p. 188).

[37] See endnote to § 46 of the edition.

The similarities between *O Oes Gwrtheyrn* and the 'Llywelyn ab Iorwerth genealogies' are noted below, and indicate that both texts were part of the same historical endeavour, perhaps the work of the same author. It has been suggested that these genealogies show the influence of Einion ap Gwalchmai, a poet and probably an official of the royal court of Llywelyn ab Iorwerth.[38] The evidence of the text of *O Oes Gwrtheyrn* itself, however, points strongly to Aberconwy in terms of its mention of the monastery's patrons, the geographical focus of the narrative, and its chronicle sources. The focus of the narrative on secular figures, albeit patrons of the monastery, could be taken as indicative of non-monastic authorship. However, it would be speculative to postulate a link between *O Oes Gwrtheyrn* and Einion on this basis, and all evidence points to Aberconwy as the chronicle's place of composition.

Context

The establishment of the chronicle's provenance enables us to consider the work as a product of Aberconwy in more depth. Consideration of other texts known or suspected to have been written or transmitted at Aberconwy will enable the chronicle to be set in the context of the intellectual activity undertaken at that monastery.

Recent work on the lost Hengwrt 33 manuscript, also entitled *Hanesyn Hen*, by Ben Guy is invaluable in considering the texts known at Aberconwy. Guy has established on the basis of manuscripts derived from Hengwrt 33 that this manuscript was probably written at Valle Crucis Abbey in the first half of the fourteenth century. He has also argued that some of this manuscript's contents were derived from Aberconwy.[39]

---

[38] Ben Guy suggested this possibility, since the genealogies favour the family. Einion was a poet and well-connected with the royal court, perhaps serving both as *Ynad Llys* and as *Bardd Teulu*, but there is no further connection between Einion and Aberconwy. Ben Guy, 'Medieval Welsh Genealogy: Texts, Contexts and Transmission', 2 vols (unpubl. doctoral thesis, University of Cambridge, 2016), I, 168; David Stephenson, *Political Power in Medieval Gwynedd: Governance and the Welsh Princes* (Cardiff: University of Wales Press, 2014), pp. xlix n. 20, 14.

[39] This is argued partially on the basis of the above evidence for *O Oes Gwrtheyrn*'s provenance, but also because Guy argues that the Llywelyn ab Iorwerth genealogies, which travel along with *O Oes Gwrtheyrn*, were produced in Aberconwy between 1216 and 1223. He also notes that Adda Fras, the only named poet whose work was included in *Hanesyn Hen*, was buried at the monastery's fourteenth-century site, Maenan. See Guy, 'A Lost Medieval Manuscript', pp. 84–91; Guy, 'Medieval Welsh Genealogy', I, 99–189, esp. 161–75.

Hengwrt 33 is fundamentally a Valle Crucis compilation, and it is difficult to determine with certainty which texts were derived from Aberconwy. At least one of the texts mentioned above, the chronicle *Oed yr Arglwydd*, was compiled at Valle Crucis in the early fourteenth century using material derived from an Aberconwy text, *O Oes Gwrtheyrn*.[40] Another of the works, the 'Llywelyn ab Iorwerth' genealogies, is extremely likely to have been compiled at Aberconwy around the same time as *O Oes Gwrtheyrn*.[41]

Some of the poetry of Hengwrt 33 was also perhaps derived from Aberconwy. The manuscript contained a poem by Adda Fras, who was buried at Maenan, the site to which Aberconwy was moved following the Edwardian conquest.[42] Two of the other poems are associated with the legendary Taliesin, and it may be significant that one of them, *Anrheg Urien*, associates Urien, Taliesin's patron, with Gwynedd and mentions Llyn Geirionydd in connection with Taliesin. Llyn Geirionydd lies about a mile from Aberconwy's property at Trefriw, and fairly close to the abbey's final site at Maenan.

The line of *Anrheg Urien* in question, 'Minneu Dalyessin | o iawn llyn geirionnyd', should be emended to read *llin geirionydd* and translated as 'I, Taliesin, of the true metre of heaven', rather than referring to the lake in particular.[43] Nevertheless, the mistaken insertion of this place name may indicate the interests of an Aberconwy scribe. *Anrheg Urien* was not only included in the Hengwrt 33 collection but also occurs in *Llyfr Coch Hergest*. The fact that the latter manuscript also included a version of *O Oes Gwrtheyrn* suggests that its version of *Anrheg Urien* may have derived from Aberconwy along with the chronicle.[44] More tangentially, an interest in Taliesin might be expected at

---

[40] Guy, 'A Lost Medieval Manuscript', pp. 84, 86–88.

[41] Guy, 'A Lost Medieval Manuscript', pp. 71–83; Guy, 'Medieval Welsh Genealogy', I, 168–75.

[42] Dafydd Johnston, 'Monastic Patronage of Welsh Poetry', in *Monastic Wales: New Approaches*, ed. by Janet Burton and Karen Stöber (Cardiff: University of Wales Press, 2013), pp. 177–90 (p. 187). For an edition, see Guy, 'A Lost Medieval Manuscript', pp. 97–98.

[43] Ifor Williams, *Canu Aneirin* (Cardiff: University of Wales Press, 1938), p. 206; Manon Bonner Jenkins, 'Aspects of the Welsh Prophetic Verse Tradition in the Middle Ages: Incorporating Textual Studies of the Poetry from *Llyfr Coch Hergest* (Oxford, Jesus College, MS cxi) and *Y Cwta Cyfarwydd* (Aberystwyth, National Library of Wales, MS Peniarth 50)', (unpubl. doctoral thesis, University of Cambridge, 1990), pp. 139–40; Marged Haycock, *Legendary Poems from the Book of Taliesin*, 2nd edn (Aberystwyth: CMCS, 2015), p. 15.

[44] It should be noted that the mistake *llyn* for *llin* occurs in the *Llyfr Coch Hergest* text of *Anrheg Urien*. I am unaware of any copies of *Anrheg Urien* derived from the lost Hengwrt 33 text.

Aberconwy, given the monastery's close proximity to Degannwy, a site which came to be associated with the legendary poet's competition with the bards of Maelgwn Gwynedd.[45]

While the association of some of these texts with Aberconwy is less secure than others, they demonstrate distinctive types of intellectual activity at the monastery. *O Oes Gwrtheyrn* indicates that chronicling activity was undertaken and shows a particular interest in the royal house of Gwynedd. The Llywelyn ab Iorwerth genealogies demonstrate that this interest at Aberconwy included the keeping of royal genealogies. The Taliesin poem, which describes his patron, Urien, as one of 'tri theyrn ar dec o'r Gogled' ('thirteen kings of the North') and locates the legendary poet in the locality of the abbey at Llyn Geirionydd, demonstrates an interest in the legendary past, and along with the poetry of Adda Fras shows an interest in vernacular poetry at the abbey.[46]

The prominence of vernacular literature above reflects the greater survival rate for vernacular manuscripts in Wales and the difficulty of attributing Latin manuscripts to Welsh monasteries.[47] There is however one medieval Latin historical work for which an Aberconwy provenance has been suggested. This is the curious Arthurian text *Vera historia de morte Arthuri*, which has been attributed to Aberconwy on grounds of both content and of the provenance of manuscripts.

It is a strange text which elaborates upon and sometimes contradicts Geoffrey of Monmouth's account of the death of Arthur, relocating his last days to a small church dedicated to the Virgin Mary in Gwynedd.[48] The earliest manuscripts

---

[45] While the earliest full witness to this story is the sixteenth-century chronicle of Elis Gruffydd, it is also referred to by court poets of the early thirteenth century, and there are several references to this story in the poems of *Llyfr Taliesin*. Juliette Wood, 'Maelgwn Gwynedd: A Forgotten Welsh Hero', *Trivium*, 19 (1984), 103–17 (p. 111). It should also be noted that a suggested identification for another site associated with Taliesin, *Caer Seon*, is Conwy mountain or one of its hillforts, located just to the west of the monastery's pre-conquest site. Haycock, *Legendary Poems*, pp. 345–46.

[46] The poem perhaps misread the *teyrn aerueda6c* of Triad 25. *Trioedd Ynys Prydein: The Triads of the Island of Britain*, ed. by Rachel Bromwich, 3rd edn (Cardiff: University of Wales Press, 2005), pp. 48–49.

[47] Daniel Huws, *Medieval Welsh Manuscripts* (Cardiff: University of Wales Press, 2000), p. 3.

[48] Michael Lapidge, 'An Edition of the *Vera historia de morte Arthuri*', *Arthurian Literature*, 1 (1981), 79–93, and Michael Lapidge, '*Update*: Additional Manuscript Evidence for the *Vera historia de morte Arthuri*', *Arthurian Literature*, 2 (1982), 163–68. For discussion, see Richard Barber, 'The *Vera historia de morte Arthuri* and its Place in Arthurian Tradition', *Arthurian Lit-*

of this work both have very tangential associations with Aberconwy. One (London, Gray's Inn, MS 7) is an early fourteenth-century manuscript which came into the possession of the Franciscan convent of Chester. Three other medieval manuscripts from the same convent were donated to Gray's Inn by the Franciscan Richard de Conway, although Gray's Inn, MS 7 itself was given by 'frater W Gyn'.[49] The second manuscript (London, BL, MS Cotton Cleopatra D III) dates to the turn of the fourteenth century and comes from Hailes Abbey, a monastery with which Aberconwy had some connection in the 1480s.[50] The text itself has been interpreted as containing a veiled reference to Aberconwy, in its reference to a small church in Gwynedd dedicated to the Virgin Mary — Aberconwy, like all Cistercian monasteries, had this dedication.[51]

The association of the *Vera historia* with Aberconwy is therefore uncertain. Indeed, it could be argued that a reference to a small church in Gwynedd dedicated to the Virgin Mary makes the Cistercian monastery of Cymer in Meirionydd at least as likely a candidate as Aberconwy as a place of authorship. The text notes that after Camlan, Arthur was taken to Gwynedd to prepare for his journey to the isle of Avalon, and Cymer lies midway between an area now known as Camlan on the boundaries of Gwynedd and near a coastline which faces Ynys Enlli.[52] It has also been argued that the text was written before 1190 or 1191, as it shows no knowledge of the discovery of Arthur's tomb in

---

erature, 1 (1981), 62–78; Siân Echard, *Arthurian Narrative in the Latin Tradition* (Cambridge: Cambridge Universtiy Press, 1998), pp. 80–85; Scott Lloyd, *The Arthurian Place Names of Wales* (Cardiff: University of Wales Press, 2017), pp. 29–30.

[49] Barber, 'The *Vera historia de morte Arthuri*', pp. 69–71.

[50] The Hailes Chronicle of MS Cotton Cleopatra D III, which contains the *Vera historia*, was a source for the text later erroneously known as the *Aberconwy Chronicle*, but this does not reveal anything regarding the source of the *Vera historia*. Stephenson, *The Aberconwy Chronicle*, pp. 13–16. For additional manuscripts of the *Vera historia*, see Lapidge, '*Update*'.

[51] Barber, 'The *Vera historia de morte Arthuri*', pp. 71–72.

[52] The Camlan in question is where the A470 crosses the Dyfi near Dinas Mawddwy, and is first named in 1571: Lloyd, *Arthurian Place Names*, p. 193. Enlli was seen as an island for burial, particularly of holy men, by the early twelfth century, when Bishop Urban transferred the remains of Saints Dyfrig and Elgar from there to his new church at Llandaf: *The Text of the Book of Llan Dâv: Reproduced from the Gwysaney Manuscript*, ed. by J. Gwenogvryn Evans, with John Rhys (Oxford: Evans, 1993), pp. 1–2, 85–86. Around the same period Meilyr Brydydd requested to be buried there in his *marwysgafn* ('death-bed poem'): *Gwaith Meilyr Brydydd a'i Ddisgynyddion*, ed. by J. E. Caerwyn Williams, with Peredur Lynch, Cyfres Beirdd y Tywysogion, 1 (Cardiff: University of Wales Press, 1994), p. 101 (poem 4, l. 38).

Glastonbury.⁵³ Between 1186 and 1192, however, Aberconwy was in between moving from its initial site of Rhedynog Felen and its later site at the mouth of the river Conwy.⁵⁴ It might rather be thought that the *Vera historia* was a Welsh response both to the ambiguities of Geoffrey of Monmouth's account of the death of Arthur and to the purported resolution of this at Glastonbury.

If it were an Aberconwy text, it would indicate an interest in Arthurian and British history echoed by *O Oes Gwrtheyrn*. It has been noted elsewhere that this Latin text has an atmosphere and incidents reminiscent of vernacular Welsh prose tales such as the Four Branches of the Mabinogi, and may therefore demonstrate a close relationship between the conventions of vernacular and Latin literature.⁵⁵

One particularly curious feature of the work is its mention of two bishops, Urien or Uriam of Bangor and Urbegen or Urgenu of Glamorgan.⁵⁶ It is curious that these names preserve two different forms of the Welsh name Urien, one with a compositional vowel.⁵⁷ There is no recorded bishop of either name; indeed Urien seems to have been a relatively unique name in Welsh sources, found only in reference to Urien Rheged ap Cynfarch, patron of Taliesin.⁵⁸ If the *Vera historia* was written at Aberconwy, which is possible rather than probable, the reference to Urien might be indicative of a general interest in Taliesin material at the monastery, as noted above with reference to Hengwrt 33. The

---

⁵³ Echard, *Arthurian Narrative*, pp. 80–81.

⁵⁴ P. Leopoldus Janauschek, *Originum Cisterciensium*, 2 vols (Vienna: Hoelder, 1877), I, 186–87; Gresham, 'The Aberconwy Charter', pp. 314–16; Insley, 'Fact and Fiction', pp. 236–38; Rhŷs W. Hays, *The History of the Abbey of Aberconway, 1186–1537* (Cardiff: University of Wales Press, 1963), pp. 5–6.

⁵⁵ Echard, *Arthurian Narrative*, pp. 81–83; Barber, 'The *Vera historia de morte Arthuri*', p. 72.

⁵⁶ The two spellings are derived from Gray's Inn, MS 7 and London, BL, MS Cotton Titus A XIX respectively. Lapidge, 'Update', p. 166.

⁵⁷ A trisyllabic alternative form of the name Urien, retaining the middle vowel, was certainly known to Cynddelw, who uses both *Urien* and *Uruoen* (*Urfoen* in modern orthography) in a poem to Owain Cyfeiliog. *Gwaith Cynddelw Brydydd Mawr I*, ed. by Nerys Ann Jones and Ann Parry Owen, Cyfres Beirdd y Tywysogion, 3 (Cardiff: University of Wales Press, 1991), pp. 192, 213 (poem 16, ll. 95–106); *Trioedd Ynys Prydein*, p. 509; Ifor Williams, 'Notes on Nennius', *BBCS*, 7 (1933–35), 380–89 (p. 388).

⁵⁸ *Trioedd Ynys Prydein*, p. 508. Richard Barber suggests that this is a reference to Urban of Llandaf, who held some form of authority over Bangor during the vacancy of the see between the episcopacies of Hervé and David the Scot, between 1109 and 1120. This is possible, but it should be noted that Urban's Welsh name was Gwrgan rather than Urien. Barber, 'The *Vera historia de morte Arthuri*', p. 73.

Vera historia was a creative Latinate response to Geoffrey's *De gestis Britonum*, which expanded his account whilst also revising it. The bishop of Bangor one would expect from *De gestis Britonum* would be Daniel or Deiniol, but we might see in these two invented bishops a playfulness with historical accuracy which sets this imitative work firmly in the Galfridian tradition.[59]

Such Galfridian influences are also perceptible in *O Oes Gwrtheyrn*, the closing section of the chronicle indicating considerable influence from Geoffrey's history. The succession of historical milestones which are dated in relation either to 1211 (ABFG) or 1255 (CDE) include the settlement of Britain by the Welsh, their conversion under Lles ap Coel, the arrival of the English, and the arrival of the Normans. The first two, and to a lesser extent the third, show the influence of Galfridian historiography. If these are part of the original composition of *O Oes Gwrtheyrn* not long after 1212, then the work is a relatively early example of the combination of Galfridian history and Welsh annalistic writing. One potentially significant and creative detail is the fact that the term *Cymry* is used from the settlement of Britain down to the present day, implying a rejection of Geoffrey's distinction between *Britones* and *Gualenses*.[60]

The texts discussed above indicate a definite interest in genealogical writing at Aberconwy, as well as a possible interest in vernacular poetry and Latin pseudo-historical writing. What *O Oes Gwrtheyrn* adds to this picture is evidence of Aberconwy as an active centre of contemporary chronicling. Its reliance on the St Davids annals, presumably derived from its mother house of Strata Florida, sets this chronicling in the context of the collaboration and sharing of material between Welsh Cistercian houses, something also apparent in the later transmission of *O Oes Gwrtheyrn* to Valle Crucis. It lies, however, outside the main stream of vernacular chronicling in that its independent material finds no parallel in any version of *Brut y Tywysogyon*.

While the exact relationship between the different versions of the *Brut* and their own relationship with a purported Latin original is ripe for reinvestigation, it is nevertheless clear that much of the content of *Brut y Tywysogyon* was originally compiled in Latin and translated into Welsh by the early years of the fourteenth century.[61] But *O Oes Gwrtheyrn* indicates a different process.

---

[59] Geoffrey of Monmouth, *The History of the Kings of Britain: An Edition and Translation of De gestis Britonum [Historia Regum Britanniae]*, ed. by Michael D. Reeve, trans. by Neil Wright (Woodbridge: Boydell, 2007), pp. 252–55.

[60] Geoffrey of Monmouth, *History*, p. 281.

[61] For a survey of views, see Ben Guy, Chapter 3, above.

There is no textual evidence that the chronicle was originally written in Latin.[62] Furthermore, the discussion of intellectual activity at the abbey suggests that the chronicle was originally compiled in Welsh. The contents of Hengwrt 33 indicate that it travelled alongside genealogical tracts, which were written in Welsh from an early date, and vernacular poetry.

There are other signs of the possible importance of Aberconwy as a centre of vernacular copying and translation. The first half of the thirteenth century saw the translation, retranslation, and editing of several vernacular versions of Geoffrey of Monmouth's *De gestis Britonum*, all in manuscripts with northern or mid-Wales associations.[63] To the closeness between Welsh and Latin writing indicated above can be added the suggestion that the biography of Gruffudd ap Cynan was translated into Welsh in Gwynedd in the early thirteenth century.[64] Daniel Huws has suggested that the later thirteenth-century manuscript which contains this text (Aberystwyth, NLW, MS Peniarth 17) was a product of Aberconwy. The same scribe also copied a volume of religious texts and the enormously important early poem *Y Gododdin*.[65] While it is important not to overstate the importance of a single monastery as a result of copying or tangential connections, *O Oes Gwrtheyrn* does demonstrate that the monastery saw the composition of innovative vernacular texts and the extension of the genres of medieval Welsh prose.

It is worth considering in more detail the relationship of the chronicle with the genealogical collection which Ben Guy has termed the 'Llywelyn ab Iorwerth genealogies'. This relationship is an extremely close one, particularly with regard to the transmission of the texts.[66] Guy has convincingly argued that

---

[62] I refer to the compilation of *O Oes Gwrtheyrn* itself and its original chronicling — the source material for its earlier sections was certainly in Latin. Other vernacular chronicles contain indications of translation from Latin such as the retention of case-endings for proper nouns. John Edward Lloyd, *The Welsh Chronicles*, The Sir John Rhŷs Memorial Lecture, British Academy (London: Milford, 1928), pp. 9–13; *BT (Pen. 20 trans.)*, p. xxxvi.

[63] Owain Wyn Jones, 'Historical Writing in Medieval Wales' (unpubl. doctoral thesis, Bangor University, 2013), pp. 352–56.

[64] The Latin biography was probably written at St Davids, and the greater focus of the Welsh version on Gwynedd is a strong argument for composition there. In terms of date, Gwynedd under Llywelyn ab Iorwerth in the early thirteenth century can be considered an appropriate context for such a translation, supported by the fact that Geoffrey's history was being translated at the same time. The earliest (fragmentary) manuscript of the Middle Welsh version dates to the second half of the thirteenth century. *Vita Griffini*, pp. 3, 33–34, 43–49.

[65] Huws, *Medieval Welsh Manuscripts*, p. 75.

[66] Guy, 'A Lost Medieval Manuscript', pp. 84–91.

the Llywelyn ab Iorwerth genealogies were written sometime between 1215/16 and 1223 and that they were written at Aberconwy. The date and provenance of the genealogies is therefore much the same as that of the basic text of *O Oes Gwrtheyrn*, written after 1212.[67]

As Guy has demonstrated, this genealogical corpus is a conscious work of historical composition. As such, it has some striking parallels with *O Oes Gwrtheyrn*, in particular its use of the formula *yn oes* [...] to contextualize a series of historical genealogies. For example, figures of the legendary past are described as living 'yn oes Vaelgwn' ('in the time of Maelgwn [Gwynedd]'), used as a generic representative of the heroic age.[68] Later on, in the discussion of the *gwehelaethau*, 'noble lineages', those belonging to the remote past are described as existing from 'oes Arthur hyt yn oes veibion Rodri Mawr' ('the time of Arthur to the time of the sons of Rhodri Mawr').[69] This, of course, parallels the opening formula of *O Oes Gwrtheyrn*, which sets the chronological outline which follows in relation to the legendary past in exactly the same way.

While these verbal formulae are common, in two texts so intimately connected as *O Oes Gwrtheyrn* and the Llywelyn ab Iorwerth genealogies they reveal a striking similarity in ways of thinking about the past, further evidence that both works were composed at the same time in the same institution. In fact, given the focus of both texts on the family of Llywelyn ab Iorwerth, they also both serve the same historical agenda, albeit in different genres. One was written in the more established vernacular genre of the pedigree, whereas the other may have been a new departure, an attempt to compile a vernacular chronicle.

There are several other parallels between *O Oes Gwrtheyrn* and the Llywelyn ab Iorwerth genealogies. Both texts show some interest in the battle of the Conwy in 881, and both have information which is additional to that in most other sources.[70] Both texts note the blinding of hostages in Coed Ceiriog by

---

[67] Guy, 'Medieval Welsh Genealogy', I, 161–68, 174–75.

[68] Guy, 'Medieval Welsh Genealogy', I, 151; II, 350.

[69] Guy, 'Medieval Welsh Genealogy', I, 157; II, 369.

[70] Guy, 'Medieval Welsh Genealogy', II, 365; Thomas M. Charles-Edwards, *Wales and the Britons 350–1064* (Oxford: Oxford University Press, 2013), pp. 490–91; *Annales Cambriae, A.D. 682–954: Texts A–C in Parallel*, ed. and trans. by David N. Dumville (Cambridge: Department of Anglo-Saxon, Norse and Celtic, University of Cambridge, 2002), pp. 12–13; *Brenhinoedd y Saeson, 'The Kings of the English', A.D. 682–954: Texts P, R, S in Parallel*, ed. and trans. by David N. Dumville (Aberdeen: Department of History, University of Aberdeen, 2005), pp. 30–31.

Henry II in 1165, the genealogies noting that a son of Owain Gwynedd was blinded there.[71] Both texts also used chronicle material originating at St Davids as a source.[72] These parallels mark both texts as part of the same historical endeavour.[73]

Its close relationship with this Welsh genealogical text is a strong argument in favour of *O Oes Gwrtheyrn*'s composition in Welsh. This could also explain some of its idiosyncrasies, most notably its chronological calculations. Its use of relative chronology and occasional chronological anchors suggests an author who was experimenting with a method to transfer the conventions of Latin chronicle writing to vernacular prose. This is an important development in the context of vernacular historical writing in Europe, and demonstrates the importance of an international monastic order, the Cistercians, in the development and extension of Welsh writing. It is important to note the interplay here between a genre with a more established vernacular tradition associated with the poets, the royal genealogy, and one closely associated with Latin monastic writing, the chronicle.[74] It was at a monastery which belonged to a network of pan-European scale but which had cultivated close links with native political culture that the transition from Latin to Welsh in the latter genre was attempted.

Beyond Wales, Irish already had an established tradition of vernacular chronicling.[75] In England, the gradual decline of Old English chronicling was reversed

---

[71] Guy, 'Medieval Welsh Genealogy', II, 357.

[72] Guy, 'Medieval Welsh Genealogy', I, 182–84; Ben Guy, 'A Second Witness to the Welsh Material in Harley 3859', *Quaestio Insularis: Selected Proceedings of the Cambridge Colloquium in Anglo-Saxon, Norse and Celtic*, 15 (2014), 72–91. More tangentially, both texts also show an interest in Scandinavian affairs, O Oes Gwrtheyrn with regard to Herlant Pic, discussed below, and the Llywelyn ab Iorwerth genealogies in the context of the genealogy of Gruffudd ap Cynan's mother, Rhanillt. Guy, 'Medieval Welsh Genealogy', II, 359–61; for an exploration of those links, though unaware of the early thirteenth-century date of this genealogical material, see Marie Therese Flanagan, '*Historia Gruffud vab Kenan* and the Origins of Balrothery, Co. Dublin', *CMCS*, 28 (1994), 71–94.

[73] For the possibility that the Llywelyn ab Iorwerth genealogies may have been influenced by Einion ap Gwalchmai, see above, and Guy, 'Medieval Welsh Genealogy', I, 168.

[74] For Gerald of Wales's comments on the poets' vernacular genealogical books, see Gerald of Wales, *Descriptio Kambriae*, I. 3, ed. by James F. Dimock, Giraldi Cambrensis Opera, 6 (London: Longmans, Green, Reader, and Dyer, 1868); trans. by Lewis Thorpe, *Gerald of Wales: The Journey Through Wales/The Description of Wales* (London: Harmondsworth, 1978), p. 223.

[75] Use of Irish in the annals of Ireland became dominant in the course of the tenth century: David N. Dumville, 'Latin and Irish in the *Annals of Ulster*, A.D. 431–1050', in *Ireland in Early Medieval Europe: Studies in Memory of Kathleen Hughes*, ed. by Dorothy Whitelock, Rosa-

and redefined in the course of the twelfth century as older chronicles and Galfridian historical texts were translated into verse: first into French, and by the thirteenth century into Middle English.[76] Vernacular historical writing in Norse had been established a hundred years before in the early twelfth century, but these decades saw a considerable extension of this with the composition of more expansive Kings' sagas of foundational importance, such as *Sverris saga*, leading eventually to the great works of Snorri Sturlusson.[77] It is purely speculative to link the composition of the short vernacular chronicle *O Oes Gwrtheyrn* directly to these wider developments in vernacular European writing. Nevertheless, the coincidence of these developments with the establishment of an interconnected, international monastic order in Gwynedd offers room for speculation.

The second decade of the thirteenth century saw conflict between the prince of Gwynedd and the English king and the increasing dominance by Gwynedd of the politics of native Wales. In this context, someone at the favoured monastery of the rulers of Gwynedd made the bold step of writing a chronicle in Welsh. Even in the context in which prose historical narratives were being translated, the composition of a vernacular chronicle may have been a new departure. The careful calculation of a chronological framework which related the text to the

---

mond McKitterick, and David N. Dumville (Cambridge: Cambridge University Press, 1982), pp. 320–41.

[76] The vibrant Anglo-Norman French *Brut* tradition of Gaimar and Wace informed the work of Laȝamon around the turn of the thirteenth century, although Laȝamon is somewhat isolated from later Middle English translations such as Robert of Gloucester's *Chronicle*, from the late thirteenth century. Chris Given-Wilson, *Chronicles: The Writing of History in Medieval England* (London: Hambledon and London, 2004), pp. 137–38; W. R. J. Barron, Françoise Le Saux, and Lesley Johnson, 'Dynastic Chronicles', in *The Arthur of the English: The Arthurian Legend in Medieval English Life and Literature*, ed. by W. R. J. Barron, 2nd edn (Cardiff: University of Wales Press, 2001), pp. 11–46 (esp. pp. 32–33); Françoise Le Saux, *Laȝamon's 'Brut': The Poem and its Sources* (Cambridge: Brewer, 1989), pp. 1–10, 24–26; Laȝamon, *Brut or Historia Brutonum*, ed. and trans. by W. R. J. Barron and S. C. Weinberg (Harlow: Longman, 1995); Robert of Gloucester, *The Metrical Chronicle*, ed. by William Aldis Wright, 2 vols (London: Her Majesty's Stationery Office, 1887).

[77] Theodore M. Anderson, 'Kings' Sagas', in *Old Norse-Icelandic Literature: A Critical Guide*, ed. by Carol J. Clover and John Lindow, Islandica, 45 (Ithaca, NY: Cornell University Press, 1985), pp. 197–238. It is interesting to note that an important development in the creation of 'official' royal sagas involved the abbot of the Icelandic monastery of Þingeyrar, Karl Jónsson, writing *Sverris saga* under the personal supervision of King Sverre, another instance of the role of monastic patronage in the definition of vernacular historiography. Sverre Bagge, *From Gang Leader to the Lord's Anointed: Kingship in Sverris saga and Hákonar saga Hákonarsonar* (Odense: Odense University Press, 1996), pp. 15–16.

Latin chronicle on which it drew was followed by some fuller, contemporary recording. This fuller account was not maintained beyond 1212, but it was later updated, and now presents a fragmented but important Venedotian perspective on some events of the thirteenth century. Some of these events will now be considered in more detail.

Herlant Pic

The most significant event recorded in *O Oes Gwrtheyrn* is undoubtedly the raid in 1209 on Llanfaes in Môn. Record of this event is unique to the chronicle and has to my knowledge never been discussed before. It is worth quoting the chronicle's brief report to begin, which comes immediately after an entry relating Llywelyn ab Iorwerth's role in King John's 1209 campaign in Scotland:

> Nos 6yl Sim6nd a Iuda yn y 6loythyn honno y doeth ystiward llys brenhin Llychlyn, Herlant Pic y en6, a chweych her6log ganta6 hyd yn Llanuaes y yspeila6 y tref a'e llosgi, a e llas Herlant Pic a'e oreugw[y]r.

> On the eve of St Simon and St Jude in that year, the steward of the court of the King of Norway, named Herlant Pic, came with six raiding ships to Llanfaes to despoil the town and burn it, and Herlant Pic was killed along with his best men.

This short, cursory notice brings the chronicle briefly into the wider politics of Northern Europe. The appearance of a Norwegian steward on Anglesey is somewhat unexpected, and his unfamiliar name certainly caused confusion to later Welsh copyists of the text, but the chronicler here is in fact very well informed. Herlant Pic's name is known, his status is described, and the exact number of ships which took part in the Llanfaes raid is noted. Three questions immediately suggest themselves. Firstly, who was this Herlant Pic who fell in the Llanfaes raid, and is the chronicle's description of his status accurate? Secondly, what was the purpose and wider political context of this event? Thirdly, why is the chronicler so well-informed about the identity and status of this Norse leader?

The first question necessitates a search through historical sources for Herlant Pic, and fortunately this reveals a near-contemporary mention of him in *Bǫglunga Sǫgur*, an Old Norse history detailing part of the Norwegian Civil Wars.[78]

---

[78] *Soga om Birkebeinar og Baglar: Bǫglunga sǫgur*, ed. by Hallvard Magerøy (Oslo: Solum, 1988), pp. 119–21; *Early Sources of Scottish History, A.D. 500 to 1286*, ed. and trans. by Alan Orr Anderson, 2 vols (Edinburgh: Oliver and Boyd, 1922), II, 378–88.

These wars dominated the second half of the twelfth century in Norway, with the last decades of that century seeing the rise to power of the charismatic Sverrir Sigurðarson (r. 1177–1202).[79] These years saw a polarization between Sverrir and his followers, the *Birkibeinar* or 'Birchlegs', and the followers of his rival Magnús Erlingsson and his successors (r. 1161–1184), the *Baglar* or 'Croziers', who had the support of most of the Norwegian church.[80] These wars petered out gradually rather than coming to any definite conclusion, but a significant step in this process was a peace treaty agreed in 1208. After describing this treaty, *Bǫglunga Sǫgur* describes a joint westward expedition planned by the two previously-opposing factions:

> Þá gerðisk kurr í hvárutveggja liðinu af þeim mǫnnum, er félausir váru ok hǫfðu þó nafnbœtr. Var þá þat ráðgert, at eptir um várit skyldu þeir herja til Suðreyja ok afla sér fjár. Ætluðusk þá til menn af hvárutveggja liðinu [...] Þat sumar fóru þeir í víking í Suðreyjar Þormóðr þasrámr ok Þormóðr fylbeinn, Óskapk suðreyski. Þessir váru af Birkibeinum. En af Bǫglum var Eiríkr Tófason ok Eiríkr of Erlendr píkr, Bergr maull, Nikolás gilli. Þeir hǫfðu .xij. skip.
>
> Then arose a murmur in both armies among those men who had no riches, yet had rank. Then this plan was made, that in the following spring they should plunder in the Hebrides and procure wealth for themselves. Men from both armies then purposed to do this [...] [The following] summer, Þormóðr Þasrámr, and Þormóðr foal's leg, and Óspakr suðreyski, went on piracy into the Hebrides; these were Birkibeinar. And of the Baglar were Eírikr Tófason, and Eírikr, and Erlendr píkr, Bergr maull, Nikolás gilli. They had twelve ships.[81]

Erlendr píkr is of course the same as *O Oes Gwrtheyrn*'s Herlant Pic, the latter being a straightforward Cambricization of the Old Norse name. Before discussing what the evidence of *O Oes Gwrtheyrn* adds to this picture, it would be well to summarize the current state of knowledge surrounding these events.

---

[79] Sverre Bagge, *From Viking Stronghold to Christian Kingdom: State Formation in Norway c. 900–1350* (Copenhagen: Museum Tusculanum, 2010), pp. 50–64; Knut Helle, 'The Norwegian Kingdom: Succession Disputes and Consolidation', in *The Cambridge History of Scandinavia*, ed. by Knut Helle, E. I. Kouri, and Torkel Jansson, 3 vols (Cambridge: Cambridge University Press, 2003–), I: *Prehistory to 1520*, ed. by Knut Helle (2003), pp. 369–91; for a close study of Sverrir in particular, see Bagge, *From Gang Leader*.

[80] Ian Beuermann, 'Masters of the Narrow Sea: Forgotten Challenges to Norwegian Rule in Man and the Isles, 1079–1266' (unpubl. doctoral thesis, University of Oslo, 2006), pp. 298–99.

[81] *Bǫglunga sǫgur*, p. 119; translation in *Early Sources of Scottish History*, II, 379.

Bǫglunga Sǫgur itself survives in both a longer and a shorter version, and the exact relationship between these versions has been a matter of some discussion. Nevertheless, both versions were written within a decade or two of the events described.[82] The short version of the saga, from which comes the above quote, ends shortly afterwards, but the narrative of the longer version continues after this point.[83] Taking the testimony of both the longer and the shorter versions together offers the following narrative. A peace deal agreed in 1208 in Norway established Ingi Bárðarson, favoured by the Birkibeinar, as the overall King of Norway based in the Trøndelag, but his authority was shared with Philippús Símonsson, favoured by the Baglar, who ruled over eastern Norway. The agreement therefore divided rule over Norway between two rival factions, both of whom agreed to lead a joint expedition to the Hebrides in the following year. The purpose of this campaign was to secure riches for those on both sides who had lost it in the war, and because the kings in the Hebrides were involved in a civil war among themselves.

The expedition was only partially successful. The participants raided in the Hebrides, and after plundering Iona they fell out and parted. Those who were not slain in various places were rebuked for their piracy by the bishops on their return. The longer version of the saga notes however that the king's officers went with the expedition to Orkney and Shetland, implying that the re-establishment of Norwegian royal authority over these areas following the civil wars was another purpose for the campaign. In the wake of the expedition, Reginald, King of Man, also travelled to Norway to swear fealty to King Ingi.[84]

To corroborate these events, the *Chronicle of the Kings of Man and the Isles* notes Reginald's absence from Man in 1210, when King John sent a fleet from Ireland to attack the island.[85] It would appear that the King of Man's journey to Norway led to a punitive expedition by John, in the same year that John also moved against Llywelyn of Gwynedd with Ranulf of Chester's attack on Degannwy, as noted in *O Oes Gwrtheyrn*. The Icelandic annals also corroborate

[82] Bagge, *From Gang Leader*, pp. 16–17.

[83] The shorter version is extant in Old Norse in two manuscripts, *Eirspennill* (s. xiv¹) and *Skálholtsbók yngsta* (s. xiv^med). The longer version survives in three medieval fragments, but is complete only in the form of a Danish translation by Peder Claussøn Friis from around 1600. Beuermann, 'Masters of the Narrow Sea', pp. 246–47.

[84] For a detailed discussion of the accounts of these events in all sources except for *O Oes Gwrtheyrn*, see Beuermann, 'Masters of the Narrow Sea', pp. 246–47, 278–95.

[85] *Chronica Regum Manniæ et Insularum: The Chronicle of Man and the Sudreys*, ed. by Peter Andreas Munch (Christiania: Brøgger and Christie, 1860), pp. 15–16.

the events described in *Bǫglunga Sǫgur*, noting the preparation of the expedition in 1209 and the pillaging of Iona in 1210.⁸⁶

The testimony of *O Oes Gwrtheyrn* is of considerable use in clarifying the events above and in adding to our knowledge of the expedition. What can be said with certainty is that its account demonstrates close knowledge of these events in naming one of the leaders of the expedition. The specific number of ships reported, six, chimes well with the twelve ships reported in *Bǫglunga Sǫgur*, as it is a possibility that this represents a split in the expedition between the Baglar and Birkibeinar, a likelihood considering how recently these factions had been at war. It seems likely, therefore, that the raid on Llanfaes took place after the raid on Iona and subsequent disagreement noted in *Bǫglunga Sǫgur*, and that therefore this raid on Iona should be dated to 1209 rather than the 1210 of the Icelandic Annals, given the detailed knowledge and near-contemporaneity of this section of *O Oes Gwrtheyrn*, as well as the exact date of 27 October. Erlendr píkr is therefore one of the men who, the saga notes, 'were slain in various places'.⁸⁷

Erlendr píkr is named in *Bǫglunga Sǫgur* as one of the Baglar, therefore we might further suppose that it was this group in the six ships which attacked Llanfaes. Interpreting the Norse evidence together with that of *O Oes Gwrtheyrn*, the various sources support the following summary of events. The joint expedition set off in 1209 with twelve ships. Iona was raided and then there was disagreement. Half the number of ships recorded at the start of the expedition then raided Anglesey, suggesting that this disagreement was a factional one between the Birkibeinar and the Baglar.

From these few facts and inferences, at least two possible explanations for a Norwegian raid on Llanfaes can be postulated. The first is political; the second is opportunistic. The political explanation must take into account the wider context of Irish Sea and Northern European politics in the previous decade. The important factors here are King John's earlier support for King Sverrir, whose Birkibeinar followers eventually supported Ingi Bárðarson in the decade after his death; and Llywelyn ab Iorwerth of Gwynedd's switch of alliance from a marriage with the daughter of the King of Man, Reginald Godredson, to King John's illegitimate daughter, Joan.

---

⁸⁶ *Islandske Annaler indtil 1578*, ed. by Gustav Storm (Christiania: Grondahl, 1888), pp. 123, 182; *Early Sources of Scottish History*, II, 378, 381–82; Beuermann, 'Masters of the Narrow Sea', p. 286.

⁸⁷ *Bǫglunga sǫgur*, p. 119; *Early Sources of Scottish History*, II, 379.

This political explanation envisages the raid on Llanfaes as a reprisal of the Baglar faction against Llywelyn. Llywelyn was, in 1209, a close ally of King John, having accompanied John on his Scottish campaign earlier in the year. Some years previously, John had supported King Sverrir, leader of the rival Birkibeinar faction, with Welsh mercenaries.[88] These facts may have influenced the Baglar decision to target Llanfaes, the most important commercial centre of Llywelyn's kingdom.

In addition, it can also be postulated that Reginald of Man, who agreed to travel to Norway to pay tribute to the Birkibeinar king, Ingi Bárðarson, may have harboured a grudge against Llywelyn, who had, a few years previously, turned his back on an already-formulated plan of alliance when he separated from Reginald's daughter in favour of an alliance with King John.[89] Reginald had previously been allied with Llywelyn's uncle and rival Rhodri ab Owain, who was betrothed to Reginald's daughter.[90] After his uncle's death in 1195, Llywelyn petitioned the Pope in 1199 for permission to marry Reginald's daughter, Rhodri's widow, on the grounds of non-consummation, suggesting a planned alliance between Reginald and Llywelyn.[91] However, by 1205 Llywelyn had instead married Joan, King John's illegitimate daughter, further strengthening the peace agreed between the ruler of Gwynedd and the English king, which was to last until 1210.[92]

Reginald's relationship with King John in the first decade of the thirteenth century was less consistent than Llywelyn's. Although 1205 saw an agree-

---

[88] The mercenaries were sent in 1201. Although they may largely have been from John's lordship of Morgannwg, mercenaries from Gwynedd had been used by the English King in 1186. They may be the men noted as a distinct group in *Sverris saga*. *The Great Roll of the Pipe for the Third Year of the Reign of King John, Michaelmas 1201 (Pipe Roll 47)*, ed. by Doris M. Stenton (Lincoln: Ruddock, 1936), pp. 128, 137, 264; Ifor W. Rowlands, '"Warriors Fit for a Prince": Welsh Troops in Angevin Service, 1154–1216', in *Mercenaries and Paid Men: The Mercenary Identity in the Middle Ages*, ed. by John France (Leiden: Brill, 2008), pp. 207–30 (pp. 213, 215, 226); *Sverrissaga: The Saga of King Sverri of Norway*, ed. by John Sephton (London: Nutt, 1899), pp. 224–25.

[89] *HW*, II, 616–17; Huw Pryce, *Native Law and the Church in Medieval Wales* (Oxford: Clarendon Press, 1993), pp. 84–85.

[90] It was the presence of Reginald's Manx troops on Anglesey in 1193 which led the *O Oes Gwrtheyrn* chronicler to describe this period as 'haf y Gwyddyl' ('the summer of the Irish'). R. Andrew McDonald, *Manx Kingship in its Irish Sea Setting 1187–1229: King Rognvaldr and the Crovan Dynasty* (Dublin: Four Courts, 2007), pp. 101–07; *HW*, II, 588; *BS*, p. 188.

[91] Pryce, *Native Law*, p. 85.

[92] *Acts of Welsh Rulers*, p. 26.

ment between John and Reginald, it also saw Reginald continue to support his brother-in-law, John de Courcy, in Ulster. The relationship between John and Reginald had certainly broken down by 1210, when John sent his army to attack Man, but it is difficult to establish the health of this relationship in 1209.[93] It is likely that Reginald's agreement to pay tribute to the Norwegian king was the most important element in this breakdown.

Reginald's co-operation with the Norwegians could have involved an agreement that the Baglar in the expedition raided Llanfaes as a reprisal against Llywelyn, who had turned his back on a Manx alliance by 1205 in favour of one with John. Such a raid would have been an attractive notion to men who were interested in plunder, as well as to men whose Birkibeinar enemies had been aided by King John some years previously in the civil war.

Such an explanation would see the raid on Llanfaes as part of a network of alliances and rivalries across Northern Europe. King John's support for the Birkibeinar reflected French support for the Danes, cemented by the marriage of Philip II of France and Ingeborg of Denmark, the Danes and French in turn supporting the Baglar faction in the Norwegian Civil Wars.[94] It is attractive to put this event in such a wide political context, though this might put too much weight on fragmentary evidence in a period when the politics of the Irish Sea were extremely changeable.[95]

Another explanation would see the raid as more opportunistic. Whereas *Bǫglunga Sǫgur* states that the aim of the expedition was plunder, the clear political motivation of re-establishing Norwegian hegemony over Orkney and Man should be given equal weight. The re-establishment of this authority may have been less important to the Baglar members of the expedition, since the king to whom the earl of Orkney and the king of Man would pay tribute and

---

[93] R. Costain-Russell, 'The Reigns of Guðrøðr and Rögnvaldr, 1153–1229', in *A New History of the Isle of Man*, 5 vols (Liverpool: Liverpool University Press, 2000–), III: *The Medieval Period 1000–1406*, ed. by Seán Duffy and Harold Mytum (2015), pp. 78–96 (p. 91). The last note of friendly relations comes in the close rolls of 1207, with nothing then until Reginald performed fealty to John at Lambeth in 1212. *Monumenta de Insula Manniæ; or, a Collection of National Documents Relating to the Isle of Man*, ed. by John Robert Oliver, 3 vols (Douglas: Manx Society, 1860–62), II (1861), 25–32.

[94] For a survey of these links, and in particular the breakdown of English support to Norway after the accession of a Baglar, Danish-supported king after 1204, see Jenny E. M. Benham, 'Philip Augustus and the Angevin Empire: The Scandinavian Connection', *Medieval Scandinavia*, 14 (2004), 37–50 (esp. p. 49); Bagge, *From Viking Stronghold*, p. 50.

[95] For an extremely comprehensive and detailed discussion of the changeable politics of the Irish Sea in this period, see Beuermann, 'Masters of the Narrow Sea'.

fealty was supported by their Birkibeinar rivals. Reginald of Man's agreement to travel to Norway, perhaps after the raid on Iona, would have satisfied the political objectives of the Norwegian king, but for those less interested in this aim it would have deprived them of the opportunity of plundering Man. The decision of these Baglar to attack Llanfaes may still have had something to do with Reginald's resentment of Llywelyn ab Iorwerth, but it may simply have been due to its position as an important trading centre on a rich island outside the authority of Norway or Man.

The second of the two explanations above is the simpler, although not necessarily the correct one. What can be said with certainty is that this episode in *O Oes Gwrtheyrn* adds considerably to the historical record in clarifying and extending our knowledge of this Norwegian expedition and its place in the politics of Northern Europe. It also illuminates Gwynedd's place in a Northern European world which involved Man and Norway as well as England and Ireland. This is apparent from another unique entry in the chronicle, which names the period of Manx mercenary activity on Anglesey in 1193 as 'haf y Gwyddyl' ('the summer of the Irish').[96] In this sense, the chronicle presents a somewhat different perspective to other Welsh chronicles, which are overwhelmingly associated with Deheubarth, south-western Wales. In this sense, we can compare *O Oes Gwrtheyrn* to the earlier *Vita Griffini filii Conani*, the biography of King Gruffudd ap Cynan of Gwynedd. Although this may have been written at St Davids, in its focus on Gwynedd it demonstrates the manifold connections of that kingdom with the Hiberno-Norse world better than most other sources.[97]

This to some extent answers the third question posed at the beginning of this discussion of Erlendr píkr, why the chronicler was so well-informed. Manx affairs were clearly important in the politics of Gwynedd in the period, and consequently Norwegian politics would have been of some significance. This wider context was also important to anyone who would understand the policy of rulers like King John in the Irish Sea world. The clear northern interest of the closely-related Llywelyn ab Iorwerth genealogies revolves around the figure of Gruffudd ap Cynan and the dynastic origins of Gwynedd, but *O Oes Gwrtheyrn* demonstrates also the contemporary significance of such Hiberno-

---

[96] McDonald, *Manx Kingship*, pp. 101–07; *HW*, II, 588.

[97] *Vita Griffini*; Emily Winkler, 'The Latin *Life of Gruffudd ap Cynan*, British Kingdoms and the Scandinavian Past', *Welsh History Review*, 28 (2017), 425–56; the latter argues, at p. 430, for a Venedotian authorship, and explores the role of Scandinavian history in this context.

Scandinavian links. Add to this the fact of Welsh mercenary service in Norway a decade previously and Gwynedd appears more integrated into this northern world than other Welsh sources suggest.

To bring this close discussion of the 1209 entry to an end, this part of the chronicle features a first and a last. The mention of Llanfaes is to my knowledge the first reference to it as a town, and therefore the earliest evidence for the economic significance of this settlement, which became, in the course of the thirteenth century, the most important commercial centre in Gwynedd. As for lasts, the fact that the shorter version of *Bǫglunga Sǫgur* describes this expedition as *víking* means that the attack on Llanfaes in 1209 can confidently be termed the last known viking raid on Wales, its surprisingly late date explicable in terms of the Manx/Norwegian political context briefly outlined above.[98] This short chronicle entry not only gives an insight into the place of Gwynedd in wider Northern European politics, it also marks the final end of the Viking Age in Wales, bringing the developments of four centuries to a close.

Sources

Having discussed a particular unique event in some detail, attention will finally be given to the uniqueness or otherwise of the other entries of *O Oes Gwrtheyrn* and their relationship to other sources. It is clear that the source for most of the entries in *O Oes Gwrtheyrn* is closely related to the common source for a number of Welsh chronicles up to the late twelfth century, a chronicle kept at St Davids.[99] More detailed discussion of these chronicles can be found elsewhere in this volume, and here I will restrict myself to commenting on the similarities and differences between them and *O Oes Gwrtheyrn*.

The events found in the chronicle up to the late tenth century are clearly derived from the chronicle kept at St Davids.[100] That this chronicle or a derivative of it was used as a source at Aberconwy's mother house of Strata Florida suggests a simple route of transmission. The most significant difference between *O Oes Gwrtheyrn* and other accounts which derive from the St Davids chronicle is the specific reference to Anarawd of Gwynedd's presence at the bat-

---

[98] *Bǫglunga sǫgur*, p. 119.

[99] The most comprehensive survey of these chronicles is still Hughes, *Celtic Britain*, pp. 67–85.

[100] For this chronicle to 954, see *Annales Cambriae*, ed. and trans. by Dumville, and *Brenhinoedd y Saeson*, ed. and trans. by Dumville.

tle of the Conwy in 881, a fact which has been assumed but is not explicitly stated in any other Welsh chronicles.[101] The sparse nature of the entries does not enable us to specify which version of the St Davids chronicle the source of *O Oes Gwrtheyrn* most resembled, but the mention of Anarawd indicates that this was not dependent on any surviving version.[102] The obituary of Caradog the monk in the twelfth century further underlines this point, as it relates to a figure associated with St Davids but who is not mentioned in any other Welsh chronicle.

There are far more unique events noted in the chronicle from the mid-twelfth century onwards. Many of these are discussed in more detail in the notes to the text, but they include: the taking of Aberteifi around 1138; the location of the battle at Tal Moelfre; the birth of Llywelyn ab Iorwerth; the name Gwern y Virogl; the naming of the events of 1193 as *Haf y Gwyddyl*; the battle of Coedanau; Llyweyn ab Iorwerth's capture of Mold; the viking attack on Llanfaes discussed above; Ranulf of Chester's attack on Degannwy and the barn of Creuddyn; and the capture of Penarlâg by Llywelyn ap Gruffudd.

The chronicler therefore had access both to sources now lost to us and to his own information. The frequency of relatively unique events from the mid-twelfth century may indicate that, having established a chronological framework from the fifth century onwards, the compiler of *O Oes Gwrtheyrn* was particularly concerned to note events which did not appear in other chronicles. He probably had access to a Welsh Cistercian chronicle by this point, perhaps from the abbey's mother house of Strata Florida, and it may be that he is noting events which did not already appear in this text, explaining why more entries concerning Gwynedd that were present in the parent chronicle were not included.[103]

But it was only in the first decade of the thirteenth century that the chronicle assumed the character of a full narrative, and this coincided with a period

---

[101] Charles-Edwards, *Wales and the Britons*, pp. 490–91; *Annales Cambriae*, ed. and trans. by Dumville, pp. 12–13; Brenhinoedd *y Saeson*, ed. and trans. by Dumville, pp. 30–31.

[102] It should be noted that, considering the Welsh Latin chronicles, there are a couple of instances where *O Oes Gwrtheyrn* is closer to the Cottonian chronicle (C) than to the Breviate (B). These are the fact that B fails to mention the burning of Degannwy in 811, and the fact that both *O Oes Gwrtheyrn* and C note events at Aberteifi in 1138. For the 811/12 entries, see *Annales Cambriae*, ed. and trans. by Dumville, pp. xi–xii.

[103] For suggestions regarding the process of sharing annals between monasteries, see Stephenson, 'The Chronicler at Cwm-Hir Abbey', pp. 34–35.

of increasing significance for the monastery and a time of conflict in Gwynedd. The previous decades had seen the establishment and gradual consolidation of the monastery, from an initial foundation at Rhedynog Felen in Arfon to a more permanent location, by 1192, at the mouth of the river Conwy.[104] The site may have been chosen because it lay between the lands controlled by rivals for the rule of Gwynedd, Dafydd, and Rhodri ab Owain, and indeed the dynasts involved in the foundation of the monastery and the conflict of the 1190s over Gwynedd are prominent in *O Oes Gwrtheyrn*.[105]

The clear victor of this conflict was Llywelyn, and the first decade of the thirteenth century saw him consolidate his power in Gwynedd, founded on his domination of Welsh rivals and his concord with King John. The reason for the breakdown in relations between John and Llywelyn is unclear, but it is around this time that *O Oes Gwrtheyrn* was compiled. These interesting times may have spurred an Aberconwy monk to historical writing, and it may be fitting that the 1211 campaign of King John and the consequent exchange of hostages was used as the initial chronological anchor at the end of the chronicle. The threat of conquest must have been apparent to the monks of Aberconwy, where John's army encamped.[106] On the other hand, this date might simply mark the stage at which the monastery was sufficiently well-established to begin making its own contribution to the chronicle writing undertaken at Welsh Cistercian houses. *O Oes Gwrtheyrn* forms part of the network of chronicle writing which is concerned primarily with secular affairs and which is an aspect of the involvement of the Cistercian order in contemporary Welsh politics, particularly with the princes of Gwynedd. Nevertheless, the likelihood that it was initially compiled in Welsh would make it a new departure in terms of vernacular historical writing. As this study has indicated, despite its brevity, *O Oes Gwrtheyrn* is a unique and significant piece of medieval historical writing.

---

[104] See above, n. 52.

[105] Gresham, 'The Aberconwy Charter', p. 316; Insley, 'Fact and Fiction'. For this conflict in general, see Charles Insley, 'The Wilderness Years of Llywelyn the Great', *Thirteenth Century England*, 9 (2001), 163–73; and *Acts of Welsh Rulers*, pp. 24–26.

[106] For the significance of the 1211 campaign, see R. Rees Davies, *Conquest, Coexistence, and Change: Wales 1063–1415* (Oxford: Oxford University Press, 1987), pp. 295–96.

Summary

To summarize the proposed development of the text, a chronicle related to *Annales Cambriae* and *Brut y Tywysogyon*, which contained material derived ultimately from a St Davids chronicle, became available at Aberconwy Abbey, coming probably from its mother house of Strata Florida (*S*). This was used to provide a chronological framework, consisting of brief notices of significant events combined with notices of events in Gwynedd and concerning the abbey's patrons. These notices prioritized details not found in the existing chronicle (*S*). This occurred after 1212, and it may be that *S* had reached the abbey fairly recently. The text created here (*G1*) from the combination of chronological notes from *S* and information from Gwynedd was the basic text of *O Oes Gwrtheyrn*, written in Welsh, and formed part of the same historiographical endeavour as the 'Llywelyn ab Iorwerth genealogies'. *G1* was updated during the late 1260s in a fairly superficial way to form *G2*. The updater added information concerning the death of Llywelyn, his wife Joan, his sons, Gruffudd and Dafydd, and some events from the early career of Llywelyn ap Gruffudd. This was in keeping with previous interest of the work in the dynasty of Gwynedd if not with the detail of the latest parts of the original work. *G2* is essentially the text of *O Oes Gwrtheyrn* as it survives in ABFG. At some later date, the series of general chronological calculations with which the work closes was updated to relate to the battle of Bryn Derwin rather than to 1211 to form *G3*, and this is *O Oes Gwrtheyrn* as it survives in CDE.

G3 was included in the now-lost Hengwrt 33 manuscript, along with other material from Aberconwy, and primarily circulated in north-east and mid-Wales.[107] *G2*'s circulation was more southern, and came to be included in manuscripts associated with Hywel Fychan and Hopcyn ap Tomos, such as *Llyfr Coch Hergest* (A) and the *Llyfr Teg* (B).

Chronology

Absolute dates are given only three times in the text, at 1055, 1133, and 1255, and this complicates its chronology. Even these present some difficulties, as in the disagreement between the date given as AD 1133 and the date of this annal in terms of the relative chronology of the work (see notes). The 1255 and 1055 chronological anchors both indicate that the starting date of the chronicle

---

[107] Guy, 'A Lost Medieval Manuscript'.

would be AD 400, but taking the date of the battles of Badon and Camlan from the Welsh Latin chronicles, 516 and 537, suggests a starting date of 388.[108] Given the considerable discrepancies within the text, it has been decided only to give dates for those events attested independently of Welsh chronicles, the texts generally referred to under the umbrella titles *Annales Cambriae* and *Brut y Tywysogyon*. These are given in the margin of the text. Dates have not been emended on historical grounds, although some have been emended from the reading of the base text (B) on textual critical grounds. It is hoped that the following chart (Table 1) will clarify the dating of the text, both in relative and in absolute terms. The first column gives shortened references to the entries, whilst the second gives the relative dating of the events to each other, with each number indicating the gap between its event and the event before. The third column gives the AD dates if the starting-point is taken to be AD 400, whilst the fourth gives the three absolute dates given in the body of the text. The fifth column gives dates when they are ascertainable from sources apart from Welsh chronicles, for example the *Anglo-Saxon Chronicle*, Irish annals, or Anglo-Norman histories, and these are the dates that appear alongside the translation of the text. The reason for giving only these dates rather than those from Welsh chronicles is to avoid the assumption that differences in dating between *O Oes Gwrtheyrn* and the dating consensus arrived at with regard to Welsh chronicles must indicate error on the part of this work. Other Welsh chronicles are, however, consulted in the notes to the text itself.

Editorial Method

MS Peniarth 32 (or B) is the basis for this edition, on the grounds that it is has fewer errors than A on the whole, and A's incomplete nature makes B the oldest near-complete copy. The text is a critical one insofar as B has been emended wherever errors are traceable with the help of variant readings from ACDEFGHIJ.[109] Whenever such errors occur, the corrected reading is given in square brackets, the correct reading often taken from A, with the original read-

---

[108] By comparison, the Harleian chronicle (or 'A-text' of *Annales Cambriae*) starts in AD 445. Egerton Phillimore, 'The *Annales Cambriae* and the Old-Welsh Genealogies from *Harleian MS.* 3859', *Y Cymmrodor*, 9 (1888), 141–83 (p. 152). Phillimore followed an earlier error in giving the first year as 444, but for the accuracy of 445, see Ben Guy, 'The Origins of the Compilation of Welsh Historical Texts in Harley 3859', *Studia Celtica*, 49 (2015), 21–56, at pp. 40–42.

[109] H and I are used occasionally, but their incompleteness restricts their use.

7. O OES GWRTHEYRN: A MEDIEVAL WELSH CHRONICLE

Table 7.1: The relative and absolute chronology of *O Oes Gwrtheyrn*

Event (summary)	Years since previous entry	AD date within text's relative chronology	AD date given in text	Date of event (if known independently)
Gwrtheyrn		400		
Badon	128	528		
Camlan	22	550		
† Maelgwn	10	560		
Arfderydd	25	585		
† Gwrgi & Peredur	7	592		
Caerleon	9	601		
Meigen	14	615		633
† Cadwaladr	48	663		
Offa	128	791		796
Degannwy	20	811		
† Merfyn	33	844		
† Rhodri	27	871		878
Conwy	3	874		
† Merfyn	17	891		
† Cadell	10	901		909
† Anarawd	6	907		916
Rome	18	925		
† Hywel	19	944		950
Carno	7	951		
Meibion Idwal	1	952		
† Owain	24	976		
Cnut	27	1003		1016
Machafwy	42	1045		1056
† Gruffudd	9	1054	1055	
Hastings	5	1059		1066
† Bleddyn	8	1067		
Mynydd Carn	6	1073		1081

Table continued on the following page

Table 7.1 *(cont.)*: The relative and absolute chronology of *O Oes Gwrtheyrn*

Event (summary)	Years since previous entry	AD date within text's relative chronology	AD date given in text	Date of event (if known independently)
† Rhys ap Tewdwr	13	1086		1093
† William Rufus	7	1093		1100
† Caradog	25	1118		
† Cadwallon	8	1126	1133	1132
Aberteifi	6	1132		
Tal Moelfre	20	1152		
Coed Ceiriog	8	1160		1165
Rhuddlan	2	1162		1167
† Owain	5	1167		1170
Llywelyn's birth	2.5	1169.5		
Gwern Firogl	14	1183.5		
Hâf y Gwyddyl	7	1190.5		
Castell Paen	5	1195.5		1198
† Gruffudd ap Cynan	2	1197.5		
† Dafydd ab Owain	1	1198.5		1203
Interdict	5	1203.5		1208
Scotland	1	1204.5		1209
Degannwy	1	1205.5		1210
Aber	1	1206.5		1211
Gruffudd Released	5	1211.5		
† John	3	1214.5		1216
† Siwan	20	1234.5		1237
† Llywelyn	3	1237.5		1240
† Gruffudd	4	1241.5		1244
† Dafydd	2	1243.5		1246
Derwin	11	1254.5	1255	1255
Diserth	10	1264.5		1263
Penarlâg	1	1265.5		

ing of B as well as the variant readings of ACDEFGHIJ given in the apparatus. The absence of a reference to a particular manuscript where others are given is indicative of the lack of an alternative reading from that manuscript. Some additions are made to the text when there is sufficient support to do so from ACDEFGHIJ, and these cases appear in square brackets with no reading from B given in the apparatus. Three dots (...) represent lost text, largely due to tears in the case of G.

Differences of orthography and small differences of phrasing in the other manuscripts are generally ignored, apart from in the case of some proper nouns. Obvious errors are emended (e.g. ymla6d = ymlada6d) and abbreviations extended (Arth' = Arthur) silently. Any significant divergences, such as additional events, words, and sentences, different chronological information, or sentences missing from any of the other manuscripts are noted in the apparatus. Some dates are given with the translation, discussed above. Historical aspects of the chronicle are discussed in the endnotes. Punctuation and capitalization have been changed to conform with modern conventions.

EDITION

§ 1 [O]¹¹⁰ oes G6rtheyrn G6rtheneu hyt weith 6adon ydd ymlada6d Arthur¹¹¹ a'r Sayson, ac y gor6u Arthur,¹¹² C. xx. viij. blyned.

§ 2 O 6eith 6adon hyd Gamlan, [xxij].¹¹³ blyned.

§ 3 O Gamlan hyd 6ar6 Maelgon, x.¹¹⁴ blyned.

§ 4 O 6ar6 Maelgon hyd y gweith Arderyd, [xxv].¹¹⁵ blyned.¹¹⁶

§ 5 O'r g6eith Arderyd hyd pan las G6rgi a Phared6r, vij. blyned.¹¹⁷

§ 6 O'r pan las G6rgi¹¹⁸ hyd 6eith Kaer Lleon, ix. blyned.

§ 7 O 6eith Kaer Lleon hyd 6eith 6eigen, xiiij.¹¹⁹

§ 8 O 6eith 6eigen hyd ual yd aeth Kad6aladr 6endigeid R6ein, [xlviij].¹²⁰ blyned.

§ 9 O Kad6aladr 6endigeid hyd a'r Opha 6renhin, C. xxviij. blyned.

§ 10 O Opha 6renhin hyd pan losges tan o nef Dygan6y yn oes Y6ein ab Mered6d, xx. blened.

§ 11 Or pan losges¹²¹ Dygan6y hyd 6ar6 Mer6yn 6rych, xxxiij. blyned.

---

¹¹⁰ Initial in B wrongly written in as J.

¹¹¹ *ae hyneif* A.

¹¹² *ae hyneif* A.

¹¹³ *lxij* B; *d6y vlyned ar hugeint* A; *ij* C; *xxii* D; *xxij* E; *22* F; *xx–22* G; *dwy vlynedd ar hugain* H; *dwy flyned arugeint* J.

¹¹⁴ *dwy* H.

¹¹⁵ *l. xv* B; *xxv* C; *pum mlynedd ar hugain* D; *pum mlynedd ar ugain* E; *xxv–25* G; *pumlynedd ar hugain* H; *pym mlyned arugeint* J.

¹¹⁶ *Gwaith Arderyd de quo in Confess Merdhin a Gwendhyd 25* F.

¹¹⁷ *O var6 maelg6n hyt weith arderyd pan las g6rgi a phared6r; seith mlyned* A.

¹¹⁸ *a pharedur* ADEFJ.

¹¹⁹ *iiij* C.

¹²⁰ *xxviij* B; *wyth mlyned a deugeint* A; *iid* C, with *d* probably a mistake for *l*; *wyth mlynedd a deugaint* D; *xlviij* E; *48* F; *xlviij–48* G; *saith mlynedd a deugain* H; *wyth mlyned a deugeint* J.

¹²¹ *pan losges y dywededic dan degann6y* A.

7. *O OES GWRTHEYRN*: A MEDIEVAL WELSH CHRONICLE

§ 12 O ỽarỽ Merỽyn hyd pan las Rodri y ỽab, xxvij.

§ 13 O'r Rodri hyd pan dialỽys Anar[a]ỽdr y ỽab, iij. blyned.[122]

§ 14 O ỽeith Konoy yny las Merỽyn ỽab Rodri,[123] xvij blyned.

§ 15 O ỽarỽ Merỽyn hyd ỽarỽ Kadell ap Rodri, x blyned.[124]

§ 16 O ỽarỽ Kadell hyd ỽarỽ Anaraỽd, vj. blyned.

§ 17 O Anaraỽd hyd pan aeth Hyỽel ab Kadell Rỽein, xviij. blyned.

§ 18 O'r pan aeth Hỽel Rỽein yny ỽu ỽarỽ, xix. blyned.

§ 19 O ỽarỽ Hyỽel hyd ỽeith Karno, vij. blyned.

§ 20 O ỽeith Karno hyd ỽeith ỽeibon Idỽal, i. blỽydyn.[125]

§ 21 O ỽeith meibon Idỽal hyd ỽarỽ Yỽein ab Hyỽel Dda, xxiiij. blyned.

§ 22 O ỽarỽ Yỽein yny ỽledychỽys Cỽnt ỽab Yỽein,[126] xxvij. blyned.

§ 23 O Gỽnỽt urenhin hyd ỽachaỽy yn y orỽu Grufut ab Llywelyn a y llas esgob y Sayson, xxxxij. blynet.

§ 24 O ỽeith Machaỽy hyd pan las Grufut ab Llywelyn,[127] ix blynet.[128]

---

[122] *O rodri yny dialaỽd anaraỽt y vab ef; teir blyned* A; *o hynny hyd pann ddialwyd rrodri y mab iij* C; *O rodri hyd pan ddialodd Rodri i vab ef. iii. blynedd* D; *O Rodri oni ddialws rrodri i vab ef iij blynedd* E; *Ony dhialawdh Anarawt 13* F; *O rodri oni ddialodd anarawd i vab xiij–13* G; *O hynny oni ddialwyd Rodri tair blynedd* H; *O Rodri, yny dialws Rodri y vap ef teir blyned* J.

[123] *merỽyn y ỽab rodri* B; *meruyn vab Rodri* ADEFGHJ; *o hynny hyd waith konwy pan las mervryn ap rrodri* C.

[124] *wyth mlynedd* H.

[125] *iiij* C, presumably a misreading of *un*.

[126] *cnut vab owein* A; *kwnt ap ywain* C; *kwnt ap Iaen* D; *cwnt mab owain* E; *Canutus vrenin* F; *Cunt frenin* G; *gwnt i vab* H; *Cwnt map ywein* J.

[127] Only B and F provide a patronymic for Gruffudd: in F Gruffudd's name is glossed with *ap lhen ap Sitsylht*.

[128] CDE do not give the amount of years here, whereas H gives *naw kant mlynedd*. This perhaps indicates an obvious mistake in the exemplar of H, which was then excised by the scribe of Hengwrt 33, the ultimate source of CDE.

§ 25 O'r pan deuth Crist yg cana6t[129] hyt y 6loythin honno,[130] xv. a [deugeint] a mil mlynet.[131]

§ 26 O'r pan las Grufut yny doeth Gwilym 6astard y'r ynys hon, v. mlynet. Ac. xxi. mlynet y g6ladych6ys.[132]

§ 27 O Wilym 6astard yny las Bledyn uab Kynuyn, viij.[133] mlynet.

§ 28 O Uledyn hyd weith Mynyt Carn, vj. mlynet. Odyna Grufut ab Kynan a Rys ab Tewd6r a or6uant yna ar Tryhaearnn ab Karada6c.[134]

§ 29 O 6eith Mynyt Carn yny las Rys ab Tewd6r, xiij. mlynet.

§ 30 O'r pan las Rys yny las Gwilym 6renhin coch, vij. mlynet. Xiij. Y gwledych6ys.[135]

§ 31 O'r brenhin coch hyd 6ar6 Karada6c[136] uynach, [xxv].[137] mlynet.

§ 32 O Garada6c uynach hyd uar6 Kadwalla6n uab Grufut, ac y bu uar6 Maredut ab Bledyn, viij. mlenet.

§ 33 O'r pan doeth Crist yg cana6t hyt y 6loythyn [honno, teir blyned ar dec ar hugeint a chant a mil].[138]

---

[129] This should perhaps be emended to *cna6t*. An epenthetic vowel in this initial position is rare in Middle Welsh, and otherwise only recorded once for *cna6t*. It is, however, used consistently in B, below at § 33 and § 62. D. Simon Evans, *A Grammar of Middle Welsh*, Mediaeval and Modern Welsh Series, Supplementary Volume (Dublin: Dublin Institute for Advanced Studies, 1964), p. 13, § 16 (b).

[130] *Or pan ddaeth krist ynghnawd hyd y flwyddyn ir aeth kydwaladr Vendigaid i ryfain* H.

[131] *xv a deucant a mil* B; *pymtheng mlynedd a deugeint a mil* A; *lv a mil* C; *pymthengmlynedd a deugain a mil* D; *M. lv* E; *pymthec mlyned a deugeint a mil* J. FG have no corresponding entry.

[132] *Or pan las gr ap lln hyd yr amsser i daeth wiliam Basdart ir ynys honn un flwyddyn ar hugain i gwledychodd wiliam Basdart* H; G does not give the length of William's reign.

[133] *viij* B; *seith* A; *vj* C; *saith* D; *7* F; *vij–7* G; *ssaith* H; *seith* J. Missing in E, which gives *O wilym vastart hyd waith mynydd karn. vj.* For reasons for accepting B's reading of eight, rather than ADFGHJ's seven, see the endnote to § 24.

[134] C does not describe Mynydd Carn.

[135] *Or pan laddwyd wiliam goch a thair blynedd ar ddeg i gwledychodd y brenin* H. H ends here.

[136] *kriadoc* C.

[137] *xxij* B; *pum mlyned ar hugeint* A; *xxv* C; *pumlynedd ar hugain* D; *xxv* E; *25* F; *xxv* G; *pum mlyned ar ugeint* J.

[138] *hon. M. CCCC. xvj. mlynet* B, written in a later hand of 1416. Text given here from A.

7. O OES GWRTHEYRN: A MEDIEVAL WELSH CHRONICLE

§ 34 O dechreu byd hyd pan las Kadwalla6n, vj. mil. CCC. xxxij. mlynet.[139] A'r rif h6nn6 diameu y6.

§ 35 O'r pan las Kadwalla6n yny dorres Y6ein a Chadwaladyr[140] Aber Tei6i, vj. mlynet.

§ 36 O'r pan dorred Aber Tei6i yny las y Frennig yn Tal Moel6re, xx. mlyned.

§ 37 O'r ymalat yNhal Moel6re yny dall6yd[141] y g6ystlon yg Choed [Keirya6c],[142] viij. mlynet.

§ 38 O Ghoed [Keirya6c] yny dorres Y6ein a Chadwaladyr Rudlan, ii. 6lynet.

§ 39 O'r pan dorred Ru[d]lan yny 6u 6ar6 Y6ein, v. mlenet, ac o 6yl Clemens hyd nos ynyht a bl6ythyn y bu [6yu][143] Kadwaladyr gwydy Y6ein.

§ 40 O'r pan 6u 6ar6 Y6ein yny anet Llywelyn ab Iorwerth, d6y ulynet a hanner.

§ 41 O'r pan anet Llywelyn ab Iorwerth yny las Y6ein ab Mada6c yn ymlat Gwern 6irogyl, xiiij mlyned.

§ 42 O'r pan las Y6ein hyd haf y G6ydyl, vij. mlyned, a'r 6l6ydyn rac 6yneb y bu 6r6ydyr y Choedaneu.[144] Y trydet 6l6ydyn y bu 6ar6 Rodri ab Y6ein.

§ 43 O haf y G6ydyl hyd Castell Paen, v. mlynet.[145] Y gayaf rac 6yneb y torres Llywelyn yr 6ydgruc.[146]

---

xxxiij a C a mil C; *tair blynedd ar ddeg ar hugain a chant a mil* D; *M. C xxxiij* E; *teyr blyned ar dec ar ugeynt a chant a mil* J. In F, the number *1133* is simply written in the margin next to the notice of Cadwallon's death. Not present in G.

[139] *xij a CCC a vi mil* C; *deuddengmlynedd ar ugaint a thrychant a chwemil* D; *deuddec blwyddyn ar ugaint a thry chant a chwemil* E; *6332* G; *deudec mlyned ar ugein a thrychant a chwe mil* J. Not present in AF.

[140] *ywain ap kydwaladr* C; *Owain ap kadwaladr* D; *ywain ap kadwaladr* E; *Owain a Chadwaladr* AFGJ.

[141] *dalywyt* A; *ddaliwyd* C; *ddallwyd* D; *ddaliwyd* E; *dhaliwyd* F; *ddallwyd* G; *dallwyt* J.

[142] *clefyta6c* B; *keirya6c* A; *keirioc* C; *keiriawg* D; *keiriawc* E; *Ceirioc* F; *keirioc* G; *Ceyriawc* J.

[143] *6uy* B; *var6* A; *vyw* C; *vyw* D; *vyw* E; *vyw* G; *vuw* J.

[144] *coettaneu* A; *koectanau* C; *koet taneu* D; *koetane* E; *Coetaveu* F; *koed aneu* G; *Coetauen* J.

[145] C does not give the amount of years.

[146] The information about Llywelyn and yr Wyddgrug is missing in G.

§ 44 D6y ulyned g6edy Castell Paen y bu uar6 Grufut ab Kynan.

§ 45 Y 6loythyn g6edy mar6 Grufut y bu uar6 Dauyd ab Y6ein.

§ 46 O'r pan 6u uar6 Dauid uab Ywein yny wahard6yt effereneu [dros Loegyr a Chymry][147] o [annundeb][148] Ieuan urenhin ac Ysteuyn archesgob Keint, v. mlyned. A'r [g6ahard h6nn6 a vu][149] seith mlyned dros Loygyr a phum mlened dros Gymry.

§ 47 Yn y 6loythyn nessaf yr 6n y gwahard6yt yr yffereneu yt aeth [Llywelyn vab Iorwerth a Hywel uab Gruffud][150] y gyd a Ieuan urenhin Lloegyr hyd ymBrydyn y darest6c brenhin Prydyn[151] y Ieuan urenhin Lloygyr. Nos 6yl Sim6nd a Iuda[152] yn y 6loythyn honno y doeth ystiward llys brenhin Llychlyn, Herlant Pic[153] y en6, a chweych her6log canta6 hyd yn Llanuaes y yspeila6[154] y tref a'e llosgi, a e llas Herlant Pic[155] a'e oreugw[y]r.[156]

§ 48 Ac yn y 6loythin rac 6yneb y aeth Ieuan urenhin y Ywerthon, ac y doeth R6nd6lf iaryll Caer [y] Dycan6y yn erbyn Ieuan urenhin,[157] ac a

---

[147] *y lloegyr* B; *dros loegyr a chymry* ACDEFGJ.

[148] *anuunideb* B; *annuundeb* A; *anghytundeb* C; *Anundeb* D; *anundeb* E; *anuudeb* G; *anuhundeb* J. Missing in F.

[149] *gwaharda6n* B; *g6ahard h6nn6 a vu* A; *gwahardd hwnnw a vu* C; *gwardd hwnnw a vu* D; *gwahardd hwnw afu* E; *gwahard hwnnw a fu* J. Missing in FG.

[150] *llywelyn ab iorwerht a hywel y uab* B; *llywelyn vab Iorwerth a howel vab gruffud* A; *lln ap jer' ap ho ap gruff* C; *llywelyn ap Ior' a hywel ap gruff* D; *lln ap Ior' a hol ap Gruff* E; *Lhywelyn ap Jorwerth a Howel ap Grufyth* F; *lly ap Io' ap ho ap g'* G; *llywelyn map Iorwerth, a Hywel map Gruffut* J.

[151] *hyt yn ruuein y darost6ng y brenhin* A; *i brydain i ddarostwng brenin prydain* C; *i ddarystwng brenin prydyn* D; *hyd ymprydyn i ddarostwng brenhin prydyn* E; *hyd ym Prydyn y dharestwng brenhin Prydyn* F; *hyd ymhrydyn i ddarostwng brenin prydyn* G; *hyt ym Prydyn y darystng brenhyn Prydyn* J.

[152] ABG date the raid to the feast of Saints Simon and Jude, missing in CDEJ. F does so in a marginal note.

[153] *Herlaut Pic* B; *heralt pic* A; *herlang pic* C; *herlaut pic* D; *herlant pic* E; *Herlanc Pik neu Herald Pie* F; *herlan pik* G; *Herlaut Pic* J.

[154] I begins here, with the slightly confused rendering of *y dref ai llosci ag yna y penaethaid pen ai wyr*.

[155] *Herlaut Pic* B; *heralt pic* A; *ef* C; *herlond pic* D; *herlant pic* E; *herlan pik* G; *Herlaut Pic* J.

[156] *oreugwr* B; *oreugwyr* ACDEFJ; *penaethaid pen ai wyr* I.

[157] A ends here.

[gynatlassei]¹⁵⁸ ac ef yno ac a gauas Dycan6y gwedy y thorri o Lywelyn rac Ieuan urenhin, ac y cadarnha6ys R6nd6lf Dycan6y o wyt yscuba6r y Creudyn.¹⁵⁹

§ 49 Y 6loythyn rac 6yneb y doeth Ieuan urenhin a dygyuor Freinc a Lloygyr a Prydyn hyd yn Aber, ac y dellyg6ys y Brabanseid¹⁶⁰ y losgi Bangor. Ac yna [y daliassant]¹⁶¹ Robert esgob ac y dugant ygharchar, hyd pan y rydha6ys y brenhin yr esgob. Ac yna y kymodes Llywelyn a'r brenhin, ac e rodes Gruffut y uab ygwystyl, a phe[d]war gwystyl arr igeint o ueibyon gwyrda y am hyny,¹⁶² ac yd ymhoeles¹⁶³ y brenhin dracheuyn y Loygyr.

§ 50 Y 6loythyn rac 6yneb, nos Sad6rn Sulgwyn,¹⁶⁴ y bu 6ar6 Maredut ab Kynan.

§ 51 Pum mlynet y bu Grufut ab Llewelyn ygharchar Ieuan urenhin, ac yna o nerth Du6 a chygor Ysteuyn, archescob Keint, y ryda6yt.

§ 52 Ympen y teir blynet gwedy rythau Grufut uab Llewelyn y bu 6ar6 Ieuan urenhin. Ac y bu 6ar6 Hywel ap Grufut.¹⁶⁵

§ 53 O'r pan 6u 6ar6 Ieuan brenhin yn[y] 6u uar6 yr argl6ytes, g6reic Llewelyn ab Iorwerth, xx. mlynet.

---

¹⁵⁸ *ymlatyssei* B; *gynatlassodd* FJ, missing in others (see below).

¹⁵⁹ *doeth Randwlff iarll kaer digannwy yni erbyn ac i kavas ddygannwy ai lu ac ai kydarnhaodd o waith ysgubor y kreuddun* C; *doeth randwlf iarll kaer dygannwy yn i erbyn ag y kavas Degannwy Gwedy i thorri o lywelyn yna y kadarnhaodd Randwlf dygannwy o wyth ysgubawr y kreuddyn* DE; *doeth Randulph Jarll Caer y dhygannwy yn erbyn Jevan vrenin a gynatlassodh ac ef ac y Cavas Dygannwy gwedi ey thorri o Lewelyn rac Jevan vrenin. Ac y Cadarnhaodh Randulph Dhygannwy o wydh yscubor y Creudhyn* F; *doeth rannddwlff Ia...yn erbyn Ien frenin ac...ac y kafas dygannwy wedi...ean ac y kadarnhaodd ranndwlff...yskuborue y kreuddyn* G; *doeth randwlff jarll kaer deganw yn i erbyn i gadarnhau* I; *doeth Randulf iarll Caer Dyganwy yn erbyn Ieuan frenhyn a gynatlassodd ag ef eno, ac y cafas Dyganwy gwedy y thorry o Lywelyn [rac Ieuan frenhyn] ac y cadarnhaus Randwlf Dyganwy o wyth [neu wyd] ysgubaur y Creudyn* J.

¹⁶⁰ *ire beuseth* C; *vrebansieid* D; *vrebansiaid* E; *Brabansieid* F; *frebanssiaut* G; *vrebansieith* J; missing in I.

¹⁶¹ *yd adalasant* B; *y daliwyd saint* C; *y daliassant* DEFGIJ.

¹⁶² *am hynny* C; *am ben hynny* D; *y am hynny* E; *am hynny* J.

¹⁶³ *ymchwelws* CEJ; *yd dymchwelodd* DFI; *y dychwelodd* G.

¹⁶⁴ The dating to the Saturday of Whitsun is unique to B.

¹⁶⁵ *lln ap Gruff* E; Hywel ap Gruffudd's obituary is missing from DI.

§ 54 O'r pan ƀu ƀarƀ yr arglƀytes yny ƀu ƀarƀ Llywelyn uab Iorwerth, teir blynet.[166]

§ 55 O'r pan ƀu ƀarƀ Llywelyn ab Iorwerth yny ƀu ƀarƀ Grufut y uab, iiij mlynet.

§ 56 O'r pan ƀu ƀarƀ Grufut yny ƀu ƀarƀ Dauyd ab Llewelyn, ij. ƀlynet.

§ 57 O'r pan ƀu ƀarƀ Dauid ab Llywelyn hyd y ƀrƀydyr yNerwin yrrƀg Ywein a Llewelyn ab Grufut, xj. mlynet.

§ 58 O'r ƀrƀydyr yNerwin yny las y Freinc yn y Kymereu, ij. ƀlynet.

§ 59 O'r ƀrƀydyr yN[erwin][167] yny tored castell y Diserth, x. mlynet. Yn yr ƀn kynhayaf y caffad Dycanƀy.

§ 60 O gael Dycanƀy hyd gael Penard Dylaƀc,[168] blƀythyn.[169]

§ 61 O dechreu byt yny ƀu y ƀrƀydyr [yNerwin],[170] [chwe mil. CCCC. liiii].[171]

§ 62 O'r pan deuth Crist yg canaƀt hyd y ƀrƀydyr yNerwin, mil. cc. l. v.[172]

§ 63 O'r pan doeth Kymry gyntaf y ynys Prydyn yny doeth Ieuan urenhin Aber, ac yny aeth Grufut ab Llewelin ygwystyl, ij. m. cccc. xvj.

§ 64 O'r pan doeth cred gyntaf y Gymry y gan Eletirius pap yn oes Lles ab Coel brenhin Kymry, hyd y ƀloytyn...

---

[166] ...4 G.

[167] *y kymereu* B; *derwyn* CDEFGIJ.

[168] *pennarddylak* C; *Pennardd y lawg* D; *peneilardalauc* E; *Penardhlac* F; *penardlyawc* G; *ffenarddylac* I; *Penardaluauc* J.

[169] From Derwin until this point, G reads: *Or frwydr yny derwyn oni ddistrowiwyd kastell y ddisserth x. O bann gad tygannwy oni gad penardlyawc- 1*. F finishes here.

[170] *yn herwyn* C; *yn y derwyn* D; *yn derwyn* E; *y derwin* G; *yn Derwyn* J.

[171] *chwe. mil CCCC lxxiiii* B; *liiij a CCCC a vi mil* C; *pedair blynedd ar ddeg a deugaint a phedwarkant a chwemil* D; *pedair blynedd ar ddec a deuaint a CCCC a chwemil* E; *vj mil ccccliiij* G; *pedayr blynedd ar ddeg a deugain a phedwar kant a chwemil* I; *pedeir blyned ar dec a deugeint a phedwarcant a chwe myl* J.

[172] *pymthec mlynedd a ddeugaint a ddeukant a mil* E.

The text of B breaks off at this point. This final section is also damaged in G (MS Peniarth 212), B's closest relative to continue to this point. The remaining part of G is now given, with any gaps filled with readings from J given in square brackets:

…pan aeth Gruffudd yngwystl, 1040 – mil xl.

§ 65 O bann ddoeth y Saesson gyntaf i ynys Brydain oni aeth Gruffudd yngwystl, 552 – ccccclij.

§ 66 O bann ddoeth Normynn [gyntaf y ynys] Brydain oni aeth Gruffudd yn [gwystel, dwy flynedd ar bymthec a deugein a chant].

The CDEI branch date this closing section with reference to the battle of Derwin rather than to Gruffudd's taking as a hostage. The text of D is given here from entry 63, as it is fuller than C, which omits and shortens.

§ 63A O'r pan ddoeth Kymry gyntaf i'r ynys hon hyd y vrwydr yn y Derwyn, saith mlynedd a thrigaint CCCC a dwyvil.[173]

§ 64A O'r pan ddoeth kred Gymry y gan Eleutherius bab yn amser Lles ap Koel hyd y vrwydyr yn y Derwyn, naw mlynedd a phedwarugain a mil.[174]

§ 65A O'r pan ddoeth Saeson i ynys Prydain hyd vrwydr yn y Derwyn, un blwyddyn a chwe chant.

§ 66A O'r pan ddoeth Norddmyn gyntaf yr ynys hon hyd brwydyr y Derwyn, chweblynedd a chwechant.[175]

J dates to both the battle of Derwin and Gruffudd ap Llywelyn's captivity, making it clear that the exemplars used by J belonged to both branches of the textual tradition. It agrees in all instances with either G or D, though it includes the portions now damaged or missing in G, given in square brackets.

---

[173] *lxvj a CCC a ii mil* C; *lxj CCCC a dwy vil* E; *wyth mlynedd ar hugain a phedwarkant a dwyvil* I; *seith mlyned a thrugeint a phedwar cant a dwy fil* J. These readings suggest D to be correct overall, with I's *mmccccxxviii* derived from a misreading of *mmcccclxvii*.

[174] *xj a C* C; *M lxxxix* E; *naw mlynedd a phedwar ygain a mil* I; The *xj* of C here is almost certainly a misreading of *mil*. Lles/Lucius was thought to have died in 156, so 1100 years would give 1256.

[175] *un flwyddyn a chwechant a…* E; *chwe blynedd a vi c* I.

TRANSLATION

The dates alongside the text are those ascertainable from other sources, not those given in the chronicle itself.

§ 1 From the time of Gwrtheyrn Gwrthenau until the battle of Badon where Arthur fought with the English and Arthur prevailed, one hundred and twenty-eight years.

§ 2 From the battle of Badon until Camlan, twenty-two years.

§ 3 From Camlan until the death of Maelgwn, ten years.

§ 4 From the death of Maelgwn until the battle of Arfderydd, twenty-five years.

§ 5 From the battle of Arfderydd until Gwrgi and Peredur were killed, seven years.

§ 6 From when Gwrgi was killed until the battle of Caer Lleon (Chester), nine years.

§ 7 (633) From the battle of Caer Lleon until the battle of Meigen, fourteen [years].

§ 8 From the battle of Meigen until Cadwaladr Fendigaid went to Rome, forty-eight years.

§ 9 (796) From Cadwaladr Fendigaid until King Offa, one hundred and twenty-eight years.

§ 10 From King Offa until fire from heaven burned Degannwy in the time of Owain ap Maredudd, twenty years.

§ 11 From when Degannwy was burned until the death of Merfyn Frych, thirty-three years.

§ 12 (878) From the death of Merfyn until his son Rhodri was killed, twenty-seven [years].

§ 13 From Rhodri until Anarawd his son avenged him, three years.

§ 14 From the battle of Conwy until Merfyn ap Rhodri was killed, seventeen years.

§ 15 (909) From the death of Merfyn until the death of Cadell ap Rhodri, ten years.

§ 16 (916) From the death of Cadell until the death of Anarawd, six years.

§ 17 From Anarawd until Hywel ap Cadell went to Rome, eighteen years.

§ 18 (950) From when Hywel went to Rome until his death, nineteen years.

§ 19 From the death of Hywel until the battle of Carno, seven years.

§ 20 From the battle of Carno until the battle of the sons of Idwal, one year.

§ 21 From the battle of the sons of Idwal until the death of Owain ap Hywel Dda, twenty-four years.

§ 22 (1016) From the death of Owain until Cnut son of Swein reigned, twenty-seven years.

§ 23 From King Cnut until Machafwy when Gruffudd ap Llywelyn prevailed and the Bishop of the English was killed, forty-two years.

§ 24 From the battle of Machafwy until Gruffudd ap Llywelyn was killed, nine years.

§ 25 From when Christ became flesh until that year, one thousand and fifty-five years.

§ 26 (1066) From when Gruffudd was killed until William the Bastard came to this island, five years. And he reigned twenty-one years.

§ 27 From William the Bastard until Bleddyn ap Cynfyn was killed, eight years.

§ 28 (1081) From Bleddyn until the battle of Mynydd Carn, six years. There Gruffudd ap Cynan and Rhys ap Tewdwr prevailed over Trahaearn ap Caradog.

§ 29 (1093) From the battle of Mynydd Carn until Rhys ap Tewdwr was killed, thirteen years.

§ 30 (1100) From when Rhys was killed until William the Red King (William Rufus) was killed, seven years. He reigned thirteen years.

§ 31 From the Red King until the death of Caradog the monk, twenty-five years.

§ 32 (1132) From Caradog the monk until the death of Cadwallon son of Gruffudd, and Maredudd ap Bleddyn died, eight years.

§ 33 From when Christ became flesh until that year, one thousand one hundred and thirty-three years.

§ 34 From the beginning of the world until Cadwallon was killed, six thousand three hundred and thirty-two years. And that number is without doubt.

§ 35 From when Cadwallon was killed until Owain and Cadwaladr destroyed Aberteifi, six years.

§ 36 From when Aberteifi was destroyed until the French were killed in Tal Moelfre, twenty years.

§ 37 (1165) From the fighting in Tal Moelfre until the hostages were blinded in Coed Ceiriog, eight years.

§ 38 (1167) From Coed Ceiriog until Owain and Cadwaladr destroyed Rhuddlan, two years.

§ 39 (1170) From when Rhuddlan was destroyed until the death of Owain, five years, and Cadwaladr lived after Owain from the Feast of St Clement to Shrove Tuesday and a year.

§ 40 From the death of Owain until the birth of Llywelyn ab Iorwerth, two and a half years.

§ 41 From the birth of Llywelyn ab Iorwerth until Owain ap Madog was killed in the fight at Gwern Virogl, fourteen years.

§ 42 From when Owain was killed until the summer of the Irish, seven years, and the next year was the battle of the Coedanau. In the third year Rhodri ab Owain died.

§ 43 (1198) From the summer of the Irish to Castell Paen (Painscastle), five years. The next winter Llywelyn destroyed yr Wyddgrug (Mold).

§ 44 (1203) Two years after Castell Paen died Gruffudd ap Cynan.

§ 45 The year after Gruffudd's death died Dafydd ab Owain.

§ 46 (1208) From when Dafydd ab Owain died until masses were suspended in England and Wales because of the disunity of King John and Stephen, Archbishop of Canterbury, five years. And that interdict was seven years over England and five years over Wales.

§ 47 (1209) In the year after the one when the masses were suspended, Llywelyn ab Iorwerth and Hywel ap Gruffudd went with King John of England to Scotland to subject the King of Scotland to King John of England. On the eve of St Simon and St Jude in that year, the steward of the court of the King of Norway, named Herlant Pic, came with six raiding ships to Llanfaes to despoil the town and burn it, and Herlant Pic was killed along with his best men.

§ 48 (1210) And in the next year King John went to Ireland and Ranulf, Earl of Chester, came to Degannwy to meet King John, and he conferred with him there and got Degannwy after its breaking by Llywelyn against King John, and Ranulf fortified Degannwy with the timber of the barn of Creuddyn.

§ 49 (1211) In the next year, King John came and mustered France and England and Scotland as far as Aber, and released the Brabançons to burn Bangor. And there they captured Bishop Robert and imprisoned him until the King released the Bishop. And then Llywelyn made peace with the King and he gave his son Gruffudd as a hostage for that reconciliation along with twenty-four hostages, the sons of noblemen, and then the King returned to England.

§ 50 The next year on the Saturday of Whitsun died Maredudd ap Cynan.

§ 51 Gruffudd ap Llywelyn was five years in King John's prison and then through the strength of God and the counsel of Stephen, Archbishop of Canterbury, he was released.

§ 52 (1216) Three years after Gruffudd ap Llywelyn's release, King John died. And Hywel ap Gruffudd died.

§ 53 (1237) From the death of King John until the death of the lady, the wife of Llywelyn ab Iorwerth, twenty years.

§ 54 (1240) From the death of the lady until the death of Llywelyn ab Iorwerth, three years.

§ 55 (1244) From the death of Llywelyn ab Iorwerth until the death of his son Gruffudd, four years.

§ 56 (1246) From the death of Gruffudd until the death of Dafydd ap Llywelyn, two years.

§ 57 (1255) From the death of Dafydd ap Llywelyn until the battle in Derwin between Owain and Llywelyn ap Gruffudd, eleven years.

§ 58 From the battle in Derwin until the French were killed in the Cymerau, two years.

§ 59 (1263) From the battle in Derwin until Diserth Castle was destroyed, ten years. Degannwy was captured in the same harvest.

§ 60 From the taking of Degannwy until the taking of Penarlâg (Hawarden), a year.

§ 61 From the beginning of the world until the battle in Derwin, six thousand four hundred and fifty-four years.

§ 62 From when Christ was made flesh until the battle in Derwin, one thousand two hundred and fifty-five years.

§ 63 From when the Welsh first came to the island of Britain until King John came to Aber and until Gruffudd ap Llywelyn was taken hostage, two thousand five hundred and sixteen years.

§ 64 From when belief in Christ came first to the Welsh from Pope Eleutherius in the time of Lles ap Coel, King of the Welsh, until the year…

G

…when Gruffudd was taken hostage, one thousand and forty years.

§ 65 From when the English first came to the island of Britain until Gruffudd was taken hostage, five hundred and fifty-two years.

§ 66 From when Normans [first came to the island of] Britain until Gruffudd was taken [hostage, one hundred and fifty-seven years].

D

§ 63A From when the Welsh first came to this island until the battle in Derwin, two thousand four hundred and sixty-seven years.

§ 64A From when belief in Christ came to Wales from Pope Eleutherius in the time of Lles ap Coel until the battle in Derwin, one thousand and eighty-nine years.

§ 65A From when the English came to the island of Britain until the battle in Derwin, six hundred and one years.

§ 66A From when Normans first came to this island until the battle in Derwin, six hundred and six years.

Notes

§ 8. **Kad6aladr 6endigeid** The dating of Cadwaladr's death to 664 may show the influence of *Historia Brittonum*, but it is likelier to be thanks to *O Oes Gwrtheyrn*'s misdating of the battle of Meigen to 615. If the correct date of Meigen (itself misdated in *Annales Cambriae* A), 633, is used, the date for Cadwaladr's death is 681, approximately the same as given in other Welsh chronicles, for which see *Annales Cambriae*, ed. and trans. by Dumville; *Brenhinoedd y Saeson*, ed. and trans. by Dumville.

§ 10–§ 11. While the burning of Degannwy and the death of Merfyn bear the accurate dates of 811 and 844 within the relative chronology of the text, the fact that both the preceding and succeeding events (the deaths of Offa and Rhodri, respectively) are inaccurate makes the significance of this difficult to determine.

§ 13–§ 14. **dial6ys Anar6dr [...] 6eith Konoy** *O Oes Gwrtheyrn*'s statement that Anarawd was present at the battle of the Conwy is unique among Welsh chronicles, but it is also implied in the 'Llywelyn ab Iorwerth Genealogies'. Guy, 'Medieval Welsh Genealogy', II, 365.

§ 19. **6eith Karno** The battle of Carno is usually dated to the year of Hywel Dda's death (*Brut y Tywysogyon*) or the year after (Welsh Latin annals). *Annales Cambriae*, ed. and trans. by Dumville, pp. 16–17; *Brenhinoedd y Saeson*, ed. and trans. by Dumville, pp. 40–41.

§ 19. **vii** My reading here differs from that of *RG* <http://www.rhyddiaithganoloesol.caerdydd.ac.uk/cy/ms-page.php?ms = Pen32&page = 230> [accessed 13 March 2018], where this is read as *6 n*.

§ 22. **C6nt 6ab Y6ein** The representation of Cnut as son of an Owain may have arisen from misreading the *S* of *Swein* as *I* or *Y*, as well as contamination from the mention of Owain ap Hywel Dda above, at some point after the text's composition. However, given the focus of the text generally on Venedotian history, the misinterpretation of Cnut as son of Owain ap Hywel Dda was probably the work of the original compiler, hence its anomalous inclusion against the general tendency of the chronicle to focus on Welsh events.

§ 23. **6acha6y yn y or6u Grufut ab Llywelyn a y llas esgob y Sayson** The event referred to here may be Gruffudd ap Llywelyn's defeat of Bishop Leofgar of Hereford in 1056, noted in the C-version of the *Anglo-Saxon Chronicle*. A. O. H. Jarman discusses the relationship of this mention of Machafwy to references in the Myrddin poetry in 'Perchen Machreu', *Llên Cymru*, 2 (1954), 115–18. For the battle, see *The Anglo-Saxon Chronicle: A Collaborative Edition*, ed. by David N. Dumville and Simon Keynes (Woodbridge: Brewer, 1983–), v: *MS C*, ed. by Katherine O'Brien O'Keeffe (2001), pp. 116–17; *HW*, II, 367–68; Lloyd, 'Wales', pp. 135–36.

§ 24. **Grufut ab Llywelyn** Only B gives a patronymic for Gruffudd, and, taking him to be Gruffudd ap Llywelyn, his death is misdated to 1055 in the text. 1055 saw the death of Gruffudd ap Rhydderch of Morgannwg at Gruffudd ap Llywelyn's hands, and this is perhaps what led to the chronological confusion here. It is likely that the original text included obituaries of both Gruffudd ap Rhydderch and Gruffudd ap Llywelyn, given the discrepancy between the two chronological anchors at 1055 and 1133. Working forward from 1055, William the Bastard's arrival (1066) is dated to 1060, Rhys ap Tewdwr's death (1093) to 1087, and the year the chronicle notes as 1133 would be 1126. If we work backwards from 1133, Rhys ap Tewdwr's death is given as 1093 and William the Bastard's arrival as 1066 (according to B; 1067 according to ADGJ). This makes it seem likely that this chronological confusion is due to the conflation of the two obituaries of Gruffudd ap Rhydderch (d. 1055 or 1056) and Gruffudd ap Llywelyn (d. 1063). Given that the previous entry, the battle of Machafwy, should be dated to 1056 according to the *Anglo-Saxon Chronicle*, it may be that the 1055 date was originally attached to a notice of the death of Gruffudd ap Rhydderch and the battle of Machafwy in the same year. It would have then been accidentally interpreted as relating to the death of Gruffudd ap Llywelyn, although this fails to explain the misdating of the battle of Machafwy to 1045.

Although the above is a solution to the difficulties of this particular section, particularly the inaccurate AD dating for 1133 (which should, within the relative dating of the text, be 1126), inserting the six years needed to balance the chronology of this section adversely affects the later parts of the chronicle. Six years is the additional amount needed to make the chronological anchor at 1055 correspond to that year when counting backwards from the chronological anchor at 1133, rather than the actual number of years between the deaths of the two Gruffudds. With regard to the section around 1208–1212, that is, the section which it has been argued was contemporary with the text's composition, the dating works best with the insertion of four or five years (the uncertainty with regard to the exact amount being due to the two and a half years given between Owain Gwynedd's death and Llywelyn ab Iorwerth's birth). The later part of the chronicle works better with the insertion of three years with regard to the obituaries of Llywelyn ab Iorwerth and his immediate family, and with the addition of no years with regard to the dating of the battle of Bryn Derwin.

§ 31. **Karada6c uynach** This Caradog is known from a *Life* originally written by Gerald of Wales and now only known from a summary. He was a favourite courtier and harpist of

Rhys ap Tewdwr, King of Deheubarth, who, after losing two of the king's favourite hunting dogs, chose an ascetic life perhaps in order to escape the king's anger as much as for religious reasons. He eventually settled in Rhos in Dyfed and was buried in St Davids. That *O Oes Gwrtheyrn* is the only Welsh chronicle to provide us with a record of his death is interesting as it suggests that the annals that the Aberconwy compiler could draw on preserved material not contained in any surviving versions of *Annales Cambriae*, the death of Caradog unlikely to be one of the things an Aberconwy annalist would add. One would think that the C version of *Annales Cambriae*, with a St Davids provenance, would be more likely to contain such an obituary. *HW*, II, 591–93; *Nova Legenda Angliae: As Collected by John of Tynemouth, John Capgrave, and Others, and First Printed, with New Lives, by Wynkyn de Worde, A.D. MDXVI*, ed. by Carl Horstman, 2 vols (Oxford: Clarendon Press, 1901), I, 174–76.

§ 32. **Kadwalla6n uab Grufut** Cadwallon was killed in 1132, his death being noted in the Breviate chronicle, *Brut y Tywysogyon*, and the Annals of Chester. *HW*, II, 467.

§ 35. **dorres Y6ein a Chadwaladyr Aber Tei6i** The castle of Aberteifi or Cardigan was not taken in these years, but if the 'breaking' referred to is that of the town, this may be Owain and Cadwaladr's 1136 campaign which culminated in the battle of Crug Mawr and the breaking of the bridge over the Teifi. Alternatively, the reference may be to Owain and Cadwaladr's attack on Cardigan with the aid of a Hiberno-Norse fleet, recorded only in the 'C-text' of *Annales Cambriae* under 1138, though this records a truce rather than the capture of the fortress. *HW*, II, 472–73, 476; *AC*, p. 41; *Annales Cambriae, the C text, from London, British Library, Cotton MS Domitian A. i, ff. 138r–155r*, ed. by Henry W. Gough-Cooper (Welsh Chronicles Research Group, 2015), p. 35, § c459.1 <http://croniclau.bangor.ac.uk/documents/AC%20C%20first%20edition.pdf> [accessed 29 June 2018].

§ 36. **Tal Moel6re** For this battle, see *HW*, II, 498–99. Its exact location is given uniquely in *O Oes Gwrtheyrn*.

§ 37. **dall6yd y g6ystlon yg Choed [Keirya6c]** The hostages were blinded rather than, as in ACE, captured. This event is also noted in the 'Llywelyn ab Iorwerth genealogies'. *HW*, II, 517; Guy, 'Medieval Welsh Genealogy', II, 357.

§ 38. **dorres Y6ein a Chadwaladyr Rudlan** The taking of Rhuddlan in 1167 was achieved with the help of Rhys ap Gruffudd after a three-month siege, and gave Owain Gwynedd control of Tegeingl. *HW*, II, 519–20.

§ 40. **anet Llywelyn ab Iorwerth** *O Oes Gwrtheyrn* is the main source for the date of Llywelyn Fawr's birth, which, given its dating in relation to the death of Owain Gwynedd on 23 November 1170, is placed in the first half of 1173. *HW*, II, 522 n. 136, 587 n. 61.

§ 41. **ymlat Gwern 6irogyl** Lloyd identifies this place with Gwern y Figyn near Carreg Hofa. In giving this location, *O Oes Gwrtheyrn* offers independent detail that can be set alongside *Brut y Tywysogyon*'s account that this happened at Carreghofa. *Gwern y Virogl* should be read here rather than Lloyd's *Gwern y Vinogl*, which he derived from A. *HW*, II, 565 n. 153; *BT (Pen. 20)*, p. 130.

§ 42. **haf y G6ydyl** This refers to Rhodri ab Owain Gwynedd's use of the troops of his ally, Reginald Godredson, King of Man, to seize Anglesey from his nephews, Gruffudd and Maredudd ap Cynan. The author of *O Oes Gwrtheyrn* shows some interest in these events, recording the deaths of Rhodri and the sons of Cynan. McDonald, *Manx Kingship*, pp. 101–07; *HW*, II, 588; *BS*, p. 188.

§ 42. **6r6ydyr y Choedaneu** *O Oes Gwrtheyrn* here provides support for Cynddelw Brydydd Mawr's account of the battle of Coedanau, *contra* Insley, 'Wilderness Years', p. 170. *Gwaith Cynddelw Brydydd Mawr II*, ed. by Nerys Ann Jones and Ann Parry Owen, Cyfres Beirdd y Tywysogion, 4 (Cardiff: University of Wales Press, 1995), pp. 241, 247 (poem 13, l. 26).

§ 43. **Castell Paen** Gwenwynwyn ab Owain Cyfeiliog's failed attack on Painscastle in July and August 1198 has traditionally been interpreted as a decisive blow to his attempts to secure dominance in the Middle March (*HW*, II, 586). For a recent reassessment, see David Stephenson, *Medieval Powys: Kingdom, Principality and Lordships, 1132–1293* (Woodbridge: Boydell, 2016), pp. 85–88.

§ 43. **torres Llywelyn yr 6ydgruc** This battle has been identified both with the battle of *Bro Alun* described in Prydydd y Moch's *Canu Mawr* (*Gwaith Llywarch ap Llywelyn: 'Prydydd y Moch'*, ed. by Elin M. Jones and Nerys Ann Jones, Cyfres Beirdd y Tywysogion, 5 (Cardiff: University of Wales Press, 1991), p. 215 (poem 23, l. 79)) and a siege of Mold described in the Annals of Chester for 1198 (*Annales Cestrienses: Or, Chronicle of the Abbey of S. Werburg at Chester*, ed. by Richard Copley Christie, Lancashire and Cheshire Record Society, 14 ([London]: Record Society, 1887), p. 44). The Chester chronicle records the capture of Mold by Llywelyn following, or as a result of, a defeat of his men. It is not necessary to emend the text in order for it to agree with *O Oes Gwrtheyrn* here, *contra HW*, II, 590. See further Rhian M. Andrews, 'The Nomenclature of Kingship in Welsh Court Poetry 1100–1300, Part II: The Rulers', *Studia Celtica*, 45 (2011), 53–82 (p. 66 n. 77), and Insley, 'Wilderness Years', pp. 167–69.

§ 44. **Grufut ab Kynan** The son of Cynan ab Owain Gwynedd who had been involved in the struggle for Anglesey in 1193 died at Aberconwy, having assumed the habit of the Cistercian order. *BT (Pen. 20)*, p. 145; *BT (RB)*, p. 182; *BS*, p. 196.

§ 45. **Dauyd ab Y6ein** *O Oes Gwrtheyrn* dates Dafydd ab Owain's death to five years before the interdict, that is 1203, in agreement with *Brut y Tywysogyon* (*BT (Pen. 20)*, p. 149; *BT (RB)*, pp. 184–86; *BS*, p. 198). However, that would mean that he died three years after Gruffudd ap Cynan ab Owain, who died in 1200 according to *Brut y Tywysogyon*. Dafydd was certainly dead by 27 March 1203. *Acts of Welsh Rulers*, p. 25.

§ 46. **wahard6yt effereneu** The Papal Interdict of England began in March, 1208, and ended in May, 1213, but the dispute over the appointment of the archbishop of Canterbury which was its primary cause began in 1205 and subsequently worsened. The Pope raised the interdict over Wales in 1212 in recognition of the opposition of the Welsh princes to John. *HW*, II, 638; *BT (Pen. 20)*, pp. 158–59.

§ 47. **Hywel uab Gruffud** The son of Gruffudd ap Cynan ab Owain Gwynedd; his obituary is given below. He was buried, like his father, at Aberconwy.

§ 47. **hyd ymBrydyn** For the Misae Roll evidence for Llywelyn's participation in John's 1209 Scottish expedition, see Lloyd, 'Wales', pp. 135–36 n. 3. The expedition took place in the summer of that year.

§ 47. **nos 6yl Sim6nd a Iuda [...] Herlant Pic a'e oreugw[y]r** This particular event, for which *O Oes Gwrtheyrn* is our only source, is discussed above.

§ 48. **Ac yn y 6loythin [...] yscuba6r y Creudyn** This would seem to be a reference to Earl Ranulf of Chester's invasion of Gwynedd in 1210, accompanied by the Bishop of Winchester and Geoffrey fitz Peter, Justiciar of England, recorded in the Annals of Dunstable. It is impossible to reconcile the account of B with what else is known of these events, since it states that Ranulf fought with John. Ranulf remained loyal to John throughout these years and so FJ's *cynatlassodd* is preferred to B's *ymlatyssei*, though it should be emended to *cynatlassei* (3 sg plup. of *cynhadlu*), with *cynatlassodd* an attempted modernization. It is likely that B's *ymlatyssei* arose from a misreading or a mistaken correction of *acynatlyssei* to *acymlaty ssei*. *Yn erbyn* is also translated as 'to meet', rather than the more aggressive 'against', though it may be a misreading of *yn ervyn*, 'to expect'. The text may therefore depict Ranulf's campaign as a preliminary step to John's Welsh campaigns, as indeed it was. It is, however, worth noting that some of the extra details which complicate this entry are restricted to the ABFGJ branch of the tradition, and so the simpler reading of DE (given C's known tendency to abbreviate) may best reflect the original chronicle entry, for which see the apparatus. *HW*, II, 631–35; Annals of Dunstable in *AM*, III (1866), 32. Thanks to Paul Russell for advice on this section.

§ 49. **Brabanseid** Mercenaries from Brabant became famous in the twelfth century under William of Cambrai and Lobar 'the Wolf'. By this point the word could be used as a generic term for foreign mercenaries. Fredric L. Cheyette, *Ermengard of Narbonne and the World of the Troubadours* (Ithaca, NY: Cornell University Press, 2001), pp. 279–85 (esp. 279 n. 21).

§ 49. **Gruffut y uab ygwystyl** Gruffudd's first appearance in the historical record is this hostageship, also referred to in the agreement of 12 August 1211 between Llywelyn and John: *Acts of Welsh Princes*, no. 233.

§ 50. **Maredut ab Kynan** One of Rhodri ab Owain Gwynedd's opponents in 1193. Expelled from Meirionydd in 1202, nothing is heard of him until *O Oes Gwrtheyrn* provides a unique record of his death, underlining the chronicle's particular interest in the participants in the struggle for Gwynedd at the close of the twelfth century. *HW*, II, 648 n. 181.

§ 51. **Pum mlynet** This is another instance of difficult chronology in the text. We know that John's expedition, and consequently the start of Gruffudd's hostageship, was in 1211, and so this would imply a date of 1216 for his release. However, the text also states that John died three years from this release, which implies a date considerably earlier that October 1216, when John died. The release of Llywelyn's son, who must be Gruffudd, is one of the conditions of Magna Carta, so a date after June 1215 is necessary, probably very soon after. The chronological confusion in this annal is another indication of a later updating of the text after 1211, when the prominence of Gruffudd may have encouraged its expansion during the reign of his son, Llywelyn. *HW*, II, 646; J. Beverley Smith, 'Magna Carta and the Charters of the Welsh Princes', *English Historical Review*, 99 (1984), 344–62 (pp. 349–51).

§ 53. **yr argl6ytes** Siwan or Joan, mother of Dafydd ap Llywelyn. This use of her title accurately echoes the title used by Joan from around 1230, *domina Wallie*. This 'apparently unprecedented' style demonstrated her importance as a political figure, and its use here doubtless shows the closeness of the continuator to the royal court of Gwynedd: *Acts of Welsh Rulers*, pp. 77–78.

§ 54, § 55, § 56. **Llywelyn uab Iorwerth [...] Grufut y uab [...] Dauyd ab Llewelyn** Llywelyn died at Aberconwy on 11 April 1240 and was buried there; Gruffudd fell to his death from the Tower of London on 1 March 1244; Dafydd died at Aber on 25 February 1246. Matthew Paris, *Chronica Majora*, ed. by Henry Richards Luard, 7 vols (London: Longman, 1872–83), IV: *A.D. 1240 to A.D. 1247* (1877), 8, 295–96; *HW*, II, 693, 700–01, 705.

§ 57. **y 6r6ydyr yNerwin** For the significance of the proximity of Bryn Derwin to lands owned by Aberconwy Abbey, see the discussion above. The battle of Bryn Derwin was the key event in the establishment of Llywelyn ap Gruffudd's supremacy in Gwynedd Uwch Conwy, when he defeated his brothers, Owain and Dafydd. The mention of Owain can perhaps only be explained by his status as the eldest brother, and as such *Cronica de Wallia* specifies him as Llywelyn's primary enemy. '"Cronica de Wallia" and Other Documents from Exeter Cathedral Library MS. 3514', ed. by Thomas Jones, *BBCS*, 12 (1946), 27–44 (p. 40); J. Beverley Smith, *Llywelyn ap Gruffudd: Prince of Wales*, new edn (Cardiff: University of Wales Press, 2014), pp. 68–77.

§ 59. **O'r 6r6ydyr yN[erwin] yny tored castell y Diserth, x. mlynet** This must refer to the fall of Diserth on 4 August and Degannwy on 28 September 1263, especially since this destruction of Diserth seems to have ended its career as a fortress, though there is no obvious reason for the misdating of the events in the chronicle by two years. *AC*, p. 101 (MS B); *Annales Cambriae: The B Text, from London, National Archives, MS E164/1, pp. 2–26*, ed. by Henry W. Gough-Cooper (Welsh Chronicles Research Group, 2015), p. 86, § 1284.2 (AD 1263) <http://croniclau.bangor.ac.uk/documents/AC%20B%20first%20edition.pdf> [accessed 8 June 2018]; *HW*, II, 732–33.

§ 60. **Penard Dyla6c** This taking of the castle of Penarlâg or Hawarden may refer to its capture by Llywelyn in September 1265, though if so the relative chronology of *O Oes Gwrtheyrn* is again rather confused in this period. In relation to the actual date of the previous recorded events (September 1263), it should have occurred in 1264, but it is dated eleven years after the battle of Derwin (1255), so 1266. In January 1265 Henry de Montfort, son of Earl Simon, met with Llywelyn ap Gruffudd and Gruffudd ap Madog at Hawarden to confirm them in their possession of all lands and castles on the Cheshire border which had fallen to the Welsh, leaving the possibility that *O Oes Gwrtheyrn* refers to an earlier capture of the castle. Possession of Hawarden was an issue discussed in the treaty of Montgomery, 1267. The short fourteenth-century chronicle *Oed yr Arglwydd* gives an exact date of 26 September 1265 for the taking of Hawarden, and while this text used *Oes Gwrtheyrn* as a source, in this notice and others it draws on independent information. *HW*, II, 735–38; *Acts of Welsh Rulers*, no. 363; Guy, 'A Lost Medieval Manuscript', pp. 87 and 103.

§ 62–§ 66A. **O'r pan deuth Crist […] chweblynedd a chwechant** The dating of these various events is complicated, particularly when dated from Gruffudd's hostageship, which has both a relative date within the text and an actual date of 1211. Dating from Derwin is comparatively easier, since an absolute date is given within the text which corresponds to the actual date of the battle.

§ 64. **doeth cred gyntaf […] brenhin Kymry** The idea that the Britons were converted under Lucius is found in Bede and *Historia Brittonum*, though here it may be evidence of the influence of Geoffrey of Monmouth. Bede, *Ecclesiastical History of the English People*, ed. by Bertram Colgrave and Roger A. B. Mynors (Oxford: Clarendon Press, 1969), p. 24; *Nennius: British History and the Welsh Annals*, ed. by John Morris (Chichester: Phillimore, 1980), p. 64; Geoffrey of Monmouth, *History*, pp. 87–91.

§ 65. **ddoeth y Saesson** The date given in both cases seems to correspond to the mid-seventh century (653 × 659), showing a late date for the Saxon arrival which seems to contradict the AD 400 date given for Gwrtheyrn, in whose time the Saxons were supposed to have arrived. Perhaps conquest rather than arrival is meant here, and if so this would indicate an idea of a mid-seventh century conquest indebted to Geoffrey's history.

§ 66. **ddoeth Normynn** Disagreement between the two versions as to the date of this event, whether in the eleventh or seventh century, make its significance doubtful. The 1049 × 1054 date of J should perhaps be preferred, and may show awareness of the existence of Normans in England before the conquest, for which see Chris P. Lewis, 'The French in England Before the Norman Conquest', *Anglo-Norman Studies*, 17 (1994), 123–44. It may on the other hand be a simple case of misdating.

8. The Cardiff Chronicle in London, British Library, MS Royal 6 B XI

Georgia Henley

Monastic houses in the medieval Welsh March — from large centres of production to smaller local priories — were involved in the composition and compilation of historical chronicles in Latin to a degree that has not always been appreciated in studies of medieval British historical writing. Close scrutiny of Marcher monastic chronicles reveals a sophisticated blending of disparate sources, a wide-ranging knowledge of events in England and Wales, and an awareness of political contexts in a rapidly changing world following the Norman conquest of South Wales. Marcher chronicles provide valuable evidence for networks of transmission that linked high-status Anglo-Norman monasteries in counties bordering Wales, such as Tewkesbury Abbey, to monasteries in the conquest territories of Wales, such as Neath Abbey and Cardiff Priory, as well as to houses located in native Wales and/or patronized by Welsh princes, such as Whitland Abbey or Valle Crucis Abbey. An overlooked chronicle in London, BL, MS Royal 6 B XI, here edited for the first time, provides insight into the connections forged by Marcher monasteries to their neighbouring houses as well as evidence for the collection and interpretation of historical records in an environment of intense political change. I demonstrate how compilers at the Benedictine priory of Cardiff sourced valuable information about their de Clare patrons from their mother house, Tewkesbury Abbey, and combined it with other sources to form a localized record of events in Glamorgan. In turn, the Cardiff chronicle (so called for its probable provenance at Cardiff Priory) in MS Royal 6 B XI was used as a source for another important but overlooked Marcher chronicle in the Neath Abbey Breviate of Domesday. Through comparison of these two chronicles, I discuss implications

---

The Chronicles of Medieval Wales and the March: New Contexts, Studies and Texts, ed. by Ben Guy, Georgia Henley, Owain Wyn Jones, and Rebecca Thomas, TCNE 31 (Turnhout: Brepols, 2020) pp. 231–287   BREPOLS PUBLISHERS   10.1484/M.TCNE-EB.5.118539

for the broader context of the transmission of these Marcher sources into native Wales, where they found their way into vernacular Welsh historical writing. This analysis paints a broader picture of transmission patterns in the region, detailing how information circulated among Marcher houses that were linked by patronage and local interest above any monastic affiliation.

The chapter is divided into two discrete parts: (1) a discussion of the patterns of source transmission, pressures of literary patronage, and points of contact among Anglo-Norman houses in the March, as evinced by the Cardiff chronicle, and (2) a placement of this evidence within the broader network of textual transmission from the March into native Wales.

Manuscript and Contents

The Cardiff chronicle is extant in London, BL, MS Royal 6 B XI (fols 105ra–108rb, 112^{r}), an early fourteenth-century manuscript probably produced at Cardiff Priory in Glamorgan.[1] This manuscript contains twenty-three historical, theological, and epistemological works in Latin, written by a variety of hands, mostly in quires of twelve. The contents include sermons and other works of Bernard of Clairvaux, *De visitatione infirmorum* sometimes attributed to St Augustine, a verse Bible, theological and gnomic verses, *Meditationes S. Bernardi*, the *Chronicle of Popes and Emperors* by Martin of Troppau, with later continuations, the *Prouinciale Romanum*, extracts from Marianus Scottus and Nicholas Trivet on chronology, an excerpt of the letter from Ceolfrith to Nechtan of the Picts, other excerpts from Bede's *Historia ecclesiastica* and from the *Life of St Anselm*, the *Floriloquium* and *Breuiloquium* of John le Walleys, and a letter concerning the abuses of the Cluniac or perhaps the Cistercian order. The manuscript is suspected to be of a Cardiff Priory provenance 'or some other cell of Tewkesbury Abbey' because of the chronicle under discussion here.[2] The cataloguer notes that the order of texts has been disturbed, which is apparent from the quire signatures. This is also evident in the chronicle text, which appears from fols 105ra–108rb before being interrupted by a list of dioceses of the world and a list of kings (*Prouinciale Romanorum*); the chronicle concludes on fol. 112^{r}, a one-column stub.

---

[1] The presence of the chronicle in the manuscript in fact constitutes the argument for a Cardiff provenance.

[2] BL, Explore Archives and Manuscripts, Royal MS 6 B XI <http://searcharchives.bl.uk/IAMS_VU2:IAMS040-002106161> [accessed 11 March 2018].

The chronicle is written in a single Anglicana hand of the early fourteenth century. The text is in a two-column layout with lead ruling. Red ink punctuates the dates at the beginning of each entry and the capital letters in the text. Incaustum ink underlining, brief marginal additions, and the occasional scratched gloss in a later hand appear throughout the text. The chronicle appears in position in the manuscript after Martin of Troppau's *Chronicle* and is interrupted — and followed — by the *Prouinciale Romanorum*, then followed by the texts on chronology and excerpts from Bede. The chronicle is contextualized, therefore, within the history of the Christian world, Christian cosmology, and, more specifically within that frame, the history of Britain and the English people.

The chronicle covers events in English and South Welsh history from 1066, beginning with the death of Edward the Confessor and the reign of William the Conqueror, to 1268, ending with the construction of Caerphilly Castle and the capture of Gilbert son of Gilbert de Umfraville, Richard Herbert, and John Marshal in an unidentified battle. Most of the chronicle is heavily indebted to the Annals of Tewkesbury, to the extent that it is a copy of those annals for much of its narrative (which accounts for why it has never been edited separately).[3] It heavily abbreviates the Tewkesbury source, resulting in a much shorter chronicle. It is independent from 1244 or perhaps 1246 onwards.

The result is a chronicle interested in the Anglo-Norman kings of England, their activities in England and France, the elections and deaths of the archbishops of Canterbury and Worcester, the Crusades, and the earls of Gloucester. These interests are consistent with a Gloucestershire source that looks towards England, as well as with the Annals of Tewkesbury's ultimate reliance on Waverley and Worcester sources.[4] Mixed in with these national and interna-

---

[3] The Annals of Tewkesbury (*AM*, I (1864), 43–180 from London, BL, MS Cotton Cleopatra A VII), were kept at Tewkesbury in Gloucestershire. They cover the years 1066 to 1263 and take a marked interest in their de Clare patrons. The Cardiff chronicle notes the establishment of Tewkesbury Abbey in 1091, the death of its first abbot, Gerald, in 1110, and its dedication in 1123.

[4] *AM*, I, xvii. For the Winchester/Waverley source, see Neil Denholm-Young, 'The Winchester Hyde Chronicle', *English Historical Review*, 49 (1934), 85–93; Felix Liebermann, *Ungedruckte anglo-normannische Geschichtsquellen* (Strassburg: Trübner, 1879), pp. 173–202. The Annals of Tewkesbury have these sources in common with the Annals of Worcester, with which they share extensive similarities. Paul Anthony Hayward argues that the Annals of Tewkesbury and the Cardiff chronicle draw on a lost Gloucester chronicle; see *The Winchcombe and Coventry Chronicles: Hitherto Unnoticed Witnesses to the Work of John of Worcester*, ed. and trans. by Paul Anthony Hayward, 2 vols (Tempe: Arizona Center for Medieval and Renaissance Studies, 2010), I, 133–35 and 141.

tional events are additional items of local interest, such as the death of Rhys ap Gruffudd in 1197, the election of Geoffrey Prior of Llanthony as Bishop of St Davids in 1203, the election of William Prior of Goldcliff as Bishop of Llandaf in 1219, the placement of Cardiff Priory under the care of Henry Capellanus in 1221, and a dispute between Llandaf and Tewkesbury over the church of Llanbleddian in 1231. As is typical of chronicles of the period, the early entries are laconic, one- to two-sentence statements, while the later entries, beginning in the early thirteenth century, are lengthier and more discursive. Departing from its dependence on a Tewkesbury source, the Cardiff chronicle is independent from 1244 or perhaps 1246 onwards, albeit with the final sentence of s.a. 1246 matching the Annals of Tewkesbury (it cannot be said whether s.aa. 1244 and 1245 are independent from the Annals of Tewkesbury because those two entries do not survive in the only extant Annals of Tewkesbury manuscript). Whether this departure from the Annals of Tewkesbury signals the loss or conclusion of a textual source or a deliberate choice is unclear. The Annals of Tewkesbury continue to be interested in the earls of Gloucester and other regional items in this period, so the former scenario is more plausible.

The portion of the chronicle that is independent — 1244 to its conclusion in 1268 — is keenly interested in the de Clare family of Glamorgan and local events in South Wales, situating it in the context of a house under de Clare patronage. It records negative interactions with the Welsh, including an attack on Neath by Welsh people from Brecon and the burning of Keynsham in 1244, the construction and fortifications of Talyfan, Glamorgan, and Degannwy Castles in 1245, the fortification of Llantrissant in 1246, Rhys Fychan's wasting of Gower in 1256, Llywelyn's attack on Llangynwyd in 1257, and the capture of Gruffudd ap Rhys at Cardiff in 1266. These events are interspersed with ecclesiastical elections and deaths as well as records about Simon de Montfort, new currencies, the activities of the French kings, and famines. Overall, the independent portion of the chronicle takes greater interest in local political events in South Wales than the previous section, while still maintaining an international focus on events in England and the Continent.

Cardiff Priory's Origins as a Cell of Tewkesbury

It is useful to consider Cardiff Priory's relationship with its mother house, Tewkesbury Abbey, in order to understand the connections of patronage that undergird the circulation of chronicle texts between monasteries in this region. Cardiff Priory's connections with Tewkesbury Abbey and its patrons, the earls of Gloucester, originate with the Norman conquest of Glamorgan. The priory was established as a cell of Tewkesbury sometime before 1106 by Robert fitz Hamon, the first Anglo-Norman Lord of Glamorgan and Lord of Cardiff. The new cell at Cardiff, a burgeoning town that was also the seat of Robert fitz Hamon's lordship, was intended to accommodate five monks, and Robert's gift to the monastery included a number of small churches. These holdings in the Glamorgan diocese, it must be said, were the direct result of Robert's conquest of Glamorgan at an unknown date, probably sometime after the death of Rhys ap Tewdwr in 1093.[5] By the 1090s Robert had established administrative control over Glamorgan and was styling himself Lord of Cardiff and Lord of Glamorgan.[6] In common with other Norman barons conquering territory in the region, he consolidated control over his new lands through ecclesiastical jurisdiction, granting Welsh churches and their lands as daughter houses to Marcher houses already under his patronage, thus cementing ecclesiastical as well as military control. Tewkesbury Abbey became the family monastery after it was granted to Robert by William the Conqueror, and it benefited considerably during this period from his gifts: in 1102 Robert rededicated the abbey and gave it a new site on the Severn, with Abbot Gerald and his Benedictine monks moving there from Cranbourne Abbey in Dorset. Robert also granted them various tithes and properties in Wales, including the church of St Mary's Cardiff and its eight dependent chapels, the church of Llantwit Major, and some land on the west bank of the river Taf.[7] According to a confirmation

---

[5] Judith A. Green, 'Robert fitz Haimon (*d.* 1107)', *Oxford Dictionary of National Biography* <https://doi.org/10.1093/ref:odnb/9596>. *HW*, I, 275 states that Morgannwg at this time included the cantrefs of Gorfynydd, Penychen, Y Cantref Breiniol, Gwynllŵg, Gwent Iscoed, Gwent Uchcoed, and possibly Ergyng and Ewyas; see now Philip Jenkins, 'Regions and Cantrefs in Early Medieval Glamorgan', *CMCS*, 15 (1988), 31–50.

[6] J. Beverley Smith ('The Lordship of Glamorgan', *Morgannwg*, 2 (1958), 9–38 (p. 15)) questions whether he was able to 'influence the distribution' of any of the territories of Glamorgan beyond the Shire-Fee; for further discussion see John Reuben Davies, *The Book of Llandaf and the Norman Church in Wales*, Studies in Celtic History, 21 (Woodbridge: Boydell, 2003), pp. 18–26.

[7] William Dugdale, *Monasticon Anglicanum: or, The History of the Ancient Abbies, Monasteries, Hospitals, Cathedral and Collegiate Churches, with their Dependencies, in England and Wales*, new edn by John Caley, Henry Ellis, and Bulkeley Bandinel, 6 vols in 8 parts (London: Bohn, 1846), II, 67; James Bennett, *The History of Tewkesbury* (London: Longman, Rees, Orme, Brown, and Green, 1830), pp. 338–39. For an 1173 × 1183 charter of Nicholas Bishop of Llandaf, confirming Tewkesbury's properties in his diocese, see *Llandaff Episcopal Acta, 1140–1287*, ed. by David Crouch (Cardiff: South Wales Record Society, 1988), pp. 28–31, with discussion in David Crouch, 'Urban: First Bishop of Llandaff 1107–34', *Journal of Welsh Ecclesiastical History*, 6 (1989), 1–15 (p. 6); the Tewkesbury cartulary is in MS Cotton

charter, Tewkesbury's holdings around Cardiff included the parish church of St Mary's in the borough of 'Kairdif', the village of Llandough, and the churches of Newcastle, Llantwit Major, Kenfig, Ystradowen, and Llanbleddian.[8] It is not known whether this church at Cardiff was replacing an earlier site; if so, this site, the church of St Mary's, could have been founded as recently as the 1080s when Normans were first trickling into the area, or it could have been an earlier native Welsh *clas* church.

After Robert's death, Tewkesbury continued to flourish under the patronage of the earls of Gloucester, first under Robert's son-in-law, Robert of Caen (made Earl of Gloucester in 1122), then under his son, William (Earl of Gloucester from 1147 to 1183).[9] Following William's death, patronage passed to the de Clares, who held it until the untimely death of an heir in 1314, discussed further below within the context of the chronicle's composition. These aristocratic families' patronage, over the generations, of monasteries in Glamorgan and Gloucestershire allowed for the transfer of chronicle sources between the houses under their control and beyond. Below I demonstrate how close links between these families, their conquest territories, and the patterns of filiation they generated forged new lines of transmission between native Welsh and Marcher monasteries.

Cardiff as an Intermediary between Tewkesbury and Neath

Importantly in the greater context of chronicle transmission in Wales and the March, the Cardiff chronicle was used as a source for another Marcher chronicle produced at Neath Abbey in Glamorgan, an important site of historical

---

Cleopatra A VII, fols 70–106; listed in Godfrey R. C. Davis, *Medieval Cartularies of Great Britain* (London: Longmans, Green, 1958), rev. by Claire Breay, Julian Harrison, and David M. Smith (London: BL, 2010), no. 953.

[8] 'Accounts of the rectory of Cardiff and other possessions of the abbey at Tewkesbury in Glamorgan, for the year 1449–50', ed. by William Rees, *Publications, South Wales & Monmouth Record Society*, 2 (1950), 127–86 (pp. 140–43); *Llandaff Episcopal Acta*, pp. 28–31; for discussion see Crouch, 'Urban', p. 6. Later, Tewkesbury and Llandaf were involved in a dispute over control of Llanbleddian after its lease-holder, Radulf Maeloc, died; details in the Annals of Tewkesbury and the Cardiff chronicle, s.a. 1231.

[9] Robert fitz Hamon died from a spear wound and was buried at Tewkesbury. His death is reported in both the Cardiff chronicle and the Annals of Tewkesbury: see Cardiff chronicle, s.a. 1107; *AM*, I, 44. Robert of Gloucester, the patron of Geoffrey of Monmouth and William of Malmesbury, funded the remainder of Tewkesbury's construction and also founded Margam Abbey in 1147, the last year of his life. He was married to Mabel, daughter of Robert fitz Hamon.

writing and manuscript production in its own right. The Cardiff chronicle provides a key link between the chronicle at Neath Abbey and its Tewkesbury source. The chronicle at Neath Abbey, which has previously been labelled the 'Breviate annals' but for present purposes is called the Neath chronicle, was in turn a source for the Welsh vernacular chronicle *Brenhinedd y Saesson* (probably composed in South Wales but in present form in two manuscripts that are linked to Valle Crucis Abbey in north-east Wales).[10] The Cardiff chronicle can thus be taken as a key example of the transmission of Marcher and English chronicle sources into Welsh vernacular contexts through the mediating influence of the March, its interests, and patrons. In the context of this chapter, the Cardiff chronicle is considered for its significance as a source ultimately used by vernacular chroniclers in North and South Wales, demonstrating the reach and impact of monastic networks in Wales and the March.

Neath Abbey, Savigniac until sometime around 1147, when the Savigniacs joined the Cistercians, was patronized first by the de Braose family and then by the de Clares. It was one of the wealthiest abbeys in South Wales and very likely responsible for the Neath Abbey Breviate of Domesday (London, The National Archives, MS E 164/1, *s.* xiii^2).[11] Neath is a crucial transmission link between the Marcher houses so far discussed and native Welsh houses such as Valle Crucis, a Cistercian monastery near Llangollen in North Wales that was a flourishing centre of literary production. An analysis of the Cardiff chronicle's close similarities to the Neath chronicle indicates that Cardiff is a node on the line of transmission between these various houses, confirming a suggestion by Kathleen Hughes that Cardiff was an intermediary point for the transmission of Tewkesbury material to Neath.[12] This material was included in *Brenhinedd y Saesson* — the Welsh vernacular chronicle which draws together English and

---

[10] See pp. 250–51, n. 46 below for further discussion of the provenance of these two manuscripts; see David Stephenson above, Chapter 6, pp. 156, 167 for discussion of the potential use of Strata Florida annals at Valle Crucis.

[11] This manuscript, which contains the Breviate chronicle, or B-text of *Annales Cambriae*, is discussed extensively in Daniel Huws, 'The Neath Abbey *Breviate of Domesday*', in *Wales and the Welsh in the Middle Ages*, ed. by Ralph A. Griffiths and Phillipp R. Schofield (Cardiff: University of Wales Press, 2011), pp. 46–55. The abbey had an annual income of £236/1/5 in 1291.

[12] Kathleen Hughes, 'The Welsh Latin Chronicles: *Annales Cambriae* and Related Texts', *Proceedings of the British Academy*, 59 (1973), 233–58 (p. 253 n. 1). J. Beverley Smith ('Historical Writing in Medieval Wales: The Composition of *Brenhinedd y Saesson*', *Studia Celtica*, 42 (2008), 55–86 (p. 70)) voices uncertainty about whether the Neath chronicle used the Annals of Tewkesbury directly or accessed a common exemplar. The present study indicates that the Neath chronicle accessed the Cardiff chronicle as an intermediary.

Welsh sources to detail the activities of Anglo-Saxon kings, English kings, and Welsh princes from the fall of the kingdom of Britain to 1461 — which was transmitted to north-east Wales, perhaps to Valle Crucis. The Neath chronicle is therefore important for modelling the transmission of English chronicle sources into native Wales.[13] I provide a quick outline of the chronicle and its contents before demonstrating through close comparison that the Cardiff chronicle was a source for the Neath chronicle.

The Neath chronicle is a brief set of Marcher annals covering 1066 to 1298. Its use of sources from far afield, including chronicle sources from Tewkesbury, Waverley, and Winchester, constitute evidence for transmission throughout the March and England. It is decidedly not a Welsh chronicle and does not use Welsh Latin sources; rather, it is interested in English events, including the activities of the English kings and the election of the archbishops of Canterbury. It artfully combines these events with details that pertain locally to the diocese of Llandaf, the lordship of Glamorgan, and the de Clare earls of Gloucester, who, as mentioned above, controlled the lordship of Glamorgan after 1218. It mentions the Welsh princes of Deuheubarth and Gwynedd when they were involved in skirmishes with Marcher lords. Of all the nobles of the period, the chronicle is the most interested in the activities of Gilbert de Clare, Seventh Earl of Gloucester (b. 1243–d. 1295).[14]

Hughes argues that the chronicle was compiled at Neath, while H. L. Jones suggests less definitively that it was compiled 'in one of the Religious Houses of Morganwg [*sic*] or Gwent'.[15] The chronicle's greatest area of interest is Glamorgan. Its provenance is difficult to determine with certainty because it is so interested in events throughout Glamorgan, not in Neath specifically. It dem-

---

[13] The Neath chronicle is edited in 'Chronicle of the Thirteenth Century: MS Exchequer Domesday', [ed. by Harry Longueville Jones], *Archaeologia Cambrensis*, 3rd ser., 8, no. 32 (1862), 272–83. Entries from 1272–1298 are on the Medieval Swansea City Witness Project's website, with translation: Catherine Clark and others, 'Domesday Breviate', *Medieval Swansea City Witness* <http://www.medievalswansea.ac.uk/en/text/3> [accessed 9 May 2020].

[14] s.aa. 1244, 1263, 1264, 1289, 1290, 1295. For Gilbert de Clare, see Clive H. Knowles, 'Clare, Gilbert de [*called* Gilbert the Red], Seventh Earl of Gloucester and Sixth Earl of Hertford (1243–1295)', *Oxford Dictionary of National Biography* <https://doi.org/10.1093/ref:odnb/5438>.

[15] For provenance, see Hughes, 'The Welsh Latin Chronicles', p. 253; J. Beverley Smith and Thomas B. Pugh, 'The Lordship of Gower and Kilvey in the Middle Ages', in *Glamorgan County History*, ed. by Glanmor Williams, 6 vols (Cardiff: University of Wales Press, 1936–88), III: *The Middle Ages*, ed. by Thomas B. Pugh (1971), pp. 205–65 (p. 241); 'Chronicle of the Thirteenth Century', p. 272.

onstrates considerable knowledge of political and ecclesiastical affairs in the Marcher lordships and bishoprics of South Wales, mentioning Llandaf above all, but also Cardiff, Worcester, Gloucester, St Davids, Margam, Tewkesbury, Neath, Goldcliff, Monmouth, Pershore, and Swansea, as well as Dinefwr, Oystermouth, and Caerphilly Castles. A consistent distribution of places to the east of Neath, clustered around Llandaf, as well as the fact that Neath itself is mentioned just three times in the text, suggests that the chronicle used a source or multiple sources from locations to the east of Neath.

Comparison reveals that it is unlikely that the Neath chronicle used the Annals of Tewkesbury directly as a source for its thirteenth-century sections (see Table 8.1). Instead, the Neath chronicle from 1248 to 1268 is so close to the Cardiff chronicle that the latter — or its immediate exemplar — was probably used as a source. To this source the Neath compilers would have added their own localizing information.[16] The two chronicles share the greatest similarities to one another from 1248 to 1268, the section that is most interested in the de Clares and South Wales. As I explain below, several errors indicate that the direction of transmission was likely from the Cardiff chronicle to the Neath chronicle, rather than the other way around. It is clear from Table 8.1 that the Annals of Tewkesbury in this section represent a different textual tradition, and that Neath and Cardiff were not acquiring their information from the Annals of Tewkesbury for this period.

Table 8.1 on the following pages demonstrates the close correspondence between the two chronicles in a representative sample from 1258 to 1268. In this portion they share information at a level of word-for-word correspondence that is striking. The better readings of the Cardiff chronicle suggest a direction of copying, that the Neath chronicle was copying from a Cardiff source rather than the other way around.[17]

---

[16] For example, the consecration of William de Braose, a member of a junior line of the family, as Bishop of Llandaf in 1266, receives attention; the final entry describes the marriage of Alina, William VI's daughter and heir, to John de Mowbray. The conclusion of the chronicle with this marriage seems deliberate and suggests purposeful compilation for this one event: William VI's dispute over the lordship of Gower and his hereditary rights. In terms of its Cistercian interest, as expected from a Cistercian abbey, the chronicle mentions the foundation of the order s.a. 1098, the foundation of Clairvaux s.a. 1115, the death of Bernard s.a. 1153, and a tax s.a. 1282. While some of these events are widely reported and therefore generic, the tax in 1282 is less so, suggesting specific Cistercian interest.

[17] I am not suggesting that the Cardiff chronicle in the Royal manuscript is the direct exemplar for the Neath chronicle in the Breviate manuscript, but that the Neath compilers accessed a source that was very similar to the Cardiff chronicle and its sources.

Table 8.1: Close correspondence in the Neath chronicle and Cardiff chronicle entries for 1258–1268, with comparison to the Annals of Tewkesbury[18]

Date	Cardiff chronicle	Neath chronicle
1258	Dominus Willelmus de Clare et abbas Westmonasterii Londoniam ueneno interierunt. Constituti sunt .xii^{cim}. pares in Angliam, quorum consilio et iudicom [corr. iudicio] Anglia et Hybernya et Wallia regnantur. Expulsi sunt ab Anglia fratres Pictauensis, tres reges.	Dominus Willielmus de Clara et abbas Westmonasterii Londoniam veneno interierunt. Constituti sunt .xii. pares in Anglia, quorum consilio et iudicio Anglia, Ybernia et Wallia regnantur. Et expulsi sunt ab Anglia fratres Pictauenses, tres reges.
1259	Cessauit Henricus quartus rex Anglie vocari dux Normannie.	Cessauit Henricus rex .iiiius. Anglie vocari dux Normannie.
1260	*No entry*	*No entry*
1261	Obiit Alexander papa .iiii^{tus}, cui successit Vrbanus .iiii^{tus}. mense Augusti.	Obiit Alexander .iiiius. papa mense Maii, cui successit Vrbanus .iiiius. mense August[i]
1262	Obiit Ricardus de Clare comes Gloucestrie Idibus Iulii.	Obiit Ricardus de Clara comes Gloucestri[e] Idibus Iulii.
1263	Gilbertus de Clare, filius dicti Ricardi comitis Gloucestrie, .xix. annorum suscepit terram suam de Glamorgan circa festum beati Michaelis. Eodem anno festo Natiuitatis beati Iohannis Baptiste precedente, orta est guerra inter regem, Eadwardum primogenitum ipsius, et tres comites, et plures barones, atque milites Anglicos et Walenses.	Gilbertus de Clara, filius dicti Ricardi com[itis] .xix. annorum accessit ad terram suam de Glammorgan circa festum beati Michelis. Eodem anno, in festo beati I[ohannis] Baptiste Natiuitatis precedente, orta est g[uerra] magna inter dominum regem et Edwardu[m] primogenitum ipsius et tres comites et plu[res] barones et milites Anglicos et Walenses.

[18] Variant readings are underlined; text supplied by me is in square brackets, superscript letters are indicated with backslash and forward slash. Though the three texts are similar from 1248–1268, note that I have supplied only the entries from 1258–1268.

8. THE CARDIFF CHRONICLE IN LONDON, BRITISH LIBRARY, MS ROYAL 6 B XI

---

nnals of Tewkesbury[19]

Passione Domini mccxxv. anni, cicli solaris vii., cicli lunaris xix., v. indictionis lxxxv., annus ejusdem concurr. i, epactae xiv., terminus Pascalis xi. kal. Aprilis, dies Paschae ix. kal. ejusdem, luna ipsius ei xvi., litera Dominicalis F. Obiit Sewalus archiepiscopus Eboracensis, cui successit [Godefridus]. mpestas valida pluviarum inundantium, nivium, glaciei, tonitrui magni, fulguris horribilis, talis subito ersit ante festum sancti Johannis Baptistae, scilicet xii. kal. Julii, qualis, ex quo gentes esse coeperunt, n fuit, videlicet supra rivos aquarum Sabrinae a Salopesburia usque ad Bristollas [...] Isabel filia cardi de Clare primogenita nupsit domino Marchio de Ponte Ferato, mense Junii, apud Leouns, cum a transfretavit Willelmus de Bekeford monachus Theokesberiae [...][20]

ominus Henricus filius regis Johannis rex Angliae, et regina, et comes Gloucestriae, transfretavit, et r arripuit versus Franciam ad vendendum vel escambium faciendum de terra et redditu Gasconiae. vimentum appositum est in capitulo Theokesberiae de perquisitis conventus. Obiit Ranulfus de Novo stro. Obiit Jacobus de Clare, viii. kal. Junii [...][21]

entry

ius et haeres Leuwisi regis Franciae mortuus est et sepultus apud [blank] ad cujus sepulturam inter- runt dominus Henricus filius regis Johannis, Angliae rex, comes Gloucestriae, et alii nonnulli gnates Angliae, et a multis putabatur et dicebatur cum ab Anglicis esse appoisionatum [...][22]

iit vir nobilis et omni laude dignus, Ricardus de Clara comes Gloverniae et Hertfordiae, idus Julii. sepultus est apud Theokesberiam quinto kal. Augusti, ad cujus sepulturam interfuerunt episcopus gorniae Walterus de Cantilupo, et Willelmus episcopus Landavensis, et viii. abbates [...][23]

no igitur MCCLXIII exiit edictum a domino rege Angliae, quod omnes magnates et proceres gliae, una cum archiepiscopis, episcopis, abbatibus, prioribus conventualibus, apud Londoniam circa um Nativitatis beatae Mariae in unum essent congregate, ad tractandum de pacis reformatione. ibus convocatis et ibidem fere per quindenam commorantibus, et de dicta pace tractantibus, la inventa est pacis recordatio, sed diaboli instinctu nefario unusquisque contra alium, minas, um et mortis dispendium obtulerunt, et ita a Londonia, infecto pacis reformandae negotio, atriaverunt [...][24]

Table continued on the following pages

[19] *AM*, I, 162–80.

[20] The Annals of Tewkesbury's entry for 1258 in the printed edition extends for five more pages with no similarities to the other two chronicles under consideration here.

[21] The Annals of Tewkesbury's entry for 1259 in the printed edition includes another two paragraphs with no similarities to the other two chronicles under consideration here.

[22] Cf. n. 20.

[23] Cf. n. 20.

[24] The Annals of Tewkesbury's entry for 1263 in the printed edition includes another four and a half pages with no similarities to the other two chronicles under consideration here.

Table 8.1 *(cont.)*: Close correspondence in the Neath chronicle and Cardiff chronicle entries for 1258–1268, with comparison to the Annals of Tewkesbury

Date	Cardiff chronicle	Neath chronicle
1264[25]	Mense Maii d*ictu*s Gilb*ertu*s de Clare vna *die* hora *pr*ima iux*ta* Lewes accipie*n*s a d*om*ino Symone de Monte Forti com*ite* Leycest*r*ie senescallo Angl*ie* arma milita*r*ia cum pl*ur*ib*us* aliis, f*a*ct*us* est comes Glouc*estrie* et Hertford*ie*. Quo die circa horam nona*m* cep*er*un*t* in *pr*elio satis duro Hen*ricu*m regem Angl*ie*, Eadwardum *eius* primogenitum, *et* Ric*ardum* comit*em* Cornubie, regem Al[e]man*i*e uocatum, et pl*ur*es alios <u>comit*es*</u> et barones Angl*ie*, int*er*fectis ex ut*ra*que *par*te t*r*ibus milib*us*.	Mense Maii d*ictu*s Gilb*ertu*s de Clara una <u>di*erum*</u> hora *pr*ima iux*ta* Lewes, accipiens a d*om*ino Symo*n*e de Monte Forti, com*ite* Leycest*r*ie, senesc*allo* Angli*a*, arma militaria cum pl*ur*ibus aliis, f*a*ct*us* est com*es* Glouc*estrie* et Hertford*ie*. Quo die c*ir*ca horam nona*m* ceperunt in *pr*elio satis duro Hen*ricu*m regem Angl*ie*, *et* <u>Hen*ricus*</u> Edwardus *pr*imogenitus [*corr*. Edwardum *pr*imogenitum] *eius*, *et* Ric*ardum* comit*em* Cornubie regem Aliman*i*e vocatum *et* pl*ur*es alios <u>comit*em*</u> [*corr*. com*ites*] *et* baron*es* <u>*et* milit*es*</u> Angl*ie* int*er*fect*i*s ex ut*ra*que *par*te t*r*ibus milib*us*.
1265	Prid*ie* Non*as* Aug*usti* apud Euesham in prelio satis duro int*er*fect*us* e*st* d*omi*n*us* <u>Symon</u> de Monte Forti <u>comes Leycest*r*ie</u>, d*omi*n*us* Henric*us* fili*us* ei*us* <u>*pr*imog*enitus*</u>, *et* cum eo pl*ur*es <u>barones *et*</u> milites et Wal*ense*s q*u*o*ru*m n*um*er*us* nescit*ur*. Eodem anno obiit d*omi*n*us* W[illelmus] de Radenore ep*iscopu*s Land*auensis*.	Prid*ie* nonas Aug*usti* ap*u*d Euesham in *pr*elio satis duro int*er*fectus est d*omi*n*us* <u>Symon*em*</u> [*corr*. Symon] de Monte Forti *et* d*omi*n*us* Hen*ricu*s fili*us* ei*us* *et* cum e*is* pl*ur*es <u>com*item* *et* baron*em*</u> [*corr*. comit*es et* barones], milites *et* Wal*ense*s, q*u*o*ru*m n*um*erus nescit*ur*. Eodem anno *o*biit d*omi*n*us* Willelm*us* de Radenore ep*iscopu*s Land*auensis* <u>.xi. Kal*endas* Sept*embris*, consecr*atur* Willi*elmu*s de Breusa Land*auensis* ep*iscopus*.</u>[26]
1266	<u>Sexto Kal*endas* D*ecembris* consec*r*atur d*omi*n*us* Willelm*us* de Brewes ep*iscopus* Land*auensis*, *et* in crastino s*anc*ti Eadmu*n*di reg*is*, intronizat*us* e*st*</u>. Eodem die dedicacio ecclesie <u>Land*auensis*</u>. Die sabb*a*ti *p*ost <u>Epiphaniam D*om*in*i*</u>, Griffin*us* ap Rees constabul*o et* armig*er* suus cap*ti* in castro <u>d*e*</u> Kayrd*iuia*, *et* <u>d*i*ctus Griffin*us* parum post</u> missus ad <u>Hybern*iam* apud Kilbenny</u> [*corr*. Kilkenny] ad incarcerand*um*.	In crastino s*anc*ti Edmu*n*di reg*is et m*art*ir*is, W[illielm*u*s] de Breusa Land*auensis* ep*iscopus* intronizatur. Eodem die dedicacio ecclesie ei*us*dem loci. <u>Eodem anno</u> post <u>fest*um* Epiphanie die Sabati, cap*tus*</u> est Griffinus ap Reys in castro Kerdiuie. <u>Postea</u> missus ad Kilkenni ad inc*ar*cerand*um*.

[25] The Annals of Tewkesbury end at 1263.

[26] He was elected 7 March 1266 and consecrated 23 May 1266. This notice should be in the following year.

Table 8.1 *(cont.)*: Close correspondence in the Neath chronicle and Cardiff chronicle entries for 1258–1268, with comparison to the Annals of Tewkesbury

Date	Cardiff chronicle	Neath chronicle
1267	Rex Francie cruce sig*n*at*us* est, *et* <u>mu</u>lti <u>com*ites*</u> <u>barones *et*</u> milites F*r*ancie *et* Ang*lie*, *et di*ct*us* rex fecit noua*m* <u>moneta*m*</u>.	Cruce signat*us* est rex Francie, <u>com*item*,</u> <u>baron*em*</u> [*corr.* com*ites*, baron*es*] *et* milites <u>pl*ures*</u> Ang*lie et* Francie, *et di*ct*us* rex fecit noua*m*.[27]
1268	Tercio Id*us* Ap*r*ilis inceptu*m* est op*us* cast*r*i de Kayrphily. Eode*m* anno, in p*r*elio duro, <u>capt*us* est</u> Gilbertus fi*lius* Gilberti de <u>Vmf*r*amuyle</u>, Ioh*ann*es Martel, R*i*c*ardus* Herberd, *et* pl*ures* pedites. <u>Non scit*ur*</u> ueracit*er* numer*us* occis*orum*.	iii. Idus Ap*r*ilis inceptu*m* est op*us* castr*o* de Karfilli. Eode*m* anno, in p*r*elio duro, <u>capti</u> <u>su*n*t</u> Gilbe*r*tus fi*lius* Gilberti de <u>Vnif*r*auile</u> [*corr.* Vmf*r*auile], Ioh[*annes*] Martel, Ric*ardus* de He*r*be*r**t*, *et* pl*ures* p*e*dites. Nu*m*e*r*us occisio*rum* veracit*er* <u>nescit*ur*</u>.

For example, in the entry for 1264, the Neath chronicle has the incorrect reading 'Henricus Edwardus primogenitus eius' where the correct reading in the Cardiff chronicle is 'Edwardum eius primogenitum' ('Edward his firstborn [was captured]'); as well as the incorrect readings *comitem* instead of *comites*; *dierum* instead of *die*. In the entry for 1265, the Neath chronicle notices the consecration of William de Braose as Bishop of Llandaf when his election should be in (as it is in the Cardiff chronicle) the following year, on 23 May 1266, as if the copyist forgot to begin the next entry for 1266. Also in the entry for 1265, the Neath chronicle has *Symonem* where it should be *Symon* and *comitem et baronem* where it should be *comites et barones*. In the entry for 1267, the Neath chronicle reads 'rex fecit nouam' ('the king made a new') where it should be 'rex fecit nouam monetam' ('the king made a new currency'); the Neath chronicle has not copied the last word. These examples show that the text of the Cardiff chronicle in MS Royal 6 B XI is more accurate than the text of the Neath chronicle in the Breviate manuscript. Taken with evidence from the Annals of Tewkesbury discussed below, I argue that the Cardiff chronicle's immediate exemplar was an intermediary source between the Annals of Tewkesbury and the Neath chronicle. Neath may have reached out to the neighbouring Benedictine priory for information because of its intimate connection to the de Clare family seat of Tewkesbury.

---

[27] Should be *nouam monetam*, supplied from the Cardiff chronicle.

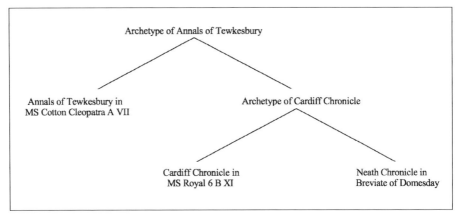

Figure 8.1: The Cardiff chronicle's relationship with the Annals of Tewkesbury. Figure by author.

Together, Tables 8.2 and 8.3 below show that the Neath chronicle could not be the intermediary between the Annals of Tewkesbury and the Cardiff chronicle. This is because (as Table 8.2 shows) the Cardiff chronicle is in closer agreement with the Annals of Tewkesbury than the Neath chronicle is,[28] and because (as Table 8.3 shows) the Cardiff chronicle is closer to the Neath chronicle in several entries. Take, for example, the Annals of Tewkesbury's abbreviation (in Table 8.3, s.a. 1169) of 'Cathaniam et alias quatuor civitates', which both the Cardiff chronicle and the Neath chronicle shorten to 'quinque ciuitates', or the error shared between the Cardiff chronicle and the Neath chronicle (Table 8.3, s.a. 1197) that names Rhys ap Gruffudd 'Resus filius Lewelini'.[29] The evidence in Tables 8.2 and 8.3 indicate that it is more likely that the Cardiff chronicle is the intermediary between the other two.

---

[28] The entries in the Cardiff chronicle that agree word-for-word with the Annals of Tewkesbury are: s.aa. 1148, 1152, 1155–1164, 1173–1190, 1192–1199, 1207–1210, 1219, 1220. The entries in the Cardiff chronicle that agree with the Annals of Tewkesbury with the exception of one- to four-word variations or interlinear additions are: s.aa. 1066, 1089, 1089, 1093, 1095, 1100, 1106, 1107, 1119, 1121, 1122, 1123, 1133, 1135, 1140, 1141, 1155, 1183, 1191, 1200, 1203, 1211, 1213–1215, 1220–1222, 1224, 1227, 1228. The variation between the Annals of Tewkesbury and the other two chronicles (the Neath chronicle and the Cardiff chronicle) suggests that the Cardiff chronicle used a variant version of the Annals of Tewkesbury as they now exist in MS Cotton Cleopatra A VII, perhaps a common exemplar shared between the two. For a diagram that illustrates this relationship, see Figure 8.1. This diagram shows Tewkesbury sources only; the Neath chronicle shows the use of other sources as well.

[29] The Annals of Winchester correctly refer to his father as *Griffinus*, while the Annals of Waverley, the Annals of Margam, and the Annals of Worcester do not mention the event.

Table 8.2: Examples of the Cardiff chronicle's closer agreement with the Annals of Tewkesbury

Date	Annals of Tewkesbury (excerpted)	Cardiff chronicle	Neath chronicle
1152	Facto divortio inter Ludovicum regem Franciae et Elienor reginam, accepit eam Henricus dux in uxorem, filius imperatricis.	Facto diuorcio inter Ludouicum regem Francie et Alianoram reginam, accepit eam Henricus dux filius imperatricis in uxorem.	Facto diuorcio inter Lodowicum regem Francorum et Helienoram reginam,[30] eam cepit Henricus dux.
1164	Rogerus consecratur in episcopum Wygorniae, x. kal. Septembris [...] Thomas Cantuariae archiepiscopus regi invisus effectus transfretavit.	Rogerus filius comitis Gloucestrie consecratur in episcopum Wygornie. Et Thomas archiepiscopus Cantuarie, regi inuisus, transfretauit.	Rogerus filius Roberti consulis eligitur pontifex Wigornie.
1208	Omne divinum interdictum est officium per totam Angliam .ix. kal. Aprilis, (unde rex dissaisiavit eclessiasticas personas ab omnibus possessionibus suis), praeter baptismum parvulorum et poenitentias morientium, propter Stephanum archiepiscopum Cantuarie et ejusdem loci conventum.	Omne diuinum officium interdictum est per totam Angliam .ix. Kalendas Aprilis, preter baptismum paruulorum et penitentias moriencium, propter Stephanum archiepiscopum Cantuarie.	Interdictum septenne in regno Anglie ab omni officio et sacramento ecclesiastico preter baptismum paruulorum et penitentias morientium et rex I[ohannes] noluit accipere archiepiscopum. Incepit interdictum mense Marcii dominica qua cantatur 'Isti sunt dies'. Iohannes[31] rex relegauit exilio Willielmum de Breusa cum vxore et filio[32] et omnia sua occupauit.
1210	Grave tallagium fecit rex super omnes ecclesias Angliae. [...] Willelmus de Breuse evasit in Franciam; uxor ejus et liberi capti et incarcerate fame perierunt. Magnum gelu fuit a vigilia Circumcisionis usque ad festum Sancti Valentini.	Graue tallagium fecit rex super omnes ecclesias Anglie. Willelmus de Breuse euasit in Franciam, et uxor eius et liberi capti et incarcerati, fame perierunt. Magnum gelu fuit a vigilia Circumcisionis usque ad festum sancti Ualentini.	Rex Iohannes transfretauit in Yberniam mense Iunii et rediit mense Septembris. Willielmus de Breusa maior fugit in Franciam. Rex incarcerauit Matildam de sancto Valerio et cum filio suo Willielmo iuniore qui fame perierunt.

[30] MS reginam *et*.
[31] MS *Ricardus*.
[32] MS filus.

Table 8.2 *(cont.)*: Examples of the Cardiff chronicle's closer agreement with the Annals of Tewkesbury

Date	Annals of Tewkesbury (excerpted)	Cardiff chronicle	Neath chronicle
1225	Concessa fuit regi quintadecima de omnibus mobilibus secularium et religiosorum.	Concessa fuit d*omi*no regi q*ui*ntadecima de omn*ibus* mobilib*us* secularium *et* religiosor*um*.	Concessa e*st* d*omi*no regi, ex [quintadeci]\ma/[33] p*ar*s secular*ium* et religiosor*um* concedi*tur* d*omi*no regi.

Table 8.3: Examples of the Cardiff chronicle's closer agreement with the Neath chronicle

Date	Annals of Tewkesbury (excerpted)	Cardiff chronicle	Neath chronicle
1169	Terraemotus magnus factus est in Sicilia, qui Cathaniam et alias quatuor civitates subvertit.	T*erremotus* magn*us* factus e*st* in Sicilia[34] q*ui* q*ui*nque ciuitates s*ub*uertit, *et* ecclesia de Keynesh*am* inchoata e*st* a Will*elmo* comite Glouc*estrie*.	Terre motus magnus factus est in Sicilia, q*ui*nque ciuitates s*ub*uertit, *et* Will*ielmus* com*es* Glouc*estrie con*struxit Keynesham.
1180	Ludovicus rex Franciae, Johannes de Saresberia episcopus Carnotensis, Robertus abbas Glastoniae, Hugo abbas Sancti Edmundi obierunt.	Obiit Ludouic*us* rex Fr*a*ncie, cui successit Ph*ilippus*.	O*biit* Lodowicus rex Fr*a*ncie, cui successit Philippus rex.
1197	Cometa apparuit tota hyeme fere. Terraemotus factus est. [...] Obiit Resus rex Walliae, et Hawisia comitissa Glocestriae, viii. kal. Maii.	Cometa app*ar*uit tota hyeme. T*erremotus* fa*ctus* est. Obiit Resus fil*ius* Lewelini, princeps Walli*e*. Obiit Hawysia com*itissa* Glouc*estrie* .viii. Kalen*das* Maii.	Cometa[35] app*ar*uit hyeme; t*er*re motus f*actus* e*st*. O*biit* filius Lewelini[36] *pr*incipis *et* Hawysia com*itissa* Glouc*estrie*.

---

[33] *Ex* \ma\ is perhaps an error here. I am supplying *quintadecima*, the reading from the Cardiff chronicle. 'Chronicle of the Thirteenth Century', p. 278 supplies *vigesima*. *Pars* in the nominative is non-sensical.

[34] MS Scicilia.

[35] MS corneta.

[36] MS Lewelin*us*.

8. THE CARDIFF CHRONICLE IN LONDON, BRITISH LIBRARY, MS ROYAL 6 B XI

Given the lack of information specific to any of the three houses, this evidence does not discount influence from other chronicles nor the possibility that all three chronicles gleaned information from a now lost source that was interested in Glamorgan generally. At certain points it is actually possible to see where the Cardiff chronicle tailored its Tewkesbury source to fit a non-Tewkesbury audience: first-person plural pronouns that are present in the Annals of Tewkesbury, addressing the community of readers there, are absent in the Cardiff chronicle, indicating that the prose was tailored to fit a non-Tewkesbury audience (Table 8.4). The changes that the Cardiff compilers made to their Tewkesbury source are evidence of the practice of refashioning of a chronicle to fit a new local context.

Table 8.4: The Cardiff chronicle's tailoring of its Tewkesbury source

Date	Annals of Tewkesbury	Cardiff chronicle
1236	**Nos concessimus** domino E[liae] Landavensi episcopo et ejusdem loci capitulo ecclesiam de Lanedern cum pertinentiis suis, retentis decimis de Lanbordan ad opus prioris de Kardif, cujus mensae pertinere dinoscuntur; actum x. kal. Maii. Circa idem tempus confirmaverunt dicti episcopus et capitulum Landavense omnia ecclesiastica beneficia quae **habemus** in dicto episcopatu, prout continetur in scripto **quod nobis confecerunt.**	Abb*as et* co*nuentus* Theouk*s*berie **conces-serun**t *domino* Elie Land*auensis* e*piscopo, et* ei*us*dem loci capit*ulo,* ecc*lesiam* de Lan*adern* cum p*ertinentiis* suis, retentis decimis de Lamforda*m* que pertinent ad mensa*m* prioris de Kairdi*via*. .x°. Kalen*das* Maii. Circa Pentecoste*m, d*o*minus* E[lyas] ep*iscopus* Land*auensis et* ei*us*dem loci cap*itulu*m *con*firmauerunt monach*is* Theouk*s*berie om*n*ia ecc*lesiastic*a beneficia que **h***aberu*nt in ep*iscop*atu Land*auense.*

Neath's copying of its Cardiff source probably occurred after 1268, when the Cardiff chronicle concludes (assuming the exemplar concluded at 1268 as well), but before c. 1300–1304, when the Neath Abbey Breviate manuscript was created according to Daniel Huws.[37] During this small window of time, a Cardiff source travelled to Neath and was used by the Neath chronicle compilers. This act could have been very nearly contemporary with the creation of the Breviate of Domesday itself, and presumably was the result of a deliberate search for sources about the de Clares.

These copying relationships indicate that Cardiff Priory, the probable site of compilation of the Cardiff chronicle, and Tewkesbury's only daughter house in the lordship of Glamorgan, was an intermediary for the transmission of thirteenth-century annalistic records from Tewkesbury to Neath, a portion of a Marcher monastic

---

[37] Huws, 'Neath Abbey *Breviate*', p. 49.

network of textual transmission not previously accounted for. This Cardiff source was probably not Neath's only source for information about Tewkesbury, as two annals in the Neath chronicle that deal with events at Tewkesbury (1187 and 1201) are not in the Cardiff chronicle.[38] Nonetheless it attests to the circulation of sources between Marcher houses interested in Glamorgan events.

The transmission of this source can be attributed to the patronage relationships that link the various houses. It makes sense that any chronicle arising from one of the many Glamorgan houses under the patronage of the de Clares — Cistercian and Benedictine alike — would focus on their lives, births, deaths, and activities[39] and that chroniclers slightly further west into the interior of Welsh lands held by Marcher lords, such as those at Neath, would look to a house like Cardiff — a degree closer to the centre of de Clare power and administration, and established a generation or so earlier than Neath — for information about their patrons.[40] The use of such a source, containing information ultimately from the Annals of Tewkesbury, by Neath chroniclers highlights the role of mutual patrons in linking geographically disparate houses in the March. Neath and Cardiff are not linked by affiliation; they were founded by different

---

[38] 'Chronicle of the Thirteenth Century', s.aa. 1178: 'Monasterium Teokesbirie cum officinis conflag[r]atur. Calixtus papa veniens ad pedes Alexandri absolutus est'; 1201: 'Combusta est ecclesia Wygornie. Obiit Alanus abbas Theoksburie et successit Walterus. Terre motus per loca Anglia.' While the entry for 1178 matches closely with the Annals of Tewkesbury (*AM*, I, 52), 1201 does not match at all.

[39] While the Cardiff chronicle reports generally on the activities of the kings of England and the archbishops of Canterbury, and on a more local level takes interest in the succession of the bishops of Llandaf and the abbots of Tewkesbury, it mentions the births, deaths, and activities of the de Clare family with the greatest regularity; see Cardiff chronicle, s.aa. 1222, 1230 (Gilbert de Clare, Fifth Earl of Gloucester); 1243, 1262 (Richard de Clare, Sixth Earl of Gloucester); 1244, 1263, 1264, 1289, 1290, 1295 (Gilbert the Red, Seventh Earl of Gloucester); 1247 (Bogo de Clare); 1258 (William de Clare).

[40] Tewkesbury was founded by Robert fitz Hamon *c.* 1102 with a new site at the confluence of the Severn and the Avon; a charter of ordination of Gerald, first Abbot of Tewkesbury, transferred from Cranborne in 1102, is in MS Cotton Cleopatra A VII, fol. 94ᵛ, printed in Dugdale, II, 81 (Appendix of Instruments, no. LXXXVII). For useful historical analysis of Robert's activities, see Ralph A. Griffiths, *Conquerors and Conquered in Medieval Wales* (New York: St. Martin's Press, 1994), pp. 22–24; Brian Golding, 'Trans-border Transactions: Patterns of Patronage in Anglo-Norman Wales', *HSJ*, 16 (2005), 27–46 (p. 35). The abbey was later patronized by the de Clare earls of Gloucester, who claimed Tewkesbury as their ancestral house. By Karen Stöber's count, this family patronized no less than sixteen religious houses by *c.* 1300: see her *Late Medieval Monasteries and their Patrons: England and Wales, c. 1300–1540*, Studies in the History of Medieval Religion, 29 (Woodbridge: Boydell, 2007), p. 164.

orders, making the point of contact all the more striking and counter to our expectations of the mutual isolation of the orders. The link between the two houses constitutes evidence for the influence of aristocratic patrons in prompting contact between otherwise geographically disparate monasteries.

Gilbert de Clare, the last de Clare Earl of Gloucester (c. 1291–1314), would have been alive at the time of the early fourteenth-century copying of the Cardiff chronicle into MS Royal 6 B XI, while his father, Earl Gilbert the Red (d. 1295), a known patron of Neath, Margam, and Tewkesbury, was alive at the time of the Cardiff chronicle's compilation around or after 1268.[41] Gilbert the Red was recently deceased when the Neath Abbey Breviate manuscript was created c. 1300–1304. It is therefore not surprising that both chronicles take such interest in their lives and that a compiler at Neath Abbey interested in the family's activities would reach eastwards for sources. In this way, de Clare patronage of this group of houses aided a significant amount of chronicling activity. Their patronage may have played a key role in the production of these contemporary Glamorgan chronicles.

It is possible to take this argument a step further and suggest that changes in the de Clare family's fortunes may have prompted the gathering of materials concerning the family at this specific time and place — Cardiff in the late thirteenth century — to record the Cardiff chronicle in MS Royal 6 B XI.[42] The end of the thirteenth century was a dire time for the family: Earl Gilbert the Red died in 1295, and his young son died prematurely, at the age of twenty-seven, at the Battle of Bannockburn in Scotland.[43] R. A. Griffiths characterizes these events as catastrophic:

> The tragic death of the last of the de Clare earls at Bannockburn on 24 June 1314 augured ill for Glamorgan. To indications, evident in Cardiff at least, that the era

---

[41] *Cartae et Alia Munimenta quae ad Dominium de Glamorgan Pertinent*, ed. by George Thomas Clarke, 6 vols (Cardiff: Lewis, 1910), III, 927; V, 1677–90; Frederick George Cowley, *The Monastic Order in South Wales, 1066–1349* (Cardiff: University of Wales Press, 1977), pp. 245–49; *The Victoria History of the County of Gloucester* (London: Victoria County History, 1907–), II, ed. by William Page (1907), pp. 61–66.

[42] In this transmission scenario, the common exemplar of the Cardiff chronicle and the Neath chronicle needs to have been written before the end of the thirteenth century, in order to make it to Neath between 1300 and 1304, when it was written into the Breviate flyleaves; Huws, 'Neath Abbey *Breviate*', p. 49.

[43] The last recorded prior of Cardiff, one Simon, is also in 1295; *The Heads of Religious Houses: England & Wales*, 3 vols (Cambridge: Cambridge University Press, 2001–08), II: *1216–1377*, ed. by David M. Smith and Vera C. M. London (2001), p. 95.

of economic prosperity was already waning, it added a certain apprehension at the prospect of royal custody of Glamorgan until the partition of the de Clare inheritance among the late earl's sisters. Moreover, some of the upland Welsh saw it as an opportunity to regain the independence they had lost.[44]

The region entered a period of chaos after Gilbert's death. The earldom of Gloucester, and along with it the patronage of Neath, Tewkesbury, and its associated monasteries, passed to the Despensers and then to the Crown. These events coincide with the date of the Cardiff chronicle's extant copy in MS Royal 6 B XI. Could the compilers' interest in the past have been stimulated by this period of uncertainty? The last section of the text is indeed most interested in the activities of Gilbert the Red, perhaps commemorating their recently deceased patron, and the copyist does not bring the chronicle up to date. The chronicle's pairing of local history with universal history places the de Clare family in the context of Christian chronology, with a focus on episodes of ecclesiastical politics (Ceolfrith's letter to the King of the Picts) and sanctity in Britain (excerpts from Bede and St Anselm) that may represent an attempt at preservation during a time of great loss and instability.

Marcher Chronicles and Native Wales

I conclude with a final note on the relevance of these chronicles to native Welsh historical writing. Close relationships bound by patronage, which resulted in textual transmission westwards from Gloucestershire to Glamorgan, had some effect on the production of historical literature in native Wales. The Neath chronicle is particularly important to studies of Welsh vernacular historical writing because it was used as a source for middle portions of the Welsh chronicle *Brenhinedd y Saesson* ('The Kings of the English'), mentioned above.[45] This continuation of Geoffrey of Monmouth's *De gestis Britonum* provides a synchronic account of Anglo-Saxons, Anglo-Normans, and Welsh to 1461.[46]

---

[44] Griffiths, *Conquerors and Conquered*, p. 345.

[45] For discussion see Smith, 'Historical Writing'; Brynley F. Roberts, '*Ystoriaeu Brenhinedd Ynys Brydein*: A Fourteenth-Century Welsh Brut', in *Narrative in Celtic Tradition: Essays in Honor of Edgar M. Slotkin*, ed. by Joseph F. Eska, CSANA Yearbook, 8–9 (Hamilton, NY: Colgate University Press, 2011), pp. 217–27; for an edition, see *BS*.

[46] The text in the earlier of the two manuscripts containing *Brenhinedd y Saesson*, London, BL, MS Cotton Cleopatra B V, part 1, fols 111ʳ–64ᵛ, is incomplete, ending at 1198. It was probably written by monks at Valle Crucis Abbey. The second manuscript, Aberystwyth, NLW, MS 7006D (*Llyfr Du Basing*) was written by two scribes, one of whom was Gutun Owain, who may

8. THE CARDIFF CHRONICLE IN LONDON, BRITISH LIBRARY, MS ROYAL 6 B XI

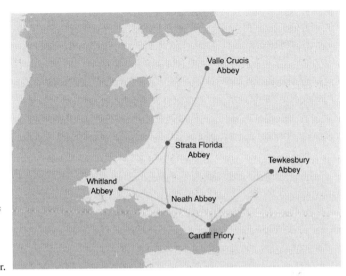

Figure 8.2: The transmission of sources from Tewkesbury to Glamorgan, and from Glamorgan to North Wales. Figure by author.

While the text's two manuscripts are probably from Valle Crucis, a place of composition somewhere in South Wales is suspected.[47] *Brenhinedd y Saesson* contains English information taken from William of Malmesbury, the Annals of Winchester, and the Neath chronicle. That these English sources were able to travel through South Wales to Valle Crucis in North Wales and appear in a Welsh-language chronicle seems nothing short of extraordinary until one understands the systems of patronage and transmission that enabled textual access in these regions (see Figure 8.2).

Figure 8.2 provides a visualization of the axes of textual transmission that enabled information to travel between native Wales and houses of the March.[48] J. Beverley Smith describes these axes as follows:

have been working at Valle Crucis and perhaps Basingwerk as well. The text is based on a lost Latin exemplar which was translated into Welsh sometime prior to *c.* 1330, the date of its earliest manuscript, MS Cotton Cleopatra B V; this manuscript also contains the Cotton Cleopatra version of *Brut y Brenhinedd*, a Welsh translation of Geoffrey's *De gestis Britonum*. For dating and provenance arguments, see Daniel Huws, *Medieval Welsh Manuscripts* (Cardiff: University of Wales Press, 2000), pp. 12 n. 21, 53, 190 n. 20. See too Huw Pryce, Chapter 1, and Barry Lewis, Chapter 5, above.

[47] Smith, 'Historical Writing', p. 56; Huws, *Medieval Welsh Manuscripts*, pp. 12 n. 21, 53; Huws, 'Neath Abbey *Breviate*'; *BS*, p. xlvi.

[48] The map in Figure 8.2 was created using Palladio, a historical data visualization tool created by Stanford Humanities + Design <http://hdlab.stanford.edu/palladio/> [accessed 23 April 2018].

One instructive axis extends between Strata Florida, where thirteenth-century annalistic work may be recognized with some assurance and Valle Crucis, where several historical texts are known to have been written at a date probably *c.* 1330. Another extends from Strata Florida to Whitland [...] A third would appear to lie between Strata Florida and the scriptorium [at Neath] [...] that was the source of an important body of historical material bound together with [...] the Breviate of Domesday.[49]

Cardiff Priory and Tewkesbury Abbey can be added to Smith's model, demonstrating how English annalistic sources were able to travel into Wales.

This chapter attests to the importance of analysing Latin chronicle sources for evidence of contact between Anglo-Norman/Marcher monasteries and Welsh ones, as well as Anglo-Norman ecclesiastical interest in and knowledge of events in Wales. It attests to a greater degree of interaction in the collection of historical sources than previously understood and demonstrates a pattern, also seen elsewhere, of cross-cultural transmission in Latin before translation into the vernacular.[50]

Notes on Text and Translation

Suspensions, abbreviations, ligatures, and brevigraphs have been expanded and marked by italics. Punctuation has been added and capital letters normalized. Letters supplied by the editor are in square brackets. Interlinear glosses and superscript letters are marked by back slash and forward slash, and marginal glosses are footnoted. The footnoes also include significant variants from the Annals of Tewkesbury (T). Underlining by a later hand in the manuscript is not noted here.

---

[49] Smith, 'Historical Writing', p. 72.

[50] I am grateful to the participants of the 'Chronicles in Medieval Wales and its Neighbours' conference at the University of Cambridge, 25–26 May 2016 for their comments on an early version of this piece, and Ben Guy and the anonymous reviewer of this volume for their very helpful suggestions and corrections. All errors are my own.

The Cardiff Chronicle: Text
London, BL, MS Royal 6 B XI, fols 105ra–108vb, 112.

[fol. 105ra]

[1066] m^mo.lxvi. Obiit Edwardus rex \Anglie .xvi. Kalendas Maii/[51] et Willelmus dux Northmanie Angliam adquisiuit.

[1087] m^mo.lxxxvii. Obiit Willelmus rex senior \v^to Kalendas Aprilis/[52] et Willelmus Rufus filius eius regnauit.

[1089] m^mo.lxxxix. Obiit Lanfrancus archiepiscopus Kalendis Aprilis, et terra mota est. Et ecclesia Sancti Petri Gloucestrie iterum renouatur.[53]

[1091] m^mo.xci. Ecclesia Sancte Marie[54] Theouksberie inchoata est Idibus Aprilibus.[55]

[1093] m^mo.xciii. Anselmus in archiepiscopum[56] eligitur .xv. Kalendas Maii.

[1095] m^mo.xcv. Obiit Wlstanus episcopus Wygornie .viii. Kalendas Aprilis.

[1100] m^mo.c. Obiit rex Willelmus iunior Kalendis Aprilis et Henricus regnauit.

[1106] m^mo.cvi. Henricus rex cepit Robertum fratrem suum .viii°. Kalendas Aprilis.

[1107] m^mo.cvii. Obiit Robertus filius Haymonis .xviii. Kalendas.[57]

---

[51] 'Anglie .xvi. Kalendas Maii', added superscript, is in the same hand as the main text.
[52] 'v^to Kalendas Aprilis', added superscript, is in the same hand as the main text.
[53] T *inchoata est*.
[54] Interlinear gloss in later hand: 'nunc Tewkesbury'.
[55] T does not have an annal entry for 1091.
[56] T *archipraesulatum*.
[57] The scribe does not supply a month for this date.

[1110] m^mo.cx. Obiit Giraldus primus abbas Theoksberie .iiii^to. Idus Aprilis, et fluvius qui uocatur Trenta apud Snotingeham a prima [mense aestatis] usque ad terciam exsiccatus est.[58]

[1119] m^mo.cxix. Terra mota est Nonis Aprilibus et pons Gloucestrie inceptus est.

[1121] m^mo.cxxi. Henricus rex desponsauit Athelizam reginam .iiii^to. Idus Aprilis.

[1122] m^mo.cxxii. [Civitas][59] Gloucestrie igne denuo \conflagratur/[60] cum abbathia Nonis Aprilibus.

[1123] m^mo.cxxiii. Dedicacio ecclesie Theoksberie .viii°. Idus Aprilis.

[1133] m^mo.cxxxiii. Robertus Curtehese dux Normannie obiit apud Kardiuiam[61] vii°. Kalendas Aprilis.

[1135] m^mo.cxxxv. Obiit Henricus rex .viii. Idus Aprilis, cui successit Stephanus nepos eius.

[1140] m^mo.cxl. Eclipsis solis facta est .viii°. Idus Aprilis.

[1141] m^mo.cxli. Stephanus rex apud Lincolniam .iii°. Kalendas Aprilis captus est, et Robertus consul Gloucestrie apud Wyntoniam, et alter pro altero redditur.

[1144] m^mo.cxliiii. Cometa apparuit.

[1147] m^mo.cxlvii. Obiit Robertus consul[62] Gloucestrie et sepul-[fol. 105rb]-tus est apud Sanctum Iacobum Bristollie, cui successit Willelmus filius eius.

[1148] m^mo.cxlviii. Eclipsis lune apparuit, et obiit Huthredus Landauensis episcopus.

---

[58] I am grateful to the anonymous reviewer for supplying this emendation.

[59] T reports 'Civitas Glaorna igne denuo conflagratur cum abbatia', 'The city of Gloucester is burnt a second time by fire, with the abbey', so I supply *civitas* here, where there is an erasure.

[60] 'conflagratur' is added superscript in the same hand as the main text. A small caret between 'denuo' and 'cum' points to the word's insertion here.

[61] This place name does not appear expanded anywhere in the text. I follow the spelling from the Neath chronicle and treat it as a first declension noun.

[62] T *illustris comes*.

[1152] m^{mo}.clii. Facto diuorcio inter Ludouicum regem Francie et Alianoram reginam, accepit eam Henricus dux filius imperatricis in uxorem.

[1154] m^{mo}.cliiii. Obiit Anastasius papa, cui successit Adrianus Anglicus, et obiit Stephanus rex .ii. Kalendas Nouembris, cui successit Henricus.

[1155] m^{mo}.clv. Alianora regina peperit Henricum.

[1156] m^{mo}.clvi. Obiit Willelmus regis primogenitus.

[1157] m^{mo}.clvii. Regina Anglie peperit Ricardum. Obiit Mabilia commitissa Gloucestrie.

[1158] m^{mo}.clviii. Regina Alianora peperit Gaufridum. Henricus rex, facta pace cum Reso, transfretauit, et Henricus filius eius duxit filiam Lodouici regis Francie in uxorem. Terremotus magnus factus est per Angliam.

[1161] m^{mo}.clxi. Obiit Theobaldus archiepiscopus Cantuarie.[63]

[1162] m^{mo}.clxii. Thomas regis Henrici cancellarius factus est archiepiscopus Cantuarie.

[1163] m^{mo}.clxiii. Rogerus filius Roberti consulis Gloucestrie eligitur ad pontificatum Wygornie.

[1164] m^{mo}.clxiiii. Rogerus filius comitis Gloucestrie consecratur in episcopum Wygornie. Et Thomas archiepiscopus Cantuarie, regi inuisus, transfretauit.

[1169] m^{mo}.clxix. Terremotus magnus factus est in Sicilia[64] qui quinque[65] ciuitates subuertit, et ecclesia de Keynesham inchoata est a Willelmo comite Gloucestrie.

[1170] m^{mo}.clxx. Henricus rex fecit coronare Henricum filium suum. Thomas archiepiscopus Cantuarie in ecclesia Christi Cantuarie occiditur .iiii^{to}. Kalendas Ianuarii.

---

[63] Throughout this text, 'Canterbury' appears abbreviated as 'Cant'. I am expanding it as 'Cantuaria', the normal form in Latin.

[64] MS Scicilia.

[65] T *Cathaniam et alias quatuor.*

[fol. 105ᵛᵃ]

[1173] mᵐᵒ.clxxiii. Grauis discordia orta est inter reges Anglie, patrem et filium. Circa mediam noctem uisum est celum rubere.

[1175] mᵐᵒ.clxxv. Henricus rex uenit in Angliam et filius eius cum eo. Archiepiscopus Cantuarie, conuocato concilio apud Londoniam, interdixit omnes prefaciones preter .xᶜᵉᵐ, quas Romana ecclesia inter missarum solempnia decantat.

[1180] mᵐᵒ.clxxx. Obiit Ludouicus rex Francie, cui successit Philippus.

[1182] mᵐᵒ.clxxxii. Corona regni Ierusalem ad regem Anglie Henricum transfertur.

[1183] mᵐᵒ.clxxxiii. Henricus rex iunior obiit. Die sancti Barnabe apostoli, obiit Willelmus comes Gloucestrie et Nicholas episcopus Landauensis et Robertus abbas Theouksberie.

[1189] mᵐᵒ.clxxxix. Obiit Henricus rex, cui successit Ricardus filius eius. Isabella comitissa Gloucestrie nupsit Iohanni comiti de Morttonie.

[1190] mᵐᵒ.clxxxx. Ricardus rex Anglie et Philippus rex Francie et Baldewynus archiepiscopus Cantuarie profecti sunt Ierusalem.

[1191] mᵐᵒ.cxci. Ricardus rex Anglie cepit Achon in terra Ierusalem. Clemens papa obiit, cui successit [Celestinus].[66] Eclipsis solis facta est.

[1192] mᵐᵒ.cxcii. Ricardus rex, audito in Siria quod Iohannes frater suus Angliam in manu forti sibi subiugasset, treugas cepit cum Saladino pagano in tres annos et rediens, captus est a duce Ostrensi et traditus Henrico imperatori Almanye.

[1194] mᵐᵒ.cxciiii. Ricardus rex Anglie rediit in Angliam solutus a capcione.

[1197] mᵐᵒ.cxcvii. Cometa apparuit tota hyeme. Terremotus factus est. Obiit Resus filius Lewelini, princeps[67] Wallie. Obiit Hawysia comitissa Gloucestrie .viii. Kalendas Maii.

---

[66] Blank space left here by the scribe; presumably he meant to come back later to fill in the name of the new pope, but never did.

[67] T rex.

[1199] m^mo.cxcix. Ricardus rex Anglie vi. Kalendas Aprilis sagittatus est apud Chaluns et obiit, cui successit Iohannes frater eius vi^to. Kalendas Iunii.

[1200] m^mo.cc^mo. Maugerius consecratur in episcopum Wygornie. [fol. 105vb] Obiit Hugo episcopus Lincolnie. Factum est diuortium inter Iohannem regem Anglie et Isabel comitissam Gloucestrie.

[1203] m^mo.cc^moiii°. Sanctus[68] Wlstanus canonizatus est Rome .x. Kalendas Maii. Gaufridus prior Lantonie consecratur in episcopum Meneuensem. Magna fames fuit in Anglia ita ut crannokus[69] frumenti uenditum fuit pro .xiiii. solidis.

[1207] m^mo.ccvii. Magister Stephanus de Langetonie electus est Rome a monachis Cantuarie in archiepiscopum Cantuarie sine assensu regis et episcoporum Anglie. Unde rex motus abegit monachos Cantuarie in exilium. Consecratur idem electus a papa Innocencio .iii°. die sancti Iohannis Baptiste. Regina Anglie peperit Henricum primogenitum.

[1208] m^mo.ccviii. Omne diuinum officium interdictum est per totam Angliam .ix. Kalendas Aprilis, preter baptismum paruulorum et penitentias moriencium, propter Stephanum archiepiscopum Cantuarie.

[1210] m^mo.ccx. Graue tallagium fecit rex super omnes ecclesias Anglie. Willelmus de Breuse euasit in Franciam, et uxor eius et liberi capti et incarcerati, fame perierunt. Magnum gelu fuit a vigilia Circumcisionis usque ad festum sancti Ualentini.

[1211] m^mo.ccxi. Walterus de Lacy ab Hybernia agitur in exilium. Otto imperator excommunicatus subiecit sibi Appuliam. Desolata Northwallia per dom-

---

[68] T Beatissimus.

[69] T quarterium. The Cardiff chronicle instead supplies crannokus: DMLBS, s.v. crannoca, crannocus, 'cf. W. crynnog, crannock, curnock, dry measure ranging from ½ quarter to 2 quarters (a) of grain or sim (b) of salt or sim'. The Annals of Tewkesbury (AM, I, 57) state 'maxima fames erat, ita ut quarterium frumenti venderetur xiv. solidis', 'a great famine happened so that a quarter [i.e. 8 bushels] of wheat was sold for fourteen shillings'. The Cardiff chronicle seems to have supplied localized vocabulary, crannocus for quarterium. The word crannocus is found in other contemporary sources, including the Account Roll of the Priory of Holy Trinity, Dublin, the Pipe Rolls, the Annals of Worcester, and the Charters and Records of Hereford Cathedral; see DMLBS for citations.

inum I[ohannem] regem Anglie, Lewelinus princeps eius cum rege pacificatur, datis obsidibus. Willelmus de Breus obiit exule.

[1213] m^(mo).ccxiii. Iohannes rex Anglie, deposito regni diademate die Ascensionis Domini, et subiciens se domino pape Innocencio, cum regno Anglie et Hibernie, coram nuncio domini pape Pandulfo, sub ann[u]o tributo m.m^a, de Anglie .dcc. m^a, de Hybernie ccc.m^a, exceptis denariis sancti Petri. Et sic absolutus est per S[tephanum] Cantuarie archiepiscopum, qui cum coexulibus suis mandatus uenerat .xiii. Kalendas Augusti. Nicholas Tusculanus uenit legatus in Angliam. Obiit Walterus abbas Theouksberie.[70]

[1214] m^(mo).ccxiiii. Interdictum Anglie generale relaxatur,[71] quod durauerat per .vi. annos et .iii. menses. Hugo [fol. 106^r a] factus est abbas Theouksberie. Isabella filia W[illelmi] Marescalli senioris nupsit Gilberto de Clare comiti Gloucestrie.

[1215] m^(mo).ccxv. Iohannes rex Anglie cruce signatur. Dissencio[72] orta est inter regem et barones Anglie.

[1216] m^(mo).ccxvi. Iohannes rex Anglie obiit apud Nowero in crastino sancte Lucie virginie. Henricus filius regis Iohannis coronatur apud Gloucestriam, W[idone] legato ei coronam regni imponente .xv. Kalendas Nouembris.[73]

[1217] m^(mo).ccxvii. Pugnante Domino pro Henrico rege et regno Anglie apud Lyncolniam die sancti Athelberti, et in mari die sancti Bartholomei inter Sandwych et insulam de Thanet, contriti sunt hostes regis et regni, ita ut Lodouicus, prestita caucione de parendo[74] iudicio ecclesie, absolutus et uiliter expulsus, rediret in Franciam. Duo soles uisi sunt die[75] sancti Marci circa uesperam. Vigilia sancti Michelis, Lodouico recedente, totum regnum pacificatur. Obiit Magister Alexander Nequam abbas Cyrencestrie. Castrum Wygornie datur monachis eiusdem loci usque ad motam turris. Baronibus obsidentibus castrum de Lincolnie, legatus et Marescallus cum magno excercitu ieurunt illuc,

---

[70] In T Walter's death is recorded in the following year, 1214.

[71] T *solutum est*.

[72] T *Turbatio magna*.

[73] Henry was crowned on 28 October [5th Kalends of November]; 'xv' is an error for 'v' in the text.

[74] MS *parando*.

[75] T *in crastino*.

et irru*m*pentes *con*gressi su*n*t cu*m* baronibus. *Et* occiso com*ite* de P*er*tico, capti sunt barones *et* Franci *et* m*u*lti magnates circit*us* .xl., *et* de militibus .ccc., *et* ampli*us* de seruientib*us* ignorat*ur* num*er*us, *et* ciuitas data e*st* in direp*er*ci*on*em.

[1219] m*mo*.ccxix. Vicesima ec*cl*esi*a*rum de t*r*ibus annis precedentib*us* dat*ur* in succ*ursum* Terre S*an*c*t*e. Capta e*st* ciuitas Damyete a *christ*ianis Non*is* Nouemb*ris* uirtute diuina. Hinc e*st* v*bi*: 'Capta fuit celeb*ris* Nonis Damieta Nouembr*is*'.⁷⁶ Hugo Foliot *con*secratur *in* episcopu*m* Hereford*ie*. Wille*lm*us p*r*ior de Goldcl*iuia*⁷⁷ [fol. 106ʳᵇ] factu*s* e*st* ep*iscopus* Landau*ensis* in Octob*re*.

[1220] m*mo*.ccxx. Nata e*st* Gileb*er*to de Clare filia no*min*e Amicia .xi. K*alendas* Iunii. Corp*us* b*ea*ti Thome m*ar*tyris t*r*anslatu*m* e*st* a Steph*ano* Cantu*ar*ie a*r*chiep*iscop*o Non*is* Iulii. Henr*icus* rex it*er*ato coronat*ur* Londoni*am* ad Pentecost*en*.

[1221] m*mo*.ccxxi. P*r*ioratu*s* de Kayrd*iuia* reu*o*c*atis* domi⁷⁸ monachis t*r*aditu*r* Henrico Capell*ano* ad firma*m*. Soror reg*is* Henr*ici* nupsit Alexandro regi Scotor*um*. Noua ecclesia Sar*um* incepta e*st* die s*an*cti Uital*is* m*a*rtyris ponente Pandulfo legato p*r*imum lapide*m* p*r*o domino papa, *secun*du*m* p*r*o rege Ang*lie*, t*er*ciu*m* p*r*o com*ite* Sa*r*esberie Will*elm*o Lungespee, q*uartum* p*r*o comitiss[a] Sa*r*esberie, quintu*m* p*r*o ep*iscop*o loci, *et* sic magnates Ang*lie et* abb*a*tes quisque p*r*o se.

[1222] m*mo*.ccxxii. Gilberto de Clare nasci*tur* filius no*min*e Ricardus .ii. Non*as* Aug*u*sti. Eode*m* anno extiteru*n*t p*l*urim*e* tempestates. Damieta, ante t*r*ienium a *Christ*ianis opten*t*a, reddit*ur* Sarascenis, in cui*us* con*m*utaci*on*e reddit*ur* *christ*ianis uera cr*ux*, *et* captiui ex ut*r*aque p*ar*te liberantur, datis treugis usq*ue* ad .vii*te*. annos. A*r*chiep*iscopu*s Cant*uar*ie tenuit sole*m*pne concilium apud Oxoni*am*.

[1224] m*mo*.ccxxiiii. Inceptu*m* e*st* nouu*m* op*us* ecclesie Wygorn*ie*. Soror reg*is* Henr*ici* nupsit Will*elm*o Marscallo iuniori. Rex cep*it* castr*um* de Bedeford *et*

---

⁷⁶ T *Decembris*. The Annals of Margam also have *Decembris*. November is the correct month.

⁷⁷ Goldcliff is not expanded elsewhere in the text, but in the Neath chronicle it appears as *Goldcliuia*, so I expand it here using that spelling. There is a gloss in the lower margin of this page, below column a, scratchy early modern hand: 'Foliat'. Gloss in inner margin, lined up with 'Hereford', incaustum *s*. xiv hand: 'Land'.

⁷⁸ T *vocatis domum*.

Falconem in exilium trusit. Pictauia se subdidit Ludouico regi Francie. Magister A[lexander] consecratur Rome in episcopum Conuentrie.

[1225] m^mo.ccxxv. Concessa fuit domino regi[79] quintadecima de omnibus mobilibus secularium et religiosorum. Omnes noue foreste per Angliam sunt deforestate. Rex[80] accinxit Ricardum fratrem suum gladio militari, et postea misit eum in Wasconiam cum comite Saresberie et magna milicia. Rex [fol. 106va] confirmauit in magno concilio apud Londoniam omnes libertates et liberas consuetudines regni, et dominus Cantuarie cum coepiscopis suis tulit sententiam in omnes qui contra uenirent ad instanciam regis.

[1227] m^mo.ccxxvii. Honorius papa obiit, cui successit Gregorius \.ix./. Henricus rex Anglie iam adultus custodiam[81] exiuit.

[1228] m^mo.ccxxviii. Gilberto de Clare nascitur filius nomine Willelmus .xv^to. Kalendas Iunii. Ricardus de Clare, frater dicti comitis, occisus est apud Londoniam die Ascensionis Domini. Gilbertus comes Gloucestrie, cum exercitu magno, profectus est in Walliam contra Walenses. Terremotus factus est per plurima loca Anglie. Stephanus archiepiscopus Cantuarie obiit, cui successit Ricardus Magnus. Henricus[82] rex Anglie adiit Muntgomery preliaturus contra Lewelinum, sed parum profecit. Ibidem captus fuit W[illelmus] de Breuse, filius Reginaldi de Breuse, et plures occisi. Magister Robertus de Bynkeham electus est in episcopum Sarum.

[1229] m^mo ccxxix. Magister Ricardus Magnus consecratus in archiepiscopum Cantuarie, Magister Robertus de Bynkeham in episcopum Sarum, Magister Rogerus in episcopum Londonie, dominus Robertus in episcopum Elyensis. Gilberto de Clare nascitur filius nomine Gilbertus .ii. Idus Septembris. Willelmus episcopus Landauensis obiit Kalendis Februarii. Magister Reginaldus de Radenore, canonicus Landauensis, eligitur in episcopum eiusdem loci, sed renuit accipere, et paulo post obiit.

---

[79] A small hole in the parchment here.

[80] This phrase is underlined. A large manicle in the same ink points to the underlined phrase. A line directs the eye towards 'religiosorum'.

[81] T *tutelam*.

[82] MS R*icardus*.

[1230] m^{mo}ccxxx. Henricus rex Anglie, pro terris suis transmarinis[83] acquirendis, cum magno exercitu transfretauit .viii°. Idus Maii. Lewelinus princeps Northwallie interfecit[84] Willelmum de Breuse \.v./. Elyas thesaurius Herefordie eligitur in episcopum Landauensis, consecratur dominica .A. prima Aduentus Domini.[85] Henricus rex Anglie reuertitur a partibus transmarinis infecto negocio. Gilbertus de [fol. 106vb] Clare comes Gloucestrie obiit apud Penros in Britannia in nocte sanctorum Crispini et Crispiniani, et legauit corpus suum sepeliendum apud Theouksberiam ubi nunc requiescit. Dominus Hubertus de Burgo iusticiarius Anglie suscepit custodiam terre Ricardi de Clare, filii Gilberti comitis Gloucestrie. Dominus rex exegit graue tallagium a uiris religiosis. Fratres predicatores construxerunt sibi oratorium in parochia Sancti Iacobi de Bristollie.

[1231] m^{mo}ccxxxi. Isabel comitissa Gloucestrie nupsit Ricardo comiti Cornubie, fratri domini Henrici regis Anglie, .iii. Kalendas Aprilis. Lewelinus princeps Wallie multum infestauit Walliam, cui dominus Henricus rex obuiauit magno uallatus excercitu, et firmauit Castrum Mahaud. Eodem tempore dominus rex admisit Ricardum Marescallum ad hereditem suam et reddidit ei omnem terram suam. Magister Radulfus Mayloc obiit Nonis Iunii. Dominus R[icardus] Cantuarie archiepiscopus obiit .ii. Nonas Augusti.[86] Dominus E[lyas] Landauensis episcopus, et capitulum eiusdem loci, concesserunt monachis Theouksberie in usus proprios ecclesiam de Lanbleuian. Nascitur Ricardo comiti Cornubie filius nomine Iohannes. Petrus abbas Theouksberie obiit .iii. Kalendas Aprilis, cui successit Robertus prior eiusdem loci.

[1232] m^{mo}ccxxxii. In crastino Pasche, recognouit dominus rex ius comitis Gloucestrie de collacione baculi pastoralis Theouksberie. Vnde dominus

---

[83] A small hole in the parchment here.

[84] T *retinuit*.

[85] The manuscript reads 'Lewelinus princeps Northwallie interfecit Willelmum de Breuse \.v./. prima Aduentus Domini. Elyas thesaurius Herefordie eligitur in episcopum Landauensis, consecratur dominica A.' A line in the inner margin is drawn (in the same ink as the main text) from the dominical letter 'a' at the end of this line to 'prima Aduentus Domini' two lines above. The scribe may have made a copying error and added 'prima Aduentus Domini' into a leftover space two lines above, or perhaps skipped ahead and wrote 'prima Aduentus Domini' too early. I have emended the text by moving 'prima Aduentus Domini' to the end of the sentence.

[86] In the middle margin next to this line is an incaustum ink (s. xiv?) gloss: 'Episcopus elyas'.

Hubertus, custodie[87] racione Ricardi de Clare dedit licenciam eligendi abbatem. Dominus Hubertus de Burgo, exutus a iusticiaria,[88] reddidit omnes custodias quas habuit de domino rege. Sed comitatum Kancie retinuit et alia ad modicum tempus, quia paulo post captus et incarceratus et multis malis afflictus est. Stephanus de Seggraua factus est iusticiarius Anglie. Randulfus comes Cestrie obiit .xvii. Kalendas Nouembris. [fol. 107ʳa] Dominus rex exigit a uiris religiosis quadragesimam omnium mobilium suorum. Truge capte fuerunt inter dominum H[enricum] regem Anglie et Lewelinum principem Wallie ad tres annos sequentes, quas Lewelinus nomine tenuit. Obiit Iohannes filius Ricardi comiti Cornubie.

[1233] mᵐᵒ.ccxxxiii. Dominus Henricus rex Anglie apud Gloucestriam accinxit gladio militari tres comites, scilicet Rogerum Bigot comitem Warewyk,[89] Hugonem de Veer, et Willelmum Lungespeh. (Accingitur gladio militari sed non sit comes Saresberie). Dominus rex misit iusticiarios itinerantes ubi non itinerauerunt .xxx. annis elapsis in Cornubiam, et concessit Ricardo comiti fratro suo omnia emolumenta. Dominus rex fecit diruere castella baronum quorundam, et terrasque eorum dedit alienis, quia tenuerunt cum Ricardo Marescallo. Dictus uero R[icardus] Marescallus, cum innotuisset ei consilium regis quod machinasset ei malum, collecto excercitu, cepit Vsk, Nouum Burgum, Berg[auenni][90] et castrum de Kayrdiuia, in cuius capcione Warinus Basset occubuit.[91] Paulo post idem Marescallus conbussit Monemutam et alia castras et uillas. Postea dominus Hubertus de Burgo per Ricardum Siward ui raptus est de ecclesia Devises et ductus apud Strigull, traditur Ricardo Marescallo. Conuocacio et episcoporum et magnatum fit apud Gloucestriam ut tractarent de pace regni in crastino sancte Katerine. Magister Eadmundus de Abyndonie canonice eligitur in archiepiscopum Cantuarie. Consecratur apud Cantuariam .iiiᵗᵒ. Nonas Aprilis. Nascitur Ricardo comiti Cornubie filia nomine Ysabella. Episcopus Wyntonie Petrus et Petrus de Riuallis amoti sunt a curia regis per archiepiscopum E[admundum]. Ricardus Marescallus comes de Penbrokie obiit in Hybernia, transfixus gladio .xvii. Kalendas Maii. et cetera.

---

[87] 'custodie' is added superscript above racione in same hand as main text. T *custos*.
[88] Modern gloss: 'justici maius'. T *exuit justiciarium*.
[89] T *Norwich*. He is actually the Earl of Norfolk.
[90] T *Bergeuem*.
[91] Gloss in inner margin, medieval hand: 'it monemuta'.

[fol. 107rb]

[1234] m^{mo}ccxxxiiii. Tercio Kalendas Iuniii pacificatur domino regi Gilbertus Marescallus cum duobus fratribus suis, Waltero et Anselmo, H[uberto] de Burgo, Ricardo Siward, Gilberto Basset, et multis aliis. Die Pentecostis G[ilbertus] Marescallus factus est comes de Penbrokia apud Wygorniam. Obiit Ysabella filia comitis Cornubie. Magister Radulfus de Maydeneston eligitur in episcopum Herefordie; consecratur apud Cantuariam in crastino sancti Martini. Magister Robertus Grosseteste canonice eligitur in episcopum Lyncolnie.

[1235] m^{mo}.ccxxxv. Dominus rex Anglie misit sororem suam Ysabellam maritandam Frederico imperatori Alemannie. Magister Robertus Groseteste consecratus in episcopum Lyncolnie .xv°. Kalendas Iulii.⁹² Circa festum sancti Barnabe, Ysabella soror dicti regis Anglie facta imperatrix Al[e]manie. Margeret soror regis Scocie nupsit Gilberto Marescallo comiti Penbrochie circa Assumpcionem beate Marie.⁹³ Nascitur Ricardo comiti Cornubie filius nomine Henricus .[i] v^{to}.⁹⁴ Nonas Nouembris. Ricardus comes Cornubie cum aliis magnatibus adiit Prouinciam ut reginam adducerent. Amicia comitissa de Wich peperit filium nomine Baldewinum in nocte Circumcicionis. Alianora filia comitis Prouincie nupsit Henrico regi Anglie apud Cantuariam .xix. Kalendas Februarii et coronatur apud Londoniam .xiii°. Kalendas Februarii.

[1236] m^{mo}.ccxxxvi. Abbas et conuentus Theouksberie concesserunt⁹⁵ domino Elie Landauensis episcopo, et eiusdem loci capitulo, ecclesiam de Lanadern cum pertinentiis suis, retentis decimis de Lamfordam que pertinent ad mensam⁹⁶ prioris de Kairdivia. .x°. Kalendas Maii. Circa Pentecostem, dominus E[lyas] episcopus Landauensis et eiusdem loci capitulum confirmauerunt monachis Theouksberie [fol. 107va] omnia ecclesiastica beneficia que haberunt⁹⁷ in episcopatu Landauense. Willelmus de Bleis episcopus Wygornie obiit .xvi°. Kalendas Septembris. In mense Iunii obiit Willelmus de Bello Campo. Iohannes abbas de Margan obiit, cui successit Iohannes La Ware. Walterus de Cantilupo eligitur

---

⁹² T *Junii*.
⁹³ T *Virginis*.
⁹⁴ MS .v^{to}.
⁹⁵ T *concessimus*.
⁹⁶ T *mensae pertinere*.
⁹⁷ T *habemus*.

in episcopum Wygornie .iii°. Kalendas Aprilis,[98] consecratur[99] die sancti Andree, intronizatur in octauis sancti Andree.

[100][1237] m^{mo}ccxxxvii. Magister Otto[101] ecclesie Romane cardinalis uenit legatus in Angliam circa festum sancti Kenelmi et celebrauit concilium apud Londoniam in crastino octauarum sancti Martini, et durauit per triduum. In Nouembre obiit Magota filia Huberti de Burgo uxor Ricardi de Clare.[102] Soror regis Anglie quondam uxor W[illelmi] Marescalli nupsit Simoni de Monte Forti .xix. Kalendas Februarii. Matilda, filia Iohannis de Lacy comitis Lincolnie, nupsit Ricardo de Clare circa Purificacionem beate Marie virginis.

[1238] m^{mo}ccxxxviii. Dominus Otto legatus apud Oxoniam constitutus a scolaribus Oxonie iniuriis afficitur, unde dominus rex commotus precepit ut clerici caperentur. Die Purificacionis dominus rex admisit Symonem de Monte Forti ad comitatum Leycestrie ad instanciam fratris dicti Symonis.

[103][1239] m^{mo}ccxxxix. Dedicata est ecclesia Theouksberie in honore sancte[104] Marie .xiiii^{to}. Kalendas Iulii a venerabile priore domino W[altero] episcopo Wygornie. Nascitur domino regi Anglie filius nomine Edwardus. Ecclesia Sancti Iacobi de Brystollie dedicata est die sancti Luce Ewangelista. Dedicate sunt eodem anno ecclesie conuentuales de Gloucestrie, Persore, et Wynchecumbie ab eodem episcopo. Eclipsis solis[105] facta est .iii°. Nonas Iunii circa horam sextam. Die Natiuitatis Domini Baldewynus de Ripariis factus est comes Insule et Deuonye. [fol. 107vb] Ysabella comitissa Gloucestrie et Cornubie obiit .xvi^{to}. Kalendas Februarii.

[1240] m^{mo}ccxl. Dominus Elyas episcopus Landauensis obiit .iii°. Idus Maii. Lewelinus princeps Wallie obiit in Aprili et Iohannes de Lacy comes Lyncolnie

---

[98] In T the April date is attached to the previous sentence. The Cardiff chronicle's reading is shared by the Annals of Worcester, which also attaches the April date to Walter's election; this would suggest that the Cardiff chronicle's reading is correct.

[99] T *benedicitur*.

[100] A manicule in the outer margin points to this entry.

[101] MS Octo.

[102] Ink change.

[103] A manicule in the outer margin points to this entry.

[104] T *Virginis*.

[105] T *sol* [...] *eclipsim*.

in Augusto. Dominus rex conuocato magno parliamento[106] apud Gloucestriam in Mayo, accinxit Dauid nepotem suum gladio militari et idem Dauid fecit domino regi homagium. Conuocato magno concilio apud Londoniam, Ricardus comes Cornubie iter arripuit uersus Ierosolimam. Mauri[ci]us archid[iaconus] Landauensis eligitur in episcopum Landauensem sed postea cassatus est. Dominus O[tto] legatus tenuit magnum concilium apud Londoniam in octabem Omnium Sanctorum, et post Natale transfretauit ad concilium domini pape, sed impediebatur per Fredericum imperatorem. Circa festum sancti Aniani,[107] obiit Eadmundus archiepiscopus Cantuarie, et sepultus est apud Pontiniacum. Margan Cham obiit in Februario. Petrus de Aqua Alba[108] factus est episcopus Herefordie. Ricardus de Clare redemit terram suam de Glamorgan datis auunculo suo Gilberto Marescallo quingentis Mª. in Februario.

[1241] m^{mo}ccxli. Alianora de Britannia, consanguinea domini regis, obiit apud Brustolliam .iiii^{to}. Idus Augusti, et sepulta fuit in ecclesia Sancti Iacobi, sed postea per preceptum domini regis, translata fuit usque Ambresbiriam. Gilbertus Basset obiit. Circa festum apostolorum Petri et Pauli, obiit Gilbertus Marescallus in torneamento apud Warem. Legati Francie et Anglie, circa Inuencionem Sancte Crucis, ab imperatore Frederico in mari capti et inprisonati sunt cum archiepiscopis, episcopis, clericis et aliis. Dominus Ricardus comes Cornubie, rediens a Terra Sancta circa festum sancte Agnetis, uenit Londoniam et cum honore susceptus est.

[1242] m^{mo}cc^{mo}xlii. Dominus rex transfretauit in Guasconiam cum magno excercitu. Willelmus de Marisco capitur apud Londoniam, et non multum post tractus [fol. 108ra] et suspensus, ad ultimum diuisus in partes, mittitur ad maiores ciuitates Anglie in signum prodicionis sue.

[1243] m^{mo}cc^{mo}xliii. Magister Senebaldus canonice[109] eligitur in summum pontificem qui uocatus est Innocencius .iiii^{to}. Hubertus de Burgo comes Kancie et Hugo comes de Arundel obierunt. Nascitur Ricardo de Claro filius nomine Gilbertus in crastino sancti Egidii abbatis. Dominus rex Anglie applicuit in Angliam apud Portesmouth die Veneris proxima ante festum sancti Michaelis.

---

[106] T *colloquio*.
[107] T *Eadmundi*.
[108] T *Egleblanchei*.
[109] T *catholice*.

Et vig*ilia* s*an*cti Mich*ae*lis, reddidit Ric*ardo*[110] de Clare totam t*e*rram suam.[111] Bonifaci*us con*firmat*ur* a d*omi*no p*a*pe in ar*ch*iep*iscopu*m Cantuar*ie*. Griffin*us* fili*us* Lewelini cadens de turri London*ie et*[112] in*te*riit.[113]P*atr*ici*us* de Chaworth duxit uxor*em* Hawisiam d*omi*nam de Vggemore. Mag*iste*r Rogerus cantor Sar*um* eligit*ur* in ep*iscopu*m Bathon*ie*. Fulco Basset *con*secrat*ur* i*n* ep*iscopu*m Londo*nie*.

[114][**1244**] m*mo*ccxliiii. In Iunio Ric*ardus* de Clar*e* infirmabat*ur* ap*ud*[115]Kard*i*uiam. Circa f*e*stu*m* s*an*ct*e* Margar*et*, uener*un*t Walenses de Breconi*a* ut pr*e*dar*e*nt t*er*ram de Neth, *sed* warnestura pat*r*ie restitit *et* q*uo*sdam ceper*un*t *et* q*uo*sdam tradider*un*t.[116] Domin*us* p*a*pa, recedens a Roma, uenit ad Geneue*n*sam ciui*ta*t*em et* fecit ibi moram p*er* aliq*ui*d t*em*pus. Walenses m*u*ltum infestabant Ric*a*rdu*m* de Clar*e et* Kenes*ham con*busser*un*t i*n* Nouemb*r*i.[117]Domin*us* Will*e*lm*us* de Burgo canon*ice* eligit*ur* in ep*iscopu*m Land*au*ensem cassato mag*ist*ro W[illelmo] de *Christi* Ecclesia. Regina Alianora pep*er*it filiu*m* nomin*e* Eadmu*n*dum .xvii. Kal*en*d*as* Ianuari*i*.

[**1245**] m*mo*cc*mo*xlv. Die Pentecost*es* s*cilicet* pr*i*die Nonas Iunii, Ric*ardus* de Clare accinct*us* est gladio militar*io* ap*u*d London*iam*. Mortuo He[r]berto fili*o* Machuti, impetit*us* est Ric*ardus* Syward de morte ips*ius et* de p*er*dic*i*one quam fecit, *et* comes saisiuit castr*um* de Taleuen [fol. 108ʳb], *et* baronia*m* de La*n*blethia*n et* p*er* paulu*m* cepit erig*er*e castr*um* de Glamorga*n*. G*e*n*er*ale *con*cilium celeb*r*atur apud Lugd*u*num ab p*a*pa Innocencio, in q*u*o *con*cilio d*omi*nus[118] p*a*pa *con*dempnauit Fredericum imp*er*atore*m*. Domin*us* rex Angl*ie*, circa festu*m* s*an*ct*i* Petri Aduin*cu*la, duxit magnu*m* exc*er*citu*m* u*er*sus

---

[110] MS Ric*ardus*.

[111] T *omnes terras suas*.

[112] This *et* is redundant. The scribe appears to be treating *cadens* as a finite verb. I am grateful to the reviewer of this volume for pointing this out.

[113] Gloss in inner margin, incaustum ink, *s*. xiv: 'P*atr*icius'.

[114] Two leaves are missing from T's manuscript here, so it is not possible to tell how much of the Cardiff chronicle's entries for 1244, 1245, and most of 1246 agree with T. From this point onward, the chronicle is independent from T.

[115] Gloss in inner margin, early modern: 'Kardyffo'.

[116] MS tr*a*dauer*un*t.

[117] Gloss in inner margin, *s*. xiv: 'Land'. It is in the same hand as 'it Monemuta' and 'P*atr*icius' previously.

[118] MS d*omi*nas.

Gannow[119] et firmauit ibi castrum, et relinquens ibi warnesturam rediit in Nouembri. Matilda comitissa Gloucestrie peperit filium nomine Thomam. Walterus Marescallus comes de Penbrokie obiit .v. Kalendas Decembris, et vigilia Natiuitatis Domini obiit Anselmus frater eius. Dauid princeps Wallie obiit et Walenses principem constituerunt Lewelinum filium Griffini fratris deinde.

[1246] m^{mo}cc^{mo}xlvi. Dominus Ricardus comes Cornubie cepit construere cenobium de Hayles. Eodem tempore Ricardus comes Gloucestrie firmauit castrum de Lantrissan, expulso Howelo filio Mereduci. Circa festum Magdalene diuisa est hereditas Marescallorum in multis partibus, tam in Anglie quam in Wallia et in Hybernia. Radulfus de Mortuo Mari obiit. Robertus episcopus Sarum obiit. Ricardus abbas Westmonasterii [obiit]. xvii. Kalendas Ianuarii apud Lugdunum, canonizatus est sanctus Eadmundus archiepiscopus. .x^{mo}. Kalendas Marcii feria .iiii^{ta}. hora diei .ix^w. factus est terremotus magnus per totam Angliam et Hyberniam.

[120][1247] m^{mo}ccxlvii. Circa festum sancti Dunstani, dominus papa In[no]cencius \.iiii./ exegit .xx^{mam}. omnium bonorum, tam a viris religiosorum quam a clericis. In crastino sancte Margarete nascitur Ricardo comite Gloucestrie filius nomine Bugo. Dominus rex precepit facere nouam monetam in Angliam. Circa Natale beate Marie, dominus rex misit ad comitatum de Kairdiuia, dominum Iohannem de Monemuta, et alios barones ut inquirerent diligenter si Ricardus Siward iuste et secundum legem terre in eodem comitatu tractaretur. In mense Aprili obiit Thomas archid[iaconus] Landauensis, cui successit Nicholas [fol. 108va] de Ledeburie. Magister Thomas Walensis confirmatur in episcopum Meneuensem. Dominus Rogerus episcopus Bathonie obiit, cui successit Magister Willelmus de Button.

[1248] m^{mo}cc^{mo}xlviii. In crastino sancti Barnabe, Ludouicus rex Francie iter arripuit uersus Terram Sanctam. Circa festum sancti Egidii, obiit Iohannes de Monemuta senior. .x^{mo}. Kalendas Ianuarii factus est terremotus per diuersa loca Anglia.

[1249] m^{mo}cc^{mo}xlix^{no}. Vigilie sancte Trinitatis, Ludouicus rex Francie cepit Damietam. Die omnium sanctorum Bonifacius archiepiscopus Cantuarie

---

[119] Degannwy; for discussion of this name see Angus McIntosh, 'Middle English "Gannokes" and Some Place-Name Problems', *Review of English Studies*, 16 (1940), 54–61.

[120] The chronicle is independent from this point forward.

intronizatur, in qua festiuitate dominus comes Gloucestrie extitit senescallus et pincerna iure hereditario. Dominus H[enricus] rex Anglie accepit crucem .ii. Nonas Marcii.

[1251] m^{mo}ccli^{oc}. Multi pastores de diuersis terris congregati ciuitatem Aurelyanum inuaserunt, et multos de clericis trucidauerunt, et apud Parisius similiter fecerunt.

[1252] m^{mo}cclii°. Tanta siccitas accidit hoc anno ut etiam maiora fluuia in pluribus locis Anglie et Wallie fere deficiarentur et segetes, prata, et pascue per siccitate aruerunt. Vi^{to}. Nonas Iulii quidam prior Campanie procurator domini episcopi Herefordie occisus fuit in quadam capella Hereford. Dominus Willelmus de Burgo episcopus Landauensis obiit.

[1253] m^{mo}ccliii°. Dominus rex transfretauit in Gwasconiam circa festum sancti Iohannis et dominus comes Gloucestrie in Hyberniam. Dominus Iohannes Laware quondam abbas de Margan consecratur in episcopum Landauensis .iii°. Idus Ianuarii.

[1254] m^{mo}ccliiii^{to}. Dominus rex contulit Gwasconiam Edwardo filio suo.

[1256] m^{mo}cclvi^{to}. Septimo decimo Kalendas Iulii, obiit dominus Iohannes episcopus Landauensis. Tercio Idus Iulii, obiit Resus filius Griffini. Sexto Kalendas Augusti, Magister Willelmus de [fol. 108vb] Radenore thesaurarius Landauensis canonice eligitur in episcopum eiusdem loci. Consecratur Londoniam in crastino Epiphanie. Intronizatur die sancte Agnece. Facto conflictu inter Walenses et Anglicos in partibus de Kermerdyn per prodicionem Resi Vauchan, multi corruerunt de Anglicis inter quos Stephanus Bauzan occiditur et multi capti fuerunt. In mense []¹²¹ venit Resus Vauchan in Goweriam cum mutitudine Walensium et totam terram uastauit, incendit, et depredauit. Et fere omnes Walenses tocius Gowerie et aliarum terrarum se subdiderunt dominio Lewelini principis Wallie, et villam de Sweyneseya conbusserunt. Sexto Idus Maii dominus Ricardus comes Cornubie coronam Al[e]manie suscepit,¹²² et coronatur apud Aquensem ciuitatem, et uxor eius similiter. Henricus filius eius ibidem accinctus est gladio militario.

---

[121] A space is left blank in the manuscript but the month was never added.
[122] A manicule in the middle margin points to this underlined phrase.

[1257] m^{mo}cclvii°. Venit dominus R[icardus] comes Gloucestrie apud Kayrdiuiam cum multitudine armatorum. Et Lewelinus fuit cum magno excercitu iuxta abbathiam de Margan. Tercio Idus Iulii accessit Lewelinus apud Langunith et conbussit castrum domini comitis et interfecit .xxiiii. homines comitis, domino comite existente cum magno excercitu apud Lanblethian.

[1258] m^{mo}cclviii°. Dominus Willelmus de Clare et abbas Westmonasterii Londoniam ueneno interierunt. Constituti sunt .xii^{cim}. pares in Angliam, quorum consilio et iudicio[123] Anglia et Hybernya et Wallia regnantur. Expulsi sunt ab Anglia fratres Pictauensis, tres reges.

[1259] m^{mo}cclix. Cessauit Henricus quartus rex Anglie vocari dux Normannie.

[1261] m^{mo}cclxi. Obiit Alexander papa .iiii^{tus}, cui successit Vrbanus .iiii^{tus}. mense Augusti.

[1262] m^{mo}cclxii°. Obiit Ricardus de Clare comes Gloucestrie Idibus Iulii.

[1263] m^{mo}cclxiii°. Gilbertus de Clare, filius dicti Ricardi comitis[124] [fol. 112^r] Gloucestrie, .xix. annorum suscepit terram suam de Glamorgan circa festum beati Michaelis. Eodem anno festo Natiuitatis beati Iohannis Baptiste precedente, orta est guerra inter regem, Eadwardum primogenitum ipsius, et tres comites, et plures barones, atque milites Anglicos et Walenses.

[1264] m^{mo}cclxiiii°. Mense Maii dictus Gilbertus de Clare vna die hora prima iuxta Lewes accipiens a domino Symone de Monte Forti comite Leycestrie Senescallo Anglie arma militaria cum pluribus aliis, factus est comes Gloucestrie et Hertfordie. Quo die circa[125] horam nonam ceperunt in prelio satis duro Henricum regem Anglie, Eadwardum eius primogenitum, et Ricardum comitem Cornubie, regem Al[e]manie uocatum, et plures alios comites et barones Anglie, interfectis ex utraque parte tribus milibus.

---

[123] MS iudicom.

[124] An early modern hand in the lower margin notes 'Supplm. pa. 112 infra'. The order of contents in the manuscript has been disturbed. The chronicle is interrupted on fols 109–11 by a copy of the *Provinciale Romanum*, a list of the dioceses of the world. The chronicle picks up again for a single remaining folio, fol. 112^r, in a single column of text (instead of the two-column layout of the rest of the chronicle). This folio has been trimmed; it is about two inches narrower than the rest of the book.

[125] Gloss in inner margin parallel to this line, s. xiv: 'Lewes'.

[1265] m^mo^cclxv^to^. Pridie Nonas Augusti apud Euesham in[126]prelio satis duro interfectus est dominus Symon de Monte Forti comes Leycestrie, dominus Henricus filius eius primogenitus, et cum eo plures barones et milites et Walenses quorum numerus nescitur. Eodem anno obiit dominus W[illelmus] de Radenore episcopus Landauensis.

[1266] m^mo^cclxvi^to^. Sexto Kalendas Decembris consecratur dominus[127]Willelmus de Brewes episcopus Landauensis, et in crastino sancti Eadmundi regis, intronizatus est. Eodem die dedicacio ecclesie Landauensis. Die sabbati post Epiphaniam Domini, Griffinus ap Rees constabulo et armiger suus capti in castro de Kayrdivia, et dictus Griffinus parum post missus ad Hyberniam apud Kilkenny[128] ad incarcerandum.

[1267] m^mo^cc°lxvii°. Rex Francie cruce signatus est, et multi comites barones et milites Francie et Anglie, et dictus rex fecit nouam monetam.

[1268] m^mo^cc°lxviii°. Tercio Idus Aprilis inceptum est opus castri de Kayrphily. Eodem anno, in prelio duro, captus est Gilbertus filius Gilberti de Vmframuyle, Iohannes Martel, Ricardus Herberd, et plures pedites. Non scitur ueraciter numerus occisorum.

---

[126] Gloss in inner margin parallel to this line, possibly same hand as 'Elyas' above: 'Eueshium'.

[127] Gloss in inner margin parallel to this line, possibly same hand as 'Kardyffo' above: 'Land~'.

[128] MS Kilbenny.

The Cardiff Chronicle: Translation[129]

1066. Edward King of England died on 16 April, and William Duke of Normandy obtained England.

1087. King William the elder died on 28 March, and William Rufus his son reigned.

1089. Archbishop Lanfranc died on 1 April, and an earthquake happened. And the church of St Peter's Gloucester is restored again.

1091. The church of St Mary's Tewkesbury was established on 13 April.

1093. Anselm is elected as Archbishop [of Canterbury] on 17 April.

1095. Wulfstan Bishop of Worcester died on 25 March.

1100. King William the younger died on 1 April, and Henry reigned.

1106. King Henry captured his brother Robert on 25 March.

1107. Robert fitz Hamon[130] died on the 18th Kalends.[131]

1110. Gerald, first Abbot of Tewkesbury, died on 10 April, and the river which is called Trent, at Nottingham, was dried up from the first month of summer up to the third.

1119. An earthquake happened on 5 April and the bridge of Gloucester was begun.

---

[129] Personal and place names are translated from Latin where they are known. Modern dates for fixed feasts and calendar days are supplied in brackets.

[130] Conqueror of Morgannwg; became first Lord of Glamorgan in 1075; founded Tewkesbury Abbey in 1092, and gave it a new site on the Severn in 1102. He granted Tewkesbury the chapel at Cardiff Castle, the church of Llantwit, and the church of St Mary's Cardiff (which became Cardiff Priory, founded *c.* 1106); he also granted to Gloucester the church of Llancarfan between 1095 and 1100. See Green, 'Robert fitz Haimon'.

[131] No month is supplied for this date, and it is not in the Annals of Tewkesbury. Green ('Robert fitz Haimon') says he died in March. As there is no 18th Kalends of April falling in March, the scribe could be in error here. Perhaps the correct reading is 17th Kalends of April (16 March).

1121. King Henry married Queen Adeliza on 10 April.

1122. [The city] of Gloucester, with the abbey, is burnt again by fire on 5 April.

1123. Dedication of the church of Tewkesbury on 6 April.

1133. Robert Curthose Duke of Normandy died at Cardiff on 26 March.

1135. King Henry died on 6 April, to whom succeeded his nephew Stephen.

1140. An eclipse of the sun happened on 6 April.

1141. King Stephen was captured at Lincoln on 30 March, and Robert Earl[132] of Gloucester was captured at Winchester, and one is returned for the other.

1144. A comet appeared.

1147. Robert Earl of Gloucester died and was buried at St James's Bristol, to whom succeeded his son William.

1148. An eclipse of the moon appeared, and Uhtred Bishop of Llandaf died.

1152. With a divorce having taken place between Louis King of France and Queen Eleanor, Duke Henry, the son of the Empress,[133] took her as wife.

1154. Pope Anastasius died, to whom succeeded Hadrian the Englishman, and King Stephen died on 31 October, to whom succeeded Henry.[134]

1155. Queen Eleanor bore Henry.

1156. William, the firstborn son of the King, died.

1157. The Queen of England bore Richard. Mabel Countess of Gloucester died.[135]

---

[132] *Consul* and *comes* are synonyms for earl in post-Conquest England; see *DMLBS*, s.v. consul, 5a and s.v. comes, 4a. Documents referring to Robert seem to favour the word *consul* over *comes*. I am grateful to Ben Guy for pointing this out to me.

[133] Empress Matilda.

[134] This date is not correct: King Stephen died on 25 October.

[135] Daughter and sole heiress of Robert fitz Hamon; wife of Robert, First Earl of Gloucester (d. 1147).

8. THE CARDIFF CHRONICLE IN LONDON, BRITISH LIBRARY, MS ROYAL 6 B XI

1158. Queen Eleanor bore Geoffrey. King Henry, having made a peace with Rhys, crossed the Channel,[136] and his son Henry took the daughter of Louis King of France as his wife. A great earthquake happened throughout England.

1161. Theobald Archbishop of Canterbury died.

1162. Thomas, chancellor of King Henry, was made Archbishop of Canterbury.

1163. Roger, son of Robert Earl of Gloucester, is elected as Bishop of Worcester.

1164. Roger, son of the Earl of Gloucester, is consecrated as Bishop of Worcester. And Thomas Archbishop of Canterbury, hated by the King, crossed the Channel.

1169. A great earthquake happened in Sicily which destroyed five cities, and the church of Keynsham[137] was founded by William Earl of Gloucester.[138]

1170. King Henry had his son Henry crowned. Thomas Archbishop of Canterbury is killed in Christ Church Canterbury on 29 December.

1173. A terrible quarrel arose between the kings of England, father and son. Around midnight the sky was seen to redden.

1175. King Henry came to England with his son. The Archbishop of Canterbury, having convened a council at London, forbade all of the prefaces except for ten, which the Roman Church chanted during the *missa solemnia*.

1180. Louis King of France died, to whom succeeded Philip.

1182. The crown of the kingdom of Jerusalem is brought to Henry King of England.

1183. King Henry the younger died. On the day of St Barnabas the apostle [11 June], William Earl of Gloucester and Nicholas Bishop of Llandaf and Robert Abbot of Tewkesbury died.

---

[136] *DMLBS*, s.v. transfretare, 1c: 'to cross the English Channel'.

[137] Keynsham Abbey in Somerset.

[138] William fitz Robert, Second Earl of Gloucester (d. 1183).

1189. King Henry died, to whom succeeded his son Richard. Isabella Countess of Gloucester was married to John, Count of Mortain.[139]

1190. Richard King of England and Philip King of France and Baldwin Archbishop of Canterbury set out for Jerusalem.

1191. Richard King of England captured Acre in the land of Jerusalem. Pope Clemens died, to whom succeeded [Celestine].[140] An eclipse of the sun happened.

1192. King Richard, having heard in Syria that his brother John had taken England for himself by force, made a truce with Saladin the pagan for three years and, returning, was captured by the Duke of Austria and given over to Henry the Emperor of Germany.

1194. Richard King of England, freed from captivity, returned to England.

1197. A comet appeared all winter. An earthquake happened. The Prince of Wales, Rhys son of Llywelyn, died.[141] Hawise Countess of Gloucester died on 24 April.

1199. Richard King of England was shot at Châlus[142] on 27 March and died, to whom succeeded his brother John on 27 May.

1200. Mauger is consecrated as Bishop of Worcester. Hugh Bishop of Lincoln died. John King of England and Isabella Countess of Gloucester were divorced.

1203. St Wulfstan was canonized in Rome on 22 April. Geoffrey Prior of Llanthony is consecrated as Bishop of St Davids. A great famine happened in England so that a crannock of wheat was sold for fourteen shillings.

1207. Master Stephen Langton was elected in Rome by the monks of Canterbury as Archbishop of Canterbury without the assent of the King or the bishops

---

[139] The future King John, then Count of Mortain in Normandy.

[140] Blank space left here by the scribe; presumably he meant to come back later to fill in the name of the new pope, but never did.

[141] This is an error: Rhys was the son of Gruffudd, not Llywelyn.

[142] A castle in Aquitaine.

of England. For which reason the King was angry and sent the monks of Canterbury into exile. The same bishop-elect is consecrated by Pope Innocent on the third day of St John the Baptist [26 June]. The Queen of England bore Henry, the firstborn.

1208. Every divine service was forbidden throughout all England on 24 March, except for the baptism of infants and the penances of the dying, because of Stephen Archbishop of Canterbury.[143]

1210. The King instituted a heavy tax on all the churches of England. William de Braose escaped into France, and his wife and children, having been captured and imprisoned, died of hunger. A great frost took place from the eve of the Circumcision [30 December] all the way to the Feast of St Valentine [14 February].

1211. Walter de Lacy is driven from Ireland into exile. Otto the excommunicated emperor made Apulia subject to him. With Gwynedd ravaged by Lord John, King of England, its prince, Llywelyn, makes peace with the King and gives hostages to him. William de Braose died in exile.

1213. John King of England — having laid down the crown of the kingdom on Ascension Day [23 May], and subjecting himself, with the kingdom of England and Ireland, to Lord Pope Innocent — in the presence of Pandulf, Legate to the Lord Pope, [he agreed to pay] 1000 marks in annual tribute: 700 from England [and] 300 from Ireland, excluding the *denarii* of St Peter. And thus he was absolved by Stephen Archbishop of Canterbury, who, according to instruction, had come with his co-exiles on 20 July. Nicholas of Tusculanum[144] came as an envoy to England. Walter Abbot of Tewkesbury died.

1214. The general interdict on England, which had endured for six years and three months, is relaxed. Hugh was made Abbot of Tewkesbury. Isabella, daughter of William Marshal the elder, was married to Gilbert de Clare the Earl of Gloucester.

---

[143] The interdict was actually pronounced a day earlier, on 23 March: see the Annals of Tewkesbury, in *AM*, I, 29.

[144] Tusculanum (now Toscolano-Maderno) in Brescia, Italy.

1215. John King of England takes the cross. Dissent arose between the King and the barons of England.

1216. John King of England died at Newark on the morrow of St Lucy the virgin [14 December].[145] Henry son of King John is crowned at Gloucester, with Guala[146] the Legate placing the crown of the kingdom upon him on 18 October.[147]

1217. With the Lord fighting on behalf of King Henry and the kingdom of England at Lincoln on the day of St Æthelberht [20 May], and by sea on the day of St Bartholomew [24 August] between Sandwich and the island of Thanet, the enemies of the King and of the kingdom were crushed. As a result, Louis, having given security that he would submit to the judgement of the church, was absolved and humiliatingly expelled. He returned to France. Two suns were seen on the day of St Mark [25 April] around evening. Once Louis had left on the eve of St Michael [28 September], the whole kingdom was pacified. Master Alexander Nequam Abbot of Cirencester died. The castle of Worcester is given to the monks of the same as far as the mound of the keep. With the barons besieging the castle of Lincoln, the Legate [Guala] and Marshal went there with a great army, and, breaking in, they met in battle with the barons. And with the Count of Perche[148] captured, the barons, and the French, and many magnates (around 40), and 300 soldiers were captured, and the greater number of servants [killed] was unknown, and the city was given over to plundering.

1219. A twentieth of the churches for the three years preceding is paid for the aid of the Holy Land. The city of Damietta was captured by the Christians on 5 November by divine power. From this is [a line of poetry]: 'the famous Damietta was captured on the Nones of November'. Hugh Foliot is consecrated as Bishop of Hereford. William Prior of Goldcliff was made Bishop of Llandaf in October.

---

[145] King John died on 19 October.

[146] The papal legate, Cardinal Guala Bicchieri, who took an active role in English politics during the First Baron's War.

[147] Henry was crowned on 28 October (5th Kalends of November); 'xv' is an error for 'v' in the text.

[148] Perche, a county between Normandy and Maine. Thomas, Count of Perche, was the commander of French forces at the battle of Lincoln in 1217.

1220. A daughter named Amice was born to Gilbert de Clare on 22 May. The body of blessed Thomas the martyr was translated by Stephen Archbishop of Canterbury on 7 July. King Henry is crowned a second time at London on Pentecost [17 May].

1221. The priory of Cardiff, with the monks of the house having been recalled, is handed over to Henry the Chaplain for rent. The sister of King Henry was married to Alexander King of Scots. The new church of Salisbury was begun on the day of St Vitalis the Martyr [28 April], with the first stone placed by the Legate, Pandulf, for the Lord Pope, the second for the King of England, the third for the Earl of Salisbury William Longespée,[149] the fourth for the Countess of Salisbury, and the fifth for the bishop of the place, and thus did the noblemen and abbots of England, each for himself.

1222. A son named Richard is born to Gilbert de Clare on 5 August. In the same year very many storms arose. Damietta, after three years of occupation by the Christians, is returned to the Saracens. In exchange for this the True Cross is returned to the Christians, and captives are freed from each side, with a truce made for seven years. The Archbishop of Canterbury held a solemn council at Oxford.

1224. New work was begun on the church of Worcester. The sister of King Henry was married to William Marshal the younger. The King captured the castle of Bedford and drove Falkes[150] into exile. Poitiers was subjected to Louis King of France. Master Alexander is consecrated in Rome as Bishop of Coventry.

1225. A fifteenth of all the movable goods belonging to secular and religious men was granted to the Lord King. All new forests throughout England were deforested. The King knighted his brother Richard and afterwards sent him to Gascony with the Earl of Salisbury and a great army. In a great council at London, the King confirmed all the liberties and free customs of the kingdom, and the Lord of Canterbury[151] with his associate bishops cast judgement on all things which would have otherwise come to the attention of the King.

---

[149] This is the French form of the name, Lungespée; Lunga Spata in Latin. He was the third Earl of Salisbury, illegitimate son of Henry II.

[150] Fulk or Falkes de Breauté did not want to return Bedford Castle to William de Beauchamp as Henry III wished.

[151] I.e. the Archbishop of Canterbury.

1227. Pope Honorius died, to whom succeeded Gregory IX. Henry King of England, now of age, left his wardship.[152]

1228. A son named William is born to Gilbert de Clare on 18 May. Richard de Clare, brother of the aforementioned Earl, was killed at London on Ascension Day [4 May]. Gilbert Earl of Gloucester with a great army set out into Wales against the Welsh. An earthquake happened throughout many locations in England. Stephen Archbishop of Canterbury died, to whom succeeded Richard the Great. Henry[153] King of England went to Montgomery in order to do battle against Llywelyn, but he accomplished very little. In that very place William de Braose, son of Reginald de Braose, was captured, and many were killed. Master Robert of Bingham was elected as Bishop of Salisbury.

1229. Master Richard the Great was consecrated as Archbishop of Canterbury, Master Robert of Bingham as Bishop of Salisbury, Master Roger as Bishop of London, [and] Lord Robert as Bishop of Ely. A son named Gilbert is born to Gilbert de Clare on 12 September. William Bishop of Llandaf died on 1 February. Master Reginald de Radnor, canon of Llandaf, is elected as Bishop of the same place, but he refused to accept, and a little bit later he died.

1230. Henry King of England, for the purpose of acquiring his lands across the sea, crossed the Channel with a great army on 8 May. Llywelyn Prince of Gwynedd killed William de Braose V. Elias, treasurer of Hereford, is elected as Bishop of Llandaf, [and] is consecrated on [Tuesday], the first day of Advent [1 December]. Henry King of England returns from overseas parts with the task unfinished. Gilbert de Clare Earl of Gloucester died at Penros in Brittany on the night of Saints Crispin and Crispianius [25 October], and he bequeathed his body for burial at Tewkesbury, where it now rests. Lord Hubert de Burgh, Justiciar of England, received custody of the land of Richard de Clare, son of Gilbert Earl of Gloucester. The Lord King exacted a heavy tax from religious men. The Dominicans constructed an oratory for themselves in the parish of St James's Bristol.

1231. Isabel Countess of Gloucester was married to Richard Earl of Cornwall, brother of the Lord King Henry of England, on 30 March. Llywelyn Prince

---

[152] Henry III took possession of his full royal powers in January 1227; see David A. Carpenter, *The Minority of Henry III* (Berkeley: University of California Press, 1990), p. 389.

[153] MS Richard.

of Wales greatly disturbed Wales, and the Lord King Henry, fortified with a great army, resisted him and secured Painscastle. At the same time the Lord King admitted Richard Marshal to his inheritance and returned all his land to him. Master Radulf Maeloc[154] died on 5 June. Lord Richard Archbishop of Canterbury died on 4 August. Lord Elias Bishop of Llandaf, and the chapter of the same place, conceded to the monks of Tewkesbury the church of Llanblethian for their own uses. A son named John is born to Richard Earl of Cornwall. Peter Abbot of Tewkesbury died on 30 March, to whom succeeded Robert the prior of the same place.

1232. The day after Easter, the Lord King recognized the right of the Earl of Gloucester to confer the pastoral staff of Tewkesbury. On which account Lord Hubert, by virtue of the wardship of Richard de Clare, granted [the community] permission to elect an abbot. Lord Hubert de Burgh, stripped of the justiciarship, returned all the offices which he held from the Lord King. But he retained the earldom of Kent and other things for a period of time, because a little bit after that he was captured and imprisoned and afflicted with many evils. Stephen de Segrave was made Justiciar of England. Ranulf Earl of Chester died on 16 October. The Lord King exacted from religious men a fortieth of all their moveable goods. Truces were undertaken between Lord Henry King of England and Llywelyn Prince of Wales for the next three years, which Llywelyn maintained in name only. John, son of Richard Earl of Cornwall, died.

1233. Lord Henry King of England knighted three earls at Gloucester, namely, Roger Bigod Earl of Warwick [*corr.* Norfolk], Hugh de Vere,[155] and William Longespée (he is knighted but he may not be the Earl of Salisbury). The Lord King sent justiciars into Cornwall, to make a circuit where they had not made a circuit for thirty years, and to his brother Earl Richard he granted all the profits. The Lord King had the castles of certain barons demolished, and gave their lands to foreigners, because they supported Richard Marshal. But the aforementioned Richard Marshal, when the King's intention to harm him had been made known to him, gathered an army and captured Usk, Newport, Abergavenny, and the castle of Cardiff. Warin Basset died during the taking

---

[154] The Maeloc family were lords of Llystalybont, a manor near Cardiff. Radulf Maeloc was holding the church of Llanblethian to farm, and after he died Tewkesbury and Llandaf fought over its ownership. In 1242 Roger Maeloc joined the dispute, claiming jurisdiction over the church; see *Cartae*, II, 434.

[155] Earl of Oxford.

of the castle. A little bit after that, the same Marshal burned Monmouth and other castles and towns. After Lord Hubert de Burgh was seized by force by Richard Siward from the church of Devizes and led to Chepstow, he is delivered to Richard Marshal. A convocation of both bishops and magnates took place at Gloucester on the morrow of St Catherine [26 November] in order to discuss the peace of the kingdom. Master Edmund of Abingdon is elected canonically as Archbishop of Canterbury. He is consecrated at Canterbury on 3 April. A daughter named Isabel is born to Richard Earl of Cornwall. Peter Bishop of Winchester and Peter de Rivaux were removed from the King's court by Archbishop Edmund. Richard Marshal Earl of Pembroke died in Ireland, pierced through by a sword on 15 April, etc.

1234. On 30 May, Gilbert Marshal with his two brothers Walter and Anselm, Hubert de Burgh, Richard Siward, Gilbert Basset, and many others makes peace with the Lord King. On Pentecost [11 June], Gilbert Marshal was made Earl of Pembroke at Worcester. Isabella, daughter of the Earl of Cornwall, died. Master Ralph de Maidstone is elected as Bishop of Hereford; he is consecrated at Canterbury on the morrow of St Martin [12 November]. Master Robert Grosseteste is elected canonically as Bishop of Lincoln.

1235. The Lord King of England sent his sister Isabella to marry Frederick Emperor of Germany. Master Robert Grosseteste was consecrated as Bishop of Lincoln on 17 June. Around the Feast of St Barnabas [11 June], Isabella, sister of the aforementioned King of England, was made Empress of Germany.[156] Margaret, sister of the King of Scotland, was married to Gilbert Marshal Earl of Pembroke around the Feast of the Assumption of Blessed Mary [15 August].[157] A son named Henry is born to Richard Earl of Cornwall on 2 November. Richard Earl of Cornwall visited Provence with many noblemen in order to fetch the queen. Amice Countess of Wight bore a son named Baldwin on

---

[156] They were married on 15 July 1235 at Worms according to the Annals of Worms (*Annales Wormatienses*, ed. by Georg Heinrich Pertz, MGH, SS, 17 (Hanover: Hahn, 1861), p. 44), 20 July according to Matthew Paris, *Chronica majora*, ed. by Henry Richards Luard, Rolls Series, 7 vols (London: Longman, 1872–83), III: *AD 1216 to AD 1239* (1876), 324.

[157] The marriage took place on 1 August according to the *Chronica de Mailros*, ed. by Joseph Stevenson, Bannatyne Club Publications, 49 (Edinburgh: Typis Societatis Edinburgensis, 1835), p. 147. See also *The Chronicle of Melrose Abbey: A Stratigraphic Edition. Volume I: Introduction and Facsimile Edition*, ed. by Dauvit Broun and Julian Harrison (Woodbridge: Boydell, 2007).

the night of the Circumcision [1 January]. Eleanor, daughter of the Earl of Provence, was married to Henry King of England at Canterbury on 14 January and crowned at London on 20 January.

1236. On 22 April, the abbot and community of Tewkesbury conceded the church of Llanedern, with its appurtenances, to Lord Bishop Elias of Llandaf and the chapter of Llandaf, with the tenths of Lamford retained, which belong to the altar of the priory of Cardiff. Around Pentecost [18 May], Lord Elias Bishop of Llandaf and the chapter of Llandaf confirmed to the monks of Tewkesbury all the ecclesiastical benefices which they held in the bishopric of Llandaf. William de Blois Bishop of Worcester died on 17 August. In the month of June William de Beauchamp died. John Abbot of Margam died, to whom succeeded John La Ware. Walter de Cantilupe is elected as Bishop of Worcester on 30 March, consecrated on St Andrew's Day [30 November], [and] enthroned on the octave of St Andrew [7 December].

1237. Master Otto, cardinal of the church of Rome, came as legate to England around the Feast of St Kenelm [17 July] and convened a council at London on the morrow of the octave of St Martin [19 November], and it endured for three days. In November, Margaret, daughter of Hubert de Burgh and wife of Richard de Clare, died. The sister of the King of England, formerly the wife of William Marshal, was married to Simon de Montfort on 14 January. Matilda, daughter of John de Lacy Earl of Lincoln, was married to Richard de Clare around the Purification of the Blessed Virgin Mary [2 February].

1238. Lord Otto the Legate, when staying at Oxford, was subjected to injuries by the scholars of Oxford, for which reason the Lord King in anger commanded that the clerics be seized. On Purification Day [2 February] the Lord King admitted Simon de Montfort to the earldom of Leicester at the urging of Simon's brother.

1239. The church of Tewkesbury was dedicated in honour of St Mary on 19 May by the venerable prior, Lord Walter Bishop of Worcester. A son named Edward is born to the Lord King of England. The church of St James's Bristol was dedicated on the day of St Luke the Evangelist [18 October]. In the same year, the conventual churches of Gloucester, Pershore, and Winchcombe were dedicated by the same bishop. An eclipse of the sun happened on 5 July around the hour of Sext [12 pm]. On the Day of Nativity [25 December], Baldwin de Redvers was made Earl of the Isle of Wight and Devon. Isabella Countess of Gloucester and Cornwall died on 17 January.

1240. Lord Elias Bishop of Llandaf died on 13 May. Llywelyn Prince of Wales died in April and John de Lacy Earl of Lincoln in August. The Lord King, with a great parliament convened at Gloucester in May, knighted his nephew Dafydd and the same Dafydd paid homage to the Lord King. When a great council had been convened at London, Richard Earl of Cornwall hastened on a journey towards Jerusalem. Maurice the Archdeacon of Llandaf is elected as Bishop of Llandaf but the election was quashed afterwards. Lord Otto the Legate held a great council at London on the octave of All Saints [8 November], and after Christmas he crossed the Channel heading to a council of the Lord Pope, but was impeded by Emperor Frederick. Around the Feast of St Aignan [17 November], Edmund Archbishop of Canterbury died, and he was buried at Pontigny. Morgan Gam died in February. Peter de Aigueblanche was made Bishop of Hereford. Richard de Clare bought back his land in Glamorgan, with 500 marks given to his uncle Gilbert Marshal in February.

1241. Eleanor of Brittany, related by blood to the Lord King, died at Bristol on 10 August, and was buried in the church of St James, but at a later time, on the order of the Lord King, she was translated to Amesbury. Gilbert Basset died. Around the Feast of the Apostles Peter and Paul [29 June], Gilbert Marshal died in a tournament at Ware. The Legates of France and England, around the Invention of the Holy Cross [3 May], were captured at sea and imprisoned by Emperor Frederick, along with archbishops, bishops, clerics, and others. Lord Richard Earl of Cornwall, returning from the Holy Land around the Feast of St Agnes [21 January], came to London and was received with honour.

1242. The Lord King crossed the Channel into Gascony with a great army. William Marsh is captured at London, and not long afterwards he was drawn and hanged, and finally, divided into parts, and sent to the major cities of England as a sign of his treason.

1243. Master Sinibaldo is elected canonically as supreme pontiff and named Innocent IV. Hubert de Burgh Earl of Kent and Hugh Earl of Arundel died. A son named Gilbert is born to Richard de Clare on the morrow of St Giles the abbot [2 September]. The Lord King of England came ashore in England at Portsmouth on the nearest Friday before the Feast of St Michael [25 September]. And on the eve of St Michael [28 September], he restored to Richard de Clare all his land. Boniface is confirmed by the Lord Pope as Archbishop of Canterbury. Gruffudd ap Llywelyn falls from the Tower of

London and is killed. Patrick de Chaworth[158] took Hawise lady of Ogmore[159] as his wife. Master Roger cantor of Salisbury is elected as Bishop of Bath. Fulk Basset is consecrated as Bishop of London.

1244. In June Richard de Clare was taken ill at Cardiff. Around the Feast of St Margaret [20 July], the Welsh came from Brecon in order to plunder the land of Neath, but the garrison of the country resisted and seized some and handed some over. The Lord Pope, leaving Rome, came to the city of Geneva and stayed there for some time. The Welsh greatly harassed Richard de Clare and burned Keynsham in November. Lord William de Burgh is elected canonically as Bishop of Llandaf, with [the election of] William of Christ Church quashed. Queen Eleanor bore a son named Edmund on 16 December.

1245. On Pentecost, namely, the day before 4 June, Richard de Clare was knighted at London. With Herbert fitz Mathew having died, Richard Siward was attacked because of Herbert's death and because of the destruction which he [Siward] had wrought, and the Earl took possession of the castle of Talyfan and the barony of Llanblethian and for a short while he set about building the castle of Glamorgan. A general council is convened at Lyon by Pope Innocent. In this council the Lord Pope condemned Emperor Frederick. The Lord King of England, around the Feast of St Peter in Chains [1 August], led a great army against Degannwy and fortified a castle there, and leaving a garrison there, he returned in November. Matilda Countess of Gloucester bore a son named Thomas. Walter Marshal Earl of Pembroke died on 27 November, and on the eve of the Nativity of the Lord [24 December], his brother Anselm died. Dafydd Prince of Wales died and the Welsh appointed Llywelyn son of Dafydd's brother Gruffudd as their prince henceforth.

1246. Lord Richard Earl of Cornwall began to construct the monastery of Hailes. At the same time Richard Earl of Gloucester fortified the castle of Llantrissant, having expelled Hywel ap Maredudd. Around the Feast of Mary Magdalene [22 July] the inheritance of the Marshals was divided into many parts, both in England and in Wales and Ireland. Ralph de Mortimer died. Robert Bishop of Salisbury died. Richard Abbot of Westminster died. On 16 December at Lyon, St Edmund the Archbishop was canonized. On 20 February, a Wednesday, in the ninth hour of the day, a great earthquake happened throughout all of England and Ireland.

---

[158] Lord of Kidwelly by marriage to Hawise.

[159] Hawise de Londres. Ogmore is in Glamorgan.

1247. Around the Feast of St Dunstan [19 May], the Lord Pope Innocent IV demanded a twentieth of all goods, as much from men of religious orders as from clerics. On the morrow of St Margaret [21 July], a son named Bogo is born to Richard Earl of Gloucester. The Lord King ordered the making of new currency in England. Around the Nativity of the Blessed Mary [8 September], the Lord King sent word to the county court of Cardiff, Lord John of Monmouth, and other barons, asking that they inquire diligently if Richard Siward was being treated justly and according to the law of the land in the county court. In the month of April, Thomas Archdeacon of Llandaf died, to whom succeeded Nicholas of Ledbury.[160] Master Thomas the Welshman is confirmed as Bishop of St Davids. Lord Roger Bishop of Bath died, to whom succeeded Master William of Bitton.[161]

1248. On the morrow of St Barnabas [12 June], Louis King of France started on a journey to the Holy Land. Around the Feast of St Giles [1 September], John of Monmouth the elder died. On 23 December an earthquake happened throughout various locations in England.

1249. On the eve of Holy Trinity [29 May], Louis King of France captured Damietta. On All Saints' Day [1 November], Boniface is enthroned Archbishop of Canterbury, during which festivity the Lord Earl of Gloucester acted as seneschal and cupbearer by hereditary right. Lord Henry King of England took the cross on 6 March.

1251. Many shepherds, having come together from diverse lands, invaded the city of Orléans, and massacred many clerics, and at Paris they did similarly.[162]

---

[160] *Fasti Ecclesiae Anglicani* does not have a record of him until 1260. Is this a unique mention of his election in 1247? See M. J. Pearson, 'Archdeacons: Llandaff', in *Fasti Ecclesiae Anglicanae 1066–1300: Volume 9, the Welsh Cathedrals (Bangor, Llandaff, St Asaph, St Davids)*, ed. by M. J. Pearson (London: Institute of Historical Research, 2003), pp. 17–20, *British History Online* <https://www.british-history.ac.uk/fasti-ecclesiae/1066-1300/vol9/pp17-20> [accessed 9 May 2020].

[161] Bitton is in Gloucestershire.

[162] The chronicle here refers to the Shepherds' Crusade of 1251, when shepherds and other labourers, or *pastoreaux*, invaded several French cities after Louis IX of France's defeat on crusade in Egypt; see Malcolm C. Barber, 'The Crusade of the Shepherds in 1251', in *Crusaders and Heretics, 12th–14th Centuries*, ed. by Malcolm C. Barber, Variorum Collected Studies Series, 498 (Aldershot: Ashgate, 1995), essay ix, pp. 1–23.

1252. So great a drought happened in this year that even great rivers in many locations in England and Wales are nearly dried up, and fields of corn, meadows, and pastures withered by drought. On 2 July a certain prior of Champagne, steward of the Lord Bishop of Hereford, was killed in a certain chapel in Hereford. Lord William de Burgh Bishop of Llandaf died.

1253. The Lord King crossed the Channel to Gascony around the Feast of St John and the Lord Earl of Gloucester crossed into Ireland.[163] Lord John La Ware, formerly Abbot of Margam, is consecrated as Bishop of Llandaf on 11 January.

1254. The Lord King granted Gascony to his son Edward.

1256. On 15 June, Lord John Bishop of Llandaf died. On 13 July, Rhys ap Gruffudd[164] died. On 27 July, Master William de Radnor, treasurer of Llandaf, is elected canonically as Bishop of the same place, and consecrated in London on the day after Epiphany [7 January]. He is enthroned on the day of St Agnes [21 January]. With a conflict between the Welsh and the English in the region of Carmarthen caused by the betrayal of Rhys Fychan, many of the English fell, among whom Stephen Bauzan is killed, and many were captured. In the month of [ ][165] Rhys Fychan came into Gower with a multitude of Welshmen and wasted, burned, and pillaged the whole land. And nearly all the Welsh of the whole of Gower and other lands made themselves subject to the lordship of Llywelyn Prince of Wales, and they burned the town of Swansea. On 10 May, Lord Richard Earl of Cornwall received the crown of Germany, and he is crowned at the city of Aachen, and his wife as well. His son Henry was knighted in the same place.

---

[163] I am not sure about the date here. Henry left England on 6 August and arrived on 24 August, but the Feast of St John the Baptist is on 24 June and St John the Evangelist on 27 December. Perhaps the Cardiff chronicler was uncertain. The Annals of Tewkesbury do not mention a date at all, though they do say that Richard de Clare goes to Ireland around the Feast of the Translation of St Benedict, which is 11 July.

[164] Rhys ap Gruffudd ab Ifor, Lord of Senghennydd.

[165] A space is left blank in the manuscript but the month was never added; for discussion see J. Beverley Smith, *Llywelyn ap Gruffudd: Prince of Wales* (Cardiff: University of Wales Press, 1998), p. 95 n. 19. Rhys Fychan is said to have burnt the town of Swansea in the same year; *BT (RB)*, pp. 248–49.

1257. Lord Richard Earl of Gloucester came to Cardiff with a multitude of armed men. And Llywelyn with a great army was next to the abbey of Margam. On 13 July, Llywelyn approached Llangynwyd and burned the castle of the Lord Earl and killed twenty-four of the Earl's men, with the Lord Earl situated with a great army at Llanblethian.

1258. Lord William de Clare and the Abbot of Westminster died from poison in London. Twelve peers[166] were set up in England, by the counsel and judgement of whom England and Ireland and Wales are governed. The Poitevin brothers, three kings, were expelled from England.

1259. Henry IV King of England ceased to be called Duke of Normandy.

1261. Pope Alexander IV died, to whom succeeded Urban IV in the month of August.

1262. Richard de Clare, Earl of Gloucester, died on 15 July.

1263. Gilbert de Clare, son of the aforementioned Richard Earl of Gloucester, nineteen years old, received his land in Glamorgan around the Feast of Blessed Michael [29 September]. In the same year, after the Feast of the Nativity of Blessed John the Baptist [24 June], a war arose between the King, his firstborn Edward, and three earls, and many barons and English and Welsh soldiers.

1264. One day in May, in the hour of Prime [6 am], near Lewes, the aforementioned Gilbert de Clare accepted military arms from Lord Simon de Montfort, Earl of Leicester and Seneschal of England, as did many others. Gilbert was made Earl of Gloucester and Hertford. On that day, around the hour of Nones [3 pm], they captured in a very harsh battle Henry King of England, Edward his firstborn, and Richard Earl of Cornwall, called King of Germany, and many other earls and barons of England, with three thousand men from each side killed.

1265. On 4 August at Evesham in a very harsh battle, Lord Simon de Montfort Earl of Leicester was killed, [along with] Lord Henry his firstborn son, and with him many barons and soldiers and Welshmen of unknown number. In the same year Lord William de Radnor Bishop of Llandaf died.

---

[166] *DMLBS*, s.v. par, 13: 'person matched in status (in legal context with reference to judgment by peers)'.

1266. On 26 November, Lord William de Braose is consecrated Bishop of Llandaf, and on the morrow of St Edmund the King [14 October] he was enthroned. The dedication of the church of Llandaf [was] on the same day. On the Saturday after Epiphany [9 January], Gruffudd ap Rhys and his armour-bearer were captured in the castle of Cardiff by the constable, and the aforementioned Gruffudd a little while afterwards was sent to Ireland, to Kilkenny, for imprisonment.

1267. The King of France took the cross, and many earls, barons, and knights of France and England [with him], and the aforementioned King made new currency.

1268. On 11 April, work was begun on the castle of Caerphilly. In the same year, in a harsh battle, Gilbert son of Gilbert de Umfraville, John Marshal, Richard Herbert, and many foot-soldiers were captured. The number of dead is not truly known.

9. The Chronicle of Gregory of Caerwent

Joshua Byron Smith

On 29 October 1237, the monks of St Peter's Abbey, Gloucester, received into their community a novice named Gregory of Caerwent.[1] The abbey had grown substantially over the course of the twelfth century, recovering from its nadir in the late Anglo-Saxon period, and by 1237 it had the scholarly resources expected of a healthy Benedictine abbey.[2] Amid the well-read volumes of Augustine and the familiar standards of the liberal arts curriculum, Gregory found enough historical documents to compose a chronicle that ran from 681 to his own day. Though not as verbose as some contempo-

---

[1] See the edition below, s.a. 1237.

[2] For an overview of the abbey's history, see 'Houses of Benedictine Monks: The Abbey of St Peter at Gloucester', in *The Victoria History of the County of Gloucester* (London: Victoria County History, 1907–), II, ed. by William Page (1907), pp. 53–61, *British History Online* <http://www.british-history.ac.uk/vch/glos/vol2/pp. 53-61> [accessed 16 March 2018]; David Bates, 'The Building of a Great Church: The Abbey of St Peter's, Gloucester, and its Early Norman Benefactors', *Transactions of the Bristol and Gloucestershire Archaeological Society*, 102 (1984), 129–32; Rodney Thomson, 'Books and Learning at Gloucester Abbey in the Twelfth and Thirteenth Centuries', in *Books and Collectors 1200–1700*, ed. by James P. Carley and Colin G. C. Tite (London: BL, 1997), pp. 3–26; *The Original Acta of St. Peter's Abbey, Gloucester c. 1122 to 1263*, ed. by Robert B. Patterson, Gloucestershire Record Series (Gloucestershire: Bristol and Gloucestershire Archeological Society, 1998), pp. xxi–xxxii; Christopher Brooke, 'St Peter of Gloucester and St Cadoc of Llancarfan', in *Celt and Saxon: Studies in the Early British Border*, ed. by Nora Chadwick (Cambridge: Cambridge University Press, 1963), pp. 258–332 (repr. in Christopher N. L. Brooke, *The Church and the Welsh Border in the Central Middle Ages*, ed. by David N. Dumville and Christopher N. L. Brooke (Woodbridge: Boydell, 1986), pp. 50–94); Richard Sharpe, *A Handlist of the Latin Writers of Great Britain and Ireland before 1540*, Publications of the Journal of Medieval Latin, 1 (Turnhout: Brepols, 1997), p. 154.

rary chroniclers, Gregory nonetheless produced a good synthesis of the available history of Gloucester and its environs, and he continued writing from his entrance into the novitiate in 1237 until his apparent death in 1290, when the chronicle suddenly stops. Gregory composed a modest chronicle, one that is mainly concerned with his own abbey, other Severn valley religious communities, Marcher nobility, and Wales. Its scope is generally local, often regional, and only occasionally national. This chapter presents the first edition and translation of the chronicle of Gregory of Caerwent.[3]

Gregory's chronicle almost suffered the same fate as other medieval works, haunting us only as an enigmatic title in John Bale's *Index* with no surviving medieval manuscript.[4] Thankfully, the chronicle was captured for posterity in London, BL, MS Cotton Vespasian A V, a composite manuscript written by the antiquaries William Lambarde and Laurence Nowell. Gregory's chronicle belongs to the second portion of this manuscript, which contains Nowell's transcriptions of various medieval chronicles.[5] Whatever manuscript Nowell used is now lost to us, and his copy of the chronicle is the sole remaining witness of Gregory's labour.

We can be reasonably certain as to when Nowell copied the chronicle. In March 1567, Nowell left England for the Continent to pursue his studies, never to return.[6] Before he left, he bequeathed all of his books to Lambarde,

---

[3] A preliminary study was carried out in Michael Hare, 'The Chronicle of Gregory of Caerwent: A Preliminary Account', *Glenvensis: The Gloucester and District Archaeological Research Group Review*, 27 (1993), 42–44. Hare intended to produce an edition himself, but he has informed me that it will not come to fruition, and he graciously gave his blessing to this project. I have found his brief account useful and can confirm all of his observations about Gregory's chronicle. Although the chronicle has not received a previous edition, it has on occasion been consulted. Some notable examples are: Thomson, 'Books and Learning', pp. 4–9; *The Chronicle of John of Worcester*, ed. by R. R. Darlington and Patrick McGurk, trans. by Jennifer Bray and Patrick McGurk, 3 vols (Oxford: Clarendon Press, 1998), III, pp. xxx–xxxi; *The Winchcombe and Coventry Chronicles: Hitherto Unnoticed Witnesses to the Work of John of Worcester*, ed. and trans. by Paul Anthony Hayward, 2 vols (Tempe: Arizona Center for Medieval and Renaissance Studies, 2010), I, 124–30; and Patrick Sims-Williams, *Religion and Literature in Western England, 600–800* (Cambridge: Cambridge University Press, 1990), pp. 35 n. 92, 38 n. 116, 122 n. 40, 123 n. 45, 124.

[4] John Bale, *Index Britanniae Scriptorum*, ed. by Reginald Lane Poole, with Mary Bateson (Oxford: Clarendon Press, 1902), pp. 98–99.

[5] Nowell wrote fols 93–203.

[6] Among the many studies of Nowell's life and work, see Retha Warnicke, 'Nowell, Laurence (1530–c. 1570), antiquary', in *Oxford Dictionary of National Biography* <https://doi.org/10.1093/ref:odnb/69731>; Carl T. Berkhout, 'Laurence Nowell (1530–ca. 1570)',

whom he had named as the executor of his estate; he must have therefore copied the chronicle before his departure. Establishing a *terminus a quo* is more difficult: Nowell's interest in Gregory's chronicle almost certainly postdates 1561, the year in which he turned his attention to the antiquities of England and accomplished his most famed antiquarian scholarship. Thus it would seem that Nowell copied the chronicle of Gregory of Caerwent during the period of his life in which he worked diligently on the English past, but before he left England and his books. It seems prudent to date Nowell's copy of Gregory's chronicle in MS Cotton Vespasian A V to *c.* 1561 × *c.* 1567.

After Nowell left England, Lambarde made good use of his friend's work. For example, Lambarde's *Archaionomia* (1568), only the second printed book to contain Old English, heavily relied on Nowell's copies and editions of Anglo-Saxon legal documents. In a similar spirt, Lambarde worked his way through Nowell's transcription of the chronicle of Gregory of Caerwent and the other attendant historical texts now in MS Cotton Vespasian A V. We know this because Lambarde left marginalia throughout the chronicle. Judging by these marginalia, he read the chronicle primarily for its toponyms, as the margins of the manuscript are filled with place names in Lambarde's hand, allowing him later to find particular locales with ease. This is unsurprising, since toponyms were of great interest to Lambarde, especially between 1567 and 1577, when he was working on his *Alphabetical Description of the Chief Places in England and Wales, with an Account of the Most Memorable Events that have Distinguished Them*.[7] Lambarde's reading and annotation of the chronicle of Gregory of Caerwent thus probably dates to this period.

Lambarde's involvement in MS Cotton Vespasian A V raises a few questions. Of chief importance is the chronicle's title, which in the manuscript reads 'Ex Chron. Gloucest' gregorii Caerguent' ('From Gregory of Caerwent's Chronicle of Gloucester').[8] I suspect one reason that this chronicle has received only passing attention is the appearance of this *Ex* in the title, which gives the

---

in *Medieval Scholarship: Biographical Studies on the Formation of a Discipline*, 3 vols (New York: Garland, 1992–2000), II: *Literature and Philology*, ed. by Helen Damico, with Donald Fennema and Karmen Lenz (1998), pp. 3–16, which contains a useful bibliography; and Patrick Wormald, 'The Lambarde Problem: Eighty Years On', in *Alfred the Wise: Studies in Honour of Janet Bately*, ed. by Jane Roberts and Janet L. Nelson, with Malcolm Godden (Cambridge: Brewer, 1997), pp. 237–75.

[7] Rebecca Brackmann, *The Elizabethan Invention of Anglo-Saxon England: Laurence Nowell, William Lambarde and the Study of Old English* (Cambridge: Brewer, 2012), p. 122.

[8] Fol. 195ʳ.

impression that what Nowell did was merely transcribe excerpts, and that what survives in MS Cotton Vespasian A V is only a partial representation of the medieval manuscript. Indeed, reluctance to credit Nowell and too much reliance on Lambarde's erroneous title has meant that the chronicle of Gregory of Caerwent has been described merely as 'notes' and 'extracts' in the two studies that explore the relationship between it and other chronicles at any length.[9] However, both of these critical impulses are mistaken.

Importantly, the title is in Lambarde's hand — not Nowell's.[10] I would suggest that Lambarde wrote the title at the same time that he wrote his marginalia, so sometime between 1567 and 1577.[11] Crucially, what this means is that Lambarde did not know what exactly he was annotating, since Nowell had almost certainly already left England. Moreover, Lambarde was likely tempted to insert the *Ex* because the first few lines of the chronicle are imperfect and begin confusingly in the middle of a passage, which might have given him the impression that Nowell was picking and choosing what passages to include (as discussed below, I believe he was not). At any rate, whenever Lambarde used Nowell's notebooks for his own projects, he was occasionally led astray by what he was reading, since he did not have Nowell on hand to clarify matters. For instance, in his *Archaionomia*, Lambarde occasionally mistakes some of Nowell's own Old English compositions, conflations, and editorial work as genuine, causing considerable frustration for later scholars of Anglo-Saxon law.[12] I would suggest that his assessment of the chronicle of Gregory of Caerwent was similarly flawed. The misleading *Ex* should be struck from the title.

Furthermore, there is little reason to doubt that we have anything but the full chronicle. The content is thematically varied and does not reflect any dis-

---

[9] *The Chronicle of John of Worcester*, III, p. xxx; *The Winchcombe and Coventry Chronicles*, I, 125–30.

[10] I would like to thank Adam V. Doskey, Curator of Rare Books and Manuscripts at the University of Illinois, for providing me with images of Lambarde's handwriting.

[11] Lambarde's marginal annotations and the title seem to be written in the same ink, which lends further support to this belief. Another telling difference is the spelling of 'Caerwent'. The title and a marginal annotation on fol. 201ʳ both have 'Caerguent', while the body of the chronicle shows 'Kairwent'. Given Lambarde's interest in ancient toponyms, it is no surprise that the title and marginal annotation display a more archaic form of the word, with the unmarked lenition of 'gwent'. The body of the text, which I take to be more indicative of what Gregory himself actually wrote, displays the common contemporary thirteenth-century spelling 'Kairwent'.

[12] For a brief overview of the extensive literature on this subject, see Berkhout, 'Laurence Nowell', pp. 11–13.

cernable editorial bias on Nowell's part. After the seven annals for Anglo-Saxon England, which seems to have been the extent of local knowledge of the Anglo-Saxon past at Gloucester, the chronicle never has a gap of more than a few years. In the period from 1072–1290, there are just under one hundred and forty annals, or roughly one for every year and half, coverage that is consistent with other brief monastic chronicles. Moreover, the span of the chronicle, from 681 to 1290, matches the scope of a copy at King's College, Cambridge, from the sixteenth century.[13] Therefore, even if Nowell did pick and choose what excerpts to copy, he did not alter the general scope of the chronicle.

Due to Nowell's status as a founding figure of Anglo-Saxon studies, his trustworthiness as a transcriber of medieval manuscripts has been examined in some detail.[14] In general, Nowell copied manuscripts with care and did not practice any brazen antiquarian 'inventio'. Patrick Wormald succinctly claims that 'Nowell's *verbal* fidelity to his originals has been vindicated'.[15] Even when working with Old English, a language whose subtleties were not yet fully grasped, Nowell produced transcriptions that can be relied upon with the appropriate caution.[16] The unproblematic familiarity of Latin means that Nowell's Latin transcripts are even more accurate than his Old English ones. Indeed, we occasionally catch Nowell's medieval exemplar peeking through in his Elizabethan copy. Nowell writes '12411' instead of 1242, surely influenced by the Roman numeral MCCXLII of his exemplar. He also at times preserves what appear to be medieval scribal errors, another mark of trustworthiness. For instance, somewhere in the transmission of the chronicle, several thorns (þ) were misread: *Egelfleda* for *Eþelfleda* appears in the annal for 910, and in the annals for 1282 and 1283, what must have originally been *Roþelan* (Rhuddlan) appears nonsensically as *Eoyelan* and *Eopelan*. Of course, it is risky to conjecture when exactly a scribal error was made, but I would suggest that Nowell, one of the best Anglo-Saxonists of his day, would have had little trouble with the letter þ. But more to the point, the fact that he does not correct *Egelfleda*, a rather obvious error and one found in other later medieval chronicles, bolsters

---

[13] As noted below, Bale (*Index Britanniae Scriptorum*) states that the *Chronicle* at King's College ends at 1291.

[14] See, for example, Raymond J. S. Grant, *Laurence Nowell, William Lambarde, and the Laws of the Anglo-Saxons* (Amsterdam: Rodopi, 1996), esp. pp. 27–29.

[15] Wormald, "The Lambarde Problem', p. 145.

[16] Most of the errors that modern scholars have identified in Nowell's Old English transcriptions are explained by spelling conventions, the unfamiliarity of insular scripts, or Nowell's attempts at editing Old English.

the case for generally crediting Nowell's transcription of the chronicle. Access to Gregory's chronicle does not seem to have been an issue. Although it will remain impossible to pinpoint the location where Nowell found his copy of the chronicle without additional bibliographic evidence, an extant copy did exist in his day at King's College, Cambridge, and William Dugdale seems to have had access to the chronicle as well.[17] On the whole, Nowell's copy presents few textual problems, and it seems that the exemplar he used, wherever he found it, was a decent one.

Like so many other medieval authors, Gregory of Caerwent will remain an obscure figure. What we know of him comes from his own chronicle; the rest we must infer. His agnomen 'de Kairwent', his entry into the novitiate in 1237 at St Peter's, and his own self-identification as the author of the chronicle are the meagre foundations for the speculation that must necessarily follow. Gregory's status as the chronicle's author even rests on unstable ground, since the entry for 1237 presents some interpretative difficulties:

> Anno 1237 Gregorius de Kairwent recepit habitum monachalem in ecclesia sancti Petri Glocestriae ab Henrico Foliot abbate quarto kalendas Nouembris, qui huius libri hucusque scripsit.

The last clause, 'qui huius libri hucusque scripsit' (who has written [...] of this book up to this point) seems to be lacking an object, upon which *huius libri* would depend. Something like *a principio huius libri* ('from the beginning of the book') makes for a better sentence, but even if a scribal error is assumed here, ambiguity remains. If Gregory compiled the chronicle up to 1237, did he do so immediately after his entry into the novitiate? Are the post-1237 entries also by Gregory? That Gregory claims Caerwent as his place of origin might help in this regard, but it immediately raises a host of questions about his ethnicity. In the preceding century, before the Cistercians had been established in Wales, 'a few Welshmen favoured by "birth or brilliance" could find admittance to one of the larger abbeys along the border'.[18] But Gregory was admitted into St Peter's Abbey, Gloucester, in 1237, and thus the option of a 'native' Welsh

---

[17] Bale, *Index Britanniae Scriptorum*, pp. 98–99. Although Bale records the incipit, the first few sentences of Gregory's chronicle are lacking in MS Cotton Vespasian A V, which makes comparison impossible. Curiously, Bale notes that Gregory's chronicle ends in 1291, not 1290 as we have it. However, Poole notes that 1291 is a correction in Bale's manuscript; there may be some confusion here. For Dugdale, see Hare, 'The Chronicle of Gregory of Caerwent', p. 43.

[18] Frederick George Cowley, *The Monastic Order in South Wales, 1066–1349* (Cardiff: University of Wales Press, 1977), p. 46.

monastery was certainly available to him. Perhaps he was of Anglo-Norman descent and purposefully chose — if indeed he had a choice at all — St Peter's Abbey to suit his own cultural leanings? But this is well and truly speculation, and it is far more likely that geographical proximity and Gloucester's own widespread interests in south-eastern Wales are enough to explain the (probably unremarkable) presence of a man from Caerwent at St Peter's Abbey. Whatever Gregory's ethnicity was or was not, after 1237 the chronicle keeps a close eye on Wales and the southern Marches, as around half of the post-1237 entries concern Wales in some fashion.

The chronicle records some of the major events of the Edwardian conquest of Wales: Edward's invasion of Wales in 1277; Llywelyn's marriage to Eleanor in 1278; Dafydd ap Gruffudd's attack against Roger Clifford in 1282; Edward's invasion of Wales and the death of Llywelyn in 1282; Dafydd ap Gruffudd's capture and execution in 1283; the establishment of English laws in Wales in 1284; and Rhys ap Maredudd's campaign in 1287. The chronicle's description of these events suggests that it viewed the English conquest of Wales in relatively neutral terms, neither heaping scorn on Llywelyn nor lending particular support to his cause. Tellingly, the chronicle wields none of the anti-Welsh rhetoric in which many English contemporaries indulged. Nonetheless, it describes Dafydd ap Gruffudd as behaving 'treacherously' ('dolose'), has Rhys ap Maredudd 'rebelling' ('rebellans'), and recounts that Hervey de Chaworth 'was cruelly slain by the Welsh' ('crudeliter occisus est a Wallensibus').[19] And English nobility generally attract more of the chronicle's attention than the Welsh. But this is generally balanced by annals like 1256, where Llywelyn's harrying of England is explained as the result of Edward I's bailiffs insulting the Welsh. In other words, the chronicle shows the ambivalence that we might expect from Gregory, who came from one of the places in Wales that had been under Anglo-Norman rule the longest, and who seemingly spent the majority of his life at a large English abbey. The chronicle also follows the Marcher aristocracy: the de Braose dynasty, the de Lacys, Gilbert Marshal, and the Chaworths — all important Marcher names — make up the bulk of the post-1237 references to secular lords. Finally, the chronicle takes note of the ecclesiastical comings and goings in the dioceses of Llandaf and St Davids in the mid-thirteenth century. The chronicle notes three bishops of St Davids (Thomas Walensis, Iorwerth, and Richard Carew) and three bishops of Llandaf (William de Burgh, John de la Warre, and William de Radnor).

---

[19] s.a. 1282, 1287, 1276.

But keeping track of the two southern Welsh bishoprics would not have been of interest to Gregory alone. St Peter's Abbey had extensive and important interests in both dioceses, and the appearance of these Welsh bishops in a Gloucester chronicle is thus unsurprising.[20] Overall, it is hard to escape the conclusion that after beginning the chronicle shortly after his entrance into the novitiate, Gregory kept a running chronicle from 1237 to 1290 that reflects independent accounts of topics that mattered most to the author: St Peter's Abbey, Marcher nobility, and Wales.[21]

Gregory, however, did not start his work *de novo*. Instead, he worked from available sources to write the earlier portions of his work. It is worth asking what those sources might have been and examining their relationship with the other surviving historical documents from St Peter's Abbey, Gloucester. The major source for the history of the abbey is the *History of St Peter's Abbey*, compiled during the abbacy of Walter Froucester (1382–1412), which has a close textual relationship with Gregory's chronicle.[22] Froucester's *History* also contains an index of the abbey's holdings and a brief account of how it acquired them. There are also surviving charters from St Peter's Abbey, and the relationship between these charters and Froucester's *History* is complex, to say the least.[23] However, it is clear that both Gregory's chronicle and Froucester's *History* made use of common Gloucester sources, since the verbal correspondences are often exact. However, these shared annals only occur in the pre-1231 portion of Gregory's chronicle.[24] On the other hand, Froucester's *History* shows no knowledge of Gregory's post-1237 annals, which strongly suggests that Gregory's chronicle was not used as a source when Abbot Froucester created his recension of

---

[20] See Joshua Byron Smith, *Walter Map and the Matter of Britain* (Philadelphia: University of Pennsylvania Press, 2017), pp. 107–39.

[21] It is impossible to prove that Gregory worked on his chronicle until his death, but the consistency of topics and the continuation of style throughout the 1237–1290 annals suggest to me that he did just that.

[22] I will refer to this *History* as 'Froucester's *History*' for the sake of clarity, since Abbot Froucester oversaw its creation. The *History*, index, and cartulary are all edited in *HC*. The *History* exists in three manuscripts: Gloucester Cathedral Library, MS 34, fols 1ʳ–43ᵛ; London, BL, MS Cotton Domitian A VIII, fols 145ᵛ–60ᵛ; Oxford, The Queen's College, MS 367, pp. 65–125. Hart based his edition on Queen's College, MS 367 and he was unaware of Gloucester, MS 34, which the chapter bought in 1879.

[23] See Brooke, 'St Peter of Gloucester'.

[24] Hare, 'The Chronicle of Gregory of Caerwent', p. 42.

Gloucester history around the year 1400.[25] The shared entries, therefore, point to common Gloucester sources and not direct borrowing. A comparison of the two chronicles shows that most of Gregory's pre-1231 annals have precedent in their shared Gloucester sources.

There are, of course, some exceptions. Gregory records the martyrdom of St Kenelm in 821, the translation of St Oswald in 910, and the Welsh uprising after Henry I's death in the annals for 1136 and 1137. None of these are present in Froucester's *History*. Gregory's annals for 821 and 910 seem to have their origin in William of Malmesbury's *Gesta regum Anglorum*. Compare Gregory's account of St Oswald's translation to William's below:

> Ossa sancti regis Oswaldi de Bardeneia in Merciam translata sunt, in cuius honore Elfredi regis filia Eþelfleda cum coniuge suo Etheredo monasterium Glocestriae construxit, cuius monachi usque tempora Danorum ibi permanserunt.

> The bones of King Oswald the Saint were translated from Bardney to Mercia, and in his honour Æthelflæd, daughter of King Alfred, together with her husband Æthelred built the monastery of Gloucester, whose monks remained there until the time of the Danes.

> Decessit ante germanum quinquennio sepultaque in monasterio sancti petri Gloecestrae, quod ipsa cum uiro Etheredo ingenti cura extruxerat eoque ossa beati Oswaldi ex Bardenia transtulerat, sed illo tempore Danorum destructo, aliud, quod nunc in eadem ciuitate precipuum habetur, Aldredus archipiscopus Eboracensis instaurauit.

> She [Æthelflæd] died five years before her brother, and was buried in the monastery of St Peter's at Gloucester which she herself and her husband Æthelred had built with great exertions, translating to it the bones of St Oswald from Bardney; but that having been destroyed at the time of the Danes, another, now regarded as the chief church in that city, was put in its place by Ealdred, Archbishop of York.[26]

---

[25] See *The Winchcombe and Coventry Chronicles*, I, 127 for the opposing view that Froucester used Gregory's chronicle for the intervening period and then relied on other material. I find this view overly complicated: we would have to assume a situation in which the redactors of Froucester's *History* used Gregory's chronicle alongside a common source, but put Gregory's chronicle aside at exactly the moment that it began to contain information not present in the shared Gloucester source.

[26] William of Malmesbury, *Gesta regum Anglorum*, ed. and trans. by Roger A. B. Mynors, completed by Rodney M. Thomson and Michael Winterbottom, 2 vols (Oxford: Clarendon Press, 1998–99), I (1998), 198–99.

Both link the translation of Oswald's relics with the Danes. In addition to the general correspondence, both passages share the spelling 'Ethered', a name which more commonly appears as 'Ethelred', and indeed Gregory writes it as such in the very next annal. On its own, that is not much, but Gregory's passage for the martyrdom of St Kenelm also shares a variant spelling with William's *Gesta*: 'martirizatur hoc anno Kenelmus qui Winchelcomba iacet' ('in this year, Kenelm is martyred and lies at Winchcombe'). Neither Gregory's chronicle nor Froucester's *History* spell 'Winchcombe' with an internal *l*, although William's *Gesta* does. To be sure, 'Ethered' and 'Winchelcomba' are otherwise attested, but their appearance in the only two passages from the Anglo-Saxon portion of Gregory's chronicle with no corresponding entries in Froucester's *History* suggests that Gregory was using something other than the common Gloucester source here. William of Malmesbury, however, does not give the date for St Oswald's translation. For that, Gregory is dependent on another source.

The Gloucester continuation of the chronicle of John of Worcester (also called the *Chronicula*) not only dates the translation of Oswald to the year 910 — as opposed to 909 in the Anglo-Saxon Chronicle — but is also the ultimate source for Gregory's annals of 1136 and 1137.[27] And while this text was certainly at St Peter's Abbey, Gloucester, since that is where it originated, it nonetheless does not appear to be the direct source for Gregory's annals. Instead, Paul Anthony Hayward has postulated a lost Gloucester chronicle, completed around 1181, which itself was at least partially dependent on the Gloucester continuation of John of Worcester.[28] It was this lost Gloucester chronicle that Gregory consulted, but he was not alone. Hayward shows that this lost chronicle was used in the second phase of the Winchcombe chronicle, and I would add that this lost chronicle was consulted by the compilers of the Osney Abbey chronicle as well.[29] What this means for the present discussion is that Gregory's chronicle, the Winchcombe chronicle, and the Osney Abbey chronicle all have cognate entries for the Welsh revolts of 1136 and 1137. A comparison of all three strongly suggests a common source and not direct borrowing.

Interestingly, the Osney Abbey chronicle and Gregory's chronicle show the closest affinity, even though the Osney Abbey chronicle omits material present

---

[27] Edited in *The Chronicle of John of Worcester*, III. See pp. xl–l for the continuations.

[28] *The Winchcombe and Coventry Chronicles*, I, 124–30.

[29] Edited in *AM*, IV (1869), 3–352. For a recent study, see Antonia Gransden, *Historical Writing in England*, 2 vols (London: Routledge and Kegan Paul, 1974–82; repr. 1996), I: *c.550 to c.1307* (1996), 429–32.

in Gregory's. Compare part of Gregory's annal for 1136 above with the chronicle from Osney Abbey below:

> Graue bellum exarsit in<ter> Normannos et Walenses apud Guer, cesis millia quingentis sedecim

> A terrible battle flared up between the Normans and the Welsh in Gower and one thousand five hundred and sixteen perished.

> Grave bellum inter Normannos et Walenses, caesis militibus quingentis sexdecim.

> A terrible battle between the Normans and the Welsh, and five hundred and sixteen soldiers perished.[30]

This close similarity occurs again in the entry for 1137:

> Fit pugna grauis apud Cairdigan et tanta strages edita est ut de captiuatis mulieribus 1000 remanentur ad decimam.

> There is a terrible fight at Cardigan and such slaughter issued forth that from captured women a thousand were left for the tithe.

> Grave bellum apud Kardigan, et tanta strages hominum facta est, ut de captivis mulieribus mille remanerent ad decimam.

> A terrible war at Cardigan and such slaughter of men was made that from captured women a thousand were left for the tithe.[31]

The Osney chronicle runs from the foundation of the abbey in 1016 to 1293 and was written in distinct phases. For the twelfth century, the chronicle follows various early sources, one of which might have been a version of the lost Gloucester chronicle that Hayward postulates. It is difficult to explain the above similarities in 1136 and 1137 otherwise. Even if Gregory somehow had access to an early version stage of the Osney Abbey chronicle, it is impossible that he used it as his sole source, since he records the deaths of Richard fitz Gilbert and Payn fitz John in 1136 and 1137 respectively, while the Osney chronicle does not (moreover, it seems needlessly complicated to suggest that Gregory used a chronicle from Osney when similar entries were present at Gloucester). On the other hand, it just might be possible that at the last stage of composition the Osney Abbey

---

[30] *AM*, IV, 20.
[31] *AM*, IV, 21.

chronicle used Gregory's chronicle — but this point cannot be proven at present. However, it seems most likely that their similarities result from a shared Gloucester source, perhaps another recension of the lost Gloucester chronicle suggested by Hayward. Whatever the case may be, Gregory includes Welsh material for 1136 and 1137 that Abbot Froucester's recension does not.

In spite of heavy reliance on prior sources, the pre-1231 portion of Gregory's chronicle still occasionally contains information that is not present elsewhere.[32] In 1157 Gregory records the obit of Gregory, a pious monk who wrote many volumes in the abbey's library.[33] While both Froucester's *History* and Gregory's chronicle record the death of Abbot Peter in 1114, only Gregory preserves an amusing anecdote: the monastery's gratitude for Abbot Peter's gracious allowance of new riding cushions, wardrobes in the dormitory, and a third day of phlebotomy. Gregory is also the only source to record Abbot William's death at Llanbadarn Fawr in 1131, after having retired on account of illness the year before. Moreover, the exact date for Robert fitz Hamon's gift of the church of St Cadog to St Peter's has remained unknown, but Gregory gives it as 1126, though that date must be incorrect because Robert died in 1107.[34] It is interesting to note that several of those episodes lacking in Froucester's *History* but present in Gregory's chronicle concern Wales, which suggests either that Gregory paid more attention to Welsh matters, or that Froucester omitted them out of distaste. There are other differences between the two, many of them slight, and Gregory's chronicle is occasionally off by one year in comparison to other sources.[35] Reading Froucester's *History* side by side with Gregory's chronicle can be instructive as well, and it makes one suspect that at times Froucester's recension takes some liberties with details. For instance, in 1095, both sources record the Archbishop of York's return of properties to the abbey. Gregory says that the Archbishop repented 'that he had held them unjustly for so long' ('quod tam diu eas inuste tenuerat'), a phrase also present in Froucester's *History*, but perhaps aggrandized by the addition that the Archbishop did so while 'harshly blaming himself, beating his breast, and bending his knee' ('semetipsum grav-

---

[32] Hare ('St Peter of Gloucester') provides several such instances.

[33] Hare, 'The Chronicle of Gregory of Caerwent', p. 43; Thomson, 'Books and Learning', pp. 4–9.

[34] For the uncertainty regarding the date, see Brian Golding, 'Trans-Border Transactions: Patterns of Patronage in Anglo-Norman Wales', *HSJ*, 16 (2005), 27–46 (pp. 35–36); Brooke, *The Church and the Welsh Border*, pp. 64–65.

[35] Hare, 'The Chronicle of Gregory of Caerwent', p. 43. Generally speaking, Gregory's chronicle often helps confirm points made by Brooke.

iter inculpando, pectus tundendo, genu flectendo).³⁶ In light of its absence in Gregory's chronicle, this passage and others read like Abbot Froucester's imaginative embellishments.

I have not set out to unravel all of the questions that arise when Gregory's chronicle is compared to other Gloucester sources, only to offer a way forward for those who may wish to do so in the future. One major obstacle is that William Hart, in his edition of Froucester's *History*, was unaware of the presence of a third manuscript, which must be consulted if any firm conclusions are to be drawn about the relationship between the two texts.³⁷ Nonetheless, the chronicle of Gregory of Caerwent serves as a useful addition to the history of St Peter's Abbey, and it can now be used in fruitful combination with other surviving Gloucester sources.

In the following edition, I have erred on the conservative side. I have retained incorrect years and even some readings that are surely incorrect. Emendations are limited and always noted, and I have tended to emend proper names only if they give nonsense. If, however, a reading is comprehensible, I generally let it stand, even if it disagrees with other sources. I have done so in order to give an accurate representation of Gregory's text. At any rate, almost all of the events in the chronicle are attested elsewhere in the historical record, so the chief interest of readers of Gregory's chronicle will often be in these variations. I have also provided references to Froucester's *History*, its index, and only occasionally relevant charters. These references are not exhaustive, but point to where I have identified the closest verbal parallels. Anyone wishing to make further study of the relationship between Gregory's chronicle and Froucester's *History* would do well to consider these references as merely guideposts, to be used in conjunction with Hart's generous index. The translation generally presents few problems. I have relied on *The Historical Gazetteer of England's Place-Names* and Hart's extensive index to give modern versions of place names, and when I am uncertain, or when there are multiple possibilities, I have retained the Latin form in quotation marks.³⁸ Stylistically, I have done little to depart drastically from the Latin, though I typically transform Latin subordinate clauses into more felicitous English sentences.³⁹

---

[36] *HC*, I, 11.

[37] Gloucester, MS 34.

[38] *The Historical Gazetteer of England's Place-Names* <http://placenames.org.uk/index.php> [accessed 16 March 2018].

[39] I would like to thank an anonymous reader of this chapter who caught many errors, provided excellent advice, and suggested several pertinent references.

Edition of Ex Chronico Gloucestriae Gregorii Caerguent

Anno 681[40] [...] et quinto Æthelredi regis Merciorum. Dedit idem rex duobus ministris suis et fratribus Osrico et Oswoldo partem quandam terrae suae: Osrico uidelicet, qui postea effectus est rex Northanhumbrorum, trecentum tributariorum in Glocestria; Oswaldo uero trecentum casatorum in Persora. Hic Osricus consensu regis primum fundauit monasterium sancti Petri Claudeae ciuitatis, et eidem praefecit abbatissam Kineburgam sororem suam, cui successit Edburga abbatissa cognata eis. Et post eam Ena abbatissa quae praefuit tres et trigenta annos et acquisiuit multas terras: in Alra, uiginti hidarum; in Pendeswelle, uiginti hidarum; extra urbem, uiginti et centum hidarum. Et postea subregulus Hwicciorum Aldredus dedit haereditatem suam ecclesiae, hoc est in Culna sexagenta manentes. Et Burgreda dedit in Faireford decem hidarum, in Wiarchanstona quindecim hidarum, in Cheddeswurtha in terra montana quindecim hidarum, in Numedesfelda tres manentes. Omnes istas terras dedit et concessit Aldredus subregulus Hwicciorum. Item Ethelmundus de Geldinges dedit triginta hidarum in Oure et quinque et triginta in Leche.[41]

Anno 729[42] Ethelricus filius Eadmundi,[43] cum consensu synodali, de<dit> triginta manentia[44] in Oura sancto Petro Glocestriae.

Anno 821[45] Beornulfus rex Merciorum dedit 15 hidas in Esneburie,[46] id est Stanedis. Martirizatur hoc anno Kenelmus qui Winchelcomba iacet.

---

[40] Cf. *HC*, I, 3–4. The beginning of the chronicle has been cut short, but, judging from *HC*, it seems that only a few introductory sentences have been left out, perhaps damaged in the copy that Nowell examined. I suspect the 'quinto' here parallels the beginning of the *HC*: 'Anno ab Incarnatione Domini sexcentesimo octogesimo primo Ethelredus rex Merciorum quartus a Penda primo rege, in eodem anno regni sui uicesimo quinto' in *HC* and that the phrase in Gregory's chronicle originally read something like 'in eodem anno uicesmio quinto Æthelredi regis Merciorum' ('in the same year, the twenty-fifth of Æthelred King of the Mercians'). As numerous commentators have pointed out, this dating, which the chronicle shares with *HC*, is in error. See *HC*, I, 3 n. 2. Cf. Sawyer 70 <http://www.esawyer.org.uk/charter/70.html> [accessed 20 January 2019].

[41] Leche] Lethe MS.

[42] Cf. *HC*, I, 104.

[43] Eadmundi] Edelmundi *HC*.

[44] manentia] manentes *HC*.

[45] Cf. *HC*, I, 111.

[46] Esneburie] Cf. 'sub Ezimbury', *HC*, I, 111.

Anno 862[47] Burgredus rex Merciorum confirmauit donationes antecessorum, et cum consensu episcoporum et optimatum eandem ecclesiam fecit liberam et omnia loca ad eam pertinentia ab omni terreno negotio et seruitio praeter orationem deuotionis in regali consilio apud Wellesburn.

Anno 910[48] Ossa sancti regis Oswaldi de Bardeneia in Merciam translata sunt, in cuius honore Elfredi regis filia Eþelfleda[49] cum coniuge suo Etheredo monasterium Glocestriae construxit, cuius monachi usque tempora Danorum ibi permanserunt.

Anno 981[50] Regnante rege Ethelredo, fratre sancti Edwardi, soror eius dedit ecclesiae sancti Petri Hynetune tunc incultam. Cumque ab ea exigerentur quinque homines in regis expeditionis nec inuenire possit, prostrauit se ad pedes regis et obtinuit ut deinceps libera et quieta esset possessio illa.

Anno 1058[51] Aldredus episcopus Wigorniensis ecclesiam sancti Petri dedicauit et Wulstanum Wigorniensem monachum ibidem abbatem constituit.

Anno 1072[52] <Obiit> Wulstanus abbas quinto idus Februarii cui successit dompnus abbas Serlo primum Abracacensis kanonicus[53] et deinde <...>

Anno 1077[54] Monochatus[55] est Odo celerarius cuius labore et industria in terris et possessio<n>ibus magnopere creuit Glocestriae ecclesia.

Anno 1080[56] Walterus de Lacy reddidit sancto Petro Ledenam cum filio Waltero octo annorum.

---

[47] Cf. *HC*, I, 9–10, 121–22. For discussion, see H. P. R. Finberg, *The Early Charters of the West Midlands*, 2nd edn (Leicester: Leicester University Press, 1972), pp. 153–66.

[48] Cf. William of Malmesbury, *Gesta regum Anglorum*, I, 198–99.

[49] Eþelfleda] Egelfleda MS.

[50] Cf. *HC*, I, 87.

[51] Cf. *HC*, I, 9.

[52] Cf. *HC*, I, 10. This entry is cut short, but the original was surely something similar to *HC*: 'deinde monachus in ecclesia sancti Michaelis, de Monte Tumba'.

[53] kanonicus] monachus kanonicus MS.

[54] Cf. *HC*, I, 11.

[55] monochatus: my thanks to an anonymous reviewer for suggesting that *monochatus* could be a spelling of *monachatus* influenced by Greek words beginning in *mono-* (one).

[56] Cf. *HC*, I, 92.

Anno 1081[57] Ernulfus de Hartinges[58] dedit sancto Petro Linkenholt, Willhelmo rege seniore concedente apud Salesburiam in purificatione sanctae Mariae.

Anno 1085 Walterus[59] de Laci sexto kalendas Aprilis obiit, qui fuit fundator beati Petri Herfordiae. Iamque pene confirmata ecclesia, scalam ascendens, cum ad trabes peruenisset, subito pede lapso, corruens spiritum exhalauit, et[60] in capitulo Glocestriae sepultus est quinto kalendas Aprilis in cena Domini. Tunc uxor eius Ermelina dedit eidem ecclesiae pro redemptione animae uiri sui uillam unam quinque hidarum, id est Duntesburne. Hoc[61] anno Willemus de Auco dedit sancto Petro molendinum de Stanhuse cum una uirgata terrae.

Anno 1087[62] In descriptione totius Angliae Rogerus senior de Berkleye fecit Nimedesfeld describi ad mensam regis subdole nesciente abbate Serlone.

Anno 1088[63] Bernadus de Nouomercato dedit sancto Petro Glasburiam cum omnibus pertinentibus liberam et quietam et totam decimam dominii de Brekonio, scilicet annonae, pecorum, caseorum, uenationis et mellis. Item ecclesiam de Corre cum decima et unam hidam quae uocatur Bache. Obiit idibus Februariis.

Anno 1089[64] Serlo abbas inchoauit mo<n>asterium sancti Petri in die apostolorum Petri et Pauli, Roberto Herefordiensi episcopo primum lapidem in fundamento ponente, agente dompno Serlone abbate.

Anno 1091[65] Rogerus senior de Berkeleye in festo sancti Sebastiani sub Serlone abbate monachus effectus reddidit sancto Petro Sothesoram liberam et quietam quam diu iniuste tenuerat. Et mortuus est eodem anno tertio decimo kalendas Julii.

---

[57] Cf. *HC*, I, 93.

[58] Hartinges] Hedyng *HC*.

[59] Walterus de Laci [...] Duntesborne] Cf. *HC*, I, 73.

[60] et] ~~corruens sp~~ et MS.

[61] Hoc anno [...] terrae] Cf. *HC*, I, 111, 122.

[62] Cf. *HC*, I, 101.

[63] Cf. *HC*, I, 80.

[64] Cf. *HC*, I, 11.

[65] Cf. *HC*, I, 112.

Anno 1094 Rogerus[66] de Berkeley iunior dedit sancto Petro terrulam Clehungre[67] concessu Willhelmi regis iunioris anno octauo regni eius, et abstulit Nimedesfeld. Obiit Wulstanus episcopus Wigorniensis octauo kalendas Aprilis.

Anno 1095[68] Thomas archiepiscopus Eboracensis reddidit ecclesiae sancti Petri Lecche, Otintonus, Stanedis, Bertonus, paenitens quod tam diu eas inuste tenuerat.

Anno 1096 Miles[69] quidam nomine Robertus Curtus dedit ecclesiae sancti Petri unam hidam in Herefordshire, Aspertonus[70] uocatam, concedente Willhelmo iuniore. Item[71] Hugo de Portu uicecomes[72] Wintoniae in obitu suo monachus factus dedit ecclesiae Litelton in Hamptonshire, aurum quoque multam et argentum et cetera. Item[73] Hugo filius Gamelini[74] dedit Plumtrw in Deuenshire pro anima sua. Samson consecratus est Wigorniensis episcopus.

Anno 1098[75] Rogerus de Buleleya cum coniuge Muriele dedit sancto Petri Clifford, concedente Willhelmo iuniore.

Anno 1099 Obiit Rogerus de Buleleya quarto idus Januarii.

Anno 1100[76] Ecclesia sancti Petri dedicata est a quattor episcopis, scilicet Sampsone Wigorniensi, Gundulfo Rouensiensi, Gerardo Hereford, et Herueo Bangor.

Anno 1101 Rex[77] Henricus dedit Maismor sancto Petro liberam, sicut ipse habuit. Confirmauit[78] etiam Brokþrop quam dederat Aedelina uxor Rogerus de Ibreio,

---

[66] Rogerus [...] Nimedesfeld] Cf. *HC*, I, 72.
[67] Clehungre] *HC*; de Hungre *MS*.
[68] Cf. *HC*, I, 11–12.
[69] Miles [...] iuniore] Cf. *HC*, I, 58.
[70] Aspertonus] *sic*.
[71] Item [...] cetera] Cf. *HC*, I, 93.
[72] uicecomes] uicarius *HC*.
[73] Item [...] sua] Cf. *HC*, I, 74.
[74] Hugo filius Gamelini] Odo filius Gamalielis *HC*.
[75] Cf. *HC*, I, 68, 123.
[76] Cf. *HC*, I, 12.
[77] Rex [...] habuit] Cf. *HC*, I, 12.
[78] Confirmauit [...] Ibreio] Cf. *HC*, I, 62.

et[79] duos radknihtes,[80] quam Rogerus de Glocestria dedit pro anima fratris sui Huberti.[81] Et[82] ecclesiam sancti Petri de Herford cum omnibus pertinentibus quam hoc anno Hugo de Laci dedit, scilicet decem uillanos in[83] decem uillis: Vnum in Stoke in Herefordshire, unum in Stanton in Shropscire, unum in Stoke in Shropshire, unum in Welbeia,[84] unum <in> Brihtmarefromer, quinque in Glocestershire, unum in Cueninton, unum <in> Stratton, unum <in> Wica, unum <in> Duntesburne, <unum> in Hama. Ecclesiam etiam sancti Audueni in Herford.

Anno 1102 Willhelmus[85] de Pomeria dedit sancto Petro uillam de Biri, pro qua frater eius Gosleynus excambiauit nobis Seldenam in Deuenscire. Anno tertio Henrici regis, ecclesia[86] sancti Petri Glocestriae cremata est cum ciuitate undecimo kalendas Junii.

Anno 1104[87] Abbas Serlo obiit anno aetatis circa sexaginta octo, quinto nonas Martii.

Anno 1105[88] Rogerus de Gloucestria apud Felesiam grauiter uulneratus dedit sancto Petro Culne.

Anno 1107[89] Petrus prior nonis Augusti suscepit regimen Glocestriae ecclesiae.

Anno 1108[90] Grandis altercatio inter abbatem et Remelinum[91] episcopum Herefordiae coram rege et Anselmo archiepiscopo pro corpore Radulfi filii Asketilli,

---

[79] et [...] Huberti] Cf. *HC*, I, 119.
[80] radknihtes] radenithes MS; cf. rodkny3tes *HC*.
[81] Huberti] Herberti *HC*.
[82] Et [...] Herford] Cf. *HC*, I, 85, 123.
[83] in] et in MS.
[84] Welbeia] Webbelia *HC*.
[85] Willhelmus [...] regis] Cf. *HC*, I, 65, 88.
[86] Ecclesia [...] Junii] Cf. *HC*, I, 88.
[87] Cf. *HC*, I, 13.
[88] Cf. *HC*, I, 69.
[89] Cf. *HC*, I, 13.
[90] Cf. *HC*, I, 13–14.
[91] Remelinum] *HC*; Reymundum MS.

quod episcopus abstulerat, et dirationatum est ut corpus difoderetur et redderetur, et indicatum ut in posterum omnes haberent liberam potestatem se ubicumque uiui disposuerant sepeliendi, consentientibus omnibus episcopis. Episcopus igitur omnes quaerelas contra abbatem demisit, excepta pulsatione signorum ante canonicos,[92] tantum ne corpus defoderetur. Hac de causa corpus remansit.

Anno 1109 Robertus[93] de Baskeruille dedit sancto Petro optimam hidam extra muros urbis. Item[94] Gunnildis de Loges nobilis faemina dedit duo hidas in Gutinges. Item[95] Willhelmus de Euerous dedit unam hidam in Vrchenfeld, Westwude[96] nomine.

Anno 1111[97] Gilbertus filius Ricardi dedit sancto Petro ecclesiam sancti Paterni cum pertinentibus et decimam omnium rerum suarum spectantum ad castelluum suum de Penwedich cum capella de Penwedich.

Anno 1112 Thomas[98] de sancto Johanne reddidit terram de Rugge. Item[99] Robertus Gernun dedit ecclesiam de Wynturborne[100] super Thamisiam. Item[101] Radulfus Bluet dedit manerium suum in fore<s>ta, Rudele nomine. Obiit Samson episcopus Wigornensis.

Anno 1113[102] Henricus rex confirmauit sancto Petro ecclesiam de Wynturborne[103] et ecclesiam de Lankeston[104] quas dederat Robertus Gernun.

---

[92] canonicos] *sic*; perhaps *canonicas <horas>* is the better reading.
[93] Robertus [...] urbis] Cf. *HC*, I, 124.
[94] Item [...] Gutinges] Cf. *HC*, I, 80–81.
[95] Item [...] nomine] Cf. *HC*, I, 118.
[96] Westwude] *HC*; wertwude MS.
[97] Cf. *HC*, I, 106.
[98] Thomas [...] Rugge] Cf. *HC*, I, 109.
[99] Item [...] Thamisiam] Cf. *HC*, I, 118.
[100] Wynturborne] *HC*; Witebi MS.
[101] Item [...] nomine] *HC*, I, 110.
[102] Cf, *HC*, I, 118.
[103] Wynturborne] see above s.a. 1112; Witebi MS.
[104] Lankeston] Lauerstoke *HC*.

Anno 1114 Petrus[105] abbas occurrens regi de Normania uenienti apud Eynsham obiit sexto decimo kalendas Augusti, cui successit Willhelmus prior. Hic concessit tertium diem fleubotomationis, et calcitra tenuia ad equitand<um> et perticas in dormitorio.

Anno 1115 Theolfus consecratus est episcopus Wigorniensis qui Willhelmum abbatem[106] consecrauit.

Anno 1117[107] Obiit Hawisa de Aula Regis, magnae probitatis maetrona, pro cuius anima uir suus Wybertus, custos Aulae Regis, dedit terram de Peraga iuxta Alnouestun.[108]

Anno 1119 Pons magnus Glocestriae coepit exordium idibus Maii.

Anno 1120 Mortuo[109] Rogero Baiocensi concessit rex sancto Petro tenere in dominio suo totam terram quam Rogerus tenuit de Thoma archiepiscopo Eboraco de manerio sancti Petri de Standiche: Mortoun, Ryndewike. Helias[110] Giffard dedit syluam de Lockholt.[111]

Anno 1122 Ecclesia[112] sancti Petri secundo cremata est cum ciuitate octauo idus Martii. Moises[113] et uxor eius dederunt unam hidam in Ameneye.[114]

Anno 1123 Obiit Odo celarius et Theulfus episcopus Wigorniensis.

Anno 1125 Obiit[115] Adealis contessa quarto idus Mai<i>, quae dedit domos et reditus suos quos h<ab>uit in Anglia. Item[116] Wahanus filius Willhelmi de

---

[105] Petrus [...] prior] Cf. *HC*, I, 14.
[106] abbatem] episcopum MS.
[107] Cf. *HC*, I, 106.
[108] Peraga iuxta Alnouestun] Cf. 'terram [...] juxta Aulam regis ubi est Bertona sua' *HC*.
[109] Mortuo [...] Ryndewike] Cf. *HC*, I, 100–01; II, 108 no. 599.
[110] Cf. *HC*, I, 62–63.
[111] Lockhold] Bocholt *HC*.
[112] Ecclesia [...] Martii] Cf. *HC*, I, 14–15.
[113] Moises [...] Ameneye] Cf. *HC*, I, 60.
[114] Ameneye] *HC*; Ameuel *MS*.
[115] Obiit [...] Anglia] Cf. *HC*, I, 81, 125.
[116] Item [...] alteri] Cf. *HC*, I, 62.

Bolega et fratres Walterus et Rogerus terram quam pater eorum dederat, cultello posito super altari. Simon consecratur episcopus Wigorniensis.

Anno 1126 Ricardus filius Nigelli, die qua filius fuit monachus, dedit molendinum et decimas quasdam. Item[117] Robertus filius Walteri cum uxore Auelina concesserunt ecclesiam de North. Rex[118] confirmauit dominium ecclesiae de Kynemarefforde,[119] quod Patricius de Cadurcis[120] dedit cum terris quas Ernulfus de Hastinges[121] <dedit>. Item ecclesiam de Heythrop.[122] Winebaldus[123] de Balun dedit Rodeford. Patricius[124] de Cadurcis[125] molendinum in Kinemarfford. Ranulfus[126] Peuerel dedit ecclesiam sancti Martini Londoni. Robertus[127] filius Hamonis ecclesiam sancti Cadoci in Lancaruan cum terra de Penhun.

Anno 1128 Robertus[128] filius Erchenbaldi et Matilda[129] uxor dedit dimid<ium> hidae in Condicont. Helewisa[130] uidua Arnulfi de Ebreus Hidam in Herforschire. Item[131] Agnes relicta Turstini Flandrensis et Eustachius filius dederunt unam hidam in Penecumbe, Southenhale. Adelicia[132] filia Askytilli[133] de Swindon decimam de Scipton. Willhelmus[134] de Ebrois unam hidam in

---

[117] Item [...] North] Cf. *HC*, I, 103.
[118] Rex [...] Heythrop] Cf. *HC*, I, 89.
[119] Kynemarefforde] *HC*; Kinesiuarsford MS.
[120] Cadurcis] *HC*; Caduus MS.
[121] Hastinges] Cf. Hesdyng *HC*.
[122] Heythrop] *HC*; Hanthorp MS.
[123] Winebaldus [...] Rodeford] Cf. *HC*, I, 77.
[124] Patricius [...] Kinemarfford] Cf. *HC*, I, 90–91.
[125] Cadurcis] *HC*; Cadacis MS.
[126] Ranulfus [...] Londoni] Cf. *HC*, I, 94.
[127] Robertus [...] Penhun] Cf. *HC*, I, 93.
[128] Robertus [...] Condicont] Cf. *HC*, I, 69.
[129] Matilda] *HC*; Matildis MS.
[130] Helewisa [...] Herforschire] Cf. *HC*, I, 88.
[131] Item [...] Southenhale] Cf. *HC*, I, 107, 114–15.
[132] Adelicia [...] Scipton] Cf. *HC*, I, 112.
[133] Askytilli] *HC*; Anrecilli MS.
[134] Willhelmus [...] Hereford] Cf. *HC*, I, 223.

Hereford. Robertus[135] de Oleo iunior filius Nigelli de Oleo decimam de Chestertun. Henricus rex confirmauit donationes Bertona, Toffeleia,[136] quas Osbernus Exonensis episcopus dederat Serloni abbati. Item[137] de Frouecestria, Scostelouera,[138] Boxwella, Addworth, Colna sancti Ailwini, Hineton, Bucland, Hammum,[139] Preston in Warewicshire, Alnoduston. Willhelmus[140] constubularius dedit terram quandam apud Doninton in Vrchenfeld, quandam terram quae fuit Willhelmi filii Normanni et aliam quae fuit Hermanni de Druiwes. Ranulfus[141] Bigod decimam de Forrusethe. Ranulfus[142] filius Walteri decimam de Keterigreham. Turstinus[143] filius Widonis decimam de Felingeham. Johannes[144] filius Ricardi decimam de Sexhingham. Hugo[145] de Laci decimam de Mumowell in Oxfordscire. Robertus[146] de Beckford decimam apud Haicoton. Willhelmus[147] Riuellus terram in Horton.[148]

Anno 1129 Serlo[149] presbiter filius Syredi et Leofleda mater eius dederunt terram suam in Glocestria. Wido[150] Flandrensis ecclesiam sancti Mariae de Deugledi, terram montis sanctae Mariae, et syluam[151] Dengort.[152]

---

[135] Robertus [...] Chestertun] Cf. *HC*, I, 70.
[136] Toffeleia [...] abbati] Cf. *HC*, I, 116.
[137] Item [...] Alnoduston] Cf. *HC*, I, 349 no. 347.
[138] de Frouecestria, Scostelouera] Frouecestria*m*, Scostelouera*m* MS.
[139] Hammam] *HC*; Hammum aliae Haimmum MS.
[140] Willhelmus [...] Druiwes] Cf. *HC*, I, 105.
[141] Ranulfus [...] Forrusethe] Cf. *HC*, II, 127.
[142] Ranulfus [...] Keterigreham] Cf. *HC*, I, 92.
[143] Turstinus [...] Felingeham] Cf. *HC*, I, 79.
[144] Johannes [...] Sexhingham] Cf. *HC*, I, 114.
[145] Hugo [...] Oxfordscire] Cf. *HC*, I, 100.
[146] Robertus [...] Haicoton] Cf. *HC*, I, 89.
[147] Willhelmus [...] Horton] Cf. *HC*, I, 88.
[148] Horton] Hamptone *HC*.
[149] Serlo ...] Glocestria] Cf. *HC*, I, 81.
[150] Wido [...] Dengort] Cf. *HC*, I, 108, 266 no. 207.
[151] syluam] syluulam MS.
[152] et syluam Dengort] et siluam quae uocatur Gengod *HC*.

9. THE CHRONICLE OF GREGORY OF CAERWENT

Anno 1130 Vir eximie religionis cenobita Glocestriae Renaldus eligitur abbas Eueshamensis, et a Symone episcopo Wigorniensi consecratur Wigorniae sexto kalendas Februarii. Abbas[153] Willhelmus Glocestriae infirmitate depressus,[154] pastoralem curam deponens, eam domino Walter de Laci tradidit, qui a Symone Wigorniensi episcopo tertio nonas[155] Augusti consecratus est.

Anno 1131 Obiit[156] Willhelmus quondam abbas Glocestriae apud <ecclesiam> sancti Paterni in Wallia tertio nonas Februarii. Robertus de Betun prior Lantoniae in Wallia fit episcopus Hereford.

Anno 1133[157] Obiit Robertus Curta Ocrea filius regis tertio nonas Februarii apud Caerdif, et in ecclesia sancti Petri ante altare principale honore sepultus est.

Anno 1134 Hugo[158] filius Willhelmi Normanni dedit sancto Petro <ecclesiam> Dauid de Kilpeck cum capella de sancta Maria[159] de castello, confirmante hoc Henrico suo herede.

Anno 1135 Obiit Helias Giffard idibus Februarii, et rex Henricus quarto nonas Nouembris.

Anno 1136 Nobilis ille Ricardus filius Gilberti Walensium preuentus insidiis septimo decimo kalendas Maii peremptus est, sepultus in capitulo Glocestriae. Graue bellum exarsit in<ter>[160] Normannos et Walenses apud Guer, cesis millia quingentis sedecim.[161]

Anno 1137 Paganus filius Johannes, miles strenuus, dum Walenses praedantes occidere tenderet, capite perforatus lancea septimo idus Julii occubuit. Et in capitulo Glocestriae sepultus est a Roberto episcopo Hereford et Waltero

---

[153] Abbas [...] est] Cf. *HC*, I, 15.

[154] depressus] depressit MS.

[155] nonas] idus nonas MS.

[156] Obiit [...] Februarii] Cf. *HC*, I, 15.

[157] Cf. *HC*, I, 15.

[158] Hugo [...] castello] Cf. *HC*, I, 16.

[159] Maria] Marie MS.

[160] in<ter>] Cf. *AM*, IV, 20: 'Grave bellum inter Normannos et Walenses'.

[161] millia quingenti sedecim] Cf. *AM*, IV, 20: 'militibus quingentis sexdecim'; *The Chronicle of John of Worcester*, III, 218: 'quingenti et sedecim'.

abbate. Fit pugna grauis apud Cairdigan et tanta strages edita est ut de captiuatis mulieribus mille remanentur ad decimam.[162]

Anno 1139 Obiit[163] abbas Walterus sexto idus Februarii, cui, procurante Milone constabulario, successit Gilbertus cognatus eius, monachus Cluniacencis, eximiae sapientiae uir. Wigorniae ab episcopo Hereford Roberto installatus est quinto idus Junii. Obiit Rogerus episcopus Sarum castellorum fundator precipuus.

Anno 1143[164] Milo constabularius comes Hereford uenandi causa Dene adiens a quodam milite suo sagitta[165] corde percussus idibus Januarii obiit. Sepultus Lantoniae cuius ecclesiam a fundamentis construxerat. Petiti<o>ne tum trium episcoporum qui affuerant et filii Rogeri postea Hereford comitis et aliorum plurium, iacuit ipsum[166] corpus eius inhumatum quattuor diebus, abbate Gilberto multis astipulatio<n>ibus ill<u>d sui esse asserente. Lis tandem sedata est ea conditione ut filius Rogeri et uxor eius et omnes haeredes et posteri et dominus castelli Glocestriae, quicumque futurus esset, iuri cederet ecc<lesi>ae sancti Petri Glocestriae. In huius confirmationem Simon episcopus Wigorniensis Rogerum comitis filium abbati Gilberti per manum assignauit.

Anno 1144 Obiit Robertus uir eximiae pietatis pridie idus Octobris. Ille Robertus prior de Euwenni, postquam prioratus officium susceperat anno 1141 super duas ecclesias, quas Mauricii de Londino, qui obiit idibus Januarii sub eodem tempore, sancto Petro Gloucestriae dederat, predictus Robertus locum illum monachis fecit habitabilem. Item[167] miles quidam Walterus de Clifford nomine dedit sancto Petro Estlenche in escambio pro Glaseburie et dedit etiam monachis Maluernie. Facta est coniunctio ecclesiae sancti Petri Hereford et sancti Guthlaci in castello, et in unum corpus rediguntur, procurante Roberto Herefordiensi episcopo, confitente Rogero de Portu quod inuste tam diu tenuerat ecclesiam sancti Guthlaci in castello, quia laicus erat et possessio<n>es indigne distribuerat.

---

[162] ut [...] decimam] Cf. *AM*, IV, 21: 'ut de captivis mulieribus mille remanerent ad decimam'; *The Chronicle of John of Worcester*, III, 220: 'ut, exceptis uiris in captivitatem abductis, de mulieribus captiuatis decies centum decimae remanerent'.

[163] Obiit [...] est] Cf. *HC*, I, 17–18.

[164] Cf. *HC*, I, pp. lxxv–lxxvii.

[165] sagitta] sagitte MS.

[166] ipsum] *dub*.

[167] Item [...] Maluernie] Cf. *HC*, I, 80, 311 no. 275.

9. THE CHRONICLE OF GREGORY OF CAERWENT

Anno 1146 In ecclesia sancti Petri Glocestriae plurima miracula gloriose ostensa sunt. Rogerus[168] de Berkleye dedit sancto Petro ecclesiam sancto Leonardie de Stanley, assensu Sabrihtsii[169] tunc eiusdem loci prioris, per manum Simonis Wigorniensis episcopi.

Anno 1148 Nicholaus monachus uir religiosus ad episcopatum Lendauensem est assumptus. Obiit[170] ut creditur sanctus Robertus de Betun Herford episcopus ad concilium Remis, cui successit abbas Glocestriae Gilebertus, et ei in abbatia successit eiusdem loci prefectus Hamelinus, qui a Simone Wigorniensi episcopo nonis Decembris consecratus est.

Anno 1149 Obiit Reginaldus abbas Eueshamensis.

Anno 1150 Obiit Simon Wigorniensis episcopus cum sedesset[171] annis uiginti sex.

Anno 1151 Abbas[172] Hamelinus aduersus Henricum Eboracensem archiepiscopum Romam iuit[173] pro Bertonia, Standiche, Northlece, etc.

Anno 1155 Abscedit rex Bruge et cepit Rogerum comitem Hereford, qui obiit monachatus <in monasterio> sancti Petri.[174] Sepultus est in capitulo Glocestriae. Canonici[175] de Bromfeld dederunt ecclesiam suam et seipsos ad monachatum sancti Petri Glocestriae per manus Gilberti Hereford episcopi, auctoritate Theobaldi archiepiscopi Cantuariensis et apostolice sedis legati.

Anno 1156 Rogerus[176] de Berkleye dedit ecclesiam de Camme[177] cum pertinentibus ecclesiae sancti Leonardi de Stanleye.

---

[168] Rogerus [...] episcopi] Cf. *HC*, I, 113.
[169] Sabrihtsii] Tabrithri *HC*.
[170] Obiit [...] est] Cf. *HC*, I, 18–19.
[171] sedesset] *sic*.
[172] Cf. *HC*, I, 19.
[173] iuit] init MS.
[174] <in monasterio> sancti Petri] .s.p. MS.
[175] Canonici [...] legati] Cf. *HC*, I, 19–20.
[176] Cf. *HC*, I, 114.
[177] Camme] *HC*; Thamme MS.

Anno 1157 Obiit piae memoriae Gregorius monachus Glocestriae, cuius sancti exercitii testes sunt multi libri in ecclesia nostra sua manu scripti.

Anno 1158 Thamesis Londoni adeo exiccata est ut siccis pedibus transiretur.

Anno 1160 Vir religiosus et eruditus prior Glocestriae Bernardus ad abbatiam de Borouton[178] super Trent assumitur.

Anno 1163 Gilbertus episcopus Hereford prius abbas Glocestriae ad sedem Londonensem tran<s>fertur.

Anno 1164 Cecidit turris sancti Petri Glocestriae.

Anno 1167[179] Helias Giffard et Berta uxor eius dederunt Sancto Petro octo libratas terrae in Olingewyke, et monachi reddiderunt eis Chronham[180] quam pater suus monachis quando monachatum suscepit <dedit>.

Anno 1171 Henricus prior factus est abbas Winchicumbae.

Anno 1173 Obiit Bernardus abbas de Borouton quonda<m> prior Glocestriae. Alexander[181] papa confirmauit prioratui[182] de Stanleye totam terram in Stanleye Rogeri de Berkley. Item cursum fontis de Carwelle. Item ecclesiam de Chanme cum pertenentibus. Item ecclesias de Stanbruge, Stanescumbe, Durseley, Osleworth, Aston, Cudberleye, Erlingham cum pertinentibus, uirgatem terrae cum hominibus et nemoribus in Cotepenne et Longhepenne et sexaginta acras terrae in Berkleye hurdnes,[183] scilicet Hardacrae.

Anno 1174 Obiit abbas Hamelinus sexto idus Martii cui successit Thomas Carbonelis, tunc prior Hereford, decimo quinto kalendas Octobris installatus.

Anno 1180 Osbernus prior sancti Petri factus est abbas Malmesburie.

---

[178] Borouton] Boroutlʒon MS.
[179] Cf. *HC*, I, 117.
[180] Chronham] *HC*; thronetun MS.
[181] Alexander […] Hardacrae] Cf. *HC*, I, 113–14.
[182] prioratui] *supra* monachis MS.
[183] hurdnes] *recte* 'hurnes'?

Anno 1181 Obiit Henricus prior Winchecomb quondam prior Glocestriae sexto idus Nouembris, et Osbernus abbas Malmesburie decimo sexto kalendas Aprilis.

Anno 1183 Nicholaus Landauensis, episcopus monachus olim Glocestriae, tertio nonas Junii obiit.

Anno 1184 Ugonulus Armorice[184] episcopus dedicauit capellam sancti Bridgidae Glocestriae sexto idus Octobris.

Anno 1187 Obiit Gilbertus Londinensis episcopus quondam abbas Glocestriae duodecimo kalendas Martii.

Anno 1190[185] Quinto idus Maii emersit incendium in Glocestria maxi<m>am partem uillae incenerans cum quibusdam officinis sancti Petri atque ecc<les>ias sanctae Mariae ante portam abbatiae et sancti Oswaldi muro tenus comburens.

Anno 1196 Preficitur abbatiae de Winchecumbe Robertus de Haseltun professus sanctus.

Anno 1198 Factum est prelium inter dominum Willhelmus de Breusa et Gwenunwen in Eluail.

Anno 1205 Obiit[186] dominus Thomas Carbonel abbas Glocestriae duodecimo kalendas Augustii, cui successit Henricus prior Glocestriae, qui a Maugerio[187] Wigorniensi episcopo tertio idus[188] Octobris consecratus est et sexto nonas eiusdem installatus.

Anno 1208 Interdictum[189] generale coepit per totam Angliam.

---

[184] Armorice] *dub.*; Armorīe MS.
[185] Cf. *HC*, I, 22.
[186] Cf. *HC*, I, 23.
[187] Maugerio] *HC*; Mangerio MS.
[188] idus] idbus MS.
[189] Cf. *HC*, I, 23.

Anno 1209 Interdictum[190] partim relaxatum <est>, concessa unius tantum missae caelebratione in ecclesiis conuentalibus per singulas ebdomas.

Anno 1210[191] Johannes rex in Junio Hyberniam petit et rediit circa assumptionem Mariae. Regina Isabella peperit filiam sua<m> Johannam Gloucestriae quam abbas Henricus presente Petro de Roches episcopo Wintoniae baptizauit. Calices abbatiae Glocestriae uenduntur pro inaudito talagio facto a rege super omnes ecclesias Angliae omne[192] genus ita ut leprosi non fuerint immunes nec mulieres[193] curiales. De abbatia Glocestriae cepit rex quinque mille et duas caretas cum equis.

Anno 1214 Villa[194] Glocestriae tota cremata est in die sancti Albani Martyris. Interdictum relaxatum est. Egidius[195] episcopus Hereford obiit in abbatia Glocestriae idibus Nouembris, qui remisit abbatiae centum marcas de debito sibi.

Anno 1216[196] Henricus filius Johannis quinto kalendas Nouembris coronatur Glocestriae in ecclesia sancti Petri a Petro de Roches episcopo Wintoniensi, auctoritate Gualae legati.

Anno 1218 Sueta de Chartres dedit in elemosynam sancto Petro terram suam quae fuit inter murum uillae et lardarium abbatiae. Willhelmus etiam Rosel suam terram ibidem dedit.

Anno 1219 Obiit Hugo de Mappenore episcopus Herford. Successit Hugo Foliot.

Anno 1220 Turris Glocestriae erecta est.

Anno 1221 Obiit Robertus abbas Wincicumbae monachus sancti Petri Glocestriae sexto idus Januarii.

---

[190] Cf. *HC*, I, 23.
[191] Cf. *HC*, I, 24.
[192] omne] oīe MS.
[193] mulieres] mulierculae *HC*.
[194] Villa [...] est] Cf. *HC*, I, 24.
[195] Egidius [...] sibi] *recte* anno 1215?
[196] Cf. *HC*, I, 24.

Anno 1222 Kalendas[197] Augusti incensa est tota parochia beatae Mariae ante portum abbatiae Glocestriae et pars pistrini et bracini et domus inter portam et stabulum.

Anno 1224 Obiit[198] Henricus abbas Glocestriae decimo kalendas Septembris, cui sucessit Thomas de Bredonn, prior eiusdem loci. Thomas de Berkeley dedit Lorewinche prioratui de Stanleye.

Anno 1226 Obiit Reginaldus de Breusa, cui successit Wilhelmus filius, qui eodem anno captus fuit in Kery.

Anno 1227 Capella[199] beatae Mariae in cimiterio sancti Petri Glocestriae ex sumptibus Randulphi de Willtonia est consummata. Magister Eadmundus de Abindonn predicauit de cruce apud Glocestriam.

Anno 1228 Obiit[200] Thomas de Bredon abbas Glocestriae quinto idus Maii, cui successit Henricus Foliot prior Bromfeld.

Anno 1230 Obiit Willhelmus Landauensis episcopus et Geruasius Meneuensis episcopus.

Anno 1224[201] Rex Henricus cepit castrum de Hereford de hominibus Fulconis fortiter resistentibus.

Anno 1230 Obiit Gilbertus comes Glocestriae ultra mare. Leuelinus princeps Walliae fecit suspendi Willhelmum de Breusa juniorem subdole ut dicitur. Obiit Gilbertus de Lacy filius Walteri septimo kalendas Nouembris.

Anno 1231[202] Henricus abbas Glocestriae constituit uiginti marcas annuas de ecclesia sancti Gundley de Nouo Burgo ad caritates inueniendas conuentui de uino Gallico.

---

[197] Cf. *HC*, I, 26.
[198] Obiit [...] loci] Cf. *HC*, I, 26–27.
[199] Capella [...] consummata] Cf. *HC*, I, 27.
[200] Cf. *HC*, I, 27–28.
[201] Anno 1224] *sic*.
[202] Cf. *HC*, I, 28.

Anno 1232[203] Concessa est cantaria fratribus hospitalis sancti Bartholomei inter pontes Glocestriae a monachis sancti Petri.

Anno 1234 Ricardus Marescallus filius Williami senioris quarto nonas Aprilis apud castrum de Kildare in Hybernia proditione suorum interfectus est ab illis. Eadmundus Cantuariensis archiepiscopus remouit a consilio regis Petrum de Roches episcopus Wintoniae, Petrum de Oriual, et Stephanum de Segraue, eo quod rex et negotia sua per eos male tractarentur, et reconsiliauit regi Gilbertum Marescallum, Hubertum de Burg, et Ricardum Siward in abbatia Glocestriae, et dictum Gilbertum Marescallum constituit comitem Penbrochiae, et omnia quae patris fuerant restituit. Obiit Hugo de Welles episcopus Lincolniae; successit Robertus Grosseteste. Obiit Hugo Foliot episcopus Hereford; successit Radulfus de Maineston.

Anno 1236 Sabrina supra modum excrescens multa mala fecit. Obiit Wilhelmus de Blois episcopus Wigorniensis.

Anno 1237 Gregorius de Kairwent recepit habitum monachalem in ecclesia sancti Petri Glocestriae ab Henrico Foliot abbate quarto kalendas Nouembris, qui <a principio> huius libri hucusque scripsit.[204]

Anno 1238 Quidam clericus de familia Willhelmi de Marisco militis uolens prodere regem ingressus est noctu cubiculum eius apud Wodstocke per fenestram; ubi captus a uigilibus, membratim discerptus est.

Anno 1239 Dedicata[205] est ecclesia Glocestriae a Waltero de Cantilupo episcipo Wigorniensi. Aduentus fratrum predicatorum Glocestria.

Anno 1240 Obiit Leuelinus princeps Walliae; successit Dauid filius, qui in abbatia Gloucestriae fecit homagium regi auunculo suo. Petrus de Aqua Blanca fit episopus Herefordiae.[206]

Anno 1241 Obiit Gilebertus comes Penbrochiae. Obiit Walterus de Laci kalendas Martii.

---

[203] Cf. *HC*, I, 245.

[204] See the introduction above for a discussion of this passage.

[205] Dedicata [...] Wigorniensi] Cf. *HC*, I, 28.

[206] Herefordiae] Wigorniensis MS.

Anno 1242[207] Willhelmus de Marisco propter seditionem quam in regum machinauerat Londini membratim distinctus est, et membra in uariis Angliae urbibus suspensa.

Anno 1243 Obiit Henricus Foliot abbas Glocestriae, cui successit Walterus de sancto Johanne prior Gloucestriae. Eodem anno obiit Walterus abbas, cui succesit Johannes de Felda precentor Glocestriae.

Anno 1244 Magna strages aedita est Anglorum a Walensibus in Glamorgantia, inter quos cecidit miles clarissimus Herbertus filius Maii.[208] Walterus[209] de Cummelia dedit sancto Petro terram suam in Litleton.

Anno 1245[210] Turris occidentalis a parte australi perfecta est.

Anno 1246 Ricardus comes Cornubia fundauit abbatiam de Hailes.

Anno 1247 Terremotus per uniuersam Angliam decimo kalendas Martii inter sextam et completorii horam. Rex fecit nouam monetam.

Anno 1251 Dedicata est ecclesia de Hailes a Waltero de Cantilupo episcopo Wigorniensi.

Anno 1252 Obiit Ricardus episcopus Cicestriae, cui successit Johannes biscop.

Anno 1253 Obiit Wilhelmus de Burgo episcopus Landaf, cui succesit Johannes de la Ware quondam abbas de Morgan. Obiit Robertus Grossetest episcopus Lincolniae; successit Henricus de Lexintonia.

Anno 1255 Obiit Thomas Walensis episcopus Meneuensis.

Anno 1256 Venit in Angliam Ricardus de Careu[211] consecratus episcopus Meneuensis a papa. Obiit Johannes de la Ware episcopus Landauensis, cui successit Wilhelmus de Radenore. Emerserunt de finibus suis Walenses cum princ-

---

[207] 1242] 12411 MS.
[208] Maii] *recte* Matthei?
[209] Walterus [...] Litleton] Cf. *HC*, I, 99.
[210] Cf. *HC*, I, 30.
[211] Careu] Carleu MS.

ipe suo Lewelino iuuene destruentes confinia Walliae caede et incendio propter iniuriam eis illatam a balliuis Edwardi filii regis.

Anno 1257 Fit ingens strages nobilium militum ab incursione Wallensium apud Landilauuaur quorum militum princeps fuit Stephanus Vaughan.

Anno 1258 Sabrina apud Glocestriam duodecies alueo suo excessit et prata cooperuit, et tam in aestate quam hieme continue pluebat; ita quod minima fuerunt interualla inundationis, adeo ut semina plurima perierunt et uina etiam asportata acida fuerunt et uiridea, ac si essent Anglica. Patricius de Caurcis apud Kilgaran fuit a Walensibus occisus propter suas fraequentes irruptiones contra eos tempore treugarum. Fit iusticiarius Angliae Hugo de Bigod comes Warenniae.

Anno 1259 Obiit Wilhelmus de Clara frater Ricardi comitis Glocestriae. Obiit Henricus de Lex<i>ntonia episcopus Lincolniensis; successit Ricardus de Grauesond thesaurarius Herefordiae.

Anno 1262 Obiit Ricardus comes Glociestriae idibus Julii, sepelitus Teuksburiae. Baldwinus de Insula comes Deuonia nepos eiusdem Ricardi comitis obiit.

Anno 1263 Obiit Johannes de Felda abbas, cui successit Regi<n>aldus de Homme capellanus eius. Post Pascho oritur bellum baronum.

Anno 1264 Capta est uilla Glocestriae a domino Edwardo primoge<n>ito regis et Godwino de Clare comite idibus Iulii. Pridie deinde nonas Augusti fit caedes apud Euesham. Obiit Willhelmus episcopus Landauensis et Walterus de Cantilupo episcopus Wigorniensis, cui successit Nicholas de Hely quondam regis cancellarius.

Anno 1267 Ventus terribilis.

Anno 1268 Gelu maximum incepit.

Anno 1269 Sabrina, ut numquam antea, excreuit, ut et caetera omnia flumina Angliae, domusque et pontes prostrauerunt.

Anno 1272 Obiit Ricardus rex Alemaniae tertio nonas Aprilis et conditur apud Hailes.

Anno 1273[212] Moritur Adam de Elmley monachus Glocestriae, sepultus cora<m> altari sanctae Crucis ubi miraculis claret[213] ante natale durauitque ad purificationem Mariae.

Anno 1275 Obiit Johannes Brutun episcopus Hereford, cui successit Thomas de Cantilupo. Robertus Burnel, regis cancellarius, fit episcopus Bathoniae. Terremotus ad horam primam tertio idus Septembris. Obiit Hunfredus de Bonn comes Hereford et Lantonae sepelitur.

Anno 1276 Dominus Herueus de Cadurcis crudeliter occisus est a Wallensibus, quare et eorum irruptionibus ruptum est foedus.

Anno 1277 Rex Edwardus ad festum sancti Johannis in Walliam ingressus est, in qua mansit et persequutus Lewelinum principem usque ad quadragesimam. Lewelinum coepit et totam Walliam subiugauit et tributariam constituit. Lewelino pacificatur qui cum suis Londinum ad parliamentum uenit et magnum celebrauit conuiuium. Quamdiu rex fuit in Wallia, scaccarium eius fuit Salopia.

Anno 1278 Inaudita lues ouium grassatur, quae o<mn>es fere sustulit. Aleonora filia Simonis de Monteforti Wigorniae traditur in uxorem Lewelino principi Walliae.

Anno 1280 Inaudita inundatio per totam Angliam.

Anno 1281 Edmundus comes Cornubiae fundauit Oxonii cenobium Cisterciensum.

Anno 1282 Dauid frater principis Walliae undecimo kalendas Aprilis die palmarum apud Haurden cum exercitu coepit dolose Rogerum de Clifford seniorem et quattuor milites interfecit, quorum unus fuit Fulco Tregor.

Anno 1282 In festo Pentecostes rex tenuit parliamentum Wigorniae. Deinde in Walliam cum infesto exercitu profectus est ad festum Beati Petri ad Vincula. Deinde octo idus Nouembris apud pontem de Anglesey dominus Lucas Thayny

---

[212] Cf. *HC*, I, 32.
[213] *Sic.*

et dominus Rogerus de Clifford junior cum multitudine militum ignota[214] submersi sunt. Septimo decimo kalendas Nouembris obiit Rogerus de Morto Mari. Octo kalendas Septembris obiit Thomas de Cantilupo episcopus Hereford, cui successit magister Ricardus de Swinfeld archidiaconus Londoni. Tertio idus Decembris Lewelinus princeps Walliae lancea perforatus occubuit; caput amputatum ad regem perfertur apud Rothelan,[215] inde super summam Londoni turrim fixtum.

Anno 1283 Dauid frater Lewelini iuxta castellum Kaernaruan a Wallis captus, Rothelan[216] ad regem perducitur et Salopiae condemnatus ut sit tractus, suspensus, decollatus, uisceribus conbustis in quattuor diuisus et in uaria loca distributus.

Anno 1284 Idibus Septembris obiit Reginaldus abbas Glocestriae uir prudens qui domum suam tempore belli strenue rexit. Ei successit dominus Johannes[217] de Gamages prior Herefordiae die sancti Andreae installatus. Rex statuit in Wallia leges Anglicanas ordinales, comitatus, iusticiarios.

Anno 1285 Edmundus de Morto Mari cingulo militari donatur et in natale beatae Mariae Wintoniae coepit in uxorem Margaretam filiam domini Wilhelmi de Fenes consanguineam reginae, et facta sunt statuta quae dicta sunt Additamenta Glocestriae.

Anno 1286 Cecidit horrenda tempestas quae, incipiens in Wallia a montibus de Morrugge transiens per Elinien et Lodelow usque Wigorniam, multa animalia, ut lepores, et alia uaria ac uolatilia interfecit; domus discoperie\<n\>s et arbores eradicans, multum nocuit.

Anno 1287 Circa Pentecostem Reis filius Ameredyth[218] rebellans terras regis in Wallia oppugnat, quod audiens Edmundus comes Cornubiae, tunc custos Angliae, exercitu collecto Walliam ingreditur. Castrum de Drossel obsedit. Murus uero machinis suffossus cecidit et oppressit uiros nobiles: dominum

---

[214] ignota] ignata MS.

[215] Rothelan] Eoyelan MS.

[216] Rothelan] Eopelan MS.

[217] Johannes] N. MS.

[218] *Ameredyth* is a contracted form of *ap Meredyth* and may imply an oral Welsh source here.

Wilhelmum de Muntchanesy et dominum Gerardum de Insula et dominum de Stafford et alios plures de exercitu.

Anno 1288 Maxi\<m>a copia annonae; summa uendebatur pro decem denariis. Maxi\<m>us calor et siccitas in estate precipue in autumno quo multi perierunt.

Anno 1290 Gilbertus de Clare comes Gloucestriae ducit in uxorem Westmo\<n>asterii die dominica post festum sancti Marci eu\<an>gelistee dominam Johannam de Acres filiam regis Edwardi. Ad festum omnium sanctorum, Judei omnes ex Anglia[219] eiiciuntur.

Translation of the Chronicle of Gregory of Caerwent

681. [...] and fifth of Æthelred, King of the Mercians. And the same king granted to his two ministers and brothers, Osric and Oswald, a certain part of his land: to Osric, who was later made King of the Northumbrians, he gave three hundred hides in Gloucester, and to Oswald three hundred hides in Pershore. With the consent of the king, Osric founded the city of Gloucester's first monastery of St Peter, and he appointed his sister Cyneburh as its abbess, and their sister Eadburh succeeded her. And after her the abbess was Ena who was in charge for thirty-three years and who acquired many lands: twenty hides in Alre; twenty hides in Pinswell; and 120 hides outside the city. And afterward Aldred, the subregulus of the Hwicce, granted his inheritance to the church, that is the sixty inhabitants of Culne. And Burgred granted ten hides in Fairford, fifteen hides in Wyarkeston, fifteen hides in hilly land in Chedworth, and three hides of Nympsfield. Aldred, the subregulus of the Hwicce, granted and bestowed all of these lands. In the same year, Æthelmund of Geldinge granted thirty hides in Overe and thirty-five in Leach.

729. Æthelric son of Edmund, with the consent of a church council, granted thirty hides in Overe to St Peter's Gloucester.

821. Beornwulf, King of the Mercians, granted fifteen hides in Esneburie, that is, Standish. In this year, Kenelm is martyred and lies at Winchcombe.

---

[219] Anglia] Angliae MS.

862. Burgred, King of the Mercians, confirmed the gifts of his ancestors, and, with the consent of bishops and nobles in a royal council at Wellesbourne, he made this very church and all places belonging to it free from all earthly imposition and service, except for devotional prayer.

910. The bones of King Oswald the Saint were translated from Bardney to Mercia, and in his honour Æthelflæd, daughter of King Alfred, together with her husband Æthelred built the monastery of Gloucester, whose monks remained there until the time of the Danes.

981. During the reign of King Æthelred, the brother of St Edward, his sister gave to St Peter's Church Hinton, which was at that time uncultivated. And when five men were required from her for military service and she could not find them, she cast herself at the king's feet and she managed to make it so that that possession would hereafter be free and quit.

1058. Aldred the Bishop of Worcester dedicated the church of St Peter's, and he appointed Wulfstan, a monk of Worcester, as abbot there.

1072. On 9 February Abbot Wulfstan died, and Lord Abbot Serlo, who had before been a canon of Avranches and then later […] succeeded.

1077. Odo the cellarer was made a monk, and with his labour and diligence regarding lands and possessions the church of Gloucester grew greatly.

1080. Walter de Lacy returned Upleadon to St Peter's and gave with it Walter, his eight-year-old son.

1081. Ernulf de Harting gave Linkenholt to St Peter's, with the consent of King William I at Salisbury on the Feast of the Purification of St Mary.

1085. On 27 March Walter de Lacy died; he was the founder of Blessed Peter's in Hereford. And at the point when the church had almost been established, he climbed a ladder, and when he had reached the crossbeams his foot suddenly slipped, and as he crashed down he breathed his last, and he was buried in the chapter house of Gloucester on 28 March on the Mass of the Lord's Supper. Then his wife Ermelina for the redemption of her husband's soul granted to the same church one estate of five hides, that is, Duntisbourne Abbots. In this year William de Auco granted to St Peter's the mill at Stonehouse with one virgate of land.

1087. In the survey of all of England,[220] Roger of Berkeley Senior had Nympsfield deceitfully described as owing provision for the king's table, without the knowledge of Abbot Serlo.

1088. Bernard de Neufmarché granted Glasbury to St Peter's, free and quit with all its appurtenances, and the entire tithe of the lordship of Brycheiniog, namely of grain, livestock, cheeses, hunting, and honey. He also granted the church of Much Cowarne with its tithe and one hide which is called 'Bache'. He died on 13 February.

1089. Abbot Serlo began the monastery of St Peter's on the Feast of Saints Peter and Paul, with Robert the Bishop of Hereford laying the first stone on the foundation and with Lord Serlo the abbot conducting the proceedings.

1091. Roger of Berkeley Senior was made a monk under Abbot Serlo on 20 January, on the Feast of St Sebastian, and he returned Shoteshore to St Peter's free and quit, which he had held unjustly for a long while. And he died this same year on 19 June.

1094. Roger of Berkeley Junior gave to St Peter's a small plot of land, Clingre House, with the consent of King William II in the eighth year of his reign, and he took away Nympsfield. Wulfstan bishop of Worcester died on 25 March.

1095. Thomas the Archbishop of York returned to the church of St Peter's Lethe, Oddington, Standish, and Barton, repenting that he had held them unjustly for so long.

1096. A certain knight named Robert the Short granted to the church of St Peter's one hide in Herefordshire, called Ashperton, with the consent of William II. In the same year Hugh de Port, sheriff of Winchester, became a monk on his deathbed, and he gave to the church Littleton in Hampshire, as well as a lot of gold and silver, etc. In the same year, Hugh fitz Gamelin granted Plymtree in Devon for the sake of his soul. Samson was consecrated Bishop of Worcester.

1098. Roger de Bulley and his wife Muriel granted Clifford to St Peter's, with the consent of William II.

---

[220] I.e. Domesday Book.

1099. Roger de Bulley died on 10 January.

1100. The church of St Peter's was dedicated by four bishops: Samson of Worcester, Gundulf of Rochester, Gerard of Hereford, and Hervey of Bangor.

1101. King Henry granted Maisemore to St Peter's, free just as he himself held it. He also confirmed Brookthorpe, which Adeline, the wife of Roger d'Ivry, had granted, and the service of two radknights[221] that Roger of Gloucester granted for the sake of his brother Hubert's soul. And he confirmed the church of St Peter's Hereford with all its appurtenances which Hugh de Lacy granted in that year, namely ten villeins in ten manors: one in Stoke in Herefordshire, one in Stanton in Shropshire, one in Stoke in Shropshire, one in Weobley, one in 'Brihtmarefromer' [Castle Frome?], five in Gloucestershire, one in Temple Guiting, one in Stratton, one in Wyck, one in Duntisbourne Abbots, and one in Hamme. And he also confirmed St Owen's in Hereford.

1102. William de la Pomeroy gave to St Peter's the estate of Berry, which his brother Goscelin exchanged with us for Sheldon in Devonshire. In King Henry's third year, the church of St Peter's Gloucester was burned along with the city on 22 May.

1104. Abbot Serlo died around the age of sixty-eight on 3 March.

1105. Roger of Gloucester, having been gravely wounded at Falaise, granted Culne to St Peter's.

1107. Peter the Prior took control of the church of Gloucester on 5 August.

1108. A great dispute arose between the Abbot and Reinhelm, Bishop of Hereford, before the King and Archbishop Anselm over the body of Ralph fitz Asketil, which the Bishop had stolen, and it was decided that his body should be dug up and given back, and it was made known that in posterity everyone should have unconstrained choice of being buried wherever they had decided when they were alive, and all of the bishops gave their consent. Therefore, the Bishop dropped all of the complaints against the Abbot, except for the ringing

---

[221] A radknight was a class of freeman particularly common in Western Mercia. The term 'radknight' was favoured in the southern March, while 'radman' was common farther north.

of bells before the canons, so long as the body was not dug up. For that reason, the body stayed put.

1109. Robert of Baskerville granted to St Peter's a very good hide outside the walls of the city. Likewise, the noblewoman Gunnild de Loges granted two hides in Guiting. And William de Everous granted one hide in Archenfield named Westwood.[222]

1111. Gilbert fitz Richard granted to St Peter's the church of St Padarn (Llanbadarn) with all its appurtenances and the tithes of all his properties pertaining to his castle of Penweddig[223] with the chapel of Penweddig.

1112. Thomas of St John returned the land of The Ridge. In the same year, Robert Gernun gave the church of Winterbourne on Thames. In the same year, Ralph Bluet granted his manor in the forest named Ruddle. Samson the Bishop of Worcester died.

1113. King Henry confirmed for St Peter's the church of Winterbourne and the church of 'Lankeston', both of which Robert Gernun had granted.

1114. Abbot Peter, meeting the King at Eynsham as he was coming from Normandy, died on 17 July. William the Prior succeeded him. He consented to a third day of phlebotomy, and thin cushions for riding, and *perticas*[224] in the dormitory.

1115. Theulf was consecrated the Bishop of Worcester, and he consecrated Abbot William.

1117. Hawise of Kingshome, a woman of great integrity, died, and for the sake of her soul her husband Wybert, the warden of Kingshome, granted the land of 'Peraga iuxta Alnouestun'.

---

[222] St Peter's already had a large estate in Westwood at the time of Domesday Book. William's grant is apparently an addition. See *Domesday Book: A Complete Translation*, ed. by Ann Williams and Geoffrey Haward Martin (London: Penguin, 2002), p. 499 (fol. 181a).

[223] Presumably the precursor to Aberystwyth Castle. See *HW*, II, 426. The following 'chapel of Penweddig' probably refers to the chapel of this castle.

[224] 'Pertica' (pole, rod; perch) refers to a wardrobe-like structure in a monastic dormitory. See Terryl N. Kinder, *Cistercian Europe: Architecture of Contemplation* (Grand Rapids, MI: Eerdmans, 2002), p. 272.

1119. The great bridge of Gloucester was begun on 15 May.

1120. After Roger of Bayeux died, the King gave his consent for St Peter's to hold in its lordship all the land that Roger held from Thomas Archbishop of York from the manor of St Peter's Standish: Morton and Randwick. Elias Giffard granted the forest of Lockholt.

1122. The church of St Peter's was burnt a second time along with the city on 8 March. Moises and his wife granted one hide in Ampney Crucis.

1123. Odo the cellarer died, as did Theulf the Bishop of Worcester.

1125. Countess Adeliza died on 12 May; she granted her houses and rents that she held in England. In the same year, Wyhan fitz William de Bulley and his brothers Walter and Roger also granted the land that their father had granted, and they placed a knife on the altar. Simon is consecrated Bishop of Worcester.

1126. Richard fitz Nigel, on the day his son became a monk, granted a mill and some tithes. In the same year, Robert fitz Walter and his wife Avelina ceded the church of North. The King confirmed the lordship of the church of Kempsford, which Patrick de Chaworth granted, along with the lands that Ernulf de Hastinges granted. Likewise, the church of Hatherop. Winnebald de Balon granted Rudford. Patrick de Chaworth granted a mill in Kempsford. Ranulph Peverel granted the church of St Martin's London. Robert fitz Hamon granted the church of St Cadog's in Llancarfan along with the land of Pennant.[225]

1128. Robert fitz Erchenbald and his wife Matilda granted half a hide in Condicote. Heloise the widow of Arnulph de Evreux granted Hyde in Herefordshire. In the same year Agnes the widow of Thurston of Flanders and Eustace their son granted one hide in Pencombe, Sothenhale. Adeliza daughter of Asketil de Swindon granted the tithe of Shipton. William de Evreux granted one hide in Hereford. Robert de Oilly the younger, son of Nigel de Oilly, granted the tithe of Chesterton. King Henry confirmed the gifts of Berton and Tuffeley, which Osborn the Bishop of Exeter had granted to Abbot Serlo. He

---

[225] Robert fitz Hamon died in 1107, so an error of some sort has been introduced at some point in transmission. Given that this donation occurs in the entry for 1126 — that is, at least some twenty years after it was made — I suspect that the error was made in the copying of an earlier charter, or in the initial assembly of Gregory's chronicle. It is unlikely that Nowell himself shifted the donation so drastically.

also confirmed Frocester, Shotover (?), Boxwell, 'Addworth', Oddington, Coln St Aldwyn's, Hinton, Buckland, Ham, Preston in Warwickshire, and Ayleston. William the constable granted a certain land at Donnington in Archenfield, a land that belonged to William fitz Norman and another that belonged to Herman de Druiwes. Ranulph Bigod granted the tithe of Furset. Ranulph fitz Walter granted the tithe of Ketteringham. Thurston fitz Guy granted the tithe of Finingham. John fitz Richard granted the tithe of Saxlingham. Hugh de Lacy granted the tithe of Moneswell in Oxfordshire. Robert of Beckford granted the tithe at 'Haicoton'. William Revel granted land in Horton.

1129. Serlo the priest, son of Syred, and Leofled his mother granted their land in Gloucester. Wizo of Flanders[226] granted the church of St Mary in Daugleddau, land of the mountain of St Mary, and the forest of 'Dengort'.

1130. Reginald, a monk of Gloucester and a man of remarkable devotion is chosen as the Abbot of Evesham, and he is consecrated at Worcester by Simon the Bishop of Worcester on 27 January. Abbot William of Gloucester, laid low by sickness, gave up his pastoral office. He handed it over to Lord Walter de Lacy, who was consecrated by Simon the Bishop of Worcester on 3 August.

1131. William, the former Abbot of Gloucester, died at Llanbadarn Fawr in Wales on 3 February. Robert de Béthune, the Prior of Llanthony in Wales, becomes the Bishop of Hereford.

1133. Robert Curthose, the King's son, died on 3 February at Cardiff, and he was buried in St Peter's church before the principal altar with honour.

1134. Hugh, son of William Norman, gave to St Peter's St David's of Kilpeck along with the chapel of St Mary in the castle, with the confirmation of Henry his heir.

1135. Helias Giffard died on 13 February and King Henry on 2 November.

1136. The nobleman Richard fitz Gilbert was caught in an ambush by the Welsh and died on 15 April, and he was buried in the chapter house at Gloucester. A terrible battle flared up between the Normans and the Welsh in Gower and 1516 perished.

---

[226] Wizo, the Flemish settler who build the castle of Wiston. See *HW*, II, 425.

1137. Payn fitz John, a valiant knight, on his way to slay the marauding Welsh, was pierced in the head by a lance and died on 9 July. And he was buried in the chapter house at Gloucester by Robert the Bishop of Hereford and Abbot Walter. There is a terrible fight at Cardigan and such slaughter issued forth that a thousand captured women were left for the tithe.[227]

1139. Abbot Walter died on 27 January, and, through the effort of Miles the constable, Gilbert his relative succeeded him, a monk of Cluny and a man of remarkable wisdom. He was installed at Worcester by Robert the Bishop of Hereford on 9 June. Robert the Bishop of Salisbury, an exceptional founder of castles, died.

1143. Milo the constable, Earl of Hereford, had gone to the Forest of Dean to hunt and he was struck in the heart by an arrow from one of his own knights and died on 13 January. He was buried at Llanthony, whose church he had built from the ground up. At the request of three bishops who were present, of his son Roger who would later be the Earl of Hereford, and of many others, his body lay unburied for four days, since Abbot Gilbert claimed, with many arguments, that it was his. Finally the quarrel was settled on the condition that Roger's son and his wife and all his heirs and descendants and whoever might be the lord of Gloucester Castle should cede to the right of St Peter's church. In confirmation of this, Simon the Bishop of Worcester in his authority entrusted Roger, the Earl's son, to Abbot Gilbert.

1144. Robert, a man of remarkable piety, died on 14 October. This Robert, Prior of Ewenny, after he had taken up the office of the prior in 1141 over the two churches which Maurice de Londres, who died on 13 January in the same year, had given to St Peter's Gloucester, this very Robert made that place habitable for the monks. In the same year, a knight by the name of Walter de Clifford granted Eastleach to St Peter's in exchange for Glasbury, and he also granted Malvern to the monks. The churches of St Peter's Hereford and St Guthlac's in the castle were joined, and they were rendered into one body through the effort of Robert the Bishop of Hereford, and Roger de Port confessed that he had held the church of St Guthlac's in the castle unjustly for a long time, since he was a layman and had distributed its possessions undeservedly.

---

[227] This passage is probably corrupted; see the introduction for two parallel passages from other sources.

1146. In the church of St Peter's Gloucester many miracles were gloriously revealed. Roger of Berkeley granted to St Peter's the church of St Leonard's at Stanley, with the assent of Sabriht the Prior of the same place, by the hand of Simon Bishop of Worcester.

1148. Nicholas, a monk and a pious man, took up the bishopric of Llandaf. Robert de Béthune, the Bishop of Hereford — who is believed to have been a saint — died at the Council of Rheims, and Gilbert the Abbot of Gloucester succeeded him, and Hamelin, the prefect of that same place, succeeded Gilbert in the abbacy, and he was consecrated by Simon the Bishop of Worcester on 5 December.

1149. Reginald the Abbot of Evesham died.

1150. Simon the Bishop of Worcester died when he had held the office of bishop for twenty-six years.

1151. Abbot Hamelin went to Rome against Henry the Archbishop of York for Berton, Standish, Northleach, etc.

1155. The King withdrew from Bridgnorth and seized Roger Earl of Hereford who died after he was made a monk in St Peter's monastery. He was buried in the chapter house at Gloucester. The canons of Bromfield granted their church and themselves to the community of monks of St Peter's Gloucester, with Gilbert the Bishop of Hereford attesting, and through the authority of Theobald, the Archbishop of Canterbury and legate of the papal see.

1156. Roger of Berkeley granted the church of Cam with its appurtenances to the church of St Leonard's at Stanley.

1157. Gregory, a monk of Gloucester of pious memory, died, and the many books in our church that were written by his hand are testaments to his holy labours.

1158. In London the Thames was so dried up that it could be crossed with dry feet.

1160. Bernard, the Prior of Gloucester, a devout and learned man, is promoted to the abbacy of Burton upon Trent.

1163. Gilbert the Bishop of Hereford, formerly the Abbot of Gloucester, is transferred to the bishopric of London.

1164. The tower of St Peter's Gloucester fell down.

1167. Elias Giffard and his wife Berta granted to St Peter's eight librates of land in Ullingswick, and the monks returned Cranham to them, which their father had given the monks when he had become a monk.

1171. Henry the Prior was made Abbot of Winchcombe.

1173. Bernard the Abbot of Burton, formerly the Prior of Gloucester, died. Pope Alexander confirmed for the priory of Stanley all of Roger of Berkeley's land in Stanley, as well as the course of the spring of 'Carwell' and the church of Cam with its appurtenances. He also confirmed the churches of Stonebridge, Standcombe, Dursley, Ozleworth, Astone, Cubberley, and Arlingham with their appurtenances, as well as a virgate of land with men and forests in Cotepenne and Longpenne, and sixty acres of land in Berkeleye Harness, that is 'Hardacrae'.

1174. Abbot Hamelin died on 10 March, and Thomas Carbonel, who was at that time the Prior of Hereford, succeeded him and was installed on 27 October.

1180. Osbern, the Prior of St Peter's, became Abbot of Malmesbury.

1181. Henry the Prior of Winchcombe, who had formerly been the Prior of Gloucester, died on 8 November, and Osborn the Abbot of Malmesbury died on 17 March.

1183. Nicholas the Bishop of Llandaf, who had once been a monk of Gloucester, died on 3 June.

1184. Hugues of Brittany dedicated the chapel of St Brides to Gloucester on 10 October.[228]

1187. Gilbert the Bishop of London and former Abbot of Gloucester died on 18 February.

---

[228] Hugues, the Bishop of Dol. My thanks to Barry Lewis for helping with the identification of this bishop.

1190. On 11 May a fire rose up in Gloucester, burning the greater part of the city to the ground, along with some of St Peter's buildings, and destroying the churches of St Mary before the gate of the abbey and of St Oswald next to the wall.

1196. Robert of Hazleton, who was declared a saint, took charge of the abbacy of Winchcombe.

1198. And a battle was fought between Lord William de Braose and Gwenwynwyn in Elfael.

1205. Lord Thomas Carbonel, Abbot of Gloucester, died on 21 July, and Henry the Prior of Gloucester succeeded him, and he was consecrated by Mauger the Bishop of Worcester on 13 October and was installed on 2 October.

1208. A general interdict began for all of England.

1209. The interdict was relaxed in part, allowing the celebration of only one mass in conventual churches each week.

1210. King John went to Ireland in June, and he returned around the Feast of the Assumption. Queen Isabella gave birth to their daughter Joan at Gloucester, and Abbot Henry baptized her in the presence of Peter des Roches, Bishop of Winchester. The chalices of Gloucester Abbey are sold on account of an unheard-of tallage levied by the King on all churches of England, every kind, so that not even lepers or courtly women were spared. From Gloucester Abbey the King seized five thousand, and two wagons along with some horses.

1214. The city of Gloucester was completely burnt on the Feast of St Alban the Martyr. The interdict was relaxed. Giles, the Bishop of Hereford, died in Gloucester Abbey on 13 November, and he remitted one hundred marks of the abbey's debt to him.

1216. On 28 October, Henry the son of John was crowned in Gloucester in the church of St Peter's by Peter des Roches, the Bishop of Winchester, with the authority of Guala the legate.

1218. Sueta de Chartres granted in alms to St Peter's her land which was between the wall of the town and the abbey's larder. William Rosell also granted his land at the same time.

1219. Hugh de Mappenore, the Bishop of Hereford, died. Hugh Foliot succeeded him.

1220. The tower of Gloucester was built.

1221. Robert the Abbot of Winchcombe, a monk of St Peter's Gloucester, died on 8 January.

1222. On 1 August, the parish of St Mary's before Gloucester Abbey's gate was completely burned up, and a part of the bakery, the brewhouse, and the house between the gate and the stable.

1224. Henry the Abbot of Gloucester died on 23 August, and Thomas of Bredon, the Prior of the same place, succeeded him. Thomas of Berkeley granted Lorridge to Stanley Priory.

1226. Reginald de Braose died, and William his son succeeded him, and he was captured in Kerry in the same year.

1227. St Mary's chapel in the cemetery of St Peter's Gloucester was completed at the expense of Ranulph of Willington. Master Edmund of Abingdon preached the Crusade at Gloucester.

1228. Thomas of Bredon, Abbot of Gloucester, died on 11 May, and Henry Foliot, the Prior of Bromfield, succeeded him.

1230. William the Bishop of Llandaf and Iorwerth the Bishop of St Davids died.

1224. King Henry took Hereford Castle from Fulk's men, who bravely resisted.

1230. Gilbert the Earl of Gloucester died overseas. Llywelyn the Prince of Wales had William de Braose the younger hanged, treacherously so they say. Gilbert de Lacy, Walter's son, died on 26 October.

1231. Henry the Abbot of Gloucester designated twenty marks per year from the church of St Gwynllyw's, Newport, for providing festive allowances of French wine for the convent.

1232. The monks of St Peter's granted the chantry between the bridges of Gloucester to the Knights Hospitaller of St Bartholomew.

1234. Richard Marshal, the son of William the Elder, was killed by his own men at Kildare Castle in Ireland through their betrayal.[229] Edmund, the Archbishop of Canterbury, removed from the King's council Peter des Roches, the Bishop of Winchester, Peter de Rivaux, and Stephen Segrave, because they handled the King and his affairs badly. And in Gloucester Abbey he reconciled Gilbert Marshal, Hubert de Burgh, and Richard Siward with the King, and he made the said Gilbert Marshal the Earl of Pembroke and restored everything which had been his father's. Hugh of Wells, the Bishop of Lincoln, died; Robert Grosseteste succeeded him. Hugh Foliot, Bishop of Hereford, died; Ralph of Maidstone succeeded him.

1236. The Severn overflowed its normal bounds and caused great injury to many things. William de Blois, Bishop of Worcester, died.

1237. Gregory of Caerwent received the monastic habit in the church of St Peter's Gloucester from Abbot Henry Foliot on 29 October, and he has written from the beginning of the book up to this point.

1238. A cleric from the household of the knight William de Marisco wished to betray the King and at night entered his room at Woodstock through the window. When he was caught by the guards, he was torn limb from limb.

1239. The church of Gloucester was dedicated by Walter de Cantilupe, Bishop of Worcester. The arrival of the Dominicans in Gloucester.

1240. Llywelyn the Prince of Wales died; Dafydd his son succeeded him, and he did homage to his uncle the King in Gloucester Abbey. Peter d'Aigueblanche is made Bishop of Hereford.

1241. Gilbert the Earl of Pembroke died. Walter de Lacy died on 1 March.

1242. William de Marisco, on account of the sedition that he had devised against the king, was torn limb from limb at London and his limbs were hung in different English cities.

---

[229] For English misrepresentation of Richard Marshal's death, especially the apparent treachery of his men, see G. H. Orpen, *Ireland under the Normans 1216–1333*, 3 vols (Oxford: Clarendon Press, 1920), III, 66–72.

1243. Henry Foliot, Abbot of Gloucester, died, and Walter of St John, Prior of Gloucester, succeeded him. In the same year Abbot Walter died, and John de Felda, Precentor of Gloucester, succeeded him.

1244. A great slaughter of the English was effected by the Welsh in Glamorgan, and among those who died was Herbert fitz Mai,[230] a very illustrious knight. Walter de Comely granted his land in Littleton to St Peter's.

1245. The western tower was completed on the southern side.

1246. Richard the Earl of Cornwall founded the abbey of Hailes.

1247. An earthquake throughout all of England on 20 February between sext and compline. The King minted new money.

1251. The church of Hailes was dedicated by Walter de Cantilupe, Bishop of Worcester.

1252. Richard the Bishop of Chichester died, and John Bishop[231] succeeded him.

1253. William de Burgh, Bishop of Llandaf, died, and John de la Warre, formerly the Abbot of Margam, succeeded him. Robert Grosseteste, Bishop of Lincoln, died; Henry of Lexington succeeded him.

1255. Thomas le Waleys, Bishop of St Davids, died.

1256. Richard Carew, after he was consecrated the Bishop of St Davids by the Pope, came into England. John de la Warre, Bishop of Llandaf, died, and William de Radnor succeeded him. The Welsh emerged from their territories with their young prince Llywelyn and ruined the borders of Wales with slaughter and fire on account of the insult done to them by the bailiffs of Edward, the King's son.

---

[230] Probably Herbert fitz Matthew.

[231] John Climping, whose surname is also recorded as Bishop and Arundel. See Michael Ray, 'Climping, John of', in *Oxford Dictionary of National Biography* <https://doi.org/10.1093/ref:odnb/98256> [accessed 20/01/19].

1257. There is a great slaughter of noble knights from a Welsh attack at Llandeilo Fawr, and the chief of those knights was Stephen Bauzan.[232]

1258. At Gloucester the Severn surpassed its normal course twelve times and covered fields, and it rained continuously in summer as well as winter; the intervals between floods were extremely small, so that many seeds perished, and even the imported wines were sour and immature, as if they were English. Patrick de Chaworth was slain by the Welsh at Cilgerran on account of his frequent attacks against them in the time of truce. Hugh Bigod, Earl of Norfolk, becomes Justiciar of England.

1259. William de Clare, brother of Richard, the Earl of Gloucester, died. Henry of Lexington, the Bishop of Lincoln, died, and Richard of Gravesend, treasurer of Hereford, succeeded him.

1262. Richard the Earl of Gloucester died on 15 July, and was buried at Tewkesbury. Baldwin de L'Isle,[233] Earl of Devon and nephew to the same Earl Richard, died.

1263. Abbot John de Felda died, and Reginald de Homme, his chaplain, succeeded him. After Easter the barons' war arose.

1264. The town of Gloucester was captured by Lord Edward, the King's firstborn, and by Earl Godwin de Clare on 15 July. Then on 4 August there is a slaughter at Evesham. William the Bishop of Llandaf died, as did Walter de Cantilupe, the Bishop of Worcester, and Nicholas of Ely, who had formerly been the King's chancellor, succeeded him.

1267. A frightful wind.

1268. A great frost began.

1269. The Severn, as never before, flooded, just as all the other rivers of England, and they destroyed houses and bridges.

---

[232] The Battle of Cadfan, in which Rhys Fychan defeated Stephen Bauzan's forces. The Latin text seems to witness some confusion between these two similar surnames, 'Vaughan' (i.e. Fychan) and Bauzan.

[233] Baldwin de Redvers, Seventh Earl of Devon and Lord of the Isle of Wight.

1272. Richard, the King of Germany,[234] died on 3 April and he is interred at Hailes.

1273. Adam of Elmley, a monk of Gloucester, dies, and he was buried before the altar of the Holy Cross, where it shone with miracles before Christmas and lasted until the Feast of the Purification of the Virgin Mary.

1275. John Breton, Bishop of Hereford, died, and Thomas de Cantilupe succeeded him. Robert Burnell, the King's chancellor, becomes Bishop of Bath. An earthquake at prime on 11 September. Humphrey de Bohun, Earl of Hereford, died and is buried at Llanthony.

1276. Lord Hervey de Chaworth was cruelly slain by the Welsh, and for that reason and for their attacks the treaty was broken.

1277. At the Feast of St John, King Edward entered into Wales, and he remained there and harrassed Prince Llywelyn until Lent. He captured Llywelyn and subjugated all of Wales and made it a tributary. He made peace with Llywelyn, who with his men came to London, and he convened a great feast. As long as the King was in Wales, his Exchequer remained in Shropshire.

1278. A plague against sheep, the likes of which had never been heard of before, prowls through the land, and it took away almost all of them. Eleanor, the daughter of Simon de Montfort, was given as a bride to Llywelyn, Prince of Wales, at Worcester.

1280. A flood, the likes of which had never been heard of before, through all of England.

1281. Edmund the Earl of Cornwall founded a Cistercian monastery at Oxford.

1282. On 22 March, Palm Sunday, Dafydd the brother of the Prince of Wales with his army at Hawarden treacherously seized Roger Clifford Senior and slew four knights, one of whom was Fulk Tregor.

1282. On Pentecost, the King held parliament at Worcester. And then he entered into Wales with a hostile army on the Feast of St Peter in Chains. And

---

[234] Richard, First Earl of Cornwall.

then on 6 November at the bridge of Anglesey, Lord Lucas de Towny and Lord Roger Clifford Junior were drowned with an unknown number of soldiers. On 16 October, Roger de Mortimer died. On 25 August, Thomas de Cantilupe, the Bishop of Hereford, died, and Master Richard Swinefield the Archdeacon of London succeeded him. On 11 December, Llywelyn the Prince of Wales was pierced by a lance and died. His head was cut off and is brought to the King at Rhuddlan and then was attached on the highest tower of London.

1283. After Dafydd the brother of Llywelyn was captured by the Welsh near the castle of Caernarfon, he is brought to the King at Rhuddlan, and he was condemned to be drawn, hung, decapitated at Shrewsbury, and to be divided, after his innards were burnt up, and distributed in different places.

1284. On 13 September, Reginald the Abbot of Gloucester, a wise man who ruled his house effectively in a time of war, died. Lord John de Gamages, Prior of Hereford, succeeded him and was installed on St Andrew's Day. The King established English common law, counties, and judges in Wales.

1285. Edmund de Mortimer is given the belt of knighthood, and at Winchester on the Feast of the Nativity of Mary he took as a wife Margaret, the daughter of Lord William Fiennes and kinswoman to the queen, and the statutes called the 'Additamenta Glocestriae'[235] were made.

1286. A dreadful storm struck, which began in Wales in the mountains of Morugge and moved through Elinien[236] and Ludlow all the way to Worcester, and it killed many animals like rabbits and other types of animals and birds. Removing buildings and uprooting trees, it caused great harm.

1287. Around Pentecost, Rhys ap Maredudd rebels and attacks the King's lands in Wales, and Edmund Earl of Cornwall, who was at that time the guardian of England, hearing about that, gathers an army and enters Wales. He besieges Dryslwyn Castle. And the wall, having been undermined from below with

---

[235] I.e. the Second Statute of Westminster.

[236] Morugge [...] Elinien] 'Elinien' probably stands for 'Elinid' (Mod. W. 'Elenydd'). For discussion, see *Pedeir Keinc y Mabinogi*, ed. by Ifor Williams (Cardiff: University of Wales Press, 1951), p. 259 n. 71.5 and J. Beverley Smith, *Llywelyn ap Gruffudd: Prince of Wales*, new edn (Cardiff: University of Wales Press, 2014), p. 560 n. 170. My thanks to Paul Russell and an anonymous reviewer for these references.

machines, fell and crushed some noblemen: Lord William de Munchensy, Lord Gerard de L'Isle, and the Lord of Stafford, along with many others from the army.

1288. A great abundance of produce; a quantity is sold for ten pence. A great heat and drought in summer and especially in autumn, in which many died.

1290. Gilbert de Clare, Earl of Gloucester married Joan of Acre, the daughter of King Edward, at Westminster on the Sunday after the Feast of St Mark the Evangelist. At the Feast of All Saints, all the Jews are cast out of England.

10. A Forgotten Welsh Chronology in Aberystwyth, National Library of Wales, MS 5267B, in MS Peniarth 50, and in the Red Book of Hergest

Rebecca Try

Y *Casgliad Brith* or Aberystwyth, NLW, MS 5267B (formerly Dingestow 7) is a small, unornamented bilingual compilation manuscript containing twenty-eight texts, five of which are in Latin.[1] The core hand has been identified by Daniel Huws as that of Siancyn ap Dafydd ap Gruffudd, a scribe working in the first half of the fifteenth century, probably in or near to Cwm Tawe (the Swansea Valley).[2] A date given in a set of Latin annals included in the manuscript suggests that it was probably written in 1438.[3] *Y Casgliad Brith* (henceforth referred to as *CB*) contains a miscellany of prose texts, some of which are well known from other collections, such as *Breuddwyd Pawl* and *Ystorya Adaf*, while others are less well evidenced, such as *Natur y missoed yn y vl6ydyn*, which seems not to be found in any earlier manuscripts and may be the only surviving version. The manuscript has a rich mixture of text types, ranging through science, geography, religion, and history, and in this it has much in common with other later medieval Welsh manuscript compilations.

---

[1] The title *Y Casgliad Brith* seems to have been given at the National Library, probably because of the speckled appearance of the vellum in the latter half of the manuscript. The size is 190 × 135 mm.

[2] This information is taken from Daniel Huws's unpublished catalogue entry for the manuscript, kindly supplied by Dr Ann Parry Owen.

[3] The date has been worked out in a modern hand on a flyleaf at the beginning of the manuscript. This is based on an entry in the Latin chronology found on fol. 42ᵛ, which appears to read 'anno domini milmo ccccxxxviii' (with 'milmo' probably an abbreviation for 'milesimo'), although the reading is somewhat impaired by damage to the manuscript.

CB is a production of South Wales. Daniel Huws suggests that Siancyn was working in Cwm Tawe, which was shared between Glamorgan in the east and Gower in the west, and I see no reason to dispute this.[4] Various orthographical features within the manuscript point to a South Walian origin and many of the texts appear to have a South Walian focus.[5] Furthermore, the manuscripts with which *CB* shares the most texts, namely Aberystwyth, NLW, MSS Llanstephan 27 and Peniarth 50, are South Walian in origin.

After its probable creation in or around Cwm Tawe, it appears to have stayed nearby, as can be inferred from the insertion of two glosses in the hand of the poet Dafydd Benwyn, on fols 52ᵛ and 84ᵛ. Dafydd Benwyn 'o Vorgannwc' ('from Glamorgan') was a poet from Llangeinor, Glamorgan, who was active in South Wales during the second half of the sixteenth century. Little is known of *CB*'s history in the seventeenth and eighteenth centuries, but the manuscript later came into the hands of the Bosanquet family of Dingestow Court in Monmouthshire, located around fifty miles from Cwm Tawe, before it was acquired by the National Library of Wales.

Situated between *Py del6 y dyly* and *Breuddwyd Pawl*, about two-thirds of the way through the manuscript, is a Welsh chronology, recorded in the *Handlist of Manuscripts in the National Library of Wales* as 'Chronology to 1321', although Huws refers to it in his forthcoming catalogue as 'Annals from Adam to 1321'.[6] The same text also appears in two other Middle Welsh manuscripts (discussed in further detail below); the catalogue for those manuscripts calls it 'Chronicl'.[7] For ease of reference, here the text will be referred to by its opening words, 'Blwydyn eiseu', or *BE*.

BE is composed of two stylistically different sections. The first is a section of eighteen lines that form a brief account of Britain from Adam to the arrival of 'William Bastart' (William the Conqueror), including the taking of Britain, first by Brutus and then by Hors and Hengist; these are prosaic in form. The rest of *BE* is a collection of formulaic annals, set out as a date followed by the event which occurred in that year. This distinction in style between the first

---

[4] Daniel Huws, *A Repertory of Welsh Manuscripts and Scribes* (forthcoming), s.n. NLW 5267B.

[5] For example, loss of -*i*- in stems as in *bryttaneit* in *Blwydyn Eiseu* line 9 (see Appendix A below).

[6] NLW, MS 5267B, fols 56ᵛ–57ᵛ; *Handlist of Manuscripts in the National Library of Wales*, 9 vols (Aberystwyth: NLW, 1940–2003), II (1951), 81; Huws, s.n. NLW 5267B.

[7] The name 'Chronicl' is that given in *RG* <http://www.rhyddiaithganoloesol.caerdydd.ac.uk/en/ms-home.php?ms = Jesus111> [accessed 18 December 2017].

and second sections seems to suggest that *BE* was originally compiled from two (or more) stylistically different texts.

The second section covers the period of history from the death of Thomas of Canterbury (Thomas Becket) in 1170 to the death of Thomas of Lancaster in 1321, recording forty events of note within that timeframe. These events are geographically centred, for the most part, on Wales, although some entries focus on events more firmly rooted in English or Scottish history, but which would have been of interest in Wales. These include the Battle of Lewes (referred to in *BE* as the Battle of Offam) in 1264 and the Battle of Bannockburn (referred to in *BE* as the Battle of Stirling) in 1314.[8] The events from Wales are mostly centred around the south and south-east (e.g. Carmarthen, Neath, Builth Wells), referring to places and events of local significance such as Neath Castle and the breaking of Carmarthen Bridge, and point to a South Wales origin for the text.[9] This focus on events in the south, despite general references to the princes of Gwynedd, suggests that the composition or compilation of *BE* can be localized to the area in or around Glamorgan.

The *CB* version features a large number of spellings that probably emanated from a Latin original, such as 'Neth' for 'Nedd' and 'Dauid' for 'Dafydd'. Also, the dates in the annalistic section are rendered in Roman numerals, although the first eighteen lines of *BE* utilize a mixture of Roman numerals and dates written out in Welsh. This suggests that the original compiler of the events in *BE* may have been working from a Latin chronicle whose influence has survived in the orthography of these place names, although this cannot be said with any degree of certainty.

BE is extant in two other versions, only one of which definitely pre-dates *CB*.[10] The earlier version is found on fols 125^r–25^v of Oxford, Jesus College, MS 111 (the Red Book of Hergest, henceforth RBH), in the hand of Hywel Fychan. Called '*Chronicl*' by the editors of *Rhyddiaith Gymraeg*, the online collection of Welsh prose from 1300 to 1425, its readings agree with those of *CB*

---

[8] *CB* dates the Battle of Lewes to 1265 and the Battle of Bannockburn to 1312.

[9] NLW, MS 5267B, fols 56^v–57^v.

[10] Just prior to the publication of this chapter, I was informed of two other instances of the text in the manuscripts Aberystwyth, NLW, MSS Peniarth 27ii and Peniarth 267, in addition to further instances where the text prefaces the Annals of Owain Glyndŵr. Unfortunately, due to this late discovery, it has been impossible to include a discussion of these versions within the chapter, and they will require further investigation in the future. For now, see the List of Chronicles in the Appendix to the present volume, items 14 and 21.

relatively closely.[11] The second version is found in MS Peniarth 50, a manuscript which was being written intermittently from 1425 to 1456; *BE* is found on pages 171–73. It is not possible to know whether the copy of the text in this manuscript was written prior to that found in *CB*. I have chosen not to transcribe the version in RBH as there is an accurate and accessible version online provided by the *Rhyddiaith Gymraeg* collection.[12] The appendices to the present chapter include transcriptions and translations of both the *CB* (Appendix A) and MS Peniarth 50 (Appendix B) versions of the texts, as well as a dates comparison which covers all three versions (Appendix C).

For each of the events recorded in *BE*, I have attempted to corroborate the details elsewhere, using Welsh chronicles where possible (see Appendix C). I have primarily utilized Jones's editions of *Brut y Tywysogyon* (henceforth referred to as *BT*), which chronicles the history of Wales from *c.* 682 to 1282 with an extension in one version to 1332; versions of *BT* are found both in RBH and in Aberystwyth, NLW, MS Peniarth 20.[13] All numbering of annals refers to the numbering system used in Appendix C.

Comparison: Dating Differences

The three versions of *BE* are similar, but none is identical to another. Each suffers from scribal interference, whether through editing or through error, and these differentiate them enough to suggest that none could have been directly copied from the other.

A key difference that sets the RBH version apart from the others is the way in which the dates are recorded. All the dates in *CB* and MS Peniarth 50 are rendered in Roman numerals, whilst the RBH version expands these dates and writes them fully in Welsh. Simon Rodway speaks of Hywel Fychan, the scribe of this part of RBH, as a scribe who was 'consistently modifying his source to make it easier to understand' by changing linguistic constructions which would

---

[11] See above, n. 7.

[12] The transcription for RBH can be found here: *RG* <http://www.rhyddiaithganoloesol.caerdydd.ac.uk/en/ms-page.php?ms = Jesus111&page = 125r&l = c516l28> [accessed 19 December 2017].

[13] *BT (RB)*; *BT (Pen. 20)*; *BT (Pen. 20 trans.)*. The *RB* version of *BT* stops in 1282; it is only the Peniarth 20 version of *BT* that continues to 1332. The text of the MS Peniarth 20 *BT* is available at RG <http://www.rhyddiaithganoloesol.caerdydd.ac.uk/en/ms-page.php?ms = Pen20&page = 65> [accessed 18 December 2017] and a digitized version of the manuscript can be found on the NLW website <http://hdl.handle.net/10107/475463> [accessed 16 January 2019].

not have been understood by his audience; it is possible that this is what is happening here.[14] Perhaps, at least in part, as a result of this translation, each of the three texts suffers from errors in dating different annals. RBH has the most errors at eight incorrect dates, with *CB* following at seven and MS Peniarth 50 at three. Most of the errors in *CB* and MS Peniarth 50 can be explained as misreadings or miscopyings by the scribes, though this is not necessarily the case in RBH. Of these, annals 2, 3, 4, and 7 are dates which are wrong in all three manuscripts (as corroborated by other annalistic sources, including *BT*), and annals 14 and 18, which do not appear in RBH, are incorrect in both *CB* and MS Peniarth 50.

In *CB* the errors which differ from the readings given in MS Peniarth 50 or RBH can be found in annals 7, 11, 18, 21, 22, 26, and 28. All but number 7, for which the correct date is uncertain, can be explained by scribal error or confusion on the part of Siancyn. Annals 11, 26, and 28 are all missing just one or two Roman numerals, which would render the readings correct. Annal 11, for example, gives the date for the 'haf tessa6c' ('hot summer') as 1250 ('mccl'). The correct reading of 1252, which is given by MS Peniarth 50 and corroborated by *BT*, is rendered in MS Peniarth 50 as 'mcclii', a difference of only two characters. It appears that Siancyn here missed or could not read the two 'i' figures.[15] With this annal in particular, RBH also gives an incorrect reading (1202), which would again have been only one character different, if rendered in Roman numerals, to MS Peniarth 50s reading. It is thus possible, although not provable, either that there was some illegibility in the exemplar of *CB* and RBH, if they were the same, or that one branch of the text's transmission contained some confusion here and that MS Peniarth 50 was working from a separate branch. It seems more likely, then, that the error was simply scribal, as is the case for the other three annals of this type.

Table 10.1: Annals 21 and 22 in *CB*

No.	Annal	Date given	Actual date
21	mcclxxxi y ryfela6d Res ap Mereduth	1281	1287
22	mcclxxxvii y collet acrys	1287	1291

---

[14] Simon Rodway, 'The Red Book Scribe of *Culhwch ac Olwen*: A Modernising Scribe at Work', *Studi Celtici*, 3 (2004), 93–161 (p. 129).

[15] An alternative possibility for the reading in annal 11 is discussed below, p. 353.

The relationship between annals 21 and 22 appears to be somewhat more complex (see Table 10.1). I would argue that the error between these two annals may be the result of an eyeskip. Annal 22 dates the fall of Acre to 1287 ('mcclxxxvii y collet acrys') rather than 1291, which was when the city of Acre actually fell. 1287 is the correct date for the preceding annal 21, rather than 1281 ('mcclxxxi y ryfelaόd Res ap Mereduth'). In the case of annal 21, it is possible that the discrepancy could have arisen from one or two missing characters: annal 21's date of 1281 ('mcclxxxi') would need only two more characters to read 1287 ('mcclxxxvii'), so perhaps the exemplar correctly dated annal 21 to 1287. However, the shift in annal 22 from the correct 1291 ('mccxci') to the incorrect 1287 ('mcclxxxvii') seems too large to suggest that missing characters caused the error. Thus, the most likely cause of the error in annal 22 is an eyeskip involving the correct date of annal 21.

Thus, almost all of the chronological errors in *CB* can be classified as scribal miscopyings. Likewise, the two chronological errors in MS Peniarth 50 (again, excluding annal 7 which will be discussed later) also seem to have arisen from the MS Peniarth 50 scribe forgetting a character. Annal 1, which in MS Peniarth 50 reads 1071 ('mlxxi'), is only one character different from the correct reading of 1171 ('mclxxi'). Again, in annal 18, MS Peniarth 50 reads 1268 ('mcclxviii'), whereas it reads 1278 ('mcclxx6iii') in *CB*. The event in question (the moving of the mint) actually occurred in 1279, and I would suggest here that the error is the result of the use of a March to March calendar. As the error in MS Peniarth 50 is only one character different to *CB*, it is probable that it was the text's archetype which was a year out, and that this error has been absorbed by both readings, with the additional error of the missing 'x' in MS Peniarth 50.[16]

RBH has the most errors, and these again seem to be mostly miscopyings or mistakes that have been taken over into the Welsh translations of the dates. With annals 1, 11, 12, and 15 the dates would be only one or two characters out if RBH's date were rendered in Roman numerals. Annal 12, for example, is rendered in RBH as 'Ch6e blyned a|deugeint a|deucant a|mil', which would read 'mccilvi' (1246) in numerals. In both *CB* and MS Peniarth 50, the date reads 'mcclvi', and so it appears that Hywel Fychan has read an extra 'i' where there is none, or that there was an existing error in his exemplar. Two other annals, 16 and 19, also appear to have suffered from a misreading as opposed to a miscopying. RBH gives the date for annal 16 as 1228 ('Wyth mlyned ar|hugeint a|deucant a|mil'), which would read 'mccxxviii' in Roman numerals. The date

---

[16] This annal does not appear in RBH.

given by the other two manuscripts is 'mcclxviii'. What appears to have happened here is that Hywel or his exemplar misread the 'l' for an 'x', and this is reflected in the translation. Similarly, annal 19 is dated to 1277 ('Dwy ulyned ar|bymthec a|thrugeint a|deucant mil') in RBH, which would read 'mcclxxvii' in Roman numerals. Annal 19 is dated to 1282 ('mcclxxxii') in the other manuscripts. Here, the final 'x' has been misread as a 'v', leading to the error in RBH.

The only error in RBH which does not seem to have an easily visible explanation is annal 4. RBH here gives 1263 as the date ('Teir blyned a|thrugeint a|deucant a mil'), which would be rendered in Roman numerals as 'mcclxiii'. In the other manuscripts it is given as 1218, which is 'mccxviii'. For the mistake here to be the result of a miscopying of Roman numerals, it would require the 'xv' in 1218 to have been read as 'lx', which, whilst not impossible, seems unlikely. It is interesting to note that this event is difficult to corroborate in *BT*, although it seems likely that it relates to William Marshall's battle at Carmarthen Bridge against Gruffudd ap Llywelyn in 1223. 1223 would be rendered in numerals as 'mccxxiii' and again the difference here lies in those central characters 'xx'. What seems to have happened is that, at some point in the text's transmission, the characters at the centre of the numeral have become obscure or unclear. Both *CB* and Peniarth 50 seem to have been following a tradition that read 'xv', whilst Hywel was either working from an exemplar that read 'lx' or from the original obscure version, which has caused his difference in translation compared with the other two manuscripts.

Of the dates which each version of the Chronicle gives incorrectly, three (annals 3, 14, and 18) appear to be a year out when compared to the dates in corroborating sources, which could be the result of the change from the 'Old Style' calendar (wherein the year ran from March to March) to the 'New Style', which began the year in January and followed the adoption of the Gregorian calendar. Recording annals in this way was not unusual; indeed, *BT* itself suffers from similar inconsistencies in dating. Jones suggests that this inconsistency reflects the varying dates for commencement in the texts used in the original compilation of the Latin version of *BT*.[17] This could also be the case for this text, as the sources being compiled to create it would probably have followed different dating systems.

Annal 2, the annal relating the slaughter at Painscastle, is given incorrectly in each of the three manuscripts, which all agree in their reading of 1188 ('mclxxxviii') where *BT* gives the year as 1198 ('mcxcviii'). The difference in

---

[17] *BT (Pen. 20 trans.)*, pp. lxiv–lxv.

this date when rendered in Roman numerals is only the loss of an 'x'. It appears, then, that either the original text or the archetype from which these three manuscripts descend had incorrectly rendered the date in Roman numerals.

Annal 7 is arguably the most complex of those contained in the chronology. The annal records a battle between Dafydd ap Gruffydd and his brother Llywelyn. In *CB* the date is given as 1251, in RBH it is 1216, and in MS Peniarth 50 it is 1241. The date is not possible to corroborate definitively in other sources, as there was much contention between the brothers in the second half of the thirteenth century. However, given that Dafydd was only born in 1238, it seems likely that both RBH and MS Peniarth 50 are wrong here. Whether or not *CB* is correct is unclear; the first recorded battle between the brothers was at Bryn Derwin in 1255. Whilst it is not unlikely that there may have been contention between them just four years earlier, it seems that this may be another example of illegibility in an exemplar causing reading difficulties for each of the copyists. *CB*'s date of 1251 is rendered in Roman numerals as 'mccli', whereas RBH would be 'mccxvi', and Peniarth 50 is 'mccxli'. Each of these dates is very similar, and in each the error lies in the middle section of the numeral, with each copyist reading it differently as either 'l', 'xv', or 'xl'.[18] If this entry was originally referring to the battle of Bryn Derwin in 1255, the year would have been rendered as 'mcclv' and it is not inconceivable that an illegible exemplar could read 'mcclv' and still be interpreted in these three ways. Although it is not possible to work out for certain what the original date for annal 7 was, what is shown by this annal is that it would not have been possible for any of the three manuscripts to have been copying directly from another, as otherwise one would see the error replicated in at least one of the other manuscripts, rather than three separate readings. That *CB* and MS Peniarth 50 are so similar, being only one character different, adds perhaps some further credence to the possibility that the two were working from the same branch of the manuscript transmission, as suggested by the readings of annal 4. On the other hand, the different readings in annal 7 might suggest that the three witnesses were working from a single exemplar that was partially illegible. It is possible that Siancyn edited his date in *CB* to one more likely, based on his knowledge of the 1250s.

The dates comparison may show that there were at least two different branches of textual transmission for the chronology, with *CB* and MS Peniarth

---

[18] Alternatively, in the case of RBH, the date 1216 may an error caused by the process of translation, due to the similarity of the Welsh words 'pumdeg' (50) and 'pymtheg' (15).

50 descending from one branch, and RBH descending from another. However, the evident difficulties caused by the copying of the Roman numerals render such a conclusion premature.

Comparison: Omissions

There are five annal entries which are not common to all versions. Four of these are annals that do not appear in RBH, and one is an annal that does not appear in *CB*. There is a further sequence of four annals in RBH that suffers from a lacuna in the manuscript. MS Peniarth 50 is not missing any of the annals which are contained in the other versions. The four annals that appear in *CB* and MS Peniarth 50 but not RBH are as shown in Table 10.2.

Table 10.2: The four annals that appear in *CB* and MS Peniarth 50 but not RBH

Annal in *CB*	Translation	Actual year	Event referenced
mccxvi y g6naethp6yt creuyd y brodyr pʳgethwyr	*In 1216 the Order of the Preaching Brothers was created.*	1216	The foundation of the Dominican order.
mcclxv y bu y lladua yn offam	*In 1265 was the slaughter at Offham.*	1264	The Battle of Lewes at Offham Hill.[19]
mcclxxviii y synmuda6d y vath a dorrit[20]	*In 1278 the mint that had been broken was moved.*	1279	In 1279 Edward had new money struck and the mint was moved to London.[21]
mcccxxi y pan Thomas o lancastyr	*1321 was when Thomas of Lancaster [was killed] [...]*	1321	The seizure and execution of Thomas Earl of Lancaster in 1321.[22]

[19] 1264 in MS Peniarth 20, pp. 277–81 <https://viewer.library.wales/475463#?c = 0&m = 0&s = 0&cv = 283&xywh = -45%2C0%2C1843%2C2668> [accessed 18 January 2019]; *BT (Pen. 20 trans.)*, pp. 113–14.

[20] MS Peniarth 50 dates this to 1268.

[21] In MS Peniarth 20, pp. 289–91, the event is recorded as taking place in 1279: <https://viewer.library.wales/475463#?c = 0&m = 0&s = 0&cv = 295&xywh = -19%2C0%2C1852%2C2679> [accessed 18 January 2019]; *BT (Pen. 20 trans.)*, p. 119.

[22] Appears in the Peniarth 20 version of *BT*, pp. 296–98 <https://viewer.library.wales/475463#?c = 0&m = 0&s = 0&cv = 300&xywh = 0%2C-21%2C1854%2C2684> [accessed 18 January 2019]; *BT (Pen. 20 trans.)*, p. 124.

It is possible that Hywel Fychan was choosing to omit entries in RBH which he did not understand or deem to be important; crucially, none of these annals refers to Wales. If he was the editing scribe that Rodway suggests, it is perhaps possible to explain why these annals were omitted from RBH.[23] Each appears in *CB* and MS Peniarth 50, though often rendered in slightly different ways. The annal 'y gonaethpoyt creuyd y brodyr p^rgethwyr' (*CB*), for example, contains a superscript 'r' between the 'p' and 'g', indicating the reading 'p*re*gethwyr'. This annal is referring to the creation of the Dominican Order, or the Order of the Preachers. MS Peniarth 50 includes this annal, but does not include the word 'p*re*gethwyr', instead omitting all but the 'p'. It is possible that the exemplar was here difficult to read, which resulted in a different response for each of the three copyists. The superscript *r* is a common Latin abbreviation which can indicate *re*. That Siancyn uses and recognizes the abbreviation shows that he was familiar with such abbreviations in a way which the other two scribes perhaps were not. It seems here that both Hywel Fychan and the MS Peniarth 50 scribe have omitted what they did not understand, rather than making an attempt to discern what the exemplar was referring to.

Similarly, the entries on 'Offam' and the mint could have proved problematic for a copyist. 'Offam' is an unusual name given in the text for the Battle of Lewes, which took place in 1264 upon Offham Hill. References to the Battle of Lewes in Welsh vernacular chronicles appear only in various manuscript copies of *BT*, wherein the battle is referred to as 'leaws', 'leos', or 'lowys'.[24] The battle is

---

[23] Rodway, 'The Red Book Scribe', pp. 93–131.

[24] For example, in MS Peniarth 20, p. 279, it is referred to as 'leaws' (*RG* <http://www.rhyddiaithganoloesol.caerdydd.ac.uk/en/ms-page.php?ms = Pen20&page = 279> [accessed 14 February 2018]; <https://viewer.library.wales/475463#?c = 0&m = 0&s = 0&cv = 285&xywh = -45%2C0%2C1838%2C2659> [accessed 18 January 2019]; *BT (Pen. 20 trans.)*, p. 113), while Aberystwyth, NLW, MS 3035 (Mostyn 116) and RBH call it 'leos' (NLW, MS 3035, fol. 206^r, at *RG* <http://www.rhyddiaithganoloesol.caerdydd.ac.uk/en/ms-page.php?ms = NLW3035&page = 206r> [accessed 14 February 2018]; Jesus College, MS 111, fol. 88^r, at *RG* <http://www.rhyddiaithganoloesol.caerdydd.ac.uk/en/ms-page.php?ms = Jesus111&page = 88r> [accessed 14 February 2018]); it is 'Lowys' in Aberystwyth, NLW, MS Peniarth 19 (MS Peniarth 19, fol. 125^v, at *RG* <http://www.rhyddiaithganoloesol.caerdydd.ac.uk/en/ms-page.php?ms = Pen19&page = 125v> [accessed 14 February 2018]). According to Jones, there is a marginal addition to MS Peniarth 20 which calls it 'kyfranc lews', although this is not entirely legible in the digitized version of the manuscript (*BT (Pen. 20 trans.)*, p. 215). I have been unable to find reference to it elsewhere in published editions of Welsh chronicles; however, it is possible that references have escaped my notice, or that there are references to the battle in as yet unpublished chronicles.

also referenced in the *Cronica de Wallia*, where it is called 'bellum apud lewes', with no mention of Offam.²⁵ Even in non-Welsh chronicles, it has proved difficult to find reference to the battle as 'the Battle of Offam'; in the Chronicle of Melrose, whose section on the Battle of Lewes is likely to be contemporary, it is referred to as 'Bello de Lewys', and similarly in the *Chronicon Willelmi de Richanger* (a contemporary account of the Second Barons' War, in which the Battle of Lewes took place), it is 'Bello de Lewes'.²⁶ It is unclear, therefore, where this reference to 'Offam' originated, though I think it would be safe to assume that a 'lladua yn Offam' may not have been familiar or recognizable as a reference to the Battle of Lewes for a Welsh audience.²⁷ Given that Hywel Fychan, the scribe of RBH, was a modifying scribe, it stands to reason that if Hywel did not recognize the 'lladua yn Offam' he may have decided not to include it in order to clarify the text for his Welsh audience, much as he seems to have done with the exclusion of other annals, such as annal 18.

Annal 18 refers to the moving of the mint in 1278/79 and is not clear in its meaning, nor is it explicit to which event it refers. It is thus perhaps not surprising that it would be misunderstood by the scribe. This event is described in *Brut y Tywysogyon* as follows:

> Blwydyn wedy hynny y gwnaeth Edward vrenhin symudaw y vwnei ac y gwnaethpwyt y dimei ar fyrdling yn grynnyon. ac yna y bu wir dewindabaeth verdin pan dywawt ef a hollir furyf y gyfnewit a|y|hanner a vyd krwnn.

> A year after that, King Edward had his money changed and the halfpenny and the farthing were made round. And then was verified the soothsaying of Merlin when he said, 'The form of exchange shall be split and its half shall be round.'²⁸

---

²⁵ *Annales Cambriae: The E Text, from Exeter Cathedral Library MS 3514, pp. 507–19*, ed. by Henry W. Gough-Cooper (Welsh Chronicles Research Group, 2016), p. 23, § e56.3 <http://croniclau.bangor.ac.uk/documents/AC_E_First_Edition%20%20.pdf> [accessed 18 December 2017].

²⁶ *Chronica de Mailros*, ed. by Joseph Stevenson (Edinburgh: Typis Societatis Edinburgensis, 1835), p. 192; *The Chronicle of William de Rishanger, of the Barons' War, the Miracles of Simon de Montfort*, ed. by James Orchard Halliwell-Phillipps (London: Camden Society, 1840), p. 2.

²⁷ *BE*'s contents seem too localized to south-east Wales (the references to Castell Buellt, Carmarthen Bridge, and certain Marcher lords, for example) to have been composed outside Wales. However, it is possible that the source text was composed in Wales but not in Welsh.

²⁸ MS Peniarth 20, p. 290 <https://viewer.library.wales/475463#?c = 0&m = 0&s = 0&cv = 296&xywh = -1%2C-14%2C1857%2C2686> [accessed 18 January. 19]; *BT (Pen. 20 trans.)*, p. 119.

The entry in *CB* is very generic and non-specific; it is perfectly understandable that Hywel Fychan may not have understood this reference and may have left it out, assuming that his patron would not miss it.

A significant omission from RBH is the omission of the final annal, referencing Thomas of Lancaster. The annal in *CB* reads 'mcccxxi y pan Thomas o Lancastyr', presumably referring to the imprisonment and execution of Thomas of Lancaster in 1321. In MS Peniarth 50, this annal reads 'M cccxxi dat pan las Thomas o lancastyl'.[29] The grammatical structure of the annal in *CB*, however, is unusual, and at first sight it appears that part of the sentence is missing, as it contains no verb. The error, however, may be one of miscopying rather than omission. A simplified standard structure for the annal as found in *CB* would be as follows:

[date] [verb] [subject]

e.g. [mclxxi] [y llas] [thomas o gaer geint]

However, where we would expect to see a verb in the final annal, we have 'y pan'. If we substitute *llas* for *pan* we get a possible reading: 'mcccxxi y llas Thomas o Lancastyr'. Alternatively, the annal might have read 'mcccxxi y bu pan las Thomos o Lancastyr', or perhaps 'mcccxxi oed pan las Thomas o Lancastyr', if it were following conventions similar to those used in the 'pan' dating clauses of *BT* (MS Peniarth 20).[30] It does not appear, then, that the sentence has broken off or been left unfinished. It may be that the verb in the exemplar was unclear. If so, this would explain the presumed misreading in *CB*, and perhaps even the omission made by Hywel Fychan in RBH, if they are copying from the same exemplar.

MS Peniarth 50 includes this annal, but the copyist here appears to have made an attempt to edit the annal and make it more comprehensible. Although this does not follow a typical grammatical pattern, it is comprehensible and now includes a verb, with the inclusion of 'las'. Again, what this suggests is that the exemplar at this point was unclear in its reading, or simply did not make sense, and that this caused the three scribes to react in different ways: Siancyn copied it exactly, the scribe of MS Peniarth 50 attempted to edit it or had an

---

[29] MS Peniarth 50, p. 173.

[30] See, for example, the first entry in MS Peniarth 20: 'Pedwar vgein mlyneð a chwe chant ac vn oyd oed krist pan vv varwolaeth vawr yn y ynys brydein', MS Peniarth 20, p. 65, col. 1, at *RG* <http://www.rhyddiaithganoloesol.caerdydd.ac.uk/en/ms-page.php?ms = Pen20&page = 65> [accessed 21 November 2018]).

exemplar which was perhaps clearer, but still incorrect, and Hywel Fychan chose to ignore it. If it were the case that the scribe of MS Peniarth 50 edited this annal in an attempt to correct it, it is possible to see a little of the personalities of the scribes shining through in their redactions of this text.

The annal that appears in RBH and MS Peniarth 50 but not *CB* reads, in MS Peniarth 50, 'M ccl y bu vr6ydyr r6g ll ap Gruff ae vrod' ('In 1250 there was a battle between Llywelyn ap Gruffudd and his brothers', annal 10 in the table in Appendix C).[31] The content of annal 10 is almost identical to annal 7, just a few entries earlier, which reads, in *CB*, 'mcc li y bu y vr6ydyr r6ng dauid ap gr a ll' ('In 1251 was the battle between Dafydd ap Gruffudd and Llywelyn').[32] The differences here are minimal: a different date (1250 and 1251, respectively), a difference in word order, the naming of Dafydd, and the lack of a patronymic for Llywelyn in the latter. The overall meaning remains mostly the same. At first, it seems possible that this may have been the same incident copied twice in RBH and MS Peniarth 50, but correctly copied only once in *CB*. However, this does not in fact seem to be the case. The following annal (11) refers to 'yr haf tessa6c' ('the hot summer'). MS Peniarth 50 dates this to 1252 and *CB* to 1250, whereas RBH has 1202.[33] What appears to have occurred here in *CB* is eyeskip, wherein Siancyn missed a line of the text, resulting in the date for annal 10 (1250) being attributed to annal 11 ('yr haf tessa6c'). This explanation accounts for the difference in date for the 'haf tessa6c' entry and suggests that *CB*'s missing annal was present in the exemplar for this text.

It is unfortunate that the bottom right-hand corner of RBH's fol. 125ʳ is missing, as this means there is a section that cannot be compared to the other witnesses. In this space, both *CB* and MS Peniarth 50 include four annals which may or may not have been in RBH. These record the death of Dafydd ap Gruffudd and the birth of Edward of Caernarfon in 1283, the campaign of Rhys ap Maredudd in 1287, the loss of Acre in 1291, and the execution of Rhys in 1292. As these annals occur in both other extant versions of *BE*, it seems safe to suggest that this lacuna in RBH may once have held these same four annals.

There is an omission of a single word in MS Peniarth 50, which could be significant. In annal 29, both *CB* and RBH record that 'ryuela6d ll brenn y

---

[31] MS Peniarth 50, p. 172.

[32] Compare RBH, fol. 125ʳ, col. 517: 'vn ul6ydyn ar|bymthec a|deucant a mil y bu vr6ydyr r6ng dauyd ap gruffud a|llywelyn', and MS Peniarth 50, p. 172: 'M ccxli y bu vr6ydyr r6g dd ap Gruff a llywelyn'.

[33] RBH, fol. 125ʳ, col. 517; MS Peniarth 50, p. 172; *CB*, fol. 57.

morgann6c' ('Llywelyn Bren waged war in Glamorgan'), but MS Peniarth 50 does not include the reference to Glamorgan. This could indicate that the scribe of MS Peniarth 50 chose to omit this because he did not deem it necessary to include the localization, perhaps because his audience would not need it. As it is likely that both *CB* and RBH were produced in or near Glamorgan, and that the text itself seems to have been southern, this further corroborates the argument of scholars such as Helen Fulton that MS Peniarth 50 was a manuscript compiled in Glamorgan by someone who had access to texts native to the region.[34]

Orthography

Each of the three versions renders the text in slightly different orthography, which could indicate the dialectal differences of the scribe, and perhaps help to localize the three manuscripts. The orthographies utilized in each manuscript are not hugely different. The differences occur mainly with proper nouns.

Where the orthography of personal and place names in RBH and MS Peniarth 50 uses common South Walian forms, some of the orthography of *CB* appears to indicate anglicized or Latinate forms, perhaps retained from one of the original sources.[35] One example of this is the rendering of Neath Castle, which is written 'kestyll neth' in *CB*, 'kestyll nethuet' in MS Peniarth 50 (both with an unnecessary plural form of *castell*), and 'castell ned' in RBH. The texts refer to Neath, a town which would have been local to both Siancyn and Hywel Fychan, and possibly to the scribe of MS Peniarth 50, who may have been working at Neath Abbey.[36] If the three versions of *BE* all derive from the same archetype independently, with MS Peniarth 50 and *CB* showing fewer deviations from the original than RBH, then the archetype must have originally followed the plural reading of 'kestyll'. Ben Guy has suggested that this points to a dependency, for this annal at least, on the version of *BT* found in RBH.[37] The same event in the RBH version of *BT* has the reading 'kestyll Ned', whereas the Peniarth 20 version has the singular form, 'kastell Ned'.[38] Thomas Jones explains

---

[34] Helen Fulton, 'The Geography of Welsh Literary Production in Late Medieval Glamorgan', *Journal of Medieval History*, 41.3 (2015), 325–40 (pp. 327–32).

[35] For more on the southern dialect of Middle Welsh, see Peter Wynn Thomas, 'Middle Welsh Dialects: Problems and Perspectives', *BBCS*, 40 (2006), 17–50.

[36] *RMWL*, I (1898), 389.

[37] Ben Guy, personal correspondence [23 November 2017].

[38] *BT (RB)*, pp. 228–29; MS Peniarth 20, pp. 254–57 <https://viewer.library.

the plural form in RBH as a misinterpretation of the same event as found in the *Cronica de Wallia*, a Latin chronicle of Wales covering the years 1190–1266, which likely represents the original reading of the Latin *BT*.[39] The Latin reads 'castella de Nech [read 'Neth'] et de Kedwelli [...]', using the plural to refer to the castles both at Neath and Kidwelly.[40] This would suggest that the reading of 'kestyll' in the RBH *BT* comes from a misinterpretation by a scribe who saw 'castella' as referring only to Neath, and it is likely that the plural form in *CB* and MS Peniarth 50 draws on this same misinterpretation of a Latinate form.

It seems, therefore, that the copyists working on *CB*, MS Peniarth 50, and RBH were copying from a Welsh version of a chronicle which had originally been written in a language which was not Welsh but probably Latin (particularly likely, given the presence of a Latin chronicle text earlier in *CB* and MS Peniarth 50 which bears some similarity to *BE*). However, it seems unlikely that Hywel Fychan, Siancyn, and the scribe of MS Peniarth 50 were independently translating an original non-extant chronicle, as the copies are too similar to allow for this possibility; one would expect differences in vocabulary and word order in three separate translations of the same text. Thus, it seems more likely that the three were working from a Welsh text which retained some Latinate forms and may have been dependent upon the RBH version of *BT*. In most cases, *CB* and MS Peniarth 50 have retained these forms, whilst Hywel Fychan has continued to act in the role of the modifying and modernizing scribe, choosing to prioritize comprehension for his audience over preserving an exact replica of the text. The other two versions, however, appear to be more concerned with preserving the original text as much as possible, only emending discreetly.

The Original Text

The earliest possible date for the composition of the original text is 1321, although it is likely that its sources could have been considerably earlier. It seems unlikely that this was a chronicle which was being added to continuously, due to its lack of chronological order. Instead, it seems more likely that the text was compiled from one or more other texts at some point in the fourteenth century,

---

wales/475463#?c = 0&m = 0&s = 0&cv = 260&xywh = 0%2C-47%2C1902%2C2753> [accessed 18 January 2019]; *BT (Pen. 20 trans.)*, p. 102.

[39] *BT (RB)*, pp. xli–xlii.

[40] *Annales Cambriae: The E Text*, p. 15, § e30.1.

prior to its incorporation into the Red Book of Hergest (*c.* 1400). Although one of these texts may have been in Latin — to account for the Latinate spellings found in *CB* — the first section, at least, seems to have drawn on a text which was written in Welsh.

The style of this first section is significantly different from the style of the second. Its opening lines detail the conquerors of Wales and the prophecies of Myrddin/Merlin, evocative of the openings of *Brut y Brenhinedd* and *BT*. The format of dating used in this section, which verbosely dates events in relation to the birth of Christ rather than giving the year in numerals, is also similar to that used in *BT*. The RBH version of *BT*, for example, begins 'Petwar ugeint mlyned a whe chant oed oet crist pan vu y uar6olyaeth ua6r [...]' and includes the prophecies of Myrddin in line 10.[41] A possible further indicator of Welsh origin for this section is the name given to William the Conqueror. In *BE* he is named as 'Wilem Bastart', a moniker used for the King only in Welsh and other non-Norman sources.[42] Although this does not mean that the text has to be of Welsh origin, only non-Norman, it makes a Welsh origin more probable than an Anglo-Norman or English one. Given the similarity of *BE* to the Welsh *Brut* texts, it seems likely to have been composed in a non-Anglo-Norman context.

In terms of geographical purview, *BE* covers the whole of Wales, and the events which do not take place in Wales involve the Welsh to a great degree. There are far fewer events which are particularly North Walian, and the focus seems to be on mid- and South Wales. The versions of the text discussed in this chapter are all found in manuscripts of Glamorgan, which could suggest that the text was mostly a southern one, with a limited circulation. However, several of the new versions of the text not discussed here (see footnote 10) are found in northern manuscripts and further investigation of these texts at a future date could illuminate the nature of *BE*'s transmission and circulation.

BE does not offer a very coherent or chronologically consistent survey of the twelfth to fourteenth centuries. The entries between 1171 and 1281 are not necessarily in chronological order. For example, the *CB*-text jumps from the taking of Neath Castle in 1230 to the breaking of the bridge at Carmarthen in 1218, and then to the death of Llywelyn ab Iorwerth in 1239 before returning to 1216 and the creation of the 'pregethwyr' ('preachers').[43] This indicates that

---

[41] *BT (RB)*, p. 2.

[42] David Bates, 'William I [*known as* William the Conqueror] (1027/8–1087)', in *Oxford Dictionary of National Biography* <https://doi.org/10.1093/ref:odnb/29448>.

[43] Interestingly, *BE*'s references to the taking of the bridge and to the death of Llywelyn

this section of *BE* is likely to have been compiled from one or more sources, rather than compiled chronologically over time. Furthermore, the inclusion of two separate versions of the same event supports the idea that this text was constructed from various different sources that may have been recording the same events. The later section, which proceeds chronologically from 1281 to 1321, may have been recorded contemporaneously in one of *BE*'s sources, or it may have been original to *BE*.

Both *CB* and MS Peniarth 50 contain a Latin text, called *Chronology and Annals* by the *Repertory*, which shares some of the events found in *BE*.[44] In *CB* this text occurs on fols 41ʳ–42ᵛ (thirteen texts before *BE*), and in MS Peniarth 50 it is the text directly preceding *BE*.[45] The Latin text is not a direct translation of the annals, but in both manuscripts it ends with the death of Thomas of Lancaster. It is possible that this was one of the texts from which *BE* was derived. However, certain events which do occur in both are referred to using different terms; the Battle of Lewes, for example, is referred to by that name, rather than as the Battle of Offham, as in *BE*. *BE* also includes some events which are not present in the Latin texts. Thus, if it were indeed a source text for *BE*, it was not the only one.

There are instances of scribal error in all the witnesses. These are separative errors, which make it impossible for any of the witnesses to have been copied directly from any of the others. Several of these are the annals which are missing from one of the three copies; of the three copies, MS Peniarth 50 is the only one to include all the annals extant in the other two, but this manuscript is too late to have been an exemplar for either of the other versions. Furthermore, the Welsh dates that are utilized in RBH do not match the Roman numerals in either *CB* or MS Peniarth 50, meaning that it would not have been possible for either *CB* or MS Peniarth 50 to have been working with RBH as an exemplar.[46]

---

ab Iorwerth both occurred later than the text records. The breaking of the bridge mentioned in 1218 probably refers to William Marshall's battle at Carmarthen in 1223 (MS Peniarth 20, pp. 248–50 <https://viewer.library.wales/475463#?c = 0&m = 0&s = 0&cv = 254&xywh = -1%2C-54%2C1910%2C2763> [accessed 18 January 2019]; *BT (Pen. 20 trans.)*, p. 99). The death of Llywelyn ab Iorwerth occurred in April 1240, not 1239 (MS Peniarth 20, pp. 257–59 <https://viewer.library.wales/475463#?c = 0&m = 0&s = 0&cv = 263&xywh = -34%2C0%2C1849%2C2675> [accessed 18 January 2019]; *BT (Pen. 20 trans.)*, p. 103).

[44] Huws, s.n. NLW 5267B.

[45] NLW, MS 5267B, fols 41ʳ–42ᵛ; MS Peniarth 50, pp. 169–71.

[46] See the discussion above.

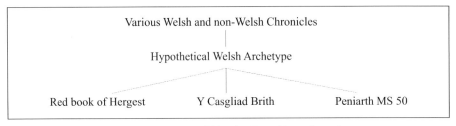

Figure 10.1: Stemma of *Blwydyn Eiseu*. Figure by author.

Thus, given the problematic nature of any argument based on the copying of Roman numerals, as discussed above, it seems safest to conclude that the three copyists were all working independently from the same exemplar. The exemplar may have been obscure in meaning or have suffered some damage, making it difficult to read in places, resulting in some of the scribal errors found in the three copies. The text itself was compiled and translated between 1321 and *c.* 1410, the *terminus ante quem* for the RBH. Of the three copies, *CB*'s copy could be argued to be closest to the exemplar, as it seems to have undergone less editing, whether through deliberate omission or through standardization of orthography. A stemma for the text should therefore be illustrated as in Figure 10.1.

Therefore, what we have here is a case of *recentiores, non deteriores*; despite not being the oldest copy, the copy in *CB* shows the fewest signs of scribal interference and as a result is probably closer to the archetype, although MS Peniarth 50 is arguably the most complete of the three. Reconstructing the archetype may be possible through a more in-depth comparison of the three versions, alongside an analysis of the possible influences — namely the version of *BT* in RBH and the Latin chronicle found in *CB* and MS Peniarth 50 — and the additional witnesses to the text recently identified in the National Library of Wales.[47] Ultimately, the above discussion has highlighted the importance of this previously unknown chronology, as well as shed some light on manuscript circulation and networks of medieval Glamorgan. It is clear that *BE* was drawing on other local texts and may indeed have influenced others. The discussion also provides further evidence for Rodway's argument that Hywel Fychan, the copyist of this section of RBH, was an editing scribe. Possible routes for further analysis of questions posed by this discussion are the correspondence between *BE* and its possible sources, as well as the interesting use of 'Offam' to refer to the Battle of Lewes. This forgotten Welsh chronology sits within the context of a great many Welsh chronicles and offers new insights into the development of chronicles and annals in South Wales during the Middle Ages.

[47] See above, n. 10.

Appendix A: Transcription and Translation of NLW, MS 5267B (CB), fols 56ᵛ–57ᵛ

Blwydyn Eiseu appears on fols 56ᵛ–57ᵛ and is bookended in the manuscript by *Py delw y dyly*, which takes up the preceeding three folios, and *Breuddwyd Pawl*, which occurs on the following two folios.

The text begins halfway down fol. 56ᵛ with a decorated initial 'B', which is interwoven with the large initial 'G' occuring towards the top of the page in *Py delw*. The decoration fills most of the left-hand margin and may once have been ornate, although this has now faded. The text has rubricated punctuation marks throughout.

There is an erased gloss at the bottom of fol. 57ʳ which is illegible. It appears to have been in a hand similar to that of the main scribe.

Word division follows that of the original manuscripts and is indicated with either a + or a | sign. A + sign indicates that the word begins at the end of one line and continues onto the next, whereas | is used to separate words which are written together in the manuscript but which would be separated today by either spaces or apostrophes.

1 **Bl6ydyn eiseu o deucant a phumil a vu o|r amser**
There were 5200 years but one from the time

2 **y g6naethp6yt adaf hyt yn deuth crist yngna6t**
that Adam was made until Christ came in man's flesh.

3 **dyn. m cc xxx kyn geni krist y deuth brutus y|r y+**
1230 years before the birth of Christ, Brutus came to

4 **nys honn a|thrychanllog yn la6n o niuer y gyt ac ef.**
this island with 300 ships filled by an army along with him.

5 **ac ef a vu o|lin ef gwedy ef petwar brenhin ar|dec**
And of his lineage after him there were 74 kings

6 **a|thrugeint kyn dyuot crist yngna6t. cccc x gwe+**
before Christ came in flesh. 410 after

7 **dy geni crist y proff6yda6d myrdin o acha6s ymlad**
the birth of Christ Myrddin prophesied about the fighting of

8 y dreigeu. gwedy dyuot hors a hengys y|r ynys honn
dragons after Hors and Hengist first came to this island

9 gyntaf a llad cccc tywyssa6c o|r bryttaneit yng|haer
and killed 400 princes of the Britons in Caer

10 garada6c tr6y d6yll. c lvi gwedy geni crist y herbyn+[48]
Caradoc through treachery. 156 after the birth of Christ

11 na6d y brytanyeit gristynogaeth yn oes lles vab koel
the Britons recieved Christianity in the age of Lles son of Coel

12 brenhin y brytanneit. Dcii mlyned gwedy geni crist
King of the Britons. 602 years after the birth of Christ

13 yd erbyna6d y saeson gristynogaeth y gan seint austin.
the Saxons recieved Christianity from St Augustine.

14 Ac ef a vu o anedigaeth du6 hyt at gatwaladyr
And there were from the birth of God to Cadwaladr

15 vendigeit tri brenhin ar dec ar|hugeint ol yn ol. Ac
the Blessed 33 successive kings. And

16 ef a vu o gatwaladyr vendigeit hyt at wilym bas+
there were from Cadwaladr the Blessed to William the Bastard

17 tart vgeint brenhin corona6c o saeson ol yn ol. A|thrych+
20 successive crowned kings of the English. And for 300

18 ant mlyned y buant yn tywyssya6 yr ynys. Mclxxi y llas
years they ruled the island. In 1171

19 thomas o gaer geint mc lxxxviii y bu y lladua yng|has+
Thomas of Canterbury was killed. In 1188 there was the slaughter at Painscastle.

20 tell paen mccxxx y kahat kestyll neth. mcc xviii y
In 1230 the castles of Neath were taken. In 1218

---

[48] End fol. 56ᵛ.

10. A FORGOTTEN WELSH CHRONOLOGY

21 torret pont gaer vyrdin. mcc xxxix y bu var6 ll ap
Carmarthen Bridge was broken. In 1239 Llywelyn ab

22 Ioruerth yn|g6yned. mcc x6i y g6naethp6yt creuyd y bro+
Iorwerth died in Gwynedd. In 1216 the order of the

23 dyr pr̄gethwyr. mcc li y bu y vr6ydyr r6ng dauid ap gr
preaching brothers was created. In 1251 was the battle between Dafydd ap Gruffudd

24 a ll. mcc xlvi y bu var6 dauid ap ll ac y doeth y llu
and Llywelyn. In 1246 Dafydd ap Llywelyn died and the black host came.

25 du Mcc xlvii y cryna6d y dayar. mccl y bu y haf
In 1247 the earth shook. In 1250 was the hot summer.

26 tessa6c. mc[c]lvi[49] y bu y lladua yn y kymereu. mcclx
In 1256 was the slaughter at Cymerau. In 1260

27 y kahat kastell buellt. mcclxv y bu y lladua yn
the castle of Builth was taken. In 1265 was the slaughter at

28 offam mcclxvii y rodes ll ap Gruffuth p6mmil ar
Offham. In 1267 Llywelyn ap Gruffudd gave 25,000

29 hugeint o vorkeu y edwart vrehin a|e 6rogaeth.
marks and his homage to King Edward.[50]

30 mcc lx6iii yd|aeth Edward vrēhin y acrys. mcc
In 1268 King Edward went to Acre. In 1275

31 lxxv y cryna6d y daear yr eilweith. mcclxx6iii y
the Earth shook for the second time. In 1278

32 symuda6d y vath a dorrit. mcclxxxii y llas ll ap
the mint that had been broken was moved. In 1282 Llywelyn ap

---

[49] The manuscript here reads 'mc lvi', which appears to be a scribal error. It should read 'mcclvi', so the second 'c' has been supplied by the editor.

[50] It should be noted that it was with King Henry III that Llywelyn ap Gruffudd made the Treaty of Montgomery in 1267, and not his son Edward I.

33 gruffuth tywyssa6c kymry. mcclxxxiii y dihenydy+
Gruffudd, Prince of Wales, was killed. In 1283

34 6yt dauid yn am6ythic a|r vl6ydyn honno y ganet
Dafydd was executed in Shrewsbury, and in that year was born

35 edwart yn y gaer yn aruon. mcc lxxxi y ryuela6d
Edward in Caernarfon. In 1281

36 Res ap Mereduth mcclxxxvii y collet acrys. mcc[51]
Rhys ap Maredudd waged war. In 1287 Acre was lost. In 1292

37 lxxxxii y merthyr6yt Rees. mcclxxxxvi y reuela6d mada6c
Rhys was cruelly put to death. In 1296 Madog

38 ap ll ac y kysegr6yt dauid. mcclxxxx6iii y bu y lladua va+
ap Llywelyn waged war and Dafydd was consecrated. In 1298 there was the great slaughter

39 6r ar yr yscotyeit. mcccvi y bu var6 edwart hen ac y kyse+
of the Scots. In 1306 the elder Edward died and his son was

40 gr6yt y vab. mcccxii y llas pyrs o ga6ston. mcccxii y bu
anointed. In 1312 Piers Gaveston was killed. In 1312 was

41 y lladua ar y saeson yn ystrilig yn y gogled ac y llas iarll
the slaughter of the English at Stirling in the north and the Earl

42 clar. mcccxv y ryuela6d ll brenn y morgann6c. mcccxviii
of Clare was killed. In 1315 Llywelyn Bren waged war in Glamorgan. In 1318

43 y rodes y brenhin y cantref ma6r y hu spenser ieuang mcc
the King gave Cantref Mawr to Hugh Spencer the Younger.

44 cxxi y pan thomas o lancastyr
1321 was when Thomas of Lancaster [was killed].[52]

---

[51] End fol. 57ʳ.

[52] For this annal, see the discussion above, pp. 352–53.

Appendix B: Transcription and translation of MS Peniarth 50, pp. 171–73

1 Bly6ddyn eisseu o ddeucant a phum mil a
There were 5200 [years] but one

2 6u or amser y gwnaethp6yt addaf yny
from the time that Adam was made until

3 ddeuth crist yngnawt dyn. M ccxxx kyn
Christ came in man's flesh. 1230 [years] before

4 geni crist y deuth Brutus y|r ynys hon a thry+
the birth of Christ, Brutus came to this island with 300

5 can llog yn lla6n o niuer gyt ac ef. Ac ef a vu
ships filled by an army along with him. And of his

6 gwedy ef o|e lin ef petwar brenhin a|ddec a thru+
lineage after him there were 74 kings

7 geint kyn dyuot Crist yngna6t. Ccccx mlyned
before Christ came in flesh. 410 years after

8 gwedy geni Crist y prof6yda6dd myrddin o acha6s
the birth of Christ Myrddin prophesied about

9 ymladd y dreigeu g6edy dyvot hors a hengist y|r[53]
the fighting of dragons after Hors and Hengist first came to this

10 y|r ynys hon gyntaf a lladd. cccc tywyssa6c o|r bruta+
island and killed 400 princes of the Britons

11 nyeit yg kaer garada6c dr6y d6yll. clvi gwedy ge+
in Caer Caradoc through treachery. 156 after the

12 ni Crist yt erbynya6dd y brytanyeit gristynogaeth yn
birth of Christ the Britons recieved Christianity in

---

[53] End p. 171.

13 oes lles vab coel brenhin y brytanyeit. Dcii 6ly+
the age of Lles son of Coel King of the Britons. 602 years

14 nedd gwedy geni Crist yd erbynna6dd y ssaesson gristo+
after the birth of Christ the Saxons recieved Christianity

15 nogaeth y gan Seint Austin. Ef a vu o anediga+
from St Augustine. There were from the birth

16 eth Crist hyt at Gatwaladyr vendigeit tri brenhin ar
of Christ to Cadwaladr the Blessed 33 successive kings.

17 ddec ar|ugeint ol yn ol. Ef a vu o katwaladyr ven
There were from Cadwaladr the Blessed

18 digeit hyt at wilim Bastart ugein brenhin coronoa6c
to William the Bastard 20 successive crowned kings

19 o|r saesson olynol. A|thrycant mlyned y buon yn ty+
of the Saxons. And for 300 years they ruled

20 wyssa6 yr ynys. M lxxi y llas Thomas o gaer
the island. In 1071 Thomas of Canterbury

21 geint. M c lxxx6iii y bu y lladua yg castell paen.
was killed. In 1188 there was the slaughter at Painscastle.

22 M ccxviii y torret pont kaer veyrdin. M cc
In 1218 Carmarthen Bridge was broken.

23 xxx y kahad kestyll nethuet. M ccxxxix y
In 1230 the castles of Neath were taken. In 1239

24 bu var6 lln ap ioruth yg6y. m ccx6i y gwnaeth
Llywelyn ap Iorwerth died in Gwynedd. In 1216 the

25 p6yt creuydd y brodyr p. m ccxli y bu vr6ydyr
order of the preaching brothers was created. In 1241 there was a battle

26 r6g dd ap Gruff a llywelyn. M ccxlvi y bu
between Dafydd ap Gruffudd and Llywelyn. In 1246

10. A FORGOTTEN WELSH CHRONOLOGY

27 var6 dd ap ll ac y doeth y llu du. M ccxl6ii y cry+
Dafydd ap Llywelyn died and the black host came. In 1247 the

28 na6d y ddaear. M ccl y bu vr6ydyr r6g ll ap
earth shook. In 1250 there was a battle between Llywelyn ap

29 Gruff ae vrod. M cclii y bu yr haf tessa6c.
Gruffudd and his brothers. In 1252 was the hot summer.

30 M cclvi y bu y llatua yn y kymereu. M cclx
In 1256 was the slaughter at Cymerau. In 1260

31 y kahat kastell buellt. M cclxv y bu y lladua
the castle of Builth was taken. In 1265 was the slaughter

32 yn Offam. M cclxvii y roddes ll ap Grufft
at Offham. In 1267 Llywelyn ap Gruffudd

33 pum mil ar|ugeint o vorkeu y Ed vrenhin a|e wra+
gave 25,000 marks to King Edward and his wife.

34 ged. M cclxviii yt aeth Ed vrenhin y acrys.
In 1268 King Edward went to Acre.

35 M cclxx6 y cryna6dd y ddaear yr eilweith. M
In 1275 the Earth shook for the second time.

36 cclxviii y symuda6dd y vath a dorrit. Mcc[54]
In 1268 the mint that had been broken was moved.

37 lxxxii y llas ll ap Grufft tywyssa6c kymry.
In 1282 Llywelyn ap Gruffudd, Prince of Wales, was killed.

38 M cclxxxiii y dihenyddy6yt dd yn am6ythic
In 1283 Dafydd was executed in Shrewsbury,

39 A|r vl6yddyn honno y ganet Edward yn y gaer
and in that year was born Edward in

---

[54] End p. 172.

40 yn aruon. M cclxxxvii y Ryela6d Rys ap
Caernarfon. In 1287 Rhys ap

41 medyth. M cclxxxxi y collet Acrys. M cc
Maredudd waged war. In 1291 Acre was lost.

42 lxxxxii y merthyr6yt Rys. M cclxxxxvi
In 1292 Rhys was cruelly put to death. In 1296

43 y ryuela6dd mad ap ll ac y kyssegr6yt dd. M
Madog ap Llywelyn waged war and Dafydd was consecrated.

44 cclxxxxviii y bu llatua va6r ar y|scotyeit.
In 1298 there was the great slaughter of the Scots.

45 M cccvii y bu var6 Edward hen ac y kysse+
In 1307 the elder Edward died and

46 gr6yt y vab. M cccxii y llas prys o ga6st6n.
his son was annointed. In 1312 Piers Gaveston was killed.

47 M cccxiiii y bu y lladdua ar y saesson yn ys+
In 1314 was the slaughter of the English at

48 triflig yn y gogledd ac y llas iarll clar. M ccc
Stirling in the north and the Earl of Clare was killed. In

49 x6 y bu ryuel ll bren. M cccxviii y rodes
1315 Llywelyn Bren waged war. In 1318

50 y brenhin y Cantref ma6r y hu spenser ieuank
the King gave Cantref Mawr to Hugh Spencer the Younger.

51 M cccxxi dat pan las Thomas o lancastyl.
1321 was when Thomas of Lancaster was killed.

Appendix C: Dates Comparison

The table on the following pages shows a comparison of the dates in the three primary witnesses to *Blwydyn Eiseu*.

Table 10.3: A comparison of the dates in the three primary witnesses to *Blwydyn Eiseu*

No.	*CB*	Date	RBH
1	Mclxxi y llas thomas o gaer geint	1171	Un vl6ydyn ar|dec ar hugeint a|chant a|mil y|llas thomas o|gaer geint.
2	mc lxxxviii y bu y lladua yng|hastell paen	1188	Wyth mlyned a|phedwar ugeint a|chant a|mil y bu y|lladua yg|kastel paen
3	mccxxx y kahat kestyll neth	1230	Deng mlyned ar|hugeint a|deucant a|mil y kahat kastell ned
4	mcc xviii y torret pont gaer vyrdin	1218	Teir blyned a|thrugeint a|deucant a mil y|tor·ret pont kaer vyrdin
5	mcc xxxix y bu var6 ll ap Ioruerth yn|g6yned	1239	Pedeir blyned ar|bymthec ar|hugeint a|deucant a|mil y|bu uar6 ll6elyn ab Jorwoerth yg g6yned
6	mcc x6i y g6naethp6yt creuyd y brodyr p^rgethwyr	1216	Not in RBH
7	mcc li y bu y vr6ydyr r6ng dauid ap gr a ll	1251	vn ul6ydyn ar|bymthec a|deucant a mil y bu y vr6ydyr r6ng dauyd ap gruffud a|llywelyn
8	mcc xlvi y bu var6 dauid ap ll ac y doeth y llu du	1246	Chwe blyned a deugeint a|deucant a|mil y bu uar6 dauyd ap llywelyn. ac y|doeth y llu du
9	Mcc xlvii y cryna6d y dayar	1247	Seith mlyned a|deugeint a|deucant a|mil y cryna6d y|dayar.
10	Not in *CB*		Deng mlyned a|deugeint a|deucant a|mil y bu vr6ydyr r6ng llywelyn ab gruffud a|e vrodyr

[55] *Annales Cambriae: The C Text, from British Library Cotton MS Domitian A. i. ff. 138r–155r*, ed. by Henry W. Gough-Cooper (Welsh Chronicles Research Group, 2015), p. 51 (c568.1) <http://croniclau.bangor.ac.uk/documents/AC%20C%20first%20edition.pdf> [accessed 4 April 2018].

10. A FORGOTTEN WELSH CHRONOLOGY

Date	MS Peniarth 50	Date	Date corroboration
1131	M lxxi y llas Thomas o gaer geint	1071	1171, *BT*.
1188	M c lxxx6iii y bu y lladua yg castell paen	1188	1198, *BT*.
1230	M cc xxx y kahad kestyll nethuet	1230	Neath Castle razed by Llywelyn the Great in 1231, *BT*.
1263	M ccxviii y torret pont kaer ve^yrdin	1218	Probably William Marshall's battle at Carmarthen Bridge against Gruffudd ap Llywelyn in 1223, *BT*.
1239	Mccxxxix y bu var6 ll ap ioruth yg6y	1239	1240, *BT*.
	M ccx6i y gwnaethp6yt creuydd y brodyr p	1216	The Dominican Order, also known as the Order of Preachers (Latin *Ordo Praedicatorum*), was approved by Pope Honorius III in 1216.
1216	m ccxli y bu vr6ydyr r6g dd ap Gruff a llywelyn	1241	In 1241, Dafydd would have only been three years old, so it seems unlikely that this is the correct date. 1251 is more likely, although he was only 13 in 1251, and the first recorded 'battle' between the brothers was Bryn Derwin in 1255. It is not unlikely that there was contention before this time.
1246	m ccxlvi y bu var6 dd ap ll ac y doeth y llu du	1246	Dafydd ap Llywelyn died in 1246, *BT*.
1247	M ccxl6ii y cryna6d y ddaear	1247	*Annales Cambriae* C, s.a. 1247: 'Terremotus magnus fuit in britannnía et ybernía . quo terremotu magna pars ecclesie meneuensis . corruít . et plura edificia in patria . et rupes scisse sunt . xi°. kalendas martíí.'⁵⁵
1250	M ccl y bu vr6ydyr r6g ll ap Gruff ae vrod	1250	This cannot be corroborated exactly, but by 1250 Llywelyn had been ruling Gwynedd with his brother Owain for four years, and with three brothers it is not unlikely that there was contention in 1250.

Table continued on the following page

Table 10.3 *(cont.)*: A comparison of the dates in the three primary witnesses to *Blwydyn Eiseu*.

No.	*CB*	Date	RBH
11	mccl y bu y haf tessa6c	1250	D6y ulyned a deucant a mil y bu yr haf tessa6c
12	mc[c]lvi y bu y lladua yn y kymereu	1256	Ch6e blyned a|deugeint a|deucant a|mil y bu y|lladua yn|y kymereu
13	mcclx y kahat kastell buellt	1260	Trugein mlyned a|deucant a|mil y|kahat castell
14	mcclxv y bu y lladua yn offam	1265	Not in RBH
15	mcclxvii y rodes ll ap Gruffuth p6mmil ar hugeint o vorkeu y edwart vrehin a|e 6rogaeth	1267	Pump mlyned a|thrugeint a deucant a|mil y rodes llywelyn ab gruffud pump mil ar hugeint o vorkeu y etwart urenhin a|e 6rogaeth
16	mcc lx6iii yd|aeth Edward vrēhin y acrys	1268	Wyth mlyned ar|hugeint a|deucant a|mil. yd|aeth etwart urenhin y ackrys
17	mcclxxv y cryna6d y daear yr eilweith	1275	Pymthec mlyned a|thrugeint a|deucant a mil. y|cryna6d y|dayar yr eilweith
18	mcclxx6iii y symuda6d y vath a dorrit	1278	Not in RB
19	mcclxxxii y llas ll ap gruffuth tywyssa6c kymry	1282	Dwy ulyned ar|bymthec a|thrugeint a|deucant mil. y llas llywelyn ab gruffud kymry
20	mcclxxxiii y dihenydy6yt dauid yn am6ythic a|r vl6ydyn honno y ganet edwart yn y gaer yn aruon	1283	Legibility in RBH impaired
21	mcc lxxxi y ryuela6d Res ap Mereduth	1281	

---

[56] *The Acts of Welsh Rulers 1120–1283*, ed. by Huw Pryce (Cardiff: University of Wales Press, 2005), nos 363, 378, 380.

10. A FORGOTTEN WELSH CHRONOLOGY

Date	MS Peniarth 50	Date	Date corroboration
202	m cclii y bu yr haf tessa6c	1252	1252, *BT*. It seems that the date in *CB* was a scribal error made by Siancyn.
246	m cclvi y bu y llatua yn y kymereu	1256	1256, *BT*.
260	m cclx y kahat kastell buellt	1260	Llywelyn ap Gruffudd took the castle at Builth in 1260, *BT*.
	M cclxv y bu y lladua yn Offam	1265	The Battle of Lewes was in 1264, *BT*.
265	m cclxvii y roddes ll ap Gruff pum mil ar|ugeint o vorkeu y Ed[ward] vrenhin ae wraged	1267	It is possible that this refers to the events prior to the Treaty of Montgomery, *BT*. Although the treaty was contracted between Llywelyn and Henry III, most of the 25,000 marks was not paid by the time of Henry's death in 1272. 5000 were meant to be paid in the first year, and 3000 each subsequent year, but Llywelyn was certainly in arrears by 1273.[56]
228	M cclxviii yt aeth Ed vrenhin y acrys	1268	In 1268 Edward began raising troops and funds for the Ninth Crusade, travelling towards Acre.
275	M cclxx6 y cryna6dd y ddaear yr eilweith	1275	1275, *BT*.
	M cclxviii y symuda6dd y vath a dorrit	1268	1279, *BT*. The difference here may be the result of the use of a March to March calendar. MS Peniarth 50 is missing an additional *x*, probably scribal error.
277	Mcclxxxii y llas ll ap Gruff tywyssa6c kymry	1282	1282, *BT*. The error in RBH is difficult to determine.
	M cclxxxiii y dihenyddy6yt dd yn am6ythic. A|r vl6yddyn honno y ganet Edward yn y gaer yn aruon	1283	1283, *BT*.
	Mcclxxxvii y Ryela6d Rys ap medyth	1287	1287; *BT*. Error likely scribal in *CB*.

Table continued on the following page

Table 10.3 *(cont.)*: A comparison of the dates in the three primary witnesses to *Blwydyn Eiseu*.

No.	*CB*	Date	RBH
22	mcclxxxvii y collet acrys	1287	
23	mcclxxxxii y merthyr6yt Rees	1292	
24	mcclxxxxvi y reuela6d mada6c ap ll ac y kysegr6yt dauid	1296	vn vl6ydyn ar bymthec a phedwar ugeint a deucant a|mil. y ryuela6d mada6c uab llywelyn
25	mcclxxxx6iii y bu y lladua va6r ar yr yscotyeit	1298	Teir blyned ar|bymthec a|phedwar ugeint a deucant a|mil y|bu y lladua ua6r ar yr yscottyeit
26	mcccvi y bu var6 edwart hen ac y kysegr6yt y vab	1306	Seith mlyned a|thrychant a|mil. y bu uar6 hen edwart. ac y|kyssegr6yt y uab
27	mcccxii y llas pyrs o ga6ston	1312	Deudeg mlyned a|thrychant y|llas pyrs o garst6n
28	mcccxii y bu y lladua ar y saeson yn ystrilig yn y gogled ac y llas iarll clar	1312	Pedeir blyned ar|dec a|thrychant a mil y bu y lladua ar y|saeson yn ystriflin yn|y gogled. ac y llas iarll clar.
29	mcccxv y ryuela6d ll brenn y morgann6c	1315	Pymtheg mlyned a|thrychant a mil y ryuela6d llywelyn brenn ym morgann6c
30	mcccxviii y rodes y brenhin y cantref ma6r y hu spenser ieuang	1318	Teir blyned ar|bymthec a|thrychant a|mil. y rodes y brenhin y kantref ma6r y|hu y sp6nsaer ieuanc. ~ ~ ~
31	mcccxxi y pan thomas o lancastyr	1321	Not in RBH

[57] See Robert T. Jenkins, 'Rhys ap Maredudd (d. 1292), lord of Dryslwyn in Ystrad Tywi', in *Dictionary of Welsh Biography* <https://biography.wales/article/s1-RHYS-APM-1291> [accessed 15 March 2019].

[58] See Thomas Jones Pierce, 'Madog ap Llywelyn, Rebel of 1294', in *Dictionary of Welsh Biography* <https://biography.wales/article/s-MADO-APL-1294> [accessed 15 March 2019].

[59] See *Fasti Ecclesiae Anglicanae 1066-1300. Volume 9: The Welsh Cathedrals (Bangor, Llandaff, St Asaph, St Davids)*, ed. by M. J. Pearson (London: Institute of Historical Research, 2003), pp. 45–50. Available online: <http://www.british-history.ac.uk/fasti-ecclesiae/1066-1300/vol9> [accessed 9 June 2018].

Date	MS Peniarth 50	Date	Date corroboration
	M cclxxxxi y collet Acrys	1291	In 1291 the city of Acre fell to the Saracens. As this was the last city in the Holy Land remaining in Christian hands, its loss signalled the end not just of the Ninth Crusade but arguably of the Crusades as a whole.
	M cclxxxxii a merthyr6yt Rys	1292	Rhys ap Maredudd, died 1292.[57] Note the interesting use here of the verb *merthyr6yt*, the primary meaning of which is 'was martyred'.
1296	M cclxxxxvi y ryuela6dd mad ap ll ac y kyssegr6yt dd	1296	This refers to Madog ap Llywelyn, who led the revolt of 1294–1295.[58] The *dauid* is probably the David Martin who was consecrated as Bishop of St Davids in 1296.[59]
1298	M cclxxxxviii y bu llatua va6r ar y|scotyeit	1298	The Battle of Falkirk was fought in 1298.
1307	M cccvii y bu var6 Edward hen ac y kyssegr6yt y vab	1307	The King died in 1307, *BT*. The error in *CB* is likely scribal.
1312	M cccxii y llas prys o ga6st6n	1312	1312; *BT*.
1314	M cccxiiii y bu y lladdua ar y saesson yn ystriflig yn y gogledd ac y llas iarll clar	1314	1314; Battle of Bannockburn at Stirling Castle.
1315	M cccx6 y bu ryuel ll bren	1315	1315; *BT*.
1318	M cccxviii y rodes y brenhin y Cantref ma6r y hu spenser ieuank	1318	Hugh Despenser killed Llywelyn Bren in 1318 and was made royal chamberlain in the same year. He was also granted the lordship of Cantref Mawr.
	M cccxxi dat pan las Thomas o lancastyl	1321	1321; *BT*.

11. *Brut Ieuan Brechfa*: A Welsh Poet Writes the Early Middle Ages

Ben Guy

In the second volume of the *Myvyrian Archaiology of Wales*, published in 1801, Owen Jones (alias 'Owain Myfyr') and his colleagues printed six vernacular texts bearing the title *Brut*, which purported to reproduce various pieces of historical prose from surviving medieval Welsh manuscripts.[1] This was the first major modern attempt to publish historical works written in medieval Welsh, and, considering the magnitude of the enterprise, the editors achieved their goal commendably. Although some of the texts were later found to contain substantial interpolations by the infamous antiquarian and literary forger Edward Williams (alias 'Iolo Morganwg'), the *Myvyrian Archaiology* at least succeeded in placing before a general readership important versions of the two most influential historical accounts produced in medieval Wales: *Brut y Brenhinedd* (the Welsh translation and adaptation of Geoffrey of Monmouth's *De gestis Britonum*, commonly known as *Historia regum Britanniae*) and *Brut y Tywysogyon* (the 'Chronicle of the Princes', a well-known annalistic chronicle surviving in multiple versions).[2] But in doing so, the *Myvyrian Archaiology* left

---

[1] *MA*, II (1801), 81–582; repr. as *MA²*, pp. 432–720. All further references to the *Myvyrian Archaiology* are to the 1870 single-volume edition (*MA²*).

[2] For Iolo Morganwg's approach to historical matters, see Prys Morgan, 'Iolo Morganwg and Welsh Historical Traditions', in *A Rattleskull Genius: The Many Faces of Iolo Morganwg*, ed. by Geraint H. Jenkins (Cardiff: University of Wales Press, 2005), pp. 251–68. For the context of the publication of Iolo's forgeries, see Geraint Phillips, 'Forgery and Patronage: Iolo Morganwg and Owain Myfyr', in *A Rattleskull Genius*, ed. by Jenkins, pp. 403–23. For the reception of Iolo's forgeries in the nineteenth and early twentieth century, see Marion Löffler, *The Literary and Historical Legacy of Iolo Morganwg, 1826–1926* (Cardiff: University of Wales Press, 2007), ch. 4 (pp. 82–83 for the *Myvyrian Archaiology*). For an introduction to *Brut y*

behind an enduring conundrum for those who strive to understand the conception and transmission of historical ideas, for all too often the relationship between the texts filling its voluminous pages and the medieval manuscripts claimed as its sources is difficult to define precisely.

Two of the *Myvyrian Archaiology*'s six *Brutiau* were versions of *Brut y Brenhinedd*: one entitled *Brut Tysilio*, taken from Oxford, Jesus College, MS 28, and the other entitled *Brut Gruffudd ab Arthur*, a composite text taken from many sources.[3] The other four were versions of *Brut y Tywysogyon*.[4] The first, entitled *Brut y Tywysogion*, reproduces the important version in the Red Book of Hergest, with variants from David Powel's 1584 *Historie of Cambria* and from a manuscript closely related to Aberystwyth, NLW, MS Llanstephan 172.[5] The second, entitled *Brut y Saeson*, was the version of *Brut y Tywysogyon* now known as *Brenhinedd y Saesson*, taken from its earliest manuscript, London, BL, MS Cotton Cleopatra B V.[6] The final two, entitled *Brut y Tywysogion* and *Brut Ieuan Brechfa*, lack the respectable credentials of the others. The first of these, known otherwise as *Brut Aberpergwm* or the 'Gwentian Chronicle', is teeming with late interpolations, as was demonstrated as early as 1858 by Thomas Stephens, and transpired to be largely the concoc-

---

Brenhinedd, see Patrick Sims-Williams, *Rhai Addasiadau Cymraeg Canol o Sieffre o Fynwy* (Aberystwyth: University of Wales Centre for Advanced Welsh and Celtic Studies, 2010); this can be found abbreviated and translated into English, with additions and corrections, as Patrick Sims-Williams, 'The Welsh Versions of Geoffrey of Monmouth's "History of the Kings of Britain"', in *Adapting Texts and Styles in a Celtic Context: Interdisciplinary Perspectives on Processes of Literary Transfer in the Middle Ages. Studies in Honour of Erich Poppe*, ed. by Axel Harlos and Neele Harlos (Münster: Nodus Publikationen, 2016), pp. 53–74. For *Brut y Tywysogyon*, see now Owain Wyn Jones, '*Brut y Tywysogion*: The History of the Princes and Twelfth-Century Cambro-Latin Historical Writing', *HSJ*, 26 (2014), 209–27.

[3] Brynley F. Roberts, 'Brut Gruffudd ab Arthur', *BBCS*, 24 (1970–72), 14–23; cf. *Brut Dingestow*, ed. by Henry Lewis (Cardiff: University of Wales Press, 1942), p. xix. For *Brut Tysilio*, see Brynley F. Roberts, *Brut Tysilio* (Swansea: University College of Swansea, 1980).

[4] For a summary of the four versions of *Brut y Tywysogyon* in the *Myvyrian Archaiology*, see *BT (Pen. 20 trans.)*, pp. xxvii–xxviii.

[5] *BT (RB)*, pp. xiii–xvii.

[6] *BS*, p. xv. The text misleadingly called '*Brut y Saeson*' in the *Myvyrian Archaiology* is not to be confused with the text to which the name *Brut y Saesson* is applied in the manuscripts, the version of which preserved in the Red Book of Hergest was published in *The Text of the Bruts from the Red Book of Hergest*, ed. by John Rhŷs and J. Gwenogvryn Evans (Oxford: Evans, 1890), pp. 385–403. See Egerton Phillimore, 'The Publication of Welsh Historical Records', *Y Cymmrodor*, 11 (1890–1), 133–75 (pp. 160–61 n. 3); *Text of the Bruts*, p. xxiii; *BS*, p. xxv.

tion of Iolo Morganwg.⁷ The second, *Brut Ieuan Brechfa*, has likewise been treated with suspicion, though it has hitherto lacked any detailed critical treatment. Instead, it has been consigned to footnotes and offhand remarks, which generally follow the tenor of Thomas Jones's statement that '*Brut Ieuan Brechfa* shows signs of being a similar forgery by Iolo Morganwg'.⁸

The purpose of the present chapter is to show that, whilst Iolo Morganwg certainly interpolated his own material into the *Myvyrian Archaiology* text of *Brut Ieuan Brechfa*, the text is by no means a complete forgery, and nor is its claimed connection with Ieuan Brechfa a figment of Iolo Morganwg's undoubtedly overactive imagination. Three other manuscripts, one of the sixteenth century and two of the eighteenth, all bear witness to this. Each of these three manuscripts, it is argued, derives from the same lost manuscript by Ieuan Brechfa, probably written in the decades around 1500. The chronicle in Ieuan Brechfa's manuscript was essentially a reproduction of the Red Book version of *Brut y Tywysogyon* for the years 720 to 1079, supplemented by various other sources, including genealogies, a law manuscript, and a chronicle of the *Annales Cambriae* family. Whilst the importance of Ieuan Brechfa's chronicle as a direct witness to events of the early Middle Ages is limited, its interest as a product of the historical scholarship of a poet of South Wales in the early Tudor period is great, and it should rank alongside the comparable works of Ieuan Brechfa's more prolific North Walian contemporary, Gutun Owain.⁹

---

⁷ Thomas Stephens, 'The Book of Aberpergwm, improperly called The Chronicle of Caradoc', *Archaeologia Cambrensis*, 3rd ser., 4, no. 13 (1858), 77–96; John Edward Lloyd, *The Welsh Chronicles* (London: Humphrey Milford, 1928), pp. 10–11; Griffith John Williams, 'Brut Aberpergwm: A Version of the Chronicle of the Princes', *Glamorgan Historian*, 4 (1967), 205–20. For the context of Stephens's work, see Löffler, *The Literary and Historical Legacy*, pp. 134–37.

⁸ *BT (Pen. 20 trans.)*, p. xxxiv n. 2; similarly on p. xiii. Cf. John Edward Lloyd, 'Geoffrey of Monmouth', *English Historical Review*, 57 (1942), 460–68 (p. 462, 'the jejune "Brut Ieuan Brechfa"'); *BT (RB)*, p. xiv n. 1; Griffith John Williams, *Iolo Morganwg* (Cardiff: University of Wales Press, 1956), p. 308; Thomas Jones, 'Historical Writing in Medieval Welsh', *Scottish Studies*, 12 (1968), 15–27 (p. 16); David Ewan Thornton, 'Locusts in Ireland? A Problem in the Welsh and Frankish Annals', *CMCS*, 31 (1996), 37–53 (p. 41); David Ewan Thornton, *Kings, Chronologies and Genealogies: Studies in the Political History of Early Medieval Ireland and Wales* (Oxford: Unit for Prosopographical Research, Linacre College, 2003), p. 11; Phillips, 'Forgery and Patronage', p. 419; Löffler, *The Literary and Historical Legacy*, p. 80; Ffion Mair Jones, *"The Bard is a Very Singular Character": Iolo Morganwg, Marginalia and Print Culture* (Cardiff: University of Wales Press, 2010), p. 26. Nonetheless, G. J. Williams ('Brut Aberpergwm', p. 209) was prepared to allow that Ieuan Brechfa really wrote a chronicle of some kind.

⁹ For Gutun Owain's historical writing, see Huw Pryce, Chapter 1, above.

The Manuscripts

At the beginning of the *Myvyrian Archaiology* copy of *Brut Ieuan Brechfa*, there appears the following statement about the source of the work:[10]

> Brut Ieuan Brechfa [...] a dynnwyd o lyfrau Caradawc Llancarfan ac eraill o hen lyfrau cyfarwyddyd. A ysgrifenodd Ieuan Brechfa. O Lyfr Rhys Thomas Argraphydd.
>
> *Brut Ieuan Brechfa* [...] taken from the books of Caradog of Llancarfan and other old history books. Ieuan Brechfa wrote it. From the book of Rhys Thomas, Printer.

Similarly, at the end of the text is the following statement:[11]

> O Lyfr Ieuan Brechfa, gan Rhys Thomas, Argraffydd, o'r Bont Faen ym Morganwg, 1780.
>
> From the Book of Ieuan Brechfa, in the possession of Rhys Thomas, Printer, from Cowbridge in Glamorgan, 1780.

Judging by these statements, the *Myvyrian Archaiology* text was taken ultimately from a transcript, made in 1780, of a certain *Llyfr Ieuan Brechfa* then in the possession of the printer Rhys Thomas. There was, however, at least one intermediary stage, because the immediate source for the *Myvyrian Archaiology*'s text of *Brut Ieuan Brechfa* (including the notice of Rhys Thomas's *Llyfr Ieuan Brechfa*) was a manuscript in the hand of Iolo Morganwg: Aberystwyth, NLW, MS 13121B (Llanover C 34), pages 24–36.[12] On page 36 of the latter manuscript, one finds more information about the source of the text than is printed in the *Myvyrian Archaiology*. At the beginning of the source was allegedly the title 'Llyfr Cyfarwyddyd ar achoedd, a buadau, a dosparthau Cerdd Dafod' ('The book of history and genealogies, and past events, and classifications of poetry'). Ieuan Brechfa then apparently gave his own genealogy back two generations ('Ieuan Brechfa ab Ierwerth ab Llywelyn'), in addition to the pedigrees of his paternal grandmother Gwenllian and other female ancestresses. He went on to explain that Henry VIII had given him 'awdurdawd mewn ysgrifen' ('authority in writing') to keep the genealogies of the noblemen of Wales in his 'llyfrau yn warantedig' ('authorized books'). G. J. Williams rightly dismissed much of this

---

[10] *MA²*, p. 716.

[11] *MA²*, p. 720.

[12] Williams, *Iolo Morganwg*, p. 398; *Handlist of Manuscripts in the National Library of Wales*, 9 vols (Aberystwyth: NLW, 1940–2003), IV (1962), 403.

as Iolo's invention; for example, the word *buadau* ('past events') seems to have been coined by Iolo himself, and so could not have appeared in a manuscript written by Ieuan Brechfa 300 years beforehand.[13] Williams was prepared to allow that many of the individual elements of *Brut Ieuan Brechfa* could have been drawn from historical fragments in manuscripts made known to Iolo by Rhys Thomas, and that some of these manuscripts may have contained various records, especially genealogies, linked to the name of Ieuan Brechfa, but he suggested that Iolo's decision to attribute the entire composition to Ieuan Brechfa rested ultimately on a statement by Lewys Dwnn.[14] Immediately before the text of *Brut Ieuan Brechfa* in Iolo's manuscript NLW, MS 13121B are a series of excerpts from Dwnn's works. Firstly, on pages 13–18 are the introductions to Dwnn's 1586 and 1606 works, as printed in Samuel Rush Meyrick's *Heraldic Visitations*.[15] Following these are two lists: one of those who had written about the genealogies and deeds of the Welsh, and the other of the authoritative poets who had written about Wales, both allegedly taken from another work of Lewys Dwnn. Third in the list of authoritative poets is Ieuan Brechfa, who is said to have written 'am dair Talaith Cymru' ('about the three provinces of Wales').[16] According to Williams, such a statement would have been enough to prompt Iolo to attribute a chronicle of his own devising to Ieuan Brechfa. Perhaps a similar process caused Iolo to credit Ieuan Brechfa with a role in the transmission of the *Myvyrian Archaiology*'s spurious 'third series' of triads.[17]

However, the plot is further complicated by the existence of another eighteenth-century copy of *Brut Ieuan Brechfa*, surviving in a manuscript written by Evan Evans.[18] The manuscript is now the first part (folios 1–14) of London, BL, MS Additional 15031, a collection of the papers of Owen Jones (Owain

---

[13] *Geiriadur Prifysgol Cymru Online* (Aberystwyth: University of Wales Centre for Advanced Welsh and Celtic Studies, 2014), s.v. buad <http://www.geiriadur.ac.uk> [accessed 10 October 2017].

[14] Williams, *Iolo Morganwg*, pp. 308, 398–99.

[15] Lewys Dwnn, *Heraldic Visitations of Wales and Part of the March between the Years 1586 and 1613, under the Authority of Clarencieux and Norroy, Two Kings at Arms*, ed. by Samuel Rush Meyrick, 2 vols (Llandovery: Rees, 1846), I, 7–10.

[16] Ieuan Brechfa is also listed in the preface to Dwnn's 1586 work, along with Gutun Owain and Hywel Swrdwal, as one of the three poets who had written 'am holl Ynys Prydain yn fanol' ('about the whole of the island of Britain in detail') in the generation preceding Dwnn's: *Heraldic Visitations*, I, 7–8.

[17] *MA²*, p. 411; Williams, *Iolo Morganwg*, pp. 395–97.

[18] *BT (RB)*, p. xxxv n. 1; Williams, *Iolo Morganwg*, p. 398 n. 18.

Myfyr). Folios 1ʳ–9ᵛ contain, in the words of Thomas Jones, 'garbled extracts from some corrupt and interpolated copy of RB [i.e. the Red Book of Hergest version of *Brut y Tywysogyon*]'.[19] A substantial amount of the text is identical to that of *Brut Ieuan Brechfa* in the *Myvyrian Archaiology*, though it lacks the parts of the latter most obviously attributable to Iolo's fanciful invention. Williams suggested that the manuscript allegedly borrowed by Iolo from Rhys Thomas the printer contained something very similar to the manuscript copied by Evan Evans. He also pointed out that there appears in Evan Evans's manuscript, immediately following the text of the chronicle, a tract that begins 'Llyma enwau y nawnyn a diriwys gyntaf yn fforest Glynn Cothi' ('These are the names of the nine people who first settled in the forest of Glyn Cothi'), which is attributed to Ieuan Brechfa in a genealogy that immediately follows. This tract is best known through the copy found in the early seventeenth-century manuscript Aberystwyth, NLW, MS 3042B (Mostyn 134), which was printed by Gwenogvryn Evans in his *Report on Manuscripts in the Welsh Language*.[20] The tract might have been another factor, so Williams suggested, for Iolo's decision to attribute the chronicle to Ieuan Brechfa. The genealogy accompanying the tract is identical in most respects to the genealogical passage copied at the end of *Brut Ieuan Brechfa* in Iolo Morganwg's manuscript (NLW, MS 13121B), showing that Iolo did indeed have before him a copy of *Llyma enwau y nawnyn* with the accompanying genealogy, and manipulated it for his own purposes.

With regard to the version of the chronicle in Evan Evans's manuscript (MS Add. 15031), Thomas Jones claimed that some of the entries 'I have seen nowhere else except in *Brut Ieuan Brechfa*'.[21] But this cannot have been so. Jones had previously noted that the chronicle in MS Add. 15031 is 'similar' to the version of *Brut y Tywysogyon* in a further manuscript: Aberystwyth, NLW, MS Llanstephan 100 (pages 4–9), which was written around 1700. Jones characterized the text of the *Brut* in MS Llanstephan 100 as 'merely a series of garbled excerpts from

---

[19] *BT (RB)*, p. xxxv n. 1.

[20] *RMWL*, I (1898), 117. This is the copy quoted by the following: Egerton Phillimore, in *The Description of Penbrokshire* [sic] *by George Owen of Henllys, Lord of Kemes*, ed. by Henry Owen, Cymmrodorion Record Series, 1, 2 vols in 4 parts (London: Clark, 1892–1936), II, pt 2 (1936), 395; *WG 1*, I, 'Cydifor Fawr 18'; John Langton, 'Land and People in Late Sixteenth-Century Glyn Cothi and Pennant Forests', *Welsh History Review*, 28 (2016), 55–86 (pp. 59 n. 27, 70 n. 72).

[21] *BT (RB)*, p. xxxv n. 1.

RB [...] of no importance'.²² In fact, the relationship between MS Add. 15031 and MS Llanstephan 100 goes beyond similarity; the chronicles in each are practically identical, including the entries that MS Add. 15031 shares with Iolo Morganwg's *Brut Ieuan Brechfa*. One can go further, for the same text is again found in Aberystwyth, NLW, MS Llanstephan 12 (pages 49–62 and 33–37), a manuscript of the mid-sixteenth century.²³ MS Llanstephan 12 is another manuscript listed by Jones as one of the witnesses to the Red Book of Hergest version of *Brut y Tywysogyon*, but his only comment about it is that 'the text is defective at the beginning and the end, shows omissions, and is of no importance'.²⁴ He does not mention that the text is almost identical to the texts in MS Llanstephan 100 and Evan Evans's MS Add. 15031. Rather startlingly, on his stemma of the manuscripts containing versions of *Brut y Tywysogyon* derived from the Red Book of Hergest, he depicts MS Llanstephan 12 (Y) and MS Llanstephan 100 (Z) as deriving from the Red Book independently.²⁵ Considering the unique additional text that they share, this simply cannot be correct. One can only assume that Jones paid little heed to the contents of these manuscripts because they were relatively poor witnesses to the archetype of the Red Book version of *Brut y Tywysogyon*. This was presumably the measure by which they were 'of no importance'.

A close examination of the two Llanstephan manuscripts reveals that the entirety of MS Llanstephan 100 was copied, probably directly, from MS Llanstephan 12. MS Llanstephan 12 is now badly mis-bound, but the original order can largely be reconstructed using the remnants of the scribe's own foliation, alongside the evidence of MS Llanstephan 100, which was copied while MS Llanstephan 12 was still bound in its proper order. The original order of Llanstephan 12 (with reference to the modern pagination) was 1–8, 49–62, 33–48, 89–189, 9–32, and 65–87, although it is clear that various folios have now been lost entirely.²⁶ When MS Llanstephan 12 was copied into MS Llanstephan 100, the scribe of the latter was generally faithful to his exemplar, though he sometimes omitted sections of text (such as the genealogies in MS Llanstephan 12, pages 10–25) or repositioned them (such as the

---

²² *BT (RB)*, p. xxxv. For a very brief list of the contents of MS Llanstephan 100, see *RMWL*, II, pt 2 (1903), 563.

²³ *RMWL*, II, pt 2, 445–48.

²⁴ *BT (RB)*, p. xxxv.

²⁵ *BT (RB)*, p. xxxvii, stemma 3.

²⁶ I have not been able to place the folio comprising pp. 63–64, which is a stray damaged leaf containing genealogies of *uchelwyr*.

'Twenty-Four Knights of Arthur's Court', positioned after *Brut Ieuan Brechfa* in MS Llanstephan 12 but after genealogies of *uchelwyr* in MS Llanstephan 100).[27] Occasionally, MS Llanstephan 100 preserves texts, or parts of texts, that are now lost or lacunose in MS Llanstephan 12, due to the various folios missing in the latter. These include, on page 21 of MS Llanstephan 100, the tract *Llyma enwau y nawnyn* followed by the genealogy of Ieuan Brechfa, just as in Evan Evans's MS Add. 15031 and the better-known NLW, MS 3042B (Mostyn 134). The text of this tract in MS Llanstephan 100 (B), page 21 reads as follows (punctuation added, proper nouns capitalized, expansions in italics, text supplied by MS Add. 15031 (C), fols 9^v–10^r and NLW, MS 3042B (M), fol. 51^v in angular brackets, text supplied by me in square brackets):

> Llyma enwau y nawnyn[28] y diriws yn gyntaf yn fforest Glyn Cothi:[29]
>
> 1 Kyntaf oedd Gronwy Go*ch*[30] yn Fforest y Penint.[31]
>
> 2 Madog Saethydd[32] yn y Llystyn.

---

[27] For the latter text, see especially Rachel Bromwich, 'Pedwar Marchog ar Hugain Llys Arthur', *THSC*, 1956, 116–32; *Trioedd Ynys Prydein: The Triads of the Island of Britain*, ed. by Rachel Bromwich, 4th edn (Cardiff: University of Wales Press, 2014), pp. cx–cxiii, 266–69.

[28] y diriws B; a diriwys C; y diriwyd M. The verb *tirio* usually means 'to land, come ashore, disembark' rather than 'to settle', as seems to be implied here.

[29] Phillimore (*Description*, II, pt 2, 395) says the following of the places named: 'Llystin and Crofft are near Fforest, and so is also a place called *Hendre Fadog*; Esgair Hir is up the Brechfa Marlas; Brithdir is a mile W. of the church of Llanfihangel Rhôs-y-Corn (a chapel to Llanllwni) and Pwll Cymbyd is a few miles further to the N. E., just within Llan-y-bydder parish'.

[30] Probably the father of the Gruffudd ap Goronwy Goch who was the forester's bailiff for Glyn Cothi and Pennant forests in 1307–09: Ralph A. Griffiths, *The Principality of Wales in the Later Middle Ages: The Structure and Personnel of Government. I. South Wales, 1277–1536* (Cardiff: University of Wales Press, 1972), p. 393. His genealogy may be found at *WG 1*, II, 'Elystan Glodrydd 50'. Bartrum's index (*WG 1*, VI, 266) shows that Gruffudd ap Goronwy Goch's genealogy is recorded only in Ieuan Brechfa's genealogical manuscript (Aberystwyth, NLW, MS Peniarth 131, pt viii, pp. 225, 257, 305) and in two of Gruffudd Hiraethog's genealogical manuscripts.

[31] Penint B; Pennant C; Penaint M. Note that Pennant was originally Pennaint: cf. Langton, 'Land and People', p. 55 n. 1 and the references in *Archif Melville Richards, Place-Name Research Centre, Bangor University*, s.v. 'Pennaint' (county 'Carmarthenshire') <http://www.e-gymraeg.co.uk/enwaulleoedd/amr/cronfa_en.aspx> [accessed 26 October 2017].

[32] Madog Saethydd BC; Madoc ap Saethydd M. The probable error in M was responsible for Phillimore's multiplication of men named Madog: *Description*, II, pt 2, 395; cf. *WG 1*, I, 'Cydifor Fawr 18'.

3 Ieu*an* ap Ierwerth ap Tegern[33] yn y Kefen Brith.[34]

4 Madog Vychan ap Madog[35] Saethydd yn yr Escer Ver.[36]

5 Madog Velyn ap Madog Saethydd[37] yn y Brithdîr.

6 Morwyn Vair Vaerwrig[38] yn y Voel Golorog.

7 Kynwrig Vinarrwth[39] <yMyarth>[40] <Llywin>.[41]

8 Y lleidir <wynebwyn>[42] yMhwll Kymbyd.

9 D*afyd*d Meilir[43] yn yr Esceir Hir.

Rhent y brenin yn yr amser hwnw[44] oedd triugain ar bob un o'r nawnyn hyny,[45] sef oedd[46] hyny triugain a dwy bynt.

---

[33] Tegern B; Tegerin C; Tegri M. A dot above the *n* in B might imply that *Tegerin* was the intended word, as in C. However, it is possible that the Ieuan of number 3 should be identified with Ieuan ab Iorwerth ap Trahaearn, whose grandfather Trahaearn was associated with Rhydodyn (Edwinsford) near Llansawel (*WG 1*, II, 'Eidio 5'). If so, *Tegern* could be an error prompted by an abbreviation for *Trahaearn*.

[34] y Kefen Brith B; y Cefn Brith C; y Crofft M. Phillimore identified the latter as Crofft near Fforest: *Description*, II, part ii, 395. Possibly Cefn Brith was another name for the same place.

[35] BM add *ap*, which is not present in C.

[36] Escer Ver B; Escair Faer C; Esgair Verr M. Compared to BC, M reverses the order of numbers 4 and 5.

[37] Madog Saethydd BC; Madoc ap Saethydh M.

[38] B; Morwin Vair Vaerwraig C; Morwin Vaerwraic M.

[39] B; Cynwrig Fin Arrwth C; Kynvric Vinrwth M.

[40] M; yn y Varch BC.

[41] C; Llywm B; Llwin M.

[42] C; Nebwin B; Melyn M. In B, immediately before *nebwin* there is a word that has been struck through, which seems originally to have read *penwyn*. Perhaps *pen* was the error, and *wyn* was wrongly struck through during the process of correction.

[43] Possibly Dafydd ap Meilyr ap Rhys Llwyd, whose descendants were associated with Dyffryn Corrwg, Llanllawddog: *WG 1*, IV, 'Rhydderch ap Tewdwr 2'. This Dafydd's great-great-grandson, Dafydd Dew, married Lleucu ferch Einion, great-granddaughter of the Ieuan ab Iorwerth ap Trahaearn, who might be equated with the subject of number 3 (see n. 33 above).

[44] BC; hynny M. M adds *ar y nawnyn hyn am dir y fforrest*.

[45] BC; – M.

[46] BC; yw M.

Myfi, Ifan Brechfa ap Ierwerth, a scrifenais⁴⁷ o'r⁴⁸ gyfrwydd<yd>⁴⁹ yma y ddwyn kof am yscrifeny ychwaneg o achoedd <a'r>⁵⁰ cyfrwyddyd.⁵¹

M*am* fy nhad i⁵² oedd Wenllian v*er*ch Ieu*an* ap Gwallter [ap]⁵³ Madog Vycha[n] ap <Madog>⁵⁴ Saethydd. Y [fam ynte]⁵⁵ oedd Werfyl⁵⁶ v*er*ch D*afy*dd <ap>⁵⁷ Madog Voel ap Kydwgan ap Einon ap Owain ap Rudd*erch* ap⁵⁸ Tewdwr ap Einon⁵⁹ ap Ho*w*ell Dda.⁶⁰ Mam [Werfyl]⁶¹ v*er*ch D*afy*dd oedd Wenllian v*er*ch Wion Benarw.

Here are the names of the nine people who first settled in the forest of Glyn Cothi:

1 The first was Goronwy Goch in Pennant forest.

2 Madog Saethydd in Llystin.

---

⁴⁷ Myfi, Ifan Brechfa ap Ierwerth, a scrifenais B; Myfi, Ieuan Brechfa ap Iorwerth, a yscifennais C; Ievan Brechva ap Ierorth a sgrivennodd M. M adds *hynn*. Note that M has changed the first-person voice to third-person. The first-person voice is retained in Iolo Morganwg's NLW, MS 13121B.

⁴⁸ BC; o M. NLW, MS 13121B has *y*.

⁴⁹ CM; gyfrwydd[..] B. In B, this word occurs at the edge of a damaged page. At first sight, the word appears to be *gyfrwydd*, but the tail of a following *y* might just be visible, confirming the reading of CM.

⁵⁰ a'r C; y B. NLW, MS 13121B reads *a*.

⁵¹ yma [...] cyfrwyddyd BC; – M.

⁵² M*am* fy nhad i BC; Mam y dâd ef M. Note that, again, M has changed the first-person voice to third-person. The first-person voice is retained in Iolo Morganwg's NLW, MS 13121B.

⁵³ – BC; y M. *ap* is present in NLW, MS 13121B.

⁵⁴ C; – B; Madoc ap M. NLW, 13121B has *Madog Saethydd*.

⁵⁵ My emendation; B reads *y mam hithe*, C reads *ei mam hithau*, M reads *y mam hithe*, and NLW, MS 13121B reads *a'i mam hithau* ('her own mother'). Gweurfyl ferch Dafydd was the mother of Madog Saethydd, the last-named figure in the preceding pedigree, and not mother of Gwenllian ferch Ieuan: see *WG 1*, I, 'Cydifor Fawr 18' and IV, 'Rhydderch ap Tewdwr 6'.

⁵⁶ BC; Mirfil M. NLW, MS 13121B has *Wyrfyl*.

⁵⁷ C; – B; y M. NLW, MS 13121B has *ap*.

⁵⁸ BC; – M. NLW, MS 13121B has *ap*.

⁵⁹ M adds *ap Owain*.

⁶⁰ Note that this version of Gweurfyl ferch Dafydd's pedigree omits Cadwgon's father Iorwerth, Tewdwr (Mawr)'s father Cadell, and Einion's father Owain (except in M): see *WG 1*, I, 42 and IV, 'Rhydderch ap Tewdwr 1'.

⁶¹ My emendation; BCM read *Wenllian*. This is presumably a copying mistake for Gweurfyl, the subject of the preceding genealogy: see *WG 1*, IV, 'Rhydderch ap Tewdwr 6'. NLW, MS 13121B has *Wyfyl*, but this might be a correction by Iolo.

3 Ieuan son of Iorwerth son of *Tegerin* in Cefn Brith.

4 Madog Fychan son of Madog Saethydd in Esgair Faer.

5 Madog Felyn son of Madog Saethydd in Brithdir.

6 Morwyn Fair Faerwraig ['the Dairywoman'] in Moel Golorog.

7 Cynwrig Finarwth in Buarth Llywin.

8 The white-faced thief in Pwllcymbyd.

9 Dafydd Meilyr in Esgair Hir.

The king's rent at that time was sixty [pence] for each one of those nine people, that is, sixty [pence] and two pounds.

I, Ieuan Brechfa son of Iorwerth, wrote about this matter in order to bring to mind further writing about genealogies and history.

The mother of my father was Gwenllian daughter of Ieuan son of Gwallter [son of] Madog Fychan son of Madog Saethydd. [The latter's] mother was Gweurfyl daughter of Dafydd son of Madog Foel son of Cadwgon son of Einion son of Owain son of Rhydderch son of Tewdwr son of Einion son of Hywel Dda. The mother of [Gweurfyl] daughter of Dafydd was Gwenllian daughter of Gwion Benarw.

Reading the tract and the genealogical colophon together, it becomes clear that the tract was composed by Ieuan Brechfa partially to show that he was descended from two of the 'first' settlers of Glyn Cothi Forest: Madog Saethydd and his son Madog Fychan, agnatic ancestors of his paternal grandmother Gwenllian.[62] Through Madog Saethydd's mother, furthermore, Ieuan Brechfa could trace his ancestry back to the famous law-giver, Hywel Dda. Ieuan Brechfa shows additional interest in Madog Saethydd elsewhere in his work. In his extant genealogical manuscript, Aberystwyth, NLW, MS Peniarth 131,

---

[62] The idea of the nine first settlers of Glyn Cothi Forest remained current in the sixteenth century: Langton, 'Land and People', pp. 70–71. A record from 1582, arising from a dispute over the nature of the landholding in Glyn Cothi Forest, preserves the attestations of various locals as to the origins of the forest's tenancies (London, The National Archives, MSS E 134/23 and 24 Eliz I/Mich 4, fols 1–5; cf. Langton, 'Land and People', p. 56 and n. 7). One local resident recalled hearing that 360 years ago nine persons were established as the first inhabitants in Glyn Cothi Forest, holding estate of Rhys Gryg son of the Lord Rhys ap Tewdwr (though Rhys Gryg's father was really the Lord Rhys ap Gruffudd). He did not know who was descended from these nine persons. Another resident recalled that nine persons, including eight men and one woman (as in the tract), were first placed as tenants in the forest of Glyn Cothi, Pennant, and Bwlchymbyd, but he dated them to the time of Edward IV. My thanks to Jack Langton for providing me with additional information from this record.

part viii, he records a version of the William Tell folk story that features Madog Saethydd as its main character.[63] The story is embedded within a genealogy traced back through Madog Saethydd.[64] In this version of the story, Madog Saethydd is compelled to shoot an apple off the head of his son, Madog Fychan, by 'Malld Walbri arglwyddes Brychainioc' (i.e. Maud de St Valéry (d. 1210), wife of William de Braose (d. 1211), Lord of Brecknock among other territories). The story explains that, following the incident, Madog Saethydd and his cousin, y Rhingyll Du, captured *Malld Walbri* and hanged her and her son in their own tower. Madog and his cousin then fled to Madog's mother's kin in Glyn Cothi Forest, explaining how he came to be established there. On the other hand, it is striking how little interest Ieuan Brechfa shows in his own patriline, which the genealogy above does not trace back beyond his father Iorwerth. It is likely that Ieuan Brechfa's agnatic ancestors were of comparatively low status; other genealogical manuscripts provide information about only three further generations of agnatic ancestors.[65]

It should now be apparent that Iolo Morganwg, in his manuscript NLW, MS 13121B and in the *Myvyrian Archaiology*, drew upon a manuscript with contents very similar to Evan Evans's MS Add. 15031, the sixteenth-century MS Llanstephan 12, and the copy of the latter made in *c.* 1700, now MS Llanstephan 100. Iolo used the chronicle in this source as the basis for his *Brut Ieuan Brechfa*, which he augmented with new passages of his own devising. He also used Ieuan Brechfa's genealogy (which in his exemplar probably accompanied the tract *Llyma enwau y nawnyn*) for the extended colophon in NLW, MS 13121B. All these manuscripts must go back to the same common archetype, which was written no later than the mid-sixteenth century, when MS Llanstephan 12 was penned.

A comparison between the various copies of the chronicle contained in these manuscripts serves to confirm this proposition. The original text is found in MS

---

[63] For this story, see Phillimore, in *Description*, II, pt 2, 394–95; Thomas Jones, 'Y Stori Werin yng Nghymru', *THSC*, 1970, 16–32 (pp. 26–28). It is printed in *RMWL*, I, 819.

[64] This pedigree by Ieuan Brechfa is one of only two pedigrees in the primary genealogical sources consulted by Peter Bartrum for the pedigree of Madog Saethydd: *WG 1*, VI, 374. The other, by Lewys Dwnn, is found in *Heraldic Visitations*, I, 155.

[65] Cf. *WG 2*, III, 'Cydifor Fawr 18(A, B), 19(A)'. Ieuan Brechfa's grandfather Dafydd and Dafydd's father and grandfather are found only in Aberystwyth, NLW, MS Peniarth 133, p. 48, by Gruffudd Hiraethog: *WG 1*, VII, 540 and *WG 2*, XV, 34. MS Peniarth 133 omits Ieuan Brechfa's father Iorwerth, and consequently claims that Gwenllian daughter of Ieuan was Ieuan Brechfa's mother, rather than his father Iorwerth's mother.

11. BRUT IEUAN BRECHFA: A WELSH POET WRITES THE EARLY MIDDLE AGES

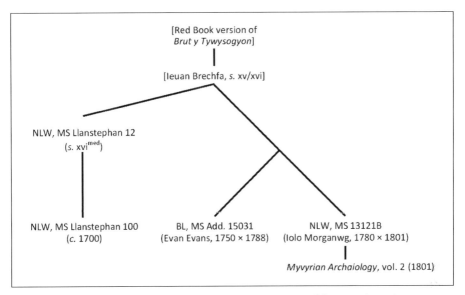

Figure 11.1: A stemma of the witnesses to *Brut Ieuan Brechfa*. Figure by author.

Llanstephan 12, MS Llanstephan 100, and MS Add. 15031; this text consists chiefly of extracts from the Red Book of Hergest version of *Brut y Tywysogyon* for the years 720 to 1079, supplemented by notices derived from other sources, as is discussed below. A collation of the text in these three manuscripts against the expanded version found in NLW, MS 13121B and the *Myvyrian Archaiology* enables Iolo Morganwg's additions in the latter two to be identified with ease. At the beginning of the text, Ieuan Brechfa's chronicle is followed fairly closely, but then as the text progresses Iolo's additions become more numerous. Sufficient correspondence remains between passages in the original version of the text and passages in Iolo's expanded version to allow one to ascertain that neither Iolo nor Evan Evans drew on each other's transcripts, or on the two earlier Llanstephan manuscripts. There are, though, a few hints that Iolo's and Evans's texts are closer to one another than to the Llanstephan texts, suggesting, as might be expected for two contemporaries in contact with one another, that Iolo and Evans ultimately had access to the same exemplar.[66] The resulting relationships are shown in Figure 11.1.

---

[66] For example, in the decade from 910, both omit the epithet *ap Cadell* after Clydog's name, even though it appears in MS Llanstephan 12 and in the Red Book *Brut*; in the decade from 1030, both omit the word *veibion* from the death notice of 'veibion Gynan ap Sesyll', creating the impression that it was Cynan who had died, even though Cynan's death had been

A more nuanced understanding of the relationships between these manuscripts can be gained by considering their genealogical contents, which are far more extensive than the chronicle. A significant proportion of the genealogies are part of the corpus that I call the 'Llywelyn ab Iorwerth genealogies', a body of genealogical text that originated in the early thirteenth century.[67] Particular correspondences between the genealogical sections in MSS Llanstephan 12/ Llanstephan 100, MS Add. 15031, and other manuscripts show that neither Evan Evans's MS Add. 15031 nor the sixteenth-century MS Llanstephan 12 were copied directly from the common source that they ultimately share.[68] MS Llanstephan 12 is closely related to Aberystwyth, NLW, MS Brogyntyn I 15 (Porkington 1), pages 381–97. MS Brogyntyn I 15 is a set of transcripts made by George Owen Harry (*c*. 1553–*c*. 1614) for the antiquarian George Owen of Henllys (1552–1613) in the last decade of the sixteenth century.[69] The section of that manuscript related to MS Llanstephan 12 is contained between two blank pages, 380 and 398, which demarcate changes in the exemplars used by the copyists. The text in MS Brogyntyn I 15, pages 381–97 corresponds closely with everything in MS Llanstephan 12, pages 11–32 and 65–85 (the end of that manuscript according to its original order), the chief difference being that MS Brogyntyn I 15 is generally fuller. The text is close enough to suggest that both manuscripts were copied from the same exemplar, with more of that exemplar's text being included in MS Brogyntyn I 15 than in MS Llanstephan 12 (just as various parts of MS Llanstephan 12 were omitted when it was copied into MS Llanstephan 100). Unfortunately, the part of the common exemplar containing

mentioned earlier; and in the decade from 1070, both omit the article *y* from 'y vrwydyr rrwng Gronwy ap Llwelyn', found in both MS Llanstephan 12 and the Red Book *Brut*.

[67] For a brief introduction to the Llywelyn ab Iorwerth genealogies, see Ben Guy, 'A Lost Medieval Manuscript from North Wales: Hengwrt 33, the *Hanesyn Hên*', *Studia Celtica*, 50 (2016), 69–105 (p. 77). This genealogical collection encompasses the bulk of the material edited by Peter C. Bartrum as four separate 'tracts' under the titles 'Plant Brychan', 'Bonedd yr Arwyr', 'Achau Brenhinoedd a Thywysogion Cymru', and 'Hen Lwythau Gwynedd a'r Mars': 'Bonedd yr Arwyr', *BBCS*, 18 (1958–60), 229–52; 'Achau Brenhinoedd a Thywysogion Cymru', *BBCS*, 19 (1961–62), 201–25; 'Hen Lwythau Gwynedd a'r Mars', *NLWJ*, 12 (1962), 201–35; *Early Welsh Genealogical Tracts* (Cardiff: University of Wales Press, 1966), pp. 75–120.

[68] For a table comparing the contents of all relevant manuscripts, see Ben Guy, *Medieval Welsh Genealogy: An Introduction and Textual Study* (Woodbridge: Boydell, 2020), pp. 299–301.

[69] Evan David Jones, 'The Brogyntyn Welsh Manuscripts, X', *NLWJ*, 7 (1951), 85–101; Bertie George Charles, 'George Owen of Henllys: Addenda', *NLWJ*, 23 (1983), 37–44 (pp. 42–44).

Brut Ieuan Brechfa, corresponding to MS Llanstephan 12, pages 49–62 and 33–37, was not copied into MS Brogyntyn I 15.

Similarly, the genealogical sections of Evan Evans's MS Add. 15031 correspond very closely to pages 601–03 of Aberystwyth, NLW, MS Peniarth 118, part ii, the great compilation of texts written by the physician and grammarian Siôn Dafydd Rhys between the 1580s and his death around 1619.[70] The manuscript used by Siôn Dafydd Rhys was possibly the same one that Evan Evans and Iolo Morganwg would draw upon two centuries later. The fact that the genealogical sections of MS Peniarth 118 and MS Add. 15031 contain textual innovations that are absent from MSS Llanstephan 12/Llanstephan 100 implies that MS Peniarth 118 and MS Add. 15031 share a common exemplar that was derived from the earlier common exemplar shared with MSS Llanstephan 12/ Llanstephan 100. The hints of shared textual innovations in the text of *Brut Ieuan Brechfa* in MS Add. 15031 and the *Myvyrian Archaiology*, as mentioned above, suggest the same conclusion. It is clear that there were once many copies of this compilation which no longer survive.

The earliest manifestations of the particular version of the Llywelyn ab Iorwerth genealogies found in all of the manuscripts discussed so far are preserved in the surviving products of Ieuan Brechfa's own hand. These include MS Peniarth 131, part viii, a genealogical manuscript written by Ieuan Brechfa for Master Harri ap Hywel ap Gwallter, Archdeacon of Carmarthenshire, between 1494 and 1509.[71] This manuscript also contains the earliest extant copy of the genealogical tract *Plant yr Arglwydd Rhys*, found too in MS Llanstephan 12 and MS Llanstephan 100.[72] Another of Ieuan Brechfa's surviving products is a genealogical roll: London, College of Arms, MS Muniment Room 12/16.[73] The roll depicts the extended family connections of Sir Rhys ap Thomas (d. 1525) and his son Sir Gruffudd ap Rhys (d. 1521), and was probably created between 1501, when Gruffudd became a Knight of the Garter, and 1509, when Henry VIII succeeded to the throne.[74] Ieuan Brechfa seems to have written

---

[70] For the date of his death, see R. Geraint Gruffydd, 'The Life of Dr. John Davies of Brecon', *THSC*, 1971, 175–90 (p. 189).

[71] The dedication to Master Harri ap Hywel is on p. 276. For Master Harri's career, see *Gwaith Syr Phylib Emlyn, Syr Lewys Meudwy a Mastr Harri ap Hywel*, ed. by M. Paul Bryant-Quinn (Aberystwyth: University of Wales Centre for Advanced Welsh and Celtic Studies, 2001), pp. 113–16.

[72] Peter C. Bartrum, 'Plant yr Arglwydd Rhys', *NLWJ*, 14 (1965–66), 97–104 (p. 97).

[73] Michael Powell Siddons, *Welsh Pedigree Rolls* (Aberystwyth: NLW, 1996), pp. 6, 39.

[74] For the family of Sir Rhys ap Thomas, see Ralph A. Griffiths, *Sir Rhys ap Thomas and his*

other things for the family of Sir Rhys ap Thomas. According to Lewys Dwnn, Ieuan Brechfa wrote a *llyfr parssment du* ('black parchment book') for Sir Rhys ap Thomas, part of which Dwnn copied.[75] Interestingly, the pedigree diagrams drawn onto MS Muniment Room 12/16 are interspersed with extracts of prose taken, for the most part, from the version of the Llywelyn ap Iorwerth genealogies found in both Ieuan Brechfa's MS Peniarth 131, part viii and in relatives of the *Brut Ieuan Brechfa* manuscripts. A further manuscript by Ieuan Brechfa, written in 1513, formed the basis for another of the transcripts preserved in MS Brogyntyn I 15, on pages 269–343, as we learn from a colophon on page 271.[76] Extracts of the Llywelyn ab Iorwerth genealogies preserved in this transcript (pages 283 and 297–98) again comply with the version associated with Ieuan Brechfa, and agree especially closely with MS Llanstephan 12.

It is abundantly clear that Ieuan Brechfa was responsible for a significant number of genealogical and historical manuscripts produced between *c*. 1490 and *c*. 1520, and that these manuscripts and their immediate derivatives contained copies of the chronicle used by Iolo Morganwg as the basis for his *Brut Ieuan Brechfa*. We shall see in the next section that the original version of *Brut Ieuan Brechfa* yields internal evidence suggesting that it was not only copied by Ieuan Brechfa, but was actively compiled by him.

The Text

The 'original' text of *Brut Ieuan Brechfa*, without Iolo Morganwg's interpolations, is edited and translated at the end of this chapter. The base text is provided by MS Llanstephan 12 or, when that manuscript is lacunose, by its copy MS Llanstephan 100. From this point on, the term '*Brut Ieuan Brechfa*' refers primarily to this edited text: namely, the 'original' text, rather than the interpolated version published in the *Myvyrian Archaiology* in 1801.

For the period covered by *Brut Ieuan Brechfa* (720–1079), the chronological apparatus is essentially the same as that of the Red Book of Hergest version of *Brut y Tywysogyon*. The beginning of each decade is marked with the *anno domini* date written out in full, and the events within that decade are then listed in succession, without any indication of the time elapsed between each

---

Family: A Study in the Wars of the Roses and Early Tudor Politics (Cardiff: University of Wales Press, 1993).

[75] *Heraldic Visitations*, I, 27.

[76] Jones, 'Brogyntyn Welsh Manuscripts', pp. 99–100.

event. Due to the tendency of *Brut Ieuan Brechfa* to skip over various events found in the Red Book *Brut*, it sometimes happens that the first event listed after the date signifying the beginning of the decade did not occur in that year. Thus, for example, the first event listed in the decade labelled 950 is the battle of Llanrwst (called here the battle of Aberconwy), which is thought to have taken place around 954.[77] Since the significance of *Brut Ieuan Brechfa* lies predominantly in its being a work of early Tudor historiography, rather than a primary source for the eighth to eleventh centuries, I have considered it best to refrain from introducing a modern annalistic dating structure to the text, as found, for example, in Thomas Jones's editions of *Brut y Tywysogyon*; instead, I have largely left the text as it would have been read by contemporary readers.

Nonetheless, in order to aid comprehension, it has been deemed necessary to add to the text's rudimentary chronological apparatus the (uncorrected) dates given in the Red Book of Hergest version of *Brut y Tywysogyon* for the beginning of each decade. These dates have been added in square brackets, as in [**R: 720**]. This is because, following the decade for 890, which is labelled correctly, the dates given in *Brut Ieuan Brechfa* diverge exponentially from the generally accurate dates of the Red Book *Brut*. The date of the decade beginning in 910 is given as 970, sixty years too late, and from this point onwards *Brut Ieuan Brechfa*'s dates deviate further and further from the dates of the Red Book *Brut* until the decade beginning in 1030, which is labelled as 1130. Thereafter, the remaining dates are consistently 100 years too late. The original error might have been caused by the accidental insertion of *a lx* ('and 60', or the prose equivalent *a thrugain*) into the date for 910, which is written out as 'x a lx ag ix^c' ('10 and 60 and 900'). Similarly, in order to correct the date for the following decade, which is written out as 'xiii a lxxx a ix^c' ('13 and 80 and 900'), *a lxxx* should probably be removed, leaving the date at which Hywel went to Rome as 913, as might have been indicated in the legal source used to supplement this section (as discussed below). So as to avoid confusion about the dating of events mentioned in the discussion below, the dates used are, unless otherwise stated, those of the Red Book *Brut*, whether or not *Brut Ieuan Brechfa* has accurately reproduced them.

The Red Book of Hergest version of *Brut y Tywysogyon* was the main textual source for *Brut Ieuan Brechfa*, as Thomas Jones implied when he included MS

---

[77] Kari L. Maund, 'Dynastic Segmentation and Gwynedd c. 950–c. 1000', *Studia Celtica*, 32 (1998), 155–67 (pp. 157–58); cf. Egerton Phillimore, 'The *Annales Cambriæ* and the Old-Welsh Genealogies from *Harleian MS. 3859*', *Y Cymmrodor*, 9 (1888), 141–83 (p. 144).

Llanstephan 12 and MS Llanstephan 100 in his list of the manuscripts containing that version of the text.[78] This is shown by many textual details, such as the inclusion of *Castell Baldwin* as the target of viking raiders in the decade from 890, and by the omission of the phrase 'y gyt a'r Saeson' ('together with the English') from the notice of Anarawd ap Rhodri's raid on Ceredigion in the same decade.[79] Occasionally, however, omissions and defects in manuscripts of the Red Book of Hergest version of the *Brut* are corrected in *Brut Ieuan Brechfa*, implying that another similar chronicle has been systematically compared with the Red Book-type base text. For example, in the decade from 970, *Brut Ieuan Brechfa* correctly names Edgar as the English king who led a host into South Wales, agreeing with other versions of *Brut y Tywysogyon* against the Red Book version, which mistakenly names the king as Edward. Likewise, in the decade from 1030, the Red Book version of the *Brut* omitted text from the end of the annal for 1034 and the beginning of the annal for 1035, thereby ignoring the roles of the sons of Rhydderch in the battle of Hiraethwy and Maredudd ab Edwin as the victim of the sons of Cynan; these details have been restored in *Brut Ieuan Brechfa*.

Further evidence suggests that the additional chronicle used in the composition of *Brut Ieuan Brechfa* was something akin to the Cottonian chronicle, the 'C-text' of the family of Welsh Latin chronicles generically known as *Annales Cambriae*, 'The Annals of Wales'.[80] At the beginning of the decade from 990 is a notice of Owain ab Einion ravaging the kingdom of Maredudd ab Owain. This 'Owain ab Einion' is a mistake for 'Edwin ab Einion', and the same mistake is also found in the Cottonian chronicle.[81] Similarly, the Cottonian chronicle is the only one of the extant *Annales Cambriae* chronicles that could have supplied the correct name of the king who led a host into South Wales in 973, rec-

---

[78] *BT (RB)*, p. xxxv.

[79] See *BT (RB)*, p. 276, notes to p. 9, lines 32–33 and p. 11, line 2. For a convenient comparison between the three versions of *Brut y Tywysogyon* for this period, see *Brenhinoedd y Saeson*, 'The Kings of the English', A.D. 682–954: Texts P, R, S in Parallel, ed. by David N. Dumville (Aberdeen: Department of History, University of Aberdeen, 2005), pp. 30–31.

[80] For the origin of this title, and a summary of scholarship on this family of chronicles, see my chapter above (Chapter 3), and cf. Ben Guy, 'The Origins of the Compilation of Welsh Historical Texts in Harley 3859', *Studia Celtica*, 49 (2015), 21–56 (pp. 25–27).

[81] *Annales Cambriae: The C Text, from London, British Library, Cotton MS Domitian A. i, ff. 138r–155r*, ed. by Henry W. Gough-Cooper (Welsh Chronicles Research Group, 2015), p. 24, § c314.1 <http://croniclau.bangor.ac.uk/documents/AC%20C%20first%20edition.pdf> [accessed 10 October 2017].

tifying the error in the Red Book *Brut*.⁸² Other deviations from the Red Book *Brut* again imply that some version of *Annales Cambriae* was used to supplement *Brut Ieuan Brechfa*, but do not indicate the specific version used. In the decade from 940, the murder of King Edmund appears in the text; this is not included in either the Red Book or Peniarth 20 versions of *Brut y Tywysogyon*, and only appears in the related *Brenhinedd y Saesson* as an extended interpolation from another source, but it is found in the Harleian, Breviate, and Cottonian chronicles (the A-, B-, and C-texts of *Annales Cambriae*) in a form very similar to that found in *Brut Ieuan Brechfa*.⁸³ With regard to the omission in the Red Book *Brut* of the name of Maredudd ab Einion as the victim of the sons of Cynan in the 1030s, as mentioned above, either the Cottonian chronicle or the Breviate chronicle could have provided the correction. However, neither of the latter chronicles could have supplied the participants of the battle of Hiraethwy, another omission in the Red Book *Brut* that is restored in *Brut Ieuan Brechfa*.⁸⁴ Overall, therefore, it is likely that the compiler of *Brut Ieuan Brechfa* supplemented the Red Book-style base text with readings taken from a version of *Annales Cambriae*, and, of the extant versions of the latter, the Cottonian chronicle would appear to be closest to *Brut Ieuan Brechfa*'s source. The Cottonian chronicle, in its extant form, is a thirteenth-century copy of a chronicle maintained at St Davids, and Ieuan Brechfa certainly cultivated connections that would have granted him access to a St Davids text: for example, he wrote MS Peniarth 131, part viii for Master Harri ap Hywel, an archdeacon of the diocese.⁸⁵ It may be significant that another chronicle, almost identical to the Cottonian chronicle, was seen and copied by John Leland in St Davids in

---

⁸² *Annales Cambriae: The C text*, p. 22, § c297.1.

⁸³ The three versions of this annal can be compared in *Annales Cambriae, A.D. 682–954: Texts A–C in Parallel*, ed. and trans. by David N. Dumville (Cambridge: Department of Anglo-Saxon, Norse and Celtic, University of Cambridge, 2002), pp. 16–17. The verb used in the Harleian and Breviate texts, *iugulatus est* ('was slaughtered, had [his] throat cut'), is more likely to have appeared in *Brut Ieuan Brechfa*'s source than the verb in the Cottonian text, *occiditur* ('was killed, was slain'). The former is probably the reading of the common source, the latter an innovation. See n. 223 to the translation below.

⁸⁴ *Annales Cambriae: The C Text*, p. 26, § c357.1, § c358.1; *Annales Cambriae: The B Text, from London, National Archives, MS E164.1, pp. 2–26*, ed. Henry W. Gough-Cooper (The Welsh Chronicles Research Group, 2015), p. 48, § b1055.1, § b1056.1 <http://croniclau.bangor.ac.uk/documents/AC%20B%20first%20edition.pdf> [accessed 10 October 2017].

⁸⁵ See above, n. 71. For the Cottonian chronicle as a St Davids record, see Lloyd, *The Welsh Chronicles*, pp. 14–15; Kathleen Hughes, *Celtic Britain in the Early Middle Ages*, ed. by David N. Dumville (Woodbridge: Boydell, 1980), pp. 73–76.

the first half of the sixteenth century.[86] Perhaps, therefore, the second annalistic source used for *Brut Ieuan Brechfa* was a relative of the Cottonian chronicle.

Brut Ieuan Brechfa's extracts from the Red Book version of the *Brut* end, perhaps poignantly, with Rhys ap Tewdwr's acquisition of rule in Deheubarth, an event which the Red Book *Brut* places towards the end of the decade from 1070.[87] The reason for this may well have been Rhys ap Tewdwr's well-known role in late medieval and early modern historiography as the founder of the royal house of Deheubarth.[88] Some confusion about the ending of the chronicle, perhaps reflecting a problem in the archetypal manuscript, is implied by MS Llanstephan 12's interlinear insertion of a new and spurious date for the rule of Rhys ap Tewdwr (AD 600!) and MS Add. 15031's dotted gap between 'Oed Crist' ('The age of Christ') and 'arglwydd Rhys ap Tewdwr Mawr yn dywysog Deheubarth' ('the lord Rhys ap Tewdwr Mawr was prince of Deheubarth').

Following the notice of Rhys ap Tewdwr is a curious coda regarding the three 'daughters' of Llywelyn ab Iorwerth and their various marriages. The daughters are actually a mixture of the daughters of Llywelyn ab Iorwerth and King John. The first and third daughters are those of John (Isabella and Eleanor), who married respectively Frederick II, the Holy Roman Emperor, and Simon de Montfort, Earl of Leicester. The second daughter is Llywelyn's (Angharad), who married Maelgwn Fychan ap Maelgwn ab yr Arglwydd Rhys (not Maelgwn Mawr ap Rhys ap Tewdwr, as the text states). The text then ends on a rather optimistic note, with the statement that there was peace for a time between the Welsh and the English, implied to be the result of a marriage between Llywelyn's 'daughter' and Simon de Montfort. Perhaps this is a confused recollection of the alliance between Llywelyn ab Iorwerth's grandson, Llywelyn ap Gruffudd, and Simon de Montfort (d. 1265), and the later marriage between Llywelyn ap Gruffudd and Simon de Montfort's daughter, also called Eleanor, in 1278.

---

[86] Caroline Brett, 'John Leland, Wales, and Early British History', *Welsh History Review*, 15 (1990), 169–82 (pp. 178–79). Leland's copy may be found in *The Itinerary of John Leland in or about the Years 1535–1543*, ed. by Lucy Toulmin Smith, 5 vols (1964), IV, 168–77.

[87] Cf. *BT (RB)*, pp. 30–31, where Jones dates the event to 1079.

[88] The version of the tract *Pump Brenhinllwyth Cymru* ('The Five Royal Dynasties of Wales') that became canonical from the late fifteenth century onwards, which includes 'Rys ap Tewdwr Mawr yn Nehevbarth' ('Rhys ap Tewdwr Mawr in Deheubarth'), is printed in Peter C. Bartrum, 'Pedigrees of the Welsh Tribal Patriarchs', *NLWJ*, 13 (1963–64), 93–146; 15 (1967–68), 157–66 (pt 1, p. 125). It seems probable that the list was originally compiled by Gutun Owain.

There are four additions to the text that cannot be explained by the use of any chronicle, because they seem to have been drawn from non-annalistic sources. Some of these sources can be connected particularly closely with Ieuan Brechfa. Each one is discussed in turn below.

The text refers twice to a certain Morudd ap Llywarch Lwyd, called King of Ceredigion. The first reference is to his death in the decade from 830, and the second is to his being the father of Gwgon, the King of Ceredigion who drowned in the decade from 870. Both references are obvious additions to the text; the first seemingly replaces the obituary of Sadyrnfyw, Bishop of St Davids, who is usually said to have died in 831, and the second replaces Meurig, Gwgon's real father.[89] The only other references to Morudd ap Llywarch Lwyd known to me are found in two genealogical sources, both concerning the family of Gwynionydd-is-Cerdin in southern Ceredigion. One reference is in the eighteenth-century pedigree of David Lewis of Dinas Cerdin and Blaen Cerdin, traced back to one Llywelyn ap Hoedlyw, Lord of Is Cerdin, whom Peter Bartrum estimated to have lived in the thirteenth century.[90] Among Llywelyn's ancestors is said to be 'Morydd, king of Cardigan, Anno Domini 830, ab Llywarch Llwyd'.[91] The appearance of the date implies some connection with *Brut Ieuan Brechfa*, which places Morudd's obituary in the decade from 830. *Brut Ieuan Brechfa* may have been a source for the pedigree, since the pedigree is late, appearing only in eighteenth-century manuscripts deriving from the work of David Edwardes of Rhyd-y-Gors, Carmarthenshire (d. 1690).[92]

---

[89] *Annales Cambriae*, ed. and trans. by Dumville, pp. 10–11; Harleian genealogies, § 26, in Guy, *Medieval Welsh Genealogy*, p. 337.

[90] Bartrum, 'Pedigrees', pt 1, pp. 111, 132–33. The genealogy of David Lewis's grandfather, another David Lewis, is given in *WG 3*, 'Pedigrees', 'L – LL', 'Llywelyn ap Hoedlyw', 'Llywelyn ap Hoedlyw (B)/1' [on CD]. This is traced back to the genealogies in *WG 2*, vii, 'Llywelyn ap Hoedlyw (A, B)' and *WG 1*, iii, 'Llywelyn ap Hoedlyw'.

[91] Bartrum, 'Pedigrees', pt 1, p. 111.

[92] The manuscripts are Aberystwyth, NLW, MS 14214B (the Dale Castle manuscript), printed in *The Dale Castle Manuscript: Pedigrees of Carmarthenshire, Cardiganshire and Pembrokeshire*, ed. by Thomas Phillipps ([n.pl.]: [n.pub.], 1859) (Is Cerdin pedigree at p. 26); NLW, MS Peniarth 156 (a copy of NLW, MS 14214B), printed in *West Wales Historical Records*, 1 (1910/11), 1–96; 2 (1911/12), 1–103 (Is Cerdin pedigree at pt 1, 37); and NLW, MS Peniarth 120 (Is Cerdin pedigree at p. 588). See Bartrum, 'Pedigrees', pt 1, pp. 99, 111; pt 2, p. 157; *RMWL*, i, 733–40, 941–42. For David Edwardes, see Peter C. Bartrum, 'Notes on the Welsh Genealogical Manuscripts', *THSC*, 1968, 63–98; 1976, 102–18; 1988, 37–46 (pt 1, pp. 91–92; pt 2, p. 114; pt 3, pp. 45–46); Francis Jones, 'An Approach to Welsh Genealogy', *THSC*, 1948, 303–466 (pp. 419–21).

However, Morudd ap Llywarch Lwyd appears in an earlier Is Cerdin pedigree, headed *Ricert Kerdin* and beginning with one Owain ap Rhys ap Ricard, sixth in descent from Llywelyn ap Hoedlyw. This survives only in MS Llanstephan 12, pages 91–92, and MS Llanstephan 100, page 19, and so probably derives from the genealogical work of Ieuan Brechfa.[93] Why Morudd ap Llywarch Lwyd in particular was added to the chronicle, alone of the very many early figures who appear in contemporary genealogies, is uncertain.

A second, more substantial addition appears in the decade beginning, according to the Red Book *Brut*, in 920, or, according to *Brut Ieuan Brechfa*, in '993' (possibly for 913). The addition concerns the supposed attempt by Hywel Dda to gain papal approval for his codification of Welsh law. The account is modelled on a historical pilgrimage to Rome undertaken by Hywel Dda in 928.[94] An interesting feature of the account is the naming of the three bishops who accompanied Hywel to Rome as *Mart* of St Davids, *Mordaf* of Bangor, and *Teibyr* of St Asaph. The names are based on those given in an epilogue to the Welsh law manuscripts that first surfaces in London, BL, MS Additional 22356 (Welsh law manuscript S), written in the mid-fifteenth century, where they appear as *Lambert*, *Mordaf*, and *Chebur*.[95] Certain textual correspondences suggest that *Brut Ieuan Brechfa* drew directly on an account like the epilogue in S for its passage about Hywel Dda's visit to Rome. In both accounts, Hywel travels to Rome 'i edrych' ('to see') if his law is 'yn erbyn kyfraith Dduw' ('against God's law'). In S, the date for this visit is given specifically as 914.[96] A similar date in a related text may be the origin of the corrupt date given in *Brut Ieuan Brechfa* as 'xiii a lxxx a ix^c' ('13 and 80 and 900'). As already men-

---

[93] Bartrum seems to have been aware only of the version in MS Llanstephan 100: *WG 1*, v, 142, 160; vii, 708.

[94] *Annales Cambriae*, ed. and trans. by Dumville, pp. 16–17.

[95] Huw Pryce, 'The Prologues to the Welsh Law Books', *BBCS*, 33 (1986), 151–87 (pp. 164–65); Morfydd E. Owen, 'Royal Propaganda: Stories from the Law-Texts', in *The Welsh King and his Court*, ed. by Thomas M. Charles-Edwards, Morfydd E. Owen, and Paul Russell (Cardiff: University of Wales Press, 2000), pp. 224–54 (pp. 226–29, 246–49). A full critical edition and study of law manuscript S is now available online: Christine James, *Machlud Cyfraith Hywel: Golygiad Beirniadol ac Eglurhaol o Lsgr. BL Add. 22356 (S)* (Cambridge: Seminar Cyfraith Hywel, 2013) <http://cyfraith-hywel.cymru.ac.uk/en/machlud-cyf-hyw.php> [accessed 25 October 2017]. The text of the epilogue is on p. 114. The first two names were probably plucked out of a chronicle, but the origin of *Chebur* of St Asaph is uncertain: Pryce, 'The Prologues', pp. 164–65; James, *Machlud Cyfraith Hywel*, pp. 146–47.

[96] 914 is also the date given in the version of the epilogue in Aberystwyth, NLW, MS Peniarth 259B, fols 57^v–58^r (law manuscript Z).

tioned, the addition of *a lxxx* is probably an error, meaning that the implied date may originally have been 913. The date is significant as the only attempt by *Brut Ieuan Brechfa* to offer a date that is not the beginning of a decade, as is always the practice in the source text, the Red Book *Brut*, which dates Hywel's journey with reference to the decade beginning in 920. The deviation might be explained by *Brut Ieuan Brechfa*'s use of an account like that of S, an account which might have included either the date 913 or 914.

A law manuscript very similar to S seems to have been in use in Carmarthenshire in 1510, during the period when Ieuan Brechfa was active in the same region, because quotations from such a manuscript (in Latin) were included in a record of an appeal about a case from Kidwelly, heard on 5 November 1510.[97] More strikingly, S itself seems to have originated in the vicinity of the *cwmwd* of Gwynionydd-uwch-Cerdin, very close to the home of the family of Owain ap Rhys ap Ricard of Gwynionydd-is-Cerdin, whose ancestor Morudd finds a place in the chronicle.[98] One wonders if the composition of the chronicle was linked especially closely with the family of Gwynionydd-is-Cerdin. Considering that the pedigree of the Is Cerdin family was included in Ieuan Brechfa's genealogical writings, perhaps Ieuan Brechfa was patronized by the family, and redacted the chronicle for their use.

A third major addition to the text concerns Hywel, son of Owain Gwynedd, and his Irish mother. The reason for the inclusion of the passage is not at all clear. It is found in the decade from 950. In this decade, the Red Book *Brut* records the ravaging of Holyhead by 'meibion Abloec' ('the sons of Olaf'), the Olaf in question probably being either Olaf Cuarán or Olaf Guthfrithsson.[99] In *Brut Ieuan Brechfa*, 'meibion Abloec' have been replaced by 'feibion Eidwal Dyfed' ('the sons of Idwal Dyfed'), the latter being the name used in the text for Idwal Foel ab Anarawd. The epithet *Dyfed* seems to have arisen through a misunderstanding of the Red Book *Brut*, which records, in its annal for 950, that 'diffeithawd Jago ac Ieuaf meibon Jdwal Dyfet dwyweith' ('Iago and Ieuaf, sons of Idwal, ravaged Dyfed twice'). Here, the personal name Idwal and the place name Dyfed are juxtaposed, even though they are not in apposition.

---

[97] Dafydd Jenkins and Morfydd E. Owen, 'Welsh Law in Carmarthenshire', *The Carmarthenshire Antiquary*, 17 (1982), 17–28 (p. 25); Pryce, p. 164 n. 4.

[98] James, *Machlud Cyfraith Hywel*, pp. xlii–xliv, lviii; Christine James, 'Llyfr Cyfraith o Ddyffryn Teifi: Disgrifiad o BL. Add. 22,356', *NLWJ*, 27 (1992), 383–404 (pp. 394–95).

[99] *BT (RB)*, pp. 14–15; Thomas M. Charles-Edwards, *Wales and the Britons 350–1064* (Oxford: Oxford University Press, 2013), pp. 539–40.

Immediately after the mention of 'feibion Eidwal Dyfed', *Brut Ieuan Brechfa* goes on to state that 'ef a wnaeth y Owain Gwynedd briodi gwyddeles, merch arglwydd Iwerddon: Pyfog y henw' ('he caused Owain Gwynedd to marry an Irish woman, a daughter of the lord of Ireland: Pyfog was her name'). The *ef* in question would appear to be Idwal 'Dyfed', despite the fact that he lived some two hundred years earlier than Owain Gwynedd (d. 1170). It is then explained that Owain and Pyfog had a son called Hywel, who, following the death of his mother, went to Ireland to claim his territory, thus initiating the tradition whereby the Britons claimed to own a lot of land in Ireland. The latter statement may have been prompted by knowledge of the lands around Dublin held by various descendants of Gruffudd ap Cynan, though it may also have been inspired by a more general perception that the events of 1169 and afterwards more commonly known as the 'Anglo-Norman' conquest of Ireland was really a 'Welsh' conquest of Ireland.[100] The Hywel concerned is Hywel ab Owain Gwynedd, the 'poet-prince' who was killed by his younger brother Dafydd in 1170, shortly after the death of their father, Owain Gwynedd.[101] According to the thirteenth-century Llywelyn ab Iorwerth genealogies, Hywel's mother was a certain 'Ffynnot Wydeles' ('Ffynnod the Irishwoman'). This is probably the same character who appears in *Brut Ieuan Brechfa* as either *Pyfog* or *Ffyfog*. One can see how a form like *Ffyfog* may have arisen from *Ffynnot*, through an *n* being misinterpreted as a *u* for /v/ (later spelled *f*) and the final *t* being misread as a *c* for /g/ (later spelled *g*). In this regard, the variation shown across copies of the Llywelyn ab Iorwerth genealogies is significant. Many copies have a reading very similar to *Ffynnot*, but five copies are closer to *Ffyfog*. Three of these five form a related group; these are Gutun Owain's London, BL, MS Additional 14919 (1493), which has *Ffinoc*, Syr Thomas ab Ieuan ap Deicws's Aberystwyth, NLW, MS Peniarth 127, part i (1510), which has *Ffinioc*, and Roger Morris's Aberystwyth, NLW, MS 3032B, part i (1580 × 1600), which

---

[100] This perception is explored in Seán Duffy, 'The Welsh Conquest of Ireland', in *Clerics, Kings and Vikings: Essays on Medieval Ireland in Honour of Donnchadh Ó Corráin*, ed. by Emer Purcell and others (Dublin: Four Courts Press, 2015), pp. 103–14. For the descendants of Gruffudd ap Cynan in Ireland, see Marie Therese Flanagan, '*Historia Gruffud vab Kenan* and the Origins of Balrothery, Co. Dublin', *CMCS*, 28 (1994), 71–94.

[101] *HW*, II, 533–34, 549. For Hywel, see *Hywel ab Owain Gwynedd: Bardd-Dywysog*, ed. by Nerys Ann Jones (Cardiff: University of Wales Press, 2009). Hywel's poems are edited by Kathleen Anne Bramley, 'Gwaith Hywel ab Owain Gwynedd', in *Gwaith Llywelyn Fardd I ac Eraill o Feirdd y Ddeuddegfed Ganrif*, ed. by Kathleen Anne Bramley and others, Cyfres Beirdd y Tywysogion, 2 (Cardiff: University of Wales Press, 1994), pp. 101–88.

likewise has *Ffinioc*. The two others, however, were written by Ieuan Brechfa: MS Peniarth 131, part viii, which has the corrupt form *Ffumoe*, probably a miscopying of *Ffinnoc*, and the genealogical roll MS Muniment Room 12/16, which has *Finoc*, closest to *Brut Ieuan Brechfa*'s *Pyfog/Ffyfog*. The form of the name *Pyfog/Ffyfog* may thus be further evidence for the role of Ieuan Brechfa in compiling *Brut Ieuan Brechfa*.

The fourth and final addition to the text to be discussed here concerns *Brut Ieuan Brechfa*'s account of the reign of Llywelyn ap Seisyll. Compared to the same passage in the Red Book *Brut*, the account has two significant additions. Firstly, *Brut Ieuan Brechfa* seems to say that Llywelyn ap Seisyll shared rule in Dyfed with a certain Hywel ap Seisyll, who is otherwise unknown. Secondly, a new passage is introduced claiming that war grew between Hywel ap Seisyll and his family at some point before the battle of Abergwili. There is, however, another text which associates Llywelyn ap Seisyll and the battle of Abergwili with a certain Hywel ap Seisyll, and this may be the key to interpreting the additions. The text in question is the Jesus College 20 genealogies, sections 32–33 of which read as follows:[102]

> Howel ac Adam a Phylib a Thrahaearn, Iorwoerth a Meilyr, Gruffud a Chadѳgaѳn a Ridyt, meibyon Seissyll m. Llewelyn m. Kadѳgaѳn. m. Elstan. A mam Seissyl oed Ellelѳ.
>
> Ellelѳ mam Seissyll m. Llewelyn o Vuellt. Merch oed Ellelѳ honѳ y Elidyr mab Llywarch m. Bledri m. Mor mab Llowarch m. Gѳgaѳn <vab>[103] Keneu Menrud, a vu neidyr vlѳydyn am y vonѳgyl. Y Gѳgaѳn hѳnѳ a wnaeth Aber Gѳyli, ac yno y lladѳyt ef a Llewelyn m. Seissyll, tat Gruffud m. Llewelyn.
>
> Hywel and Adam and Phylib and Trahaearn, Iorwerth and Meilyr, Gruffudd and Cadwgon and Rhiddid, sons of Seisyll son of Llywelyn son of Cadwgon son of Elystan. And Seisyll's mother was Ellelw.
>
> Ellelw, mother of Seisyll ap Llywelyn of Buellt. That Ellelw was the daughter of Elidyr son of Llywarch son of Bleddri son of Mor son of Llywarch son of Gwgon son of Cenau Menrudd, who had a snake around his neck for a year. That Gwgon built Abergwili, and there he and Llywelyn ap Seisyll, father of Gruffudd ap Llywelyn, were killed.

---

[102] The text is taken from my edition in *Medieval Welsh Genealogy*, p. 343. Cf. *Early Welsh Genealogical Tracts*, p. 48.

[103] This reading is taken from the other copy of the text preserved in NLW, MS 3042B, fol. 17ʳ: see below.

The text claims that Gwgon son of Cenau Menrudd, an ancestor of Ellelw, mother of Seisyll ap Llywelyn of Buellt, built Abergwili, where both Gwgon and Llywelyn ap Seisyll were killed. According to the preceding section, Seisyll ap Llywelyn of Buellt had nine sons, the first of whom is listed as Hywel. In reality, Hywel and his brothers probably lived in the first half of the twelfth century, in the vicinity of Buellt. Although none of the brothers appears in contemporary records, the Breviate chronicle records that Hywel's nephew, one *Meuruc filius Adam filius Seisil de Buellt*, was killed by a relative in 1170.[104] But an early reader of a passage like that in the Jesus College 20 genealogies may not have realized this. The author of *Brut Ieuan Brechfa* may have inserted Hywel ap Seisyll, son of Seisyll ap Llywelyn of Buellt and reputed descendant of the founder of Abergwili, into the narrative about Llywelyn ap Seisyll in order to create a plausible context for the battle of Abergwili, which Hywel ap Seisyll's ancestor allegedly founded. If a passage like that in the Jesus College 20 genealogies does indeed lie behind the chronicle, it might imply that the intended meaning of the chronicle's notice of Llywelyn ap Seisyll's death ('*yno* i lladdwyd Llwelyn ap Sesyllt') was that Llywelyn ap Seisyll was killed 'there' (i.e. at Abergwili) rather than 'then', as this is what the Jesus College 20 genealogies explicitly state.[105] In reality, Llywelyn fought the battle of Abergwili against the mysterious Rhain the Irishman, but the text of *Brut Ieuan Brechfa* does not mention Rhain.[106] It may be significant that the only other manuscript known to contain the passage about Gwgon son of Cenau Menrudd and Abergwili is the early seventeenth-century NLW, MS 3042B, mentioned above as the only manuscript aside from the *Brut Ieuan Brechfa* manuscripts known to preserve the tract *Llyma enwau y nawnyn* along with Ieuan Brechfa's genealogical colophon.[107]

Before concluding, it is worth briefly drawing attention to the language and orthography of the text. In MS Add. 15031 and the *Myvyrian Archaiology*, the text has, to a large extent, been standardized to the norms of eighteenth-century literary Welsh. But in MS Llanstephan 12 and MS Llanstephan 100,

[104] *Annales Cambriae: The B Text*, p. 63, § b1192.2 [1170].

[105] Welsh *yno* can bear either meaning.

[106] For Rhain the Irishman, see David Ewan Thornton, 'Who was Rhain the Irishman?', *Studia Celtica*, 34 (2000), 131–48, but cf. Jones, '*Brut y Tywysogyon*', pp. 213–14.

[107] Bartrum, 'Notes on the Welsh Genealogical Manuscripts', pt 1, pp. 64–65. On fol. 17ʳ of NLW, MS 3042B, the relevant passage is headed 'Ach y gwr y naeth Abergwili' ('The genealogy of the man who built Abergwili') (cf. *RMWL*, I, 115).

which are used as base texts for the edition, the language and orthography are overwhelmingly southern in orientation. Obvious southern phonological traits include the occasional absence of the glide vowel yod /i/ from word endings (*Brycheinog*, *meibon*, *varfolaeth*) and the use of the third singular masculine conjugated preposition *gantaw* rather than *ganthaw*.[108] A notable orthographic feature indicative of southern manuscripts of this period is the abundance of spellings in *y*, including the use of *y* for /ʉ/ (*by*, *Morydd*, *dyon*, probably because /ʉ/ had fallen together with /i/, usually spelled *y*) and for /i/ in the diphthongs presently spelled *ae* (*may*, *lodraythy*, *aython*), *eu* (*Deheybarthwyr*, *Meyryg*, *goreygwyr*), and *oe* (*doyth*). Other spellings are modelled on colloquial pronunciation. There are examples of word-final *-ae* and *-ai* shortened to *-e* (*gwydde*, *weddie*, *ymladde*, *vyse*), the diphthong *oe* shortened to *o* (*odd*, *rryfelodd*), and *y* for /ə/ omitted before the semi-vowel /w/ (*Hwel*, *Llwelyn*, *dwedyd*). A similar range of features has been identified in other texts preserved in southern manuscripts of the early modern period, such as the version of the romance *Iarlles y Ffynnon* in NLW, MS Llanstephan 58.[109]

It is hoped that the foregoing study has provided ample evidence to support the conclusion that the chronicle text *Brut Ieuan Brechfa*, as found in MS Llanstephan 12, MS Llanstephan 100, and MS Add. 15031, was produced by the poet and scholar Ieuan Brechfa, sometime in the decades around 1500. The text was based on the Red Book of Hergest version of *Brut y Tywysogyon* but was embellished with details taken from a number of other sources, including a chronicle related to the Latin Cottonian chronicle, the genealogy of the family of Gwynionydd-is-Cerdin, a law manuscript similar to law manuscript S, and a genealogical text similar to the section of the Jesus College 20 genealogies concerned with the family of Seisyll ap Llywelyn of Buellt. The resulting chronicle was then copied numerous time in the sixteenth century as part of

---

[108] Peter Wynn Thomas, 'Middle Welsh Dialects: Problems and Perspectives', *BBCS*, 40 (1993), 17–50; Patrick Sims-Williams, 'Variation in Middle Welsh Conjugated Prepositions: Chronology, Register and Dialect', *Transactions of the Philological Society*, 111 (2013), 1–50 (pp. 32–39, 44).

[109] R. L. Thomson, 'Iarlles y Ffynnon: The Version in Llanstephan MS. 58', *Studia Celtica*, 6 (1971), 57–87 (p. 57); Sioned Davies, 'O Gaer Llion i Benybenglog: Testun Llanstephan 58 o "Iarlles y Ffynnon"', in *Cyfoeth y Testun: Ysgrifau ar Lenyddiaeth Gymraeg yr Oesoedd Canol*, ed. by R. Iestyn Daniel and others (Cardiff: University of Wales Press, 2003), pp. 326–48 (pp. 329–30); Henry Lewis, 'Modern Welsh Versions of the Seven Wise Men of Rome', *Revue Celtique*, 46 (1929), 50–88 (pp. 50–52); J. E. Caerwyn Williams *apud* Thomas Jones and J. E. Caerwyn Williams, 'Ystori Alexander a Lodwig', *Studia Celtica*, 10/11 (1975/76), 261–304 (pp. 275–77).

a wider compilation of materials derived from the work of Ieuan Brechfa, the best witness to which is the mid-sixteenth-century MS Llanstephan 12. In the second half of the eighteenth century, one copy of this compilation was in the possession of Evan Evans, who reproduced the text of the chronicle carefully in the manuscript that became the first part of MS Add. 15031. It was perhaps the same copy which, by 1780, had fallen into the hands of Iolo Morganwg, who set about transforming it into the text incorporated into the *Myvyrian Archaiology of Wales* as *Brut Ieuan Brechfa*.[110]

An Edition and Translation of Brut Ieuan Brechfa

The base text for the edition has been taken from MS Llanstephan 12, so far as it is available. Where MS Llanstephan 12 is wanting, the base text has been taken from MS Llanstephan 100, which was copied from MS Llanstephan 12 before some pages of the latter were lost. The sigla for the variants are as follows:

A: Aberystwyth, NLW, MS Llanstephan 12, pp. 49–62, 33–37 (*s.* xvi^{med}).

B: Aberystwyth, NLW, MS Llanstephan 100, pp. 4–9 (*s.* xvii/xviii).

C: London, BL, MS Additional 15031, part i, fols 1^r–9^v (Evan Evans, 1750 × 1788).

D: *MA²*, pp. 716–20.

Where A is available to provide the base text, variants are not ordinarily given for B. Full variants have been given for C. Selected variants only have been given for D, because of the extent to which D varies from the other witnesses. Readings from the following versions of *Brut y Tywysogyon* and *Brenhinedd y Saesson* are also occasionally given for comparative purposes, sometimes in order to ascertain which of the witnesses to *Brut Ieuan Brechfa* best preserve the reading of the archetype:

P: *BT (Pen. 20); BT (Pen. 20 trans.).*

R: *BT (RB).*

S: *BS.*

---

[110] My thanks to Rebecca Thomas for her helpful comments on a draft of this chapter, and to David Callander for suggesting corrections to the translation.

Words in the main text drawn from witnesses other than the base texts are placed in angular brackets < >. Text supplied by the editor is placed in square brackets [ ]. Numerals in square brackets in normal type indicate the page numbers of the manuscript providing the base text. Numerals in square brackets in bold type show the more accurate AD dates found in R. Capitalization and punctuation have been regularized. Expansions are in italics. Historical commentary is provided in the footnotes to the translation.

Text (Llanstephan 100, 4)

Llyma fryt y tywsogion, fal y by ryvelodd, <dialedd>,[111] a rhyfeddod.

[**R: 720**] 720 odd oed Crist pan fy'r haf tesog, ag y bu farw Beli mab Elffin.

[**R: 750**] 750 pan fy farw Tewdwr ap Rodri, brenin y Britaniaid.

[**R: 760**] 760 pan fy'r frwydyr rhwng y Britaniaid a'r Saeson am waith Henffordd, ag y by farw Dyfnwal <ap>[112] Tewdwr.

[**R: 770**] 770 pan symydwyd pasc y Brytaniaid, ag y bu farw Fferinol[113] fab Eidwal, ag y by ddistriw ar y Deheybarthwyr gan y brenin y hûn, [**R: 780**] ag y gorfy ar y <deau>[114] ladd y brenin yn amser haf.

[**R: 800**] Oed Crist 800 pan laddodd y Saeson Cradog, frenin Gwynedd, ag y marw Arthyr, frenin Credigion, a Rhydderch, frenin Dyfed, a Chadell, frenin Powys, ag <Elbod>,[115] archesgob Gwynedd, ag y by ddiffig ar yr hayl.

[**R: 810**] Oed Crist 810 pan duodd y lloyad <duw>[116] Natalic, ag y llosgodd Manaw, ag y bu farwolaeth ar <yr>[117] anifeiliad, ag y lloscodd Tegonwy

---

[111] C; a oedd B.
[112] CD; a B.
[113] BC; Ffermael D. The correct name is *Fernuail* (R).
[114] C; deyan B; Deheuwyr D.
[115] CD; Esbod B.
[116] CR; ddydd B; diw D.
[117] C; – BD. R has *varwolaeth yr anifeileit*, but manuscript T reads *ar yr* instead of *yr* (BT (RB), p. 6 n. 1).

gan dân llyghed [gwy]lltion,[118] ag y by waith Llan Faes, ag y tylodod brenhiniaeth Fon a brenhiniaeth Dyfed oblegid rhyfel a fy rhwng Hwel Fychan,[119] ag y gorfy Hwel Ynys[120] Fôn.

[**R: 820**] <Oed Crist ugain ag wythgant pan ddestrywiwyd castell Teganwy gan y Saeson, ag i dygodd y Saeson frenhiniaeth Powys rhag y Brytanniaid, ag i bu farw Hywel Fychan.>[121]

[**R: 830**] Oed Crist <830>[122] pan vy diffig ar y lloyad yr wythfed [Llanstephan 12, 49] dydd o vis Rragvyr, ag i by varw Morydd ap Llwarch Lwyd vrenin Credigion.

[**R: 840**] Oed Krist trigaint[123] ag viii^c pen wledychodd Meyryg esgob Myniw, ag i by waith Fferyll,[124] ag y marw[125] Merfyn Vrych, ag i llas Ithel vrenin Gwent gan wyr Brycheinog.

[**R: 870**] Oed Crist trigain ag viii^c penn i torres y peganiaid Gaer Alclyd, ag i boddes Gwgan vab Morydd vab Llwarch Lwyd brenin Credigion, ag i by waith Bangor, ag i by varw'r esgob,[126] ag i lladdodd y Saeson Rodri Mawr a [50] Gwerydyr i vrawd.

[**R: 890**] Oed Crist x a lxxx ag viii^c pen ddoyth y Normaniaid Dyon i Gastell Baldwin,[127] ag i by varw Henydd vab Bledri,[128] ag i doyth Nynyawd[129] i ddiffeithiaw Credigion ag Ystrad Towi, ag i diffeithiwyd y Normaniaid

---

[118] [...]lltion B; gwylltion CD.

[119] D adds *a Chynan ei frawd*, probably from another source. This text is missing in BC.

[120] BD; yn y C.

[121] C; – B. Similar text is found in D.

[122] C; 833 B; wythgant a deg ar hugain D; deg mlyned ar hugein ac wythgant R.

[123] ACD. The correct reading is *deugein* (R).

[124] AC; Fferyllwg D.

[125] A; bu farw C.

[126] ag i by varw'r esgob A; – C. D has similar text but specifies the bishop as *Einiawn Escob Mynyw*, as in P.

[127] ACD. This agrees with R against PS.

[128] AD; Rhodri C. In A, *rrodri* was written first but then immediately erased, and *bledri* was written after it.

[129] AC; Nynawd D. The correct reading is *Anarawt* (R). The omission of the text *y gyt a'r Saeson* after the name agrees with R against PS.

Dyon yn Lloeger a Brycheinog a Gwent, ag a ddyffygiodd bwyd yn Iwerddon kanys pryfed dierth[130] ar wedd gwydde, a day ddant gan bob vn ohanynt, a'r rrai hyny a vwytaodd yr holl lafyr, a thrwy weddie a theilyng-dawd y bobl i gwrthladdwyd.

[R: 910] [51] Oed Crist x a lx ag ix^c pan vy varw Anarawd ap Rrodri Mawr, brenin y Brytaniaid, a'r amser hwnw y lladdodd Moyryg ap Kadell y vrawd a elwid Kelydog ap Kadell,[131] ag o'r achos hyny i by ryfel rrwng kidgenedl.

[R: 920] Oed Crist xiii a lxxx a ix^c pen aeth Howel Dda vab Cadell vrenin i Ryfain, a chidag ef tri esgob, nid amgen Mart esgob Myniw, a Mordaf esgob Bangor, Teibyr esgob saint Asa[ff],[132] ag oll defnydd y dernas y [52] gidag ef. Sef achos ir aeth ef[133] [i][134] Ryfain: i edrych rrag bod y gyfraith a wnaethoedd ef a'e ddoethion yn y Ty Gwyn ar Daf yNyfed rag i bod yn erbyn kyfraith[135] Dduw a chyfraith y dinasoedd ereill. Ag o achos yr ymladde a vyse rrwng kenhedloedd o'r blaen y gwnaeth ef y gyfraith, o achos bod yn kamarfer yn erbyn kyfraith Dyfnwal. A'r am*ser* hwnw i by varw El6n gwraig Howel Dda ap Kadel[l].[136]

[R: 940] [Llanstephan 100, 5] Oed Crist 1000 pan fy farw Kadell ap Rodri ag Eidwal ap Rodri, ag y lladdodd y Saeson Elysed ap Rodri a Lwmbart esgob Mynyw, ag yspeilwyd Ystrad Llyr[137] gan y Saeson, ag yno y tag-wyd Edmwnd brenin y Saeson, a'r amser hwnw y marw Ho*w*ell Dda <ap Cadell>,[138] a Chadwgan ap Owen a laddwyd gan y Saeson, ag y by <gwaith>[139] Garno rhwng meibon Eidwal Dyfed a meibon Howel Dda.

---

[130] AD; dieithr C.
[131] ap Kadell A; – CD.
[132] Asa[..] A; Assaff BCD.
[133] ir aeth ef A; ir aeth C; ei fyned D.
[134] [...] A; y BCD.
[135] AD; – C.
[136] Kadel[.] A; Kadell BC; – D.
[137] B; Hlur C; Lur D.
[138] CD; – B.
[139] CD; – B.

[**R: 950**] [6] Oed Crist 1030 pan fy laddfa fawr rhwng meibon Eidwal Dyfed a meibon Howell Dda ynhylch <gwaith>[140] Aberkonwy, a'r amser hwnw y diffeithiodd meibon Eidwal Dyfed Gredigion, <ag i bu farw Owain ap Hywel>,[141] ag y bu'r haf tesog, <ag>[142] y diffeithwyd Kaer Gibi gan feibon Eidwal Dyfed. Ef[143] a wnaeth y[144] Owain Gwynedd briodi[145] gwyddeles, merch arglwydd[146] Iwerddon, Pyfog y he[n]w,[147] a honno oedd fam[148] [Llanstephan 12, 53] Howel ap Owen Gwynedd, ag i damchweinodd yr arglwyddiaeth i Howel yn ol marfolaeth Ffyfog[149] y vam, ag yna ir aeth Howel ap Owain i[150] Iwerddon i oresgyn i gyfoeth; dyna'r achos y may y Brytaniaid yn dwedyd may hwynt a bie llawer o dir Iwerddon yn dragywyddawl o hyny allan.

[**R: 960**] Oed Crist xl a mil pen laddwyd Eidwal ap Rodri gann [54] y Saeson, ag y distrywid y Towyn, ag yna i by varw Meyryg ap Kadfan, ag yna i henillodd y Saeson arglwyddiaeth meibion Eidwal, ag i lladdwyd Rodri ap Eidwal, ag i diffeithiwyd y Berffro, ag yn ol hyny i dalodd Iago ap Eidwal i vrawd Ifan[151] ap Eidwal ag a'y rroes efo yngharchar, ag yna i krogodd ef Ifan[152] i vrawd a ddwesbwyd[153] ychod, ag yna i rryfelodd Einon [55] ap Owain[154] ag i lladdawdd ef[155] Vark ag Eyrlaid.

[140] CD; gnaith B.

[141] C; Owen ap [GAP] B.

[142] C; – B.

[143] B; sef C.

[144] B; – C.

[145] B; briod C.

[146] C *adds* o.

[147] hew B; henw C.

[148] B writes *Howell ap Owen Gwynedd* twice, probably because its exemplar, A, had this phrase at the end of one page and the beginning of the next (the latter being the present p. 53).

[149] A; Pyfog C.

[150] A; i'r C.

[151] AD; Ieuan C.

[152] A; Ieuan C.

[153] A; ddywedpwyd C.

[154] Einon ap Owain AD; Owain ap Einion C.

[155] A; – CD.

[**R: 970**] Oed Krist l a mil[156] penn ddiffeithiodd Gotbrig ap Eyrlaid Von, ag ef a wnaeth ddirfawr drafael y'r ynys, ag yna[157] i doyth <Etgar>[158] brenin y Saeson a dirfawr ly gantaw yn erbyn holl Gymry hyd yNghaer Lleon ar Wysg, ag yna i gwrthladdwyd Iago vab Eidwal o'e gyfoeth, ag i gwledychawdd Howell ap Eidwal ef[159] a Meyryg ap Eidwal gan vy[56]ddygoliaeth, ag i by varw Morgan ap Eidwal,[160] ag i by varw <Etgar>[161] brenin y Saeson, ag yno i dalwyd Iago ap Ifan[162] ap Eidwal ag i gorfy Howel ap Eidwal ag i goresgynodd i gyfoeth ef, ag yna i lladdwyd[163] Eidwal, ag yna i gorfy Kystenin ap Iago yn erbyn Howel ap Ifan.[164]

[**R: 980**] Oed Crist lx a mil penn ddoyth Gotbrig ap Eyrlaid y Ddyfed ag i Vyniw, a'r amser hyny[165] i by waith Llan Wenog, a'r amser hwnw[166] i diffeithiwyd Brechein[57]oc a'e holl gyfoeth gan y Saeson, ag i lladdodd y Saeson Howel ap Ieu*an* ap Eidwal trwy dwyll, ag yna i goresgynawdd Kadwallon ap Ieu*an* trwy vyddygoliaeth y gyfoeth[167] yn erbyn y Saeson, nid amgen Ynys Von a Meirionnydd a holl wladoedd Gwynedd,[168] a hyny trwy ddyal[169] a synwyr, a'r amser hwnw i tynwyd llygaid [58] Llwarch ap Owain, ag yna y doyth Gotbric ap Eyrlaid a'r lly dy gidag ef y Ynys Von ag y dalwyd dwy fil o ddynion, a'r dryll arall a ddyg Mr*ed*ydd ap Owain gantaw i Gredigion ag i Ddyfed, ag i by varfolaeth ar <anifeiliaid>[170] dros Ynys

---

[156] l a mil A; 1051 C; nawcant a deuddeg a thrugain D.

[157] AD; – C.

[158] CD; Etgor A.

[159] A; – C.

[160] ag i by varw Morgan ap Eidwal A; – C.

[161] CD; Etgor A.

[162] AD; Ieuan C.

[163] AD; lladdodd C.

[164] AD; Ieuan C.

[165] A; hwnnw C.

[166] A; hynny C.

[167] trwy vyddygoliaeth y gyfoeth A; trwy fuddugoliaeth C; ei gyfoeth ef drwy fuddugoliaeth D.

[168] A repeats *Gwynedd* erroneously.

[169] A; ddeall CD. Cf. R: 'o diruawr ystryw a challder' ('through great craft and cunning').

[170] CD; nefeiliaid A.

Brydain, ag i by varw Ieu*an* ap Eidwal ag Owen ap Howel, ag yna <i>[171] <diffeithiodd y cenedloedd>[172] Llann Badarn a Myniw a Llann Yllytyd a Llann Garmon [59] a Llann Dydoch, ag i by ddirvawr varwolaeth yn Ynys Brydain, ag yn yr ams*er* hwnw y bu drydaniaeth yn Ynys Brydain[173] megis i by <farw>[174] pobl gan newyn.

[R: 990] Oed Krist iiii igain a mil pyn ddiffeithiodd Owen ap Einon vrenhiniaeth M*redy*dd ap Owen, nid amgen Dyfed a Chredigion, a'r amser hwnw i by ddirfawr newyn ynghyfoeth M*redy*dd, ag i by vrwydyr rrwng meibion Meyryg a M*redy*dd yn emyl Llann Gwm ag i gorfy meibion[175] [60] Meyryg yn erbyn M*redy*dd, ag yna i lladdwyd Tewdwr ap Einon ap Owen[176] ap Howel Dda vab Cadell.

Oed Crist mil a chant pyn ddoyth Ll*wely*n ap Sesyllt i lodraethy[177] Dyfed, a Howel ap Sesyllt gorychaf a ffenaf vrenin Gwynedd a brenin yr holl Vrytaniaid, ag yn i amser ef i by gyfoeth mawr gan y Brytaniaid, ag yna i tyfodd rryfel rrwng Howel ap Sesyllt a'i rieni, ag i doyth Ysgotiaid ar draws y[178] Kymry, ag i by vaes yNglan [61] Gwili, ag yno i lladdwyd Ll*wely*n[179] ap Sesyllt, ag i doyth Rydd*erch* ap Iestyn i lodraythy'r[180] deay, ag yna i lladdwyd Kynan ap Sesyllt.

[R: 1030] Oed Crist mil a chant a xxx pen laddwyd Rydderch ap Iestyn gan Ysgotiaid, ag[181] yna i kynhaliodd Iago ap Eidwal lywodraeth y deay, a'r amser hwnw i by waith Hiraythwy rrwng meibion Rydderch ap Iestyn a meibion <Edwin>,[182] ag yna i lladdwys meibion Gynan ap Sesyllt veibion

---

[171] C; a A; y D.

[172] C; diffeithiwyd kenedlaeth AD. R agrees with C.

[173] ag yn yr ams*er* hwnw y bu drydaniaeth yn Ynys Brydain A; – C. Almost identical text is found in D.

[174] CD; rarw A.

[175] A repeats *meibion* at the beginning of the next page.

[176] ap Owen AD; – C.

[177] A; lywodraeth CD.

[178] A; – C.

[179] A; Owain C.

[180] A; lywodraeth y C.

[181] A repeats *ag*.

[182] C; Edwim A.

Edwin,[183] ag yna i lladdodd y Saeson veib[62]ion[184] Gynan ap Sesyll, ag yna y doyth Gry*ff*ydd ap Ll*wely*n ap Sesyllt i lodraythy'r deay, ag <i>[185] ryfelodd yn erbyn y Saeson, ag i rroes Gryffydd vaes yn erbyn y Saeson yn emyl Rryd y Groes ar Hafren, ag i kafas Gry*ff*ydd y vyddygoliaeth, a'r amser hwnw i by waith Pen Kadair, ag yna i by ddi[r]fawr[186] dwyll a brad rrwng Gry*ff*ydd ap R*ys* a meibion Rydderch ap Iestyn yn erbyn Gry*ff*ydd ap Ll*wely*n ap [33] Sesyllt, ag yna i lladdwyd amgylch saith igain <o oreugwyr>[187] Gry*ff*ydd ap Ll*wely*n o wyr Ystrad Towi a Dyfed, ag yna i bu ddirfawr eira dduw[188] kalan Ionawr heb doddi hyd wyl Badrig. Yn yr amser hwnw i by ddifaith holl Deheybarth.

[**R: 1050**] Oed Crist mil a chant a l pen ddoyth y lly o Iwerddon y Ddeheybarth, ag aython gida Gry*ff*ydd ap Llwelyn ap Sesyllt yn erbyn y Saeson, [34] ac yn Henffordd i by faes rryngthynt a'r Saeson, ag i kavas Gry*ff*ydd y vyddygoliaeth, ag yna i by lawer o ladd a llosgi.

[**R: 1060**] <Oed>[189] Crist mil a chant a lx pan vy varw Gry*ff*ydd ap Llwelyn ap Sesyllt, penn a tharian ag ymddiffynwr yr holl Vrytaniaid, ag yna i doeth Willi*a*m Bastart twsog Normandi yn gynkwerwr i Loeger trwy groelonder gwedi marw Edwart vrenin y Saeson, [35] ac yn yr amser hwnw i by anvndeb mawr rrwng Bleddvn ap Kynfyn a Rriwallawn ap Kynvyn yn erbyn Mredydd ap Ithel, ag yna i by varw M*redy*dd ap Ithel rog annwyd yn kilo rog Bleddyn ap Kynfyn,[190] ag yno i heddychodd Bleddyn a Rriwallawn ap Kynfyn, ag i kynhelis Bleddyn ap Kynfyn gyfoeth Gwynedd a Ffowys yn erbyn Rriwallon ap Kynvyn a M*redy*dd ap Owen ap Edwin a gynhelis Deheybarth, [**R: 1070**] ag yn ol hyny i by [36] y[191] vrwydyr rrwng Gronwy

---

[183] ag yna i lladdwys meibion Gynan ap Sesyllt veibion Edwin A; – C.

[184] A; – CD.

[185] C; a A.

[186] ddi[.]fawr A; ddirfawr BC.

[187] CD; o'r goreygwyr A.

[188] A; ddydd CD.

[189] C; O A.

[190] a Rriwallawn [...] Bleddyn ap Kynfyn A; – C. Similar text appears in D. The text was probably omitted from C due to eyeskip.

[191] A; – CD.

ap Ll*wely*n a meibion Gydwgan ap Gr*yffy*dd, ag yn ol hyny i by'r[192] arglwydd R*ys* ap Tewdwr Mawr yn dywsog Deheybarth.

Arglwydd Lywelyn ap Ierwerth Drwyndwn yn dywsog yNgwynedd, ag yna i priodes yr arglwydd Lywelyn v*erc*h Ieu*an* vrenin Lloeger, a thair merch*e*d a vy iddaw ef o'r wraig hon. Vn o'r merched a roed i [37] Vedric amherawdr Rryfain, a'r ail i Vaelgwn Vawr ap yr arglwydd R*ys* ap Tewdwr, a'r drydedd i Simwnt Mwnffwrt Iarll Elystyder, ag yna i heddychwyd rrwng[193] Kymry a'r Saeson dros amser.

<Terfyn y dryll hwnn o hanes.>[194]

Translation

This is the chronicle of the princes, how there were wars, vengeance, and wonders.

- [**R: 720**] 720 was the age of Christ when there was the hot summer, and Beli ab Elffin died.
- [**R: 750**] 750 when Tewdwr ap Rhodri,[195] King of the Britons, died.
- [**R: 760**] 760 when there was the conflict between the Britons and the English at the battle of Hereford, and Dyfnwal ap Tewdwr died.
- [**R: 770**] 770 when the Easter of the Britons was moved, and Ffernfael ab Idwal died, and destruction was brought upon the men of Deheubarth by their own king,[196] [**R: 780**] and the south was forced to kill the king in summertime.

---

[192] ag yn ol hyny i by'r A; Oed Crist ... . C. Interlinear insertion in A: Oed Crist cccccc a by.

[193] C adds *y*.

[194] C; – A.

[195] The obituaries of Tewdwr ap Beli and Rhodri have been merged in BC, as printed above. D has the correct text, probably taken from another source: '[...] Tewdwr ab Beli a Rhodri [...]'.

[196] This is ambiguous; if *y hûn* is taken to be modern *eu hun*, the translation above can stand, but if it is taken to be modern *ei hun*, it might be translated as 'by the king himself'. In other texts, it is Offa of Mercia who devastates the men of Deheubarth.

[**R: 800**] 800 was the age of Christ when the English killed Caradog, King of Gwynedd, and Arthur,[197] King of Ceredigion, Rhydderch,[198] King of Dyfed, Cadell, King of Powys, and Elfodd, Archbishop of Gwynedd, died, and there was an eclipse of the sun.

[**R: 810**] 810 was the age of Christ when the moon darkened on Christmas day, and the Isle of Man[199] burned, and there was a mortality upon the animals, and Degannwy burned with the fire of wild lightning strikes, and the battle of Llanfaes took place, and the kingdoms of Anglesey and Dyfed[200] were impoverished because of a war between Hywel Fychan [and Cynan his brother], and Hywel of Anglesey prevailed.

[**R: 820**] Eight hundred and twenty was the age of Christ when the castle of Degannwy was destroyed by the English, and the English took the kingdom of Powys from the Britons, and Hywel Fychan died.

[**R: 830**] 830 was the age of Christ when there was an eclipse of the moon on 24 November,[201] and Morudd ap Llywarch Lwyd, King of Ceredigion, died.[202]

[**R: 840**] Eight hundred and sixty was the age of Christ when Meurig, Bishop of St Davids, began to reign, and the battle of Fferyll[203] took place, and

---

[197] The name should be Arthen.

[198] The name should be Rhain.

[199] This should be *Mynyw* (St Davids) rather than *Manaw* (the Isle of Man).

[200] The destruction of Dyfed, perpetrated by Coenwulf of Mercia, should be a separate event.

[201] For this date, *Brut Ieuan Brechfa* follows the Red Book version of *Brut y Tywysogyon*. However, the Red Book version's reading, 'yr wythuet dyd o vis Racuyr' ('the eighth day from the month of December', i.e. 24 November, as above) is an error for 'yr wythuet dyd o vis Tachwed' ('the eighth day from the month of November', i.e. 25 October). Modern scientific data shows that the correct date for the eclipse is 24/25 October, as given in *Brenhinedd y Saesson* ('viii kalendas Nouembres' = 25 October): Erik Grigg, '"Mole Rain" and Other Natural Phenomena in the Welsh Annals: Can *Mirabilia* Unravel the Textual History of the *Annales Cambriae*?', *Welsh History Review*, 24 (2009), 1–40 (p. 24). No precise date is given for the eclipse in the Peniarth 20 version of *Brut y Tywysogyon* or in any Welsh Latin chronicles.

[202] The obituary of Morudd ap Llywarch Lwyd, unique to this text, replaces that of Sadyrnfyw, Bishop of St Davids. Morudd and Llywarch Lwyd have been taken from the genealogy of the family of Gwynionydd-is-Cerdin (see above, pp. 395–96).

[203] This is a misreading of *Ketyll* (R), possibly influenced either by *Fferyll*, the Welsh name for Virgil, or by *Fferyllwg*, a late name for Hereford. See *HW*, I, 282.

Merfyn Frych died, and Ithel, King of Gwent, was killed by the men of Brycheiniog.

[**R: 870**] Eight hundred and sixty was the age of Christ when the pagans broke the fortress of Alclud, and Gwgon ap Morudd ap Llywarch Lwyd,[204] King of Ceredigion, drowned, and the battle of Bangor[205] took place, and the Bishop[206] died, and the English killed Rhodri Mawr and Gwrydr[207] his brother.[208]

[**R: 890**] 890 was the age of Christ when the Black Northmen came to Baldwin's Castle, and Hyfaidd[209] son of Bleddri died, and *Nynyawd*[210] came to ravage Ceredigion and Ystrad Tywi, and the Black Northmen were destroyed[211] in England and Brycheiniog and Gwent, and food failed in Ireland on account of strange creatures in the form of geese,[212] every one of which had two teeth, and they ate the entire harvest, and through the prayers and praiseworthiness of the people they were driven away.

[**R: 910**] 970[213] was the age of Christ when Anarawd ap Rhodri Mawr, King of the Britons, died, and at that time Meurig ap Cadell killed his brother,

---

[204] Gwgon's patronymic is spurious; the real name of his father was Meurig, as is stated in R (see above, p. 395).

[205] R reads *Bangoleu*, following other chronicles (cf. *BT (Pen. 20 trans.)*, p. 137, note to p. 5, l. 7).

[206] R specifies that *Meuryc* was the name of the bishop. The silence here may reflect the variation in the name of this bishop as seen across multiple chronicles: see *BT (Pen. 20 trans.)*, p. 137, note to p. 5, ll. 8–9.

[207] The name should be Gwriad, as in R.

[208] *Brut Ieuan Brechfa* follows R and other versions of *Brut y Tywysogyon* in calling Gwriad the brother of Rhodri. Gwraid was more probably Rhodri's son: see David Dumville, 'The "Six" Sons of Rhodri Mawr: A Problem in Asser's *Life of King Alfred*', *CMCS*, 4 (1982), 5–18 (p. 8).

[209] The spelling of Hyfaidd used here, *Henydd*, derives ultimately from the Old Welsh form *Himeyd*. The latter caused difficulty elsewhere too: *BT (Pen. 20 trans.)*, p. 139, note to p. 5, l. 29.

[210] The name should be Anarawd.

[211] This is a reversal of the usual sense of this passage, whereby the Northmen ravage the places named.

[212] The reading should be *gwadd* ('mole') rather than *gwydd* ('goose').

[213] The addition of *a lx* ('and 60') to this date throws the chronology of the remainder of the chronicle out of line with that of R.

who was called Clydog ap Cadell, and for that reason there was war among the same kindred.[214]

[**R: 920**] 993 was the age of Christ when King Hywel Dda son of Cadell went to Rome,[215] and with him were three bishops, namely *Mart*,[216] Bishop of St Davids, Mordaf, Bishop of Bangor, and *Teibyr*,[217] Bishop of St Asaph, along with everyone of substance in the kingdom. This is the reason that he went to Rome: to check in case the law that he and his wise men had made in the White House on the Taf in Dyfed should be against the law of God and the law of the other cities. And he made the law because of the fighting that there had been among kindreds beforehand, because they were abusing the law of Dyfnwal.[218] And at that time Elen, wife of Hywel Dda ap Cadell, died.

[**R: 940**] 1000 was the age of Christ when Cadell ap Rhodri[219] and Idwal ap Rhodri[220] died, and the English killed Elise ap Rhodri and *Lwmbart*, Bishop of St Davids,[221] and Ystrad *Llyr*[222] was despoiled by the English, and then Edmund, King of the English, was strangled,[223] and at that time

---

[214] This last statement is an addition to R's text, designed to complement the addition in the following section.

[215] Everything from this point to the notice about the death of Elen is an addition to R's text, based on the epilogue to law manuscripts like BL, MS Add. 22356 (Welsh law manuscript S).

[216] An error for *Lwmbart*, as in the next section.

[217] In the epilogue to the law books the name is *Chebur*.

[218] This is a reference to Dyfnwal Moelmud, who promulgates a law code for the Britons in Geoffrey of Monmouth's *Historia regum Britanniae*, and who is mentioned in the same capacity in *Cyfraith Hywel Dda*. See Owen, 'Royal Propaganda', pp. 229–32, 250–51.

[219] The patronymic should be *vab Arthuael* (R).

[220] Idwal 'ap Rhodri' (properly Idwal Foel, grandson of Rhodri) was really killed by the English alongside his brother Elise in the incident recounted in the next clause.

[221] The notice of *Lwmbart*'s death was been incorrectly associated with the conflict between Elise 'ap Rhodri' and the English.

[222] The correct reading is *Ystrat Clut* (R), 'Strathclyde'.

[223] The murder of King Edmund is missing from R and P and appears in S only as an extended addition from another source. It is present, however, in the three Latin *Annales Cambriae* chronicles, in a form comparable to the notice given here. The verb *tagwyd* might imply a closer association with the wording of the Harleian and Breviate chronicles, *iugulatus est* ('was slaughtered, had [his] throat cut'), than with the *occiditur* ('was killed, was slain') of the Cottonian chronicle. Perhaps Ieuan Brechfa did not know that *iugulare* could have the more general meaning 'to kill violently'.

Hywel Dda ap Cadell died, and Cadwgon ab Owain was killed by the English, and the battle of Carno took place between the sons of Idwal Dyfed[224] and the sons of Hywel Dda.

[**R: 950**] 1030 was the age of Christ when there was a great slaughter between the sons of Idwal Dyfed and the sons of Hywel Dda in the area of Aberconwy,[225] and at that time the sons of Idwal Dyfed ravaged Ceredigion, and Owain[226] ap Hywel died, and the hot summer occurred, and Holyhead was ravaged by the sons of Idwal Dyfed.[227] He caused Owain Gwynedd to marry an Irish woman called Pyfog,[228] the daughter of the lord of Ireland, and she was the mother of Hywel ab Owain Gwynedd, and the lordship fell to Hywel after the death of Pyfog his mother, and then Hywel ab Owain went to Ireland to conquer his territory; that is the reason for the Britons saying that it is they who have the perpetual right to much of Ireland's land from that time onwards.[229]

[**R: 960**] 1040 was the age of Christ when Idwal ap Rhodri was killed by the English,[230] and Tywyn was destroyed, and then Meurig ap Cadfan died, and then the English won the lordship of the sons of Idwal,[231] and Rhodri ab Idwal was killed, and Aberffraw was ravaged, and after that Iago ab Idwal seized his brother Ifan[232] ab Idwal and put him in prison, and then

---

[224] Idwal's epithet *Dyfed* seems to have arisen from a misreading of R. See above, p. 397.

[225] This battle happened in Llanrwst. R has 'yg gweith Conwy yn Llan Wrst' ('in the battle of Conwy at Llanrwst').

[226] This is a mistake for *Etwin* (R). Perhaps the error was facilitated by a reading such as that in the Breviate chronicle, which has *guin* for *etguin*.

[227] It was actually the sons of one Olaf who ravaged Holyhead. The Olaf in question was probably either Olaf Cuarán or Olaf Guthfrithsson: Charles-Edwards, *Wales and the Britons*, pp. 539–40.

[228] In the Llywelyn ab Iorwerth genealogies, Hywel's mother is called *Ffynnot Wydeles*: Guy, *Medieval Welsh Genealogy*, p. 364 (LlIG 12.9); *Early Welsh Genealogical Tracts*, p. 97 ('ABT' 2l).

[229] This story about Hywel ab Owain Gwynedd and his Irish mother is unique, though the implied historical connection between Idwal Foel and Owain Gwynedd is anachronistic.

[230] This is the only text to specify Idwal's killers. It may be a deduction from the following statement about the English attacking the sons of Idwal.

[231] According to other texts the English ravaged the kingdoms of the sons of Idwal ('diffeithawd y Saesson [...] vrenhinaetheu meibon Idwal' in R), but they did not win them.

[232] That is, Ieuaf.

he hanged Ifan his brother who was mentioned above, and then Einion ab Owain waged war and he killed Mark and *Eyrlaid*.[233]

[R: 970] 1050 was the age of Christ when Guthfrith son of *Eyrlaid* ravaged Anglesey, and he caused great hardship for the island, and then Edgar,[234] King of the English, came with a great host against all the Welsh as far as Caerleon-on-Usk, and then Iago ab Idwal was expelled from his territory, and on account of his victory Hywel ab Idwal[235] ruled over him and Meurig ab Idwal, and Morgan ab Idwal[236] died, and Edgar, King of the English, died, and then Iago ab Ifan[237] ab Idwal was seized and Hywel ab Idwal[238] prevailed and conquered his territory, and then Idwal was killed, and then Custennin ab Iago prevailed against Hywel ab Ifan.[239]

[R: 980] 1060 was the age of Christ when Guthfrith son of *Eyrlaid* came to Dyfed and to St Davids, and at that time the battle of Llanwenog took place, and at that time Brycheiniog, with all its territory,[240] was ravaged by the English, and the English killed Hywel ab Ieuan[241] ab Idwal through treachery, and then through victory Cadwallon ab Ieuan[242] took possession of his territory in opposition to the English,[243] namely Anglesey and

---

[233] *Eyrlaid* is the text's version of Harold. Two consecutive events have been merged in this notice. In R, Einion ab Owain ravages Gower, and then Mark son of Harold (*ag* 'and' in *Brut Ieuan Brechfa* is an error for *ap* 'son (of)') ravages Penmon. 'Mark' is an error for 'Maccus'. Among the Welsh chronicles, only S preserves an approximately correct form of the name (*Mactus*): *BT (Pen. 20 trans.)*, p. 143, note to p. 8, l. 18.

[234] By naming this king as Edgar, *Brut Ieuan Brechfa* agrees with PS against R, which mistakenly has *Edwart* for *Edgar*.

[235] Both references to Hywel ab Idwal in this section should refer to Hywel ab Ieuaf (or Ifan), as in the final notice. 'Idwal' is a misreading of Old Welsh *Iouab*.

[236] This is the only chronicle that specifies Morgan's patronymic. It is probably spurious, because the Morgan concerned is likely to have been Morgan ab Owain, King of Morgannwg.

[237] That is, Ieuaf. Other chronicles do not specify this Iago's ancestry.

[238] See n. 235 above.

[239] That is, Ieuaf. It was actually Hywel ab Ieuaf who defeated and killed Custennin ab Iago.

[240] It is usually said to be Brycheiniog and the territory of Einion ab Owain that were ravaged by the English.

[241] That is, Ieuaf.

[242] That is, Ieuaf.

[243] This is the only chronicle suggesting that Cadwallon ab Ieuaf contended with the English for possession of Gwynedd. This is probably no more than a supposition arising from the

Meirionydd and all the lands of Gwynedd, and that was done through vengeance and cunning, and at that time the eyes of Llywarch ab Owain were removed, and then Guthfrith son of *Eyrlaid* came with the black host to Anglesey and two thousand men were seized, and Maredudd ab Owain took the remainder with him to Ceredigion and to Dyfed, and there was a mortality upon the animals across the island of Britain, and Ieuan[244] ab Idwal and Owain ap Hywel died, and then the gentiles ravaged Llanbadarn, St Davids, Llanilltud, Llangarmon,[245] and Llandudoch, and there was a great mortality in the island of Britain, and in that time there was a famine in the island of Britain with the result that people died from hunger.

[**R: 990**] 1080 was the age of Christ when Owain[246] ab Einion ravaged the kingdom of Maredudd ab Owain, namely Dyfed and Ceredigion, and at that time there was great hunger in the territory of Maredudd, and there was a battle between the sons of Meurig and Maredudd near Llangwm and the sons of Meurig prevailed against Maredudd, and then Tewdwr ab Einion ab Owain ap Hywel Dda ap Cadell was killed.

1100[247] was the age of Christ when Llywelyn ap Seisyll came to govern Dyfed, and Hywel ap Seisyll[248] was the supreme and foremost King of Gwynedd and King of all the Britons,[249] and in his time the Britons had

previous notice of Hywel ab Ieuan (Ieuaf), King of Gwynedd, being killed by the English. In any case, R's statement that Cadwallon ab Ieuaf took possession of Gwynedd, upon which *Brut Ieuan Brechfa* based its supposition, is probably an incorrect rendering of an annal preserved more accurately in other chronicles, which states that Maredudd ab Owain slew Cadwallon ab Ieuaf and gained possession of his territory. See *BT (RB)*, p. 279, note to p. 17, ll. 20–23.

[244] That is, Ieuaf.

[245] The correct reading is *Llan Garban* (R), meaning Llancarfan.

[246] This is a mistake for *Etwin* (R). The same mistake is found in the Cottonian chronicle (*Owein*). The error in both was probably caused by a reading such as that in the Breviate chronicle, which has *guin* rather than *etguin*.

[247] There is no equivalent notice in R for the beginning of the decade starting in 1020 (*BT (RB)*, p. lvi), but the following events, which *Brut Ieuan Brechfa* broadly shares with R, are dated by Thomas Jones to 1022–1027. *Brut Ieuan Brechfa* omits all the events given in R for the two preceding decades starting in 1000 and 1010.

[248] The two appearances of Hywel ap Seisyll are additions to the text of R. This character may ultimately be based on a twelfth-century figure found in the Jesus 20 genealogies: see above, pp. 399–400.

[249] In other chronicles, which do not mention a Hywel ap Seisyll, this description applies to Llywelyn ap Seisyll.

great power, and then war grew between Hywel ap Seisyll and his kin, and the Irish came across to Wales, and there was a battle in Glan Gwili, and there[250] Llywelyn ap Seisyll was killed, and Rhydderch ab Iestyn came to govern the south, and then Cynan ap Seisyll was killed.

[**R: 1030**] 1130 was the age of Christ when Rhydderch ab Iestyn was killed by the Irish, and then Iago ab Idwal took hold of the government of the south,[251] and at that time the battle of Hiraethwy took place between the sons of Rhydderch ab Iestyn[252] and the sons of Edwin, and then the sons of Cynan ap Seisyll killed the sons of Edwin,[253] and then the English killed the sons of Cynan ap Seisyll,[254] and then Gruffudd ap Llywelyn ap Seisyll came to govern the south,[255] and he warred against the English, and Gruffudd gave battle to the English near Rhyd-y-Groes on the Severn, and Gruffudd had the victory, and at that time the battle of Pencader took place, and then there was a great deceit and treachery between Gruffudd ap Rhys[256] and the sons of Rhydderch ab Iestyn against Gruffudd ap Llywelyn ap Seisyll, and then around seven score of Gruffudd ap Llywelyn's foremost men were killed by the men of Ystrad Tywi and Dyfed,[257] and then there was a very great snow on the first of January which did not melt until the Feast of Patrick. In that time all Deheubarth was waste.

---

[250] For the interpretation of *yno* as 'there' rather than 'then' in this case, see above, p. 400.

[251] This should be 'Wyned' (R) rather than 'y deay'. The error has resulted from an eyeskip from 'llywodraeth Wyned' to 'llywodraeth y Deheu' (R).

[252] The text here agrees with PS against R, which by error does not name the opponents of the sons of Edwin in the battle. The Latin chronicles do not name the participants of the battle. Cf. *BT (RB)*, pp. xlvi–xlvii.

[253] Due to an error, R does not name the victim of the sons of Cynan. PS, in agreement with the Latin chronicles, name the victim specifically as Maredudd ab Edwin.

[254] Other chronicles report that it was Caradog ap Rhydderch who was killed by the English, rather than the sons of Cynan ap Seisyll.

[255] Again, 'the south' has been substituted for 'Gwynedd' (see n. 251 above). In R, it is clear that Gruffudd ap Llywelyn succeeded Iago ab Idwal, so the present error presumably stems from the preceding error whereby Iago ab Idwal was made to govern the south rather than Gwynedd.

[256] The introduction of a 'Gruffudd ap Rhys' to this part of the chronicle is due to a slight alteration of R's text, which reads 'Ruffud a Rys meibon Ryderch'.

[257] In R only the men of Ystrad Tywi are said to be responsible for the treachery. The appearance of Dyfed is probably due to an eyeskip to R's next sentence, which states that Gruffudd avenged his men by ravaging *Ystrat Tywi a Dyfet* (R).

[**R: 1050**] 1150 was the age of Christ when the host came from Ireland to Deheubarth, and they went[258] with Gruffudd ap Llywelyn ap Seisyll against the English, and in Hereford there was a battle between them and the English, and Gruffudd had the victory, and then there was lots of killing and burning.

[**R: 1060**] 1160 was the age of Christ when Gruffudd ap Llywelyn ap Seisyll died, the head and shield and defender of all the Britons, and then William the Bastard, Prince of Normandy, became the conqueror of England through cruelty after the death of Edward, King of the English, and in that time there was great discord among Bleddyn ap Cynfyn and Rhiwallon ap Cynfyn against Maredudd ab Ithel,[259] and then Maredudd ab Ithel died of cold while fleeing from Bleddyn ap Cynfyn, and then Bleddyn and Rhiwallon ap Cynfyn restored peace, and Bleddyn ap Cynfyn held the territory of Gwynedd and Powys in opposition to Rhiwallon ap Cynfyn[260] and Maredudd ab Owain ab Edwin held Deheubarth, and after that the battle between Goronwy ap Llywelyn and the sons of Cadwgon ap Gruffudd took place,[261] and after that the Lord Rhys ap Tewdwr was Prince of Deheubarth.

Lord Llywelyn ab Iorwerth Drwyndwn [was] Prince in Gwynedd, and then the Lord Llywelyn married the daughter of John, King of England, and he had three daughters with that wife.[262] One of the daughters was given to Frederick,

---

[258] In other chronicles the Irish fleet is said to have foundered four or five years before Gruffudd ap Llywelyn's attack on Hereford.

[259] The text should read *Maredud ac Ithel* ('Maredudd and Ithel') (R).

[260] Other chronicles claim that Rhiwallon ap Cynfyn was killed in the battle just described, after which Maredudd died of cold in flight.

[261] The names of the participants in this battle have become confused. Compare the text of R: 'Ac yna y bu y vrwydyr yg Kamdwr rwg Goronw a Llywelyn meibon Kadwgawn a Charadawc vab Gruffud gyt ac wynt a Rys vab Ywein a Ryderch vab Caradawc' ('And then was the battle in the Camddwr between Goronwy and Llywelyn, sons of Cadwgon, and Caradog ap Gruffudd along with them, and Rhys ab Owain and Rhydderch ap Caradog'). In *Brut Ieuan Brechfa*, Llywelyn has become Goronwy's father, Cadwgon has replaced Caradog as the son of Gruffudd, and Rhys ab Owain and Rhydderch ap Caradog have been omitted entirely.

[262] This list confuses the daughters of Llywelyn ab Iorwerth and his father-in-law, King John. The first is Isabella, daughter of John, who married the Holy Roman Emperor Frederick II; the second is Angharad, daughter of Llywelyn, who married Maelgwn Fychan ap Maelgwn ap yr Argwlydd Rhys ap Gruffudd; and the third is Eleanor, daughter of John, who married Simon de Montfort.

Emperor of Rome, the second to Maelgwn Mawr son of the Lord Rhys ap Tewdwr, and the third to Simon de Montfort, Earl of Leicester, and then peace was made between Wales and the English for a while.

The end of this part of history.

Appendix: List of the Chronicles of Medieval Wales and the March

The following is a list of chronicles known to have been composed in Wales and the March from the earliest times to the sixteenth century. Chronicles written in Latin, Welsh, and, in the case of Humphrey Llwyd's *Cronica Walliae*, English have been included. The texts are ordered according to their approximate dates of composition, judging for the most part by the dating of their final annal. There is admittedly room for debate about the exact ordering, especially for the chronicles finalized in the 1280s (nos 6–9, and possibly 4), but the list should serve as a rough guide. The information for each chronicle is provided in three sections:

- YRS: The years covered by the chronicle. Sometimes additional information is given about the date of the chronicle's composition, if this is not sufficiently indicated by the years covered.
- MSS: The principal manuscripts of the chronicle. Derivative manuscripts are excluded, as are later manuscripts when they are of little textual importance (e.g. the many later manuscripts of the Red Book of Hergest version of *Brut y Tywysogyon*). The dates of the Welsh vernacular manuscripts have been checked against Daniel Huws's forthcoming *Repertory of Welsh Manuscripts and Scribes*. Abbreviations have been employed for the two most important archives: BL = London, British Library, and NLW = Aberystwyth, National Library of Wales.
- EDS: The principal published editions of the chronicle, with preference given to those in which the text may be found in full. This section is not intended to be comprehensive; for further editions, including parallel editions, see the works cited in Chapter 3 above.

It should be noted that the list is not quite comprehensive, owing to the numerous chronicles and sets of annals surviving in early modern Welsh manuscripts that have yet to be studied.[1]

---

[1] For the comments by Huw Pryce and Ben Guy above, see p. 24 and pp. 105–06.

1. The Harleian chronicle (A-text of *Annales Cambriae*).

YRS: 445–954.

MSS: BL, MS Harley 3859, fols 190ʳ–93ᵛ (s. xi/xii).

EDS: Egerton Phillimore, 'The *Annales Cambriæ* and the Old-Welsh Genealogies from *Harleian MS. 3859*', *Y Cymmrodor*, 9 (1888), 141–83; *Annales Cambriae: The A Text, from British Library, Harley MS 3859, ff. 190r–193r*, ed. by Henry W. Gough Cooper (Welsh Chronicles Research Group, 2015) <http://croniclau.bangor.ac.uk/documents/AC_A_first_edition.pdf> [accessed 18 December 2017].

2. The Annals of Margam (*Annales de Margan*).

YRS: 1066–1232; Grace Dieu continuation 1232–1235.

MSS: Cambridge, Trinity College, MS O.2.4, fols 1–16 (c. 1232); Trinity College Dublin, MS 507, fols 2ʳ–13ᵛ (s. xiii²/⁴).

EDS: *AM*, I (1864), 1–40; Marvin L. Colker, 'The "Margam Chronicle" in a Dublin Manuscript', *HSJ*, 4 (1992), 123–48.

3. *O Oes Gwrtheyrn*.

YRS: 400–1265.

MSS: Oxford, Jesus College, MS 111, fols 254ʳ–54ᵛ (Red Book of Hergest; s. xiv/xv,>1382); NLW, MS Peniarth 32, fols 114ᵛ–16ᵛ (*Y Llyfr Teg*; c. 1404); NLW, MS Llanstephan 28, pp. 86–92 (Gutun Owain, 1456); NLW, MS Peniarth 182, pp. 24–34 (Huw Pennant, 1509 × 1513); NLW, MS Peniarth 135, pp. 66–71 (Gruffudd Hiraethog, 1556–1564); Cardiff, Central Library, MS 3.11, pp. 149–54 (David Powel, 1561–c. 1580); NLW, MS Peniarth 212, pp. 514–23 (Wiliam Cynwal, 1565 × 1587); etc.

EDS: Owain Wyn Jones, Chapter 7 above.

4. *Cronica de Wallia* (E-text of *Annales Cambriae*; *Cronicon de Wallia*).

YRS: 1190–1266.

MSS: Exeter Cathedral Library, MS 3514, pp. 507–19 (*c.* 1285).

EDS: '"Cronica de Wallia" and Other Documents from Exeter Cathedral Library MS. 3514', ed. by Thomas Jones, *BBCS*, 12 (1946), 27–44; *Annales Cambriae: The E Text, from Exeter Cathedral Library MS 3514, pp. 507–19*, ed. by Henry W. Gough-Cooper (Welsh Chronicles Research Group, 2016) <http://croniclau.bangor.ac.uk/documents/AC_E_First_Edition%20%20.pdf> [accessed 18 December 2017].

5. The Annals of Cardiff.

YRS: 1066–1268.

MSS: BL, Royal 6 B XI, fols 105^r–108^v (*s.* xiv^{in}).

EDS: Georgia Henley, Chapter 8 above.

6. *Cronica ante aduentum Domini*
(D-text of *Annales Cambriae*; *Cronica de Anglia*).

YRS: 1132 BC–AD 1285.

MSS: Exeter Cathedral Library, MS 3514, pp. 523–28 (*c.* 1285).

EDS: *Annales Cambriae: The D Text, from Exeter Cathedral Library MS 3514, pp. 523–28*, ed. by Henry W. Gough-Cooper (Welsh Chronicles Research Group, 2015) <http://croniclau.bangor.ac.uk/documents/AC%20D%20first%20edition.pdf> [accessed 18 December 2017].

7. The Breviate chronicle (B-text of *Annales Cambriae*;
PRO chronicle; Annals of Strata Florida).

YRS: 1 AM–AD 1286.

MSS: London, The National Archives, MS E 164/1, fols 1^r–13^r (*c.* 1300).

EDS: *Annales Cambriae: The B Text, from London, National Archives, MS E164/1, pp. 2–26*, ed. by Henry W. Gough-Cooper (Welsh Chronicles Research Group, 2015) <http://croniclau.bangor.ac.uk/documents/AC%20B%20first%20edition.pdf> [accessed 18 December 2017].

8. Extracts from Welsh annals.

   YRS: 1095–1287.
   MSS: London, The National Archives, MS E 164/1, fols 237^v–238^r (c. 1300).
   EDS: None.

**9. The Cottonian chronicle
(C-text of *Annales Cambriae*; Annals of St Davids).**

   YRS: 1 AM–AD 1288.
   MSS: BL, MS Cotton Domitian A 1, fols 138^r–55^r (c. 1286–1288).
   EDS: *Annales Cambriae: The C Text, from London, British Library, Cotton MS Domitian A. i, ff. 138r–155r*, ed. by Henry W. Gough-Cooper (Welsh Chronicles Research Group, 2015) <http://croniclau.bangor.ac.uk/documents/AC%20C%20first%20edition.pdf> [accessed 18 December 2017].

10. The Neath chronicle (the Glamorgan chronicle; the Breviate annals).

   YRS: 600, 1066–1298.
   MSS: London, The National Archives, MS E 164/1, fols 14^v–17^v (c. 1300).
   EDS: 'Chronicle of the Thirteenth Century: MS. Exchequer Domesday', [ed. by Harry Longueville Jones], *Archaeologia Cambrensis*, 3rd ser., 8, no. 32 (1862), 272–83.

11. *Brut y Tywysogyon*, Red Book of Hergest version.

   YRS: 682–1282 (finalized after 1307).
   MSS: NLW, MS Peniarth 18 (s. xiv^{med}); NLW, MS 3035B, fols 142^r–206^v (Mostyn 116; s. xiv^2); Oxford, Jesus College, MS 111, fols 58^r–89^v (Red Book of Hergest; s. xiv/xv, >1382); NLW, MS Peniarth 19, fols 99^v–153^r (s. xiv/xv); etc.
   EDS: *BT (RB)*.

12. *Oed yr Arglwydd*.

YRS: 540–1307.

MSS: NLW, MS Llanstephan 28, pp. 92–94 (Gutun Owain, 1456); NLW, MS Peniarth 182, pp. 34–37 (Huw Pennant, 1509 × 1513); NLW, MS Cwrtmawr 453, pp. 27–31 (Robert Vaughan, *c*. 1615 × 1630); etc.

EDS: Ben Guy, 'A Lost Medieval Manuscript from North Wales: Hengwrt 33, the *Hanesyn Hên*', *Studia Celtica*, 50 (2016), 69–105.

13. The Tintern chronicle (i).

YRS: 1131–1320.

MSS: Cambridge, Corpus Christi College, MS 210, p. 4 (William Worcestre, 1478); BL, MS Cotton Vespasian D XVII, fols 60^r–61^v (Thomas Talbot, *s*. xvi^2).

EDS: Julian Harrison, 'The Tintern Abbey Chronicles', *The Monmouthshire Antiquary*, 16 (2000), 84–98.

14. *Blwydyn Eiseu*.

YRS: 1 AM–AD 1321.

MSS: (to 1318) Oxford, Jesus College, MS 111, fols 125^r–25^v (Red Book of Hergest; *s*. xiv/xv, > 1382); NLW, MS 5267B, fols 56^v–57^v (*Y Casgliad Brith*; 1438); NLW, MS Peniarth 50, pp. 171–73 (*Y Cwtta Cyfarwydd*; Davyd, *c*. 1445); (to 1315) NLW, MS Peniarth 27, pt ii, pp. 49–51 (*s*. xv^2); NLW, MS Peniarth 267, pp. 4–10 (John Jones, 1635–1641).

EDS: Rebecca Try, Chapter 10 above.

15. The Tintern chronicle (ii).

YRS: 1305–1323.

MSS: BL, MS Royal 14 C VI, fols 254^r–59^r (*c*. 1323).

EDS: *Flores Historiarum*, ed. by Henry Richards Luard, 3 vols (London: Her Majesty's Stationery Office, 1890), III, 328–48.

16. *Brut y Tywysogyon*, Peniarth 20 version.

YRS: 682–1332.

MSS: NLW, MS Peniarth 20, pp. 65–302 (*c.* 1330).

EDS: *BT (Pen. 20)*; *BT (Pen. 20 trans.)*.

17. Abergavenny annals.

YRS: 1265–1348.

MSS: Trinity College Dublin, MS 212, fol. 89^v.

EDS: Eric St John Brooks, 'The *Piers Plowman* Manuscripts in Trinity College, Dublin', *The Library*, 5th ser., 6.4–5 (1951), 141–53; trans. by David Stephenson, Chapter 6 above.

18. *Epitome historiae Britanniae*.

YRS: 1230 BC–AD 1375.

MSS: NLW, MS Peniarth 32, fols 112^v–14^v (*Y Llyfr Teg*; *c.* 1404); BL, MS Cotton Titus D XXII, fols 22^r–37^r (1429); BL, MS Cotton Nero A IV, fols 2^r–7^v (*s.* xv/xvi); NLW, MS Peniarth 383, pp. 267a–h (*s.* xvii^1).

EDS: (MS Peniarth 32) Diana Luft, 'The NLW Peniarth 32 Latin Chronicle', *Studia Celtica*, 44 (2010), 47–70; (MS Cotton Titus D XXII) *Lives of the Cambro British Saints*, ed. and trans. by William J. Rees, Society for the Publication of Ancient Welsh Manuscripts, [4] (Llandovery: Rees, 1853), pp. 278–86, 612–22; (MS Cotton Nero A IV extracts) *Cartae et Alia Munimenta quae ad Dominium de Glamorgan Pertinent*, ed. by George Thomas Clarke, 6 vols (Cardiff: Lewis, 1910), III: *1271–1331*, pp. 1087–89, item DCCCCIII.

19. *Brut y Saesson*.

YRS: 850–1382.

MSS: Oxford, Jesus College, MS 111, fols 248^v–53^v (Red Book of Hergest; *s.* xiv/xv, >1382); NLW, MS Peniarth 19, fols 153^r–55^v (*s.* xiv/xv); NLW, MS Peniarth 32, fols 125^v–32^v (*Y Llyfr Teg*; *c.* 1404).

EDS: *The Text of the Bruts from the Red Book of Hergest*, ed. by John Rhŷs and J. Gwenogvryn Evans (Oxford: Evans, 1890), pp. 385–403.

20. The Chronicle of Adam Usk.

YRS: 1377–1421.

MSS: BL, MS Additional 10104, fols 155^r–76^v + the Belvoir quire (1401–1421).

EDS: *The Chronicle of Adam Usk 1377–1421*, ed. and trans. by Chris Given-Wilson (Oxford: Clarendon Press, 1997).

21. Annals of Owain Glyndŵr (a continuation of 14. *Blwydyn Eiseu*).

YRS: 1 AM–1422.

MSS: NLW, MS Peniarth 135, pp. 49–65 (Gruffudd Hiraethog, 1556–1564); NLW, MS Cwrtmawr 453, pp. 91–109 (Robert Vaughan, *c.* 1615 × 1630); NLW, MS 2023B, pp. 409–19 (John Owen, *c.* 1758); NLW, MS 1992B, pp. 210–29 (Panton 23; Evan Evans, *c.* 1775); (1400–1415) NLW, MS 1991B, fols 1–4 (Panton 22; Evan Evans, *c.* 1776).

EDS: (1400–1415) J. E. Lloyd, *Owen Glendower* (Oxford: Clarendon Press, 1931), pp. 147–54; (1400–1415) *Owain Glyndŵr: A Casebook*, ed. by Michael Livingston and John K. Bollard (Liverpool: Liverpool University Press, 2013), pp. 172–75, 371–79.

22. Oswestry annals.

YRS: 1400–1461.

MSS: NLW, MS Peniarth 26, pp. 97–98 (1456).

EDS: (Extract) J. R. S. Phillips, 'When Did Owain Glyn Dŵr Die?', *BBCS*, 24 (1970–72), 59–77.

23. *Brenhinedd y Saesson*.

YRS: 682–1461 (the version in MS Cotton Cleopatra B V, lacking its ending, would have originally finished with some year between 1197 and the date at which the manuscript was written).

MSS: BL, MS Cotton Cleopatra B V, pt 1, fols 109^r–62^v (*s.* xiv^1); NLW, MS 7006D, pp. 199–308 (Black Book of Basingwerk; Gutun Owain and another, *s.* xv^2, >1461).

EDS: *BS*.

24. *Teyrnassedd y Saesson*.

YRS: 682–1461.

MSS: Oxford, Jesus College, MS 141, fols 48ᵛ–123ᵛ + NLW, MS 1585D, fol. 132 (Gutun Owain, *s.* xv², >1471).

EDS: (Extract) J. R. S. Phillips, 'When Did Owain Glyn Dŵr Die?', *BBCS*, 24 (1970–72), 59–77.

25. *Brut Ieuan Brechfa*.

YRS: 720–1079 (redacted *c.* 1490–*c.* 1520).

MSS: NLW, MS Llanstephan 12, pp. 49–52, 53–62, 33–37 (*s.* xvi^med); NLW, MS Llanstephan 100, pp. 4–9 (*s.* xvii/xviii); BL, MS Additional 15031, pt i, fols 1ʳ–9ᵛ (Evan Evans, 1750 × 1788).

EDS: Ben Guy, Chapter 11 above.

26. The chronicle of Elis Gruffydd.

YRS: 1 AM–AD 1552.

MSS: NLW, MS 5276D (Elis Gruffydd, *c.* 1550); NLW, MS 3054D (Mostyn 158; Elis Gruffydd, *c.* 1552).

EDS: Extracts in the following: (NLW, MS 5276D,[2] fols 41ʳ–63ʳ) Thomas Jones, 'Ystorya Erkwlf', *BBCS*, 10 (1939–41), 284–97; 11 (1941–44), 21–30, 85–91; (fols 76ᵛ–80ᵛ) Bryn F. Roberts, 'Ystori'r Llong Foel', *BBCS*, 18 (1958–60), 337–62; (fols 230ʳ–33ᵛ) Thomas Jones, '"Credo'r Apostolion" yn Gymraeg', *NLWJ*, 4 (1945–46), 75–82; (fols 329ʳ–30ʳ) Thomas Jones, 'Chwedl Huail ap Caw ac Arthur', in *Astudiaethau Amrywiol a gyflwynir i Syr Thomas Parry-Williams*, ed. by Thomas Jones (Cardiff: University of Wales Press, 1968), pp. 48–66; (fols 342ʳ–43ʳ) Thomas Jones, 'Chwedl Myrddin a'r Farwolaeth Driphlyg yng Nghronicl Elis Gruffudd', *BBCS*, 16 (1954–56), 184–88; (fols 353ʳ–71ʳ) *Ystoria Taliesin*, ed. by Patrick K. Ford (Cardiff: University of Wales Press, 1992); (fols 362ᵛ–63ᵛ) Thomas Jones, 'Gwraig Maelgwn Gwynedd a'r

---

[2] Note that this manuscript was refoliated in 1985, due to the erratic nature of the previous foliation. While earlier publications follow the old foliation, the present list employs the 1985 foliation.

Fodrwy', *BBCS*, 18 (1958–60), 55–58; (fols 395ᵛ–99ᵛ) Thomas Jones, 'The Story of Myrddin and the Five Dreams of Gwenddydd in the Chronicle of Elis Gruffudd', *Études celtiques*, 8 (1958–59), 315–45; (NLW, MS 3054D, fols 90ʳ–91ᵛ) Thomas Jones, 'Hanes Llywelyn ap Iorwerth a Chynwrig Goch o Drefriw: Dau Fersiwn o Chwedl Werin', *NLWJ*, 3 (1943–44), 151–57; (fols 418ʳ–33ᵛ) Thomas Jones, 'Disgrifiad Elis Gruffudd o'r Cynadleddau a fu rhwng Harri VIII a'r Ymherodr Siarl V a rhyngddo a Ffranses I, Brenin Ffrainc, yn 1520', *BBCS*, 18 (1958–60), 311–37; (fols 441ʳ–48ʳ) Thomas Jones, 'Disgrifiad Elis Gruffudd o Ymgyrch Dug Suffolk yn Ffrainc yn 1523', *BBCS*, 15 (1952–54), 267–79; (fols 451ʳ–51ᵛ) Thomas Jones, 'A Sixteenth Century Version of the Arthurian Cave Legend', in *Studies in Language and Literature in Honour of Margaret Schlauch*, ed. by Mieczysław Brahmer, Stanisław Helsztyński, and Julian Krzyżanowski (New York: Russell & Russell, 1971), pp. 175–85; (fols 466ʳ–69ʳ) Thomas Jones, 'Disgrifiad Elis Gruffudd o Ymweliad y Cardinal Wolsey â Ffrainc yn Haf 1527', *BBCS*, 21 (1964–66), 219–23; (fols 485ᵛ–87ʳ) Thomas Jones, 'Mynd drosodd i Ffrainc', in *Rhyddiaith Gymraeg: Y Gyfrol Gyntaf. Detholion o Lawysgrifau 1488–1609*, ed. by Thomas H. Parry-Williams (Cardiff: University of Wales Press, 1954), pp. 31–36.

27. *Cronica Walliae* (Humphrey Llwyd).

YRS: 688–1295 (completed 1559).

MSS: NLW, MS Llanstephan 177, fols 21ʳ–247ᵛ (1559 × 1573); BL, MS Cotton Caligula A VI, pt i, fols 1–221 (*c.* 1578); NLW, MS 23202B, fols 1–165 (Thomas Powell, 1559 × 1588).

EDS: Humphrey Llwyd, *Cronica Walliae*, ed. by Ieuan M. Williams and J. Beverley Smith (Cardiff: University of Wales Press, 2002).

Index of Manuscripts

Aberystwyth, National Library of Wales

Bodewryd 103: 177
Brogyntyn I 15 (Porkington 1): 388–90
Cwrtmawr 453: 172, 175, 176, 178, 425, 427
Llanstephan 1: 18 n. 65, 148–49, 153
Llanstephan 12: 381–82, 386–90, 392, 394, 396, 400–02, 428
Llanstephan 27 (Red Book of Talgarth): 342
Llanstephan 28: 149 n. 131, 149–50, 170, 171, 173, 176, 422, 425
Llanstephan 58: 401
Llanstephan 74: 177
Llanstephan 80: 172, 176
Llanstephan 100: 380–82, 386–89, 392, 396, 400–19, 428
Llanstephan 172: 376
Llanstephan 177: 429
NLW 1585D: 26 n. 100, 28 n. 108, 29 n. 109, 428
NLW 1984B (Panton 15): 172, 176
NLW 1991B (Panton 22): 24 n. 88, 427
NLW 1992B (Panton 23): 172, 176, 427
NLW 2008B (Panton 40): 24 n. 91
NLW 2023B (Panton 56): 427
NLW 2024B (Panton 57): 172, 176
NLW 3032B (Mostyn 113): 398–99
NLW 3035B (Mostyn 116): 350 n. 24, 424
NLW 3042B (Mostyn 134): 380, 382, 399–400
NLW 3054D (Mostyn 158): 428
NLW 4973B: 172, 175, 178
NLW 5267B (*Y Casgliad Brith*): 341–62, 368–73, 425
NLW 5276D: 428
NLW 7006D (Black Book of Basingwerk): 25, 27, 27 n. 102, 29, 85–86, 148 n. 5, 250 n. 46, 427
NLW 9092D: 24 n. 90

NLW 13121B (Llanover C 34): 378–79, 386–87
NLW 14214B (Dale Castle manuscript): 395 n. 92
NLW 23202B: 429
Peniarth 16: 140
Peniarth 17: 191
Peniarth 18: 83–84, 84 n. 57, 85, 424
Peniarth 19: 23 n. 85, 100 n. 132, 350 n. 24, 424, 426
Peniarth 20: xiv, 11, 18, 19 n. 66, 22, 26, 80, 80 n. 45, 81–85, 87, 350 n. 24, 352 n. 30, 426
Peniarth 23: 20
Peniarth 26: 103, 427
Peniarth 27: 343 n. 10, 425
Peniarth 32 (*Y Llyfr Teg*): 23 n. 85, 105, 171, 173, 205, 206, 422, 426
Peniarth 44: 153
Peniarth 50 (*Y Cwtta Cyfarwydd*): 342, 344–58, 363–73, 425
Peniarth 118: 150, 150 n. 34, 152, 389
Peniarth 120: 395 n. 92
Peniarth 127: 150 n. 32, 398
Peniarth 131: 385–86, 389–90, 399
Peniarth 135: 23 n. 88, 171, 173, 422, 427
Peniarth 137: 150 n. 34, 152, 172, 175, 178
Peniarth 138: 106
Peniarth 156: 395 n. 92
Peniarth 182: 149 n. 30, 171, 173, 176, 422, 425
Peniarth 183: 150 n. 34, 152, 172, 174, 178
Peniarth 212: 105, 172, 174, 217, 422
Peniarth 267: 343 n. 10, 425
Peniarth 383: 426
Wynnstay 12: 177

Cambridge, Corpus Christi College
210: 425
339: 83

Cambridge, Trinity College
O.2.4: 101, 422

Cardiff, Central Library
1.363: 148
3.11: 170, 172, 174, 422
3.242: 152
3.77: 149 n. 29

Dublin, Trinity College
212: 426
507: 101, 422

Exeter, Cathedral Library
3514: 15, 70, 87, 90, 94, 423

Gloucester, Cathedral Library
34: 296 n. 22

London, British Library
Additional 10104: 427
Additional 14919: 398
Additional 15031: 379–82, 386–89, 394, 400–02, 428
Additional 22356: 396
Cotton Caligula A III: 149 n. 27
Cotton Caligula A VI: 429
Cotton Cleopatra A VII: 233 n. 3, 235 n. 7, 244, 244 n. 28, 248 n. 40
Cotton Cleopatra B V: 19 n. 66, 21–22, 26–27, 73, 84–86, 100 n. 132, 250 n. 46, 376, 427
Cotton Cleopatra D III: 188
Cotton Domitian A I: 75, 107 n. 1, 424
Cotton Domitian A VIII: 296 n. 22
Cotton Nero A IV: 105, 426
Cotton Titus D XXI: 105, 426
Cotton Vespasian A V: 290
Cotton Vespasian D XVII: 425
Cotton Vespasian E IV: 89, 95 n. 105, 110, 110 n. 20, 123 n. 8, 123 n. 13, 123 n. 15, 124, 128 n. 67
Egerton 3088: 102
Harley 848: 110
Harley 3859: 2, 75, 107 n. 1, 422
Royal 6 B XI: 231, 232, 243, 244, 249, 250, 423
Royal 13 D II: 94
Royal 14 C VI: 425

London, College of Arms
Muniment Room 12/16: 389–90, 399

London, Gray's Inn
7: 188

London, The National Archives
24 Eliz I/Mich 4: 385 n. 62
E 134/23: 385 n. 62
E 164/1: 75, 107 n. 1, 237, 423, 424

Manchester, John Rylands Library
Welsh 1: 28

Northampton, Northamptonshire Archives
FH7: 172, 178–79

Oxford, Jesus College
20: 399–400
111 (Red Book of Hergest): 11, 73, 75, 79–80, 82, 85, 170, 171, 172, 175, 176, 186, 205, 343–58, 368–72, 422, 424, 425
141: 26, 26 n. 99, 27, 27 n. 101, 27 n. 102, 28 n. 104, 28 n. 108, 29 n. 109, 29 n. 110, 29 n. 111, 30 n. 114, 103, 428

Oxford, The Queen's College
367: 296 n. 22

Lost
Hengwrt 33 ('Hanesyn Hen'): 149–50, 151, 152, 174, 175, 176–77, 178, 185, 189, 191, 205

General Index

Aachen: 268, 285
Abbo of Fleury, *Passio* of St Edmund: 45
Aberconwy, battle of *alias* battle of Llanrwst: 391, 406, 414
Aberconwy Abbey: 9–10, 105, 202, 226, 228
   and the 'Aberconwy chronicle': 104, 182
   copying of vernacular texts at: 191
   and Hengwrt 33: 185–87
   and the Llywelyn ab Iorwerth genealogies: 10, 185–86, 187, 192
   and *O Oes Gwrtheyrn*: xiv, 9–10, 104, 169, 180–82, 183, 185, 187, 204, 205, 207–08, 225
   production of chronicles at: 190
   and *Vera historia de morte Arthuri*: 187–89
Aberffraw: 406, 414
Abergavenny: 262, 279
Abergavenny Priory, chronicle of: 24, 157–59, 426
   comparison with the Peniarth 20 continuation of *Brut y Tywysogyon*: 159–61
Abergele, northern Welsh chronicle from: 3, 93
Abergwili, battle of: 399–400, 408, 417
Abergwyngregyn: 141 n. 5
Aberllwchwr Castle: 128
Aberpergwm *Brut* see *Brut Aberpergwm*
Aberteifi: 208, 213, 220, 225, 312, 330
   see also Cardigan
Aberystwyth Castle: 307, 327 n. 223
Abraham, Bishop of St Davids: 133 n. 81
Abraham (Old Testament): 62
Absalon, Archbishop of Lund: 52
Acre: 33, 46 n. 51, 345–46, 353, 361–62, 365–66, 370–71

Acts of Union: 15
Adam (Old Testament): 342, 359, 363
Adam of Bremen: 44–47, 58, 59, 63
Adam of Elmley: 321, 338
Adam Usk: 103
   Chronicle of: 103, 427
Adela of Blois: 52 n. 82
Adeliza, countess: 308, 328
Adeliza, Queen of England: 254, 272
Admont Abbey: 53 n. 93
Adda Fras: 186, 187
Ælfhere, Ealdorman of the Mercians: 136 n. 2
Aeneas: 20, 39
Æthelflæd, Lady of the Mercians: 297, 303, 324
Æthelred, Ealdorman of the Mercians: 297–98, 303, 324
Æthelred, King of the Mercians: 302, 323
Æthelred the Unready, King of the English: 134 nn. 11–12, 303, 324
Æthelsige: 137 n. 13
Alban, St: 64, 316, 333
   Life of: 54
Alberic of Troisfontaines: 37, 40, 45–46, 49–50, 57–58
Alclud: 404, 412
Aldred, Bishop of Worcester: 303, 324
Alexander, Bishop of Coventry: 260, 277
Alexander II, King of Scots: 259, 277
Alexander III, Pope: 123 n. 9
Alexander IV, Pope: 240, 269, 286
Alexander the Great: 36, 38
Alexander Nequam, Abbot of Cirencester: 258, 276
Ambrose: 35, 37
Amice, Countess of Wight: 263, 280

Amphibalus, St: 64
Anarawd ap Gruffudd ap Rhys: 126, 127
Anarawd ap Rhodri Mawr, King of Gwynedd: 202–03, 207, 211, 211 n. 122, 218, 219, 223, 392, 404, 405, 412 and n. 210
Angharad ferch Llywelyn ab Iorwerth: 394, 418 n. 262
Anglesey, *Môn*: 20, 136 n. 6, 137 n. 14, 169, 195, 198, 201, 226, 321, 339, 404, 407, 411, 415–16
Anglo-Norman *Brut*: 28, 194 n. 76
Anglo-Saxon Chronicle: 50, 206, 224, 298
Anjou, counts of: 44, 125 n. 12
Annales Cambriae: xiv, 2, 7, 171, 179, 182, 183, 205, 206, 377, 393, 413 n. 223, 422–24
 chronology of: 112–15, 124–37
 editing of: 69–70, 75–79
 nomenclature of: 70, 77
 recent scholarship on: 92–97, 100–04
 relationships between versions of: 75–78, 80–82, 86, 99–100, 107–37
 sources of: 88–93, 98–101, 110–11, 119–24
 see also Breviate chronicle; Cottonian chronicle; Harleian chronicle
Anselm, Archbishop of Canterbury: 253, 271, 306–07, 326
Anselm, *Gesta episcoporum Leodiensium*: 57
Anselm Marshal: 112
Anskar, St: 59
Antenor: 61 n. 129
Archenfield, *Ergyng*: 307, 310, 327, 329
Arfderydd, battle of: 207, 210, 210 n. 116, 210 n. 117, 218
Armagh: 137 n. 19
Arthen (*alias* 'Arthur'), King of Ceredigion: 403, 411
Arthur, king: 5, 16, 18, 19 n. 66, 52, 170, 179, 187, 188, 189, 192, 210, 218
Arthur, King of Ceredigion *see* Arthen, King of Ceredigion
Arthur of Brittany: 114, 119–21
Arwystli: 13 n. 45, 98
Assyria: 61, 62
Attila: 49, 58, 59, 61 n. 130
Augustine of Canterbury, St: 7 n. 21, 360, 364

Augustine of Hippo, St: 35, 36, 37, 37 n. 19, 37 nn. 21–22, 42, 47, 54, 232
Aulus Gellius: 35
Austria: 59

Badon, battle of: 5, 170, 206, 207, 210, 218
Baldwin, Archbishop of Canterbury: 121, 256, 274
Baldwin de Redvers, Earl of the Isle of Wight and Devon: 264, 281, 320, 337
Bale, John: 290
Bangor: 215, 221
 bishops of: 396, 405, 413
 see also Hervé, Bishop of Bangor; Robert, Bishop of Bangor
Bangor, battle of (*recte Bangoleu*): 404, 412
Bannockburn, battle of: 160, 249, 343, 362, 366, 372–73
Bardsey *see* Ynys Enlli
Bartholomew, Bishop of Exeter: 123 n. 12
Bartholomew, St: 55
Beaumaris Castle: 156, 156–57 n. 6
Bede: 51, 233
 as a source: 44, 75, 229
 De temporibus: 9, 10 n. 34, 93
 death of: 5
 and Dionysian tables: 133
 Historia ecclesiastica: 232
Bedford Castle: 113, 260, 277
Beli ab Elffin, King of Alclud: 403, 410
Benedictines: 6, 14, 31, 235
Beornwulf, King of the Mercians: 302, 323
Berkeley family *see* Roger I of Berkeley; Roger II of Berkeley; Roger III of Berkeley; Thomas of Berkeley
Bern of Reichenau: 48
Bernard, Bishop of St Davids: 125 n. 10, 127
Bernard de Neufmarché: 304, 325
Bernard of Clairvaux: 232
Bible, as source and model for chronicles: 35, 40–42, 47, 60, 62, 65, 67
 see also Old Testament; New Testament
Bleddyn ap Cynfyn, King of Gwynedd: 100, 207, 212, 219, 409, 418
Bleiddudd, Bishop of St Davids: 133 n. 81
Blwydyn Eiseu: 23, 341–73, 425
 edition and translation of: 359–73
 stemma of the manuscripts of: 358
Bodo and Gwynnin, church of: 141 n. 5

Boethius: 37 n. 19, 42
Bǫglunga Sǫgur: 195, 196, 197, 198, 200, 202
Bogo de Clare: 163
Bohemia: 37, 41–43, 66
Bonedd y Saint: 139–54, 174
  archetype of: 139–40, 146–47, 151, 152, 153
  different branches of: 148–49, 151, 152
  entries, format of: 139–41
  manuscripts of: 139, 146, 151–52
  Peris, St, entry on: 140, 142–43, 146, 148, 151; *see also* Peris, St
  relationship with *Brenhinedd y Saesson*: 143, 147
  revised at Valle Crucis Abbey: 140, 148, 151, 153
Boniface, Archbishop of Canterbury: 266, 267, 282, 284
Brecon: 234, 266, 283
Brenhinedd y Saesson: xiv, 17, 21–22, 104, 168, 402, 411 n. 201, 427
  called *Brut y Saeson* in the *Myvyrian Archaiology*: 73, 76, 376
  and Dafydd ap Maredudd Glais: 20–21
  date: 11, 146–48
  editions of: 71–73
  and Gutun Owain: 25–30
  manuscripts of: 85
  name of: 80 n. 43, 100 n. 132
  recent scholarship on: 94, 97
  relationship with other chronicles: 19 n. 66, 21–22, 81–86, 143, 147, 393
  underlying sources: 22, 76, 97 n. 120, 143, 147, 237, 250, 251
  Welsh text created at Valle Crucis Abbey: 148, 153
  see also under Bonedd y Saint
Breuddwyd Pawl: 173, 341–42, 359
Breviate annals *see* Neath chronicle
Breviate chronicle (B-text of *Annales Cambriae*): xiv, 83 n. 55, 101 n. 134, 148, 225, 400, 423
  editions of: 79
  manuscript of: 7–9, 16, 90–91, 94, 97, 102, 109, 122
  recent scholarship on: 95–97, 100–01
  relationship with other chronicles: 7, 17, 78, 86, 89–97, 107–37

  sources of: 8–9, 75, 80–82, 89–93, 96–97, 119–37
  see also Annales Cambriae
Brian Boru: 134 n. 10, 134 n. 14
Bridgnorth: 313, 331
Brigit, St (Ffraid): 5, 149 n. 28
Britons: 3, 5, 10, 13–15, 18–24, 56, 105, 126, 398, 406, 409, 414, 418
  conversion of: 360, 363–64
Bromfield, canons of: 313, 331
Bromfield and Yale, lordship of: 162, 164, 166
Brothen, St, church of: 141 n. 5
Brut Aberpergwm: 73–74, 77 n. 31, 80, 376
Brut Gruffudd ab Arthur: 376
Brut Ieuan Brechfa: xv, 73–74, 375–419, 428
  see also Ieuan Brechfa
Brut Tysilio: 376
Brut y Brenhinedd: 1, 18–22, 25–26, 72, 84, 85, 148–49, 151, 153, 191, 250 n. 46, 375–76
Brut y Saesson: 23, 79, 80 n. 43, 172, 376 n. 6, 426
  see also under Brenhinedd y Saesson
Brut y Tywysogyon: xiv, xv, 11–19, 21–22, 25–26, 69, 71–87, 95, 104, 171, 176, 179, 182, 183–84, 190, 206, 225, 344, 351–52, 356, 375–76, 392, 402, 424, 426, 427
  editions of: 72, 75–76
  Latin source of: 11–14, 76, 80, 97, 148, 153, 190
  and loss of sovereignty: 18–19
  Peniarth 20 continuation of: 153, 155–57, 161–64, 166–68, 182, 344 n. 13
  Peniarth 20 version: 22, 80–83, 144, 393, 411 n. 201, 426
  Red Book of Hergest version: 25–26, 80–83, 144, 380–81, 387, 391–93, 396, 399, 401, 411 n. 201, 421, 424
  relationship with other chronicles: 9, 17–19, 19 n. 66, 21–22, 26, 80–87, 90, 92, 97, 100, 143, 184, 205, 354–55, 377, 392
Brutus: 23, 28, 105, 342, 359, 363
Brycheiniog: 136 n. 2, 304, 325, 386, 404, 405, 407, 412, 415

Bryn Derwin, battle of: 171, 177, 180, 181–82, 205, 208, 216, 217, 222, 223, 224, 228, 229, 348, 369
Buellt, *Builth*: 343, 361, 365, 370–71, 399–401
Burchard, Bishop of Worms: 44
Burgred, King of the Mercians: 303, 324
Burgundy: 57
Burton upon Trent Abbey: 314, 331–32
Bury St Edmunds, chronicle of: 90, 94

Cadell ab Arthfael (*alias* Cadell ap 'Rhodri'): 405, 413
Cadell ap Brochfael, King of Powys: 403, 411
Cadell ap Gruffudd: 127, 128
Cadell ap Rhodri *see* Cadell ab Arthfael
Cadell ap Rhodri Mawr: 207, 211, 219
Cadfan, St: 141
Cadfan ap Cadwaladr: 127, 128
Cadfarch of Llŷn, St: 149 n. 28
Cadwaladr ap Gruffudd ap Cynan: 127, 213, 220, 225
Cadwaladr Fendigaid (the Blessed) ap Cadwallon: 18–19, 23, 27, 80, 105, 118, 207, 210, 212 n. 130, 218, 223, 360, 364
Cadwallon ap Gruffudd: 208, 212, 212 n. 138, 220, 225
Cadwallon ab Ieuaf, King of Gwynedd: 136 n. 5, 407, 415 and n. 243
Cadwgon ap Gruffudd: 410, 418 and n. 261
Cadwgon ap Madog ab Idnerth: 127
Cadwgon ab Owain: 405, 414
Caer Caradoc: 360, 363
Caergybi, *Holyhead*: 397, 406, 414
see also Elfod of Holyhead, St
Caerleon-on-Usk: 207, 407, 415
Caernarfon Castle: 322, 339, 362, 366, 370–71
Caerphilly Castle: 232, 239, 243, 270, 287
Caerwent: 294–95
see also Gregory of Caerwent
Cambrai: 48
Camlan, battle of: 5, 171, 188, 206, 207, 210, 218
Canterbury: 8, 60, 120, 121, 226, 233
Cantref Mawr: 362, 366, 372–73
Caradog ap Meirion, King of Gwynedd: 403, 411

Caradog of Llancarfan: 21, 71–73, 80
Cardiff: 239, 254, 272, 279 n. 154, 311, 329
  castle: 128 n. 67, 262, 270, 279, 287
  priory: 6, 231, 232, 234–36, 247–48, 251, 252, 259, 263, 277, 281
  St Mary's Church: 235, 236, 271 n. 130
Cardiff chronicle: xiv, 7 n. 21, 90, 232, 252, 423
  and the Annals of Tewkesbury: 233, 234, 237, 244, 245–46, 247
  edition and translation of: 253–87
  manuscript of: 232
  and the Neath chronicle: 239, 240, 242–43, 244, 245–46, 247, 248–49
  possible context for: 249–50
  scope of: 233
  source for other chronicles: 236–37
  tailoring of source material: 247
Cardigan: 117, 158, 225, 299, 312, 330
  see also Aberteifi
Cardigan Bay: 141
Carmarthen: 91, 117, 127, 268, 285, 343, 356, 361, 364, 368–69
Carmarthenshire: 395, 397
Carno, battle of: 207, 211, 219, 223, 405, 414
Cassiodorus: 35
Castell Baldwin: 392, 404, 412
Castell Paen, *Painscastle*: 208, 213, 220, 226, 347, 360, 364, 368–69
Castile: 48, 65
Catalonia: 66
Cenau Menrudd: 399
Ceolfrith, letter to Nechtan, King of the Picts: 232, 250
Ceredigion: 8, 12, 13, 14, 126, 127, 128, 137 n. 13, 151, 392, 395, 403, 404, 406, 407, 408, 411, 412, 414, 416
Ceri, *Kerry*: 317, 333
Chad, St: 149 n. 28
Champagne: 33, 46
Charlemagne: 46
Chebur, Bishop of St Asaph: 413 n. 217
  see also Teibyr, Bishop of St Asaph
Chester
  annals of: 225, 226
  battle of: 210, 218
Chronicle of Ireland: 3, 92–93
Chronicle of the Kings of Man and the Isles: 197

Chronicon Roskildense: 45, 63, 66
Chronicon Willelmi de Richanger: 351
Cicero: 35, 36, 37, 37 n. 19, 38, 62
Cilgerran: 120, 320, 337
Cistercians: 6–9, 11–18, 25, 31, 50, 57, 67, 78, 89, 96, 96 n. 112, 102, 104, 105, 153–54, 169, 183, 183 n. 32, 190, 193, 204, 239 n. 16
   see also Aberconwy Abbey; Cwm-hir Abbey; Cymer Abbey; Dore Abbey, annals of; Grace Dieu Abbey; Hailes Abbey; Heiligenkreuz Abbey; Llantarnam Abbey; Margam Abbey; Neath Abbey; Strata Florida Abbey; Strata Marcella Abbey; Tintern Abbey, chronicle of; Valle Crucis Abbey; Waverley Abbey, annals of; Whitland Abbey; Zwettl Abbey
Cîteaux: 111
Clairvaux: 111
clas churches: 153–54, 236
classical authors, use in medieval chronicles: 35–39, 43, 52, 60, 64, 66, 67
Clemens, Pope: 256, 274
Clement, Abbot of Brevnov: 53
Clement, St: 213, 220
Clonmacnoise
   annals of: 3
   recension of the Chronicle of Ireland: 92
Cluny Abbey: 47, 55, 312, 330
Clwyd, Vale of: 149 n. 28
Clydog ap Cadell: 405, 413
Cnut, King of the English:
   134 n. 9, 134 n. 11, 134 n. 16, 207, 211, 211 n. 126, 219, 223–24
Coed Ceiriog: 208, 213, 220
Coenwulf, King of the Mercians: 411 n. 200
Coleshill, battle of: 125 n. 13
Columba, St: 5
computus fragment in Old Welsh: 132 n. 74
Conwy
   battle of: 5, 192, 202–03, 211, 211 n. 123, 218, 223
   castle: 156–57 n. 6
Cornwall: 262, 279
Cosmas of Prague, *Chronica Boemorum*: 36, 41–42, 53
Cottonian chronicle (C-text of *Annales Cambriae*): xiv, 17, 75, 79, 148, 225, 369, 392, 401, 424

chronological restructuring of source: 9, 93–94
English perspective of: 8, 75, 76
interleaved with annals from Worcester: 76, 95, 115
lost Latin sources of: 9, 89, 107–37
relationship with other versions: 75–76, 78, 82, 86, 89, 93, 100, 107–37, 392
and St Davids: 7, 81, 90, 98, 225
see also *Annales Cambriae*
Cowbridge: 378
Cranbourne Abbey: 235
Croatia: 33, 58
Cronica ante aduentum Domini: 70, 87–88, 90, 92, 101, 148, 423
Cronica de Wallia: 9, 11, 14, 87–90, 92, 99, 112, 228, 350–51, 355, 423
Croyland Abbey: 48
Crusades: 233, 317, 334, 371, 373
Custennin ab Iago: 407, 415
Cwm Tawe: 341–42
Cwm-hir Abbey: 8, 89, 96, 111, 137
Cydweli, *Kidwelly*: 128, 137 n. 13, 397
   castle: 355
Cyfeiliog: 125 n. 14, 125 n. 15, 127, 128
Cyfraith Hywel (Welsh Law): 396–97, 401, 405, 413
Cymer Abbey: 188
Cymerau, battle of: 361, 365, 370–71
Cynan ap Hywel, King of Gwynedd: 134 n. 3, 134 n. 6
Cynan ap Maredudd: 160
Cynan ab Owain Gwynedd: 127, 226
Cynan ap Seisyll: 387 n. 66, 408–09, 417
Cynan Dindaethwy: 404 n. 119, 411
Cynddelw Brydydd Mawr: 226
Cynhafal, St: 149 n. 28
Czechs: 42, 62

Dafydd ap Bleddyn, Bishop of St Asaph: 162
Dafydd ap Gruffudd, Prince of Wales: 156 n. 6, 228, 295, 321, 338, 348, 353, 361, 362, 364–65, 368–69, 370–71
Dafydd ap Llywelyn, Prince of Wales: 208, 216, 222, 228, 265, 267, 282, 283, 318, 335, 361, 364–65, 368–69
Dafydd ap Maredudd Glais: 20, 21
Dafydd ap Meilyr ap Rhys Llwyd: 383 n. 43, 385

Dafydd ab Owain Gwynedd: 204, 208, 214, 220, 221, 226, 398
Dafydd Benwyn: 342
Dafydd Dew: 383 n. 43
Damietta: 112, 117, 259, 267, 276, 277, 284
Danes: 55, 56, 58 n. 117, 59–62, 298, 303, 324
Daniel ap Sulien: 13, 98
Dares Phrygius, *De excidio Troiae historia*: 15, 17, 19, 25, 37–40, 43, 65
Daugleddau: 310, 329
David, King of Scots: 125 n. 14, 125 n. 15, 128
David, St: 5
  Life of: 13
David (Old Testament): 40–41
David Edwardes of Rhyd-y-Gors: 395
David fitz Gerald, Bishop of St Davids: 123 n. 1, 127
David Lewis of Dinas Cerdin and Blaen Cerdin: 395
David Martin, Bishop of St Davids: 362, 366, 372–73
David Powel: 174, 422
  Historie of Cambria: 72–73, 376
De Braose family *see* Gower; Maud de Braose; Neath Abbey; Reginald de Braose; William de Braose
De Clare family: 162–63, 236, 238, 239, 243, 247, 248, 248 n. 40, 249, 250
  see also Bogo de Clare; Gilbert de Clare; Gilbert fitz Richard de Clare; Glamorgan; Godwin de Clare; Richard fitz Gilbert de Clare; Richard de Clare; William de Clare
De Lacy family: 114, 120, 295, 303–04, 310, 324, 329
  see also Gilbert de Lacy; Hugh de Lacy; John de Lacy; Walter de Lacy
decennovenal cycles: 117, 118, 123 n. 4, 124, 128, 131–33, 134 n. 1, 134 n. 8
Degannwy: 182, 207, 210, 210 n. 121, 214–15, 216, 218, 221, 222, 223, 228, 234, 266, 283, 403–04, 411
Deheubarth: 137 n. 13, 160, 201, 225, 238, 394, 403, 409, 410, 417, 418
Denbigh: 106
Denmark: 33, 43, 45, 46, 57, 59, 66
Despenser family: 250
  see also Hugh le Despenser

Dinefwr Castle: 127, 239
Dingestow Court: 342
Diserth Castle: 208, 216, 222, 228
Disgrifiad o Ynys Brydain: 26–27
Domesday Book: 304, 325
  Breviate of: 16, 90, 94, 97, 102, 109, 122, 137, 231, 237, 247, 249, 252
Dominican order: 318, 335, 349–50, 356, 361, 364, 368–69
Dore Abbey, annals of: 102
Dryslwyn Castle: 322, 339
  see also Rhys ap Maredudd, Lord of Dryslwyn
Dudo of St Quentin: 45, 58 n. 117, 61 n. 129
Dugdale, William: 294
Dumbarton *see* Alclud
Dunstable, annals of: 227
Durham: 55 n. 104, 57
Dyfed: 8, 134 n. 4, 137 n. 13, 225, 399, 403, 404, 405, 407, 408, 409, 411, 413, 415, 416, 417
Dyfnwal ap Tewdwr, King of Alclud: 403, 410
Dyfnwal Moelmud: 405, 413

Eadmer of Canterbury: 60
Eadric Streona: 134 n. 9
Ealdred, Archbishop of York: 297
Easter, dating of: 3–5, 31, 94, 132, 403, 410
Ecgberht, King of the West Saxons: 27
eclipses: 115, 123 n. 5, 123 n. 13, 125 n. 3
Edgar, King of the English: 136 n. 1, 392, 407, 415 and n. 234
Edmund, Earl of Cornwall: 322, 339
Edmund, King of the English: 393, 405, 413
Edmund de Mortimer: 322, 339
Edmund of Abingdon, Archbishop of Canterbury: 262, 265, 267, 280, 282, 283, 317, 318, 334, 335
Edward I, King of England: 2, 8, 83, 104, 110, 111 n. 22, 111 n. 23, 232, 240, 242, 243, 253, 264, 268, 269, 271, 281, 285, 286, 295, 320–23, 336–40, 349, 361–62, 365–66, 370–73
  daughter of *see* Joan of Acre
  expels Jews from England: 323, 340
Edward II, King of England: 16, 156, 158, 159, 160, 353, 362, 365–66, 370–71

Edward IV, King of England: 26, 28, 385 n. 62
Edward VI, King of England: 105
Edward Balliol: 22
Edward Seymour, Duke of Somerset: 106
Edward the Confessor, King of the English: 7, 7 n. 21, 27, 409, 418
Edwin ab Einion (*alias* 'Owain' ab Einion): 137 n. 13, 392, 408–09, 416, 417
Edwin ap Hywel (*alias* 'Owain' ap Hywel): 406, 414
Egyptians: 61
Einion ap Gwalchmai: 149 n. 28
Einion ab Owain: 136 n. 2, 136 n. 3, 406, 415, 415 n. 233, 415 n. 240
Eleanor, Countess of Leicester, daughter of King John: 394, 418 n. 262
Eleanor de Montfort, Princess of Wales, daughter of Simon de Montfort: 321, 338, 394
Eleanor of Aquitaine: 245, 255, 272, 273
Eleanor of Brittany: 119, 265, 282
Eleanor of Provence: 263, 266, 281, 283
Elen ferch Llywarch, wife of Hywel Dda: 405, 413
Elenydd: 322, 339
Eleutherius, Pope: 216, 217, 222, 223
Elfael: 175, 315, 333
Elfod of Holyhead, St: 149 n. 28
Elfoddw, Archbishop of Gwynedd: 3–4, 403, 411
Elias, Bishop of Llandaf: 247, 261, 263, 264, 278, 279, 281, 282
Elis Gruffydd: 103, 187 n. 45
  chronicle of: 428
Elisabeth of Schönau: 49
Elise ab Anarawd ap Rhodri Mawr (*alias* Elise ap 'Rhodri'): 405, 413
Elise ap Rhodri *see* Elise ab Anarawd ap Rhodri Mawr
Ellelw ferch Elidyr: 399–400
England
  chronicles of: 7, 35–36, 43–45, 46, 48–51, 56, 58, 60, 66, 71, 94, 106, 193–94
  and Gruffudd ap Cynan: 40–41
  Gutun Owain's interest in: 25, 27–29
  and Llywelyn ap Gruffudd: 15
  Norman conquest of: 7, 409, 418
  Ralph de Diceto's portrayal of: 44–45
  Welsh chronicles' interest in: 8, 11, 17, 19, 21–23, 25, 27–30, 72, 75–76, 94, 97, 110–11, 119–21, 124, 125, 126, 161, 233, 405, 409, 410, 412, 418
  see also Wales, Edwardian conquest of
English people: 5, 10 n. 34, 56
  conversion of: 5, 7 n. 21, 360, 364
  see also Saxons
Epitome historiae Britanniae: 155 n. 1, 426
Erfyn, Bishop of St Davids: 133 n. 81
Ergyng *see* Archenfield
Erlendr píkr (Herlant Pic): 169, 193 n. 72, 195, 196, 198, 201, 214, 221
Estoria de Espanna: 65
Europe, common tradition of historical writing in: xiv, 4, 33–34, 40, 43–67
Eusebius: 4, 37 n. 19, 39, 44, 59
Evans, Evan: 176, 379–80, 386–89, 402, 427, 428
Evans, J. Gwenogvryn: 79, 83, 104, 105, 151, 170
Evesham
  abbots of: 311, 313, 329, 331
  battle of (1264): 270, 286, 320, 337
Eyrlaid see Guthfrith son of Harold; Maccus son of Harold
Ezekias: 40

Falaise: 306, 326
Falkirk, battle of: 362, 366, 373
Ffernfael ab Idwal: 403, 410
Fferyll, battle of: 404, 411
Ffynnod Wyddeles, mother of Hywel ab Owain Gwynedd *see* Pyfog, mother of Hywel ab Owain Gwynedd
Flanders: 57
Flodoard of Rheims: 37 n. 21
Florus, *Epitome bellorum annorum*: 47
Forest of Dean: 312, 330
France: 16, 30, 37, 61, 66, 111, 117, 233, 243, 245, 258, 270, 276, 287
Franks: 5, 56
Fredegar: 64
Frederick II, Holy Roman Emperor: 263, 265, 266, 280, 282, 283, 418–19
Frederick Barbarossa: 51, 55
Frisians: 56
Fulk Basset: 266, 283
Fulk Tregor: 321, 338

Gallus Anonymus, *Gesta principum Polonorum*: 36, 66
Gascony: 260, 265, 268, 277, 282, 285
Gauls: 56, 61, 62
Gebhard, Abbot of Windberg: 47 n. 57
Geffrei Gaimar: 50
genealogies: xiv, 2, 10–11, 15, 25, 27–28, 31, 49–50, 140–41, 175, 378–79, 399
    Jesus College 20 genealogies: 399–401
    Llywelyn ab Iorwerth genealogies: 185–86, 187, 191–93, 201, 205, 223, 225, 388–90, 398
Geneva: 266, 283
Geoffrey, Abbot of St Albans: 54
Geoffrey, Prior of Llanthony, Bishop of St Davids: 234, 257, 274
Geoffrey Clement: 158, 159
Geoffrey de Henlaw, Bishop of St Davids: 96, 114, 117, 120, 121
Geoffrey of Monmouth: 236 n. 9
    account of Arthur: 187, 189
    De gestis Britonum: 1, 6, 8–9, 11, 15, 17–22, 30, 50–52, 54, 57, 63–64, 72–73, 75, 93, 94, 105, 118, 148, 151, 190, 191, 229, 413 n. 218
    death of: 125 n. 17
    Prophetiae Merlini: 45
    see also *Brut y Brenhinedd*; Merlin
Gerald, Abbot of Tewkesbury: 233 n. 3, 235, 248 n. 40, 254, 271
Gerald of Aurillac: 38–39
Gerald of Wales: 45, 95–96, 105, 122, 193 n. 74, 224
Gerard, Bishop of Hereford: 305, 326
Gerard de L'Isle: 323, 340
Germanus, St: 141
Germany: 33, 36–37, 43, 45–46, 48, 53, 57–58, 61–62, 64, 66, 67, 134
Gervase, Archdeacon of Prague: 53
Gervase, Bishop of St Davids
    see Iorwerth *alias* Gervase, Bishop of St Davids
Gervase of Canterbury: 34
Gesta Treverorum: 49, 61–62
Gilbert Basset: 263, 265, 280, 282
Gilbert de Clare, 1st Earl of Pembroke (*alias* Gilbert fitz Gilbert, Gilbert Strongbow) (d. 1148): 125 n. 8, 125 n. 9, 127

Gilbert de Clare, 5th Earl of Gloucester (d. 1230): 258, 259, 260, 261, 275, 277, 278, 317, 334
Gilbert de Clare, 7th Earl of Gloucester (*alias* Gilbert the Red) (d. 1295): 162, 163, 238, 240, 242, 249, 250, 269, 286, 323, 340
    wife of *see* Joan of Acre
Gilbert de Clare, 8th Earl of Gloucester (d. 1314): 162, 249, 362, 366, 372–73
Gilbert de Lacy: 317, 334
Gilbert de Umfraville: 233, 242
    son of: 233, 242, 270, 287
Gilbert fitz Richard de Clare: 307, 327
Gilbert Foliot: 312, 313, 314, 315, 321, 330, 331, 332, 338
Gilbert Marshal: 117, 263, 265, 280, 282, 295, 318, 335
    brothers of: 263, 280
    wife of: 263, 280
Gilbert Strongbow *see* Gilbert de Clare, 1st Earl of Pembroke
Gildas: 5, 13, 19
Giles, Bishop of Hereford: 316, 333
Glamorgan: 6, 7, 16, 22, 23, 90, 94 n. 101, 105, 109, 158, 162, 163, 234, 235, 238, 240, 247, 248, 266, 269, 283, 286, 319, 336, 342–43, 354, 356
    Clare lordship of: 109, 162, 163, 234, 238
Glamorgan chronicle *see* Neath chronicle
Glasbury: 304, 312, 325, 330
Glastonbury Abbey: 52
Gloucester: 158, 239, 254, 262, 265, 271, 272, 280, 282, 306, 308, 316, 320, 326, 328, 333, 337
    bridges of: 318, 334
    castle of: 312, 330
    church of St Mary: 315, 317, 333, 334
    church of St Oswald: 315, 333
    church of St Peter: 315, 333
    earls of: 233, 234, 236, 250, 269, 286
    St Peter's Abbey: xv, 13 n. 45, 94–95, 98 n. 123, 128 n. 67, 131 n. 73, 253, 271, 289, 293, 296–98, 302–22, 323–39
Gloucestershire: 306, 326
Glúniairn son of Amlaíb: 136 n. 9
Glyn Cothi: 380, 382, 385 n. 62, 386
    see also *Llyma enwau y nawnyn*

Godfrey of Viterbo, 37, 46, 57, 66
  Memoria seculorum: 56
  Pantheon: 48, 49 n. 69, 51–52, 56, 64–66
Godfrey son of Harold *see* Guthfrith son of Harold
Gododdin, Y: 191
Godwin de Clare: 320, 337
Goldcliff: 239
Gomer, tribe of: 62
Goronwy ap Llywelyn: 409–10, 418 and n. 261
Goronwy ap Tudur: 163
Goscelin of St Bertin: 60
Goths: 39, 56, 58–59
Gotland: 49
Göttweig Abbey: 59
Gower: 91, 137 n. 13, 415 n. 233
  De Braose lords of: 8, 16, 91, 109, 120, 122, 237
  lordship of: 109, 234, 239 n. 16, 268, 285, 299, 311, 329, 342
Grace Dieu Abbey: 102, 422
Gregory, monk and scribe of St Peter's Abbey, Gloucester: 314, 331
Gregory IX, Pope: 260, 278
Gregory of Caerwent: 289–301, 318, 335
Gregory of Tours: 37 n. 21, 44
Gregory the Great, St: 36, 37, 37 n. 19, 37 n. 22
Gronwy (Goronwy) Goch: 382, 384
Gruffudd ap Cynan ab Iago, King of Gwynedd: 1, 40–41, 126, 181, 193 n. 72, 201, 212, 219, 398
  see also Vita Griffini filii Conani
Gruffudd ap Cynan ab Owain Gwynedd: 208, 214, 220, 226
Gruffudd ap Goronwy Goch: 382 n. 30
Gruffudd ap Llywelyn ab Iorwerth: 10, 171, 177, 180, 184, 208, 215, 216, 217, 221, 222, 227, 228, 229, 266, 282
Gruffudd ap Llywelyn ap Seisyll, King of Wales: 207, 211, 211 n. 127, 219, 224, 399, 409, 417, 418
Gruffudd ap Rhydderch: 224
Gruffudd ap Rhys: 409, 417 and n. 256
Gruffudd ap Rhys, Lord of Senghennydd: 234, 242, 270, 287
Gruffudd ap Rhys ap Tewdwr: 126
Gruffudd ap Rhys ap Thomas, Sir: 389–90

Gruffudd ap Sulhaearn: 130
Gruffudd Hiraethog: 103, 105 n. 159, 150, 173, 422, 427
Guala Bicchieri, papal legate: 316, 333
Guthfrith son of Harold (*alias* Guthfrith son of *Eyrlaid*): 136 n. 6, 407, 415–16
Gutun Owain: xiii, 2, 17, 21–22, 24–31, 85, 103, 149, 150, 152, 173, 250 n. 46, 377, 398, 422, 425, 427, 428
Gwenllian ferch Ieuan ap Gwallter: 378, 384–85, 386 n. 65, 394 n. 88
Gwent: 136, 158, 159, 238, 404, 405, 412
Gwentian *Brut see Brut Aberpergwm*
Gwenwynwyn ab Owain Cyfeiliog, Prince of Southern Powys: 226, 315, 333
Gweurfyl ferch Dafydd: 384 and nn. 55 and 60, 385
Gwgon ap Meurig (*alias* Gwgon ap 'Morudd'), King of Ceredigion: 395, 404, 412
Gwgon ap Morudd *see* Gwgon ap Meurig
Gwladus Ddu ferch Llywelyn: 112
Gwrgi ab Eliffer Gosgorddfawr: 207, 210, 210 n. 117, 218
Gwriad ap Rhodri Mawr (*alias* 'Gwrydr, brother of Rhodri Mawr'): 404, 412
Gwrydr, brother of Rhodri Mawr *see* Gwriad ap Rhodri Mawr
Gwrtheyrn *see* Vortigern
Gwyddfarch of Meifod, St: 141
Gwynedd: xiv, 2–4, 9, 10 n. 34, 13, 15, 27 n. 103, 28, 40, 104, 134 n. 3, 136 n. 5, 137 n. 14, 145, 167, 169, 180, 181–82, 186, 187, 188, 194, 199, 201, 202, 203, 204, 205, 223–24, 227, 228, 238, 257, 275, 343, 403, 407, 408, 409, 410, 411, 415 n. 243, 416, 417 n. 251, 417 n. 255, 418
Gwynhoedl, church of: 141 n. 5
Gwynionydd-is-Cerdin: 395–97, 401, 411 n. 202

Hailes Abbey: 105, 319, 320, 336, 338
Hamburg, archbishops of: 44–45
Hamelin, Abbot of St Peter's, Gloucester: 313, 331
Hardy, Thomas Duffus, Sir: 74

Harleian chronicle (A-text of *Annales Cambriae*): xv, 107–08, 422
  chronology of: 4
  compilation of: 2–3, 75
  editions of, 71, 75, 75 n. 21, 79
  geographical scope of: 4, 6
  interest in Christianity: 5
  interest in secular politics: 5
  linguistic ability of compilers: 5
  relationship with other chronicles, 18, 78
  sources of: 3
  and St Davids: 7, 80
  see also Annales Cambriae
Harold II, King of the English: 163
Harold Bluetooth, King of Denmark: 59
Harri ap Hywel ap Gwallter, Archdeacon of Carmarthenshire: 389 and n. 71, 393
Hastings, battle of: 207
Hawarden *see* Penarlâg
Hawise, Countess of Gloucester: 246, 256, 274
Hawise, Lady of Ogmore: 266, 283
Hawise of Kingshome: 308, 327
Hebrews: 118
  see also Israelites
Hebrides: 196, 197
Heiligenkreuz Abbey: 53 n. 93
Heimo of Bamberg, *De decursu temporum*: 39, 56, 58–59
Heimskringla: 59, 64
Hélinand of Froidmont, *Chronicon*: 57
Helmold of Bosau: 59
Hendy-Gwyn ar Daf: 405, 413
  see also Whitland Abbey
Hengist and Horsa: 342, 360, 363
Henry, Abbot of St Peter's, Gloucester (d. 1224): 315–17, 333–34
Henry, Abbot of Winchcombe: 314, 316, 332, 334
Henry, Archbishop of York: 313, 331
Henry, Bishop of Exeter: 120
Henry I, King of England: 41, 50, 110 n. 20, 125 n. 1, 126, 126 n. 66, 128, 130, 131, 253, 254, 255, 271, 272, 273, 297, 305, 307, 310–11, 326, 327, 328–29
Henry II, King of England: 44, 121, 123 n. 8, 123 n. 10, 123 n. 13, 124 n. 64, 125 n. 11, 125 n. 12, 193, 245, 255, 256, 272, 273, 274

Henry III, King of England: 115 n. 39, 117, 242, 257, 258, 259, 260, 261, 262, 268, 269, 275, 276, 277, 278, 279, 284, 286, 316, 317, 333, 334, 371
  sister of: 263, 280
Henry IV, King of England: 240
Henry V, King of England: 30
Henry VI, Holy Roman Emperor: 51, 256, 274
Henry VI, King of England: 23, 29
Henry VIII, King of England: 15, 105, 378, 389
Henry Capellanus: 234
Henry Foliot, Abbot of St Peter's, Gloucester (d. 1243): 294, 317, 318, 319, 334, 335, 336
Henry of Huntingdon, *Historia Anglorum*: 15, 21, 45–46, 50, 58, 60
Henry of Lexington, Bishop of Lincoln: 319, 320, 336, 337
Henry of Livonia: 47 n. 59, 52
Henry the Young King: 123 n. 11
Herbert fitz Mathew: 266, 283, 319, 336 n. 230
Hereford: 158, 268, 285
  battle of: 403, 409, 410, 418
  castle of: 317, 334
  St Owen's Church: 306, 326
Herefordshire: 306, 326
Herlant Pic *see* Erlendr píkr
Hertford: 269, 286
Hervé, Bishop of Bangor: 305, 326
Hervey de Chaworth: 295, 321, 338
Hincmar of Rheims: 54
Hiraethwy, battle of: 392–93, 408, 417
Historia Brittonum: 1–4, 10, 10 n. 34, 63, 88, 91, 93, 145, 223, 229
Historia Gruffud vab Kenan
  see under *Vita Griffini filii Conani*
Historia Norwegie: 45, 63
History of St Peter's Abbey
  see under Walter Froucester
Holy Roman Empire: 59, 66
Holyhead *see* Caergybi
Homer: 39
Honorius III, Pope: 260, 278, 369
Honorius Augustodonensis: 45
Hopcyn ap Tomos: 205
Horace: 36, 37, 37 n. 19, 37 n. 20, 42, 47

Horns of Hattin, battle of: 122, 123 n. 15
Hospitaller, Knights: 318, 334
Hubert, Archbishop of Canterbury: 114, 120
Hubert de Burgh, Justiciar of England: 261, 262, 263, 265, 278, 279, 280, 282, 318, 335
  daughter of: 264, 281
Hugh, Abbot of Tewkesbury: 258, 275
Hugh, Bishop of Lincoln (d. 1200): 257, 274
Hugh Bigod, Justiciar of England: 320, 337
Hugh Foliot, Bishop of Hereford: 259, 276, 316, 318, 334, 335
Hugh de Lacy: 306, 310, 326, 329
Hugh de Mappenore, Bishop of Hereford: 316, 334
Hugh de Mortimer: 127
Hugh de Vere, Earl of Oxford: 262, 279
Hugh le Despenser: 158, 160, 162, 362, 366, 372–73
Hugh of Fleury: 44, 52 n. 82, 57
Hugh of St Victor: 43
Hugh of Wells, Bishop of Lincoln (d. 1234): 318, 335
Hugues, Bishop of Dol: 315, 332 n. 228
Humbert of Silva Candida: 57
Humphrey de Bohun, 2nd Earl of Hereford: 321, 338
Humphrey de Bohun, 4th Earl of Hereford: 160 n. 15
Humphrey Llwyd
  Britannicæ descriptionis commentariolum: 170
  Cronica Walliae: xv, 72, 72 n. 9, 421, 429
Hundred Years War: 30
Hungarians: 39, 43, 46, 56, 58, 61–63, 66
Huns: 49, 56, 59, 61, 61 n. 130, 63–65
Huw Pennant: 149, 150, 173, 422, 425
Hwicce: 302, 323
Hyfaidd ap Bleddri, King of Dyfed: 404, 412
Hywel ap Caradog (*alias* Hywel 'Fychan'), King of Gwynedd: 404, 411
Hywel ap Gruffudd ap Cynan ab Owain Gwynedd: 215, 221, 226
Hywel ab Idwal *see* Hywel ab Ieuaf
Hywel ab Ieuaf (*alias* Hywel ab 'Idwal', Hywel ab 'Ifan', Hywel ab 'Ieuan' ab Idwal), King of Gwynedd: 136 n. 2, 136 n. 4, 407, 415 and n. 243

Hywel ab Ifan *see* Hywel ab Ieuaf
Hywel ab Ieuan ab Idwal *see* Hywel ab Ieuaf
Hywel ap Madog ab Idnerth: 127
Hywel ap Maredudd ap Bleddyn: 127
Hywel ap Maredudd ap Caradog, Lord of Meisgyn: 267, 283
Hywel ap Maredudd ap Rhydderch: 127
Hywel ab Owain Gwynedd: 127, 128, 397–98, 406, 414
Hywel ap Seisyll: 399–400, 408, 416–17
Hywel Dda ap Cadell, King of Deheubarth and Gwynedd: 207, 211, 219, 223, 384–85, 391, 396–97, 405–06, 413–14
  see also Cyfraith Hywel
Hywel Fychan: 205, 343, 346–47, 350–55, 358

Iago ab Idwal ap Meurig, King of Gwynedd: 408, 417, 417 n. 255
Iago ab Idwal Foel, King of Gwynedd: 406–07, 414–15
Iago ab Ieuaf ab Idwal (*alias* Iago ab 'Ifan' ab Idwal): 407, 415
Iago ab Ifan ab Idwal *see* Iago ab Ieuaf ab Idwal
Iarddur of Bardsey: 134 n. 9
Iarlles y Ffynnon: 401
Iceland: 37, 43
Icelandic annals: 197–98
Idwal (d. 979/80): 407, 415
Idwal ap Meurig: 136 n. 18
Idwal ap Rhodri *see* Idwal Foel ab Anarawd ap Rhodri Mawr
Idwal ap Rhodri (d. 962): 406, 414
Idwal Dyfed *see* Idwal Foel ab Anarawd ap Rhodri Mawr
Idwal Foel ab Anarawd ap Rhodri Mawr (*alias* Idwal ap 'Rhodri', Idwal 'Dyfed'), King of Gwynedd: 207, 211, 219, 397–98, 405–06, 413–14
Ieuaf ab Idwal (d. 988) (*alias* 'Ieuan' ab Idwal): 136 n. 7, 408, 416
  see also Ieuaf ab Idwal Foel
Ieuaf ab Idwal Foel (*alias* 'Ifan' ab Idwal): 406, 414–15
  see also Ieuaf ab Idwal (d. 988)
Ieuan ab Idwal *see* Ieuaf ab Idwal (d. 988)
Ieuan ab Iorwerth: 383 n. 33, 385
Ieuan ap Sulien: 13–14

Ieuan Brechfa: xv, 25, 378–79, 382–86, 389–90, 397, 399, 401–02, 413 n. 223
  see also Brut Ieuan Brechfa
Ifan ab Idwal *see* Ieuaf ab Idwal Foel
Ifor son of Alan, King of Brittany: 18
Imhar of Waterford: 134 n. 5
Ingi Bárðarson, King of Norway: 197, 198, 199
Innocent III, Pope: 117, 257, 258, 275
Innocent IV, Pope: 265, 266, 267, 282, 283, 284
Interdict of 1208: 117, 120, 184, 208, 214, 221, 226, 245, 257–58, 275, 315–16, 333
Iolo Morganwg: xv, 74, 76–77, 375–81, 386–90, 402
Iona: 3, 197, 198
Iorwerth *alias* Gervase, Bishop of St Davids: 117, 317, 334
Ireland: 120, 197, 201, 262, 270, 280, 285, 287, 318, 335, 398, 405, 406, 409, 412, 414, 418
  conquest of: 398
  see also Chronicle of Ireland
Irish chronicles: 3, 71
  source for Welsh chronicles: 3, 75, 88, 92–93
  use of the vernacular in: 193, 193 n. 75
  see also Chronicle of Ireland; Clonmacnoise
Irish people: 5, 408, 417
Is-Aeron Castle: 128
Isabella, Countess of Gloucester: 256, 257, 258, 261, 264, 274, 275, 278, 281, 316, 333
Isabella, Holy Roman Empress, daughter of King John: 394, 418 n. 262
Isidore of Seville: 35–37, 37 n. 19, 37 n. 20, 37 n. 22, 47, 62, 75
  Chronica minora: 8, 93, 118
  Etymologiae: 109 n. 11
Israelites: 40–43
  see also Hebrews
Italians: 55–56
Italy: 37, 43, 57, 66
Ithel, King of Gwent: 404, 412

Jack Cade's rebellion: 29
Jacques de Vitry, *Historia Occidentalis*: 45

Japhet: 20
Jasper Tudor: 106
Jerome: 4, 35, 37 n. 19, 37 n. 20, 37 n. 21, 44, 62
Jerusalem: 118, 123 n. 8, 123 n. 13, 123 n. 15, 256, 265, 273, 274, 282
Jews: 123 n. 7, 125 n. 6
Joan (*alias* Siwan), daughter of King John, wife of Llywelyn ab Iorwerth: 198, 199, 205, 208, 228, 316, 333, 410, 418
Joan of Acre, daughter of Edward I: 323, 340
John, Abbot of Margam: 263, 281
John, Archbishop of Lyon: 44
John, Count of Mortain: 256, 274
John, King of England: 10, 80, 114, 115, 117, 119, 120, 180, 195, 197, 198–201, 204, 214, 215, 216, 221, 222, 226, 227, 256, 257, 258, 274, 275, 276, 316, 333, 394, 410, 418
John, Lord of Monmouth: 267, 283, 284
John ap Rhys: 175
John Breton, Bishop of Hereford: 321, 338
John Davies of Mallwyd: 175
John de Courcy: 120, 200
John de Felda, Abbot of St Peter's, Gloucester: 319, 320, 336, 337
John de Gamages, Abbot of St Peter's, Gloucester: 322, 339
John de Lacy, Earl of Lincoln: 264, 282
  daughter of: 264, 281
John de Warenne, Earl of Surrey: 164–65
John Jones of Gellilyfdy: 149, 150, 425
John La Ware, Abbot of Margam, Bishop of Llandaf: 263, 268, 281, 285, 319, 336
John le Walleys: 233
John Marshal: 233, 242, 270, 287
John of Salisbury, *Policraticus*: 45
John of Taxster: 90
John of Worcester: 44, 46, 48, 60, 298
John Oldcastle, Sir: 29
John Pecham, Archbishop of Canterbury: 20
John Prise of Brecon, Sir: 174, 177, 178
Jordanes: 46, 65
Joseph, Bishop of St Davids: 133 n. 81
Joseph of Arimathea, St: 52
Josephus: 37 n. 19, 37 n. 21, 65
Julius Caesar: 36, 64, 110 n. 17
Justin, epitome of: 62
Juvenal: 37, 37 n. 19, 37 n. 20, 37 n. 22, 42

Kenelm, St: 297–98, 302, 323
Kenfig church: 236
Kerry *see* Ceri
Keynsham: 234, 255, 266, 273, 283
Kidwelly *see* Cydweli
Kildare: 318, 335
Kilpeck, church of St David: 311, 329

La Grand Chartreuse Abbey: 54
Laȝamon: 194 n. 76
Lambarde, William: 290–92
Lanfranc, Archbishop of Canterbury: 253, 271
Lantbert, Life of Heribert of Cologne: 57
Lateran council: 117
Latin
   language: 5, 23, 24, 31, 36, 37, 49, 51, 54, 58, 60, 64–65, 72, 105, 132 n. 74
   sources for Welsh chronicles: 9, 11–13, 15, 17–18, 20–22, 76, 81–83, 86–87, 97–98, 99, 132
   and Welsh vernacular: 10, 15–17, 21, 30, 71, 97, 187, 189, 193, 252
Laurence de Hastings, Lord of Abergavenny: 159
Law, Welsh *see Cyfraith Hywel*
Leland, John: 72 n. 9, 81 n. 48, 393–94
Leo IX, Pope: 57, 61 n. 130
Leofgar, Bishop of Hereford: 224
Letard Litelking: 126
Lewes, battle of (Offham): 343, 349–51, 357–58, 361, 365, 370–71
Lewys Dwnn: 379, 390
Lewys Morgannwg: 23 n. 88
Liber pontificalis: 46, 47
Life of Gruffudd ap Cynan *see Vita Griffini filii Conani*
Life of St Anselm: 232
Lincoln: 254, 259, 272, 276
Liudprand of Cremona: 57
Livy: 37 n. 22
Llanaber: 141 n. 5
Llanbadarn Fawr: 14, 31, 136 n. 7, 300, 307, 311, 327, 329, 408, 416
   chronicle from: 12, 13, 13 n. 45, 81, 98–100, 102, 183–84
Llanbleddian church: 234, 236
Llancarfan: 136 n. 7, 309, 328, 408, 416 and n. 245

Llandaf, diocese of: 159, 234, 238, 239, 242, 295
Llanddewibrefi, Anchorite of: 84 n. 57
Llandeilo Fawr: 320, 337
Llandinam: 13 n. 45
Llandough, *Llandochau Fach*: 236
Llandudoch *see* St Dogmaels
Llanedern, church of: 247, 263, 281
Llanfaes: 169, 195, 198–201, 202, 203, 214, 221, 404, 411
Llanfihangel Rhôs-y-Corn: 382 n. 29
Llangadog Castle: 114, 120
Llangarmon *see* Llancarfan
Llangeinor: 342
Llangïan: 145
Llangwm: 137 n. 15, 408, 416
Llangynwyd: 234, 269, 286
Llanilltud Fawr *see* Llantwit Major
Llanllawddog: 383 n. 43
Llannerch: 26, 27
Llanrhystud Castle: 127, 128
Llanrwst: 391, 414 n. 225
Llanstephan Castle: 127
Llantarnam Abbey: 105
Llanthony Prima Priory: 311, 329
Llanthony Secunda Priory: 312, 321, 330, 338
Llantrisant: 234, 267, 283
Llantwit Major, *Llanilltud Fawr*: 136 n. 7, 235, 236, 271 n. 130, 408, 416
Llanwenog, battle of: 407, 415
Llanybydder: 382 n. 29
Lles ap Coel: 216, 217, 217 n. 174, 222, 223, 229, 360, 364
Lleucu ferch Einion: 383 n. 43
Llyfr Dysgread Arfau: 27
Llyma enwau y nawnyn (genealogical tract): 380
   text and translation: 382–85
   see also Glyn Cothi
Llŷn peninsula: 141 n. 5, 145
Llywarch ab Owain: 407, 416
Llywelyn, Bishop of St Asaph: 162
Llywelyn ap Gruffudd, Prince of Wales: 15, 16, 24, 29, 83 n. 55, 110, 171, 180, 182, 203, 216, 222, 228, 234, 267, 268, 269, 283, 285, 286, 295, 319–20, 321–22, 336, 338–39, 348, 353, 361–62, 364–65, 368–71, 394

Llywelyn ap Hoedlyw, Lord of Is Cerdin: 395
Llywelyn ab Iorwerth, Prince of Gwynedd: 7, 9, 10, 17, 28, 94, 117, 118, 180, 181, 185, 195, 197, 198–201, 203, 204, 205, 208, 213, 213 n. 146, 214, 215, 216, 220, 221, 222, 224, 226, 227, 257, 258, 260, 261, 262, 264, 275, 278, 279, 282, 317, 318, 334, 335, 356–57, 361, 364, 368–69, 394, 410, 418
Llywelyn ap Rhisiart *see* Lewys Morgannwg
Llywelyn ap Seisyll, King of Gwynedd and Deheubarth: 399–400, 408, 416–17
Llywelyn Bren: 158, 160, 162, 353–54, 362, 366, 372–73
Lollards: 29
Lombards: 56
London: 314, 322, 331, 339
Louis VII, King of France: 123 n. 6, 245, 246, 255, 256, 272, 273
Louis VIII, King of France: 117, 123, 258, 260, 276, 277
Louis IX, King of France: 112, 267, 284, 284 n. 162
Luard, Henry: 79, 101
Lucan: 36, 47, 62, 121
Lucas de Towny: 321, 339
Lucius III, Pope: 123 n. 9, 123 n. 14
Ludlow: 322, 339
Lund, archbishops of: 52
Lwmbart, Bishop of St Davids: 405, 413

Mabel, Countess of Gloucester: 255, 272
Mabinogi, Four Branches of the: 189
Mabudryd Castle: 127
Maccus (*alias* 'Mark') son of Harold (*alias* Eyrlaid): 406, 415
Machafwy, battle of: 207, 211, 219, 224
Macrobius: 35
Madog ap Llywelyn: xiv, 22, 163–68, 362, 366, 372–73
Madog ap Maredudd: 127
Madog Fychan ap Madog Saethydd: 383–86
Madog Saethydd: 383–86
Máel Mórda, King of Leinster: 134 n. 14
Maelienydd: 8
Maelgwn ap Rhys ap Gruffudd: 112
Maelgwn ap Rhys Fychan: 158, 160
Maelgwn Fychan (*alias* Maelgwn Ieuanc) ap Maelgwn ap Rhys: 112, 394, 418 n. 262

Maelgwn Gwynedd: 187, 192, 207, 210, 210 n. 217, 218
Maelgwn Ieuanc *see* Maelgwn Fychan
Maesyfed, *New Radnor*: 136 n. 11
Magna Carta: 227
Magnús Erlingsson: 196
Magyars: 39–40, 54, 63, 65
Mainz, printing in: 29
Malmesbury: 125 n. 11, 314, 332
Malvern: 312, 330
Man, Isle of: 137 n. 16, 200, 201, 403, 411
March of Wales
 chronicles of the: 71, 231, 236, 237, 238, 248–49
 connections with native Wales: 232, 236, 237, 252
 lordships of the: 2, 31, 235, 239
 monasteries of the: 78, 88, 95, 231, 232, 235, 252
Maredudd ap Bleddyn: 212, 220
Maredudd ap Cynan: 184, 215, 221, 226, 227
Maredudd ab Edwin: 392, 417 n. 253
Maredudd ab Einion: 393
Maredudd ap Gruffudd: 127, 128
Maredudd ab Ithel: 409, 418 and n. 259
Maredudd ap Madog ab Idnerth: 127
Maredudd ab Owain ab Edwin, King of Deheubarth: 409, 418
Maredudd ab Owain ap Hywel Dda, King of Deheubarth and Gwynedd: 100, 134 n. 2, 135, 136 n. 5, 136 n. 8, 136 n. 11, 137 n. 13, 137 n. 15, 137 n. 21, 392, 407, 408, 415 n. 243, 416
Margam Abbey: 7, 14, 239, 269, 286
 annals of: 6, 7, 79, 90–91, 91 n. 86, 94, 101–02, 422
Marianus Scottus: 43, 48, 56–57, 232
Mark *see* Maccus son of Harold
Martianus Capellanus: 35, 37
Martin of Troppau: 37, 51–52, 57, 232, 233
Matilda, Countess of Gloucester: 267, 283
Matilda, Empress: 125 n. 2, 125 n. 12
Matthew Paris: 49–50, 55, 58
Maud de Braose (*alias* Maud de St Valéry, *Malld Walbri*): 120, 386
Mauger, Bishop of Worcester: 257, 274, 315, 333

Maurice, Archdeacon and Bishop of Llandaf: 265, 282
Maurice de Londres: 312, 330
Maurice fitz Gerald: 123 n. 1
Meditationes S. Bernardi: 232
Medrawd: 5
Meifod: 13 n. 45
Meigen, battle of: 207, 210, 218, 223
Meilyr Brydydd: 188 n. 52
Meirionydd: 127, 227, 407, 416
Melrose, chronicle of: 351
Mercia: 302–03, 323–24
Merfyn ap Rhodri: 207, 211, 211 n. 123, 218, 219
Merfyn Frych, King of Gwynedd: 207, 210, 211, 218, 223, 404, 412
Merin, church of: 141 n. 5
Merlin: 18, 210 n. 116
  prophecies of: 18, 45, 356, 359–60, 363
Meurig, Bishop of St Davids: 404, 411
Meurig ap Cadell: 405, 412
Meurig ap Cadfan: 406, 414
Meurig ap Dafydd: 158, 159
Meurig ap Gruffudd: 127
Meurig ab Idwal Foel: 137 n. 14, 137 n. 15, 407, 408, 415, 416
Middle English Prose *Brut*: 28–29
Miles, Earl of Hereford: 125 n. 5, 127, 312, 330
Mold Castle, *Yr Wyddgrug*: 127
Monmouth: 239, 262, 280
Montgomery, treaty of: 228, 361 n. 50, 365, 371
Mor ap Gwyn: 134 n. 5
Mordaf, Bishop of Bangor: 405, 413
Morgan ab Idwal *see* Morgan ab Owain
Morgan ap Maredudd (d. 1177): 123 n. 3
Morgan ap Maredudd, Lord of Glamorgan: 158, 162
Morgan ab Owain (*alias* Morgan ab 'Idwal'), King of Morgannwg: 407, 415
Morgan ap Rhys: 112
Morgan Gam: 265, 282
Morgan Patta: 123 n. 2
Morgenau, Bishop of St Davids: 134 n. 2, 137 n. 21
Morgynnydd, Bishop of St Davids: 133, 133 n. 81
Morris, Lewis: 176

Mortimer family *see* Edmund de Mortimer; Hugh de Mortimer; Ralph de Mortimer; Roger de Mortimer; Roger Mortimer
Morudd ap Llywarch Lwyd, fictional king of Ceredigion: 395–96, 397, 404, 411 n. 202
Morugge, mountains of: 322, 339
Murchad son of Brian Boru: 134 n. 14
Mynydd Carn, battle of: 207, 212, 212 n. 134, 219
Myrddin *see* Merlin
Myvyrian Archaiology of Wales: 72–76, 80 n. 43, 375–80, 386–90, 400, 402

Neath: 234, 239, 266, 283, 343
  castle of: 343, 354–56, 360, 364, 368–69
Neath Abbey: 7, 109, 231, 237, 249, 250, 251, 252
  chronicle of: xiv, 6, 16, 22, 78–79, 91, 94, 96–97, 102, 147, 237, 238–39, 240, 242–43, 244, 247, 248, 251, 424
  chronicling at: 6–8, 22, 78–79, 90–91, 94, 95 n. 105, 96 n. 112, 97, 102, 109, 137, 147, 236, 354, 424
  and De Braoses: 8, 14–16, 109, 122, 237, 239 n. 16
  see also under Domesday Book
Neath Breviate *see under* Domesday Book
Nechtan son of Der-Ilei, King of the Picts: 232
Nennius *see Historia Brittonum*
Neuburg Abbey: 53 n. 93
New Radnor *see* Maesyfed
New Testament: 52, 67
Newcastle Church: 236
Newport: 262, 279, 317, 334
  St Gwynllyw's church: 317, 334
Nibelungenlied: 64–65
Nicholas, Bishop of Llandaf: 235 n. 7, 256, 273, 313, 315, 331, 332
Nicholas of Ely, Bishop of Worcester: 320, 337
Nicholas of Ledbury, Archdeacon of Llandaf: 267, 284
Nicholas of Tusculanum: 258, 275
Nicholas Trivet: 232
Niederaltaich Abbey: 53
Njáls saga: 38

Norman conquest: *see* England; Wales
Normandy: 46, 120, 121, 409, 418
Normans: 2, 40, 44–46, 48
  conquest of Ceredigion: 13
  conquest of Glamorgan: 6, 234, 235, 271 n. 130
  genealogies of: 15
Norse language: 37, 38, 64, 194, 196
Northmen, black: 136 n. 6, 136 n. 8, 404–05, 407, 412, 416
Northumbria: 3
Norway: 37, 43, 64, 169, 195, 196, 197, 201, 214, 221
Nottingham: 254, 271
Nowell, Laurence: 290–94

O Oes Gwrtheyrn: xiv, 9, 17, 80, 104, 106, 169–229, 422
  chronology of: 170–71, 179–80, 205–06
  date of: 169, 180, 205
  edition and translation of: 210–23
  Galfridian influence upon: 190
  language of: 169, 190–91, 193, 194
  and the Llywelyn ab Iorwerth genealogies: 185, 191–93, 205
  manuscripts of: 171–79
  provenance of: 169, 180–82, 185
  raid on Llanfaes, account of: 195–202
  scholarship on: 170
  seventeenth-century English translation of: 177
  sources: 202–03, 205, 225
Octavian: 118
Odense: 55
Odo, cellarer of St Peter's, Gloucester: 303, 308, 324, 328
Oed yr Arglwydd: 16, 104, 150, 173, 175, 185, 425
Offa, King of the Mercians: 207, 210, 218, 223, 410 n. 196
Offham *see* Lewes, battle of
Olaf Cuarán: 397, 414 n. 227
Olaf Guthfrithsson: 397, 414 n. 227
Old English: 291–93
Old Testament: 42–43
  Chronicles: 40
  Exodus 62
  Kings: 41
  Samuel: 40, 41

Orderic Vitalis: 44, 48–49
Orkney: 197, 200
Orléans: 268, 284
Orosius: 37 n. 19, 37 n. 20, 37 n. 21, 37 n. 22, 39, 44, 59, 62–65
Osbern, Abbot of Malmesbury: 314, 332
Osbern of Canterbury: 60
Osborn, Bishop of Exeter: 310, 328
Osney Abbey chronicle: 298–300
Oswald, St: 149 n. 28, 297, 303, 324
Oswestry
  annals: 24, 103, 427
  lordship of: 25, 162
Otto, cardinal and legate: 264, 265, 281, 282
Otto II, Holy Roman Emperor: 55
Otto IV, Holy Roman Emperor: 257, 275
Otto of Freising: 37, 39, 51, 53, 55, 55 n. 102, 57, 62 n. 134
Otto the Legate: 117
Ovid: 36–37, 37 n. 19, 37 n. 20, 42, 47
Owain ap Dyfnwal (k. 990): 136 n. 10
Owain ap Dyfnwal (k. 1015): 134 n. 15
Owain ab Einion *see* Edwin ab Einion
Owain ap Hywel *see* Edwin ap Hywel
Owain ap Hywel Dda, King of Deheubarth: 136 n. 7, 207, 211, 219, 223–24, 408, 416
Owain ap Maredudd, King of Dyfed: 210, 218
Owain ap Rhys ap Ricard: 396, 397
Owain Cyfeiliog ap Gruffudd: 127
Owain Fychan ap Madog: 213, 220
Owain Glyndŵr: 23, 24, 29
  annals of: 23 n. 88, 103, 427
Owain Goch ap Gruffudd: 216, 222, 228, 369
Owain Gwynedd: 127, 208, 213, 220, 225, 398, 406, 414
Owein see Iarlles y Ffynnon
Owen, Aneirin: 73 n. 14, 74, 81, 97, 106 n. 160
Owen, George, of Henllys: 388
Owen, John: 427
Oxford: 259, 264, 277, 281, 321, 338
Oystermouth, castle: 239

Padarn, St: 14
Padua: 61 n. 129

GENERAL INDEX

Painscastle *see* Castell Paen
Pandulf, papal legate: 258, 259, 275, 277
Pannonia: 61 n. 130
Paris: 268, 284
Patrick, St: 5, 409, 417
Patrick de Chaworth, benefactor of St Peter's Abbey, Gloucester: 309, 328
Patrick de Chaworth, Lord of Kidwelly: 266, 283, 320, 337
Paul the Deacon: 37 n. 22, 44
Payn fitz John: 299, 311, 330
Peasants' Revolt: 29
Pembroke: 318, 335
Penarlâg, *Hawarden*: 208, 216, 222, 228, 321, 338
Pencader, battle of: 409, 417
Penmon: 415 n. 233
Pennant: 309, 328
Pennant Forest: 382 n. 31, 384, 385 n. 62
Penweddig: 307, 327
Peredur ab Eliffer Gosgorddfawr: 207, 210, 210 n. 117, 218
Peris, St: 140
  cult of: 145
  name of: 145
  see also under Bonedd y Saint
Peris, St, of Llanberis: 139
Pershore: 239
Persia: 61
Peter, Abbot of Gloucester: 300, 306, 308, 326, 327
Peter, Abbot of Tewkesbury: 261, 279
Peter Comestor: 65
Peter Damian, Life of Odilo of Cluny: 57
Peter de Aigueblanche, Bishop of Hereford: 265, 282, 318, 335
Peter de Leia, Bishop of St Davids: 144
Peter de Rivaux: 262, 280, 318, 335
Peter des Roches, Bishop of Winchester: 262, 280, 316, 318, 333, 335
Peter of Clairvaux, abbot: 144
Peter of Poitiers, *Compendium Historiae in Genealogia Christi*: 20
Peter the Venerable, Abbot of Cluny: 47, 54
Petrie, Henry: 74, 76 n. 25, 106 n. 160
Philip II, King of France: 119, 120, 123 n. 6, 123 n. 7, 200, 256, 273, 274
Philippús Símonsson: 197
Philistines: 40

Phillimore, Egerton: 77, 79
Picts: 5
Piers de Gaveston: 158, 160, 362, 366, 372–73
Pindar: 39
Plant yr Arglwydd Rhys: 389
Pliny the Elder: 35, 36, 64, 65
Poitiers: 260, 277
Poitou: 117, 120
Poland: 43, 61, 66
Poles: 60–62, 66
Powell, Thomas: 429
Powys: 13, 29, 130, 403–04, 409, 411, 418
  saints of: 141
Prague: 42
Prosper of Aquitaine: 4, 64
Protestant reformation: 15
Prouinciale Romanum: 232, 233
Prudentius: 42
Prydydd y Moch: 226
Pseudo-Methodius: 15
Pughe, William Owen: 74
Py delw y dyly: 342, 359
Pyfog, mother of Hywel ab Owain Gwynedd: 398, 406, 414

radknights: 306, 326 and n. 221
Radulf Maeloc: 261, 279, 279 n. 154
Ragnar Lodbrok: 58
Rainald of Dassel: 55 n. 102
Ralph de Diceto: 44, 56, 64
Ralph de Maidstone, Bishop of Hereford: 263, 280, 318, 335
Ralph de Mortimer: 267, 283
Ralph Niger, *Chronica*: 44
Ranulf, Earl of Chester (d. 1153): 125 n. 4, 125 n. 7, 125 n. 14, 125 n. 15, 128
Ranulf, Earl of Chester (d. 1232): 182, 197, 203, 214–15, 221, 227, 262, 279
Ranulf Higden, *Polychronicon*: 27
Reginald, King of Man: 197, 198, 199–201, 226
Reginald de Braose: 260, 278, 317, 334
Reginald de Homme, Abbot of St Peter's, Gloucester: 320, 322, 337, 339
Reginald de Radnor, canon of Llandaf: 260, 278
Regino of Prüm: 36, 37 n. 19, 37 n. 21, 42, 43, 57

Reinhelm, Bishop of Hereford: 306–07, 326
Rhain (*alias* 'Rhydderch') ap Maredudd, King of Dyfed: 403, 411
Rhain the Irishman: 100, 400
Rhiwallon ap Cynfyn: 409, 418
Rhodri ap Hywel Dda: 2
Rhodri ab Idwal: 406, 414
Rhodri ab Owain Gwynedd: 199, 204, 213, 220, 226, 227
Rhodri Mawr: 5, 27, 192, 211, 211 n. 122, 218, 223, 404, 412
Rhodri Molwynog: 18, 410 n. 195
Rhos (Dyfed): 117, 118, 126
Rhuddlan: 208, 213, 220, 225, 322, 339
  Statute of: 322, 339
Rhun ab Owain Gwynedd: 127
Rhyd-y-Groes ar Hafren: 409, 417
Rhydderch, King of Dyfed *see* Rhain ap Maredudd, King of Dyfed
Rhydderch ab Iestyn, King of Deheubarth: 408, 409, 417
Rhygyfarch ap Sulien: 13
Rhŷs, John, Sir: 79
Rhys ap Gruffudd (the Lord Rhys): 125 n. 14, 125 n. 15, 128, 225, 234, 244, 256, 274
Rhys ap Gruffudd ab Ifor, Lord of Senghennydd: 268, 285
Rhys ap Hywel: 127
Rhys ap Maredudd, Lord of Dryslwyn: 156, 156 n. 6, 295, 322, 339, 345–46, 353, 362, 366, 370–73
Rhys ap Tewdwr, King of Deheubarth: 100, 207, 212, 219, 224, 225, 235, 385 n. 62, 394, 410, 418
Rhys ap Thomas, Sir: 389–90
Rhys Fychan ap Rhys Mechyll: 234, 268, 285
  see also Rhys Gryg (Rhys Fychan)
Rhys Gryg (Rhys Fychan): 114, 116, 120, 385 n. 62
Richard, Abbot of Westminster: 267, 283
Richard, Bishop of Chichester *see* Richard of Chichester, St
Richard, Earl of Cornwall: 120, 242, 261, 262, 263, 265, 267, 268, 269, 278, 279, 280, 282, 283, 285, 286, 319, 320, 336, 338
  daughter of: 262, 263, 280
  sons of: 261, 262, 263, 268, 279, 280, 285
  wife of: 268, 285
Richard I, King of England: 119, 119 n. 52, 255, 256, 257, 260, 272, 274, 277
Richard II, King of England: 23, 28, 80
Richard Carew, Bishop of St Davids: 319, 336
Richard de Clare, 6th Earl of Gloucester: 240, 259, 261, 262, 264, 265, 266, 267, 269, 277, 278, 279, 281, 282, 283, 285 n. 163, 286, 320, 337
  brother of: 320, 337
  son of: 265, 267, 282, 284
  wife of: 264, 281
Richard de Clare, 2nd Earl of Pembroke (*alias* Richard de Striguil, Richard fitz Gilbert, Strongbow): 123 n. 1
Richard de Conway, franciscan: 188
Richard fitz Gilbert de Clare (d. 1136): 299, 311, 329
Richard Herbert: 233, 242, 270, 287
Richard le Grant, Archbishop of Canterbury: 260, 261, 278, 279
Richard Marshal, 3rd Earl of Pembroke: 261, 262, 279, 280, 318, 335
Richard of Chichester, St: 319, 336
Richard of Devizes, annals of: 83
Richard of Dover, Archbishop of Canterbury: 123 n. 11
Richard of Gravesend, Bishop of Lincoln: 320, 337
Richard Siward: 263, 266, 267, 280, 283, 284, 318, 335
Richard Swinefield, Bishop of Hereford: 322, 339
Robert, Abbot of Tewkesbury: 256, 273
Robert, Bishop of Bangor: 215, 221
Robert, Bishop of Ely: 260, 278
Robert, Bishop of Hereford (d. 1095): 304, 325
Robert, Earl of Gloucester: 50–51, 125 n. 4, 125 n. 9, 127, 128, 130, 131, 236 n. 9, 254, 272
Robert, Prior and Abbot of Tewkesbury: 261, 279
Robert, Prior of Ewenny: 312, 330
Robert Burnell, Bishop of Bath: 321, 338
Robert Curthose, Duke of Normandy: 110 n. 20, 131, 253, 254, 271, 272, 311, 329

Robert de Béthune, Prior of Llanthony Prima and Bishop of Hereford: 125 n. 10, 311–12, 313, 329–30, 331
Robert de Beaumont, Earl of Leicester: 114, 120
Robert fitz Hamon, Lord of Glamorgan: 235, 236 n. 9, 248 n. 40, 253, 271, 300, 309, 328 n. 225
Robert Grosseteste, Bishop of Lincoln: 263, 280, 318, 319, 335, 336
Robert of Bingham, Bishop of Salisbury: 260, 267, 278, 283
Robert of Caen, Earl of Gloucester: 236
Robert of Torigni: 46
Robert Vaughan: 24, 169, 175, 176, 177, 425, 427, 428
Rodulfus Glaber: 57
Roger, Bishop of Bath: 266, 267, 283, 284
Roger, Bishop of London: 260, 278
Roger, Bishop of Worcester: 245, 255, 273
Roger, Earl of Hereford: 125 n. 17, 312, 313, 330, 331
Roger I of Berkeley: 304, 325
Roger II of Berkeley: 305, 325
Roger III of Berkeley: 313, 331
Roger Bigod, Earl of Warwick: 262, 279
Roger Clifford Junior: 322, 339
Roger Clifford Senior: 321, 338
Roger de Bulley: 305, 325–26
Roger de Mortimer (d. 1282): 322, 339
Roger Mortimer, Earl of March: 159, 160, 165
Roger of Gloucester: 306, 326
Romans: 14, 35, 61–62
Rome: 18, 36, 39, 41, 49, 55, 60–62, 120, 207, 210, 211, 214 n. 151, 218, 219, 257, 260, 266, 274, 277, 283, 396, 405, 410, 413, 419
Roskilde: 46, 58
Rouen: 120
Rudolf of Ems, *Weltchronik*: 64–65
Ruotger, Life of Bruno: 57
Russians: 56

Sadyrnfyw, Bishop of St Davids: 395, 411 n. 202
Saeran, St: 149 n. 28
St Albans: 49, 54–55, 61
St Asaph: 156, 157, 159, 162

bishops of: 162, 396, 405, 413
St Davids, *Mynyw*: 102, 118, 120–22, 123 n. 8, 124 n. 63, 131, 134 n. 2, 134 n. 9, 136 n. 7, 137 n. 13, 137 n. 21, 225, 239, 295, 319, 336, 407, 408, 411 n. 199, 415, 416
bishops of: 13, 96, 114, 117, 121, 123 n. 1, 123 n. 8, 125 n. 10, 127, 132–33, 134 n. 2, 137 n. 21, 295, 319, 336, 396, 405, 413
chronicles from: 2, 3, 5–10, 12, 18, 70–71, 80–81, 89–96, 98, 108–09, 115, 119–22, 131, 133, 135, 137, 179, 190, 193, 202–03, 393
St Dogmaels, *Llandudoch*: 136 n. 7, 408, 416
St Lambert's Abbey: 53 n. 93
St Peter's Abbey *see under* Gloucester
St Ulrich and St Afra's Abbey: 53 n. 93
Saladin: 256, 274
Salisbury: 304, 324
Salisbury, church of: 259, 277
Sallust: 36–37, 37 n. 19, 42
Salona: 58
Samson, Bishop of Worcester: 305, 307, 325–26, 327
Santiago de Compostella: 46
Saul: 40–42
Saxo Grammaticus, *Gesta Danorum*: 45, 52, 57, 58 n. 117, 60–63, 66
Saxons: 10, 15, 18, 21, 27, 49, 56, 60, 170, 360, 364
Scotland: 195, 208, 214, 221, 249, 343
Scots: 56
Scythians: 39, 40, 61
Seisyll ap Llywelyn of Buellt: 399–401
Seneca: 35, 36, 37 n. 19, 37 n. 20
Senefyr: 141 n. 5
Senghennydd: 162
see also Gruffudd ap Rhys, Lord of Senghennydd; Rhys ap Gruffudd ab Ifor, Lord of Senghennydd
Sens, archbishops of: 52
Serlo, Abbot of St Peter's, Gloucester: 304, 306, 325–26, 310, 328
Severn, River: 318, 320, 335, 337, 409, 417
Severus, provost of Melnik: 53
Sewal, Archbishop of York: 241
Sex aetates mundi: 10 n. 34, 71

Shetland: 197
Shirburn Castle: 106 n. 159
Shrewsbury: 322, 339, 362, 365, 370–71
Shropshire: 25, 306, 321, 326, 338
Siancyn ap Dafydd ap Gruffudd: 341, 345, 350, 352–55, 371
Sicard of Cremona: 61 n. 129
Sicilians: 56
Sicily: 49, 255, 273
Sigebert of Gembloux: 44, 48, 56–58
Simeon of Durham: 60
Simon, Bishop of Worcester: 309, 311, 312, 313, 328, 329, 330, 331
Simon de Kéza, *Gesta Hungarorum*: 39, 40 n. 34, 46, 61 n. 130
Simon de Montfort, 6th Earl of Leicester: 158, 234, 242, 264, 269, 270, 281, 286, 321, 338, 394, 410, 418 n. 262, 419
  daughter of *see* Eleanor de Montfort
  son of: 270, 286
Siôn Dafydd Rhys: 389
Sitric Silkenbeard: 134 n. 14
Siwan *see* Joan
Slavs: 59
Snorri Sturlusson: 194
Socrates: 36
Solinus: 35, 37 n. 21, 37 n. 22
Spanish: 56
Stafford, lord of: 323, 340
Statius: 64, 65
Stephen, King of England: 124, 125 n. 1, 125 n. 4, 125 n. 7, 125 n. 16, 131, 254, 272
Stephen, St: 39, 65
Stephen Bauzan: 268, 285, 320, 337
Stephen de Segrave, Justiciar of England: 262, 279, 318, 335
Stephen Langton, Archbishop of Canterbury: 120, 214, 215, 221, 245, 257, 258, 259, 260, 274, 274, 275, 277, 278
Stephens, Thomas: 376
Stigand, Archbishop of Canterbury: 142
Stirling *see* Bannockburn, battle of
Strasbourg: 49, 65
Strata Florida Abbey: 8, 10, 12, 14, 83 n. 55, 84 n. 57, 95, 102, 105, 110, 251, 252
  chronicles from: 8, 10, 12, 14–16, 75–76, 80–81, 83, 88 n. 73, 89, 89 n. 79, 90, 96, 98, 137, 156, 167, 183–84, 190, 202, 203, 205, 423
Strata Marcella Abbey: 103 n. 146
Strathclyde, *Ystrad Clud* (*alias* Ystrad 'Llyr'): 405, 413
  see also Alclud
Strongbow *see* Gilbert de Clare, 1st Earl of Pembroke; Richard de Clare, 2nd Earl of Pembroke
Sturla Þórðarson, *Íslendinga saga*: 38
Sulien ap Rhygyfarch: 13 n. 46
Sven Aggesen: 63
Sverrir Sigurðarson: 196, 198, 199
Sverris saga: 194, 194 n. 77
Swabians: 56
Swansea: 239, 268, 285, 341
Sweden: 59
Sweyn Forkbeard: 134 n. 9, 134 n. 11, 134 n. 12, 134 n. 13, 137 n. 16
Syria: 256, 274

Tal Moelfre: 208, 213, 220, 225
Talbot, Thomas: 425
Taliesin (legendary poet): 186–87, 189
Talyfan: 234, 266, 283
Tegernsee Abbey: 53 n. 93
Teibyr, Bishop of St Asaph: 405, 413
  see also Chebur, Bishop of St Asaph
Tenby, men of: 128
Terence: 42
Tewdwr ap Beli, King of Alclud: 410 n. 195
Tewdwr ab Einion: 137 n. 15, 408, 416
Tewdwr ap Rhodri: 403, 410
  see also Rhodri Molwynog; Tewdwr ap Beli
Tewkesbury: 239, 254, 272
  abbey: 231, 232, 233 n. 3, 234, 235, 238, 247, 248 n. 40, 250, 251, 252, 254, 261, 263, 264, 271 n. 130, 278, 279, 279 n. 154, 281, 320, 337
  annals of: xiv, 6, 7 n. 21, 16, 91, 94–95, 110, 233, 233 n. 3, 234, 239, 244, 245–46, 248, 252
  St Mary's Church: 253, 271
Teyrnassedd y Saesson: 428
Theobald, Archbishop of Canterbury: 255, 273, 313, 331
Theodoricus Monachus: 64
Theulf, Bishop of Worcester: 308, 327–28

GENERAL INDEX

Thietmar of Merseburg: 36–37, 64
Thomas, Archbishop of York: 305, 308, 325, 328
Thomas, Archdeacon of Llandaf: 267, 284
Thomas, Lord of Lancaster: 158, 160, 164–65, 343, 349, 352, 357, 362, 366, 372–73
Thomas, Rhys, printer: 378–80
Thomas ab Ieuan ap Deicws, 'Syr': 150, 398
Thomas ap Llywelyn ab Ithel: 106
Thomas Becket: 24, 245, 255, 259, 273, 277, 342, 360, 364, 368–69
Thomas Carbonel, Abbot of St Peter's, Gloucester: 315, 333
Thomas de Cantilupe, St, Bishop of Hereford: 321, 322, 338, 339
Thomas de Turberville: 159, 160
Thomas le Waleys, Bishop of St Davids: 267, 284, 319, 336
Thomas of Berkeley: 317, 334
Thomas of Bredon, Abbot of St Peter's, Gloucester: 317, 334
Thomas of Split: 46–47, 57–58
Thomas of Walsingham, *Gesta abbatum monasterii sancti Albani*: 54
Tiberius: 36
Tintern Abbey, chronicles of: 16, 102, 425
Tower of Babel: 61
Trahaearn ap Caradog, King of Gwynedd: 212, 219
Trebeta son of Ninus of Assyria: 61–62
Trier: 49, 61, 62
Trioedd Ynys Prydein: 151, 379
Trojans: 61–62, 61 n. 129
    Hungarian origins: 40, 43, 62
    Roman origins: 39
    Scythian origins: 40 n. 35
    Venetian origins: 58
    Welsh origins: 2, 16, 20, 23, 61, 63
Trójumanna saga: 37–38
Troy: 41, 43, 61 n. 130, 62–63
    fall of: 2, 16, 39
    in Welsh history: 2, 16, 20, 23, 25, 29
Tudno, church of: 141 n. 5
Tuscans: 56
Tudglyd of Penmachno: 141 n. 5
Tysilio, St: 141
Tywyn: 406, 414

Ufegeat, son of Ealdorman Ælfhelm: 134 n. 7
Ugrinus, Archbishop of Kalocsa: 46–47
Uhtred, Bishop of Llandaf: 125 n. 10, 127, 254, 272
Urban, Bishop of Llandaf: 188 n. 52, 189 n. 58
Urban III, Pope: 51, 123 n. 14
Urban IV, Pope: 240, 269, 286
Ursula, St: 49
Usk: 262, 279

Valerius Maximus: 35, 37, 37 n. 20
Valle Crucis Abbey: 25, 231, 237, 238, 252
    appropriation of church at Llansanffraid Glyn Ceiriog: 149 n. 28
    Black Book of Basingwerk probably written at: 25, 148, 250 n. 46, 251
    Bonedd y Saint worked over at: 140, 148, 151
    Cardiff 1.363 possibly written at: 149
    composition of the Peniarth 20 continuation of *Brut y Tywysogyon* at: 156–57, 164, 167–68, 182
    Cotton Cleopatra B V written at: 19 n. 66, 21, 250 n. 46, 251
    Hengwrt 33 put together at: 150, 185
    Llanstephan 1 almost certainly produced at: 149, 153
    Oed yr Arglwydd possibly written at: 16, 104
    Peniarth 20 written at: 19, 22, 84, 153
    transmission of *O Oes Gwrtheyrn* to: 190
    Welsh text of *Brenhinedd y Saesson* created at: 148, 153
Vandals: 56
Venantius Fortunatus: 54
Venetians: 61 n. 130
Venice: 49, 65
Vera historia de morte Arthuri: 187–90
Vincent Kadlubek: 60, 61, 66
Virgil: 36–37, 37 n. 19, 37 n. 20, 37 n. 22, 39, 42, 47, 61 n. 129, 62
Vita Griffini filii Conani: 1, 17, 40, 42, 174, 201
    Welsh translation of (*Historia Gruffud vab Kenan*): 191, 191 n. 64
Vitruvius: 35
Vortigern (Gwrtheyrn): 9, 10, 18, 19 n. 66, 170, 179, 207, 210, 218, 229

Wales: 214, 221
　drowned lands of: 141
　Edwardian conquest of: 2, 11–12, 15, 17, 22–23, 29–31, 295, 321–22, 338–39
　Normans in: 2, 6, 13, 40, 101, 231; *see also* Normans
　pre-Norman: 6, 75
Walter, Abbot of Tewkesbury: 258, 275
Walter de Cantilupe, Bishop of Worcester: 263, 264, 281, 318, 319, 320, 335, 336, 337
Walter de Clifford: 312, 330
Walter de Lacy (d. 1085): 303–04, 324
Walter de Lacy, Abbot of St Peter's, Gloucester: 311–12, 329–30
Walter de Lacy, Lord of Meath (d. 1241): 257, 275, 318, 335
Walter Froucester: 296
　History of St Peter's Abbey: 296–98, 301
Walter Marshal: 112, 117, 267, 283
　brother of: 267, 283
Walter of Châtillon, *Alexandreis*: 45
Walter of St John, Abbot of St Peter's, Gloucester: 319, 336
Wareham: 125 n. 12
Warenne Chronicle: 46
Warin Basset: 262, 279
Waverley Abbey, annals of: 8, 91–92, 96 n. 112, 110, 110 n. 19, 114, 121
Weihenstephan Abbey: 53 n. 93
Wellesbourne: 303, 324
Welsh bardic learning: 23–24 n. 88, 25, 73–74 n. 14, 76, 77, 105 n. 159
Welsh law *see Cyfraith Hywel*
Welsh saints, names of: 144
Welsh vernacular chronicles: 5, 10–13, 15, 17–19, 30–31, 71–72, 87, 169, 190–91, 193, 204, 232, 252
Weobley: 306, 326
Wessex: 3
Westminster: 323, 340
　Second Statute of: 322, 339 n. 235
Wharton, Henry, *Anglia Sacra*: 80–81
Whitland Abbey: 102, 231, 251, 252
　and chronicles: 8, 9, 88, 88 n. 73, 89, 96, 96 n. 112, 96 n. 114, 97, 102, 111, 135–37
　possible origin of Exeter 3514 in: 15, 88, 88 n. 73

Wibert, Life of Pope Leo IX: 57
Widukind of Corvey: 57
Wiliam Cynwal: 105, 174, 422
Wiliam Dyfi: 174
Wiliam Llŷn: 23
William, Abbot of St Peter's, Gloucester: 300, 308, 311, 327, 329
William, Prior of Goldcliff, Bishop of Llandaf: 234, 259, 260, 276, 278, 317, 334
William I: 212, 212 n. 132, 219, 224, 232, 235, 253, 271, 304, 324, 342, 360, 364, 409, 418
　called 'the bastard': 356
William II (William Rufus): 207, 212, 212 n. 135, 219, 253, 271, 305, 325
William Caxton: 28
William de Beauchamp: 263, 281
William de Blois, Bishop of Worcester: 263, 281, 318, 335
William de Braose (d. 1211): 120, 122, 245, 257, 258, 275, 315, 333, 386
William de Braose (d. 1230), son of Reginald de Braose: 260, 261, 278, 317, 334
William de Braose (d. 1287), Bishop of Llandaf: 242, 243, 270, 287
William de Braose (d. 1326), Lord of Gower: 147
William de Burgh, Bishop of Llandaf: 266, 268, 283, 285, 295, 319, 336
William de Clare: 240, 269, 286
William de la Pomeroy: 306, 326
William de Marisco: 318, 319, 335
William de Munchensy: 323, 340
William de Radnor, Bishop of Llandaf: 242, 268, 270, 285, 286, 295, 319, 320, 336, 337
William de Shaldeford: 165
William fitz Gerald: 127
William fitz Robert, 2nd Earl of Gloucester: 236, 246, 254, 255, 256, 272, 273
William Longespée, Earl of Salisbury: 259, 262, 277, 279
William Marsh: 265, 282
William Marshal (d. 1219), 1st Earl of Pembroke: 113, 117, 120
William Marshal (d. 1231), 2nd Earl of Pembroke: 113, 259, 264, 277, 281, 347, 356 n. 43, 369

William of Britton, Bishop of Bath: 267, 284
William of Malmesbury, 6, 48, 57, 60, 66, 236 n. 9, 251
   Gesta regum Anglorum: 21, 22, 46, 50–52, 94, 147, 297
   Life of St Wulfstan: 49
   Polyhistor: 35–36
William Worcestre: 425
Williams, Edward *see* Iolo Morganwg
Williams, Moses: 176
Williams, Taliesin: 77
Williams ab Ithel, John: 74 n. 14, 76–78
Winchcombe: 298, 302, 314, 316, 323, 332, 334
Winchcombe and Coventry chronicles: 95, 298
Winchester-Waverley chronicle: 89, 94, 110–12, 126 n. 66, 129, 131 n. 73, 233
Winchester: 254, 272, 322, 339
   annals of: 22, 76, 83, 94, 110, 110 n. 19, 114, 143, 147, 251
Wizo of Flanders: 310, 329
Wolfsdale: 117, 118
Woodstock: 318, 335
Worcester: 239, 258, 263, 276, 280, 322, 339
Worcester Cathedral: 48, 49, 52, 259, 277, 303, 312, 321, 324, 330, 338
   annals of: 95, 233 n. 4
   see also Cottonian chronicle; John of Worcester
Wulfheah, son of Ealdorman Ælfhelm: 134 n. 7
Wulfstan, Abbot of St Peter's, Gloucester: 303, 324
Wulfstan, St: 257, 274, 305, 325
Wyddgrug see Mold Castle

Y Bibyl Ynghymraec: 20, 26
Ynys Enlli, *Bardsey*: 188, 188 n. 52
   see also Iarddur of Bardsey
Ystorya Adaf: 341
Ystorya Dared: 17, 19, 20, 25, 26, 85
Ystrad *Llyr see* Strathclyde
Ystrad Meurig Castle: 128
Ystrad Tywi: 404, 409, 412, 417
Ystradowen church: 236

Zwettl Abbey: 53 n. 93

Medieval Texts and Cultures of Northern Europe

All volumes in this series are evaluated by an Editorial Board, strictly on academic grounds, based on reports prepared by referees who have been commissioned by virtue of their specialism in the appropriate field. The Board ensures that the screening is done independently and without conflicts of interest. The definitive texts supplied by authors are also subject to review by the Board before being approved for publication. Further, the volumes are copyedited to conform to the publisher's stylebook and to the best international academic standards in the field.

Titles in Series

Drama and Community: People and Plays in Medieval Europe, ed. by Alan Hindley (1999)

Showing Status: Representations of Social Positions in the Late Middle Ages, ed. by Wim Blockmans and Antheun Janse (1999)

Sandra Billington, *Midsummer: A Cultural Sub-Text from Chrétien de Troyes to Jean Michel* (2000)

History and Images: Towards a New Iconology, ed. by Axel Bolvig and Phillip Lindley (2003)

Scandinavia and Europe 800–1350: Contact, Conflict, and Coexistence, ed. by Jonathan Adams and Katherine Holman (2004)

Anu Mänd, *Urban Carnival: Festive Culture in the Hanseatic Cities of the Eastern Baltic, 1350–1550* (2005)

Bjørn Bandlien, *Strategies of Passion: Love and Marriage in Old Norse Society* (2005)

Imagining the Book, ed. by Stephen Kelly and John J. Thompson (2005)

Forms of Servitude in Northern and Central Europe: Decline, Resistance, and Expansion, ed. by Paul Freedman and Monique Bourin (2005)

Grant risee?: The Medieval Comic Presence / La Présence comique médiévale. Essays in Honour of Brian J. Levy, ed. by Adrian P. Tudor and Alan Hindley (2006)

Urban Theatre in the Low Countries, 1400–1625, ed. by Elsa Strietman and Peter Happé (2006)

Gautier de Coinci: Miracles, Music, and Manuscripts, ed. by Kathy M. Krause and Alison Stones (2006)

The Narrator, the Expositor, and the Prompter in European Medieval Theatre, ed. by Philip Butterworth (2007)

Learning and Understanding in the Old Norse World: Essays in Honour of Margaret Clunies Ross, ed. by Judy Quinn, Kate Heslop, and Tarrin Wills (2007)

Essays in Manuscript Geography: Vernacular Manuscripts of the English West Midlands from the Conquest to the Sixteenth Century, ed. by Wendy Scase (2007)

Parisian Confraternity Drama of the Fourteenth Century, ed. by Donald Maddox and Sara Sturm-Maddox (2008)

Broken Lines: Genealogical Literature in Medieval Britain and France, ed. by Raluca L. Radulescu and Edward Donald Kennedy (2008)

Laments for the Lost in Medieval Literature, ed. by Jane Tolmie and M. J. Toswell (2010)

Medieval Multilingualism: The Francophone World and its Neighbours, ed. by Christopher Kleinhenz and Keith Busby (2010)

The Playful Middle Ages: Meanings of Play and Plays of Meaning. Essays in Memory of Elaine C. Block, ed. by Paul Hardwick (2011)

Emilia Jamroziak, *Survival and Success on Medieval Borders: Cistercian Houses in Medieval Scotland and Pomerania from the Twelfth to the Late Fourteenth Century* (2011)

Normandy and its Neighbours, 900–1250: Essays for David Bates, ed. by David Crouch and Kathleen Thompson (2011)

Historical Narratives and Christian Identity on a European Periphery: Early History Writing in Northern, East-Central, and Eastern Europe (c.1070–1200), ed. by Ildar H. Garipzanov (2011)

Multilingualism in Medieval Britain (c. 1066-1520): Sources and Analysis, ed. by Judith Jefferson and Ad Putter with the assistance of Amanda Hopkins (2013)

The Social Life of Illumination: Manuscripts, Images, and Communities in the Late Middle Ages, ed. by Joyce Coleman, Markus Cruse, and Kathryn A. Smith (2013)

Stefka Georgieva Eriksen, *Writing and Reading in Medieval Manuscript Culture: The Translation and Transmission of the story of Elye in Old French and Old Norse Literary Contexts* (2014)

Keith Busby, *French in Medieval Ireland, Ireland in Medieval French: The Paradox of Two Worlds* (2017)

Medieval Francophone Literary Culture Outside France: Studies in the Moving Word, ed. by Nicola Morato and Dirk Schoenaers (2019)

Colmán Etchingham, Jón Viðar Sigurðsson, Máire Ní Mhaonaigh, and Elizabeth Ashman Rowe, *Norse-Gaelic Contacts in a Viking World* (2019)

Crossing Borders in the Insular Middle Ages, ed. by Aisling Byrne and Victoria Flood (2019)

Making the Profane Sacred in the Viking Age: Essays in Honour of Stefan Brink, ed. by Irene García Losquiño, Olof Sundqvist, and Declan Taggart (2020)